CANADIAN SIKHS
THROUGH A CENTURY
(1897-1997)

By the Same Author

English Works
1. *Canadian Society and Culture*
2. *Canadian Sikhs through a Century (1897-1997)*
3. *A History of the Sikh Misals*
4. *Maharaja Ranjit Singh and His Times*
5. *Sikh Polity in the Eighteenth and Nineteenth Centuries*
6. *Mughal Court News (Akhbar-i-Darbar-i-Mualla (1708-1718)*
7. *Persian Historians and Historiography of the Sikhs*
8. Published about ten dozen research papers
9. About 200 entries in the Encyclopaedia of Sikhism

Punjabi Works
10. *History of the Punjab (1469-1857)*
11. *History of India Part-I*
12. *History of India Part-II*
13. *Medieval Indian Institutions: social, cultural and economic*
14. *Maharaja Ranjit Singh*, Punjabi and Hindi
15. *Giani Gian Singh* (Historian)
16. *Prem Singh Hoti — His Life and Works*
17. *Rashtar Vir Guru Gobind Singh*
18. *Raja Porus*
19. *Prominent Buildings of the World*
20. About 100 entries in the World and the Punjab Encyclopaedias
    (Punjab Government Languages Department)

Translations
21. *A History of the Sikhs* (Teja Singh and Ganda Singh)
22. *The World Religions* (Harban Singh and M.L. Joshi)
23. *History of Britain* (Carter and Mears)
24. *A Short History of the British Commonwealth Part-I* (Ramsay Muir)
25. *A Short History of the British Commonwealth Part-II* (Ramsay Muir)
26. *Akbar to Aurangzeb* (W.H. Moreland)

CANADIAN SIKHS
THROUGH A CENTURY
(1897-1997)

BHAGAT SINGH
M.A., Ph.D.

FOR FUTURE CONTACT
BRAR 604-275-5700
CELL 604-644-4590
NANNAR 604-321-0715
CELL 604-657-2811

Gyan Sagar Publications
Delhi

Gyan Sagar Publications
C-143, Preet Vihar
Delhi - 110092

CANADIAN SIKHS THROUGH A CENTURY (1897-1997)
By DR BHAGAT SINGH

First published, 2001

ISBN No. 81-7685-075-6

Besides donations from others, the Canadian Sikh Study and Teaching Society, Vancouver, B.C., Canada, has also helped financially in the publication of this book.

PRINTED IN INDIA
_____

Published by Gyan Sagar Publications, Delhi - 110092
Laser Typeset by Perfect Computer Arts, Delhi -110051
Printed by Ram Printograph (India), Delhi - 110051

To

*The cherished memory of the brave and enterprising
pioneer Sikhs who underwent tremendous sufferings,
sacrificing their yesterday for our tomorrow,
to make us comfortable and affluent*

CONTENTS

PREFACE

This work on the Canadian Sikhs from 1897 to 1997 was undertaken despite my impaired health at the express instance of some Sikh scholars and Sikh societies in B.C. and some friends from Vancouver (B.C.). To write a good book is not a cakewalk, rather it is a strenuous and endless journey that exhausts the writer but writing is his lifeline. I partly agree with William Hazlitt that "a book is a bloodless substitute for life." Probably, he wants to convey that one has to shed or burn ones blood to produce a book which ultimately comprises bloodless mass of scribbled papers. But I fully agree with Milton that "a good book is the precious life-blood of a master-spirit," meaning that the author's life-blood flows freely in the body of his book. The author transfers his blood into his book otherwise it does not come to life. The author can never absent himself from his work, however objective and impersonal he may try to be. A book is born of the brain and heart of its author who puts himself in its pages. His individuality imperceptibly blends itself into his work and gradually emerges in front of the reader.

It is demanded of every writer to give his best and his best cannot be another's. Those who speak frankly are always likely to be listened to than those who speak with less candour. An author should never conceal or suppress his mind. The question of his views finding favour or disfavour with his readers is secondary but the author's primary consideration is his sincerity towards himself and towards how he feels. He should be sincere to his experiences and his views regarding the subject in his hand. Personal experience is the basis of every real work and sincerity to ones experience of life is the foundation of a good work. Experience is a good school but its fees are very high. It is hard to beat an experience of more than half a century. It is not for sale at the corner store. You have to earn it. If we could sell our experiences for what they cost us, we would all be millionaires. Generally it is gained through advancing years. No wise man ever wishes to be younger, thus losing the experience of life gained at high price. He should write as his inner spirit prompts him to write and he should not write as the others want him to write. Writing to order would be dishonesty to himself and to his readers, to which a good writer should never condescend.

In the course of writing this book this author made it his chief business to report faithfully of what he has lived, seen, thought, felt and known for himself. It is something which an honest writer should never lose sight of. If readers differ with him at places it is natural, if they never differ with him that is unnatural as no two men always think alike. Differing with one another occasionally adds flavour to the thoughts.

Style of an author, as Carlyle says, is not the coat of a writer but his very skin. When a writer has something really personal to say he will certainly not fail to find a really personal way in which to say it. A thought which is his own will hardly permit itself to be shaped into the fashion of some one else's expression.' Every spirit builds its own house.'

At places this author solicits to be too assertive in his views and experiences. As said above no two persons see a situation in the same way. Two men looked out through prison bars, one saw the mud, the other saw the stars. The aspiring men never look to the earth, they always look into the space. So do the writers look at things differently, some look with pessimism and despondency and some with hope and optimism. In this book I have said things from my own experiences and assessments but still I believe that most of the readers may tend to agree with me on most of my observations.

A century-old history of the Canadian Sikhs is marked by many stages : from sheer penury to comfortable affluence and from deprivation of all human rights to full-fledged citizenship with representation in city councils, provincial assembles and federal parliament. The process of this change had been awfully agonising and beset with hurdles which took them decades to overcome. In this study the same would be depicted faithfully. The camera shows no mercy. It cannot ignore your faults. You cannot be too cautious. A true historian is a slave to his jealous mistress—history— that never allows him to go astray. The author must be true to his inner voice. He should never be for a ban or constraint on voice. He must believe in freedom to disagree. He should be in full agreement with Voltaire, an 18th century world-renowned French philosopher who says, "I disapprove of what you say but I will defend, to the death, your right to say."

The pioneers being mostly illiterate they did not write any thing about themselves and those who could, did not find time to record it due to their over-busy daily schedules. It is well known that those who create history seldom find time to write it. Later interviews with them exposed the perpetrators of intense pain and gross injustice on them. Although those were bad times for them but were lived in the hope of good times to come, which ultimately did come. In the circle of time no stage is stationary. There is no sting in their voices and no remorse in their memories. When compelled to speak of their past, they smiled away those miserable days. Their struggle to vacate injustice was determined with undepressed spirits and relentless tirade without surrendering to the agents of fate. For a genuine cause they would rather break than bend. They never compromised over their established heritage and valuable principles of righteous conduct. In their new home-land they always meticulously upheld the intrinsic values of their religious tenets and moral discipline. These qualities made them stand firm in their odd hours in an alien, inhospitable and sometimes hostile land where ultimately they found ready recognition and ungrudging acceptance at the hands of their long-time detractors. It is my very sincere feeling that I have not been able to narrate the tearful tales of woe of the pioneer immigrants as agonisingly and distressfully as they had suffered.

I wish that these elderly pioneers who are now travelling in the fast lane of their life-journey and are locked up inside themselves must open up and divulge all their experiences before they bang into the sunset of oblivion and the treasure of history within them gets cremated or buried unknown. The preserved old stories of the pioneers will bring their remote past to the present. An investigator-historian approaches the past with one aim: "Tell me all". But they imploringly appeal to the questioner to leave their past into the past and they are unwilling to talk about it. But their life is not their's now, it is death's. Death is the penalty one pays for living. At their late 80s or 90s they have become the relics of the past.

The Sikhs are probably the most adventurous people in the world. None in the world had exhibited so strongly the indomitability of human spirit as the Sikhs. Migration from one place to another for greener pastures has been the practice of almost all the tribes of the universe right from its creation. This had been necessitated by the vagaries of geographical conditions or calamitous changes in the phenomena of nature. The economic considerations of the Sikhs pushed them out of the Punjab into various parts of the world including Canada. The Sikh diaspora has made a meaningful contribution to the Sikh faith by making it a world religion but sadly enough most of the non-Sikhs, the world over, know little about Sikh religion and culture. The Sikhs do need to tell the non-Sikhs outside India as to who they are and, despite their small numbers, how they have contributed significantly to different aspects of life in the countries they happened to inhabit permanently. To provide the readers with some basic information about the religious and cultural heritage of the Sikhs a chapter has been incorporated in this work.

The first chapter of this book narrates the situation out of which the Sikhs were born and raised before they journeyed to Canada. They carried in their blood strong germs of resistance to injustice and servitude and had preference and readiness for sacrifice when encountering ignominy. Their habit of hard work and determination to attain what they once planned to achieve always brightened their path. They possess limitless and unbounded inherent capacity to bear hardships and sufferings and under all circumstances their anxiety to rise equal to the expectations of others always keeps them prompting.

When they go to foreign lands they know what challenges they are likely to face. Odd circumstances facing them never pose any threat to their indomitable spirits and they make themselves worthy challengers of the gravest situations mentally and physically.

This book is not an admiring look at the Sikh community in Canada but an impersonal analysis of their century-long struggle for existence in their newly adopted country. We remember, more often, what has been unpleasant. I have covered all times—with one foot in the past and one foot in the future and two eyes on the present. This is what a historian is like. History is tonnes more than 'a collection of tales from the tombs' as has been ignorantly said. Voltaire's sweeping remarks are also incorrect when he says that 'history is a pack of tricks we play on the dead.' Without its study a man does not know his past, present and future and is thus reduced to the status of a semi-human being.

The Canadian Sikhs passed through a strenuous struggle in their new homeland, being unwelcome guests there. They faced horrendous opposition arising out of racism ingrained in the whites' blood. The Anglo-Saxons are white-skin-colour vanity incarnates.

This work is the story of one hundred years of self-assertion by the most virile community of the world. The Sikhs all over the decades waded through a ceaseless identity crisis and ultimately established their distinct identity clearly recognizable and acceptable everywhere on this planet.

In the early stages the whites made all efforts to exterminate the Sikh presence in Canada. The Canadian whites' enduring effort to keep Canada a white country had to be fought against on the irrefutable plea that Canada belongs as much to the Asians and Africans as to the Europeans. Canada is a land of immigrants. All inhabitants of Canada including the aboriginal settlers are immigrants whether they came here fifty years back or ten thousand years ago. Right from the beginning the well-designed immigration handicaps and hurdles put before the East Indians had to be crossed at all stages of their existence in Canada. Unfortunately the immigration problems subject them to harassment even today.

The Canadian government's policy of multiculturalism is noble in letter and spirit but the whites in private dealings have always flouted it with impunity as they took this policy as an affront to their cultural superiority and cultural imperialism to which they have been accustomed for centuries. They have been discriminating against the non-whites to the point of criminality. With the younger generation this trend is now slightly in the reverse gear. But the policy of multiculturalism came as a rescue and relief to the Asians and other non-whites.

The two major constituents of Canadian population—the Anglo-Saxon and the French, believe that the observance of their cultural heritage is their most prized privilege and all other cultures should merge into their cultures. Such thinking is an act of high-handedness and shocking injustice on the part of those who think that way. If a person loses his culture he loses his personality, his individuality and his identity without which he is reduced to a status far less than that of a dignified man.

Canada is an ethnically and culturally a diverse country. In essence, to be Canadian is to be multicultural. Cultural diversity is one of this country's most positive national characteristics. It is the belief of the sensible Canadians that more exposure to diverse cultures promotes tolerance, understanding and cooperation, giving them their Canadian identity.

The problem of preservation of Sikh identity has been constantly plaguing the minds of the Canadian Sikhs. There is no question of Sikhs becoming Canadians through some metamorphosis. The Sikhs, by virtue of their living in Canada, are fully Canadians. To keep them as such, the Khalsa Diwan Society, Vancouver's role for almost a century has been commendable and its multifarious contributions to the Sikh community has received adequate attention and discussion in this book.

The Sikhs maintaining an unalloyed identity in Canada gave them strength and distinctiveness, despite every effort to assimilate them by destroying their ancestral heritage. They integrated in the mainstream but never accepted to merge in it, surrendering their religious and moral ideas, to the perpetual chagrin of the assimilationists. When different traditions have combined together what has grown is not merely the aggregate of these traditions but the interaction has led to the emergence of something which is much more and is characterised by freshness and vigour. Among the finest fruits of this process of cultural synthesis has been the introduction of Sikhism in Canada. The Sikh religion has all the attributes and graces of major world religions.

The book is an account of the Sikhs who created a respectable place for themselves in Canada through sheer hard labour, inexhaustible vitality, a deep sense of responsibility and fairness in their dealings with others. This account manifests as to how a few enterprising Sikh individuals, starting from a scratch in a foreign land, grew into a sizeable, a dignified and one of the most eminently conspicuous communities in a country which comprises a multitude of peoples originally belonging to more than a hundred nationalities of the world.

Two major events in the history of the Canadian Sikhs, that kept them shaking to their spine, were the refusal of the passengers of the *Komagata Maru* to land in Canada in 1914 and denial of franchise in British Columbia for forty years (1907 to 1947). For their rights the Canadian Sikhs always chose to fight by peaceful and legal means. The significance of man is not in what he attains, but rather in what he longs to attain. Speaking more precisely, the greatness lies not only in achieving ones goal but also in the struggle to achieve it. Through their perseverance and persistent efforts the Sikhs, ultimately, emerged triumphant. Of course, their participation in the ghadar movement in India was based on violent means which entailed sad consequences leading to their hangings, transportation and imprisonment.

During my stay in Canada my perceptions regarding the past, present and the future generation Sikhs became clear and deeply intuitive and cognitive. I had watched and visualised the Sikh life-style, their professions, their poverty and riches very closely through living amidst them for a number of years, and by ripping open their hearts to know how they felt being in a foreign land. I studied the corporate life of the community as well as that of the individuals, producing an accumulative effect upon my mind and enabling me to evaluate them rigorously. This book is, in fact, a story of the East Indians' confrontations suffered in their past. It is an account of an unhappy memory to a good time. In an ultimate analysis, their's is a success story which every immigrant community across the globe should emulate. If you forget the past you forfeit the future. So the linkage with the past is absolutely imperative. In the course of writing my book on the 'Canadian Society and Culture', I had made an in-depth study of various aspects of the total Canadian life spectrum which stood me in good stead in producing this work.

My sources of information include those pioneers who are now on the brink of departure to a world hereafter. They have grievous and deplorable tales to tell in their stammering voices that move the listeners emotionally. Literature on the harrowing story of the *Komagata Maru* and the ghadar movement is available in abundance. The records of the Khalsa Diwan Society, Vancouver, though maintained incompletely, provide a very valuable source material regarding all phases through which the Sikh community passed in the course of their century-long existence in Canada. The manifestation of racial discrimination and the vehement opposition to the Sikh rights in Canada during the period under study can be read in the old issues of *The Daily Province* and *The Vancouver Sun*. The British Columbia press had been hostile to the East Indians for decades after decades. But the anti-Sikh and pro-Sikh speeches of the white MLAs and MPs and the records of the debates in the legislative assemblies and the Canadian parliament are also available. ' The deepest sin against the human mind is to make it believe things without evidence' (Huxley). So the evidence for every historical statement has to be produced. Lastly, but very importantly, are my observations based on my personal experiences, instinctive propensities and perceptions of the Sikh way of life in Canada and the influence of the west on their cultural and religious heritage. Let me hope that the readers will graciously excuse the author's remarks that a historian is a prophet who knows the past, understands the present and divines the future. Through this work this author has attempted to tell the Canadian Sikhs as to who they have been in the past and who they are at present and what is expected of them to become in the coming generations or what they are likely to become in the days to come. The past is dead and buried and the future which is still to come is pregnant with unknown probabilities. Therefore, future is more important than the past. I am a futurist and believe that in the days ahead our dream of the Sikh splendour in Canada will come true. They are destined to have glorious future because of their diverse noble qualities.

History is not only the study of the past for its own sake, completely divorced from the encumbrances of the present, but linked with the present and the future as well.

No work of this nature can lay claim to perfection in respect of information on the various aspects of life of the Canadian Sikhs discussed herein. There is always a scope of unearthing more relevant material for incorporation and a scope to evaluate it from a new angle. So this book may be judged from what it is and not from what it is not. For the sake of clarity, repetition at places is unavoidable.

When I undertook this work I was in India. I felt slightly disadvantaged in respect of procuring required source material for this project as no good book can be written without having access to scholarly apparatus. But I was very fortunate to thankfully receive every bit of needed information and usable material from Canada through incessant efforts of Sardar Pritam Singh Aulakh of Vancouver and Sardar Balwinder Singh Brar of Richmond (BC). But for their continuous and persistent help and follow up action, this book could not have come into being. Their immense interest in producing literature on the Canadian Sikhs was, undoubtedly, the main factor in accomplishing this work. They were kind to find time to read the manuscript very carefully and give very valuable suggestions and useful information to be incorporated in the book. I am deeply indebted to them for the same.

My two books on Canada totally consumed the restful years of my retired life and from a rocking chair they put me on a hard and hot seat. When an author is seriously engaged in his work he finds himself placed under self-imposed curfew and tied to his working desk month after month. Generally a writer uses his manuscript as his pillow as he does not know as to when a new idea or information flashes across his mind that he hastens to incorporate in his book. But I am pleased to say that through these books I gave to Canada more than I received from it. Giving is never my regret, it is always blissful. I feel that in the remaining days of my life my proudest moment will come when I hold this book in my hand.

This author is a strong admirer of the various qualities of the Sikhs not because he proudly belongs to this community but because of his having made comparative study on almost all the major communities of the world. Others are good in their own ways but the Sikhs are unique and unparalleled in many ways. Their qualities of dauntless courage, genuineness of word, superb gentleness, gracious hospitality and matchless honesty—that they brought with them as an invaluable gift to Canada— make them a people par excellence on this planet.

The author is deeply grateful to the donors of the financial assistance for the publication of this book.

—**BHAGAT SINGH**
27-Khalsa College Colony
Patiala (INDIA)

CHAPTER 1

HISTORICAL BACKGROUND

Geographic Situation of the Punjab

People envisaged in this study mainly hail from the Punjab, —a rich province of India with the highest agricultural produce and sturdiest and most virile men. It would be profitable for the reader to have a little clearer picture of the area and its inhabitants.

Punjab is the combination of two Persian words: *'punj'* and *'ab'* meaning five waters o five rivers-Satluj, Beas, Ravi, Chenab and Jhelum. In medieval ages, the Punjab was called *suba* Lahore with Lahore as its capital. During Emperor Akbar's period this province was divided into two parts and named *suba* Lahore and *suba* Multan. Under Maharaja Ranjit Singh the Punjab came to be named as Lahore Darbar. After its annexation by the British in 1849 it was renamed Punjab. After the mutiny of 1857 Delhi was also made a part of the Punjab. In 1901 the British government separated the areas across river Indus from the Punjab and named it the North-Western Frontier Province. In 1947, on the occasion of India's independence the Punjab was split up into two parts on the basis of Muslim and Sikh-Hindu population. The Muslim-dominated area of the province was joined with Pakistan and the second part remained with India. In 1966, on the linguistic basis Indian Punjab was broken into three parts: Punjab, Haryana and Himachal.

The Punjab, prior to 1800, had been the gateway of India for the invaders from its Northwest. To its north the sky-touching and snow-clad Himalayas stand as invincible guards for its security. But it was from the Khyber. Quram. Tochi and Bolan passes in the north-west that a large number of peoples as Aryans. Iranians. Greeks. Kushans. Hunas. Turks. Mughals. Duranis, etc., entered India or made repeated inroads into it.

They all had brought with them, to this land, their distinctive modes of life, religious beliefs and practices and social customs which, in a measure, added some new strands to the fabric of India's culture and civilization. The Muslims, before coming to India, in the beginning of the eleventh century, had developed a civilization of which they were very proud. They believed that their religion was the best of all in the world and they considered themselves under a solemn obligation to propagate it and bring as many people into its fold as possible. They would pay little heed to India's glory prior to their advent. They looked upon the people of India as infidels and adopted a contemptuous attitude towards them. Consequently, the Hindus and the Sikhs suffered many hardships.

Because of its geographical position, the Punjab has been the field of many battles. The intruders and invaders had to fight their way through the Punjab to the other parts of India. The Aryans, Greeks, Kushans and Hunas had to fight battles in the Punjab. Later, Sultan Mahmud, Muhammad Ghori and Babar did the same. Panipat had been the battlefield of three historic battles of 1526, 1556 and 1761. We see that the Punjab had been constantly the arena of fighting through the ages. Thus, the people of this part of the country became hardy, brave and martial in spirit. This characteristic of the Punjabis was inherited by the subsequent generations of the Punjab.

Economic Condition of the Punjab

In the later medieval times, mainly, the Punjab has been a rural-based province, agriculture being the principal occupation of the people. The land being fertile, it had been a suitable source of income or subsistence for the farmers. Francklin's writing about the eighteenth century Punjab says, "The Sikh territories are said to contain prodigious quantities of cattle, horses, oxen, cows and sheep; and grains of various kinds are produced in abundance."[1]

The land of the Punjab has been, in the past and is at present, fertile and very productive due to natural and artificial means of irrigation. Exemptions, remissions and inducements given by the state from time to time further encouraged cultivation.

According to Steinbach, the tranquility, which prevailed during the later years of the rule of Maharaja Ranjit Singh, stimulated traffic and a considerable commercial intercourse between the Punjab, British India and Afghanistan was the result. The Punjab that produced a variety of manufactures and agricultural products exported the same to different parts of India and central Asian countries. The exports of the Punjab included grains, pulses, sugar, rice, ghee, oil, salt, cotton, manufactured silk, woollen fabrics, shawls, blankets, cloth, paper, gold and silver articles and enamelled works. The Punjab imported from Afghanistan, Central Asia and hill areas, dry and fresh fruits, groceries, Persian carpets and ornamental wood-works. Punjab imported fine cotton cloth, ivory, spices, glass, copper, hardware, gold and silver, etc. , from all over India and Europe.[2] The nobles and rich courtiers of the Lahore Darbar and the Punjab chiefs procured chandeliers, mirrors, paintings and other curios from European countries and other parts of the world like Syria and China.

The horses of good breed were imported from Afghanistan and Central Asia. People of Turkistan bred horses for export to Hindustan. During this period Punjab was an independent state under Maharaja Ranjit Singh (1780-1839) and Hindustan was under the British. Apart from the military demands of the government for the supply of good horses, the animal was also commonly used for conveyance, pleasure-riding and racing particularly by the upper classes. Good horses always found a profitable market everywhere.

The Punjab had many trading centres, which included the cities of Lahore, Amritsar, Peshawar, Multan, Wazirabad, Rawalpindi, Dera Ghazi Khan, Attock and Jhang. Amritsar was known as the commercial emporium of Northern India and Lahore was called the 'Delhi of Punjab'.

Besides trade with the countries referred to above the Punjab had trade with Balkh, Khurasan, Turkistan, Persia, Russia, Tibet, Yarkand, China, Sind, Bahawalpur and Rajasthan states. Thus, once upon a time, not long back, Punjab, the land of the ancestors of the Canadian Sikhs, was economically a flourishing state where people from foreign countries aspired to settle and serve, and people lived in peace and plenty. There were more than sixty persons hailing from almost all the countries of Europe, England and the USA in the employ of Maharaja Ranjit Singh. They had come to the Punjab to better their economic prospects. They included senior army officers, J. F. Allard and C.A. Court (French), J.B. Ventura and P. D. Avitabile (Italian), Honigberger and H. Steinbach (German), J. Harlan and Kunarah (American), Foulkes and Ford (English).

Sikh Jats a Virile Community

Through their sheer Herculean strength, unbending spirits, unshaken determination and matchless intrepidity the Sikh Jats carved out their principalities in the Punjab in the 18th century throwing out the Afghan invader Ahmad Shah Durrani, the greatest military genius of the time in Asia. Ultimately under Maharaja Ranjit Singh they created a strong and compact kingdom, as large as that of France. The military achievements of the Sikhs gave them a splendid halo.

The Sikh Jats are, undoubtedly, a unique and marvellous people on this planet. Whenever they issue out of their home country they seldom look back and wherever they settle they put their whole heart and soul into their new homeland. But they always carry their cultural heritage baggage with them and keep sticking to it devotedly.

They are perfectly law-abiding citizens. They put at stake even their lives when their dignity, self-respect and honour are in jeopardy. Their qualities of superb gentleness, hospitality, honesty, large-heartedness and camaraderie make them a people par excellence.

The fundamental traits in the Jat character have been the instinct of tribal freedom and tribal kinship. Due to their strong love of freedom and warlike spirit they could no longer be denied a high place in the Sikh society that they eminently hold. The Sikh Gurus took pains to bring such a people into the pale of discipline and made them wonderful citizens of the world. How they were transformed through Sikhism has been discussed in detail in Chapter 13 of this book.

The Sikh Struggle for Independence and Assumption of Sovereignty

In the first six decades of the eighteenth century (1707-1768), the Sikhs constantly remained engaged in the struggle against the Mughal rulers of the Punjab and the foreign invaders of Afghanistan, till ultimately they assumed the rule of their land. The Sikh struggle for sovereignty can be split into four distinct stages: from 1708 to 1716; 1717 to 1747; 1748 to 1761 and 1762 to 1768. The period from 1708 to 1716 witnessed the first unsuccessful Sikh attempt to carve out an independent state under the leadership of the valiant Banda Singh Bahadur. The task set before him proved too great for him. The Mughal *raj* was deeply rooted in the soil; its power was not yet exhausted. The Mughal Emperor Bahadur Shah (1707-1712) issued an edict on 10 December 1710, ordering a wholesale genocide of the Sikhs—the worshippers of Nanak—wherever found, saying: *Nanak prastan ra har ja kih ba-yaband ba-qatl rasanand.*[3]

To the ill-luck of the Sikhs the government had at the helm of affairs in the Punjab a strong man like Abdul Samad Khan, who mustered all the resources of the province and held the Sikhs in check. But during Banda

Singh's period a will was created in the ordinary masses to resist tyranny and to live and die for a national cause. The idea of a national state working underground like a smouldering fire came out forty years later with fuller effulgence never to be suppressed again.[4]

During the period from 1717 to 1747, the Sikhs suffered horrible persecutions and martyrdoms at the hands of the Mughal governors of Lahore, but they remained as defiant as ever. They had learnt to carry their cross on their shoulders and wage their battles. The Persian invader Nadir Shah asked Zakariya Khan, the governor of Lahore, in 1739, where the Sikhs lived. Zakariya Khan said, "Their homes are on their saddles. They eat grass and claim kingship of the Punjab." Nadir Shah prophetically told him, "Take care, the day is not distant when these rebels will take possession of the country."[5]

On 1 June 1746, nearly seven thousand Sikhs were killed and three thousand made prisoners, This carnage is known as *chhota ghallughara* (the small holocaust) as compared to the *wadda ghallughara* (the big holocaust) of 5 February 1762, when massacre of ten to thirty thousand Sikhs had been estimated.

In the third stage from 1748 to 1761, the direct thrust of Ahmad Shah Durrani—the Afghan ruler, was against the Mughals and the Marathas. This provided a golden opportunity to the Sikhs to recoup and gather strength. During each invasion of the Durrani the various Sikh bands harried the retreating Afghans all the way up to river Indus, depriving them of most of their booty. The Sikh leaders moved into the vacuum created in the central Punjab by the Mughal-Afghan contest. Jassa Singh Ahluwalia took over the leadership in 1748 from the aging Kapur Singh and became the supreme commander of the Dal Khalsa.

The Afghan rule of the Punjab, from May 1757 to April 1758, was terminated by the joint action of Adeena Beg—later the governor of Lahore, the Marathas and the Sikhs. The historic battle of Panipat, fought on 14 January 1761, between the Marathas and the Afghans, sealed the fate of the Marathas in the north.

In the fourth stage, from 1762 to 1768, only two contestants, the Afghans and the Sikhs, were left in the arena of the Punjab. In this period the Sikhs suffered tremendous human losses in the great holocaust referred to above. But the Sikhs were determined to fight the Afghans to the finish. In 1763, the Sikhs defeated the Afghan general Jahan Khan. They captured Sirhind in January 1764 and entered Lahore, in April 1765. In December 1766, on the request of the Muslim citizens of Lahore, Ahmad Shah Durrani offered the *subedari* (governorship) of the capital to Lehna Singh Bhangi which the latter declined saying that accepting it from the hands of a foreign invader was against the policy and honour of his community.[6]

The Afghans in 1757,1762 and1764 had demolished the Harmandir and every time it was rebuilt from the debris left by the Afghans, making the Sikhs more and more determined against the Afghans. By 1767, the Sikhs had retaken almost the whole of the Punjab. Ahmad Shah seemingly an invincible conqueror of his time in Asia ultimately retired to Kabul, leaving the Punjab in the hands of the Sikhs. Earnest Trumpp says, "Repeatedly repulsed and dispersed, their temples desecrated and destroyed, massacred in thousands and driven to the deserts, wantonly pursued by the Mughals on the one hand and pillaged by the Durrani on the other, the Sikhs yet succeeded in erecting sovereignty of their own."[7]

The second and third quarters of the eighteenth century produced a galaxy of valiant and very competent Sikh leaders as Kapur Singh Faizullapuria, Jassa Singh Ahluwalia, Jassa Singh Ramgarhia, Ala Singh Phulkian, Tara Singh Ghaiba, Jai Singh Kanaihya, Lehna Singh and Gujjar Singh Bhangi, Charhat Singh Sukarchakia and Baghel Singh Karorsinghia. All of them had emerged from very humble origins. They were gems shinning in the dust. Their leaders picked them up. Ultimately, they liberated the Punjab from the Mughals and Afghans and carved out their principalities.

The immensity of sacrifice, in human blood, made by the Sikhs to gain mastery over their own homeland was tremendously vast. Some of the writers estimate this number as two lakhs (200,000) from the days of Guru Gobind Singh to the final ouster of Ahmad Shah Durrani from the Punjab in 1768.

The above-mentioned Sikh leaders carved out their independent principalities named Misals. Though twelve is the generally accepted number of the major confederacies, there were smaller ones also which allied themselves to one of them in need of war. The Sardars were sovereign in their areas, whatever the extent of their possessions. They had direct dealings with the neighbouring independent states.[8] Out of 12 Misals ten were headed by the Jat Sikhs.

Jassa Singh Ahluwalia (1718-1783) remained the undisputed leader of the Sikh community till his death. Jassa Singh Ramgarhia (1723-1803) would jump into the battlefield amidst booming guns, totally indifferent and insensitive to the grave hazards to his life. The founder of the Singhpuria Misal, Kapur Singh (1697-1753), possessed sharp intellect, penetrating shrewdness and power of quick grasp. Ala Singh (1695-1765) had pleased the Mughal Emperor, the Durrani invader and the Dal Khalsa to the extent of using them to his advantage. He may rightly be called the Bismarck of the Sikhs. He had three balls in his hands and by throwing them simultaneously into the air, he always caught them never allowing any one of them to fall.

The Khalsa ideals served as a beacon light for the Sikh chiefs. Whenever the people felt their leaders were likely to stray, out of ignorance, from their ideals, they showed them the right path. The Sikh chiefs dared not, therefore, defy the Sikh ideals. The *Panth* or the Khalsa commonwealth was considered by all the Sikhs as a very sacred creation of the Gurus reared into the final shape by Guru Gobind Singh.[9]

The military achievements gave the Sikhs a splendid status as soldiers. The Sikh chiefs of the eighteenth century were the generalissimos of the Dal Khalsa (the Sikh national army) and also the rulers of their Misals. Even when in the civil administration of the Misal there was not much of democracy left, the organization of the Dal Khalsa still functioned in a democratic way. The leader of the national army was elected and in times of emergency the Misal chiefs pooled their resources in the common interest of the entire Sikh community.[10]

Maharaja Ranjit Singh, who was born on 13 November 1780, succeeded his father who died in 1790. From 1799 to 1809, he directed his efforts mainly to the consolidation of his position in the central Punjab. During the second period of his rule, from 1809 to 1822, the annexation of Multan and Kashmir extended the borders of his kingdom. And during the third period, from 1822 to 1839, by annexing the valley of Peshawar, he gained control of the principal highway by which the Punjab had often been attacked through the past many centuries.

Within a period of four decades, Ranjit Singh rose from the position of a petty Sardar to that of a king of an extensive kingdom. Scores of Sikh and non-Sikh chieftains in the Punjab or on its borders accepted his suzerainty. His kingdom extended from the Himalayas in the north-east to certain important posts beyond the Indus on the south-west. "This ruler of the Sikhs was the first monarch after Anangpal who not only checked the recurring stream of invaders, which during eight hundred years had been pouring into the Punjab from the North-Western frontier, but also subdued the inhabitants of that area." He brought the scattered people of the Punjab under uniform and consistent system of government. The position of Ranjit Singh among the Sikhs may be paralleled to that of Frederick the Great, of Germany, who rose to power not so much as the king of Prussia as the one man to whom all Germans could look as likely to raise that medley of principalities and electorates into a nation. Thus, Ranjit Singh created a strong and compact kingdom with natural and dependable frontiers on all sides.

The Maharaja always made himself available to those who wanted to see him. His was a court that did not inspire any fear which made the princes and officers tremble and fall down on the ground in the Darbar of the medieval rulers. Although the Maharaja was the sole director of the state affairs and was competent and shrewd enough to run the administration without guidance from any quarter, he had at his court, a galaxy of nobles, bureaucrats and a military hierarchy whom he could consult whenever he liked. None of his subjects could defy his orders. Victor Jacquemont, a French traveller, who visited the Maharaja at Lahore, writes, "He is better obeyed by his subjects than the Mughal Emperors at the zenith of their power."[11]

The Maharaja was the most outstanding ruler of his time in the whole of Asia. Alexander Burnes, who came to Lahore to deliver to Ranjit Singh the presents of the king of England, wrote, "I never quitted the presence of a native of Asia with such impressions as I left this man: without education and without a guide, he conducted all the affairs of kingdom with surprising energy and vigour and yet he wields his power with moderation quite unprecedented in an eastern prince."[12]

Ranjit Singh's comparison with historical personages as Sher Shah Suri, Napoleon, Bismarck, Abraham Lincoln, Shivaji, Haider Ali, etc., is unreasonable, as their circumstances were different. Ranjit Singh carved out his way to a kingdom in more unfavourable circumstances than those of the above mentioned great men of history[13]. He died on 27 June 1839 in the full blaze of his glory.

He left his kingdom in the hands of imbecile, weak and incompetent successors — Kharak Singh, Sher Singh and Duleep Singh. The English, against their promises, annexed the kingdom of the Maharaja to their dominion on 29 March 1849. Thus came to a sad end the Sikh royalty that Maharaja Ranjit Singh had established with great toil and statesmanship.

The Mutiny of 1857

The outbreak of the mutiny at Meerut took place on 10 May 1857, to massacre the English and thus liberate India from foreign domination. It spread to different parts of northern India and partially to the Punjab. Th Punjab has been charged of having saved the British Empire because of their lukewarm support of the mutineers. There could be a few causes that are said to have kept the Punjabis a little inactive. The British with the help of the Poorbiya (Hindustani) soldiers had enslaved the Punjab. The Poorbiya soldiers had been looking down upon the Sikh soldiers who considered themselves to be superior. The Sikhs had a grudge against Delhi where the ninth Sikh Guru had been martyred and later Banda Singh and his hundreds of Sikh followers were killed under the orders of Emperor Bahadur Shah's ancestors. During the two Anglo-Sikh wars, the Shah of Delhi and one of his chiefs, the *Nawab* of Jhajjar, had given every aid to the British against the Sikhs. And a good portion of the spoils of the Lahore Darbar *toshakhana* had gone to the Shah's palace either through purchases or through some other means. The Sikhs believed that the Timur family, which led the mutiny, had been the traditional enemies of the Sikhs. After the annexation of the Punjab the Sikh soldiers had been completely disarmed and had been diverted to farming with a lot of facilities provided to them. This first war of independence failed because it was fought without a uniformity of purpose and unity of aim. It was a leaderless big enterprise, against a powerful alien rule, which was bound to fail.

The Sikh Diaspora

After the mutiny of 1857 was over many parts of the country faced many serious problems. Conquering a country is different from providing the people with all they need not as luxury but as ordinary or minimum requirements of everyday life. The Punjab faced famines in 1861. Orissa faced drought in 1865, South India in 1876-77, Kashmir in 1878 and in some other parts of India from 1896 to 1900 which took a heavy toll of life, poverished the people and subjected them to indebtedness. They spread out to different countries of the world especially to South East Asia, Indo-China and Indonesia. When British Parliament abolished slavery through an Act the African slaves refused to work as free labour. Many thousands indentured labour (on contract of five to seven years) was hired from 1837 to 1915 from Bihar and Eastern U.P. to work on the sugarcane farms of their British masters in Jamaica, Trinidad, Fiji, Mauritius and British Guyana. Some of them worked as petty contractors and clerks in South Africa, particularly Natal, Kenya, Uganda, Tanzania, Malaya, Singapore and Hong Kong. In 1876 about 45000 people from Calcutta and about 15000 from Madras were sent to Fiji islands alone. The records relating to the United States show that there were two persons from India in 1859, five in 1860 and six in 1861 in that country. In due course of time the number continued growing and at present, may be, a million Indians living in the United States. Many of the Punjabi Sikhs went to the Asian countries where they worked as clerks, policemen or watchmen, masons and carpenters. People from Gujarat and Sindh had also settled in those countries as traders and bankers. The South Indians, mostly Tamils ventured out to nearby Malaya, as labourers on rubber estates. Many of them went towards East Africa, North America and Great Britain. Thousands of Indians had settled abroad in about a century—from 1837 to 1915. At present, about half a million of the East Indians are settled in Canada, more than 90 percent of them are the Punjabi Sikhs, mostly from Hoshiarpur, Jalandhar and Amritsar districts. Hardly there is a district in the Punjab that does not represent in Canada.

The Sikhs, at present, have penetrated to all the countries of the world. Wherever they go they create a respectable niche for them. There are many wonderful stories of their adaptability in even very remote corners of the world. I give below only two such incidents briefly to give some idea and leave the rest to the reader's imagination.

I have a cutting from *The Daily Statesman* newspaper of 14 February 1961, preserved in my file that reads as under:

"The adaptability and enterprise of the Sikhs are justly famous; all over the world they are to be found, usually prosperous and often highly respected citizens. Of all the remarkable achievements of Indians abroad, however, perhaps Evelyn Waugh in his latest book, 'A Tourist in Africa', mentions the most startling. He writes admiringly of the Masai tribe in Tanganyika as being great fighters and hunters who kill lions with spears: ' no one has made a servant of a Masai; nor were they ever conquered. They are an intelligent people who have deliberately chosen to retain their own way of life.' Then he adds; 'In one boma (village) near Arusha I saw a headman who was by origin a Sikh.'

"Surely leadership of the aloof and forbidding Masai is infinitely more difficult of achievement than, say, election to the U.S. Senate. Can we not hear more about this remarkable son of India? Readers who have friends or relatives in Arusha might ask them to scour the slopes of Mount Kilimanjaro for this Masai chieftain from the Punjab." - 'Observer.'[14]

Dr Ganda Singh, the celebrated historian of the Punjab, once told this author that in the early twenties of the 20th century when he was in the British army, he was once sailing in the Mediterranean Sea along with some army companions. The ship developed some fault and water started leaking into it. They sighted an island and hurriedly anchored the ship on its shores and started moving on the island to find some village or habitation nearby from where they could get some help to do the necessary repairs to the ship. On the turn of the path they saw a man. in front of them. carrying a bundle of long sugarcanes on head with its upper part trailing behind on the ground. Dr Ganda Singh put his foot on the trailing part of the sugarcane. The man threw down the load from his head. The party was astonished to find that the man was a turbaned Sikh with full-grown flowing beard. On inquiry he told that he forgot the count of time, may be forty years back, when he first accidentally landed on that island. Since then he was happily living there with the other residents of the island and during all these years he never visited the Punjab. To the Sikh diaspora plans, even the sky is not the limit.

Can anyone tell me a place on this planet where the Sikhs may not be found? The over-due recognition that Sikhism is one of the world religions has been greatly facilitated by the work of the Sikh diaspora which, has made a meaningful contribution to the Sikh faith. They have made Sikhism a world religion and we should now no more keep it in the over-closed doors. Its appeal is growing and it has a glowing future in the world at large. The challenge of modernity to the Sikh religion abroad is now gradually fading away and Sikhism, in letter and spirit, is being appreciated more than ever.

The Kuka or Namdhari Movement

This movement was more or less a religious movement but the English bureaucracy dubbed it as a political movement that it was not. The government subjected the Kukas to hardships and strict surveillance.

The founder of this movement, Baba Balak Singh, was a devout follower of *Sain* Jawahar Mal who was given to deep meditation. Baba Balak Singh was deputed to Hazro to look after the Sikh congregations there. He spent most of his time in reciting the *Adi Granth*. Baba Ram Singh was one of the three most prominent disciples of Baba Balak Singh and was chosen to succeed him.

Baba Ram Singh was born on 3 February 1816, at Bhaini Araiyan, a village in the Ludhiana district. His father was a carpenter by profession. When Ram Singh grew into a young man he joined service in the Khalsa army at Lahore but later left it in 1845-46. He was a staunch follower of Sikhism and had an unshakable faith in the spiritual leadership of the Sikh Gurus. He desired the Sikhs to receive the baptism of Guru Gobind Singh and he chalked out vigorous plans for *amrit prachar*. He was against caste distinctions among his followers. He was a strong exponent of widow remarriage. He preached against the *pardah* (wearing of veil by women) system among women and was in favour of mixed congregations. His followers tied *sidhi pag* (straight turban) and kept white woollen rosary.

He, unequivocally, told his followers not to call him 'Guru' but since he was a beau ideal in religious matters, some of them took it easy to style him as the 'Guru'. In the beginning the followers of Baba Ram Singh were called *jagyasi or abhyasi*. But because in a state of ecstasy, removing their turbans from their heads, they would start dancing and shouting. They were called Kukas or shouters. Baba Ram Singh gave himself the nomenclature of Namdhari because he enjoined upon his followers to practice *naam*.

Because of his simple and easily practicable teachings Baba Ram Singh gathered a large following. Mr Macnabb, the Deputy Commissioner of Sialkot, reported on 5 April 1863, that, "an elderly Sikh of Ludhiana was going about the country with two hundred men whom he drilled at night with sticks instead of muskets, that he boasted of five thousand followers who obey no *hakam* (officer)." On 28 June 1863, he was interned in his village Bhaini by the Punjab government.

In respect of the cow, the Kukas were more orthodox believers in the sacredness of the animal than the Hindus were. In 1870 a group of enthusiastic Kukas attacked the butchers of Amritsar at the dead of night, murdering four of the butchers and injuring three of them seriously. Four of the Kukas were hanged and two of them deported for life.

On 11 January 1872, hundreds of Kukas met at Bhaini to celebrate the Lohri festival. Some of the zealot Kukas planned to murder the butchers of Malerkotla in utter contravention of the advice of their leader Baba Ram Singh. On the morning of 15 January, one hundred and twenty five Kukas, including two women, entered the palace of the *Nawab* of Malerkotla to get arms from the state armoury. In the clash that ensued in the palace both sides suffered heavy casualties. The Kukas left the town but they were overpowered by the state police and brought back to Malerkotla. On 17 January, 65 of them were tied with the guns and blown up under the orders of Mr Cowan, the Deputy Commissioner of Ludhiana and Mr Forsyth, Commissioner of Ambala Division without formal trial. Cowan was dismissed from service and Forsyth reduced in status. Baba Ram Singh was deported to Rangoon (Burma) where he died on 29 November 1884.

Baba Ram Singh was succeeded on *gaddi* by his brother Baba Hari Singh, and then by Baba Partap Singh and then by the present incumbent Baba Jagjit Singh.

The Kuka movement was basically a religious and social movement that was hampered by the activities of a handful of its over-zealous and fanatic followers. The movement would have been a marvellous success and would have found favour with a much larger population of the Sikhs if violence had not come into their actions against the butchers and the continuance of the *guru gaddi* had not been followed and propagated as a part of their creed.

The Singh Sabha Movement

The year following the persecution of the Kukas and the suppression of their movement saw the birth of the Singh Sabha (1873). The Singh Sabha movement and its activities had a much wider appeal to the Sikh masses and consequently made a far greater impact. There were certain factors that hastened its start. A flood of Christian missionaries had moved into the province after its annexation in 1849. They opened many educational institutions and societies for the propagation of their gospel. The British government took undue and unreasonable interest in their missionary activities. Queen Victoria wrote a letter to Lord Dalhousie on 24 November 1854, expressing the hope that the development of the railway communication in the country would facilitate considerably the spread of Christianity in these lands. In 1873 four Sikh students of the Amritsar Mission School offered themselves for conversion into Christianity. Though they were prevented from doing so but it alerted the leaders of the Sikh community against the proselytizing activities of the Christians.

Some Hindu missionary movements had also started to demolish the separate and distinctive identity of the Sikhs. Many practices banned in Sikhism were creeping into its fold. To stand against the threats being posed before Sikhism some leaders of the community assembled in Amritsar in 1873 and organized the Singh Sabha and decided to revive the basic Sikh philosophy. In 1876 Prof. Gurmukh Singh placed a programme before the Sikhs as under: To produce national literature in Punjabi, to impart religious education to the Sikhs, to save the Sikhs falling from their faith and to carry all such activities with the co-operation of the British government. Besides the Singh Sabha of Amritsar, Singh Sabha, Lahore, was also organized in 1879. Sir Robert Egerton, the governor of the Punjab, agreed to be its patron. The government of India expressed hearty sympathy for the promotion of social and religious programmes of the Sikhs.

The main activities of the Lahore Sabha aimed at defining the principles of the Sikh religion by bringing in the market such books as explained and adored the Sikh religion; by correcting the doubtful Sikh literature and developing Punjabi language and publishing papers and magazines in it yet saying nothing against any other religion or against the government but soliciting the support of the government.

A joint meeting of the Amritsar Sabha and the Lahore Sabha was held on 11 April 1880, and a general Sabha was established which was named the Khalsa Diwan. In due course of time more Khalsa Diwans were set up and those were ultimately converted into the Chief Khalsa Diwan.

The major contribution of the Singh Sabha movement was the creation of a network of the Khalsa schools, colleges and other centres of learning. The Singh Sabha leaders felt that the spread of education among the Sikhs needed the help and friendship of the British rulers. The Khalsa College, Amritsar, was the result of the educational activities of the Singh Sabha. Tight grip over administration of this college by the British government created bitterness among the Sikhs. Pro-British Sikh leaders like Sunder Singh Majitha who brooked the official interference in the Khalsa College, Amritsar, were branded as 'traitors'.

The Singh Sabha movement produced prominent Sikh scholars as Bhai Vir Singh, Bhai Kahan Singh, Bhai Ditt Singh, Professor Gurmukh Singh and Giani Gian Singh. They were truly among the most respected keepers of the conscience of the Sikhs. The writings of the scholars who wrote in pursuance of the objectives of the Singh Sabha exposed the evils, which had slowly crept into the Sikh social and religious life and inculcated in them a desire for reform. The growing political unrest in the province of the Punjab in the early years of the twentieth century, the influence of the nationalist press and above all the growing forces of nationalism in the country further added to the unrest among the Sikhs. This prepared the ground for the coming Akali struggle directed against the *mahants* and other vested interests in the Sikh shrines on the one hand and the British imperialism on the other.

The Singh Sabha movement rejuvenated the Sikh faith, Sikh culture, Sikh education, Sikh literature to a stage from where the Sikhs never looked back and never lost track of their distinctiveness.

India's Freedom Struggle

Indian National Congress was founded by a progressive government English Officer Alan Octavian Hume in 1885. Hume asked the young graduates of Calcutta to come forward and serve the people, be unselfish and make sacrifices to get liberated. Hume's message was a signal for the Indians to strive for their independence. But the Congress continued working in it's own way.

Against the ideology of the Congress, Indian emigrants organized the Ghadar Party outside India in 1914 and in it, the Sikhs played a dominant role. Since Canada was a part of the British Empire they shifted their revolutionary activities to the U.S. Thousands of the East Indians volunteered for terrorist work in India and funds were collected to defray the expenses of their passage. They were told, " your duty is clear, go to India, stir up rebellion in every corner of the country...., Arms will be provided for you on arrival in India. Failing this, you must ransack the police stations for rifles, obey without hesitation the commands of your leaders." Many of their leaders including Jawala Singh were arrested in India. The ghadarites continued pouring into India from Canada, the United States, China, Japan, Hong Kong and the Philippines. By the beginning of December 1914 about 6000 ghadarites had entered India.

But in India the ghadarites found that the people were not prepared to co-operate with them. The Punjab was sending the flower of their manhood to the battle-fronts. The Sikh religious organizations were opposing the ghadarites and giving them bad names. The ghadarites had a truck with the Germans who were soon disillusioned about the dishonest dealings of some of the leaders of the party. The Ghadar Party failed in its objectives on account of multiple reasons as lack of needed arms, lack of experience, bad, inefficient and dishonest leadership, failure of revolutionaries to keep secrets[15]. Other causes included the efficiency of the British intelligence service, lack of co-ordination and tension between the Germans and the ghadarites and harsh measures employed by the Punjab police to extract information from the arrested activists. And lastly, as told above, the Punjabi masses rejected it.

The next stage in India's freedom struggle was the Jallianwala Bagh Massacre on 13th April 1919 that shook the whole country to its very bottom.

During the First World War (1914-1918) in the hour of England's peril India rushed to her help with unfailing faith and loyal enthusiasm. The voice of controversy was hushed and the grievances, which the people had against the government, were laid aside. In the words of Lord Hardinge, India allowed herself to be 'bled white' and contributed freely in men and money. And in this Punjab's share was more than that of any other province or community in India. More than 100,000 Sikhs went to fight the battles of the British in different parts of the world. Of the 22 military crosses awarded for conspicuous gallantry to Indians, the Sikhs won 14. After the war, the Sikhs were pained to find that the police and the local officers continued to treat them as common rustic people instead of outstanding heroes. They came to know for the first time the full account of the maltreatment of the Sikh emigrants by the Canadian and American whites and the infamous ghadar trials resulting in the hangings, deportations and internment in their villages of nearly five thousand Sikh ghadarites.

Because of their unstinted support of the British in the war they expected to get something like self-government or dominion status within the British Commonwealth. But instead they got Rowlatt Act passed in March 1919 which gave the provincial government powers to intern any person, and the judges were allowed to try political offences with a jury in specific cases. It was indeed a draconian measure in times of peace. There was a storm of protest against the ruthless regime of Sir Michael O'Dwyer, Lieutenant Governor of Punjab. Mahatma Gandhi was leading agitation against the Rowlatt Act and on his way to Amritsar he was prohibited to enter the Punjab on 4 April 1919. Gandhi was shown the order at Palwal railway station. On his refusal to obey the order he was arrested and taken to Bombay. The organizers of demonstration at Amritsar, Dr Saif-ud-din Kitchlew and Dr Satyapal were arrested and whisked away to Dharmsala (Kangra) on 9th of April. The people of Amritsar protested against these arrests and they attacked two British banks and killed their white managers. Brigadier General Edward Harry Dyer was called from Jalandhar cantonment. He reached Amritsar on the evening of 11th April, took charge of the city and studied the situation. On 12th April, it was announced by the government that there would be no meeting on 13th April, —the Baisakhi day. But as scheduled the meeting was held at the Jallianwala Bagh at 4 p.m. Shortly thereafter General Dyer reached there with armoured cars and ordered firing without warning, killing, according to government figures, 379 people, and wounding over 2000. But according to unofficial inquiries about 1000 persons lay dead. Sir Michael O' Dwyer approving the action sent a message 'action correct'. This gory episode gave an awfully disturbing idea of the unlimited power assumed by the foreign government in terms of destructiveness. The Jallianwala Bagh is a standing monument to the arrogant and cruel firmness of the British *raj*.

Martial law was clamped on the Punjab. The Hunter Commission, giving unanimous verdict on General Dyer's action recommended his dismissal from service. Winston Churchill, later the Prime Minister of England (1940-45), said in the British Parliament in 1919, "This episode which appeared to be without parallel in the modern history of the British Empire was an extraordinary event, a monstrous event, an event which stood in singular and sinister isolation".[16]

General Dyer told the Hunter Commission that the British *raj* was not in danger at all. He wanted to teach a lesson to the people. Jawahar Lal Nehru writes in his autobiography that towards the end of the year 1919 he travelled from Amritsar to Delhi. In the morning he discovered that all his fellow-passengers were military officers. One of them was describing in an aggressive and triumphant tone his Amritsar experiences. I soon discovered that he was Dyer, the 'hero' of the Jallianwala Bagh. He pointed out how he had the whole town at his mercy and he had felt like reducing the rebellious city to a heap of ashes but he took pity on it and refrained. He was evidently coming back from Lahore after giving his evidence before the Hunter Committee of Inquiry.[17] His admirers presented him a golden sword, being the 'defender of the empire'. *The Morning Post* raised a fund for him. He received a sum of (£26,317 from his English supporters. This amount was equal to his pay for many years, much higher to the salary he was to get during the remaining period of his service. This betrays the bankruptcy of conscience of the whites for the murderer of the innocent non-whites.

Udham Singh, a Sikh, at a public meeting in London on 13th March 1940, murdered Sir Michael O'Dwyer, the Lieutenant Governor of the Punjab. Udham Singh was hanged on 13th June 1940 and this earned him martyrdom for his brave act.

During her visit to India in October 1997, Queen Elizabeth-II said at a banquet hosted in her honour at Rashtrapati Bhawan, New Delhi, on 13th October, "It is no secret that there have been some difficult episodes in our past-Jallianwala Bagh, which I shall visit tomorrow, is a distressing example. But history cannot be rewritten however much we might sometimes wish otherwise. It has its moments of sadness as well as gladness. We must learn from the sadness and build on the gladness". On 14th October 1997, the Queen visited Amritsar. Removing their shoes, the Queen and the Duke (her husband), together, placed a wreath at the 'flame of liberty' and stood in silence and then signed the visitor's book. It has been interpreted as recognition of those killed as martyrs by the British monarch.

The Akali Movement

The Gurdwaras and their properties were being misused by the *mahants* who were in occupation of the same. Despite the warnings of the Akalis, the *mahants* carried on their immoral practices on the premises of the Gurdwaras and continued misusing their income.

Nankana Sahib, the birthplace of Guru Nanak, was one of the richest shrines of the Sikhs. The Gurdwara's Udasi *mahant*, Narain Das, lived in the Gurdwara with a mistress and he called the prostitutes and dancing girls to the premises of the sacred shrine. Narain Das was asked to improve his ways. Far from that he hired 400 *gundas* or mercenary murderers to meet the Akali threat.

A *jatha* of 130 men, under the leadership of Lachman Singh entered the Gurdwara at about 6 a.m. on 20th February 1921 against the advice of the SGPC who had an idea of the designs of the *mahant*. As soon as the *jatha* stepped inside the gates of the Gurdwara, the gates were closed. The *mahant* had already alerted his gang of assassins who were armed with all types of weapons including hatchets, swords and firearms. The Akali entrants were immediately attacked and all the members of the *jatha* were cut into pieces and dragged to a pile of logs and burnt.

It was a mockery of British justice that for the murder of 130 Akalis, three men were sentenced to death and two including Narain Dass were transported for life. Of *mahant's* 400 murderers the government could arrest almost all of them. The Nankana tragedy and the inaction of the local government made the authorities in Delhi and London think that there was an urgent need to change their policy of non-interference in the religious affairs of the minority community. The Indian government felt that the Punjab government was not adequately sympathetic towards the demands of the Akali movement.

The Gurdwara was handed over to the Shiromani Gurdwara Parbandhak Committee (SGPC). National leaders like Mahatma Gandhi, Maulana Shaukat Ali, Lala Lajpat Rai and Dr Saif-ud-Din Kitchlew visited the Nankana scene of the tragedy and expressed sympathies over the loss.

Guru Ka Bagh *morcha* is another landmark in the history of the Akali movement. In this struggle for their rights the Akalis remarkably demonstrated the efficiency of the weapon of peaceful *satyagraha*. The immoral use of force on the unarmed and non-violent protesters exposed the callousness of the government.

Guru Ka Bagh was a small Sikh shrine, thirteen miles from Amritsar that had been erected to commemorate the visit of Guru Arjan Dev Ji. Adjacent to the Gurdwara was a piece of land on which acacia trees had been grown to provide firewood for the Gurdwara *langar*. The Gurdwara's possession was taken by the SGPC but the *Bagh* and the land remained in the hands of the *mahant*. On the report of the *mahant* the authorities arrested five Akalis on 9 August 1922, and put them on trial on the charges of cutting the trees, theft, riot and trespass.

To protest against the arrest and charging the Akalis with trespass and theft and for the Akalis' right to cutting the wood for the Guru's *langar, jathas* from the surrounding areas and from the different parts of the Punjab began to pour into the Guru Ka Bagh. The number of Sikh arrests began to swell. The number of the members of each *jatha* began to grow. The police, under the orders of the higher authorities, decided to use force to prevent the Akalis from reaching the Bagh. The police stopped the *jathas* and beat them with *lathis*, jack-boots and fists.

C.F. Andrews, an English Christian missionary, visited the site of the police brutalities in the afternoon of 12 September 1922. He described the official action as 'inhuman, brutal, foul, cowardly and incredible to an English man and a moral defeat of England.' "The vow they (the Sikhs) had made to God was kept to the letter. I saw no act, no look of defiance. It was a true martyrdom for them as they went forward, a true act of faith, a true deed of devotion to God." Later in the day he met the Lieutenant-Governor of the Punjab and asked him to see things for himself. He had seen with his own eyes hundreds of 'Christs' being crucified at Guru Ka Bagh. Sir Edward Maclagan arrived at Guru Ka Bagh on 13 September, and ordered the beatings to stop. The police returned from the scene four days later. The brutalities of the police on the passive resisters had continued for nineteen days. During the police action many national leaders including Swami Shardanand, Maulana Kifayat Ullah, Hakim Ajmal Khan, Pandit Madan Mohan Malaviya and Kumari Lilawanti visited Amritsar and expressed their solidarity with the movement. An American, Captain A. L. Verges, who filmed the beatings of the Akalis at the Guru Ka Bagh, prepared a short film titled 'Exclusive Picture of India's Martyrdom'. He described this *morcha* as 'a unique struggle in human history and a peaceful rebellion against the constitutional authority. During the barbaric police action 5605 Akalis had been arrested and 936 were hospitalized. The arrested were released in May 1923. The disputed property was taken from the *mahant* and handed over to the S.G.P.C. on 17 October 1923.

Jaito Morcha

There was a sharp dispute between the Nabha and Patiala states that had common boundaries. Justice Stewart of Allahabad High Court, who conducted an inquiry, gave his verdict in favour of their favourite state, Patiala. Maharaja Ripudaman Singh of Nabha also took interest in the affairs of the Sikh community and the national movement. The British government decided to take action against him. He was made to abdicate in favour of his young son. The Shiromani Gurdwara Parbandhak Committee observed 9 September 1923, as Nabha Day in protest against the removal of the Maharaja and arranged *akhandpaths* in many

Gurdwaras. The police interrupted the *akhandpath* at Gurdwara Gangsar in Jaito (Nabha State). A *morcha* was launched. The *jathas* or peaceful protest marchers to Jaito increased from twenty five each to a hundred and then to five hundred. They came from all parts of the Punjab. The Indian National Congress also expressed full sympathy with the *morcha*.

The SGPC and the Akali Dal were declared illegal. Fifty nine Akali leaders were arrested and charged with a conspiracy to wage war against the British crown. But the Akalis did not yield.

One such *jatha*, of five hundred Akalis arrived at Jaito on 21 February 1924, and on refusal to disperse was fired at by the state police, causing a heavy loss of life. The shooting aroused sympathy for the cause of the Akalis. Jawahar Lal Nehru, along with his colleagues, K. Santanam and A.T. Gidwani, came to Jaito to know the exact position of the Sikh *morcha*. They were arrested and sent to jail and later released. The *morcha* finally ended with the Akalis completing their 101 *akhandpaths* on 6 August 1925. A *jatha* of ten from Vancouver (Canada) also came to the Punjab to participate in the *morcha*.

The Babbar Akalis

The militant spirit of the Punjabis that had lain dormant since the suppression of ghadar movement was resuscitated when the radical section of the Akali reformers organized themselves into militant groups popularly known as the Babbar Akalis. This breakaway wing made its appearance during the Sikh Education Conference held at Hoshiarpur on 19-21 March 1921. They framed the program of eliminating certain officials and non-officials condemned as enemies of the Khalsa *Panth*. They wanted to teach a lesson to the toadies and to demonstrate to the government that self-respect and revolutionary spirit was very much alive in the Sikh community.

Their activities were mainly confined to the two districts of Punjab— Jalandhar and Hoshiarpur. Officialdom in the Punjab believed that they received large sums of money for revolutionary propaganda from their counterparts still in America and Canada.[18]

It was also planned to paralyse the supporters of the bureaucracy— the *zaildars, safed poshes, lambardars, patwaris* and police informers. Kishan Singh of village Birring (district Jalandhar), the retired army personnel, Havaldar Major, was the moving spirit behind the Babbar movement. He exhorted people through his speeches to give up non-violence. He also contacted the Sikh soldiers at Jalandhar cantonment with a view to obtaining arms and ammunitions.

Many individuals who were police informers or toadies were done to death by the Babbars. In a bid to capture Dhanna Singh, an important Babbar leader, on the night of 25 October 1923, five policemen were killed on the spot and one died later. A.F. Horton, Superintendent of police, Hoshiarpur, and W.N.P. Jenkin, Assistant Superintendent of police, along with four inspectors were severely injured. Horton died a few days later in hospital. A bomb blasted by Dhanna Singh concealed in his armpit caused these casualties.

By mid-June 1924, all the important Babbars had either been killed in police encounters or taken prisoners. Of the 62 Babbars put up for trial six, including Kishan Singh Birring, were condemned to death, some of them were acquitted and the rest were sentenced to varying terms of imprisonment.

The Naujawan Bharat Sabha

The Naujawan Sabha was formed in November 1924 to win India's freedom with methods of violence, as its members had no faith in the cult of non-violence. They worked away from the shadow of the Indian National Congress. Both these parties had one shared vision of their country's freedom from the foreign rule but their means to achieve it were different.

The revolutionaries unanimously elected Chander Shekhar Azad as their president. At the proposal of Bhagat Singh (1907-1931), this organisation was named Hindustan Socialist Republican Army. They manufactured bombs and procured weapons. Mistakenly, they killed Saunders, Assistant Superintendent of police at Lahore, to seek vengeance of the death of Lala Lajpat Rai. In fact, they wanted to murder Mr. Scot, the Superintendent of police. They managed to escape after killing Saunders.

On 8 April 1929, Bhagat Singh and his companions threw a bomb in the Central Assembly at Delhi and threw some pamphlets condemning the British government for the maltreatment of the Indians. The note thrown with the bomb said, "Your repression must come to an end. The brutal murder of Lala Lajpat Rai is the most heinous crime. You cannot crush a resurgent nation sustained by its faith in its ideological rectitude. With the blood of the martyrs a holy altar is gradually being built on this sacred soil which will see the end of the exploitation of man by man. Since we know the deaf can't hear our normal voice we send our message through this explosion. *Inqulab Zindabad*." The Naujawan Sabha was banned in 1930 under the Seditious Meetings Act.

For the Lahore conspiracy and Central Assembly bomb cases Bhagat Singh and some nineteen other members of their party were tried out of which Bhagat Singh, Raj Guru and Sukhdev were sentenced to death on 7 October 1930, and the others were awarded different terms of imprisonment. The three condemned to death were hanged on the evening of 23 March 1931, and their bodies were secretly taken to the banks of river Satluj near Ferozepur and cremated. The hanging of Bhagat Singh and his companions was a cruel, brutalizing and out-dated form of the British-sanctioned vengeance against those who wanted freedom for their beloved country. The names of the three martyrs became a household word. Their daring and supreme sacrifice of life inspired and boosted the sagging morale of every youth throughout the country. Their martyrdom day is solemnly observed and homage is paid to the brave sons of the soil every year at Hussainawala, the site of their cremation, and at Bhagat Singh's ancestral village Khatkal Kalan, in the present Nawanshahr district of Punjab.

World War II and INA (1939-45)

During the World War II (1939-45) Japanese armies pushed across the Thai-Malayan border and defeated the British Indian forces opposing them. One of the thousands of Indians captured was Captain Mohan Singh, of Ist/14th Punjab regiment. He offered his services to the Japanese commander. Mohan Singh was elevated to the rank of a general and was made commanding officer of the newly established Indian National Army (INA). The INA led the Japanese attack on Singapore that was captured on 15 February 1942.

About 45,000 Indian prisoners assembled at Singapore. Of the 20,000 who offered to join the INA a high proportion were the Sikhs. General Mohan Singh set up his headquarters at Singapore. He asked the Japanese Field Marshal about the role of the INA that the Japanese had in mind. Mohan Singh again demanded of the Japanese government during the Bangkok Conference, on 15 June 1942, to make a declaration of their policy towards India. The Japanese government did not react favourably. Mohan Singh's faith in the Japanese government wavered. The Japanese commander at Singapore took direct control of the INA. Mohan Singh became cold towards the Japanese. His colleague Naranjan Singh Gill, who was in charge of Burma, was arrested in 1942 and the INA weakened and Mohan Singh dissolved it.

At this stage Subash Chander Bose arrived from Germany and took charge of the situation. He set up provisional government of Azad Hind.

The Japanese became more co-operative with Subash than with Mohan Singh. Subash moved his headquarters to Rangoon and in February 1944 fought the British forces and succeeded in forcing his way into Indian Territory. By the monsoon season the INA was pushed back. It was ill-equipped and outnumbered by the British forces. In January 1945 the INA fought its second round with the British whose performance proved superior and by the middle of May 1945 the heroic drama of the INA came to an end.

Subash Chander retreated from Rangoon to Singapore and from there to Bangkok. On 18 August 1945, the plane carrying him to Tokyo crashed, ending his violently enterprising career.

Partition of the Punjab (1947)

On 22 March 1947, Lord Mountbatten took over charge from Lord Wavell as viceroy of India. He was to make arrangements for the transfer of power from the British to the Indians. The partition of India into India and Pakistan had been decided. The split of the Punjab was a matter of deep concern to all as it entailed disastrous consequences. The Sikhs and the Hindus of the Punjab wanted division of the province on the basis of numbers and property. Sir Evan Jenkins, governor of Punjab, had warned that the division of the Punjab on communal lines was fraught with serious repercussions as the Muslims, Hindus and the Sikhs were inextricably mixed in every district. The partition of the province was bound to split the population of the Sikhs into two but the Sikhs wanted to have the Punjab divided than live in Pakistan.

On 3 June 1947, Lord Mountbatten made an emotional speech in broadcast regarding the fate that was in store for the Sikhs. "We have given careful consideration to the position of the Sikhs. This valiant community forms about an eighth of the population of the Punjab, but they are so distributed that any partition of this province will inevitably divide them. All of us who have the good of the Sikh community at heart are very sorry to think that the partition of the Punjab which they themselves desire, cannot avoid splitting them to a greater or lesser extent. The exact degree of the split will be left to the Boundary Commission in which they will of course be represented."[19]

On 4 June, the viceroy said at a press conference, "There are two main parties to this plan—the Congress and the Muslim League—but another community much less numerous but of great importance—the Sikh community—have of course to be considered. I found that it was mainly at the request of the Sikh community that Congress had put forward the resolution on the partition of the Punjab, and you will remember that in the words of that resolution they wished the Punjab to be divided between predominantly Muslim and non-Muslim areas.... I must say that I was astounded to find that the plan that they had produced divided their community into two almost equal parts. I have spent a great deal of time both out here and in England in seeing whether there was any solution which would keep the Sikh community more together without departing from the broad and easily understood principle, the principle which was demanded on the one side and was conceded on the other. I am not a miracle worker and I have not found that solution."

British government appointed Boundary Commission with Sir Cyril Radcliffe as chairman. Each commission had four judges on its panel with two Muslims and two others. The Sikhs wanted the dividing line to be drawn along the Chenab river, thus keeping over 90 per cent of the Sikhs in a compact unit with most of their historical shrines with them. On the other hand Muslims demanded Lahore, Multan and Rawalpindi divisions and some tehsils in the Jalandhar and Ambala divisions. But the decision was solely in the hands of Sir Cyril Radcliffe who gave 13 districts to the East Punjab i.e. the districts of Jalandhar and Ambala divisions, the district of Amritsar and some tehsils of Lahore and Gurdaspur. 62 per cent of the total area of the province of Punjab and 55 per cent of its population was given to Pakistan.

According to new findings on the partition of the Punjab by Prof. V.N. Datta, Professor Emeritus, Modern History, Kurukshetra University, Lord Mountbatten interfered in the boundary question. He even urged the Chairman Sir Cyril Radcliffe to balance the border of the east and the west bearing the Sikh problem in mind and that any generosity to Pakistan should be more in Bengal than in the Punjab. Lord Mountbatten was concerned about the Sikhs as their most fertile lands of Lyalpur and Montgomery were being given to Pakistan. Besides awarding the Muslim majority district of Gurdaspur to India, ignoring the principle of majority population, the boundary line with respect to Ferozepore and Zira tehsils was also changed on 10 or 11 February 1947, reverting them back to India, after being awarded to Pakistan.

On 14-15 August 1947, when India and Pakistan were celebrating their independence nearly ten million Punjabis—Muslims and the Sikhs and Hindus were at each other's throats.

During the migration of population horrible atrocities were committed on both the Pakistan and Indian sides. Trains carrying refugees were attacked and bogies packed with murdered passengers were sent across the borders. Even the old and infirm, women and infants were not spared. There was never a bigger exchange of population attended by so much of bloodshed earlier in the history of the world. Lakhs of people were slaughtered on both sides like goats and sheep. Politicians could not envisage the transfer of population on such a large scale and they could not arrange it nor could they stop the senseless murders. Partition was the result of the failure of the Indian statesmanship. We may call it hastily-conceived, man-made catastrophe brought about by rash, cynical and hot-headed politicians. It's shadow still lengthens over India and Pakistan.

More than four million Muslims were left in the East Punjab and about four million Sikhs and Hindus in the West Punjab. It is generally believed that in 1947 about six million Sikhs and Hindus migrated to India from Pakistan and about the same number of Muslims migrated from India to Pakistan. This migration on both sides took place by trains, motor transport and foot convoys. On both sides of the border, thousands of people accepted conversions to save their lives. Thousands of young women were abducted; some of whom were recovered later. They lived their later lives in terrible traumatic memories that brought moments of horror shaking them to their spine till their bones cracked under the weight of years. Such tragic events could be the most shameful chapter in the history of any country of the world.

Partition of the Punjab brought about revolutionary changes in the political, social and economic structure of the Punjab. The Sikhs who were the most prosperous community was reduced to the level of other Indian communities. To earn their livelihood, they were obliged to be scattered to different parts of the country. Thousands of the Sikhs went abroad to once again better their living standards.

The Punjabi Suba

After the independence of India (15 August 1947) the main grievances of the Sikhs remained. They had no place under the sun where they could have their political and cultural expression. The states of southern India had been reorganized on the basis of language but this principle was not applied to the northern India. Even their mother tongue Punjabi was denied the status of a state language, because the Punjabi Hindus, on political reasons, opted for Hindi, both in the schools and at the census. The Sachar formula (after the name of Bhim Sen Sachar, the then chief minister of the Punjab) was evolved that suggested the teaching of Punjabi and Hindi after the third primary grade, leaving the choice of the medium of instruction to the parents. The Hindus freely opted for Hindi and the Sikhs for Punjabi. This split the communities further apart. In 1949 the Punjab University, dominated as it was by the Arya Samajists, also declared that Punjabi could not be a fit medium of instruction even if the Sikhs agreed to both Nagri and *Gurmukhi* scripts. This exasperated the situation and the Punjab became the battlefield on the language issue.

All parties accepted a compromise on Regional Formula in 1956. The Punjab was divided into two regions—Punjabi and Hindi. In the Punjabi region, Punjabi was to be the sole medium and it was to be compulsorily taught in the Hindi region and the vice versa. The Hindus never opted for it. On the other hand the Hindus launched pro-Hindi agitation.

Jawahar Lal Nehru, the Prime Minister of India, and Partap Singh Kairon, a powerful chief minister of Punjab, were against Punjabi Suba. And unfortunately the Sikhs and Hindus did not fight for it from a common platform and it became wholly a Sikh issue and Jan Sangh (the main Hindu organisation) was opposed to this demand.

Master Tara Singh, president of Shiromani Gurdwara Parbandhak Committee, launched a strong agitation for a Punjabi speaking state in 1960. He was arrested on 24 May 1960, and lodged in the Dharmsala jail. In his absence Sant Fateh Singh, the vice-president of the SGPC, went on fast unto death over this issue on the precincts of the Golden Temple at Amritsar on 18 December 1960. Under the explosive circumstances the government released Master Tara Singh in January 1961. Tara Singh met Jawahar Lal Nehru who told him that "it is not out of any discrimination against the Punjab or distrust of the Sikhs that the process of forming a linguistic state was not possible...." That "Punjabi was essentially a dominant language," of the Punjab state, common to both Hindus and the Sikhs, though it is not possible to accept the principle of purely linguistic states in the case of Punjab. He felt that in the case of Punjab's division, "it will be harmful to the Punjab, to the Sikhs as well as Hindus and to the whole of India." He did not elaborate as to why it was harmful.

Master Tara Singh asked Sant Fateh Singh to give up his fast. The people at large thought that the Sant had broken a solemn vow and betrayed their trust. Master Tara Singh was also under the gun. It was said that Tara Singh feared that he himself would have to undergo a similar ordeal in case Fateh Singh died without achieving anything. Under public pressure and government's tough attitude Master Tara Singh went on fast unto death over the issue of a 'Punjabi speaking state', on 15 August 1961. But on the assurance of the government to appoint a commission to look into the Sikh grievances Tara Singh got out of the self-inflicted ordeal on 2 October 1961.

Efforts for the Punjabi Suba continued. Jawahar Lal Nehru died on 27 May 1964. Lal Bahadur Shastri, the new Prime Minister, appointed a Parliamentary Committee under the chairmanship of its speaker Hukam Singh, a former president of the Akali Dal. The Committee unanimously recommended the linguistic division of the Punjab. But before the recommendation of the Committee reached the government, the Congress Working Committee, on the initiative of the succeeding Prime Minister Indira Gandhi, resolved with an overwhelming majority on 2 March 1966 that out of the existing state of Punjab, a state with Punjabi as the state language be formed except for Kharar tehsil which the majority of the commission wanted excluded and which the government of India decided to include in the new state.

However, the division was awfully unfair, unjust and even communally motivated. It did not demarcate the Punjabi speaking areas from the Hindi speaking ones. It only separated the Sikh dominated areas from the Hindu populated areas. Even the capital city of Chandigarh and Punjabi speaking areas of Karnal in Haryana, and Shimla and Kangra in Himachal Pradesh, were kept out of the Punjab. Kangra was 90 per cent Punjabi speaking in 1951 and had declared itself overwhelmingly Hindi speaking ten years later, due to communal reasons. Shimla was also predominantly Punjabi speaking. The Commission and government divided the Punjab into Hindu and Sikh with vengeance. Even the division of river waters became a communal rather than a national issue. To-day, we are only harvesting the crop of injustices, the seeds of which were sown in the past.

Another Commission appointed by Indira Gandhi, unreasonably recommended the productive areas of Fazilka and Abohar to be transferred to Haryana in a barter deal of transferring Chandigarh to the Punjab and this was not acceptable to the Punjab. The controversial issues are hanging fire since the creation of the Punjabi Suba. The way the Punjab was sliced into three parts—Punjab, Haryana and Himachal Pradesh and the way the Punjab was wronged against by the central government has no parallel in Indian history. It was a stunning political setback to the cause of the Punjabi Suba.

Army attack on the Golden Temple Complex
(June 1984)

Indian government believed that some Sikh extremists were staying in the Akal Takht and they needed to be flushed out. The Akalis were also said to be planning a non-co-operation movement with effect from 3rd June 1984, as their political demands were not being accepted. An army attack (officially known by the deceptively chastened appellation of Operation Blue Star) on Akal Takht was ordered. The tanks were employed to demolish the holy precincts of the Akal Takht and in the military action more than three hundred bullets struck the Harmandir—the *sanctum sanctorum*, one of the holiest of the holy temples of the world.

Under the orders of the Indian Prime Minister the army had moved to lay siege to the Golden Temple and the Akal Takht. All channels of communication between the holy complex and the rest of the world were severed. The entire state of Punjab was placed under curfew, leaving life in the Punjab in total paralysis. A most strict censorship was imposed on all newspapers in the state before Indira Gandhi, the Prime Minister, made her last minute 'appeal' to 'accept the framework of settlement the government had outlined.'[20]

As soon as she finished her speech at 9 p.m. on 2 June 1984, the All India Radio announced that all movements in the state were brought to a stand still. Kuldip Nayar and Khushwant Singh took note of this fact. "How could she first order a military operation and then suggest negotiations. And even if the Akalis were ready to talk how could they contact her? All their telephones had been cut off."[21]

It is not particularly in the above context but as a general analysis of Mrs Indira Gandhi, Nayantra Sahgal, daughter of Mrs Vijayalaxmi Pandit (sister of Jawahar Lal Nehru), wrote in her book 'Indira Gandhi's Emergence and Style' that, " Mrs Gandhi's style had reduced politics to a state of confrontation from which nothing but dictatorship could emerge". Nayantra again wrote about Indira Gandhi in a paper presented in March 1994 to a conference of 'Leadership in South Asia' that, " I came to the conclusion that we were moving inexorably towards an authoritarian order not because the Indian situation demanded it, but because of the particular character in charge of us, driven by the needs of her own nature which had very little to do with the reason and rhyme of the Indian situation".

In the beginning of June 1984 a large number of devotees had gathered at the Golden Temple complex to observe the martyrdom anniversary of Guru Arjan Dev. They could not leave the complex before the army operation started. There were thousands of casualties but the official figures claimed a total of 554 civilians/extremists dead and 121 injured during the armed action in the Golden Temple complex between 2 June and 7 June. As against this, according to the official figures again, a total of four officers, four JCOS and 84 other ranks died, while 15 officers, 19 JCOS and 253 other ranks sustained injuries in the course of the operation. A total of 4712 civilians/extremists were reported to have been arrested including 1592 from the Golden Temple complex, 796 from the other religious places and 2324 in operations in the rest of the Punjab.[22]

The army operation was also conducted against 37 other Gurdwaras in the Punjab. Everywhere the people were hunted like jungle game and the human loss rose to thousands as against the cooked small figures given above. The exact number of casualties remained controversial, as the government did not release information on the identity of those killed, wounded and arrested. By modest estimate this army attack caused the loss of over 7000 lives and enormous damage to sacred property at Golden Temple complex alone. It was indeed a great tragedy where army was used to attack the holy places and kill their own civilian population. This military operation resulted in the universal alienation of the Sikhs living in India and elsewhere in the world.

Khushwant Singh wrote, "What I protested against, by returning the *Padma Bhushan*, was that my warnings to the government, through my speeches in Parliament, had been ignored.... Any action to expel the extremists by force could result in blood-bath, which in turn, would hurt and alienate the Sikh community, a large number of whom are not concerned with politics. I am not saying that the government's action was anti-Sikh but it was directed against a shrine which is held sacred by all the Sikhs. The result of the action, and one, which I had been afraid of, has come with a vengeance. Barring a handful, almost all the Sikhs are outraged and I can say that this includes the President of India."[23]

Sikh Carnage (November 1984)

Indira Gandhi, Indian Prime Minister, was shot dead by her two Sikh body-guards on 31 October 1984, presumably because of her ordering an army attack on the Golden Temple complex and many other Gurdwaras. In retaliation the bloody carnage of the Sikhs started in Delhi, under the very eye of the Indian government, in the afternoon of 31 October, and continued till 4 November almost unabated. A fact-finding team jointly organized by the People's Union for Democratic Rights (PUDR) and People's Union for Civil Liberties (PUCL) in the course of investigation from 1 November to 10 November, came to the conclusion that the attacks, on members of the Sikh community in Delhi and its suburbs during this period, far from being a spontaneous expression of 'madness' and of popular 'grief and anger' at Indira Gandhi's assassination, as made out by the authorities, were the outcome of a well-organized plan marked by acts of both deliberate commissions and omissions by important politicians of the then ruling party at the top and by authorities in the administration. The violence that followed, was the handiwork of a determined group, which was inspired by different sentiments altogether.

The attacks on the Sikhs followed a common pattern. The uniformity in the sequence of events at every spot, even in far-flung places, proves beyond doubt that some powerful organized groups masterminded the attacks. The arson was the work of experts. There was also a definite pattern discernible in the choice of the victims made by the assailants. The Sikhs who were killed in these riots mostly belonged to the 20-50 age group. The official figures estimated killed to more than 3000 in Delhi alone. No protection was provided to trains carrying Sikh passengers, arriving from the Punjab or other parts of India. No troops were sent, with the result that every train was left to the mercy of gangsters who dragged out the Sikhs from the incoming train compartments, lynched them, threw their bodies on the platforms or the railway tracks and many were set on fire. Scores of them were done to death in the trains. Many Sikhs were killed in other cities of India.

All through the period from 31 October to 4 November—the height of the riots— the police all over the city uniformly betrayed a common behavioural pattern marked by total absence from the scene or a role of passive spectators or direct participation or abetment in the orgy of violence against the Sikhs. In certain areas while police pickets sat by idly, hundreds of young men, armed with swords, *trishuls* and iron rods blocked the main roads. The Sikh-owned shops were set on fire right under the nose of heavy para-military and police pickets. Mobs burnt the Sikh-owned factories and houses and the inmates were burnt in most barbarous manner. No help came. The administration was a mute spectator to the whole tragedy taking place before their eyes. The unfortunate remark of the slain Prime Minister's successor—her son—that 'when a big tree falls the earth trembles', was widely resented as it justified the violence and the riots that broke out after Indira Gandhi's death. When after the destruction and murders, people went to complain and file FIRs, the police, in many areas, refused to record their complaints.

Men at the top in the administration and the ruling party displayed repeatedly a curious lack of concern often bordering on deliberate negligence of duty and abdication of responsibility through period from 31 October to 4 November. It seemed that the legitimate authorities were superceded and a few ruling party leaders assumed decision-making powers. Report of a joint inquiry into the causes and impact of the riots in Delhi from 31 October to 10 November published jointly in November 1984 by Gobinda Mukhoty, President, PUDR, and Rajni Kothari, President, PUCL, under the title, 'Who are the Guilty?' has named the leaders of the anti-Sikh riots and the perpetrators of the heinous crimes. The above report discusses the roles of the police, the administration, the army, the Congress, the media and the opposition and the public. The above study gives briefly the chronology of events in Delhi from 31 October to 6 November 1984, along with a list of people who actively participated in the anti-Sikh violence.

The survivors of the victims' families are still in the position of the humble beggars of compensation, which is eluding them.

The role of the regularly constituted central government vis-à-vis the barbarous genocide of the Sikhs in the Indian capital itself leaves a big question unanswered for all these years—a decade and a half. A still greater painful thing for the community, that had been the standard bearers in India's freedom struggle, is that they have still to hear a word of regret in the Indian Parliament for what this violence did to the Sikhs.

The Sikhs who migrated to different parts of the world including Canada in the twentieth century have a very vibrant and forceful historical background. The Sikhs have never been a dormant society in any period of history and the impact of the Sikh activities, that took place in their ancestral land, on the Sikhs in their new homes abroad, has always been deep and significant as they have never forgotten their ancestral heritage. Thus, to fully understand the characteristics and mould of the foreign-based Sikhs the knowledge of their historical background is essential, that has been dealt with precisely in the preceding pages. The Sikhs are a small community with big past and bigger future.

REFERENCES

1. Francklin, *The History of the Reign of Shah Aulum*, London, 1798, p.73.

2. Steinbach, *The Punjaub*, London, 1845, p.53.

3. *Akhbar-i-Darbar-i-Mualla*, news dated 10 December 1710(Persian manuscript, Dr Ganda Singh's Private Collection, now at Punjabi University, Patiala) English version by Dr Bhagat Singh, published in *The Panjab Past and Present*, Punjabi University, Patiala, Vol. XVIII-II, October 1984, (pp.1-206), p.49.

4. Teja Singh and Ganda Singh. *A Short History of the Sikhs*, Bombay, 1950. pp. 107-08.

5.   George Forster. *A Journey from Bengal to England.* Vol. I. (1798). reprint Patiala, p.272.

6.   Ali-ud-Din Mufti, *Ibratnama* (1854), The Punjabi Adabi Academy, Lahore, Vol. I, 1961,p.240.

7.   Earnest Trumpp, Introduction, *The Adi Granth*, London, 1877.

8.   Bhagat Singh, *A History of the Sikh Misals*, Punjabi University, Patiala, 1993, p.372.

9.   Bhagat Singh, *Sikh Polity in the Eighteenth and Nineteenth Centuries*, Delhi, 1978, p.101.

10.   *Ibid.* p.70.

11.   Victor Jacquemont, *Letters from India*, Vol. I, London, 1834, p.399.

12.   Alexander Burnes, *The Travels into Bokhara*, Vol. I, London, 1834, p.33. Bhagat Singh, *Maharaja Ranjit Singh and His Times*, Delhi, 1990, p.301.

13.   *The Daily Statesman*, 14 February 1961, 'Observer.'

14.   F.C. Isemonger and J. Slattery, *An Account of the Ghadar Conspiracy*, Lahore, 1921.

15.   R. Furneaux, *Massacre at Amritsar*, London, 1963, p. 153.

16.   Jawahar Lal Nehru, *An Autobiography*, Oxford University Press, New Delhi, Reprint 1982, p.43.

17.   'Babbar Akali Case' *The Civil and Military Gazette*, 10 June 1923.

18.   Lord Mountbatten's broadcast at All India Radio, 3 June 1947.

19.   Indian Government's *White Paper*, 1984, p.108.

20.   Kuldip Nayar and Khushwant Singh, *Tragedy of Punjab: Operation Blue Star and After*, Vision Books, New Delhi, 1984, cited in 'Operation Blue Star' *The Tribune*, Chandigarh, 21 october1984.

21.   Indian Government, White Paper, Annexure, xi, p.169.

22.   Khushwant Singh. 'Khalistan's Dawn: A new chapter in Sikh History', *Gentleman.* Bombay, 15 July 1986.

CHAPTER 2

EARLY SIKH SETTLERS AND
THEIR HARDSHIPS AND SUFFERINGS

Among the first Sikhs to visit Canada were the members of the Sikh Regiment who arrived by train in Vancouver from Montreal, Quebec, during the summer of 1897, en route home from Queen Victoria's Diamond Jubilee celebrations in England. They were seen as soldiers mounted on horsebacks in the streets of Vancouver. They seemed to have been deeply impressed with the beautiful landscape, rushing brooks and streams, winding rivers and interior seas disguised as lakes. They found Canada as a land of incredible beauty. Its geography shaped it in a manner unmatched anywhere else. Heavens were made in Canada's image. These Sikhs went home and told adventurous Sikhs about the opportunities Canada could provide. They made travel plans and were soon thereafter seen in Alberta in 1903, the number of first batch of entrants is not known. It is vaguely estimated that about one hundred East Indians, mostly the Sikhs, had arrived in B.C. between 1897 and 1900. They could not settle at one place due to job uncertainties. They were shuttling between Vancouver and Victoria and were trying to find a satisfactory place to settle down. Before coming to Canada many Sikh soldiers had migrated to Malaya, Hong Kong, Shanghai, Australia, Fiji, New Zealand and Philippines which were under the British domination. They worked in those places as watchmen, policemen and caretakers. They were allured of the opportunities of prosperous life in Canada. The newspapers and the posters distributed in the villages of Punjab also impressed upon the people to go and settle in Canada.

As per the fiscal year reports of 1904-08 the number of the East Indian immigrants to Canada was as under:

Year	1904	1905	1906	1907	1908	Total
	45	387	2124	2623	6	5185

Amongst these arrivals, 98 per cent were the Sikhs and the remaining were Muslims and Hindus. Since the natives were called the red Indians, the people coming from India began to be called the East Indians. Though primarily I mean the Sikhs but when I have to include non-Sikh Indians who are hardly 5 per cent, I am obliged to use the term East-Indians. This term is a label used for persons with origins in Ceylon, India, Pakistan and Fiji also. It is also applied to persons immigrating from Africa and elsewhere who trace their ancestry to India. This often led to the mixing up and confusing identities. In the earlier Canadian government records all the Sikhs who hailed from India were wrongly stated as 'Hindus'.

All those living in India are Indians but all are not Hindus. The Indian population comprises various religious groups or communities as the Sikhs, Muslims, Hindus, Christians, etc. The religion of the Sikhs is distinct and complete in itself as those of others. I.M. Muthanna absurdly believed and indiscreetly recorded that "all those people who hailed from India were stated as Hindus, and that was perfectly correct because every non-Hindu or his father or grandfather, was once a Hindu. This applied to the Sikhs, Muslims, Christians and others who are from India and of the Indian origin."[1] He lacks even the minimum sense of history.

Regarding the names of the earlier immigrants to Canada, we have some scanty information. Vir Singh Majhail of village Gudde (district Amritsar) is said to have arrived in Vancouver in 1902. About half a dozen Sikh policemen are also believed to have come to B.C. in 1902. Ten East Indians came here in 1903. The names of many people who came to B.C. in 1906 are available in records. They include Mayo Singh Paldi, Hazara Singh Sangha, Waryam Singh Jaura, Partap Singh Johal, Duman Singh, Dasonda Singh granthi, Bhawan Singh Sihota, Bachan Singh Dhillon and Sohan Singh Bhullar.

An old picture shows some Sikh railway workers dumping truckloads of debris at Frank, Alberta, in 1903. Another picture shows the Sikhs newly arrived in Canada with their truncks and bedrolls at CPR station, Frank, Alberta, in the same year, that is, in 1903. The exact number of arrivals before 1904 is not known. The Punjabi immigrants who arrived in Vancouver in 1904 belonged to the villages of Sur Singh, Kharaudi, Gudde and Halwara. According to one recent study, the Sikhs had been in Canada by 1880 and had a Gurdwara established in Golden in BC by 1890.[2]

The presence of the Sikhs in Golden (B.C.) in the 1880s seems probable from local evidence. In the survey of the 'Churches of the Columbia Valley', on page 57 of 'Kin Basket Country', compiled by Miss Heather Miller, she quotes Rev. McRay, the Presbyterian minister in Golden (1902-13): "During the later 1880s a number of Hindus (as the Sikhs were then called) moved here to work in newly developed C.R.L mill. They built a Hindu Temple (Gurdwara) not far from where the School Board Office is now, around which most of the Hindus (Sikhs) built their houses. They were of the Sikh religion."

When the Rev. invited the Sikhs to church they would take off their shoes before entering the church as they do when entering the Gurdwara.

The above information was supplied on 4 May 1981 to Ray Hundle— a Sikh resident of Golden, by Fred Bjarnason, Secretary, Golden and District Historical Society, Golden,B.C. Ray Hundle writes that the Sikhs came to Golden in 1880 according to Golden museum records and old-timers, through Columbia River steamship. These Sikhs, in all probability, came there from a route different from the one followed by those who came to Vancouver in 1897 and following years.

In 1979 Ray Hundle interviewed an 85-year old resident of Golden, named Billey, who told him that the early Sikh workers of the mill included Surjan Singh—supervisor in a small sawmill and Hari Singh who was called doctor as he could fix the dislocated legs and arms of the mill workers. Both of these Sikhs left Golden after having worked in the mill for about two decades and Hardit Singh took over as the foreman of CRLC lumber mill. Later Hardit Singh shifted to Victoria and established there a mill named Plumper Bay Mill, Victoria, which in 1979 was being looked after by Hardit Singh's grandson Piara Singh.

45-50 Punjabis who lived in Golden had moved away from there in 1927 when their lumber mill was closed due to massive forest fire. Ray Hundle also recorded interview in 1979 with an octogenerian resident in Golden, named Norm King who remembered the names of Hardit Singh, Wattan Singh, Hari Singh, Arjan Singh and Kartar Singh who worked in the mill there. Norm King confirmed that the Sikhs lived in Golden in 1880 and the Sikh temple there. Norm King also told that at the time of leaving Golden the Sikhs dismantled the Gurdwara and gave its floor carpet to the King family.

The living of the Sikhs there from 1880 to 1927 is also supported by the police and hospital records of Golden and no Sikh lived there from 1927 to 1961. The present Sikh families settled there since 1962. Later the Sikhs of Golden demanded the site of the Old Sikh temple for constructing a new one there and they had a temple of worship of their own.

It seems that the Sikh existence in Golden in 1880s was independent of the Sikhs who came a little later in 1897 and after and settled in Vancouver Island. The handful of the Sikhs at Golden, with passive existence, belonged to a different group of immigrants, without any history to attract notice of the writers except that they entered Canada a few years earlier. But the main or the exclusive thrust of the Sikh immigrants stepping on the Canadian soil was via Vancouver Island. Whether the Sikhs of Golden had any contact with the Sikhs of Vancouver is not yet known to history. They were all good workers and good citizens as affirmed by Norm King. These were uneducated and unskilled people.

These were uneducated and unskilled people. Their intention was to make money and return to their country. A significant number of these Punjab peasants had mortgaged their land to reach Canada. These early visitors used to sleep on mattresses filled with sawdust. They brought their own quilts or blankets from India to be used in winter.

Life was very tough with cold mornings, very chilly nights and an air of distinct inhospitality. They were offered the most unpleasant jobs that no white man would accept.

In lumber mills, in the vicinity of Vancouver and Victoria, they could get $1.50 to $2.0′, a day. The lived frugally, three or four of them sharing a room and thu , saving some money. Besides, being needed at the sawmills, these hard v. orking people were wanted by the railway contractors, farmers and fruit-growers and mine contractors. They also worked in dairy farms, fish plants and forests to chop wood.

Besides the East Indians, Chinese and Japanese had also entered Canada in larger numbers and with effect from earlier dates. The Chinese were the first of the Asians to migrate to Canada in 1840. In the census of 1891 there were 9129 Chinese in the whole of Canada out of whom 8910 were in British Columbia alone. In the 1890s there were about 1500 Japanese people in British Columbia and in the first four months of the year 1900, about 400 new-comers landed on the shores of Canada. There was a great hue and cry among the different associations of workers that Canada in general and British Columbia in particular 'was being overrun by Japanese and Chinese', and total abolition of the oriental immigration was demanded through resolutions. In 1900 the total population of British Columbia was estimated at three hundred thousand out of whom 40,000 were working white men and 20,000 Asians. This was not acceptable to the working classes of the Canadians.

In the light of this situation we can easily visualise the future prospects of the newcomers, the East Indians, and the type of welcome awaiting them in Canada. From 1901 to 1904 the government of British Columbia seriously thought about restricting rather abolishing the entry of the immigrants. The Oriental Commission also recommended strict restriction on immigration. Sometime later, the Kootney sawmill's white workers refused to allow the oriental workers along with them, despite mill officials wanting to have the Asians work in the mill.

By 1906, 2556 East Indians, almost all of them Sikhs, had entered Canada. They were nearly all old soldiers. Some of the employers sympathized with them and gave them employment as they had fought for the British Empire, instead of giving work to the total aliens. Many white Canadians were keen to keep Canada a white country. They wanted the aliens to be turned out as these Chinese, Japanese and the Sikhs were not going to adapt to the Canadian way of life.

Henry Gladstone, a nephew of William Gladstone, the famous Prime Minister of England, came to Vancouver in October 1906. Earlier he had been in India for fifteen years and knew a lot about the Sikhs. He expressed his amazement over the Sikhs doing coolies' labour. "They are men of high caste in their own country and have been employed in military work. These men work in India as policemen and military patrol. Not many years ago it was against the rule of their caste to travel overseas but their work as soldiers of the empire has taken them away from the idea."[3] Henry Gladstone also told the Canadian whites that "they (the Sikhs) will not assimilate in British Columbia. If I have any knowledge of them they do not want to assimilate. They will make a little money and go back to their country." In Canada they were feeling themselves as prisoners of circumstances.

The largest contingent of Indian immigrants comprising 901 persons arrived in Vancouver on the Canadian Pacific steamer Monteagle on 12 September 1907.

The housing problem of these earlier Sikh immigrants was simply miserable and awful. Far from living in comfortable houses they had hardly a shelter that could properly protect them from the cold of Canada's winter. The city council came to their rescue. A city official said, "no one desired them to wander about in the streets with no covering for their heads save their turbans or no bed but sidewalks." The mayor of Vancouver ordered to pitch a big tent to shelter them from the unfavourable weather conditions.[4]

The Sikhs were so much pleased with the humane gesture of the city council that they decided to meet all the costs of the shelter without making the city to bear any expenses. This showed that the Sikhs were not monetarily poor but had difficulties in respect of living accommodation. In the early stages the East Indians, some times, 'spent the nights in the open air with scantiest clothes, huddled together to keep out the cold.' One Atma Singh rented accommodation near the Cemetery Road where more than 100 Sikhs 'swarmed in the stables and chicken houses'. Now and then, 'the Sikhs died of cold and these deaths were often concealed from the authorities so that the community was not disgraced for inadequate attention to the insufficiently dressed co-religionists.

Most of them lived in the fields and thick forests of B.C. and would come to the city to purchase grocery and other necessities of life. These Sikhs were victims of racism to the extent that the Sikhs who died there were not allowed to be cremated in the cemetery of the white people. They were cremated in the jungle away from the gaze of the whites at odd hours. The whites did not at all socialize with them, thus subjecting them to total aloofness and segregation from the whites. Through their treatment the whites kept the pioneers in a state of suffocation for decades together.

We are unhappy because we are afflicted with adversity. The fact is that the greatest affliction of life is never to be afflicted. It is like threshing which separates the wheat from the chaff. Afflictions purify and strengthen us. He, who wrestles with you, strengthens your muscles. The Sikhs have always fought against adversity with marvellous courage, never complaining against fate. Leighton has said, "Adversity is the diamond-dust Heaven polishes its jewels with." Bad times are a part of life. No one can escape of them. No one is an all-time favourite of God. No one can have all sunshine, and no dark, dismal clouds.

"While man sits on the cushion of advantages, he goes to sleep. When pushed, tormented, defeated, he has a chance to learn something. It is in such a situation that he learns of his ignorance, is cured of the insanity of conceit, acquires moderation and real skill" says Emerson.

Men of courage do not wait for circumstances to turn favourable; they make them favourable. An ounce of action is better than a ton of brooding. The Sikhs never keep thinking with heads hanging but act with heads raised. It is not what befalls us that matters but how we react to it. There are millions who have gone under the steamroller of the fate in one blow. But there are some that, despite repeated blows from misfortune, have stuck to their guns. They have mastered the art of rolling along with the blow. They stagger but get up. Who can say that the Sikhs are otherwise? They had to go a long way before they had a place in the Canadian sun. They lay on their backs and looked up at the stars.

The Canadian whites have been making excuses to get rid of the East Indians. Sometimes they argued that the climate of Canada was unsuitable to them, so they should go back to their country and save themselves from the vagaries of the weather, as they were accustomed to the conditions of a tropical climate. In 1908, the government told the Sikhs that "a large number of them were likely to be out of work during winter and were liable to become public charge and, therefore, measures for their deportation to Hong Kong and possibly to India, will be adopted"[5]. Their spokesman, Professor Teja Singh, holder of Master's Degree from the Harvard University (USA), an academic royalty among the Sikhs in Canada at that time, told the government that the Sikhs had fully adjusted themselves to the climate of Canada and they faced no problem from it. They belonged to Hoshiarpur, Jalandhar, Ludhiana, Ferozepur, Amritsar and Lahore districts of Punjab.

In order to save the Sikhs from unemployment some of the Sikhs under the advice of Teja Singh planned to purchase lands in B.C. and settle them in farming. Starting of an agricultural colony was contemplated with the purchase of a tract of 441 acres of agricultural land for $41,000, in North Vancouver, located between Skunk and Capilano River, in front of the English Bay. Another tract of land was also negotiated for the proposed market-gardens. The Sikhs agreed to pay the initial cash amount and the remaining amount in two instalments. What happened to these deals nothing specific is known. In the meantime, Col. Swayne, who had served in India for many years, told at a meeting in Ottawa that "Among the people in the East Indians colony on the West Coast, first place should be accorded to the Sikhs. This tribe had been the hardiest of all the Indian tribes to conquer but once subdued they had remained steadfast in their loyalty to the crown."[6] Thus, the Sikhs were always ready to face every eventuality, whether it is from the climate or from unemployment.

The Sikhs were Clean But their Living Conditions were Unclean

The Canadian whites, time and again, charged the Sikhs of being unclean which they were not. They would rise early, wash themselves and offer their prayers before going out to work. Physical or bodily cleanliness is one of the essentials of their religious code of conduct. The Sikh religion has a cult of bathing and they think cleanliness a virtue. Against them, the Canadian or European and English whites would avoid taking bath in the morning or daily and would carry the laziness of their night-sleep with them to their jobs. The turbans and un-shorn hair on head and beard bothered the narrow-minded whites to the extent of branding them unclean.

The British who came in contact with the Sikhs in India knew that keeping themselves perfectly clean was a religion with them. Henry Gladstone, answering the charge that Indians had filthy habits, said on 18 October 1906, "that the Sikhs are scrupulously clean and I regard them as a very fine race of men."[7]

Dr. S.H. Lawson, who was a ship's surgeon on the Canadian Pacific Railway steamers, *Monteagle* and *Tartar,* wrote: "It was my duty to make a thorough physical examination of each immigrant at Hong Kong and, although at first I was strongly prejudiced against them, I lost this prejudice after thousands of them had passed through my hands and I had compared them with white steerage passengers I had seen on the Atlantic. I refer in particular to the Sikhs and I am not exaggerating in the least when I say that they were one hundred per cent cleaner in their habits and free from disease than the European steerage passengers I had come in contact with. The Sikhs impressed me as a clean, manly, honest race."[8]

Col. John Smith, Political Adviser to the Maharaja of Mysore, on his way back to India after spending his holidays in England, passed through Vancouver in March 1908. He said, "Nearly all those I talked with are the Sikhs. It distressed me to hear their tales of woe. These Sikhs are a brave, sensitive and proud people. I know all these from experience in many campaigns. Have sensitive feelings for them.... In India it is a common sight in the East Indians washing at the river banks. On the average, I should say they are cleaner than the white men are.... And they are proudly sensitive to their ways of life and culture."[9]

The Sikhs always honour man's laws and also never break God's laws. The Sikhs know Plato putting laws above man and they respect these laws till they are changed.

Regarding their living conditions, undoubtedly, they lived in small and ill-equipped houses. In fact, they did not live in houses rather they lived in dirty matchboxes. As they were the new-comers it would take some time to be able to earn enough as to build good houses for themselves. In those early days they were living in Canada without their families who were back in India. Whatever little they saved, they sent it to their families who depended on them. They could not save much from their meagre wages and thus could not spend enough on themselves and naturally they could not maintain a decent standard of living. The host society was hostile and jobs were uncertain and they were living thousands of miles away from their home country. The medical officers could not but report about their quarters or shacks in bad condition, ill-ventilated, badly plumbed and damp. To live in the standard of earlier white settlers was pretty difficult for the new immigrants. The health officers were not incorrect when they reported that in the living quarters of the East Indians the air was suffocating as many men used to live in one room. The health officers sometimes recommended to the city council to destroy those unhygienic houses. The new whites arriving from Europe and the other Asians lived in no better dwellings. Most of the houses of the Chinese and Japanese were in no way better than those of the East Indians. But that provided no justification against criticism of the East Indians by the city health department.

At the mill sites the accommodation provided to the workers was equally sub-standard and unfit for healthy living. The mills' bunkhouses were awfully slummy, packed with dwellers like animals, huddled in an inadequate space. The clothes of the sawmill workers were always in very shabby condition covered and soiled with a thick layer of sawdust. They burnt wood in the kitchen. A big group of them would keep a common mess, pooled the expenses and had a simple repast. They wore simple clothes and most of them did not have sufficient warm clothes to meet the biting cold of the winter months. Anyhow, they braved all that and in due course of time a noticeable change in their condition came and they pulled themselves out of the criticism of the health officials. At present, the Sikhs can compete in living standards favourably with any section of the Canadian society. They always achieve their cherished goals through dedication, persistence and undrooping spirits. Their motto is 'never give in'. They know no defeat in their aims. They refuse to surrender.

Asiatic Exclusion League (1907)

During these times there was a strong feeling among the Canadians that Canada should be preserved as the exclusive heritage of the whites and the Asiatics should be totally banned from entry into this country. The Asiatic Exclusion League was formed on 12 August 1907. They tried to create trouble in Vancouver. Some 30 whites from Bellingham, America, a few miles from Canadian border, crossed over to Canada where they were joined by more rioters. More than the East Indians the Chinese and Japanese suffered the loss of their goods as their shops were ransacked and their dwellings set on fire, in Vancouver. The Sikh workers had to stay inside their houses and they had to go without work for some time. They avoided confrontationist postures. These riots were known as the anti-Asiatic riots of September 1907. In these days a song that became popular in British Columbia was titled as 'White Canada for Ever' — This is the voice of the West and it speaks to the world:

The rights that our fathers have given
We'll hold by right and maintain by might,
Till the foe is backward driven.
We welcome as brothers all white men still,
But the shifty yellow race,
Whose word is vain, who oppress the weak,
Must find another place.

Chorus:

Then let us stand united all
And show our father's might,
That won the home we call our own,
For white man's land we fight.
To oriental grasp and greed
We'll surrender, no never.
Our watchword be "God save the king"
White Canada for ever.

This thinking of the whites added to the woes of the Asians. The Sikhs, by their appearance were more conspicuous than the others were. In the Okanagan valley, the Sikhs already employed there, lost their work. The white labourers tried to scare them away. These pioneer settlers did not consider it proper to clash with the aggressive whites as the government always stood on the side of the whites. As a sensible step, under the unfavourable circumstances, the Sikhs bowed to the inevitable and voiced no expression of anger against anyone. Thus, tactfully they avoided the situations that were bound to damage their interests. At this stage, much against their tribal characteristic of settling the scores expeditiously, with the help of their muscles, they preferred recourse to petition and legal procedure.

Herbert H. Stevens, an alderman of the Vancouver City Council, and later an M.P., was the leader of the Asiatic Exclusion League. He was an intellectual spark plug, terribly hostile to the East Indians. His rancorous language caused deep resentment among the Indian community. He wanted these foreigners to be shipped home at all costs. He said, "We contend that the destiny of Canada is best left in the hands of the Anglo-Saxon race, and are 'unalterably and irrevocably' opposed to any move which threatens in the slightest degree this position.... As far as Canada is concerned, it shall remain white, and our doors shall be closed to the East Indians as well as other Orientals."[10]

Sir Wilfred Laurier, Canadian Prime Minister (1896-1911) also wanted in the heart of his hearts to get rid of the East Indians but his office stood in the way of his saying it openly. In a garbled language, and avoiding to look racist, he puts it as under: "The East Indians were unsuited to live in the climatic condition of British Columbia, and were a serious disturbance to industrial and economic conditions in that part of the dominion." Wilfred Laurier further remarked in a letter to Lord Minto, viceroy of India, that "Strange to say the East Indians... are looked upon by our people in British Columbia with still more disfavour than the Chinese. They seem to be less adaptable to our ways and manners than all the other oriental races that come to us." The Prime Minister had to move with his flock if he had to be in the saddle comfortably. The British Indian government endorsed all steps being proposed by the Canadian government to keep Canada a white country. The Indian government always gave a cold shoulder to the Sikh immigrants whenever they requested or petitioned for help to be out of the situation in which they were involved because of Canada government's hostile postures. Through orders-in- council in 1908 the new immigrants from India were prevented from entering Canada. The details of these orders may be studied in the chapter on immigration.

Canadian Government's plan to send the Sikhs to British Honduras

By 1908, the number of the East Indians in Canada was only 5185. But even such a small number seemed to pose a problem before the Canadian government. They wanted to get rid of them by all means. The government planned to shift them to British Honduras in the Central America. But it was a little difficult to throw them away without their consent.

William Charles Hopkinson, a Euro-Indian, in British Columbia service, working as Vancouver Immigration official and interpreter, and, co-ordinated a spy-ring within B.C.'s Indo-Canadian community, offered to contact the influential Sikhs in connection with their transfer to British Honduras. He, who was born in Delhi in 1880 of an English father and an Indian mother, was fully conversant with Punjabi and Hindi. He contacted Bhai Balwant Singh who was, at that time, the first priest at the 2nd Avenue Gurdwara. Hopkinson put the proposal before Balwant Singh, assuring him that the ex-soldiers and pensioners from India would be absorbed in the armed forces and the police in Honduras. They would also be given guard duties there and others would be provided with land to cultivate. The Sikhs will have highly paying vocations as poultry, sheep breeding, piggery and dairying. All the inquiries and objections of Balwant Singh were duly answered by Hopkinson.

In a meeting held on 18 October 1908, in Vancouver, the Sikh leaders decided to send a delegation comprising four person— J.B. Harkin, Secretary to the Interior Ministry of the federal government, William Hopkinson—the Vancouver official and interpreter, and Nagar Singh and Sham Singh, representatives of the Sikh community. The delegation reached Honduras on 25 October 1908 and returned to Vancouver on 7 November 1908.

In the British Honduras the government members of the delegation made all efforts to persuade the Sikh representatives to form a favourable opinion about their shifting to the new colony. But Nagar Singh and Sham Singh talked to about thirty Sikhs who had been residing there for the last forty years. They had been brought there from India under a contract to work on the plantations with many promises made to them. Those old people told about their pitiable lot, ill-treatment and broken promises. They had been, all through, yearning to return to India but could not, because of financial stringencies.

In the meantime, the media would not lag behind to play their anti-Sikh role. The editorial of *The Daily Province* said that sending the Sikhs to the British Honduras was an extremely good solution (of getting rid of them). The editor advised the Sikhs not to miss the opportunity. In Canada they could not compete with their rivals in the market and moreover they would be entirely without work in winter and autumn and there would be scarcely sufficient food for them for winter. The climate was warm in that colony throughout the year as they had it in India.[11]

The government representatives felt that the representatives of the Sikhs were not likely to submit a favourable report to their community about the suitability of the colony. Hopkinson, the official interpreter, unsuccessfully tried to bribe the Sikh members with a bag of $3,000, which they declined to accept. On return from the British Honduras the Sikh members reported as under:

1. The climate of the colony was unsuitable to the East Indians. The place was infested with mosquitoes and malaria was common everywhere.
2. The saltish sea-water was used for bathing and it was injurious to health.

3. Stored rain water was used for all purposes and no fresh water was available anywhere.
4. Monthly wages were between eight and twelve dollars. It was very difficult to live in that meagre income.
5. The poor residents could not get fresh milk and butter and the available cooking oil was very expensive.
6. The Indians already settled there were living a miserable life. The old Indians there wanted to go back to their country but they had no money to undertake journey.
7. Only contractual labour was available there and unless the contract matured they could not take up any other work.
8. They were offered a bribe, for a favourable report, which they spurned as sinful.

The congregation at Vancouver Gurdwara passed a unanimous resolution on 22 November 1908 to reject the offer to go to Honduras. The Sikhs, under Prof. Teja Singh's motivation who was a man of vision, a man of enormous talent and a total man of principles, hijacked this nefarious plan. By disposition he was appeasing rather than a provoking person. At times he was slightly aggressive but without being hurtful. He had a rare moral force about him, as a result of which, he foisted his personality òn the East Indians. Meeting him was some what like meeting a whole Sikh way of life such as Sikh ethos and Sikh culture. Prof. Teja Singh who had come to Vancouver, B.C., on 17 October 1908, emphatically said that the Sikhs would not go to Honduras. The climate in Canada suited them all right and more than seventy per cent of them were employed and the arrangement of work was being made for the remaining as well. They were farming people and unemployed men would be settled on farms leaving none to be a charge on the government. Any step to deport them from Canada would be fraught with bad consequences. The plan aimed at total Sikh ethnic cleansing from Canada. But due to the vehement opposition of the East Indians and their power of resistance, the government plan fizzled out with J.B. Harkin informing the government on 23 November 1908 that the Sikh delegation was against sending the Sikhs to British Honduras.

In a speech Prof. Teja Singh asserted that to work on an average of ten to twelve dollars a month under an indenture system would be strongly opposed by the Sikhs. This was akin to slavery. The Sikh delegates likened the British Honduras' conditions to that of the Andaman island, a British penal settlement in the Bay of Bengal. The Sikhs categorically told the

Canadian government that this plan might be most desirable to them but it was most disastrous for the Sikhs. Hence it was announced to be totally unacceptable to them. After knowing the strong reaction to the government's proposal of sending the Sikhs to Honduras, the official of the Interior Ministry in Ottawa informed the Sikhs in December 1908 of their decision that "No official steps will be taken to transport the unemployed Sikhs to British Honduras in view of the opposition offered to the proposition." The Sikhs considered it a victory as they emerged unscathed from the Canadian government's move to throw them into the hell. As a result to the opposition of the Sikhs to the government's plan they were threatened with deportation. "A large number of the East Indians were likely to be out of work during the winter and were liable to become public charges, and therefore, measures for their deportation to Hong Kong and possibly to India will be adopted."[12]

Brigadier Eric John Swayne, Governor of British Honduras, who met the leaders of the East Indians in Vancouver, learnt that they would not agree to the British Honduras migration proposals under any circumstances. He had known the capabilities of Sikh policemen while he was in India and had tested that they couldn't be corrupted. He told that during his visit to Vancouver, he had asked some leading Sikhs at a conference to give him twelve of their countrymen for the purpose of doing police duty at Belize, the capital city of British Honduras. He also asked for the services of ex-army men and offered them twenty dollars per month for each as salary and they would be given a pension of ten dollars per month at the conclusion of ten years service. But the Sikhs whom he met told him that none of the Sikhs would like to go to the British Honduras. Later he went to Ottawa where he reported that his trip had proved fruitless.

Proposal to raise a Sikh regiment

During his visit to British Columbia Sams Hughes, Minister for Militia, expressed a desire to form a Sikh regiment. He said that it was a pity to see such excellent material being wasted without exploiting their talents. Captain Gordon Adjutant of the 72nd Highlanders, who had served in India said that the ex-soldiers of the king who were then in Canada should have been given an opportunity to participate in the country's national life to which they were accustomed. That would also do away with much of the discontent that then existed. [13] This proposal was appreciated in the beginning but later the government got lukewarm towards it thinking that it would be a useless regiment as Canada had none to fight against. This proposal also did not find favour with the press.

But Captain Gordon vehemently supported the move of the Sikh militia. Praising the Sikh soldiers he said. "The Indian troops are second to none in the world and are really a most formidable and highly efficient body of men. They are used to fighting... and had to guard their frontiers for centuries in the North." But the proposal failed to catch the imagination of the public and the press and it fell through without any publicity. Under the stress of circumstances many of them moved to Washington, Oregon and California, where they found employment in farms and factories. In Canada, in due course of time, the number of immigrants reduced considerably.

Guru Nanak Mining and Trust Company

Prof. Teja Singh conceived an idea of starting a Trust Company for the economic welfare of the Sikhs living in Canada. Guided by Teja Singh, the Sikhs approved to register Guru Nanak Mining and Trust Company with its headquarters established at the Vancouver Sikh Temple, at 1866 West 2nd Avenue. The aim of this company was to place the East Indians in British Columbia on strong footing and enable them to live with dignity and honour. Half of the profit of the shareholders was to be donated for missionary and educational purposes.

As per company charter of September 1909, its objectives were:
1. to invest in mining to arrange employment for East Indian workers,
2. to purchase land to settle unemployed workers on farming,
3. to establish Guru Nanak Hostel for East Indian students,
4. to set up their own Trust Company to meet the banking needs of the workers,
5. to open a shopping market provisioned with Indian goods,
6. to set up a company for home builders,
7. and to establish an Indian Supply Trust Company.

In pursuance of the Company's plans they decided to buy one fourth shares of the gold mine in Jackson Ville and sent money to Mr. Crawford. The Company's by-laws were drafted and it was got registered in a week's time. With the help of Dr Knapp, a real estate man, a block of 250 acres of land was purchased for $25,000 near Eagle Harbour. A down payment of $10,000 was made for the deal. The remaining payment of $15,000 was also sent to Crawford. The whole enterprise was explained to the East Indians at a big meeting. Later, due to some misunderstanding, in respect of the funds, gold mine shares were withdrawn. The plan fell down through its alleged cracks. Crawford returned $19,000 to the Sikhs for $15,000 received from them. The members of the committee, thus closing down the whole project also sold the 250 acres of land near the harbour. Had the Sikhs remained united to run the Trust Company it would have served the community most wonderfully during their hard times and would have proved a great Sikh banking institution in Canada with the prospect of starting many of its branches all over the country.

Indian Revolutionaries enter Canada

The Indian revolutionaries were gradually entering Canada and US with plans to ultimately fight for the liberation of their country.

Guru Dutt Kumar was one of them who pursued his mission very actively. Originally he was a native of Bannu on the North West Frontier of India. After brief stints in various vocations he became an instructor in Urdu and Hindi at the National College in Calcutta. Kumar lived at Marathi Lodge in a boarding house that had been marked by CID as a gathering place for revolutionaries. He met Tarak Nath there for the first time. On Tarak Nath's suggestion Kumar migrated to Canada in October 1907 and soon thereafter set up a grocery shop in Victoria. In December 1909 Kumar opened *Swadesh Sewak*—a home where revolutionaries used to meet under the garb of Indians attending night classes in English and Mathematics.

Tarak Nath and Kumar planned to shake the loyalty of the Sikh troop in India. Kumar took up the task of publishing *Swadesh Sewak* — a monthly in Punjabi and Urdu, and sent its copies in bulk to India. It reproduced articles from such revolutionary papers of India as *Bande Mataram, Liberator* and Shyamaji Krishna Verma's *Indian Sociology* published from London, Paris or Geneva.

The Indian government placed *Swadesh Sewak* under prohibition list in March 1911. Hopkinson kept a watchful eye on the activities of Kumar and his associates but could not do any thing against them.

As usual when Stevens MP spoke against the East Indian immigrants stating that the orientals had retarded the progress of the country Guru Dutt Kumar who was Secretary, Hindustani Association, stated:

"Let Mr. Stevens study the history of the British. Where were the people of Great Britain 2000 years ago? The Anglo-Saxon race is nothing but a part of the Caucasian race which is the same as the Aryan race, and we the East Indians are proud to belong to such a race which was highly civilized when the people of Britain and Europe were mere savages.

"The East Indians have accomplished more in these five years they have been in British Columbia than any other labouring class of people of

England, Italy or Russia have done.... They are quite willing to get into the untrodden parts of Canada and cultivate the land."[14]

Tarak Nath Das, Guru Dutt Kumar and Rahim Husain were active members of the Socialist Party and always actively participated in the demands of the Khalsa Diwan Society, Vancouver. Under Kumar, Rahim and Tarak Nath the ghadar movement was considerably intensified in Canada.

To pursue his revolutionary work among the Sikhs in the Far East, Kumar left Vancouver in the spring of 1913 for Manila, a strategic base. Regarding Tarak Nath Das and Husain Rahim more information is provided in the chapter on 'Ghadar Movement'.

Armed Group Rivalry among the Sikhs

William C. Hopkinson, an official of the immigration department as referred to earlier, was always on the track of the members or supporters of the ghadar organisation. His chief informer was Bela Singh, 'the immigration dog' as he was called by the Sikhs. Bela Singh was an ex-soldier and signaller in the 20th Punjab Regiment, and, after being released, came to Canada in 1910. He was tall and straight with military bearing and was considered to be 'the handsomest Sikh' in Canada as *The Vancouver Sun* wrote on 6 November 1914. But at the same time he was the most dangerous and unreliable person. He was suspected of passing on news about the Sikhs to the immigration authorities. He was an employee in the office of the immigration department, getting $62.50 per month. He was the leader of his group and the chief tipster, misguider and back-room boy of the immigration department. He was always on the mission of espionage for which he received every help from the concerned quarters.

Bela Singh had a group of some twenty men, through whom he used to operate. A string of murders took place in the ensuing months. One Harnam Singh, Bela Singh's loyal supporter, disappeared on 17 August 1914, and a few days later his dead body was found. Within the next couple of days, a young man, who was later acquitted, accidentally killed Arjan Singh, another spy of Hopkinson. At the post-funeral service of Arjan Singh in the Gurdwara on 5 September 1914, with a criminal brute active inside him, Bela Singh mortally shot Bhag Singh, the president of the Gurdwara Committee, when the latter was kneeling forward before *Guru Granth Sahib* at the time of offering *ardas* (prayer). One Battan Singh, by some named Badan Singh, who rushed towards Bela Singh, was also shot at and mortally wounded. Bela Singh was holding pistols in both hands and seven others were also shot at. Then, in the melee Bela Singh escaped but was later arrested. The worst thing about the incident was that it took place inside the Gurdwara and in the presence of the holy *Guru Granth Sahib*. The Sikhs were awfully enraged over it.

Bela Singh was put under trial for murdering two men and injuring seven. He told the court that he did it in self-defence. On 21 October 1914, Hopkinson, 37 years old, was to appear in the court to testify that Bela Singh fired the shots in self-defence. Hopkinson was standing at the door of the Assize Court on the Georgia Street, ready to enter the court room when Mewa Singh Lopoke, 34 years old, and of robust physique and a devout Sikh, accompanied by some other Sikhs, came up to Hopkinson. He pulled two revolvers, one in each hand, and shot at Hopkinson. After the first shot the victim tried to grapple with Mewa Singh who instantly pumped into his body four more bullets and killed him on the spot and surrendered himself to the police.

Malcolm Reid, the immigration officer, was also a marked man, but he was transferred to Ottawa for security reasons.

Hopkinson was a loyal civil servant and a very valued member of the Dominion Immigration Office in Vancouver. Sometimes he disguised himself as a Sikh, and discovered their plans. He made all efforts to unearth the plans of the ghadarites. He was also instrumental in the deportation of Bhagwan Singh Giani, an active member of the ghadar party, who had returned to the United States after travelling up to Manila. Bhagwan Singh's deportation angered the Sikh community against Bela Singh and Hopkinson. A general feeling developed among the Sikhs that Hopkinson was the enemy of the Sikhs and he served the interests of the Canadian government as well as the British Indian government. He was a difficult man to figure out. Frown on his face was a permanent fixture. There were some active supporters of the ghadar movement in Canada and they felt that there were some traitors working against India, giving out their secrets to the Canadian government, and they planned that 'they had better fix them (traitors) first'. There had been plots to assassinate Hopkinson. It was alleged that he had been personally hostile to some Sikhs in Vancouver. The nature of his duty was delicate and dangerous indeed. His efforts to save Bela Singh further antagonized the Sikhs against him. Therefore, Mewa Singh decided to liquidate Hopkinson before he could speak in favour of the murderer Bela Singh and bring about his release.

Mewa Singh's trial was slated for 30 October 1914, and it lasted hardly for less than two hours (an hour and forty minutes). Mewa Singh did not offer any defence and he confessed his guilt. The jury discussed the case only for five minutes and recommended the death penalty.

Mewa Singh's confessional statement was as under:

"My religion does not teach me to bear enmity with anybody, no matter what class, creed or order he belongs to, nor had I any enmity with Hopkinson. I heard that he was oppressing my poor people very much....I being a staunch Sikh, could no longer bear to see the wrong done both to my innocent countrymen and the dominion of Canada.... And I, performing the duty of a true Sikh and remembering the name of God, will proceed towards the scaffold with the same amount of pleasure as the hungry babe does towards the mother. I shall gladly have the rope put around my neck thinking it to be a rosary of God's name...." His confession matched his action. He was goodness personified. He was a super-nice man. If one feels good after the act it is moral and if one feels bad after the act it is immoral. A brave man learns to obey his conscience. Mewa Singh felt that he had discharged his duty as a true Sikh and felt morally elevated. He remained true to his conscience, which is God's presence in man. He, who has not found a cause to die for, has not learnt how to live. Mewa Singh strongly believed that cowards die many times before their death, while the valiant never taste death but once. He had inherited a strong legacy of sacrifice against injustice and discrimination. Besides all said, he was a larger than life figure who had an enormous impact on the Sikh community. Thereby, he earned a name of heroic stature and has gone down in Canadian Sikh history as a personification of Sikh dignity, courage and sacrifice.

Justice Morrison convicted Mewa Singh and pronounced his judgement: "I sentence you to be taken back to the jail from whence you came and detained until the 11th day of January 1915, when you shall be hanged by the neck until you are dead."

Amidst utter silence of the court, Mewa Singh bowed his head and was led away. He was calm and resigned as he was convinced in his heart of hearts that he had done it in a good cause. To face the coming death, he derived strength from his intense faith in his religion and spiritual calmness from his belief that through Hopkinson's murder he had served his suffering people and saved them from an evil-minded and a hostile person's nefarious designs against them. He said that he was not afraid of death and was prepared to pay the price for a noble cause. His mission of the riddance of an enemy of the Sikhs had been accomplished. He had been in BC since 1906. He waited his date with death with perfect composure and self-possession. He was an outstanding Sikh who was big enough to measure up to the legacy of the Sikh heritage. He was hanged on 11 January 1915, at the provincial jail, New Westminster, at 8'o clock in the morning. It was a terribly cold morning and it was raining. Hundreds of people awaited his dead body outside the jail in rain. He became a Sikh martyr for a Sikh cause. History knows of a great martyr with pegs in his body. Mewa Singh's martyrdom entailed a tightening noose around his neck. When his dead body was handed over to the sorrowful and sombre crowds, deeply soaked in traumatizing anguish and tormenting agony, waiting outside the jail, a flood of tears poured out of their eyes. His funeral was largely attended. The Sikhs cremated his dead body at Fraser Mill crematorium with great honour. His martyrdom is observed every year by the Sikhs of Canada and the USA with due solemnity in Gurdwaras. In 1970, the *langar* hall of the Khalsa Diwan Society, Gurdwara, 8000-Ross Street, Vancouver, was named after Bhai Mewa Singh's name and in 1976, Akali Singh Society, 1890-Skeena Street Vancouver's Gurdwara library was named as Bhai Mewa Singh library. It was not an execution for a murder; it was a sacrifice and martyrdom for a cause that afflicted the Sikh community awfully. Mewa Singh left behind a young wife and a small baby son, to suffer and pride in the sacrifice of the young husband and a loving father respectively. May the martyr's soul rest in peace.

On a charge of instigating Mewa Singh to murder Hopkinson the Shore Committee members, Husain Rahim, Balwant Singh, Sohan Lal, Mit Singh and Kartar Singh were arrested but later the charges were withdrawn for want of sufficient testimony.

Bela Singh's trial for murdering two men and wounding seven men was taken up again, four days after the judgement was passed against Mewa Singh. His counsel made a strong plea for the acquittal of his client as he acted in self-defence as his life was in danger at the hands of his opponents. Justice Morrison strongly agreed with the defence and the defence witnesses and he said, "the prisoner (Bela Singh) was one of the men who had stood for law and order, while the opposite side were preaching sedition and importing seditious literature and trying to undermine British rule within the empire. It is a wonder to me that the authorities are allowing it. The prisoner and his side are trying to stop it but some have been killed and threats were made to kill the prisoner. They threatened and killed Inspector Hopkinson and if they could shoot him right in the corridors of the Court House how much easier must they have thought it to kill the prisoner when in the temple." On 3 December 1915, the court acquitted Bela Singh of murdering two men—Bhag Singh and Battan Singh, on the ground of self-defence. It was a strange decision totally bereft of any convincing reasons.

Bela Singh was again involved in another case along with his companion Bhagat Singh Haripur. They made a murderous attack on Lashman Singh Khurdpur on 16 April 1915 at his residence on West 2nd Avenue, Vancouver. But he escaped. Both of them were sentenced for twelve months in prison on 12 June 1915 and sent to Okkala prison farm. In 1916 when Bela Singh was released from the prison, his life in Canada seemed insecure. He was considered a high-risk resident of Canada. He was just a poor excuse for an East Indian who was every inch against his community on whom he always spied to the immigration department. And many of the East Indians were thirsting for his blood. He was advised by the government to return to India, which he did. The government paid his passage. The government rewarded him for his spying against the ghadarites with one hundred and fifty acres of fertile land in the district of Montgomery after the World War I was over. He constructed a big house in his native village of Jian in Hoshiarpur district. He was provided with an armed security guard. For eighteen long years he eluded the ghadarites. Finally in May 1934 he was hunted down on his way back to his village Jian from Hoshiarpur, and cut into pieces. Bela Singh had lived by the gun and he died by the gun.

There were many incidents of lethal attacks in 1915, on one another among the Sikhs. On 18 March 1915, one Jagat Singh shot dead Rattan Singh Kotli. On 13 April 1915, Bela Singh's men Bhagat Singh Haripur and Sewa Singh Kamane blew up Mehtab Singh's residence resulting in Mehtab Singh's death. On 16 April 1915, Bhagat Singh Haripur and his companions attacked Lachman Singh Khurdpur at his residence. On 3 October 1915, Partap Singh Tatuanwala fired two shots at Mit Singh, the priest of the Gurdwara at Abbotsford.

We see that there was a spurt of attacks on each other by the Sikhs due to their siding with groups among them. These incidents damaged the image of the Sikhs in Canada.

There is no denying the fact that almost all of the Sikhs involved in these murderous incidents were the Jat Sikhs and the avenue was generally the holy Gurdwara (the Sikh temple). Despite their deep veneration and devotion for the holy Sikh temple their rivalries originated from there. It is such a sad part of the story. The Gurdwara is the unifying institution, open not only to the Sikhs but also to all communities of the world irrespective of their colour, culture or religious barriers. History is witness to the fact that the Jat Sikhs have been known for their warlike spirit and sacrifice and with these two inalienable characteristics they have been changing the course of history again and again and in Canada or elsewhere in the world they would not do it differently. The glow of their unconquerable spirit has always been in high splendour. And they have been glorified for that over the ages. Many other peoples have been feeling like worshipping them for these qualities. Let these wonderful traits not be allowed to degenerate into personal vendetta to jump on each other's throats.

A report on the conduct of the Sikhs published in *The Daily Province* of 30th November 1913, says that "at the Sikh temple there have always been quarrels and disputes and abuses among them, and for which a charge of 'public nuisance' was laid on some of them. David Scott, the Police Inspector, declared that almost every Sunday he had to turn out his reserves to quell fights which occurred in the neighbourhood of the temple".[15] How would the Sikhs feel from this report published in a daily newspaper 85 years back? In the light of this report how will they evaluate themselves or the community in 1998? This evaluation is reader's own privilege based on his present personal experience. 11th January 1997 was a very sad day for the Sikhs when the sanctity of Guru Nanak Sikh Gurdwara in Surrey (B.C.) was desecrated with the intervention and entry of the riot police to resolve the dispute over the mode of serving of Guru's *langar* in the Gurdwara's community kitchen or free mess. Why cannot the Sikhs settle their difference of opinion through discussion and consensus without resorting to the use of cold steel? How will the Sikhs react to a white man's comment that they should try to find brotherliness and peace of mind from another religion's temple if the Gurdwara is helpless in that regard? This remark is an eye-opener for the Sikhs. Is the Gurdwara not functioning to provide deep veneration for each other and is it not upholding the spiritual and human values envisaged by the Sikh Gurus? Yes, it does in the noblest way and in a measure far beyond human comprehension. It is appealed to the blessed Sikhs of the Sat Guru to be always respectful to the all-pervading presence of the Guru in the Gurdwara. Coming down on each other's neck in the Gurdwara is deeply abhorrent to the Guru and thus unforgivably sinful.

Journey from India to Canada

When the 'through ticket order' to Canada was revoked in March 1919 the families of immigrants and other new-comers started pouring into Canada. They could change steamship en route and otherwise also could break their journey. Most of them being first-timers, faced many difficulties during their journey. Some of the men and women, who came to Canada in 1920s and 1930s and are still alive, feel pleased to share their experiences in respect of their first journey from India to this new country.

Generally their relatives or family friends accompanied the families of the Canadian immigrants to Canada. Since most of them had never gone out of their villages alone it was extremely difficult to undertake such a journey without outside help.

They travelled to Calcutta by train and from there to Hong Kong and further to Canada by ship. It took them about two months to reach their destination. The total charges of this trip were around $ 250 per person.

At Calcutta they had to cool their heels for one or two weeks before they could board a ship for their journey to Hong Kong. At a Gurdwara near Howrah in Calcutta they spent their waiting time. They were hospitably looked after without any charges for their stay and food. These people travelled by freighter ships. Either there were no passenger ships available on this route or they could not afford to travel by them. In the freighter ships the accommodation and passenger services were extremely poor. These village people travelled on the deck without grumble. On the deck they were exposed to the vagaries of weather—rain, cold, sun and high winds. If there was rain they would put up a small tent. They cooked their meals themselves, on the deck. Before leaving Calcutta they purchased groceries, utensils, stove, coal, portable beds and other necessaries of daily life for their journey. They brought their heavy quilts from home to meet the cold winter of Canada.

In the ship, undoubtedly, the living conditions were sub-standard and not suitable for human journey. Underneath the deck or in the basement of the ship, besides other goods, there was a cargo of animals that emitted bad odour. There was no help against it. The passengers or this human cargo was being exported like sacks of potatoes or wheat, perhaps not knowing that they were journeying to a hellish life, to be exploited to the hilt in sweatshops, had to live with it. When the sea was rough these poor passengers, along with their articles were tossed over from one side of the deck to the other and when the ship rolled to the other side the utensils and their baggage moved to the other side again. This was very unpleasant and upsetting experience of the passengers. Even today, in their solitary moments their minds nostalgically travel back to the earlier days. The old memories come flooding before their eyes with an uncontrolled force. We need to closely study their sentimental yearnings and not simply ignore them. We must try to have an access into their minds and converse with them that would enliven their dreary days. While dealing with the old men we have to be very sensitive. Bad things hurt the elderly more than the young, the latter being more shock-absorbing. To have peace of mind is a person's top priority in the final years of his life. These elderly people are very valuable relics and not the living or breathing fossils. When the physical frame ceases to be equal to the demands that one places on it life becomes intolerable. It is the time to quit. Termination of life at this stage is tolerable. At this time these elderly people need to be given a very venerable departure.

The important stopovers from Calcutta to Hong Kong were Rangoon (Burma), Penang (Malaysia) and Singapore. The freighters would load and unload their cargo at these ports and ordinarily they would take two or three days at each harbour. The passengers could get down at the stopovers and visit the cities for sightseeing and purchases and return to the ship before its departure. The money-changers met them on the ship itself to exchange for that country's money. The inquisitive passengers would gather information about the cities on shore, their customs and culture and Indians, if any, living there, and their living standards.

Hong Kong was the most important stop for all the immigrants to Canada. It was there that the passengers had to get their clearance to move ahead. There being no Canadian immigration office in India, all formalities regarding immigration had to be complied with at Hong Kong. Holding interviews, examining documents and conducting medical examinations had to be gone through there. Sometimes, Canadian immigrants had to stay there for quite some time. People whose formalities got pending had to stay back at Hong Kong till these were complied with. Sometimes they had to miss the ship for which they and their companions were scheduled to travel. In some cases the stay at Hong Kong was prolonged to a year or more, as they had to procure documents from India or Canada.

To save the East Indians from a lot of harassment in respect of accommodation and food a Sikh temple, at Hong Kong, looked after their needs. In the Gurdwara a Chinese man along with his wife had been appointed to welcome the new-comers. As soon as the ship docked that Chinese *sewadar* (a helping hand or volunteer) would go on board and render every possible help to shift the Sikh passengers' luggage to the Gurdwara. The Canadian Sikhs had raised some funds to furnish some rooms with beds on the lower floor of the Gurdwara for the use of the travellers journeying between India and Canada. Hong Kong being an important transit station the Gurdwara rendered excellent service to the travellers. In the Gurdwara, there was an arrangement for cooking food in large quantities. Thus, the passengers could jointly prepare meals in the Gurdwara. During their departure from Hong Kong the passengers could make a contribution to the Gurdwara if they liked. It was totally voluntary.

The Immigration officials tried to find excuses to prevent the emigrants to Canada. Medical examination was an easy means to create obstacles in the way of the passengers from India. Some other hassles regarding passports, period of their stay in India and expiry of visas, had to be faced by the Indian immigrants. The Hong Kong Gurdwara personnel helped the Punjabi immigrants in respect of language, customs and legal matters to which they were alien. They readily came forward to get expedited the matters of immigration, medical examination, financial problems and passage booking for the last stage of their long and enduring trip.

In those days many ship companies operated between Hong Kong and Canada as the Empress of Japan, the Empress of Canada, the Empress of Asia and the Empress of Russia. One of these companies was arriving in Vancouver or Hong Kong every fifteen days. Their stops were in Japan and Honolulu. On this leg of the journey the services had improved considerably. As these were passenger ships, the travellers were provided rooms furnished with beds and the food was included in the ticket fare. If the passengers did not like the Canadian or European food they could get groceries, utensils, pots, pans and stoves and other needed things from the authorities of the ship, free of any extra charges, and cook their own food.

Despite the hardships suffered on the way the first journey from India to Canada remained an indelible experience lovingly treasured in their memories. Bitter memories rather than sweet ones are more stable and they create a greater sense of relatedness since they are more poignant and pricking. When they are reminded of their early days they have the old memories relived.

REFERENCES

1.   I.M. Muthanna, *People of India in North America*, Banglore, India, 1975, p.28.
2.   Harbans Lal, 'In memory of the first Gurdwara established in North America', *The Sikh Courier International*, Spring Summer 1992, London, UK, p.20.
3.   *The Daily Province*, Vancouver, 1 October 1906.
4.   *Ibid.*, 19 November 1906.
5.   *Ibid.*, 2 December 1908.
6.   *Ibid.*, 18 December 1908.

7.   *Pacific Monthly*, Vol. 17 of 1907.

8.   R.K. Das, *Hindustani Workers on the Pacific Coast*, Walter De Gruyter and Co., Berlin, 1923, p.75.

9.   *The Daily Province*, Vancouver, 18 March 1908.

10.   *Ibid.*, November 1907.

11.   *Ibid.*, 20 October 1908.

12.   *Ibid.*, 2 December 1908.

13.   *Ibid.*, 14 November 1911.

14.   *Ibid.*, 6 May 1912.

15.   *Ibid.*, 30 November 1913.

CHAPTER 3

THE KOMAGATA MARU—
A CHALLENGE TO CANADIAN
IMMIGRATION RULES AND RACISM

The episode of the *Komagata Maru* (1914) was broadcast all over the world as it had far-reaching effects on the relations between the people of India and the British Indian Government. This episode was effectively used by the Ghadar Party to fan anti-British feelings for its negative role in the application of Canadian immigration regulations. To bring about the tragedy of the *Komagata Maru* the racial sentiment of Canadian whites was much more stronger and effective than the immigration rules that were comparatively weaker and could be challenged and defeated at higher law courts. Being the British subjects the Indians believed that they had the right to visit any British colony including Canada. An enterprising Sikh Indian businessman, Gurdit Singh, chartered the steamer to test or to challenge the Canadian rules of racial discrimination especially directed against the Indian immigrants.

Gurdit Singh, son of Hukam Singh, was born in 1859, in Sarhali village, in the district of Amritsar. He immigrated to Singapore in 1899 and started business as a contractor. He returned to India in 1909 and after a four-year stay there he went back to Singapore in 1913 and on 5 January 1914, he moved to Hong Kong where he soon gained influence in the community. At the Hong Kong Gurdwara he found many Sikhs keen to come to Canada but unable to do so because of the Canadian immigration rules that strictly banned the entry of the East Indians.

The chartering of a ship for taking the Punjabis to Canada was planned. The launching of such an enterprise was not the work of Gurdit Singh's brain alone. He was inspired and encouraged by many people from India and Canada. As held "indeed this very project is believed to have been discussed by the Sikh delegates from Canada, while in the Punjab."[1]

And also as recorded, "It is said that many Canada domiciled Sikhs, who under the instructions by Immigration Department to the shipping companies, were refused passage to this country, jointly chartered a vessel and under the management of Gurdit Singh, have headed for Vancouver."[2]

Gurdit Singh himself corroborates the above statements. "I went to Hong Kong in 1913, where a *sabha* was held in December 1913, in which a proposal of chartering a steamship of our own was discussed."[3]

In January 1914 the Guru Nanak Steamship Company was formed under the charge of Gurdit Singh. He came to Calcutta and put out a poster on 13 February 1914, announcing that a Chinese ship would be chartered from Calcutta to Vancouver via Penang, Singapore, Hong Kong and Shanghai. But the government of India did not allow him to take passengers from Calcutta and he went back to Hong Kong. He met A. Bune, a German shipping agent, to get a steamship, who arranged a steamer that was being used' for carrying coal. This ship, called *Komagata Maru*, had been built in Glasgow in 1890, for a German company that registered it under the name of *Stubbenhuk*. Later it was sold to a Japanese company from which Gurdit Singh hired it for six months at $11,000 Hong Kong per month. The terms settled were as under: The rent for the first month was to be paid at the time of signing the agreement; for the second month, within a week; the third and fourth months, within two weeks and the remaining within two months. The company or the owners would provide the captain and the crew.

Gurdit Singh appointed Daljit Singh of Muktsar as his personal secretary and Bir Singh, an assistant secretary. Earlier Daljit Singh had been an associate editor of the *Khalsa Advocate* publishing from Amritsar. Daljit Singh sold tickets at $210 Hong Kong—equal to return fare. Tickets could be sold to 165 men who were all East Indians. When the Hong Kong police came to know of it they raided Gurdit Singh's office, seized his papers and he was produced before the magistrate who released him, as there was no case against him. The ship, which had the capacity for over 500 passengers, could book only 165 from Hong Kong. The *Komagata Maru*, the Japanese vessel, was chartered on 24 March 1914. The ship was renamed Guru Nanak Jahaz. To start with, the steamer was delayed until 4 April, by the Hong Kong government which wanted to prevent the vessel from starting, as they were aware that the passengers would not be admitted to Canada. In the meantime, Gurdit Singh consulted three foremost counsels from a Hong Kong firm of lawyers—C.D.

Williamson, E.J. Orit and C.E.H. Davis. They gave the following advice: "Referring to your interview with us this afternoon when you enquired whether there were any restrictions upon Indians who wish to travel to Vancouver, so far as this country is concerned, we have to advise you that in our opinion there are no restrictions upon immigration by Indians from the colony, unless they are under contract of service."[4]

Departure of the Ship from Hong Kong

After not hearing from London despite his two urgent cables to them regarding signing a clearance for the *Komagata Maru*, F.W. May, the governor of Hong Kong, said that the ship could go. The ship steamed off on 4 April. It was decided that the ship would touch only Shanghai, Moji and Yokohama after its departure from Hong Kong. The *Komagata Maru* had started from Hong Kong with 165 passengers. It picked up 111 passengers from Shanghai where it reached on 8 April, and reached Moji on 14 April, from where it picked 86 men and it stopped at Yokohama on the 28 April, and took on board 14 passengers, thus totalling 376 passengers on the *Komagata Maru*. There were 340 Sikhs, 12 Hindus and 24 Muslims including two women and four children on the ship. One of the two women was Dr Raghunath Singh's wife and the second was Kishan Kaur Tumowal and one of the four children was Dr Raghunath's son, the second was seven-year old son of Gurdit Singh, and a son and a baby daughter of Kishan Kaur Tumowal.

Most of the passengers came from the districts of Jalandhar, Hoshiarpur, Ludhiana, Amritsar, Ferozepur, Patiala and Lahore in the Punjab. The Muslims were from Shahpur in the Western Punjab. Almost all districts of Punjab represented on the ship.

Gurdit Singh had the holy *Guru Granth Sahib* on the ship from which the Sikhs recited the hymns regularly during their journey to Vancouver and back and during their stay on the waters of the Pacific Ocean on the shores of Vancouver. They had also a *dhadi jatha* (musicians with their instruments) who sang patriotic songs to keep the passengers in high spirits.

The steerage section of the ship was in awful condition because of very bad ventilation. The passengers preferred to cook their food on the open deck and also to sleep there during the night. The ship had a few very dirty and unclean washrooms that made people sick. Every living part of the vessel was unlivable and presented an ugly look. But the passengers tolerated everything in the hope that they were shortly going to step on a celestial land provided with the amenities of life, not knowing as to what was in store for them.

During an early stage of their journey the passengers were visited on the ship by two reputed revolutionaries—Bhagwan Singh Giani, and Muhammad Barkatulla, and also Balwant Singh the priest of the Gurdwara in Vancouver, when the *Komagata Maru* had arrived in Yokohama in Japan. They delivered spirited lectures to the passengers and distributed printed material relating to the ghadar movement. It is also said that Balwant Singh met the passengers at Moji, and lectured them twice. Gurdit Singh himself often spoke to the passengers to keep them in high spirits.

The passengers of the ship were divided into two factions—one was headed by Gurdit Singh and the other by the medical officer of the ship, Dr Raghunath Singh. This friction spoiled the unity among the passengers and created ill-will and bitterness between the two groups. Dr Raghunath Singh criticized the lack of cleanliness and supply of the proper food on the ship and the financial difficulties in which Gurdit Singh himself and the passengers had landed, as the payment of the rent of the ship was in arrears. The in-charge of the ship and the passengers were not in a position to pay it off. Some of the passengers joined Raghunath Singh in accusing Gurdit Singh for all their hardships. Gurdit Singh had a much larger number of followers as compared to that of the doctor who was always apprehensive of some violence against him by the loyalists of Gurdit Singh.

The hostility hampered unanimity and consensus among the passengers to plan a strategy to meet the challenge of the Immigration Department stoutly. Gurdit Singh viewed Dr Raghunath Singh as a traitor who gave a large catalogue of complaints and charges against him to the immigration officials when anchored at Vancouver.

The Komagata Maru arrived at Vancouver

Passing through Victoria the *Komagata Maru* anchored at Burrard Inlet, opposite Vancouver City, in the early hours of 23 May 1914. The passengers were attired in their best dresses, with their bags properly packed and were getting ready to land ashore but that was not to be. The Indians already living in Canada were apprehensive of immigration law and felt that 'illegal immigrants' might not be allowed to land. But as the ship was approaching Vancouver the East Indians were eagerly waiting to extend a hearty welcome to them.

The ship was forced to anchor two hundred yards off the wharf so that the passengers might not escape into the town or might not display riotous behaviour on landing or on refusal to enter Vancouver.

As the ship anchored, the newspapers described the incident as the 'second oriental invasion of Canada.' *The Sun* declared, "Hindu (Sikh) invaders are now in the city harbour on the *Komagata Maru*." The local newspapers published editorials against them. The Indians and the white Canadians who were sympathetic to the horrible plight of the passengers were depicted as traitors to the British Empire. *The Times*, London, commented that "Asia is knocking and knocking persistently at the door of the western America." The premier of British Columbia, Sir Richard McBride said, "To admit Orientals in large numbers would mean in the end the extinction of the white peoples and we have always in mind the necessity of keeping this a white man's country."[5] Herbert H. Stevens, an M.P. from Vancouver, a strong opponent of the East Indians' entry into Canada, took an active part in preventing the passengers of the *Komagata Maru* from landing. C.E. Tisdall and Dr Maguire, the members of the provincial legislature and W. Baxter, the mayor of Vancouver, also vehemently opposed the embarkment of the passengers. The Immigration Officer, Malcolm Reid, assisted by William Hopkinson, was under instructions from the government to deal with the situation created by the *Komagata Maru* with an iron hand. Hopkinson, an Indian born, with 'a half-eastern, half western air' and taken for a half-caste was a strong and committed right hand man of Malcolm Reid. He was born in Delhi to Anglo-Indian parents and before coming to Canada he had served as police inspector at Calcutta for a few years. In Canadian immigration department he seemed to be an indispensable officer, being more loyal to Canada than the Canadians themselves.

It is said that Hopkinson demanded (£2000 as gratification to help the passengers to land. Gurdit Singh agreed to pay (£1000 in advance and the remainder after the passengers had landed. Hopkinson wanted of Gurdit Singh to keep this deal a guarded secret but the latter refused to keep it undisclosed, as he had to collect the money from the passengers. Consequently the deal collapsed. This story seems a little too hard to digest as the *Komagata Maru* affair had attracted too much of public and government attention and Hopkinson was not the authority to take the final decision in permitting the passengers to land.

Gurdit Singh though deeply worried about the fate of his enterprise but he maintained his calm. He told the press, "We are British subjects and we consider we have a right to visit any part of the empire. We were determined to make this a test case and if we are refused entrance into your country, the matter will not end here." He told Hopkinson, "What is done with this shipload of my people will determine whether we shall have peace in all parts of the British Empire."[6]

Gurdit Singh told the immigration officials, "you know I am a merchant and there is no law to prevent merchants from going on shore. You can detain the passengers, not me; you are responsible for the damages." But they were not prepared to bother about what Gurdit Singh wanted. He was put under a sort of confinement on the ship. J. Edward Bird, the lawyer, engaged to fight the case of the *Komagata Maru*, protested that 'Gurdit Singh is even more a prisoner than if he were in a penitentiary.'[7]

The immigration department over-stepped the laws entitling them to deal with the *Komagata Maru*. They had taken armed possession of the ship and posted guards that patrolled the waters around it in armed boats. They disallowed anybody from boarding the vessel including the lawyer engaged for the passengers who had legal right to get the necessary information from his clients that could help in their case at court. The passengers were treated worse than the prisoners who had been convicted of some serious crimes.

The lawyer was helpless against the policy of immigration department knowing that in the dispensation of justice the racist sentiments of the government, white majority and the judiciary were glaringly conspicuous. When the lawyer E. Bird threatened to go to court against the powers used against his clients by the immigration department, Malcolm Reid, the immigration officer, told that he would not 'pay the slightest attention to any laws of the court if any are made.' So it was not the immigration law that worked in Canada at that time, it was that intense racist feeling that prevailed in the whole white scenario. So, in this situation, the lawyers who had already been taking up the cases of Indians with great interest refused to take the cases of the passengers of the *Komagata Maru*. The racist sentiment had superceded the law.

Under the pretext of processing the passengers on the ship, the immigration officials were delaying the matter as they were up to an enormous mischief of keeping the passengers away from the Canadian soil. The medical officer spent three days to find seventy-seven cases of trachoma, which caused inflammation in the eyes and considered it to be a suitable ground for failing a person from getting admittance into Canada. There was also a hookworm bogey. The medical officer told that 90 per cent Indians were infected with hookworm disease. Such were the ploys for disqualifying the passengers of the *Komagata Maru* from gaining entry into the country.

Twenty-two passengers were already the residents of Canada. There was no objection to their landing but Gurdit Singh was not allowing them to disembark as they were a part of the whole lot of 376 passengers and all of them would leave the ship together.

The checking process of the passengers was intentionally going on at a very slow speed. In the case of European passengers two doctors would clear 300 or 400 persons in an hour. But in the case of the East Indians, many days, may be weeks, required to pass them through a full physical examination.

The resident East Indians of Vancouver appealed to Lord Hardinge, viceroy of India, and to Lord Crewe, secretary of state for India, for the admission of the passengers of the ship into Canada but to no avail. "The probable answer to them was that interference with the autonomy of the self-government dominions would not be possible."

The reaction of a London daily expressed through its editorial to the plea of the East Indians that they were the British citizens was that, "Phrases like British citizenship cannot be used as a talisman to open doors... sophistry and catch logic, the spinning of words or the reading of many books will not help her (India). And she is likely to get little profit out of enterprises like that which has sent the *Komagata Maru* to hurl its shipload of hundreds at the door of Canada."[8]

A meeting and fund-raising (31 May 1914)

Under the joint auspices of the Khalsa Diwan Society, Vancouver, and the United India League, a meeting was held in the hired Dominion Hall on the 31 May 1914. The meeting was attended by about six hundred Indians and about two dozen whites, a couple of reporters and William Hopkinson along with his stenographer. Husain Rahim, President, United India League, chaired the meeting. The speakers at the meeting included Husain Rahim, Edward Bird—lawyer of the passengers, H.M. Fitzgerald— a socialist leader, Bhag Singh—President of the Khalsa Diwan Society, Balwant Singh—Head priest of the Vancouver Gurdwara, and Sohan Lal and Rajah Singh—members of the 'Shore Committee'. They delivered spirited speeches, using very strong language as, "Get up and arm yourselves and fight to regain your liberty. Inspire your countrymen to return and sweep all the whites from India." A strong ghadar spirit prevailed at the meeting. Balwant Singh delivered the key address or the principal speech in Punjabi. Even the government official Hopkinson was recording the proceedings of the meeting. Balwant Singh's address was quite daring. He strongly believed in action and not rhetoric. He spoke of a new unity against the British, a return to the spirit of Mutiny of 1857, the coming of revolution if India was not freed within the next few years. He strongly referred to the exclusion laws in the white dominions and the weak statutes of the Indian government within the empire. In the end he talked of the

Sikh soldiers of the past years who fought three times against the British. An appeal for the funds for the *Komagata Maru* was also made. He clearly indicated the changing mood in India.[9]

Balwant Singh was a man of very high voltage. He was born with a blazing fire in his stomach. He always carried a verbal bomb within him and could explode it any time in any assembly. He always spoke to the listeners' hearts rather than to their brains. He was terribly fearless. Courage is the absence of fear, which comes from conviction. He clicked with his audience, as he knew their heartbeats. He was a whip-lasher across the backs of the Canadian and the British governments. He emerged as the Knight in the shining armour to stand up to the Canadian whites' policy of racism against the East Indian immigrants. He had a solid image among his people and his whole-hearted sincerity and dedication to the Sikh causes had added extra lustre to his image. He was later hanged on 16 March 1917 at Lahore at the age of 35, leaving behind a young wife Kartar Kaur and three small children still tied to their mom's apron strings. Through his death, there was inevitably a tremendous void created in the life and activities of the Canadian Sikhs.

Under the influence of the provocative speeches many more from this assembly wanted to speak but they could not be permitted to speak for want of time. Husain Rahim said that the meeting had been called for hard cash to keep the ship in Vancouver. Immediately after the meeting ended $5,000 in cash lay on the table with $66,000 in pledges.

The meeting also unanimously adopted an appeal to the Indian National Congress, Madras, that "Move government of India to get 376 East Indians on board the *Komagata Maru* landed at Vancouver on constitutional rights—serious pecuniary loss and dishonour to India, if ship turned away with them." Cables to the Maharaja of Patiala and Nabha were also sent saying that the *Komagata Maru* lies at Vancouver with 376 Hindus, Sikhs and Muslims—many of whom are subjects of your states. Move government of India to get them landed at once to save serious pecuniary loss and honour of India."[10]

The medical examination of the passengers was complete on 1 June 1914, and one by one their cases began to be processed in the office of Malcolm Reid by the Board of Inquiry. They started with those who were the former residents of Canada. But Edward Bird asked the Board to start inquiry with a man who had never been in Canada before.

He suggested the name of Gurdit Singh to be taken up first but there was a deadlock over the procedure for a day. The 'Shore Committee' and

Edward Bird suggested to the immigration department that a detention shed should be provided to the passengers where the coal brought by Gurdit Singh from Japan for sale in Canada to meet the expenses of the vessel, be unloaded and new cargo of timber be allowed to be loaded on the *Komagata Maru* which may be sent back to Hong Kong. In the event of the deportation of the passengers another ship may be hired to send them back. This proposal was strongly opposed by the immigration department because it was considered dangerous and expensive to guard such a big group of men, on the shore.

Gurdit Singh expressed a desire to go back to Hong Kong by the return boat but he was not allowed lest he should campaign for support for his mission from the British Indian government and London government, and arrange pressure on Canadian government and also mobilise agitation in India. He was not permitted to go back without the *Komagata Maru* and its passengers. On 9 June, Gurdit Singh allowed the twenty two passengers, who had been formerly the residents of Canada, to disembark, discontinuing the boycott.

During these days, that is, in the end of the first week and the beginning of the second week of June the passengers were going almost without food. They were in desperate need of food stuffs and other necessary supplies. Gurdit Singh sent messages to the king of England and the governor-general of Canada "No provisions for four days, Malcolm Reid (R.J.) refuses supply, charterer and passengers starving, kept prisoners."

Malcolm Reid informed his supervisor W.D. Scott through a telegram that "I will take care not to furnish any rations." Reid believed that the passengers demand of ration was just an excuse to remain anchored for longer period, otherwise they had lot of rations on board the ship. It was immoral on the part of Reid to disbelieve the woes of the starving passengers. Even the local newspapers heartlessly wrote that the passengers were telling lies to win sympathy. The doctor aboard the ship informed the Immigration Officer that ninety of the passengers were sick and some of them were seriously ill. On this information Reid agreed to the supplies for the passengers.

Some supply was sent by the Shore Committee. In response to Gurdit Singh's telegram, cable was sent from the Buckingham Palace to Canada. The governor-general of Canada wired the following reply. "Provisions supply started. Lawyers permitted to interview. Cargo allowed to unload."[11]

But action according to this telegram started much later.

A Mass Meeting of the East Indians (21 June 1914)

Another meeting of the East Indians was jointly called for 21 June by the Khalsa Diwan Society and the United India League at a Vancouver Down Town hall to discuss as to how help can be given to the passengers of the *Komagata Maru* to keep them in Canada. About 800 East Indians and 200 whites gathered in Down Town Dominion Hall.

Edward Bird, the lawyer of the passengers, was the principal speaker. He accused the immigration department of delaying to decide the issue of these newcomers "till such time as those people were starved back to their original port from whence they sailed." He spoke with deep emotion. He said, "they talk about socialists and anarchists. There is no set of anarchists in Canada like the immigration officials who defy all law and order." Through their lectures the speakers delivered a few deft kicks and provoked the audience to an ignition point. Looking at Hopkinson who was sitting there, Bird told him that they knew the plans of his department. His clients were not going to leave. "Do not blame the East Indians if you see this farce dragged on for months. If necessary they can wait a century, perhaps they will die before this thing is decided." The speech of H.M. Fitzgerald, the socialist leader, was no less spirited. Balwant Singh, Rajah Singh and Sohan Lal addressed the audience in Punjabi in strongly-worded language and very daringly. Balwant Singh always used violent language. He was a highly inflammable gas can and was mainly in the mould of Giani Bhagwan Singh who invariably always used dangerously loaded vocabulary.

After spirited speeches a resolution was drafted, copies of which were sent to the Prime Minister of Canada, and the secretary of state for India, and some others. The resolution read as under: "whereas the East Indians on the steamship, the *Komagata Maru*, are unlawfully prevented by the immigration authorities from consulting with their legal adviser and from procuring provisions and water from their East Indian friends, making their lot on board one to which cattle would not be subjected, and whereas such brutal and unlawful treatment of British subject of the same type as the East Indians would not be tolerated in India, we urge the dominion authorities under the principle of 'do unto others as you would have them do unto you' to see that the East Indians are saved without delay, from the highhanded action of the immigration department. We further protest that action of the immigration officers of Vancouver are unlawful and so provoking that the East Indians will never forget or forgive the powers that be if they do not remedy the immigration situation here."

It is amusing to note that on the receipt of the copy of the resolution in India, some English women wrote a letter to the Mayor of Vancouver that "May Canada be firm and able to hold her own against the orientals is the earnest wish and prayer of every English woman and man who knows India.... Pray God help you to be firm to the bitter end. Britain's policy towards Indians has ruined India for the white race. Take the heed of Britain's advice now."[12]

The general opinion in Great Britain was that the Canadians being the masters of their house it was up to them to decide as to who should be allowed to live in their house and who should be refused admittance.

There was a strong opposition from the white population of Vancouver. They wanted the *Komagata Maru* to be immediately sent back with all its passengers. An editorial in the local daily newspaper called on Ottawa to adopt a policy of total exclusion in regard to the East Indian passengers. There was no room for discussion, no call for argument, no need for speeches. The sentiments of the people were clear.[13] "And whereas the presence of these people would prove a serious menace to our civilization, both economically and socially, besides intensifying the present unsatisfactory labour condition."[14]

Since the arrival of the *Komagata Maru* there had been a lot of opposition from the Board of Trade and city council. In Vancouver, the labour was facing slump and it was reported by the building traders that about sixty per cent of their workers were out of job. The white labourers were demanding that the timber companies in British Columbia that had given jobs to the Indians should provide jobs to them by laying off the Indians. These whites could not tolerate the passengers of the *Komagata Maru*, the people who would worsen the job situation if allowed entry into Vancouver.

Thus, an opposition from the white public was mounting. The mayor of Vancouver said, "The East Indian is not a desirable citizen and when I say that I am backed by the public opinion."[15]

During this time *The Vancouver Sun* was printing such racist cartoons which would not be acceptable today, nor were they acceptable by the Sikhs then. It is believed that *The Vancouver Sun* must be realising today that as their professional ethics demands they should not have done what was liked by the white majority but they should have done what was right.

But there were some saner and sympathetic voices also that rose at the plight of the unfortunate passengers and expressed compassion towards them. A London weekly wrote a long article on the Indian Immigration to Canada and said, "We had hoped broader view, for more pre-science and for a truer imperial spirit on the part of Canada. The Canadians themselves are all settlers from foreign lands or descendants of such. They are intruders upon the native possessors of the country."[16]

Malcolm J. Reid, who played the maximum role in preventing the East Indians —the passengers of the *Komagata Maru,* from landing on Canadian soil, was a Scot who emigrated from Scotland at the age of 14.

E. Mannings, a critic, said that "as a city and a country, we are writing history and we are writing a very ugly page now."[17]

Wallace Wright said, "Are we not in Canada making ourselves rather ridiculous over what is called the East Indian question? The dominion has admitted and is admitting many most undesirable Europeans, Galicians, Armenians, Doukhobors, etc., yet we are keeping out men of tried loyalty who have fought for our empire in many climes and arduous campaigns."[18]

There were public meetings in several cities of the Punjab to express their sympathy with the passengers of the *Komagata Maru*. Mrs. Annie Besant took up the cause in the British press. She said, "If the empire rejects the love and disregards the loyalty of India just when she is awakening into national self-consciousness, will you be for the empire? If her sons are shut out of the colonies, if India is shut out of the empire as a self-governing country, will she be blamable?" She always delivered an electrifying speech.

But her views were criticized by the London papers. The *London Times* wrote an editorial and said, "East is east, West is west, and though we may hesitate to accept as inevitable the corollary is that never the twain shall meet; it would be futile to deny the immediate difference between them."[19]

Thus, Annie Besant had drawn a press controversy on the subject which remained enlivened for some time. Almost no notice was taken of this agitation by the Indian, British or Canadian governments.

Board of Inquiry

The Board of Inquiry functioned very slowly and it was feared that it could take months or even years to process the cases of the passengers of the *Komagata Maru*. Edward Bird, the lawyer of the passengers, thought of withdrawing from the Board. Then it was decided that Bird could choose one of the passengers' cases and present it as a test case. Munshi Singh of Hoshiarpur district was selected by Bird to be brought before the Board of Inquiry. He was a married young man of 26-year old with his wife and daughter back in India. He told the Board that he had come to Canada 'to do farming', through a broken journey as the company, he contacted to get a ticket from Calcutta to Vancouver, refused to provide him with such a ticket for continuous journey. He could not corroborate his statement by any witness. His case for entry into Canada was rejected on 25 June and was ordered for deportation immediately, on the false finding that he was a labourer and not a farmer.

Commenting on the immigration department's action Bird said, "The Board of Inquiry was a travesty of justice in which the prosecution are the judges." The Board of Inquiry was strongly prejudiced against the passengers. Of its five appointed members, Malcolm Reid, the immigration officer, and the strongest opponent of the passengers entry into Vancouver, was one himself.

Munshi Singh's lawyers, J. Edward Bird and Robert Cassidy, filed writ petition with the Court of Appeal at Victoria. The East Indian community leaders tried to hire the services of T.R.E. MacInnes, a lawyer interested in the Indian problems, but he refused. Then McCrossan and Harper, advocates earlier dealing with Indian cases, were contacted. They also declined to take up the case of Munshi Singh. They told that the whole matter of the passengers of the *Komagata Maru* had gone 'beyond the realm of legal proceedings' and had become a political question marked with a pre-decision of preventing the passengers of this ship from entering Canada with strong public racial overtones.

Robert Cassidy argued the case on 29 and 30 June before the Court of Appeal without necessary preparation. Munshi Singh could not prove that he was a farmer and intended farming in Canada and he was not a labourer.

An order-in-council, P.C.897 was passed on 8 December 1913, prohibiting the landing of labourers at specified British Columbian ports. The Board of Inquiry based their decision on the observation that 90 per cent of Indian immigrants in Canada became labourers and 10 per cent took up farming. All the five judges unanimously upheld the Immigration Act and the orders-in-council and the appeal was dismissed on 6 July 1914, on the biased interpretation of the exclusionary immigration regulations. Edward Bird's plea could not change the court's mind that Munshi Singh was really a farmer and not an objectionable labourer. That Canada could not impose the rule of continuous journey from India because Canada could not legislate as to how a British subject was to spend his time before he came to Canada. That the dominion government could no more legislate definitely to keep labourers out of British Columbia than they could keep doctors out of Nova Scotia. In other words, the rule should apply nation-wide or not at all. But the Court of Appeal ruled on 6 July that "(i) the East Indian is a native of India and as an immigrant of Asiatic race he did not possess in his own right $200 (ii) he is an immigrant who has come to Canada otherwise by continuous journey from his native country. (iii) he is an unskilled labourer."[20]

Gurdit Singh, the organizer of the *Komagata Maru*, was not a man of violent nature. He was a strongly determined person and was always for a legal fight. But the situation to which he was reduced by the immigration department made him a helpless prisoner on the *Komagata Maru*. "In the beginning Gurdit Singh had declared that he would battle right through to the highest court of appeal, the Judicial Committee of the British Privy Council. But it was not realistic to carry on. The Supreme Court of Canada would not be sitting until October and there would be immense problems in trying to go directly to the Committee of Privy Council in the current calendar year. The decision of the Court of Appeal meant defeat for the passengers and the Indian community in Canada."[21]

But Gurdit Singh won't easily give in and he always kept his spirits far from drooping. Neither he undertook this enterprise for pecuniary benefits nor with a view to permanently settling in Canada. His fight was exclusively against racial discrimination and atrocious immigration laws.

The Komagata Maru loses case and decides to return

A day after Munshi Singh's case failed Edward Bird met Gurdit Singh who asked him to negotiate the return of the *Komagata Maru*. The ship had already been co-chartered in the names of Bhag Singh and Husain Rahim, so government was supposed to deal with them. The immigration department was told that the ship could sail away in twenty four hours or in a couple of days if they paid them their fares to the tune of $20,000. But the government won't agree to do it. During the next two weeks the situation took many turns some of which were pretty dangerous both for the passengers and the Canadian government.

On 8 July, an informer of the immigration department conveyed to the immigration officers, R.J. Reid and W. Hopkinson that he had overheard a conversation between three members of the Shore Committee (formed by the East Indians to help the passengers) that these immigration officers be done away with. Reid had also learnt that some East Indians were trying to make bombs and purchase a large number of automatic pistols. Reid got scary but he would go ahead with his plans. The Superintendent of Immigration, W.D. Scott, had given him free hand to chalk out his plans to deal with the passengers of the *Komagata Maru*. For his tough and unsympathetic attitude and measures he was hated by the East Indians of Vancouver.

Dr Raghunath Singh had been interviewed by the immigration department and H.H. Stevens on 20 June 1914, in the office of Reid. He gave a long list of charges and complaints against Gurdit Singh and also promised to give a full written report about him. He became a suspect in the eyes of the passengers and their organizer Gurdit Singh. He was locked in his cabin and they were not allowing him to land. Gurdit Singh had told Reid that if he wanted peace on the ship he should stop listening to him. Gurdit Singh believed that the doctor was a Canadian government detective. Before locking him in his cabin the doctor was placed under the guard of four or five passengers. He was always complaining that his life was in danger. Later, by the special efforts of Reid, Dr Raghunath Singh, along with his wife and child, was got freed and safely taken on shore on 17 July 1914.

As needed for their return journey Gurdit Singh demanded provisions from the government. The demand was accepted on the condition that the provisions would be delivered to the *Komagata Maru* at a point away from Canada's five kilometre limit, that is about 250 kilometres from Vancouver by sea. Suspecting the intentions of the immigration department, Gurdit Singh refused to accept the offer. In the meantime the *Komagata Maru* was visited by the Health Department. It reported that the upper deck which was mostly used by the passengers for all purposes was awfully dirty. The toilets and floors needed thorough cleaning, lime-washing and fumigation, to avoid illness and epidemic.

Gurdit Singh's men had taken control of the ship and its captain Yamamoto could not move the ship without Gurdit Singh's permission. On 19 July, provisions worth 4000 to 6000 dollars were loaded on the *Sea Lion*, the largest tug, docked in the harbour. One hundred and twenty five policemen headed by their chief and equipped with revolvers and batons arrived. Thirty five armed men were already there on the beck and call of Reid, thus making an armed force of 160 men which was more than enough to deal with the unarmed half-starved passengers of the *Komagata Maru*.

A small incident took place on 19 July when during the night the searchlight of the *Sea Lion* exposed a line of passengers, over the railing of the *Komagata Maru*. They started shouting at the members of the *Sea Lion*, brandishing their clubs. One of the passengers said, "We are ready to fight. This ship is going to stay here. She is not going to move. If you start a fight the Sikhs will show you how to fight. If you make fast we will jump into your boat and fight you and take chances. The Sikhs are not afraid."[22] The police threw cold water on them with pumps and the East

Indians reacted with pieces of coal,, fire bricks and scrap metal. A few people were injured from both sides and they got disengaged soon.

Gurdit Singh writes that 'some of the policemen fired at the passengers without the slightest warning'.[23]

The news of this fight was broadcast all over the world. The Vancouver papers described it as the battle of Burrard Inlet. It aroused racial feelings. "England was informed which sanctioned the use of force to send them back."[24]

A song on this battle includes the following:

> 'Give me a box of dynamite,
> And a goodly length of fuse,
> And, believe me, I'd surely fix
> that bunch of mad Hindus.'[25]

The sad plight of their countrymen inflamed the minds of Indians everywhere. In America, Indian labourers and farm hands left their work and rushed to Vancouver. The passengers had now only two alternatives before them, to submit and go back without food and water and die of starvation on the high seas, or to defy the orders and die with the guns of the warships at the door of Canada. After discussion they decided to give a fight as far as they could, failing which they would set the ship on fire and burn themselves alive.[26]

Soon thereafter H.H. Stevens wired the Prime Minister for the *Rainbow* gun-boat, or some naval vessel to deal with the passengers who were getting defiant. The *Rainbow* was made available to Reid on 21 July, equipped with 12 machine guns and a force of forty-seven men. The situation was on razor's edge. If the trio could take action against the passengers of the *Komagata Maru* by mistake it could be just human error but if they insisted on committing a mistake it was an evil which they were intent upon. Fortunately, Martin Burrell—the Federal Minister, averted it. The Prime Minister knew that the use of the *Rainbow* could cause a lot of bloodshed and a situation that could bring condemnation on the Canadian government from the world community. The *Rainbow* could sink the *Komagata Maru* with a couple of shots. The Prime Minister, Robert Borden, did not want the use of the gunboat entirely in the hands of the trio—Reid, Stevens and Hopkinson, because they could use it without considering its far-reaching consequences. H. Stevens was a control-freak buster and R.J. Reid and W. Hopkinson followed him like a puppy. Rather he could wrap them around his finger. He called the shots in the immigration department as he controlled its levers of power in

Vancouver. He was very over-reaching and a forceful and domineering personality both, in and outside the Parliament. To leave the situation entirely in their hands was fraught with awful dangers and far-reaching consequences entailing gunfire holocaust.

Dr O.D. Skelton (biographer of Wilfred Laurier) wrote to Sir Wilfred Laurier, former Prime Minister of Canada that "By a strange irony, this nucleus of the new Canadian navy was first used to prevent the British subjects from landing on the British soil."

Martin Burrell, the federal Minister of Agriculture, was in Okanagan at that time. He was asked to immediately proceed to Vancouver and involve himself in the situation. The only point of dispute at that time was that Gurdit Singh did not want to move away from the Burrard Inlet without receiving the provisions and Reid wanted the ship to go at least five kilometres out of Canada's limit. Both the parties lacked faith on each other.

It is said that some Sikhs assembled in the Gurdwara at Vancouver in the evening of 21 July 1914, and decided that if the ship was fired at they would set fire to the city of Vancouver. Gurdit Singh later wrote, "Duties were allotted to each man so that as soon as the *Komagata Maru* is on fire, so will be the city of Vancouver and all in it."[27]

It is likely that such a step was thought of, in a fit of extreme anger and frustration, by some violent people as it was fraught with very serious consequences for the East Indians in particular and others in general. But unfortunately, the immigration department had darkened the political landscape so grievously as to compel the East Indians' imagination of indignation to take the battle to the streets.

But there is no denying the fact that the ghadarites distributed the ghadar literature among the passengers of the *Komagata Maru* when they were on their way to Vancouver. The revolutionaries made all efforts to see the passengers land in Canada. But in the event of their return journey they were supplied with automatic pistols and ammunition, probably meant to be used in India during the rebellion to be shortly launched there to liberate their mother country from the British rulers.

The *Rainbow* commander Walter Hose told Martin Burrell, the federal minister, that a hundred lives could be lost in the action to forcibly take the *Komagata Maru*. Burrell disagreed with the use of force and such a heavy loss of life and he agreed to make concessions to the passengers for the sake of peace. The trio had been issuing ultimatum after ultimatum to the passengers but they were adamant on their demands. The Shore Committee also told the minister that they would not be in a position to talk to the semi-starved people on the ship. They should be provided with food first and then the committee would talk to them."

Ultimately, on 22 July, the ship was provided with flour, pulses, curry powder, potatoes, onions, butter, rice, salt, tea, ginger, hair oil, vinegar, matches, kerosene oil, pepper, cabbage, carrots, etc., in sufficient quantity, to last at least for one month. The situation was eased and control of the ship was given to its captain Yamamoto and the *Komagata Maru* decided to leave on 23 July at 5 a.m. The decision of the *Komagata Maru* to return ripped the Sikh community asunder as they hoped against hope to get the passengers landed on the shores of Vancouver by all means. Because of this sad incident many of the Sikhs remained traumatized for quite sometime. They felt hit as if by a ton of bricks. In this hour of agony their psyche got changed in favour of the ghadar party. To submit lying down is alien to their nature. The passengers considered this day to be a 'black day', as all their efforts to land in Canada had proved abortive.

Martin Burrell, felt relieved and addressed Robie Reid, the government's legal counsel, "Mr. Reid, this is the most awful day in my life. Another day like this would kill me." All people involved in the explosive situation heaved a sigh of relief with the relaxation of tension.

Regarding Burrell's role in the situation likely to flare up any moment, A.H. MacNeill, the lawyer for the Indians, wrote to the Prime Minister, Robert Borden, on 22 July:" It was very fortunate that the Honourable Mr. Burrell was in British Columbia, and arrived on the scene at the critical moment. I can assure you that were it not for Mr. Burrell's presence here, no settlement could possibly have been arrived at. The attitude of the local immigration people and local politicians was such as not to admit of any negotiations or settlement on any terms. I think that an investigation will disclose that there never was any occasion for the night attack made by the immigration people on the *Komagta Maru*. The whole matter could have been very readily avoided by the exercise of some slight degree of diplomacy and consideration for the people who were on board, as well as their friends on shore."[28]

The Prime Minister was happy over it because the viceroy of India and the India Office, London felt that the use of force against the *Komagata Maru* passengers was likely to have a 'very bad effect in India.' Mr. Borden knew that H.H. Stevens and the local whites were not aware of the imperial dimensions of the crisis.

On 22 July, the East Indians of Vancouver were allowed to meet their relatives and friends on the *Komagata Maru* in groups of ten, each for five minutes time.

On 23 July, at 5.10 just after sunrise, the *Komagata Maru* raised its anchor and in the next few minutes the ship vanished in the vast ocean on its return voyage.

The local *Vancouver Sun* made a sharp attack on H.H. Stevens M.P. and Robert Borden's government for not settling the issue without the use of violence and the show of force by the machine-gun boat and the *Sea Lion* equipped with armed men.

Throughout the dispute between the immigration department and the *Komagata Maru*, the Khalsa Diwan Society, Vancouver, got itself actively involved on the side of the East Indian passengers. The office-bearers of the Society and the Sikhs of Vancouver and other areas of the country appealed to the government's sense of justice, requesting them to allow the newcomers to land. The Vancouver Sikhs even promised to pay the required $200 per person. But the immigration authorities did not relax their conditions. The legal fight continued for two months subjecting the Sikh community to heavy expenses that they bore ungrudgingly. The Shore Committee, which had been constituted to defend the case of the passengers of the *Komagata Maru*, spent more than $70,000 on food, supplies, and all types of expenses including charter costs. Almost all members of the Sikh community contributed towards this fund according to their resources. Local people were not allowed any contact with the passengers and the Canadian navy ruthlessly checked any communication between them.

Had the communication of the Shore Committee and the lawyer been allowed with the passengers and if some of the passengers had not fallen ill and their condition on the ship had not been that bad and if it had been possible to keep the *Komagata Maru* anchored on the Vancouver shore any further, the case would have been taken to the British Privy Council in London.

No doubt the immigration rules were weak and if challenged at higher courts as Supreme Court of Canada or the Privy Council these could be defeated but in the circumstances in which the passengers were placed they could not wait floating on sea that long.

One of the crew, a graduate of Calcutta University, addressed the court before waving a flag proudly. He said, "The disintegrating laws which a misguided diplomacy have allowed to be passed were exhaustively analyzed after being promulgated thoroughly among those interested. We decided after mature deliberation that while the dominion of Canada is not so great as India, it is still a part of the globe-encircling empire and that we were not without adequate justification in coming here to make it greater by our brawn and brain. All we ask from the deck of our prison ship is to be treated as men and brothers. Let this false race prejudice be obliterated in a flood of real patriotism and we still stand shoulder to shoulder with you in making this Canada realise the consummation of which you dream."

Indian viceroy, Lord Hardinge's subsequent statements show clearly that he had no sympathy with the Indian immigrants. In a speech to his council on 8 September 1914, he said that the voyage of the *Komagata Maru* had been undertaken without the cognizance or approval of the Indian government and was in contravention of Canadian immigration laws. He spoke of the generosity of the Canadians in supplying the *Komagata Maru* with 4000 dollars worth of provisions and not the hardships and expenses borne by the passengers. His own attitude is summed up in the following words: "The development of this incident was watched by the government of India with the closest attention; but that as the question at issue was of a purely legal character, there was no occasion for intervention."[29]

Return Journey and Killings at Budge Budge

The passengers of the *Komagata Maru* left the shores of Vancouver in bad mood and naturally so because most of them had staked all their possessions on this unsuccessful enterprise.

As observed in numerous situations, the Sikhs cope with trauma better than the whites. Even in daily life, they would be less stressed than the Westerners in the same situation. By nature, they are more stress-absorbing and more amenable to the circumstances in which they are placed. It is easy to judge them from their faces that they are comparatively more composed, stronger in their mental makeup and their tolerance level. Since they are more exposed to trying conditions in their daily lives, they would be tougher to crack. We can attribute it to their fatalistic bent of mind, their unshakable faith in God and their being deeply religious.

Ploying the rough waters for 25 days the ship reached Yokohama on 16 August 1914. Sohan Singh Bhakna, the founding member and the first president of the ghadar party, delivered two hundred automatic pistols and two thousand rounds of ammunition to the passengers of the ship. Giani Bhagwan Singh later stated that he had purchased the pistols and sent them through Baba Sohan Singh. At Yokohama, Gurdit Singh received a letter from the colonial secretary at Hong Kong that none of the passengers could land there otherwise those landing there would be arrested under the vagrancy law. Gurdit Singh wrote to the British consul, at

Yokohama that they will proceed to any port in India if provisions were supplied to them. The consul declined the demand.

When some members of the Vancouver Shore Committee including Mit Singh and Husain Rahim met Gurdit Singh on the ship a day before its departure for India, it was decided here that the ship be purchased so that the passengers could be brought to Canada direct from Calcutta, thus foiling the prohibitive immigration regulations of Canada. In Kobe (Japan) Gurdit Singh made an offer and got a letter from Sato—the agent for the company that owned the *Komagata Maru*, setting out the terms of purchase. On his arrival in Japan Gurdit Singh received thousands of dollars sent by the ghadarites from the United States and Canada and was also making all possible savings to be able to purchase the ship. But since he was not allowed to land anywhere on his way back the deal could not be finalised and the Budge Budge incident ended the plan to buy the ship.

The ship left Yokohama on 18 August and reached Kobe on 21 August where they were able to get 19,000 Yen from the Consul-General Forster for provisions on Indian government's permission after a lot of protest. Some passengers had disembarked at Yokohama and another fifteen landed at Kobe. The *Komagata Maru* left Kobe on 3 September and reached Singapore on 16 September. At Singapore no passenger was allowed to get off the ship. Even Gurdit Singh, who had been a long time resident of the Malay States and could move about freely in Singapore, was not allowed to disembark to purchase some necessary provisions. The ship left Singapore on 19 September for its next port, now in India. On 26 September the *Komagata Maru* entered Hooghly and it came opposite to Kalpi where it was thoroughly searched next day and nothing incriminating was found in it. Gurdit Singh himself writes, "all the illegitimate things with the passengers were either thrown overboard in the sea or restored to the Japanese.... The deck passengers were thoroughly searched and they found nothing objectionable in their possessions."[30]

There is no denying the fact that some passengers used firearms at Budge Budge. Where did these come from? Isemonger and Slattery write: "While there was no obstruction to the search of baggage it was impossible on the crowded ship to make this thorough."[31]

According to Michael O'Dwyer, "Unfortunately the search was perfunctory and many revolvers and much ammunition were brought ashore, either concealed on the persons or among the clothes, covering *The Granth Sahib* or Sikh *Bible*."[32]

It is also said, "that by wrapping the revolvers in cloth sheets, these were put in the water instead of oil tank and were safely hidden. Some of these revolvers got rusted because of water."[33]

On 29 September the ship reached Budge Budge about 27 kilometres from Calcutta, where the Deputy Commissioner Humphreys told Gurdit Singh that from there the passengers would be taken to the Budge Budge railway station to board train for the Punjab.

The suspected connections of the ship with the ghadarites, the outbreak of war and unemployment in Calcutta, were most probably, the excuses of the Bengal authorities to send them to the Punjab. None of the passengers of the *Komagata Maru* was considered above suspicion, including the 59 who had boarded the train for Punjab at Budge Budge before the trouble started there. Even they were interned in their villages during the years of war. Neither they could find a job nor could they do farming properly.

Gurdit Singh refused to accept the proposal telling James Donald, magistrate and chief administrative officer of the district of 24-Parganas, that the holy *Guru Granth Sahib* had to be taken to Howrah Gurdwara. Secondly, the passengers wanted to stay on in Calcutta to earn a living. Thirdly, he had to straighten some matters with the owners of the ship regarding certain cargo to be left with them. Fourthly, he suspected that the train was not gong to the Punjab but to Assam. Fifthly, he had some personal business in connection with the *Komagata Maru* and the arbitrator in Calcutta could adjust that in his presence. Sixthly, he had still to recover $25,000 from the passengers who expected to get the money from their relatives and friends in Calcutta. And seventhly, the passengers who had spent nearly six months on board wanted time to settle their accounts with each other.

The police persuaded forty-five more passengers to board the train and the remaining about 250 of them moved towards Calcutta on foot. The Commissioner of Police, Frederick Halliday, called the police from the police headquarters in Calcutta. The Superintendent of Reserve police, J.H. Eastwood, led the police force to stop the march of the passengers of the *Komagata Maru* and he brought them back to Budge Budge where they sat down around the holy *Guru Granth Sahib*. The district magistrate, Donald, called Gurdit Singh out of the assembled Sikhs but the latter asked Donald to talk to him where he was. The Superintendent of Police, Eastwood, pushed into the Sikhs to get Gurdit Singh. The police officer was knocked down by the Sikhs and firing started. Eastwood was fatally wounded. As a result of the firing and riots twenty Sikh passengers, two Europeans, two Punjabi police officers and two Indian residents of Budge

Budge were killed. Of those twenty Sikhs who died eighteen died from gun shot and one was drowned and another was injured and later died of cholera in the hospital.[34]

The appointment of a Commission of Inquiry was announced on 15 October 1914 by the government of India on the Budge Budge incident. It started work on 23 October and finished it in six weeks. The Commission declared the police not guilty and put the whole blame on the passengers of the *Komagata Maru*. The Commission comprised of three Englishmen and two Indians, Bijoy Chand, the Maharaja of Burdwan, who had already earned notoriety for his contemptuous remarks about Indian nationalists and Daljit Singh of Kapurthala who was subsequently knighted for his 'services.'[35]

The Indian members were not known for their independence. Hence the report was highly prejudiced as desired by the government.

Last days of Gurdit Singh

Many of the captured Sikhs including Gurdit Singh's seven-year old son, Balwant Singh, were detained in the jail in Calcutta and later sent to the Punjab. Twenty eight passengers including Gurdit Singh escaped. He remained at large for seven years one month and seventeen days, that is, from 29 September 1914 to 16 November 1921. He surrendered himself to police on 16 November 1921, in the presence of his son, his old father and his elder sister, on the insistence of Mahatma Gandhi. On 26 July 1922, he was sentenced to five years imprisonment after trial at Amritsar. During the period he remained underground before his surrender he met Mahatma Gandhi, Pandit Rambhuj Dutt Choudhari and many others. During the days of his hiding Gurdit Singh could not stick to one particular place for fear of being recognized and arrested. When he was sentenced to imprisonment he was sixty-three. He remained in jail for full five years. . After he came out of prison in 1927 he had some smaller repeated stints in prison.

In 1935, he contested an election to the Punjab Assembly at the age of 76 and he lost to a Sikh nationalist politician, Partap Singh Kairon, who was forty-one years his junior. In July 1939 he wrote to Ram Sharan Vidyarthi that : "I have to work very hard at an advanced age of seventy nine. I simply cannot get time to write my own biography.... I have many proofs that the government had given me a great deal of trouble and hardship for no crime of mine that is why I opposed the British government. The British government is very unjust to our countrymen and based on that I have made this the principle of my life that I am willing to uproot the government and establish independence for my country and it is for this I have suffered all kinds of hardships."[36]

In September 1951 Gurdit Singh wrote to Prime Minister Jawahar Lal Nehru that he wanted a memorial built in the memory of the passengers of the *Komagata Maru*. The Bengal government built it and Pandit Nehru unveiled it on 1 January 1952. In January 1954 Gurdit Singh came from Calcutta to Amritsar on grounds of bad health. On his request the living passengers of the *Komagata Maru* were called to Amritsar at a function arranged by the Punjab Sikh Youth Federation on 4 July 1954, presided over by Gurdit Singh. Almost completing ninety fifth year of his life the hero of the *Komagata Maru* died on 24 July 1954, after a very strenuous and chequered career.

For the last forty years of his life Gurdit Singh continued revealing the innocence of the passengers of the *Komagata Maru* who had been refused entry into Canada and fired on by the police and troops in India.

To sum up, the *Komagata Maru* episode was a challenge to racially discriminating immigration laws of Canada and it questioned as to why the Indians—the British subjects, could not enter Canada while the non-British citizens could. Besides the above immigration rules, it was the declared policy of the Canadian government, the Canadian press and the Canadian people to keep Canada a white country.

Gurdit Singh was shrewd enough to know as to what was going to happen to the *Komagata Maru* at Vancouver but he was determined to let the world know what the Canadian Immigration laws for India were and how the race and skin colour determined their immigration policy. And on that account Gurdit Singh and his companions had to make a perilous trip that involved tremendous sacrifices that they did not shirk to undergo. There can be nothing farther from truth than the view that Gurdit Singh wanted to make money out of this enterprise.

But let us believe for a moment that Gurdit Singh planned to operate a lucrative shipping service between Canada and India for purely economic considerations. What was wrong with it? In that eventuality he would have also falsified or made the 'through journey' order of the Canadian government designed to ban the entry of the Indians into Canada as null and void. But he was less of a businessman and more of a fighter for his and his people's rights. If business were his only concern he could have enough of it in Singapore, Hong Kong and Malay states where he exercised a lot of influence, before he undertook the *Komagata Maru* voyage to Canada.

Gurdit Singh said," Besides, the visions of men are widened by travel and contact with citizens of a free country will infuse a spirit of independence and foster yearning for freedom in the minds of the emasculated subjects of alien rule," as he strongly felt that India's degradation was due to lack of association with new ideas and developments outside her borders. Thus, through this enterprise, he wanted to ignite a fiery passion in the Indians' hearts for the world beyond the horizon of their country.

The overall effect of this great enterprise of the East Indians was that it caused to intensify the movement of India's freedom as it strongly reminded them of their helpless status in their own motherland. This episode had assumed the status of an international importance. If the *Komagata Maru* incident had not occurred, there would not have been such an awakening among the Indians in Canada and the United States. This episode gave a powerful stimulus to the ghadar propaganda that was already spreading among the Indians alarmingly to the disadvantage of the British and to the awakening of national consciousness in India.

The Canadian government rectified this gross racial discrimination against the East Indians as late as 1989 when on 23 July, Sikh societies across Canada commemorated the 75th anniversary of this reprehensible incident. They put a plaque with the following inscription on the shores of Vancouver at the Portal Park on Hastings Street overlooking the Burrard Inlet, on 23 May 1990, jointly by the municipal, provincial and federal governments.

THE KOMAGATA MARU 75TH ANNIVERSARY

ON MAY 23, 1914, 376 BRITISH SUBJECTS (12 HINDUS, 24 MUSLIMS AND 340 SIKHS) OF INDIAN ORIGIN ARRIVED IN VANCOUVER HARBOUR ABOARD THE *KOMAGATA MARU* SEEKING TO ENTER CANADA. 352 OF THE PASSENGERS WERE DENIED ENTRY AND FORCED TO DEPART ON JULY 23, 1914. THIS PLAQUE COMMEMORATES THE 75TH ANNIVERSARY OF THAT UNFORTUNATE INCIDENT OF RACIAL DISCRIMINATION, AND REMINDS CANADIANS OF OUR COMMITMENT TO AN OPEN SOCIETY IN WHICH MUTUAL RESPECT AND UNDERSTANDING ARE HONOURED, DIFFERENCES ARE RESPECTED AND TRADITIONS ARE CHERISHED.

There were hundreds of incidents that affected the Indo-Canadians during their one hundred years existence in Canada. Mentioned below are two events first of which gave them their biggest shock and the second gave them their biggest joy. The first happened on 23 July 1914, when the *Komagata Maru* was forced to return to India from Canadian shores and the second took place on 2 April 1947, when they were given the right to vote and become Canadian citizens.

REFERENCES

1. Isemonger, F.C. and Slattery J., *An Account of the Ghadar*
2. *Conspiracy*, Lahore, 1919, p.36.
3. Department of Commerce and Industry, Government of India, *Emigration B Proceedings*, July 1914, Nos.13-15, pp.16-17.
4. Gurdit Singh, *Voyage of Komagata Maru*, Calcutta, 1st edition, n.d., pp.15-16.
5. *Ibid.*, p.20.
6. *The Times*, London, 23 May 1914.
7. *The daily News-Advertiser*, Vancouver, 23 May 1914.
8. *The Daily Province*, Vancouver, 27 May 1914.
9. *The Times*, London, 4 June 1914.
10. Husain Rahim (edited), *The Hindustanee*, Journal, Vancouver, 1 June 1914.
11. *The Vancouver Sun*, 1 June 1914.
12. Department of Commerce and Industry, Government of India, *Emigration A Proceedings*, September 1914, Nos.13-15, p.4.
13. *The Vancouver Sun*, 26 June 1914.
14. *The Vancouver Sun*, 24 June 1914.
15. *Ibid.*, 30 June 1914.
16. *Ibid.*, 24 June 1914.
17. *Statist*, a weekly, London, 13 June 1914.
18. *Daily News-Advertiser*, 17 June 1914.
19. *Ibid.*
20. *The Times*, London, 4 June 1914.
21. *The Daily Province*, Vancouver, 29 June, 6 July 1914.
22. Hugh Johnston, *The Voyage of the Komagata Maru : The Sikh challenge to Canada's colour Bar*, 2nd edition, Vancouver, 1989, p.64.
23. *Ibid.*, p.77.
24. Gurdit Singh, *op.cit*, p. 104.
25. *Ibid.*, p.106.
26. Ferguson, *A Whiteman's Country*, Toronto, 1975, pp.116-117.
27. Gurdit Singh, *op.cit.*, p.107.

28. *Ibid.*, p.110.
29. *MacNeill to Borden*, 22 July 1914, Borden Papers quoted by Hugh Johnston, op.cit., p.86.
30. *Gazette of India*, 19 September 1914, p.973.
31. Gurdit Singh, op.cit., Part II, pp.31-34.
32. F.C. Isemonger and J. Slattery, *op.cit.*, p.81.
33. Michael O'Dwyer, *India as I Knew* it, London, 1927, p.193.
34. *Report of Komagata Maru Committee*, p.14.
35. *The Report of the Enquiry Commission*, Government of India, Home Department.
36. Khushwant Singh, *A History of the Sikhs*, Vol.2, Princeton, New Jersey, 1966, p.181.
37. Ram Sharan Vidyarthi, *Komagata Maru Ki Samundri Yatra*, Mirzapur, 1970, pp.98-99.

CHAPTER 4

GHADAR MOVEMENT IN CANADA AND AMERICA

The social, economic and political conditions were mainly responsible for changing the passive habits of the East Indians to an attitude of rebellion in the United States and Canada. When Kartar Singh Sarabha, a young man in his teens, was asked as to why he left a comfortable life in America to be rotting in an Indian jail, he replied that he was no better in America. The humiliating treatment there worked as nails in his body. The Indians were treated like animals or even worse and seen with contempt.

Ghadar Movement Originated in Canada

Ghadar literally means mutiny. The ghadar movement was started by ordinary East Indian farmers and labourers who were subjected to intolerable indignities in Canada and America and not by some extremists. In 1906, the Canadian legislature passed an Immigration Act to control the entry of Asians into Canada. In 1907 the government of British Columbia deprived the Indians of right to vote in the provincial elections. Next year, they were debarred from participating in the municipal elections also. During the next forty years they were kept outside their genuine right of franchise. And mercilessly enough, the Victoria (British Columbia) municipality even took a decision to the effect that the Indians should not be provided with any work.[1]

In 1907, W.L. Mackenzie King, Deputy Minister for Labour, Canada (later Prime Minister), visited England and met Secretary of State for India and the Foreign Secretary, in connection with preventing the Indians from entering Canada. They expressed agreement with the demand of the Canadian government. This lack of sympathy of the British government towards the British Indian subjects created bitterness in the minds of the

Indians. The two orders-in-council passed by Canada in 1908 closed the Canadian borders to the Indians. These orders have been discussed in the chapter on immigration in this book in detail. Their effect on the minds of the Indians was none other than bitter resentment. The Chinese and the Japanese were not placed under such harsh restrictions. Their governments always safeguarded their interests and on the other hand the British rulers of India were always against the interests of their Indian subjects. The Indians in Canada and America realized that unless they were a free nation, they would not have a respectful place in foreign countries. And so long as their ambassadors were not in those countries, their demands would always remain unattended, their rights would remain ignored or would remain on the mercy of the governments of those countries.

In 1908, the Canadian government tried to get rid of the East Indians by sending them to Honduras telling them fraudulently that they would be much better off there in the warm climate.

In 1906, the Khalsa Diwan Society was organized in Vancouver with branches at Victoria, New Westminster, Abbotsford, Fraser Mills, etc. The society built a Gurdwara in Vancouver on 2nd Avenue in 1908. Three years later another Sikh temple was built in Victoria (1912) and some time later smaller Gurdwaras were built in other towns. Similarly the Khalsa Diwan Society of the United States built a Gurdwara at Stockton. The Gurdwaras were the only public places where the East Indians could meet for discussing their religious, social and political problems. In due course of time, these Sikh temples became storm centres of political activity.

Lala Lajpat Rai, who visited the East Indians in Canada and the United States, said that there were three types of prejudices against the Indians, "Firstly, there is colour prejudice, secondly, there is the race prejudice, thirdly, there is the prejudice of religion."[2]

The Interests of Canadian and American Labour clashed with Indian Labour

The American and Canadian trade unions always fought against their employers for higher wages and better working conditions. In the event of a strike, by the white labourers, the Indian workers offered their services at low wages, to the detriment of the interests of the whites. It resulted in straining the relations between the white labourers and the Indian workers. The whites launched programmes to expel the Indians from their countries. From the year of 1907 onwards the legislatures of British Columbia as well as that of the state of California passed several enactments to prohibit employment of the Indians in certain industries and check the East Indian immigration. The Asiatic Exclusion Leagues were formed in both Canada and America.

In 1910, a monthly journal, *The Whiteman,* started at San Francisco, wrote in its August 1910 issue that "The economic, moral and social life of the white race in California and elsewhere must be protected. The surrender of our lands and opportunities to Asiatics is a mark of national decay. The association of white women with Mongolians, Indians and Negroes is racial pollution."[3]

An election statement of Franck McGown, candidate for Republican nomination for Attorney-General said, "For political, industrial and sociological reasons, I am unalterably opposed to Asiatic immigration."[4] Bernard J. Flood, a candidate for Republican nomination as Justice of Peace wrote, "I am decidedly opposed to making California the hunting ground of Asiatic coolies. I am opposed to the admission of Indians, Japanese and Chinese and no law could be too stringent to restrict them. This is a white man's country, let us keep it for the white man's children."[5] The East Indians felt very unhappy on such statements. They attributed it to the British government in India who did not provide them protection in their new homelands. They planned to drive out the British rulers from India and liberate their motherland from the foreign yoke.

There were many clubs and associations in Canada and America that shouted at the top of their voice that their countries were becoming the dumping ground for the most undesirable people of India whose wholesale admission to their countries was fast becoming a menace to their countries. The Indians found it again and again that the Japanese and Chinese consuls in America protected their respective countrymen from maltreatment at the hands of the Americans, but the British Indian rulers never did it.

Inspiration from the American War of Independence

Though the American War of Independence was fought against the same imperial British masters long back in 1775-76, its spirit prevailed very much there in the country. It gave encouragement to the Indians and fired their thinking that all their problems would be resolved and with India as a free country, the Indians abroad would live a life of honour and dignity. The stigma of slavery would be permanently washed away. Consequently they began to seriously think in terms of launching an armed rebellion against the British.

Contact with Russian Anarchists and Irish Patriots

The Indian patriots met the Russian anarchists and Irish patriots. The Russian anarchists told the Indians that the maltreatment meted out to them by their rulers was a part of the capitalist exploitation of the workers of different nationalities and race and colour prejudice was a sort of class snobbery. The Irish patriots taught them as to how an alien rule can be done away with, by the use of arms.

Impending war between the Great Britain and Germany

As the situation obtained, the war between Great Britain and Germany was going to flare up shortly and the ghadar or mutiny in India would be greatly instrumental in throwing the British out of India. Therefore, the Indian immigrants established contact with the Germans who gave them assurance that the German government would provide them help if they engaged in anti-British activities and organized an armed movement against the British in India. This situation hastened the preparation of armed rebellion against the British by the Canadian and American immigrants.

American Sympathy with the Indians

Some of the Americans expressed their sympathy and moral support to the Indians and desired of them to organize an armed struggle against their callous British rulers. Sohan Singh Bhakna writes in his biography that once he, along with another worker, went to a mill in search of a job. The owner of the mill told them that though he had enough of work, he would not employ them. If he had his way, he felt like shooting them. He asked Sohan Singh about the population of India. 'It was three hundred million', told Bhakna. He retorted, 'three hundred million dumb animals or human beings?' Bhakna said, 'three hundred million human beings'. The mill owner asked them if they were three hundred million people how come that they were slaves. He offered a gun to Bhakna and said, 'go back to your country and liberate it, then he would be the first to welcome them'. Bhakna instantly decided to do the needful at the earliest opportunity. It was a colossally stupendous task to fight against the British Empire that controlled and governed almost more than half the world at that time.

An extremist movement rising in India itself

A violent movement was taking birth in India itself under the leadership of Lala Lajpat Rai and Ajit Singh who belonged to the Punjab and knew the humiliation and hardships being suffered by the Punjabis abroad. They attributed it to the policies of the British rulers of India. During those days Bengal witnessed a terrorist and an extremist movement in Maharashtra led by B.G. Tilak and there was a general strike of workers in Bombay. Thus, there was a section of the national movement that was becoming militant in nature and spirit.

The above factors played a prominent role in the establishment of a Ghadar Party with its headquarters at San Francisco and branches in Canada, Japan, Philippines, Hong Kong, China, Malaya States, Singapore, Trinidad, South Africa and other countries where there were Indian communities.

Founding of the Ghadar Party

Before the Ghadar Party was formed much of the spadework had been done in Canada and America. The Khalsa Diwan Societies had adequately aroused awareness among the Sikhs in particular and the other Indians in general. Some societies worked to safeguard the economic interests of Indian workers and took up their cases with the immigration department. 'The United India League' functioned in Vancouver and 'the Hindustani Association of the *Pacific Coast*' operated in Astoria. There was a society named 'Friends of Hindustan' set up in San Francisco in 1910. Its members included a number of white ladies, one of whom was the secretary of the organisation. This club tried to secure unrestricted admission to Canada and America for the East Indians and also they wanted to advance the cause of India's freedom. A newspaper report said, "Armed with the western education, the members of 'Friends of Hindustan' society, will be in a position to fight the battles of India for the Indians".[6]

Despite all these ambitious plans, it was an extremely dangerous and a Herculean task for which they had to do a lot tightrope walking before they could dream of achieving their cherished goal.

One of the Indian students who was a member of the 'Friends of Hindustan' society told that Chemistry was his subject and he wanted to make use of his knowledge to furthering 'the cause'. Making of explosives occupied most of his attention. He also told that he was a member of a secret military organisation formed from the ranks of his fellow students of his country.

In 1912, some East Indian associations were organized in the United States. Their objectives were to arrange vernacular papers from India to keep them abreast of the events in their country, to invite students from India for education and to develop in them a nationalist outlook and to hold weekly meetings to discuss politics.

Kesar Singh as president and Balwant Singh as secretary headed an association organized at Astoria, Oregan. Guru Dutt Kumar formed an association in Portland. Thus, various associations were established with political considerations as the main objective.

Many political journals made their appearance from time to time, most of them from Canada. The East Indians were interested in politics, as they were keen to get themselves liberated from an alien rule in their mother country. Tarak Nath Das, a Bengali, had left India in 1905 for Tokyo as warrants of his arrest had been issued against him for his anti-government activities. From there he went to the USA where he became a leading revolutionary. He had earlier stayed in Vancouver also for some time where he was employed by the government as an interpreter. For his writings against the government, police inspector W.C. Hopkinson was dispatched from Calcutta to arrest and send him to India. Tarak Nath came to know of it and he managed to slip to Seattle where he started his studies and also worked for his livelihood and passed M.A. examination and later also got the citizenship of America. He continued his anti-India activities and was an active member of a secret society of his compatriots. He was one of the prominent revolutionaries and was a staunch believer of a revolution in India. Tarak Nath Das's *Free Hindustan* contained seditious writings. This journal was in circulation for three years, issued first from Vancouver and then from Seattle and later from New York. Its editor, a Bengali, was a man of very progressive views. Prominent socialists like Tolstoy and British sociologist Hyndman contributed articles to this journal. Its publication was stopped in 1912 by the American government at the instance of the British government. Tarak Nath Das who was ordered to be deported was the president of a secret society called *Samity*. He had close links with many secret organizations in India. He was sentenced to two years in jail after a trial in San Francisco.

Harnam Singh and Guru Dutt Kumar from Vancouver published *Desh Sewak in Gurmukhi* script and Urdu. This journal also reproduced many articles from such revolutionary papers of India as *Bande Matram*, *Liberator* and Shyamji Krishnavarma's *Indian Sociologist* published from London, Paris and Geneva. Guru Dutt Kumar was also a member of the Secret Society that functioned from Vancouver and Seattle. Dr Sundar Singh and Husain Rahim also became the members of that society later and delivered inflammatory speeches. They also appealed for arms and funds for a fight against the British. Once some literature regarding the manufacturing of bombs was found from the house of Husain Rahim.

Dr Sunder Singh edited an English monthly magazine *Aryan* from 1909-1912; it was very popular among the educated East Indians. Kartar Singh Akali, who came to Canada in 1911, started a Punjabi (*Gurmukhi*) monthly, *Khalsa Herald* in Vancouver and this paper was known for its radical views. Kartar Singh also edited a journal named *Sansar* in 1912, which was later merged with Sundar Singh's *Aryan*. The *Hindustanee*, the official organ of 'The United India League' began its publication from Vancouver in 1914 in English, edited by Husain Rahim. Dr Sundar Singh later edited *Canada and India* from Toronto, which continued appearing till 1917. Kartar Singh Akali also moved to Toronto from where he edited The *Theosophical News* for some years.

These efforts to produce literature aimed at political awakening among the Canadian and the American Immigrants but none of these journals could enjoy a long tenure of existence.

In March 1913, it was decided by ghadarites to give a concrete shape to their programmes against the British. Har Dayal was called to assume charge of the movement. He was a man of luminous intelligence with amazing capacity to pierce through any problem to its core. This revolutionary organisation was given the name of Ghadar Party. A meeting held on 25 March 1913, was attended by Har Dayal, Parmanand, Sohan Singh Bhakna, Jawala Singh, Kartar Singh Sarabha and many others who offered themselves to jump into the movement disregarding the consequences, however dreadful they might be. To propagate their political programme it was decided to publish a weekly newspaper called the *ghadar* meaning mutiny or rebellion. The headquarters of the party were to be located at San Francisco (California). The party office was named Yugantar Ashram or Ghadar Ashram.

Har Dayal (1884-1938) was appointed to work as editor of the *weekly ghadar*. Sohan Singh Bhakna (1870-1968) who was, then, working in a lumber mill in Oregon, was elected as president of the party and Har Dayal its secretary. Sohan Singh Bhakna was one of the outstanding leaders of the ghadar movement. He had very definite and committed political leanings towards the party he was chosen to lead. He was a very balanced man and always used very carefully chosen words. In his dealings he was as clean as fresh snow. He would never allow his sweet temper get sour. But being almost an illiterate person he lacked the imagination required for directing a movement like ghadar against the shrewd and powerful

British government. For want of supremely intelligent and efficient leader to guide the ghadar, it was destined to be unsuccessful. Bhakna had been a very active member of the Namdhari movement in India. In response to the Kuka or Namdhari movement's code of discipline he had decided, "Not to accept service with the government, not to send children to government schools, not to use courts of law but settle disputes in *panchayats* (village community courts), not to use foreign goods and not to use the government postal service."

Bhakna returned to India in pursuance of the party's mission. He was arrested, tortured and sentenced to death and later his death penalty was commuted to transportation for life. About the mid-1930s he was released from the prison. In the later years of his life he worked for the Kisan Sabha.

Unshaken in his convictions and always ready to make the maximum sacrifice for his cherished mission, Bhakna was decidedly the best choice for the post of the president of the ghadar party despite his handicap in respect of adequate education and political acumen. Har Dayal belonged to a Kayastha family of Delhi. He had his education in Delhi, Lahore and England at Oxford. After his return to India, he was sent to Paris to edit *Bande Matram*, a monthly journal issued from Geneva. Shortly thereafter he went to California in 1911. He took up the job of a lecturer in Sanskrit and Indian philosophy, at the Stanford University (USA). Later he became secretary of the San Francisco Radical Club and also organized a society of Indian students there for fomenting a revolutionary agitation in their mother-country. Later, he took up his job as the secretary of the *ghadar* party and the editorship of the weekly journal *ghadar*. He possessed prodigious memory and broke many university examination records. He was a man of uncommon commonsense. He had earned the reputation of possessing towering intellectual strength and passionate dedication to his work matchlessly, projecting a charismatic personality but later he distanced himself from the *ghadar* movement that caused noticeable erosion in his popularity. Though he came to be known as a great intellectual and a genius but his book 'Hints for Self Culture' does not reveal any signs of a genius. He was eccentric in his political views. After the First World War he moved to Sweden where he taught philosophy at Upsala.

On 1 November 1913, Har Dayal brought out the first issue of the *ghadar* in Punjabi (*Gurmukhi* script) and Urdu. In the editorial he wrote: "What is our name? Mutiny (*ghadar*). What is our work? Mutiny. Where will this mutiny break out? In India. When will it break out? In a few years. Why should it break out? Because the people can no longer bear the oppression and tyranny practised under British rule and are ready to fight and die for freedom." The message of the *ghadar* went to all associations linked with the movement and to most of the Indians who could read it. Bhag Singh, president of the Gurdwara in Vancouver, read it out to the Sikhs assembled in the Gurdwara. The East Indians in Canada and the USA were appealed to send money to the '*ghadar* Ashram' in San Francisco so that thousands of copies could be published and sent to as many people as possible.

On the front page, just beneath the name of the paper, was written, "Enemy of the British government." In the third issue of the paper that dealt with the impending war in Europe was written: "The Germans have great sympathy with our movement for liberty because they and ourselves have a common enemy (the English). In the future, Germany can draw assistance from us and they can render us great assistance also."[7]

Many poems and articles from the *ghadar* were reproduced in booklets. The following are the extracts from *ghadar-di-gunj*[8] (echoes of the mutiny):

No pundits or mullahs do we need,
No prayers or litanies we need recite,
These will only scuttle our boat.
Draw the sword; it is time to fight.   (Vol. I, No.4)

Though Hindus, Musalmans and the Sikhs we be,
Sons of Bharat are we still,
Put aside our arguments for another day,
Call of the hour is to kill.   (Vol. I, No.23)

In the course of a few months the paper began to circulate among the Indians settled in Canada, Hong Kong, China, Japan, Philippines, Singapore, South and East Africa and many other countries where Indians were living. Thousands of copies were also sent to India. And everywhere people were reading the *ghadar* with interest.

Har Dayal was arrested on 25th March 1914, in San Francisco, for his revolutionary writings through his paper *ghadar*. He was released on 1000 dollars bail but he jumped bail and went to Switzerland in April 1914. William Hopkinson kept watch over the activities of the Indian revolutionaries living in Canada and the U.S.A. He would occasionally disguise himself as a Sikh, wearing a turban. He attended meetings addressed by Har Dayal in San Francisco. In Vancouver also he attended the meetings of the East Indian immigrants, held in connection with the refusal of the government to the passengers of the *Komagata Maru* to land.

The Aims of the Ghadar Party

The conferences of the *ghadar* party at Astoria on 21st April 1913, and at Sacramento on 31st December 1913, outlined the aims of the party through the resolutions passed there. It was declared that India was to be liberated from foreign yoke by an armed rebellion. The system of self-government in India would be based on the principles of liberty, equality and fraternity. In an article published in the *ghadar*, it was laid down that "the object of this movement is that the people of India should start a mutiny, uproot and destroy the British government like a worm-eaten tree, and establish a national government."[9]

The first Mandalay conspiracy case, with reference to the paper *ghadar* observed that "from the first issue it (the *ghadar*) openly preached turning out the British and establishment of a republican government in which all communities of India will have representation."[10]

The objects of the Indian revolutionaries in the United States were, "to prepare the means for a military enterprise to be carried on from within the territory of the United States against India... to incite mutiny and armed rebellion in India and to destroy the said government and authority."[11]

The party being secular in nature, every body could join it, irrespective of caste, creed, colour or community. The party was free from any taboos of mixing, socialising and eating as it propagated international outlook. The national anthem of the party was *Bande Matram* (hail mother).

The members of the party were required to be ready for every sacrifice—physical, mental and financial, for the liberation of India. They should always keep in mind that their lives and properties were at the disposal of the party.

The Plans of the Party

Different first rank members of the party played different roles. Har Dayal, through his forceful writings, inspired thousands of readers of the *ghadar* paper. He, again and again, emphasized the need of a mutiny and expulsion of the British from India if its people had to live a life of respect and dignity in their motherland and abroad and the only way to oust them out of India was the use of force. No peaceful means could work. They should amass weapons and attend to the call of the *ghadar* party at the proper time.

Jawala Singh Thathian, Wasakha Singh and Santokh Singh had taken a big farm on contract near San Francisco. They received good returns from the farm and ran a community kitchen and served as a transit camp for the newcomers. Since they were better off, they contributed liberally to the ghadar party. They offered scholarships to import students from India and then to prepare them for the *ghadar*. In the early stages Jawala Singh worked from the background but financed the party to the best of his means. He was a great grower of potatoes and thus came to be known a 'potato king'. He became a rich man because of large-scale farming. The above trio started to organize the Khalsa Diwan Society in California and shortly thereafter built a Gurdwara at Stockton. The Gurdwaras at Vancouver and Stockton became the two nerve-centres of all types of activities relating to the Indians.

It was decided by the ghadar party to give military training to Indian immigrants in the United States. The students drawn into the movement represented all parts of the country and belonging to all communities in order to give it an all India character. These students also helped in dispatching the *ghadar* papers to different parts of the world where the pro-*ghadar* Indian people lived. Some of the students learnt the use of explosives and bomb-making, military war strategies and guerrilla warfare. Kartar Singh Sarabha received training in civil aviation. Harnam Singh Tundilat learnt the art of manufacturing a bomb from a British friend and during one of the experiments he lost one of his arms and henceforth came to be known as Tundilat. In government records he has been shown as Tunda (a man without an arm). Some of the *ghadarites* were to go to Kabul for the purpose of learning the technique of manufacturing rifles and to smuggle the same into India.

The *ghadar* party had planned very ambitious programmes to be pursued in India as to seduce the Indian troops, to infiltrate the ranks of the rural and urban youth, to distribute seditious literature, to procure and manufacture arms, to have close contacts with foreign enemies of the British, to destroy the government means of transportation and communications as railways and telephones, to liquidate loyal subjects, to break jails and release their sympathizers, to plunder the treasuries and *thanas*. Some members of the party visited India from time to time to study the situation and to do the necessary spadework.

The Komagata Maru Episode and Canadian Ghadarites

A chapter has been devoted to the *Komagata Maru* issue in this book.

It did not remain a problem confined to the Vancouver shores but attracted the attention of Indian people, British Indian government, the *ghadarites*, the London government and Ottawa government in particular and the whole world in general. This issue gave a fillip to the *ghadar* movement, as it was a symbol of inhumanities, indignities and stark racial discrimination inflicted on the British subjects by a British dominion. Bhai Parmanand writes, "If the *Komagata Maru* incident had not occurred, there would not have been such an awakening among the Indians in Canada and the United States."[12]

As the *Komagata Maru* entered the waters of Vancouver, the men who involved themselves in the ship's dispute with the immigration department included Bhag Singh, Balwant Singh, Mit Singh—the president and head priest and the secretary of the Gurdwara of Vancouver respectively, and Chagan Kairaj Varma alias Husain Rahim and Bhagwan Singh Giani. The Indian leaders in foreign lands need to be brought into historical focus to correctly analyse their role in the movement.

Bhagwan Singh had been a revolutionary of the stature of Har Dayal. He was gifted with sparkling wit and sharp intelligence. He had trouble with the police in 1907 in connection with disturbances in the Punjab. He left the country in 1908 to escape arrest. He worked as a priest of a Gurdwara in Hong Kong. He was arrested for preaching sedition to the Sikh troops and consequently he was compelled to leave Hong Kong in May 1913. Through a changed identity—as Natha Singh, an earlier resident of Canada, he arrived at Victoria, a few weeks later. He became clean-shaven and remained so for the rest of his life.

Of the poems published in the *ghadar* were those of Bhagwan Singh, which were translated from Punjabi to other languages and inflamed passions against the British rulers as nothing else could do. His writings were rapacious.

About Bhagwan Singh, the British war office wrote: "With Barkatullah was associated, at a later date, Bhagwan Singh, a dangerous ruffian whose seditious activities had secured his dismissal from the post of *granthi* (priest) at the Sikh temples at Penang and Hong Kong, and who was subsequently deported from Canada (August 1913) for entering the country under a misrepresentation".

Maulvi Mohammad Barkatullah was a professor of Urdu at the Tokyo University. The Japanese assisted him in his efforts against the British. He became a staunch revolutionary. Bhagwan Singh had a close liaison with Barkatullah. Bhagwan Singh was a very impressive, forceful and convincing speaker. Sometimes he used acid language in his speeches and writings. He fought against foreign rule at every foot of his path. He had a spine of steel.

Bhagwan Singh belonged to the village of Wrang in the Amritsar district. 'He was a powerful orator and his words came in a torrent, rich in imagery.' From Victoria he shifted to Vancouver where he addressed the weekly congregations at the Gurdwara and impressed upon the people to adopt the slogan *Bande Matram* (hail mother). Soon thereafter, he was arrested and ordered deported. He arranged bail and rehearing, but the immigration department, without caring for court orders, bundled him into the ship and locked in a cabin and he was sent away from Canada about the middle of November 1913. He was branded as a staunch seditionist. After meeting the returning *Komagata Maru* in Yokohama he reached San Francisco via Honolulu. He was the rarest of the rare species of human defiance and it was almost impossible for any government to put him in the can. He knew how to devise means to escape from any net spread to entrap him. He had a roller coaster career, facing a new situation every new morning. Within him lay a soul not at peace with himself or with others. He was, emotionally, a restless man, a man of mercurial temper. He emerged on the scene like a hurricane. After Har Dayal left for Switzerland on threat of deportation from America, Bhagwan Singh took charge of the weekly *ghadar*. Bhagwan Singh had purchased 270 pistols along with 500 cartridges from the USA and the same were managed to be delivered to the passengers of the *Komagata Maru*, through Sohan Singh Bhakna.

At a meeting held at Oxford (California) on 26th July 1914, Bhagwan Singh and Barkatullah announced that "the time for rebellion had come, and the British were to be expelled, as war in Europe had commenced."[13] Towards the end of November 1914 the main *jatha* of the ghadarites left San Francisco by the *S. S. Korea*. Bhagwan Singh came to the ship and addressed the passengers as under: "Your duty is clear. Go to India and stir up rebellion in every corner of the country. Rob the wealthy and show mercy to the poor. In this way you will win universal sympathy. Arms will be provided for you on your arrival in India. Failing this you must ransack the police stations for rifles. Obey without hesitation the command of your leaders."[14] He strongly agreed with the remarks of Fredrick Douglas that "Those who profess to favour freedom and yet deprecate agitation are men who want rain without thunder and lightning. They want the ocean without the roar of its many waters." He always favoured action and violent action. With blazing fire in his belly he could stir strongly and sway terribly his audience for action. He was a flaming sword unsheathed for India's freedom. He was a radiant charmer and the spirit of *ghadar* shone through his whole being. He visited many countries including Japan, China, Korea and Philippines for recruitment of volunteers from the Indian residents there. He settled in America and returned to India in 1958. In 1960, when he was bordering on 80 this author invited him to speak on *ghadar* party at a college where he was then teaching history. His answers to the questions from the staff members and senior students were simply superb and his presence of mind was marvellous. During his lecture he was all fire though from his outward appearance the bright flame of life seemed to have almost extinguished long back.

With the magic of his oratory he could mesmerize his audience. It was amusing to note that the fire of *ghadar* movement could not go out of his system even in nearly half a century after the event, which erupted even at the slightest provocation. His unbeaten soul and animated machine-gun-speed chatter defied his age-tortured and health-wrecked physical frame. He seemed to have taken his failures to be more important than success. His sufferings gave greater incentive to his growth and maturity. Hardships, pain and distress had revealed and redefined his character. Success and happiness generally make us lazy, feeble and flabby.

Another Sikh, a very daring speaker for the cause of the Sikhs and later turned a committed *ghadarite*, was Balwant Singh Atwal (1882-1917) who belonged to the village of Khurdpur in the Jalandhar district. After a brief stint in the army he reached Canada in 1906. He took active interest in the building of the Sikh temple at 2nd Avenue, Vancouver, and later became its first priest. He spoke and fought vigorously against the exclusionary policies of the Canadian immigration department. Balwant Singh, along with Bhag Singh and Sunder Singh, visited India in 1911 to enlighten the people about the miserable condition of the East Indians in Canada. In March 1913, he visited London with a deputation of two other delegates, Nand Singh and Narain Singh, to plead with the British government for the relaxation of restrictions unjustifiably imposed on them. They also visited India via Paris and Marseilles and during the summer of 1913 they addressed meetings at different places in the Punjab. Balwant Singh, in the course of his lectures, was becoming more and more bitter in his attacks on the Canadian and Indian governments. He was the son of a gun, always ready to discharge a bullet. India's freedom was very high on his life's agenda. He was proving to be a thorn in the flesh of the government. The delegates met the Punjab Lt. Governor Michael O'Dwyer who warned Balwant Singh to stop talking against the government otherwise he would have to suffer the consequences. The delegates also asked for an interview with the viceroy, Lord Hardinge, and they were sent on to him as well.

Michael O'Dwyer wrote in his book, *India As I knew it*, "In the summer of 1913, three Sikh delegates came from Canada to the Punjab. They were really advance agents—though we did not know this at the time—of the Ghadar Party.

"Their ostensible object was to arouse public opinion in India against the hardships created by Canadian immigration laws. They held meetings throughout the province, some of which were attended by many men of undoubted loyalty. But after a time the tone of these meetings changed. Instead of reasonable criticism of the immigration laws, the speeches became menacing and inflammatory.

"The delegates on an occasion asked for an interview with me. I had a long talk with them and repeated my warning. Two of them were oily and specious; the manner of the third seemed to be that of a dangerous revolutionary. They wished to see the viceroy, and in sending them on to him, I particularly warned the viceroy about this man.

"He was next heard of as a *ghadar* leader and a German agent in the Far East, engaged in pushing the revolutionary movement in Burma and Siam. He was arrested by the Siamese government in 1915, was deported to India, was tried in the second *Lahore Conspiracy* Case for murder, rebellion, etc., and sentenced to death."

When the *Komagata Maru* was on its way to Vancouver Balwant Singh addressed to them on the ship at Yokohama. When the passengers of the *Komagata Maru* were not allowed to land in Vancouver the Sikh community there held many meetings in the Gurdwara and in the hired halls. At every meeting Balwant Singh spoke with vehemence and without any fear. He was always very sincere to the cause he was pleading but at times he indulged in severe tongue-lashing, inviting government's ire and trouble for himself. He was a defiant lion to the end. Later, the *ghadar* party sent him on the *ghadar* mission to Shanghai, Siam and Singapore. The Siamese government arrested and deported him to Singapore from where he was shipped to the Punjab for trial. During the trial the witnesses linked him with the murder of Hopkinson. Bela Singh, an informer of Vancouver police (who was later killed by ghadarites in 1933 near Hoshiarpur, in the Punjab) and Dr Raghunath Singh, (who travelled to Vancouver, on the *Komagata Maru* and who had a secret meeting with Malcolm Reid, the immigration officer, regarding the plans of Gurdit Singh) informed the court as witnesses about the mutinous speeches of

Balwant Singh that he had given at the Vancouver Gurdwara and to the passengers of the *Komagata Maru* at Moji in Japan. Some witnesses also accused him of talking about the murder of Malcolm Reid, Hopkinson and Bela Singh. The court judged him as a ringleader and fit case to be awarded maximum penalty. After trial at Lahore he was hanged on 16 March 1917.

Bhag Singh (1872-1914) was another activist of Vancouver. He hailed from village Bhikhiwind in the present Amritsar district. Before moving to Canada he served in the Indian cavalry for five years, two and a half years in Hong Kong police and a little more than two years in Shanghai municipal police. Despite the immigration rules he brought his wife to Vancouver and fought legally against the deportation order served on her. He won and became an active opponent of the invidious regulations. He was elected the president of the Vancouver Gurdwara. He was a high-strung man, seldom found relaxed.

When the governor-general of Canada visited Vancouver in September 1912, the ex-army personnel sporting their medals participated in the military review. Bhag Singh rejected the invitation to attend the function. He refused to bow before the Canadian Mughal bureaucrats of his time. Three years after his immigration to Canada he burnt his discharge certificate from the Indian army, impressing upon his point that the service in the British Indian army was nothing short of a period of utter slavery. Desperate men do desperate things. He was a man of strong independent views. It is an ordinary man's way of life to live according to the world's opinion and an extraordinary brave man's way of life is to live according to his own independent opinion. Bhag Singh was a man of stout and brave mettle. He was a man of strong likes and dislikes. He held out to his opinion firmly. Later Gurdit Singh made him a co-charterer of the *Komagata Maru* along with Husain Rahim. He joined with Rahim and Guru Dutt Kumar in the formation of a branch of the Vancouver-based Socialist Party of Canada. Bhag Singh, Balwant Singh and Harnam Singh of Victoria were held on the American side of the border with weapons, which were purchased to be delivered to Gurdit Singh at the *Komagata Maru*. He distributed *ghadar* literature to the people in Vancouver. Unfortunately, through mutual rivalry, he was killed by Bela Singh—an informer of the Immigration Department, when he was offering prayer at 2nd Avenue Sikh temple, Vancouver, on 5 September 1914, at the age of 42.

Harnam Singh Sahri, a leading figure among the Sikh population of British Columbia and a committed revolutionary, hailed from the village of Kahri Sahri in the district of Hoshiarpur. He joined the army when he was still in his teens and resigned his job after a year. He reached Canada in 1907 and studied for three years in an institution in Vancouver. He was threatened to be deported from Canada, as he published a monthly journal *Desh Sewak*, from his residence. He was suspected of political activities. In 1911, he shifted to Berkeley for higher education and there he actively participated in the activities of the *ghadar* party. For sometime he worked as editor of the *Sansar*, a journal, and also a director of the Guru Nanak Mining and Trust Company and treasurer of the 'Shore Committee' that supported the passengers of the *Komagata Maru*. He contributed articles to the *ghadar* newspaper. He helped and incited the passengers of the *Komagata Maru* and supplied copies of the *ghadar* paper to the sympathizers of the party. Later he was deputed by the *ghadar* party to train the Sikh volunteers in Shanghai, Siam, Singapore, Malaya and Burma. While propagating the mission of the *ghadar* party among the Indian troops stationed in Rangoon he was arrested. His trial in the Mandalay conspiracy case resulted in his hanging on 14 August 1916.

Chagan Kairaj Verma, alias Husain Rahim, a middle-aged Hindu from Porbandar in Gujrat, lived in Japan for a number of years, before he absconded to Honolulu, due to having run into financial problems, under an assumed Muslim name of Husain Rahim. Hence onward he always used this Muslim name. He entered Canada as a tourist in January 1910. After his nine months stay in Canada he was ordered deported but he appealed for permission to stay on in this country. He expressed his bitterness towards the British to Hopkinson who was there at the time of his arrest. He said, "You drive us, the East Indians, out of Canada and we will drive every white man out of India." At the police station, during the search of his person he was found to be in possession of "comprehensive notes respecting the handling and treatment of nitroglycerine with references to dynamites, acids, etc., well known to chemistry of high explosives." The report also noted that Rahim had information of deadly explosives, the names and addresses of many well-known agitators against the British India rule living in India and abroad—in the United States, France, Egypt and South Africa.[15]

The immigration department marked him as a problem character and he was reported to be 'a walking text-book on explosives.' Rahim ran the Canada-India Supply and Trust Company, trading in Vancouver and suburban real estate, but he was activist first and realtor later. After a long court proceedings for nearly twenty months it was announced on 3 October 1911, that Rahim was 'a fit and proper person to reside within Canada.'

He was a lively conversationalist, sometimes showing utter disregard to any scruples for political conduct. He was charged with conspiring to murder William Hopkinson but was acquitted. He died in Vancouver in 1936.

Rahim held the Canadian government and the Canadian press in contempt. He could boldly say in a public meetings that the Japanese got admittance to preserve peace and to get justice in Canada the Indians must go back to their country with a petition where they were 330 million strong. He openly stated that in order to get due protection overseas they must get self-government in their mother-country. He became the president of the United India League. He often chaired the meetings held in Vancouver to help the passengers of the *Komagata Maru* to be able to land. He was a very effective and vocal member of the Shore Committee and pleaded the cause of the passengers very strongly and fearlessly. He was a member of the Canadian socialist party, a revolutionary and a staunch follower of the *ghadar* party. He was a reckless man who ignored all stop signs of life.

Almost all the East Indians living in Canada and America were the sympathizers and supporters of the ghadar party. They had fully come to realise that they could not have a dignified and respectful living in foreign countries till their country was liberated from foreign hands. William Hopkinson, though serving in the Canadian immigration department, was still in the service of the British Indian government. He supplied them information about the activities of the Canadian and American Indian revolutionaries. He shuttled between Canada and the U.S. in search of an up-to-date information about the plans and programmes of the ghadarites. The immigration department had engaged his services to break up the *ghadar* organisation. He was always trying to catch the snowbirds but did not have much success.

The Outbreak of World War I and the Ghadar Party in Action

The First World War broke out on 28 July 1914, between the Central Powers and the Allies. The Central powers comprised Austria, Hungary and Germany and the Allies consisted of Serbia, Belgium and the Great Britain. The ghadarites came to know that most of the British troops were being despatched out of India. They felt that it was the right time to strike. The party leaders announced that 'the time for rebellion had come and the British were to be expelled, as war in Europe had commenced.' In the issue of the *ghadar* paper of 4 August 1914, an article declared "War has started between Germany and England. Now is the chance for India's freedom— O brethren, take your freedom now. If you do not, you will remain slaves forever. So dear ones, raise your hands and start the mutiny. Go to India and incite the native troops. Preach mutiny openly. Take arms from the troops of native states, and wherever you see the British, kill them."[16]

To such a call thousands of men volunteered for terrorist work in India. Funds were collected to defray the expenses of the passage. There was a great rush to catch ships leaving for India.[17]

The first group of ghadarites led by Jawala Singh left San Francisco by *S. S. Korea* in the last week of August 1914. The second party left on 5 September 1914, from San Francisco and about the same time another group left Victoria by the *S .S. Canada Maru*. Various parties took boats for India from Manila, Hong Kong, and Shanghai.

At this critical time the *ghadar* party in the U.S. and Canada was left without its seasoned leadership. Sohan Singh Bhakna and Jawala Singh proceeded to India for revolutionary activities and Har Dayal had shifted to Switzerland. The control of the party in California was left in the hands of Ram Chandra, a Brahman from Peshawar, with whom the Sikhs had no understanding. Of the Japanese ships that took the ghadarites to India the *Tosa Maru* and the *Mishima Maru* were more important. Since there was a great influx of Indians from various countries the Indian government was not unaware of their motives and missions.

As regards the number of Indians returned to India from foreign countries the opinions slightly vary. According to the trial court of the second *Lahore Conspiracy* Case the number of Indians returned to India between the *Komagata Maru* episode and 1915, was not less than 6,000.[18]

According to Lord Hardinge, seven thousand revolutionaries returned to India from Canada and America.[19]

Michael O'Dwyer writes that during the first two years of the war the number of Indians who returned to India was eight thousand.[20]

The 'Ingress into India Ordinance', which was promulgated on 5 September 1914, gave powers to local authorities to detain any returning emigrants. The Defence of India Act, passed on 19 March 1915, authorized the governor-general to frame rules "to empower any civil or military authority to prohibit the entry or residence in any area of a person suspected to be acting in a manner prejudicial to the public safety, or to direct the residence of such person in any specified area." The Act was enforced in most of the districts of the Punjab to control the movements of the doubtful characters. To the great annoyance of the ghadarites the situation in India seemed non-conducive to revolution or armed rebellion. The people of

Punjab looked unconcerned with revolution and if at all they were slightly worried over the European War. The leaders of the National Congress were in sympathy with the British cause and even radical leaders of India's movement were against exploiting the situation. The Punjab was liberally sending the flower of its manhood to the front. The high priests of many important Sikh temples branded the ghadarites as renegades. Isemonger and Slattery wrote in 1919, "The peasantry saw nothing justifiable in these acts (i.e. the acts of violence committed by the ghadarites).... To them the revolutionaries became murderers and plunderers of honest men, the more dangerous for their organisation and arms but to be resisted by all means possible and captured."[21]

The ghadarites made frantic efforts to secure the co-operation of the peasantry. They participated in the religious festivals of the Sikhs at Amritsar, Tarn Taran and Nankana Sahib and openly appealed to the people to revolt against the British government. There was very meagre response and the ghadarites had to bank on their own resources. Not much could be achieved by them and by the end of 1914 they succeeded only in killing a police constable and a village official as per government reports.

The ghadarites held meetings at various places in November 1914 and fixed 23 November as the provisional date for starting action in different parts of the Punjab. This date was postponed to 26 November as the final date for the general uprising against the government to kill certain people and render the administrative machinery ineffective. Some of the *sawars* of the 23rd cavalry stationed at Lahore cantonment had promised the ghadarites to join them. Only a few could desert their posts and join the revolutionaries but were later arrested. On 27 November 1914, the ghadarites killed Sub-Inspector of Police posted at Moga. They also killed Zaildar Jawala Singh. But to their disadvantage most of their plans got leaked and thus foiled.

Rash Behari Bose reached Punjab in January 1915 and took over the leadership of the revolution. Receiving encouraging reports from the cantonments he fixed the night of 21 February 1915, for general rising of the Indian troops. The plan of starting the action on 21 February 1915 leaked out. Most vital thing in such plans is the maintenance of strict confidentiality that the ghadarites could not keep. Rash Behari advanced the date from 21 February to 19 February. This change of the date also leaked and the disaffected regiments were disarmed and some of the suspects were court-martialled and executed. The revolutionaries got disappointed and Rash Behari Bose also left the Punjab in utter disgust.

The ghadarites did not give up their efforts to obtain support from the peasantry. Sant Randhir Singh of Narangwal, district Ludhiana, *mahant* of Jhar Sahib, in district Amritsar, and.*mahant* Nath Singh of village Sur Singh, district Lahore, became active supporters of the revolutionaries. Whenever anybody enquired from the ghadarites as to how they would be able to overthrow such a powerful government of the British they told that they would approach the peasantry and the Indian army who were their brethren. They also told that a number of their brethren had learnt in America the craft of making airships, bombs, dynamites, ammunition and firearms and would on their arrival in India manufacture the same.

In February 1915, about 7000 men of 5th Light Infantry regiment of Singapore revolted but they were overpowered, court-martialled and 37 of them were sentenced to death, 41 suffered transportation for life and others given varying terms of imprisonment. The condemned men were publicly executed in Singapore.

Ghadar Party Rapport with Germany

The revolutionaries had conducted their propaganda from London, Paris and Berlin for at least a decade before the ghadar party was formed. During the war they shifted their activities to Berlin. The ghadarites persuaded the German government foreign minister Zimmerman to instruct the German ambassador in the United States to provide arms to the revolutionaries and arrange funds for them. The consuls-general in Bangkok and Shanghai were also asked to help the ghadarites. The German funds were with Haramba Lal Gupta and some misunderstandings cropped up regarding the use of the German money. Due to the active watch of the British navy the German weapons sent to India could not reach their destination. The quarrels of the Germans with the Indian revolutionaries weakened liaison between them and the German support to the ghadarites received a setback.

In February 1916, with the approval of the German foreign office, the Berlin-India Committee sent Dr Chandra Kant Chakravarty, a Bengali, to conduct the ghadar movement and he was provided with large amounts of money which he put to his own use and kept sending wrong reports to the Germans about his work. He was ambitious, calculating and money-target-bound or a money-spinner. When they discovered his fraud they became very rough towards Indians. The United States security men once described him as "an oily leader of an oily revolution." It is said that Chakravarty did some work, made some money and lived long. He died on 14 May 1971, in Calcutta, at the age of 94. Chakravarty misappropriated the

German money and Ram Chandra had control over the donations of the immigrants. The Sikhs who had staked everything including their lives formed the have-not group. The Sikhs could not be comfortable with money-grabbers. They would not open their arms to a person who deceived them.

The United States joined the war on 6 April 1917. Under the pressure of the British government the American police arrested 17 Indian ghadarites along with 18 Germans of consulate service and tried them for violating the neutrality of the American government. During the trial one Ram Singh shot Ram Chandra and the former was shot dead by the marshal of the court. Lajpat Rai stated, "Most of the Bengali revolutionaries I found absolutely unprincipled both in the conduct of their campaign and in the obtaining and spending of funds.... Among the Punjabis the worst cases were of Ram Chandra and Harish Chandra. The Sikhs on the whole proved to be purer, more unselfish and disciplined."[22]

Trials of the Revolutionaries

To expedite the trials, extraordinary procedures were adopted by the tribunals of three judges in each case on the recommendation of the Lieut. Governor of the Punjab, Michael O'Dywer, to the government of India. He wrote, "It is most undesirable at the present time to allow trials of these revolutionaries or of other sedition-mongers to be protracted by the ingenuity of counsel and drawn out to inordinate lengths by the committal and appeal procedure which the criminal law provides."[23]

Against the decision or the sentence of the judges there could be no further judicial appeal, though the convicts had the right to petition to the local government and the viceroy for mercy.

Lahore Conspiracy Cases Nos. I, II and III

The first group of 61 persons was tried in the *Lahore Conspiracy* Case No. I. The accused were charged with waging war against the crown, seducing troops, peasantry and students. The trial began on 26 April 1915, and the judgement pronounced on 13 September 1915. 24 persons were sentenced to death (the Viceroy changed the sentence of 17 of these to life imprisonment), 27 sentenced to transportation for life and forfeiture of their properties and some others to lesser punishments.

Kartar Singh Sarabha was tried and condemned to death in the *Lahore Conspiracy* Case No. I. In view of his young age the judge suggested to him that he could be saved from the gallows if he modified his statement, which he refused to do. He never ever showed regret for the things he had done rather regretted the things he could not have done. He was resolutely determined to prevent the unjust British Government to bleed India white, turning them out of his country by all means. The frenzied glow on the face of a revolutionary going to the gallows could be visualized by a man who could see him in his eyes moments before his last flicker of life goes out. Bhai Parmanand writes that at the time of his hanging "Kartar Singh Sarabha was in a very joyous mood and infected others with the same spirit." "Let us be hanged quickly", he would say, "so that we may, the sooner be reborn to take up work, where we dropped it." [24] He was a defiant spirit in chains. He believed that inevitability of death is a part of life. We should not be afraid of it. His death-defying courage for a cause so dear to him put his prosecutors to shame. He had a heart of fire, always burning for his country's freedom.

Under the influence of *ghadar* literature the psyche of Indian youth was oriented towards seeking self-rule by radical methods irrespective of personal loss of any magnitude. While we Indians celebrate the 50th year of India's independence. The nation must salute the brave and selfless men who contributed to their country's independence with their blood by basing their movement in foreign lands. India owes immensely and perpetually to those martyrs whose efforts brought liberation to their country but did not live to see their dreams come true. Sarabha was hanged in 1916.

In *Lahore conspiracy* Case II, 74 persons were tried. The trial started on 29 October 1915, and judgement delivered on 30 March 1916. Six were condemned to death; five of them actually executed. The punishment of others included transportation for life (to Andaman Islands, the convict colony for British India) and imprisonment.

In *Lahore conspiracy* case III there were 17 accused. The case started on 8 November 1916 and judgement declared on 4 January 1917. Six of them were sentenced to death and the sentence of one of these was changed to transportation for life and some others sentenced to imprisonment.

Balwant Singh, head priest of Vancouver Gurdwara, was convicted in *Lahore Conspiracy* case III and hanged on 16 March 1917, at Lahore.

Mandalay (Burma) Conspiracy Cases Nos. I and II

In the first conspiracy case judgement was delivered on 27 July 916. Seven of them were sentenced to death and later the sentence of one of them was changed to life imprisonment. Harnam Singh Kahri Sahri was fated to be a loser in his case against the British government and was convicted and hanged in 1916.

In the second Mandalay case the revolutionaries from Siam were tried in 1917. Out of the four tried three were sentenced to death and one for transportation for life.

Similarly there were trials of San Francisco, Chicago and Mandi cases and sentenced to varying terms of imprisonment. In the trials of Ferozeshah, Walla railway bridge, Anarkali (Lahore), Padri and Benaras cases many were sentenced to death, transportation for life and different periods of imprisonment.

Court Martial

18 persons of the 23rd Cavalry were court-martialled at Dagshai and sentenced to death. Sentences of six of them were changed into transportation for life. One soldier of 128 Pioneers was shot dead. Eleven from 12th Cavalry, Meerut, were hanged. 166 men of 5th infantry, Singapore, were court-martialled. Forty-one of them were sentenced to death in front of the cannon. Others were given lesser punishments. In the 130th Baluch Regiment four were condemned to death and fifty-nine to transportation for life. Many more were court-martialled and shot dead whose record is incomplete.

On the basis of information available from government records 145 persons were either hanged as a result of their trials or killed in police encounters. 306 were sentenced to transportation for life with their properties confiscated and 77 awarded lesser punishments. But these figures do not seem to speak correctly about the whole human loss of the revolutionaries at the hands of the government, which was larger in number and mercilessly perpetrated by the English tribunals.

Failure of the Ghadar Rebellion

The ghadar party had hardly a life of one year when it had to issue the call for action. Its members were without any experience of organizing and directing a revolutionary movement. Its branches in other foreign countries were in their early stages and without proper co-ordination between them. The revolutionaries in Canada and the USA had almost no contacts with the revolutionaries in India and they had not assured any support and sympathy to them. Certain heart-searching analysts of the ghadar party sympathizers have realized that "though the party had become popular among the Indians in foreign countries it was practically non-existent in India, even in Punjab, which ought to have been the heart and soul of the movement."

Lack of efficient leadership went a long way in harming the interests of the ghadar movement. Lala Har Dayal who was, then, away in Switzerland, far from guiding the party from his European station or residence, was writing a book on philosophy and studying Spanish language. He walked out of this revolutionary movement forever. In early stages he was the most shining jewel in the ghadar movement's crown but later it bedimmed, losing its lustre totally. It amply shows that he was hardly anything more than an armchair revolutionary. Shortly after he shifted to Europe, Har Dayal seemed to have become a pacifist and he remained so till his death in 1938 maintaining loud silence. Lajpat Rai known as an extremist nationalist could be seen no where in the movement.

The ghadarites returned to India without any planned programme. The sponsors of the movement were arrested on landing on Indian soil. They included Sohan Singh Bhakna president and Jawala Singh and Kesar Singh both vice-presidents of the party. Giani Bhagwan Singh was sent to countries as Japan, China, Korea and the Philippines to recruit volunteers for India and Barkatullah was detailed for Persia, Turky and Afghanistan on a similar mission. By assuming all powers Ram Chandra had become a sort of dictator. With the donors' money some of these leaders were living lives of comfort unworthy of the revolutionaries.

It was unfortunate that the ghadarites could not maintain secrecy of their plans. The details of their programmes and missions reached India before they landed there. Through their *ghadar* paper they had been giving publicity of their committed mission of driving out the British from their country. Tactlessly enough, Tarak Nath Das, a revolutionary, through "an open letter addressed to the British public and to His Majesty, the king; had asked: "If the loyal Indian soldiers refused to handle the muskets what would be their position? Would not the British be in trouble for this?" This letter clearly warns the British government of the mission and plans of the ghadarites and they got ready for them.

The attitude of the Indian leaders was anti-ghadar party and against their violent methods. B.G. Tilak, earlier known for his inciting people for seditious activities, had started condemning militant methods by the time the ghadar party planned its actions. Mahatma Gandhi was helping the British government during the First World War, through propaganda for recruitment to the army. G. K. Gokhale, an eminent Indian national leader, was also sympathetic to the British government during the activities of the revolutionaries. Lord Hardinge, viceroy of India, put a question,

"How would you like it, if I were to tell you that all the British officials and British troops would leave India within a month?" Gokhale replied, "I would be pleased to hear that news, but before you had all reached Aden, we would be telegraphing to you to come back again."[25]

The priestly classes of the Hindus, the Sikhs and the Muslims had been emphatically told by the government not to harbour the revolutionaries in the religious places. The Chief Khalsa Diwan disowned the Sikh emigrants through a manifesto and told their co-religionists not to follow the ghadarites.

The ghadarites did not seriously think of winning the local police to their side. Probably they did not visualise the usefulness of the police co-operation in the success of their mission. As against that, the police worked very actively in dealing with the activities of the ghadarites. *The Report on Police Administration in the Punjab* for the year 1915 contains the following remarks of the Lieut. Governor of the Punjab, "The eventful year 1915 will always be memorable in the annals of the criminal administration of the province; and no less worthy of the recollection will be the skill, courage and loyalty with which the officers and men of the police force carried out their arduous duties in circumstances of grave anxiety and often, in situations involving personal danger and self-sacrifices."[26]

The government formed Sikh committees in all the districts of the Punjab to assist them in combating the revolutionaries. The Commissioner of the Jalandhar Division, Mr. Renouf, said, "The main task of the authorities consisted in bringing the returned emigrants and would be revolutionaries under control.... It was decided to enlist the assistance of Sikh committees, these including the recognised leaders of the community. The measure of success achieved was remarkable.... In a few months the police succeeded in arresting most of the active leaders of the movement. Great credit is due to the members of the Sikh committees."[27]

The British had a very efficient and successful security system with their secret agents working in Canada, US, Hong Kong and other places and supplied instant information about the activities and planned programmes of the ghadarites. In India also the government agents had infiltrated the ranks of the revolutionaries and all their plans were leaked to the government before they could be executed into action. It displayed government's efficiency in their intelligence-gathering apparatus.

The governments of the native states of the Punjab opposed the ghadar movement. Michael O'Dwyer remarked, "My cordial thanks are due to the 'darbars' [governments of the native states] for their co-operation and assistance in the repression of seditious attempts." *The Report on Police Administration in the Punjab* for 1915 refers "to the valuable co-operation of the police of the Kapurthala State in winding up revolutionaries and assisting us in the preservation of law and order in the central Punjab."[28]

There was lack of national and political awakening and mass following in India in respect of the ghadar movement. The Commissioner of Jalandhar reported in December 1914 that "I do not think that there is any chance of disaffected Canadian emigrants receiving any measure of popular support; at least, I shall be surprised, if they do so."[29] The *jagirdars*, *sfaid poshes*, big *zamindars*, *zaildars* and *lambardars* stood firmly on the side of the government and incited the common people and peasantry against the ghadarites. In certain cases the people of the villages chased the ghadarites and after apprehending them handed them over to the police. Michael O'Dwyer, Lieut. Governor of the Punjab, wrote, "Fortunately through this anxious period the great mass of the rural population, including the Sikhs, remained staunch and loyal and continued to give, often at great risk, the most active assistance to the authorities in rounding up and bringing to justice the revolutionary gangs."[30]

Summing up in the words of Isemonger and Slattery, "Lack of organisation, bad leadership, incapacity to maintain secrecy and the Indian habit of regarding the ideal as the fact accomplished, no doubt, played their part in defeating the revolutionaries."[31]

And further in the words of Khushwant Singh, the ghadar rebellion failed for a variety of reasons including "tension between the Germans and the ghadarites, the efficiency of the British intelligence service which planted spies in the highest councils of the revolutionaries; the stern measures taken by government of India and the brutal methods adopted by the Punjab police, which compelled many of the leaders to inform against their colleagues. Above all, it failed because the Punjabi masses were not ready for it. Rich land owners assured the governor of their loyalty and set up committees in the districts to watch the movements of returning emigrants and to bring them back to the path of obedience and loyalty. Even the peasants were more concerned with the war than with the revolution."[32]

The ghadar party had planned to throw the English out of India but no Englishman was thrown out by them or killed at their hands. But the ghadar movement was important to the extent that it was the first secular movement that aimed to free the country from foreign yoke with the use of arms. The majority of the ghadarites were the Sikhs but they brought into its fold the

Hindus and also the Muslims. This movement brought about a radical change in the outlook of the Sikhs as well. Though the ghadar activities were suppressed by the government but a few years later a movement of terrorism erupted in a few districts of the Punjab under the name of Babbar movement (1922-1925) whose members were largely recruited from among the ghadarites. As the Babbar movement was started with a small number of its members and limited resources it was soon controlled by the vigorous action of the government and six of its leaders were condemned to death and many others were sentenced to varying terms of imprisonment. The men under death penalty refused to appeal for mercy and were hanged.

Observing the role of the ghadar party on the national movements of India G. S. Deol remarks that the ghadar party neither achieved its aim nor did its efforts yield any immediate results, because the people of India were generally co-operating with the British government in prosecuting the war. But immediately after the war the effects became evident, and the Akali movement in particular and the Congress movement in general benefited greatly by the example and participation of the remnants of the ghadar party and the spirit born of its patriotic activities. The ghadarites as a body raised the slogan of complete national independence and republican government in India for the first time and made sacrifices for the materialization of the slogan. It was done at a time when no other party did or could dare to do so. Thus, it can be said that it paved the way for the Indian National Congress to demand complete independence at a later stage.... The impact can also be seen in the shaking which it gave to the foreign rule and in the national awakening that followed after the trials and executions of the ghadarites. It contributed to convincing the British that it was difficult for them to silence Indians over the matter of their right to national freedom.[33]

Foresight and wisdom are more difficult to obtain than freedom. It is a lesson of history that generally a militant or a terrorist movement to oust a government is bound to fail unless it is a mass movement. Organizing an extremist mass movement is extremely difficult because generally the public thinking is against extremism. And also the government is in a strong position to adopt violent measures to crush the movement, feeling justified to take any action it pleases. Through suppression it deprives the movement of its leadership and does not allow it to raise its head again for a long time to come.

The ghadar movement was not aimless but it was certainly leaderless and without any plans. On the other hand the British *raj* was a mighty *raj* and it was well nigh impossible to defeat so deeply entrenched government by limited resources and inadequate preparation of the ghadar party.

A spectacular and miraculous success against the British could be possible only if the whole nation, to the last man, had risen against the foreign rule without which this movement was destined to meet its Waterloo not long after it was launched. When there are unequal powers peaceful but determined struggle by the weaker one could produce better results, though it may take a little longer time.

REFERENCES

1.   Waiz, S.A., *Indians Abroad*, Bombay, 1927, p.661.

2.   Lajpat Rai, *The United States of America*, Calcutta, 1919, p.459.

3.   *The Whiteman*, August 1910, Vol. I, No.2.

4.   *Ibid.*

5.   *Ibid.*

6.   *The Daily Province*, Vancouver, 5 October 1910.

7.   *Ghadar*, 15 November 1913.

8.   *Ghadar-di-Gunj*, Vol. I, Nos.4 and 23.

9.   *The Lahore Conspiracy* Case No .I, Judgement dated 13 September 1915, Part III A(3).

10.   Mandalay (Burma) Case No. I, Judgement of 27 July 1916, p.259.

11.   *San Francisco Case*, judgement of 7 July 1917, pp.2-3 (Northern district of California).

12.   Parmanand, *The story of My Life* (English rendering), Lahore, 1934, p.68.

13.   *Lahore Conspiracy* case No. I, Judgement dated 13 September 1915, Part III A(1).

14.   Quoted by F.C. Isemonger and J. Slattery, *An Account of the Ghadar Conspiracy*, Lahore, 1919, pp.44-45.

15.   *The Daily Province*, Vancouver, 28 October 1910.

16.   *Official Records* of U.S. government on Indian's activities during War, File No.9-10-3 Section 7, Memorandum on the *Ghadar*, p.8.

17.   *The Portland Telegram*, 7 August, 1914.

18.   *Lahore Conspiracy* case No. II, Judgement dated 30 March 1916, p.27.

19.   Official Reports, *Parliamentary Debates* (Lords) 1917, Vol. XXI, p.733.

20.   Michael O'Dwyer, *India As I knew it*, London, 1925, p.196.

21.   F.C. Isemonger and J. Slattery, *op.cit.*, p.45.

22.   Lajpat Rai, *Autobiographical Writings*, ed. V.C. Joshi, University Publishers. Delhi. 1965. p.218.

23.   Michael O'Dwyer, *op.cit.*, p.199.

24. Parmanand, *op.cit.*, p.93.

25. Lord Hardinge, *My Indian Years*, London, 1948, p.116.

26. *The Report on Police Administration in the Punjab* for the year 1915, p.5.

27. *Ibid.*, p.11.

28. *Ibid.*, p.22.

29. *Home Department Political Deposit, Government of India, Proceedings,* January 1915, No.43, p.12.

30. *Ibid.*, p.198.

31. F.C. Isemonger and J. Slattery, *op.cit.*, p.44.

32. Khushwant Singh, *A History of the Sikhs* Vol.2, Princeton, New Jersey, 1966, pp.189-90.

33. G. S. Deol, *The Role of the Ghadar Party in the National Movement,* Delhi, 1969, p.192. In the writing of this chapter I have made an ample use of this work.

CHAPTER 5

FIGHT FOR FRANCHISE OR
RIGHT TO VOTE

The East Indians Denied the Right to Vote

The early Sikh settlers in Canada, as British subjects, had the right to vote in all elections of the country. By 1907 their number was a little above 5000. It being a sizeable number they could pose a threat to the existing government if they chose to vote against it, and support any other party favourable to their demands and interests. To safeguard their position, the government of British Columbia passed a bill in 1907 to disenfranchise the Indians, 95 per cent of whom were the Punjabi Sikhs. The bill provided that all the East Indians, not born of Anglo-Saxon parents, would stand debarred from participating in municipal, provincial and then federal franchise, despite the fact that all of them were the British subjects. The East Indians were classed with the Chinese and Japanese who were not the British subjects and who had been denied the right to vote by the statutes of 1903 and 1904 (chapter 17). Thus, the East Indians were clubbed with the rest of the Asians.[1]

Aliens from Europe were allowed to attain full citizenship under the Naturalization Law after five years' residence in Canada, and in the case of British subjects by birth, only one year's residence was required.

Although, the East Indians were the British subjects by birth they were not only denied the privilege of becoming citizens after a year's residence they were also denied this privilege even after five years' residence. Thus, they were totally debarred from attaining citizenship under any conditions in British Columbia. And without being citizens they were not entitled to vote in any elections.

For the next forty years, the Sikhs of British Columbia remained excluded from the province's political process and from becoming Canadian citizens until 1947. The bill for disenfranchisement of the East Indians that was introduced in the provincial legislature in Victoria by Bowser, the Interior Minister, read as:

"No Chinese, Japanese or The East Indians shall have the name on the register of voters for any electoral district or be entitled to vote at any election." The House unanimously approved the plan of de-franchising the East Indians.

The British Columbia legislators had made known this fact that they had got the inspiration for introducing such an undemocratic and racial legislation from South Africa where the parliament of the Transval Colony at Pretoria legislated to stop the Hindu influx to that country and ban all Asians because they found the Indians in South Africa too smart as traders who were capable of throwing the petty white traders out.

Speaking in connection with the amendment in the Election Act the Interior Minister Bowser said," I regret exceedingly that the federal government has taken a very strong stand in regard to a legislation of this character.... But I ask the liberals of this House to break away from the party alliance in this and keep British Columbia a whiteman's country to the extent that is in power."[2]

The opposition members expressed happiness on this statement. The opposition leader, W. Macdonald, said in this connection: "I do not say what he (Mr. Bowser) takes the right view of the question. It has a very important imperial aspect. The East Indian as we all know, is a British subject, and the imperial government will look upon this kind of legislation with great care. It invites the serious consideration, both of Ottawa and London. I agree in keeping foreigners out of our voters' list. An East Indian, though a British subject, not one in one hundred among them can speak our language nor are they familiar with our laws and customs.... I would suggest that the government revise our election laws, and while depriving those East Indians and naturalized foreigners of franchise, exclude also others who are unable to read even a ballot paper. Until such action is taken I propose— I vote for this measure."

Thus, both the government and the opposition endorsed this bill to disenfranchise the East Indians. Where racial discrimination came in all the whites irrespective of their political affiliations were unanimous in their decisions during these early years of the twentieth century. With the disability slapped on the Sikhs they were not appointed to provincial public offices. Although this denial of right to vote did not restrict the Sikhs' appointment to public jobs but the denial had become a rule and universal

118 *Canadian Sikhs Through a Century (1897-1997)*

practice and the employers unjustly refused to consider them for the public jobs. The East Indians were debarred from many professions as pharmacy and law. They could not serve on juries or become trustees of schools or trustees of improvement districts.

A lot of businesses would not go in for hiring the Sikhs who were considered foreigners and had a marginal status. They could not call Canada their home till they gained this franchise. These denials were unworthy of a civilized society as the Canadians boasted to belong to.

Since the East Indians were subjected to a more serious problem of a ban on their entry into Canada through two orders-in-council in 1908 (discussed earlier), the restriction on their right to vote slipped into the background for the time being. It had become important for them to fight for their right to bring their families to Canada without which their own stay in this country was in jeopardy.

Ever since the restrictions put on voting rights of the East Indians, there had been discussions on the injustice perpetrated on them. G. D. Kumar, an educated Indian leader in Vancouver, applied for enrolment on the voter's list in October 1910, stating that he was a qualified voter but the city Act told him that no Hindu could be given the civic franchise. Kumar said that he was not a Hindu but a Buddhist and threatened the city court that in case his claim was not accepted he would appeal to the higher courts. But it had been provided in the original civil charter that no Asian would be entitled to vote at any municipal election. They made the necessary amendment, in the relevant clause by emphasizing the word Indian and stood firm on the subject of not allowing the East Indians to vote.[3]

When a deputation comprising Prof. Teja Singh, Sardar Rajah Singh, Dr Sunder Singh and Rev. L. W. Hall— a white Christian missionary, met the Canadian government officials on behalf of the Khalsa Diwan Society, Vancouver, and the United League, on 13 December 1911, in Ottawa, they submitted a forceful and effective memorandum. Their main focus was on the cancellation of the orders-in-council of 1908 but they also strongly stressed their two-fold proposal rather demand to the effect that: "Give us our wives and give us our votes," which in some quarters had been endorsed. But no body could guess in 1911 that the struggle for right to vote would extend to as distant a future as 1947.

The East Indians were the British subjects and it was unfortunate for the government of the United Kingdom and the British Indian government that they could not get this gross injustice of denial of franchise to their Indian subjects removed by exercising their influence or pressure on the

Canadian government which also owed allegiance to the British government. On 30 April 1912, it was stated in the British parliament that the Indians settled in British Columbia had been deprived of their right to vote. But the British conscience remained unstirred and unresponsive.

Husain Rahim (details about him given in chapter on Ghadar Party) came to Canada as a visitor and later declared by court as "a fit and proper person to reside within Canada." In March 1912, Rahim's arrest warrant was issued on a charge of perjury because he was 'alleged to have caste a vote in the polling'. Rahim was a well known man and a leader of the community. He contravened knowingly, the Provincial Election Act, which declared that no Indian could exercise his franchise. At the civic elections held on 28 March 1912, Rahim was alleged to have voted, when the provincial Interior Minister, Bowser declared: "I shall certainly see that the name of this man (Husain Rahim) is struck from the voters' list forthwith.... I have heard that the man was acting for the conservatives."[4]

The warrant against Rahim said that he swore falsely on 14 September 1911 before the election officer in the Vancouver electoral district. If found guilty he could be sentenced for fourteen years in jail. The court refused to accept an East Indian's surety for his bail placed at 5,000 dollars, reduced from the amount originally fixed at 10,000 dollars. Rahim's lawyer, A.M. Harper, who strongly pleaded for him, announced that his client had property in his own name in Vancouver and in India and he had the right to become a qualified voter. But his plea was not upheld by the court.[5]

He had managed to get himself enrolled as a voter and he had actually cast his vote in the election. Since the charge of his having cast his vote could not be proved and his name could not be found in the voters' list, he was acquitted of his charge. This was Rahim's expression of defiant opposition to an unjust act that the government had heartlessly inflicted on the people who had made Canada their new home. So many others were feeling likewise under this utterly discriminatory ban.

Thousands and thousands of Sikh soldiers fought on the side of the British on various war-fronts of the world during the two world wars and thousands of them laid down their lives for the British cause. But when the turn came for the British to repay even minimally or only with a word from the mouth, for all that the brave Sikh soldiers had done for them they (including the British generals who had seen the gallant Sikh soldiers sacrificing their lives before their eyes) kept their mouths locked. Facts do not cease to exist because they are ignored. Barring a very few, they could not even express their anguish over the inhuman treatment meted out to their old battlefield or wartime companions. These Sikh pioneers to

Canada were mostly the old army retirees. These Sikhs expected much from the British but they got hardly anything more than despondency and despair. The British people may be good but thanklessness is bad.

After the conclusion of the First World War, Arthur Meighen, Prime Minister of Canada, promised to restore the franchise to the East Indians at the Imperial Conference in London, but he did not honour his word.

In 1922, Shri V. S. Srinivasa Sastri visited Canada. At Victoria he argued with the British Columbia government officials about the franchise of the East Indians in the province. He told them that the proper treatment of the Indians in the British colonies would have a healthy effect in India and the denial of their rights would adversely affect the peace in that country.

Mr. Mackenzie King, in a letter to Srinivasa Sastri, promised that "at the earliest favourable moment the government will be pleased to invite the consideration of Parliament to your request that natives of India, resident in Canada, be granted a dominion Parliament franchise on terms and conditions identical with those which govern the exercise of the right by Canadian citizens generally."

During the parliamentary debate in 1922 on the franchise, MPs from B.C. insisted that Ottawa should not interfere in a 'B.C. problem'. McBride went on to stress," We have B.C. Chinamen and Japs running our stores. We have Greeks running our hotels and we have Jews running our second hand stores, and some people want to bring in the Hindus (the East Indians) to run our mills."

The promise of Mackenzie King was neither honoured in the election amendments then, nor in 1939 and 1940 amendments. After the conclusion of the Second World War, the public opinion against these racist legislations was so intense that it forced a change.

The question of giving right to vote to the Indians residing in Canada was raised in the Canadian Parliament on 29 June 1923. During the debate Mr. Jacobs emphatically impressed upon the House that as citizens of the British Empire the East Indians had every right to vote in the elections and it was the duty of the government to see that they were not deprived of their rights. Some members of the House opposed the move. However J. S. Woodsworth while replying told the House that in denying the right of vote to the Indians the Canadians were betraying their feelings of prejudice and small-heartedness. But unfortunately the majority was not in favour of including them in voters' list. The English press of Vancouver was also a victim of prejudice against the East Indians gaining franchise.

From 1908 to 1920 the main consideration before the East Indians was their getting united with their families that had remained separated from them because of the orders in council. Up to 1920 only nine Sikh women had immigrated to Canada. Most of the early settlers being uneducated they could not fully understand or would not bother about the disadvantages of their exclusion from the voters' list. Thus, vigorous efforts, for right to vote, were lacking during this period. The families of the Sikh immigrants were allowed passage to Canada with effect from 26 March 1919.

After 1920 the emphasis of the East Indians was shifted to bringing their families to Canada and the demand for franchise again remained on the back burner. 1930s were years of depression in Canada and the demand for franchise remained subdued. The Khalsa Diwan Society, Vancouver, was the only major power that could fight for the interests and rights of the Sikhs. Besides depression years in the 1930s, the Sikhs could not get an active worker and a crusader like Nagindar Singh Gill to pursue their objectives. His services as an indefatigable and unbending moving spirit behind a vigorous campaign for right to vote were available to the society in the 1940s.

Nagindar Singh Gill—Secretary of the Khalsa Diwan Society, Vancouver, was an educated, effective and well-meaning person. He was a polite, soft-spoken, and convincing speaker but at the same time firm, resolute, dynamic and fearless. He was always found determined to din the authentic voice of his community into the ears of the Canadian government. Perhaps he was the best secretary that the Khalsa Diwan Society, Vancouver, could get in its whole past life since 1907. From the recorded activities of Nagindar Singh it seems that he was indisputably the star actor in the show put up by the Sikhs on the Canadian stage in the 1940s. The entire Sikh community in B.C. reposed full trust in him and he had their full co-operation. He had the ability to generate support as he had immense personal momentum. Under the seasoned guidance of Nagindar Singh community's energy and attention was focussed on gaining franchise despite B.C. government's trying to postpone its consideration till the conclusion of the war. Ceaseless and untiring fight for the community's rights was his lifeline. He was indeed a high profile secretary of the Khalsa Diwan Society. He fought for their rights at all levels against the governments of Canada, England and India to restore self-respect of their country.

Under the National War Service Regulations the British subjects who were single men and childless widowers between the ages of 20 and 40 and who had been in Canada for at least one year, were called for compulsory military service in 1942. Many Sikhs who complied with these requirements were asked to report for training. Through the legal services of a law firm—Bird and Bird, Vancouver, the Khalsa Diwan Society pleaded on behalf of the Sikhs, eligible for military service, that they would not go to war until they were given the right to vote. The B.C. government did not join this issue with the Sikhs, as they were not readily granting the franchise to them. Consequently they were exempted from compulsory military service.

A Letter Protesting Compulsory Military Service for the Sikhs

The office of the law firm, Bird and Bird, Barristers and Solicitors, Vancouver, on behalf of the Khalsa Diwan Society, Vancouver, issued this letter.

Bird and Bird
Vancouver, B.C.
8 October 1942

Dear Sir,

We are instructed by the Khalsa Diwan Society, which body represents all the East Indians resident in British Columbia, to forward you the enclosed petition.

The East Indians of British Columbia are disqualified from voting at any election. This is the only province in Canada where the East Indians are deprived of the franchise. Nevertheless, they are liable to be called for military service. Thus, they suffer the same obligations as other British subjects, without being able to enjoy the like privileges.

It is with the object of remedying this situation that the petition, a copy of which is enclosed, has been forwarded to the proper dominion government and provincial authorities. Concurrently with the forwarding of the petition, our clients are sending to the Minister of National Defence a communication protesting against the imposition upon them of compulsory military service.

Should the petition be allowed and our clients be granted the franchise they will no longer have any objection to military service, but on the contrary, they will most gladly do their part to further the war effort.

Our clients seek assistance of the press in making public the situation referred to above. They hope that the granting to them of the franchise will have a soothing effect upon the political unrest in India. Consequently, any favourable publicity you may choose to give to this matter will be appreciated.

Yours very truly

....

The above letter is to be forwarded to the following newspapers:

The Editors, *Vancouver Daily Province*; *Vancouver Sun*; *Victoria Daily Times; Victoria Colonist; Federationist, Vancouver; Labour Statesman*; *Congress News*, Holden Building; *Columbian*, New Westminster; *Trail News*, Trail; *Canadian Press*, Vancouver; *News-Herald, Vancouver*; President American Federation of Labour, Ottawa; and President, Canadian Congress of Labour, Ottawa.

Communication regarding Franchise

Bird and Bird, Barristers and Solicitors, Vancouver, addressed a communication to H. E. Winch, M.L.A., B.C., on behalf of their East Indian clients on 20 October 1942. Harold E. Winch, leader of the Co-operative Commonwealth Federation (C.C.F) (later named NDP or New Democratic Party) was a staunch supporter of the grant of franchise to the East Indians. Bird and Bird, Vancouver, wrote:

My dear Mr. Winch,

Our clients, the East Indians, of British Columbia, are gratified to receive your communication of the 13th instant in which you stated that the C.C.F. legislative group and the Provincial Executive have endorsed the petition of the East Indians. We trust that this will mean that you will raise the question at the next sitting of the legislature. If such is the case, we feel that we can give you certain information that may be of value to you.

On 9 October 1942, we received a letter from the Honourable John Hart (Premier of British Columbia) in which he states, "this matter has been brought to the attention of the government before and the attitude has been that this is an inopportune time (because of war) to undertake any change in our 'Election Act'. On the 10th instant we received a letter from the Hon. George S. Pearson, Provincial Secretary, in which he states, "This will be placed before the Executive Council at its next meeting. Our clients feel that the provincial government is reluctant to grant the franchise to our clients and that it is likely that they will decide against the matter as they did in January of this year (1942) when the matter was raised by H.

S. Polak. Mr. Polak's efforts, on behalf of the East Indians, are referred to in the petition. Our clients are some what afraid that some sort of compromise may be forced upon them whereby such of them who have served in the last war (1914-18) or those who serve in this war (1939-45), may be entitled to vote. This sort of compromise is distasteful to our clients and they feel that the racial discrimination against them should be removed, and they, as a whole, should be entitled to exercise the franchise.

Our clients inform us that there are about 1200 East Indians resident in British Columbia of which possibly 900 would be of voting age, the balance being children. Mr. Turner has asked us to let him know how many white women are married to the East Indians. We are told that there are about six of them. There are about 300 to 400 men, who, subject to medical examination, would be liable to military service.

As we have stated in our previous communication to you and in the petition that the East Indians are subject to military service. They are also subject to National Defence tax and all the other taxes, necessary to the war efforts, but unlike other British subjects they suffer many disabilities. This letter was also sent to thirteen other MLAs.

H. E. Winch Addressed a Meeting of the Khalsa Diwan Society

Harold E. Winch MLA of CCF party spoke to a meeting of the Khalsa Diwan Society on 22 October 1942. He pointed out that fear rising from economics, social life and politics is the root of race prejudice. The example of the Soviet Union was cited as a clear example of what could be done to outlaw race prejudice. He indicated that in the USSR racial groups were encouraged to develop their culture as a part of the overall culture of the country. "We in Canada can learn a great deal from the success of the Russian racial programme," he said. He further stated, "what we seek to achieve for ourselves must be done for everybody... for the Chinese, for the East Indians and for the Africans; you have got to do it for everybody." He pointed out that progress could be made towards a better world only if we really believe in the rights of other nations and other people.

He said," Canada can give the United Nations leadership now by symbolizing world fellowship through the removal of long standing grievances and injustices." He pointed out that at the Imperial Conference in 1921 it was resolved that in the interests of the solidarity of the commonwealth it was desirable that the rights of the Indians to citizenship in the dominion be recognized.

The East Indians Meet B.C. Cabinet

A deputation of the East Indians called on Premier John Hart and the B.C. cabinet on 2 March 1943, for the provincial vote and abolition of what they termed racial barriers against them.

With them were a veteran of the 1914-18 war, Baboo Singh, wearing his service medals, and two young Sikh soldiers in the uniform of Canadian soldiers of the Second World War. Some of the delegates wore turbans in sky-blue and orange.

Sir Robert Holland of Victoria, for long a civil servant in India, led the delegation before the cabinet and spoke for the East Indians of B.C. He pointed out what they did in the last war and what they were doing for Canada in the Second World War.

The official brief of the Khalsa Diwan Society, read by Nagindar Singh Gill, asked for British justice and enjoyment of democratic rights for the East Indian community of B.C. "As long as our people have been residents in this province we have tried to live as good citizens," he said. The brief said that the East Indians were accepted for military service but were not given the right to vote.

"We the Canadian Sikhs are willing and anxious to play our part and to fight for Canada too. We want our children to grow up as good Canadians and responsible citizens, playing their part as respected members of the Canadian community," he continued. The main focus of the delegation was on gaining franchise.

Several members of the group pointed out to the cabinet that the East Indians were definitely discriminated against. They said that the East Indians, even those in uniform, were often refused admittance to theatres, cafes, dance-halls and other public places of assembly.

Before meeting the cabinet the delegation conferred with the opposition leader Harold Winch, who accompanied them to the Executive Council Chamber. The delegation included Harold Pritchett, President, International Wood Workers of America.[6]

Pearson's Derogatory Remarks Condemned

While opposing the franchise for B.C.'s East Indians, Labour Minister, George S. Pearson, made a strongly bitter attack upon these people and by inference, upon the Chinese, on 9 March 1944. He called the East Indians 'unreliable, dishonest, deceitful and non-co-operative'. He said that they avoided giving their workmen the privileges of the law and that their workmen lied rather than take a stand against their employers. He said that neither the East Indians nor the Chinese were prepared to help maintain the B.C. standard of living. For that reason he would not support a move to give them the right of citizenship. Pearson's remarks about the East Indians were deeply offensive to the basic norms of a civilized behaviour and could not be stomached without causing indigestion. In fact, their flaw was not dishonesty but extra-honesty. To an average man it is hurtful not to pay back a rival hater in his own coins. Pearson's giant-sized ego needed to be deflated but sobriety prevailed upon the East Indians and they desisted from reacting in a retaliatory manner, feeling that tolerance has greater force than the power of revengeful action.

Reading Pearson's harsh words many progressives were tempted to answer them with harsher ones. But it was felt that it would not serve any good purpose. What was needed was light, not heat. Mr. Barry of *The Daily Province*, said that it was unfair generalization to say that no East Indian or Chinese had done anything to raise the work and wage conditions of this province. "Some of the best labour men I know are the East Indians and Chinese." Commenting on Pearson's statement, a Chinese said that the Labour Minister must have spoken 'in a moment of irritation'. His words were unworthy of him.

It was left to history to pass a judgement on the deprivation of franchise of a section of the society for forty years by the British Columbia government.

Barry said, "In our hearts we know that to deny these people votes perverts every principle of democracy. We would gain in world esteem by the news that B.C. had granted citizenship rights to her East Indians as it would be a proof to the world, sadly in need of it, that at least one country means what it says in praising the Atlantic Charter. Again, in this province as elsewhere, the alternative to justice is injustice that can breed only resentment, intolerance and hatred at home—while we "strive to end these evils abroad."

W. W. Lefeaux of C.C.F. asserted that George S. Pearson, "owes an apology or an explanation for his tirade against the East Indians that was uncalled for and below his usual standard of debate." Honourable H.G.T. Perry was minister of education in the same government in which Pearson was labour minister. Perry said, "India was a member of the empire and was making a magnificent contribution to the war effort. If the East Indians were breaking labour laws, there were other groups with nothing to brag about." Britain, he said, received the blame for B.C. barring the East Indians from voting. After the war, Canada and particularly B.C. would need friends in India.

Jermeja Singh (popularly called Jerry) Hundal, a prominent young East Indian businessman and University of British Columbia graduate, commenting on Pearson's remarks while addressing the East Indians, said," It is a case of compelling you to maintain a certain standard and at the same time making it impossible for you to do so." Other groups, such as Europeans, were granted full citizenship rights without question, he pointed out. And it could hardly be expected that the East Indians would assume their full responsibility as citizens unless they had some voice in public affairs, he contended. "Who is there to speak for us now?" he asked. "If we had the vote, legislators would be more alert to our problems and then perhaps the necessity for some of the things Mr. Pearson alleges to exist would disappear." Mr. Hundal observed that "if they are trying to dodge the issue, they have certainly taken the worst possible way out."[7]

Fergus McKeen, provincial Labour-Progressive leader, whose party had been active in pressing for the wider franchise and had several East Indians in its councils, expressed regret at Mr. Pearson's attitude, stating that it was "completely out of line with principles enunciated in the Atlantic Charter."

The Khalsa Diwan Society Solicits Help from India

Nagindar Singh Gill, Secretary, Khalsa Diwan Society, Vancouver, wrote following letters dated 18 September 1944, soliciting help for obtaining franchise.

The first letter was addressed to the Shiromani Gurdwara Parbandhak Committee, Amritsar (India), in reference to their letter no.128/16 dated 5 April 1943. It was in connection with the enfranchisement of the East Indians in British Columbia. The secretary of the society told the SGPC that he did not know as to what the Indian government was doing regarding their demand. Since the society was again presenting their case in the provincial legislature in January 1945 the SGPC should exert pressure on the government of India to influence the provincial government of British Columbia to grant franchise to the East Indians in B.C.

The second letter was addressed to Dr N.B. Khare, Department of Indian Overseas and the government of India, New Delhi, India, in reference to overseas department letter No.F.72/43-O-S., dated 26 February 1942. The Khalsa Diwan Society Secretary wanted to know as to what the Indian government had done so far to get them the right to vote. Khare was asked to raise his voice in the viceroy's council and bear enough pressure on B.C. government to grant the enfranchisement to the Sikhs.

In the third letter which was addressed to Hon. Baldev Singh, Minister of Development, Punjab Government, Lahore, India, the secretary of the society referred to both the above letters and asked him to exert his pressure on the government to get their names inserted in the voters' lists. In all these letters Nagindar Singh sadly mentioned that they were not treated as British subjects in British Columbia. But there could be no help from India.

So the Sikhs decided to bank upon their Canadian resources and their unrelenting efforts. Every day they put their steps forward and they were determined on no looking back. It was a sort of peaceful *morcha* against the British Columbia government and they knew the technique of a *morcha* — not to relax their efforts.

The Sikhs are dauntless and determined fighters not only in the field of battle but also for their rights and against injustice, unmindful of the time they take to arrive at a logical conclusion. They never choose to hide in a shell. They come out in the open and give a vigorous fight for their cause. They had always displayed the strength of courage even when they were most subdued and dismayed.

To aid their fight for their right to vote the Khalsa Diwan Society started to publish a bi-monthly paper titled *The Sikh Voice*, in November 1944.

In November 1944, Mrs. Vijayalakshmi Pandit, younger sister of Jawahar Lal Nehru, a very charming and graceful lady, a real piece of work, very impressive in her discourse, was on a visit to America. The secretary of the Khalsa Diwan Society sent telegrams to people in New York to arrange her visit to Vancouver hoping that her appearance in Vancouver would aid the Indians considerably in their efforts to obtain franchise and would contribute much towards establishing a better understanding and arouse public interest in the cause of India. But due to certain circumstances she could not make it.

Harold Pritchett, President of International Wood Workers of America, told a mass meeting of the Khalsa Diwan Society in the Sikh Temple, Vancouver, on 19 November 1944, that "the East Indian people have the backing of the entire labour movement in their struggle for the franchise." As the Sikh struggle for obtaining their franchise was gaining momentum the fulfilment of their demand was approaching nearer.

The Sikh Objectives

The Sikh Voice, (the bulletin of the Khalsa Diwan Society, Vancouver,

B.C.) of first December 1944, discussed in its editorial the objectives of the British Columbia Sikhs, as under:

Ever since the first turbaned Sikhs from India set foot in their new adopted land of Canada, they had conducted an unrelenting struggle to measure up to the standards of Canadian citizens of other descents. While cheerfully discharging all those duties that were prerogative of the nationals of any democratic state, they had willingly accepted all the responsibilities that fall upon a citizen.

Yet paradoxically, the Canadian authorities had been reluctant to extend the right of franchise to a handful of the East Indians in this country, despite the fact that they were the British subjects by birth. They wanted to drown the voice of the immigrants in the cry of keeping Canada white. This situation reached the extreme point of absurdity in the case of those born in this country, who were denied the right to vote. While the Sikhs in B.C. or in India, whether on the war-front or on the production lines had strained every nerve to defeat international fascism, their efforts were retarded by lack of democratic liberties, for whose vindication the United Nations had battled.

At the next session, once again their community would present its case for franchise before the Provincial House. In the past they had received ample support from the labour and progressive circles, in their fight for democratic rights. To these forces and all other lovers of freedom and equality for different races, they appealed once again to champion their cause. The triumph of democracy for them was a victory for all the Canadian people.

It was unfortunate indeed to note that there were those who strove to make political capital out of the East Indian franchise issue. They wished to make it crystal clear lest there was any doubt or misunderstanding in any quarter that the Sikhs of B.C. were not and would not become a vehicle of any single political group or party out to catch votes or to promote its own partisan interests. They associated themselves, generally with all the democratic forces within the Canadian life, who were fighting for fuller democracy, against all types of racial, religious and political intolerance, and for a happier and freer Canada.

In December 1944, H.G.T. Perry, Minister of Education for the province of British Columbia, assured the Khalsa Diwan Society, Vancouver, of his support and advocacy of the franchise for the East Indians, in British Columbia. During this month Nagindar Singh Gill and Hazara Singh Garcha visited all of the larger centres in the province as part of the campaign. On their tour they expressed surprise that a number of the Sikhs were legal owners of property, had invested in victory loans, and had actively taken part in the work of International Wood Workers of America but they were without a right to vote.

The Sikhs of British Columbia were shocked and astounded at the reactionary attitude of Attorney General, R. L. Maitland, in failing to take immediate action on their request to extend them the franchise. The excuse that no action could be taken to redress the long-standing injustice to the East Indians in Canada because of the absence of some 50,000 B.C. citizens in the fighting services. That it was an insult to the fighting record of their people, said Nagindar Singh.[8]

A press release issued by Jack Henderson and Robert Macnicol, President and Executive Secretary respectively of the B.C. Command Canadian Legion, supported the efforts of the East Indians in British Columbia to obtain the franchise .[9]

J. E. Boyd of *News Herald* wrote on 27 December 1944, under the sub-heading 'Voice of the people' that "In consideration of their (the Sikhs') excellent record in the building of B.C. and support of the war effort despite the serious handicaps of unequal opportunities, the East Indians decidedly merit the right of franchise—now. Let us extend them a friendly helping hand."[10]

Two things that affected the Indo-Canadians most were the denial of the passengers of the *Komagata Maru* from landing on the Canadian soil, and their exclusion from the right to vote for forty years.

To the Government of the Province of British Columbia

The humble petition of the undersigned, the Khalsa Diwan Society, a society duly incorporated under the "Societies Act" of the Province of British Columbia, and representing all persons residing in the Province of British Columbia coming within the definition of "Hindu" as defined by Section 2 of the " Provincial Elections Act" of the said Province, and hereinafter referred to as " East Indian" as given below.

PETITION AS FOLLOWS:

1. That by reason of Section 5, Sub-section (a) of the said Statute "The East Indians" of the Province of British Columbia may not apply to have their names inserted in any list of voters, and are disqualified from voting at any election.
2. That Section 14, Sub-section (2) (i) of the "Dominion Elections

Act, 1938, Chapter 46 of the Statutes of Canada disqualifies and renders incapable of being registered as an elector, any person who is disqualified by reason of race from voting at an election of a member of the Legislative Assembly of the Province in which he or she resides.

That because of the provisions of the "Provincial Elections Act" enacted by the Government of the Province of British Columbia "The East Indians" residing in British Columbia suffer the following disabilities, namely:

They may not vote at any provincial election.

They may not vote at any dominion election.

Because the "Provincial Elections Act" referred to in the petition prohibits them from being entered on the voter's list; they may not be elected as members of the Legislative Assembly. ("Constitution Act," Chap. 49, Section 27).

They may not vote at any Municipal Election ("Municipal Elections Act," chap.83, Section 4).

They may not hold any municipal office for the reasons given above.

They may not serve as trustee to any municipal or rural school district. ("Public Schools Act", Chap. 253, Sections 33 and 77).

They may not serve on juries because they can not vote at elections for members of the Legislative Assembly. (Jury Act," Chap. 136, Section 4).

A contractor may not employ them for the Public Works Department by reason of Clause 45 of the Public Works Contract Form that excludes the employment of Asiatics.

It is believed that the government form of timber sale contract or lease has a similar provision.

We are informed that it is a policy of the Department of Lands that no foreshore lease be granted to an "East Indian".

We are also informed that it is the policy of the government that no East Indian may hold an Engineer's Certificate under the "Boiler Inspection Act".

They may not be called to the Bar, as they are restricted from being articled as students. (Only those on Voter's List eligible).

Restricted from being Pharmacists.

Property restrictions possible only because no voice in municipal affairs.

Have no recourse from injustice in B.C., as they are neither Indians nor Canadians. (Canadians by reason of residence only, and denied possibilities of naturalization because of being British subjects. In this respect they are more handicapped from point of view of privilege than any other racial group in Canada, including Chinese and Japanese nationals. In all, there are twenty-six restrictions based entirely upon the privilege of the franchise.

4. That the Province of British Columbia is the only Province of the Dominion of Canada which disqualifies "The East Indians" from voting at Provincial Elections.

5. That your petitioner has as its members all" The East Indians" resident in the province of British Columbia, and there are one thousand seven hundred and fifteen " East Indians" living in the said province. Schedule A hereto shows the number of " The East Indians" resident in the various cities and towns throughout the said province, and elsewhere in Canada.

6. That at a meeting of your petitioner, the Khalsa Diwan Society, held at the Sikh Temple in the City of Vancouver, province of British Columbia, the 27th day of September, 1942, the following resolution was duly passed by a unanimous vote, namely:
   "That we the "East Indians" of British Columbia, are loyal to Canada, and, if necessary are ready to lay down our lives in defence of this country against aggression.
   That a petition or memorial we sent to the Prime Minister of Canada and the premier of British Columbia and other proper authorities in Ottawa and Victoria requesting that we, the "East Indians" of British Columbia be granted our long cherished and legitimate overdue citizenship rights in British Columbia.

7. That since 1908 "The East Indians" of the province of British Columbia have been seeking the franchise now enjoyed by other British subjects or naturalized aliens (Germans, Italians and others). Shortly after the "Great War I" the Rt. Hon. Mr. Sastri, then Indian Government Agent in South Africa representing the "East Indians" of British Columbia, urged upon the authorities at Ottawa, the granting of such franchise, but without success. About 1934, Dr Anup Singh and Dr Sadhu Singh Dhami conferred with the Minister of Immigration regarding this question. Again in 1938, Dr D. P. Pandia, then a member of the Indian National Council of India, while in Canada, made similar efforts to accomplish such purpose, but with the same result. That during the months of January and February, 1942, Mr. S. L. Polack,

Barrister of London, England, and secretary of the Indians' Overseas Association personally interviewed Prime Minister W. L. Mackenzie King at Ottawa, and Dr H. L. Keenleyside of the Department of External Affairs, Ottawa, requesting on behalf of the "East Indians" of British Columbia that the government of Canada prevail upon the government of British Columbia the granting of such franchise. The Prime Minister of Canada refused such request. During such period Mr. Polack personally interviewed the Hon. John Hart, Premier of the province of British Columbia, with a view to obtaining such franchise from your government. Such efforts were unsuccessful, even when in 1943 and 1944 the Khalsa Diwan Society took a delegation including the East Indian leaders and permanent Canadian resident leaders to the authorities.

8. A hundred representative organizations of British Columbia signed support for this issue in 1945. The East Indians lost the vote by only two voting against the franchise.

    The Indian overseas Department, Delhi, was approached twice in the previous years, for support, but has not done anything on the question as yet. The Punjab government and the Shiromani Committee, upon written requests from the Khalsa Diwan Society, contacted the Indian Overseas Department and again presented the issue of the franchise.

9. That your petitioner hopes that the granting of this petition, if the same is allowed, will have in some measure, a soothing effect upon the present political unrest in India. A communication from the Prime Minister of Canada to the Viceroy of India stating that if such franchise had been granted, it would have no little effect upon the forty million voters of India, many of whom reside in the very Punjab cities, towns and villages from which they themselves originate.

Your petitioner, therefore, most humbly prays that your government be graciously pleased to grant to the "East Indians" resident in the province of British Columbia the right to vote at all elections held in the said province, and that your government will enact an amendment to the said "Provincial Elections Act" with the object of removing the disqualification of "the East Indians" under the said statute, thereby abolishing the racial restrictions preventing "the East Indians" from voting at all elections held in the said province, including elections held under the said "Dominion Elections Act", and the other disabilities referred to in paragraph 3 thereof.

And your petitioner will ever pray, etc.

Dated at the city of Vancouver, Province of British Columbia, this 24th day of January 1945.

Khalsa Diwan Society
Vancouver, B.C.
Submitted through
Barrister and Solicitors,
Birds and Birds, Vancouver.

The following circular letter was issued to a large number of well-meaning Canadians:

Khalsa Diwan Society
Head Office, Sikh Temple,
1866 East 2nd Avenue
Vancouver, B.C.
February 16th, 1945.

Dear Friend:

Our Society represents all the East Indians resident in British Columbia.

Our purpose in writing you is to enlist your aid in securing for resident East Indians the voting franchise in British Columbia. Your assistance can be given us by adopting as a resolution of your organisation the resolution following, namely:

Resolved: That the East Indians resident in the province of British Columbia be granted the right to vote at all elections held in the province of British Columbia, and that the government be urged to enact an amendment to the "Provincial Elections Act" with the object of removing the disqualification of the East Indians under the said statute, thereby abolishing racial restrictions preventing the East Indians from voting at all elections held in the province, including elections held under the "Dominion Elections Act."

A delegation of representative East Indians, together with others, among them certain Canadians of some prominence, has attended on the Hon. John Hart and the members of his cabinet, for the purpose of urging upon them the advisability of granting to the East Indians the voting franchise in British Columbia.

The actual disqualification of the East Indians occurs by reason of Section 5, Sub-section (a) of the "Provincial Elections Act", which prevents the East Indians from having their names inserted in any list of voters, and consequently results in their disqualification from voting in provincial elections. Section 14, Sub-section 2(1) of the "Dominion Elections Act" disqualifies and renders incapable of being registered as a voter any person who is disqualified by reason of race from voting at a provincial election. Thus the East Indian is also disqualified by reason of the provincial enactment from voting at a dominion election. Consequently, all that is necessary to enable the East Indians to vote at elections of the province and dominion is to amend the provincial statute.

The province of British Columbia is the only province in the dominion of Canada, which disqualifies the East Indians from voting. The disqualification exists notwithstanding the fact that the East Indians are British subjects and are subject to all laws and taxation that apply to full citizens.

This is no new thought on the part of our organisation. Ever since 1908, the East Indians have struggled unsuccessfully to secure the franchise.

We would deeply appreciate it if you would give favourable consideration to the enclosed resolution.

We would also appreciate it if you would notify our society at the above address, of your action.

Yours very truly,
KHALSA DIWAN SOCIETY
Per. (Nagindar Singh Gill)
Secretary

Workers Unions Support Franchise for the East Indians

Retallack Mine and Mill Workers Union, B.C. and Silbak Premier Mine, Mill and Smelter Workers Union, B.C. unanimously adopted the following resolution in February/March 1945 and forwarded the same to Premier John Hart:

"Resolved that the East Indians resident in the province of British Columbia be granted the right to vote at all elections held in the province of British Columbia, and that the government be urged to enact an amendment to the 'Provincial Elections Act' with the object of removing the disqualification of the East Indians under the said statute, thereby abolishing racial restrictions preventing the East Indians from voting at all elections held in the province, including elections held under the Dominion Election Act."[11]

Silbak Union further added that "Our organisation believes in equality for all mankind, regardless of race, creed or colour, and we urge you to speedily pass the necessary legislation that will help bring a better understanding between all races." Dozens after dozens of unions passed such resolutions.

On 4 March 1945, Rev. A.E. Cook spoke at the Sunday *Forum* in St. John's United Church Vancouver, on the East Indian's right to vote. He told *the Forum* that these Indians had intellectual and moral qualifications necessary to qualify them to take their place as fellow citizens of the British Empire. It was unjust to deny them the common privileges of the British people and deprive them of the full rights of Canadian citizenship. He strongly supported their right to franchise, which had been gathering dust for nearly forty years.

Through the un-relaxing campaign of the B.C. Sikhs, the tempo was building day by day for their long denied rights in B.C.

Dr Hirday Nath Kunzro, an eminent Indian leader, on his way back to India after attending the Institute of Pacific Relations Conference at Hot Springs, Virginia (United States) addressed a meeting sponsored by the Khalsa Diwan Society, Vancouver. He told the meeting that full citizenship for the East Indian population of B.C. would in no way constitute a threat to any other section of the province. He emphatically stressed on the East Indians right to vote.[12]

The leaders of the Indian community told the Canadian government again and again that the occasional and delaying tactics of half-hearted political exercise was tantamount to the blatant denial to the country's permanent residents their legal right to vote. But the government openly flouted the citizens' hopes and demonstrated a transgression upon the territory of their trust for a long period of time.

Franchise Resolution Lost

A resolution for enfranchisement of the East Indians resident in B.C. was introduced by W.W. Lefeaux (Vancouver centre) in the March 1945 session of the Legislative Assembly on 27 March 1945. Appealing to the government on grounds of justice, economics and a unified war effort, Co-operative Commonwealth Federation (C.C.F.) members fought hard for passage of the resolution. Opposition members contended that it would be hopeless to approach the peace table while prejudice and an attitude of superiority existed in this country. It was betraying the cause for which Canadians were fighting, denying the franchise to British citizens living in the province.

Education Minister Perry supported the C.C.F. in a whole-hearted appeal for decency and British fair play. But other government members whose petty objections brought defeat to the resolution undid the effect of his scholarly statement. Voting with Mr. Perry and the C.C.F. were Mrs. Nancy Hodges, Dr J. J. Gillis and Tom Uphill.

The measure was lost in the division by a vote of 20-18 and many members expressed confidence that the East Indians would win justice at the next session of the House.[13] Dwindling legislative opposition encouraged the Sikhs to garner or drum up support from all quarters to gain the right of franchise. The East Indians never gave up hope which is a step above despair. Slowly but surely they were inching towards their goal.

Southam Newspaper (Vancouver) of 28 March 1945, wrote under the sub-title of 'Votes and Citizenship' that an amendment to the Provincial Elections Act introduced in the legislature by provincial secretary Pearson gave the franchise to Indians and persons of oriental blood who had served in the Second World War or in the First World War. The dominion franchise was to follow the provincial franchise.

Amendment to the Provincial Election Act of 1945 read as:

"For every Chinese, Japanese or Hindu (East Indian) or Indian, the law provided that the provisions of the paragraph shall not disqualify or render incompetent to vote any person who has served in the Naval, Military or Air Force of Canada in the Great War of 1914 to 1918 or in the present war."

The desire to reward those Indians and Orientals who had taken up arms on behalf of the country in which they were domiciled is understandable and nothing could be said against it. At the same time, it remained true, as always, that the basis of franchise should be citizenship and not military service.

The East Indian community in British Columbia waged a vigorous struggle against the racist, exclusionary legislation from the very beginning. Many visiting foreign, particularly Indian, dignitaries and local notables had pleaded vehemently on behalf of the East Indians in B.C. both in Victoria and Ottawa unsuccessfully. As referred to earlier the promises of Arthur Meighen, Canadian Prime Minister, in London and Mackenzie King in Ottawa, to grant franchise on terms and conditions identical with white Canadians, had proved hollow.

It was one of the serious weaknesses of their political organisation in Canada that they had no proper basis of citizenship. In most countries there was a basis and a very simple one. Persons born there or persons naturalized were citizens and all citizens had the full rights of citizens, including the vote, once they reached voting age. In Canada, the birth did not confer full citizenship; nor did naturalization. In British Columbia, persons of oriental blood were not citizens, whether born in Canada or naturalized.

Canadians who were born in Canada were recognized as Canadians in the United States, but naturalized Canadians were not so recognized, and Canada did nothing about it. It allowed a foreign country to divide Canadians into two categories and the foreign country claimed to do it because Canada did it herself. Canada's failure to make a naturalized Canadian a Canadian in every sense of the word was having the effect of splitting Canadians into castes; and it ill-became a democracy to create a caste system.

The way out was plain. It was the British way and an American way. A British citizen and an American citizen had all the privileges of every other Briton or American. He could vote. He could hold office. He could own land or do business, employ or be employed. He could travel freely within his country and outside, there was no question of his being recognized as British or as American.

Every British citizen and every American citizen was recognized as on a level with every other. He laboured under no political disadvantages; he enjoyed no privileges such as exemption from military service. In Canada, they had a privileged class who did not have to defend their country. They had an under-privileged class who had no vote.

The amendment to the Election Act, which Pearson had introduced merely played with the fringes of the problem. If they wished to have a real democracy in Canada, they should build it on a solid foundation.[14]

Statement to the Press

"The Sikhs of British Columbia are thrilled at the great moral victory indicated by the narrow margin by which the bill was defeated (in 1945 session) which would have given us our long overdue rights. While naturally disappointed that the victory was not final and complete we feel sure that with the tide flowing so strongly toward justice final results will be secured within the next year.

Had but two more members voted for equal rights victory would have crowned our cause.

We feel deep gratitude, not only to the CCF group who voted for our rights solidly, but even more especially to the three government supporters who broke with the rest of the coalition for the sake of British justice and Canadian fair play. The Sikhs of Canada will remember the name of Hon. Mr. Perry long after this fight has been won.

The Sikhs challenge the attitude of one coalition minister who opposed equal rights for the Sikhs on the ground of non-co-operation in maintaining labour standards. The best answer to that unfair complaint is that our petition for full voting rights was supported in this present year (1945) by no less than 75 organizations including many of the important trades unions in B.C.

We intend to carry on the fight for our rights with more, not less ardour. The gains made in the past two years show how mightily public opinion is rising behind the demand for equal rights.

We feel sure of victory within the coming year".

Nagindar Singh Gill
Secretary,
Khalsa Diwan Society,
Vancouver.

Supporters of the East Indian Franchise

The following organizations endorsed the resolution to grant the franchise to the East Indians:

1. Junior Board of Trade, Vancouver, B.C.
2. Canadian Association of Social Workers, Vancouver, B.C.
3. Vancouver Secondary School Teachers' Association, Vancouver, B.C.
4. Vancouver General Ministerial Association, Vancouver, B.C
5. St. John's United Church ,Vancouver, B.C.
6. First United Church, Vancouver, B.C.
7. West Point Grey Presbyterian Church, Vancouver, B.C.
8. First Unitarian Church, Vancouver, B.C.
9. Civic Employees Union, Local No.28, Vancouver, B.C.
10. Prince Rupert Labour Council, Prince Rupert, B.C.
11. United Association of Journeymen Plumbers and Steam Fitters of the U.S. and Canada, Vancouver, B.C.
12. Blacksmiths and Helpers' Union of Canada, Vancouver, B.C.
13. Hotel and Restaurant Employees' Union, Vancouver, B.C.
14. Fruit and Vegetable Workers' Union, Penticton, B.C.
15. Retallack Mine & Mill Workers' Union, Retallack, B.C.

16. United Fishermen's Federal Union of B.C., Ladner, B.C.
17. Boilermakers' and Iron Shipbuilders' Union, Local # 2, Victoria, B.C.
18. United Garment Workers of America, Vancouver, B.C.
19. Michel Local Union No.7292, District 18, United Mine Workers of America, Natal, B.C.
20. Copper Mountain Miners' Union, Local No.649, Copper Mountain, B.C.
21. British Columbia Woodworkers' Union, Local No.4, Kelowna, B.C.
22. Canadian Brotherhood of Railway Employees and other Transport Workers Kamloops, B.C.
23. United Packinghouse Workers of America, Local 249, Vancouver, B.C.
24. United Brotherhood of Carpenters and Joiners, Local 452, Vancouver, B.C.
25. Brotherhood Railway Carmen of America, Lodge No.58, Vancouver, B.C.
26. Journeymen Tailors' Union of America, Local No.178, Vancouver, B.C.
27. Pioneer Miners' Union, Local No.693, Pioneer Mines, B.C.
28. National Union of Machinists, Fitters and Helpers Local No.1, Prince Rupert, B.C.
29. International Association of Machinists, No. 692, Vancouver, B.C.
30. Pile Drivers, Bridge, Dock and Wharf Builders, # 2404, Vancouver, B.C.
31. Silbak Premier Mine, Mill and Tramway Workers' Union, Local No.694, Premier, B.C.
32. United Steel workers of America, Local 2765, Vancouver, B.C.
33. International Woodworkers of America , Local 1-80, Duncan, B.C.
34. Amalgamated Association of Street, Electric Railway and Motor Coach Employees of America, Vancouver, B.C.
35. Taxicab, Stage and Bus Drivers, Local 151, Vancouver, B.C.
36. Dock and Shipyard Workers' Union of Vancouver and Dis.#2, Vancouver, B.C.
37. International Woodworkers of America, Local # 367, Mission, B.C.
38. U.A. Plumbers and Steam Fitters, Local # 170, Vancouver, B.C.

39. Fish Cannery-Reduction Plant and Allied Workers' Federal Union No.89., Vancouver, B.C.
40. Texada Island Quarry and Mine Worker Union No.816, Van Anda, B.C.
41. Okanagan Valley Labour Council, Penticton, B.C.
42. Shipwrights, Joiners & Caulkers Industrial Union, Vancouver, B.C.
43. Sointula Local of the W.F.F.U., Sointula, B.C.
44. Stenographers, Typists, Book-keepers and Assistants # 18177, Vancouver, B.C.
45. United Fisherman's Federal Union of B.C. Local 44, Albion, B.C.
46. Labour Progressive Party, Campbell River Club, Campbell River, B.C.
47. New Westminster Local of the U.F.F.U., New Westminster, B.C.
48. Silverton Mine & Mill Workers' Union Local No.662, Silverton, B.C.
49. Renfrew District Improvement Association, Vancouver, B.C.
50. CCF Vancouver Centre Constituency, Vancouver, B.C.
51. Labour Progressive Party, Kamloops, B.C.
52. Labour Progressive Club, Prince Rupert, B.C.
53. Cambie Club, Labour Progressive Party, Eburne, B.C.
54. LPP Club, Duncan, B.C.
55. Hjorth Road Club, Labour Progressive Party, New Westminster, B.C.
56. Labour Progressive Party, Vancouver, B.C.
57. United Steel workers of America, Local No.2952, Vancouver, B.C.
58. Cedar Cottage United Church, Vancouver, B.C.
59. International Wood Works of America, Vancouver, B.C.
60. H.G.T. Perry Minister of Education, Vancouver, B.C.
61. Mrs. Hodges, M.L.A., Victoria, B.C.
62. Arther J. Turner, M.L.A. Victoria, B.C.
63. C.G. MacNeil M.L.A., Victoria, B.C.
64. Bernard G. Webber, M.L.A., Victoria, B.C.
65. Colin Cameron, M.L.A., Victoria, B.C.
66. Grace MacInnis, M.L.A., Victoria, B.C.
67. Laura E. Jamieson, M.L.A., Victoria, B.C.
68. Harold E. Winch, M.L.A., Victoria, B.C.
69. Tom Uphill, M.L.A., Victoria, B.C.

70. Mr. Hugh Dalton, CmM.A., Victoria, B.C.
71. Mr. Elmore Philpott, *The Sun* writer and C.B.R. Radio commentator, Vancouver B.C.
72. B.C. Command, Canadian Legion, Vancouver, B.C.

The East Indians Ask for Voting Right

A letter had been directed to candidates of all parties contesting the provincial elections in 1946 by N. S. Gill, Secretary of the Khalsa Diwan Society, asking the position of the candidates on the question of the vote for the East Indians.

The text of the letter follows:

"The Khalsa Diwan Society which represents virtually the entire East Indian population in Canada, is anxious to learn as soon as possible your attitude on the question of granting us full voting rights in British Columbia, such as we already enjoy in all other provinces.

"You will recall that in recent years large delegations representing leaders of all walks of life in B.C. have pressed on the government the desirability of such a change. Our cause was supported by some members of all political parties represented in the legislature, and indeed lost out by one vote only in the 1945 session.

"With the victorious conclusion of the war against Hitler-Fascism and Japanese aggression we feel that democratic rights should be extended to all Canadian residents who are British subjects and of the East Indian origin on a basis of full equality with all others. Many of our kinsmen died fighting in the recent war for these principles.

"As you are a candidate in the pending provincial elections we would appreciate knowing what your attitude and stand will be if elected to the legislature. Thanking you in advance for your consideration in this matter".

—N. S. Gill

The federal or dominion franchise for the East Indians was finally addressed in 1946 but they could not vote in the federal election unless they had the provincial vote.

Provincial Franchise

The B.C. Legislative Assembly in its 1946 session made an appointment of all party Election Act Committee, comprising seven members, headed by R. H. Carson to recommend any necessary changes in the Election Act. This Committee was to hold public hearings to receive briefs and representations from the public bodies. The committee held its meetings on 31st October and 1 November 1946, at the Court House, Vancouver.

The East Indians' delegation, composed of Kapoor Singh Sidhu, Mayo Singh, Dr D. P. Pandia, Nagindar Singh Gill, Ishar Singh and Kartar Singh, met the Elections Act committee. Dr Pandia presented the brief on behalf of the East Indians. The Committee recommended extending the franchise for the East Indians, to the legislature in March 1947. The B.C. government embodied the recommendation in Bill 85, which was passed on 2nd April 1947, thereby ending the long-standing political discrimination. The provincial franchise automatically sanctioned the Sikhs the federal franchise and eliminated the attendant disabilities slapped on the East Indians. 2nd April 1947 will always be marked as a red-letter day in the history of the East Indians in Canada.

Municipal Franchise

With the exception of the municipality of the city of Vancouver all the municipalities of the British Columbia were governed by the Municipal Elections Act and were autonomous bodies in respect of civic affairs including the municipal franchise. The city of Vancouver had its own charter under the Vancouver Incorporation Act. The Municipal Elections Act and the Vancouver Incorporation Act contained clauses that excluded the East Indians from franchise. These clauses could be changed only on the recommendation of the municipal bodies and only then implemented by the provincial legislature.

The annual convention of the Union of B.C. Municipalities was slated for 15 to 17 September 1947, at Harrison Hot Springs. Kapoor Singh wrote to the Burnaby municipality and Dr Pandia to the Victoria municipality to include the East Indians franchise in the agenda of the convention. Kapoor Singh, Kartar Singh Hundal, Mayo Singh and Dr Pandia attended the convention and some representatives of Vancouver and Victoria Sikh temples were also present to provide support. Urgency created momentum. They were not going to give up or slacken their struggle for their right to vote knowing full well that quitters never win and winners never quit. They decided to undertake some magic exercise to qualify for this role. With shrewd deftness the East Indian delegates nailed the municipal councillors' ill-intentioned design to keep them out of the election process.

On the first day Dr Pandia wanted to speak at their convention. But he was not allowed to speak and was told that only aldermen and mayors could speak. The above mentioned East Indians managed to get permission for Pandia to speak next day. He pointed out that Indians were British subjects and they were taxpayers and property owners. It was the fundamental principle of democracy that there should be no taxation without representation. The Indians had contributed to economic development of Canada through lumber industry and farming. They had given half a million dollars towards the sixth victory bond issue. The provincial and federal governments had already extended franchise.

It was pointed out that the word 'Hindu' was wrongly used for the East Indians or Indians. On the resolution moved by Mayor Loutet, North Vancouver, the word 'Hindu' was recommended to be replaced by Indian in the Provincial Elections Act.

When Pandia was speaking on 16th September 1947 he pointed at Kapoor Singh and Mayo Singh that "these two men had hundreds of employees working for them. Their workers were allowed to vote and these two mill owners could not vote because they were the East Indians". It was a stroke of intelligence, which appealed to the councillors' hearts. Just then they put it to a vote and decided that the East Indians should be allowed to vote in municipal elections.

Vancouver's city council, at its meeting held on 23 October 1947, through an amendment in the city charter, bestowed upon the East Indians the right of vote in Vancouver City elections. Thus, British Columbia's East Indians obtained the triple franchise in 1947 from which they had been deprived since 1907 through an ethnically-based, discriminatory and exclusionary legislation, thus marking the end of the period of frigidity in respect of the East Indian's participation in the country's politics.

There were some strong factors that helped the East Indians to obtain franchise. There was support from many sane voices, some politicians, C.C.F. (later named NDP) and many ruling party MLAs and ministers. A large number of workers unions from Canada and America supported their cause. In later stages their claim of being British citizens solicited support from the Indian and the British governments. The coming independence of India hastened the franchise for the East Indians in B.C. The last but not the least factor was the untiring and ceaseless struggle carried out vehemently by the Khalsa Diwan Society, Vancouver, that got their franchise disqualification vacated. No body can be happy without a goal before him. And none can be happier than the man who achieves his goal. Whenever the Sikhs fight for their rights, they fight to win. To them, there is no substitute for victory. The attainment of franchise was a great occasion for the East Indians for rejuvenation. They were highly appreciative of all the organizations and individuals who supported their cause.

On this political victory Elmore Philpott, Editor of the *Vancouver News Herald* wrote in 1947:

"Like the Biblical children of Israel, who wandered homeless for forty years in the wilderness, before they crossed into the promised land, the men and women from India had to fight in Canada for over forty years for admission to citizenship and full rights of democracy".

In 1997 the Indo-Canadians observed centennial celebrations and along with it they celebrated the 50th anniversary of Indo-Canadians obtaining the right to vote. Sindi Hawkins (Satinder Kaur), B.C., MLA, thinks that the winning of franchise is not an occasion for celebration. She says that the fact that the Indo-Canadian community is century-old yet Canadians of Indian origin have had the vote for only half that time is a source of embarrassment for Canada. "We had the right to vote as British subjects when we got here and it was taken away from us", says Hawkins. "The way it was taken away was so blatantly discriminatory that I think that is something for which we are owed an apology"[15] The Indo-Canadians do not want apology, they want explanation from the executioners of the basic rights of the country's citizens for the wrong done to them for forty long years. Seeking apology and offering apology are both reprehensible and painful to a proud and self-respecting man. After deprivation of their right to vote so long, it passed into history with Indo-Canadian victory in 1947—the year of India's gaining independence from a foreign rule. History shows no mercy or forgiveness to the dominant society or its rulers for the grave injustice perpetrated on a minority.

Right to vote is an inherent right of a citizen of a country. Prolonging denial of that right for such a long time to a section of the society was a grave crime or injustice perpetrated by the government. This infliction of pain was immeasurably deep but the victims' power of bearing was marvellous. The struggle for franchise was ceaseless until the goal was achieved. No body can be happy without a goal before him. And none can be happier than the one who achieves his goal. The attainment of franchise gave immense joy to our pioneers who struggled so vigorously for so long. Do we, who enjoy the fruits of our ancestors' unfathomable labours, even realise the sacrifices they made so that we may have a comfortable and smooth sailing, free of any rough and stormy strife in our life?

REFERENCES

1.   *The Daily Province*, Vancouver, 20 March 1907.

2. The Proceedings of the B.C. Legislature, 26 March 1907.
3. The Daily Province, Vancouver,17 October 1910.
4. Ibid., 29 and 30 March 1912.
5. Ibid., 30 March and 4 April 1912.
6. The British Columbian, New Westminster, 2 March 1943.
7. The Vancouver Sun, 9 March 1944.
8. The Daily Province, Vancouver, 6 December 1944.
9. The Vancouver Sun, 11 December 1944.
10. J.E. Boyd, News Herald, Vancouver , 27 December 1944.
11. The B.C. District Union News, 10 March 1945, pp.3 and 7.
12. News Herald, 26 March 1945.
13. C.C.F. Cooperative Commonwealth Federation News, 29 March 1945.
14. Editorial, 'Votes and Citizenship', Southam Newspaper,
    Vancouver, 28 March 1945.
15. Surj Rattan, 'Looking Back', Mehfil, Vancouver, December
    1997, p.53.

CHAPTER 6
THE SIKHS AND IMMIGRATION

The history of Canada is, in large measure, the history of immigration. Whether the immigrants have been the French or Anglo-Saxons or Asians or even the aborigines people they came to this land from outside at some period of time. They were all outsiders. The earlier settlers called the later coming immigrants as intruders and undesirables. This thinking has persisted in the minds of the Canadians up to recent times.

In the early stages of their existence in Canada the East Indians were awfully handicapped in respect of their immigration. Their number in Canada was small, constantly under severe strains and stresses, no Canadians to support their genuine demands, no money to fight their cases, no judiciary to give them full justice and no government to protect their rights as British subjects. To crown all, the British Indian government listened only to the Canadian government and not the Indian immigrants and often, the Canadian government, in collusion with the Indian government, worked to the detriment of the interests of their ex-soldiers and loyal subjects.

Canadian government formulated their immigration policy vis-à-vis the Indians after holding discussions between Ottawa, London and Calcutta (then the capital of India). British Columbia was the mainly affected province with the immigration of the Sikhs who came and settled in Vancouver, Victoria and some other adjoining areas. Whenever British Columbia referred the immigration problems to their federal government, they would refer it to the British and the Indian governments. These governments agreed that the B.C. government had every right to exclude the East Indian immigrants. They only wanted that it should be done in such a way that it did not smack racial discrimination.

It is estimated that there were around 100 East Indians in Victoria and Vancouver in 1900. They did not seem settled at one place. They were constantly on the move in search of better and more suitable places and better jobs. The Chinese and the Japanese were the main Orientals at that time. According to the 1891 census there were 9,129 Chinese in the whole of Canada, out of whom 8,910 were in British Columbia alone.

The editorial of *The Daily Province* of 15 May 1900, wrote that 'the recent influx of Japanese and Chinese of coolie class has so much accentuated the dread of their over-running the province.' The trades and labour council passed a resolution for the 'total abolition' of the oriental immigration through the Alien Act that already existed. In the first four months of 1900, 4669 Japanese landed on Canadian shores. The Canadians felt very much upset by this 'oriental plague' and told the Asians that they retained the right to keep the Asians out.

From 1901 to 1904 the government of British Columbia made strenuous efforts to stem the tide of immigrants. The Oriental Commission also recommended that the Asians be kept out of Canada by imposing restrictions on their immigration. From 1904 to 1906 there was an influx of the Sikhs into Canada, and they were supplanting Chinese and Japanese working in the mills of British Columbia. According to W.L. Mackenzie King, the Deputy Minister of Labour (later Prime Minister of Canada) there were some valid reasons for the East Indians to come all the way to Canada. First, some steamship companies and agents in Calcutta and elsewhere propagated about the opportunities of good earnings in Canada. Second, some printed pamphlets in Punjabi were distributed in the Punjab villages concerning sure chances of employment in Canada.

In October 1906, the people of British Columbia impressed upon the federal government to restrict immigration from Asia. In the meantime, a ship bringing a party of the East Indians was diverted to Victoria because the mayor refused to allow it to dock in Vancouver harbour. A mass meeting was held in Vancouver Town Hall on 18 October 1906, at which resolutions were passed for banning immigration of the East Indians. They sent telegram to that effect to Winston Churchill, the then colonial secretary and to Sir Wilfred Laurier, the Prime Minister of Canada. The message sent to the Prime Minister read as: 'the city of Vancouver will not stand for any further dumping of the East Indians.'

A subtle scheme of the government Immigration Department to get rid of the Sikhs was to subject them to a difficult situation by not providing them with proper documentation when they left Canada for India to see their family members or relatives although the outgoing Chinese were duly registered. So, on their return from India, they could not prove their previous residence in Canada easily. In respect of the East Indians the

Canadian Immigration Department always followed a policy of 'human deterrence.'

After discussing the matter in the parliament Immigration Act of 1906 was passed. Some voices were raised in protest on behalf of the Sikhs. Henry H. Gladstone (nephew of the great Prime Minister of England) was among them. He had served in India for 15 years. Answering the charge that Indians had filthy habits, he wrote "the Sikhs are scrupulously clean and I regard them as a very fine race of men."[1] And some local whites called the bill discriminative.

The Pioneer Sikhs Observed Sikh Symbols

Almost all of the early Sikh immigrants to Canada were bearded and turbaned men and were disliked and the popular sentiment was to exclude these East Indians. But these picturesquely attired Sikhs, mostly ex-army soldiers, would not part with their religious symbols and code of conduct. During the 18th and 19th centuries it was essential for every Sikh to take *amrit* (baptism) prepared with the double-edged sword and to follow the Sikh *rahit* strictly before joining the Khalsa army. The British realised that the Sikh soldiers were best in their performance when they were in their true form and spirit. Hence the British emphasized the Sikh form. All the Sikhs who sought recruitment to the British army had to undergo the Khalsa baptism and uphold the five symbols of the Khalsa.

After the Lahore Khalsa Durbar army was disbanded by the British, after the annexation of the Punjab, the most important decision taken by the new rulers was to assure that the Sikhs who joined the army the traditions of the Khalsa would not be meddled with. This decision had a far-reaching effect in preserving the separate and distinct identity of the Sikhs. The British government's new regulation provided that:

"The *paol* (*pahul* or baptism) or religious pledges of Sikh fraternity, should on no account be interfered with. The Sikh should be permitted to wear his beard, and the hair of his head gathered up, as enjoined by his religion. Any invasion, however slight, of these obligations, would be construed into a desire to subvert his faith, lead to evil consequences, and naturally inspire general distrust and alarm. Even those, who have assumed the outward conventional characteristics of the Sikhs should not be permitted after entering the British army, to drop them."[2]

Lord Dalhousie, the governor-general of India, approved these regulations and said, "Soon after I entered the Punjab during the present march, I heard that the Sikhs had been enlisted, but that, in compliance I presume with existing regulations, they had been required to cut off their beards — an act to which no real Sikh can submit; or if he for a time submits to it of necessity, it is impossible that he can do so without the deepest discontent.... No true Sikh will submit to it— and the intelligence that such a regulation is enforced, rapidly spreading among the other Sikh corps in the service, may produce alarm or at best restlessness which is much to be deprecated. This point, therefore, should at once be set at rest."[3]

We see a large number of group pictures of the pioneer Sikh immigrants to Canada. Almost all of them being the ex-army soldiers strictly followed the Sikh discipline of conduct, sporting turbans and having untampered with beards. They were not 20 or 22 carat Sikhs but 24 carat Sikhs. J.B. Hobson, General Manager of Cariboo Consolidated Company remarked that if these Sikh workers had been suitably clothed and properly equipped before sending them to Cariboo, they would have done their work more efficiently than the Chinese and the Japanese. "I always liked to give employment to these old soldiers who had helped to fight for the British Empire than to entire aliens," remarked Hobson.

The East Indians Debarred from Canada

All efforts were being made to keep the Sikhs out of Canada. In 1907, a total of 120 East Indians were debarred from Canada because of their failure to fulfil the conditions laid down by the immigration department while the number of the debarred in 1906 was 18. The Canadian whites said again and again that they did not want the Sikhs in Canada. They were not the class of immigrants who would be of benefit to the country. Colonel John Smith, Political Adviser to the Maharaja of Mysore, who just passed through Vancouver in 1908 after spending his holidays in England, said, "If the people of British Columbia are true British subjects and proud of the traditions of our common empire, they will not treat the Sikhs harshly. Close your gates if you will, against the Indians, but do not humiliate, prosecute or antagonize them, for, the consequences in India may be horrible. The Sikh residents in this province (B.C.), will and possibly have already written home telling their relatives that the flag, which they have served under in India, does not protect them in Canada. It will create unrest and dissensions among the native troops and may precipitate an outlook of far greater magnitude than the Indian mutiny. The danger is there."[4]

In 1908, MacKenzie King visited London and Calcutta to present strongly the Canadian point of view. In compliance with Mackenzie King's request to ban the immigration of the East Indians to Canada, the government of India ordered shipping companies to stop advertising travel facilities and job opportunities in Canada and invoked the provisions of the Emigration Act 1883, to prevent the East Indians leaving for Canada.

The Direct Passage order (1908) and Indian Immigration

The Canadian government included in the Immigration Act of 1906 a section called the 'direct passage' without mentioning specific people but stated that "immigrants to Canada must come by direct steamship passage from the land of their origin." Since there was no 'direct passage' from India to Canada, this clause effectively prevented all immigrants from India although the Chinese and Japanese continued to come. The Japanese were exempted from the application of this order by virtue of an agreement with their government and this order was not invoked in the case of the Chinese. The above order-in-council (No.920) passed on 18 January 1908, authorized the Minister of the Interior to prohibit entry of travellers into Canada if they did not comply with the order. The government ordered the deportation of 200 East Indians who came through Hong Kong or Fiji. The deportation order was challenged in the Supreme Court. Judge Clement, giving his judgement, said that the governor-general-in-council, could not delegate his powers on immigration matters to any official, even though that official be the Minister of Interior. The discretion as to which immigrant would be admitted and which refused admission must be exercised solely by the governor-general-in-council The deportation order stood cancelled. The petitioners Bhola Singh and his 'dusky brethren, who had crowded the court room and the corridors, revealed beautiful rows of pearly teeth in smiles', commented a press reporter.

A modified order-in-council was passed as under: "All immigrants seeking entry must come to Canada by continuous journey and on 'through tickets' from the country of their birth or nationality or citizenship".

A new section 23 was added which read, "No court, and no judge or officer thereof, shall have the jurisdiction to review, quash, reverse, restrain or otherwise interfere with any proceedings, decisions or orders of the minister or any Board of Inquiry, or officer in-charge made or given under the authority in accordance with provisions of this Act relating to the detention or deportation of any ejected immigrant, passenger or other person upon any ground whatsoever, unless such person is a Canadian citizen or has Canadian domicile."

The second order-in-council (No.926) promulgated on 3 June 1908, raised the sum of the money required to be in the possession of an intending immigrant from $25 to $200. Both these orders were specifically directed against the Indians. The Chinese and Japanese immigrants were given exemption from the provision regarding the possession of $ 200.[5] The 'continuous passage' order was pointedly aimed at the Indians as it was known that no company ran ships directly from India to Canada. A transshipment at Hong Kong or Shanghai or some other port was necessary. Through these orders-in-council, the door to Canada for the East Indians was firmly shut and these orders clearly announced, "Indians keep out". The constitution or regulations of a country are like a mirror that reflects the national soul but if they debar a segment of society from its rights the mirror is bedimmed and the constitution becomes unworthy of implementation. There were wide gaps between what the constitution guaranteed and what the East Indians found in practice. Certainly, such discriminatory rules had no right to exist. The East Indians were subjects of British Indian government as were the Canadians, thus both being under the king of England. Exemptions from the application of orders-in-council were given to the Chinese and Japanese but were denied to the East Indians despite the fact that the former were not the British subjects while the latter were.

The Canadian government's explanation for putting a ban on the East Indians' entry into Canada was: first, to save the Indians from the severity of Canada's climate, second, to avoid friction between the Canadian whites and the East Indians, and third, to protect the Canadian workers whose standard of life, family obligations and civil duties were of a high order.[6]

Herbert H. Stevens, an M.P. from Vancouver, rabidly anti-Indian, who had gone wild in mobilizing the Canadian opinion against the East Indian immigrants, admitted "that the minister who drafted the order, knew, and his government knew, that there was no steamship line direct from India to Canada and, therefore, this regulation would keep the East Indians out, and at the same time render the government immune from attack on the ground that they were passing regulations against the interests of the East Indians who were British subjects."[7]

The victims of the orders-in-council included, to start with, 18 persons who had waited for the boat at Hong Kong. They were debarred because they had not come by direct passage from India. In March 1908, a ship named *Monteagle* with 200 East Indians (mostly the Sikhs) came to Vancouver. It was turned back as it did not meet the requirements of the orders-in-council.

In 1907, 2623 East Indians entered Canada but due to restrictions imposed by the orders-in-council only six East Indians could come to

Canada in 1908. And another group of 105, who had boarded the ship at Calcutta, was turned back because they could not provide proof that they were the men who had purchased the tickets at Calcutta.

In reply to the Canadian Prime Minister Sir Wilfred Laurier's letter the viceroy of India, Lord Minto, wrote on 1 March 1909, that: "We have published the conditions imposed by Canada widely, with the result that immigration has ceased altogether and we consider there is practically no chance of its being reopened.... We raised no objection to the method adopted by Canada and we have not any intention of raising any question regarding them."[8]

Lord Crewe, secretary for colonies, said in the House of Lords, London: "The question of immigration into self-governing colonies was one for the independent discretion of the colonies themselves."[9] The Canadian government also wanted to have a permanent Board of Inquiry with absolute jurisdiction in determining as to which immigrants should be liable to deportation from the post of entry.

Herbert Stevens, a violent opponent of the East Indians' immigration to Canada, ironically remarked in 1909, "The Hindu civilization is measurably older than ours; whereas they, as a race, never been known to open up a new territory or extend civilization. They came creeping into the choicest parts of our empire, seeking to pluck some of the rich rewards resulting from the labours of a hardy race of pioneers who have opened up the country and made possible a comfortable life.":

Despite the whites nursing hatred against the East Indians an interesting event took place in Vancouver during this time. One baptised Sikh, Munsha Singh married a white woman. He was renamed as, Gian Singh and his wife Annie Wright was given the name, Labh Kaur, before the marriage ceremony was performed according to the Sikh *maryada* at the Gurdwara, on Vancouver's second Avenue, on 4 April 1909. This was the first marriage between a Canadian Sikh and a white woman.

In 1910, Sir Wilfred Laurier, the Canadian Prime Minister (1896-1911), who was happy that the immigration from India had been stopped, was slightly sympathetic towards those East Indians who were already in Canada. In a speech he said, "The men from India were of the Sikh race—subjects of His Majesty—the king.... How were they to be treated? Were they to be driven back ignominiously and told that they had no right to land here—a part of the same Empire?"[10]

The government of the United States had easier methods of deporting the immigrants than the Canadian government. They would simply turn back the immigrants telling them that they were suffering from contagious diseases. Some of them were charged of violating the alien contract labour law.

The decline in the number of immigrants into Canada was due to the collusion of the governments of India and Canada regarding the ban of entry of the East Indians to Canada. The number of the East Indians that had reached 5185 between 1904 and 1908 came down to 2342 in the year 1911. One reason for this reduction was the two orders-in-council of 1908 and another reason was of the East Indians having left for Washington, Oregon and California for better prospects of work. And as a result of the above two orders only 128 East Indians could enter Canada from 1908 to 1920 i.e. in 13 years, while the influx of immigrants from other countries to Canada continued as the following table shows:

Immigration to Canada
1908-1920

Year	East Indian Immigrants	Total Immigrants[11]
1908	6	143,326
1909	10	173,694
1910	5	286,839
1911	3	331,288
1912	5	375,756
1913	88	400,870
1914	0	150,484
1915	1	36,665
1916	0	55,914
1917	0	72,910
1918	0	41,845
1919	0	107,698
1920	10	138,824

Families of the East Indian Immigrants banned entry

The hardest hit of these orders were the families of the East Indians who could not join their husbands for a numbers of years. In 1911, a Sikh woman, along with her child, accompanied by her husband named Hira Singh, a resident of Canada, came to Vancouver. Despite Hira Singh's explaining the immigration department that there was no provision of a direct passage from India to British Columbia, the woman and her child, were ordered to be deported. Hira Singh filed a habeas corpus writ with the Supreme Court of British Columbia. Within a week the federal authorities decided to drop the deportation proceedings.

In 1911, there came to Canada 11,132 Chinese and 2,986 Japanese of whom 1037 were women. Only three East Indians were allowed to land during the same period." [12]

The Sikhs have always been guided by a secret, sublime and infallible instinct to do the right thing in the right way.

Same year, a delegation of the East Indians from British Columbia went to Ottawa to plead for the entry of the Canadian immigrants' wives and children without any obstruction and to ask the federal government to hear the silenced voices of the suppressed minorities. They impressed upon the government, "Give us our wives and children." The public opinion was also mobilized to support them. The delegation comprised Prof. Teja Singh, Dr Sunder Singh, Rajah Singh and Rev., C.W. Hall, a Presbyterian missionary.

\The deputation met the government officials on behalf of the Khalsa Diwan Society, Vancouver, on 13 December 1911, in Ottawa, and submitted a memorandum from which an extract is given below:

"We are British subjects, our claim, for which we respectfully request your acceptance, is that our status in Canada is wholly distinct and differentiated from that of oriental immigrants, by the way Japanese, Chinese or others; as a matter of fact, we cannot justly be classed as aliens.

"The restriction that most presses, and needs very immediate redress, is the prohibition by regulations that make it impossible for the wives and children of the Hindustanees residing in Canada joining them. The compulsory separation of families is punitive and in itself penal, and can only lawfully be applied to criminals by any civilized nation. It is contrary to every human instinct and jeopardized the existence of the family life, which is the very foundation of the British Empire as a whole. The regulation presses (contrary to all preconceived ideas of British justice and fair-play) hardest on the weaker of the two parties concerned, namely, the mother and the child. There are no good political, economic or racial reasons why this regulation should not be abolished.... It is well to consider from an empirical standpoint, the reflex action of this regulation on the Sikh communities of India, who are so closely united, by the bonds of their religion whether it fosters loyalty or otherwise.

"The next immigration regulation is the continuous journey restriction. We would ask you to consider: "Is there any process of law or regulation that can be indirectly used to strip a loyal British subject of his inherent right to travel or reside in any part of the empire"? If not, then why this restriction? Our common sovereigns, their Majesties, have solemnly promised all subjects of the empire, regardless of race, equality of treatment.

"The other reasons we would urge are that the Hindustanees domiciled in Canada have economically made good, as citizens and as producers and that they comply with every condition in which they have been placed, intelligently and successfully. In the larger centres of British Columbia their holdings in land, houses and stocks, and their savings bank accounts for the time which they have been in the country exceed any other class of immigrants, and their faithful compliance with the law is now unquestioned.

"We claim for ourselves, while our language is different and customs are not the same, that we understand your laws and we are more ready to give intelligent obedience to them than most European immigrants and all Orientals, and above all, we are already loyal and trained subjects of the same king, and we worship the same God, moreover, that the Sikh home-life is identical in all virtues as the Christian home.

"We will give bonds to the immigration authorities that no Hindustani shall become a public charge. The questions involved in the representation are not local, as being purely Canadian they are in their very nature empire questions, and hence must be dealt with from this broad standpoint. There will either be one standard, or two, within the empire of British subjects' interests and privileges. If the latter, then it must be based on race privileges or race superiority."

Prof. Teja Singh could say and do the nastiest things in the nicest way as against the characteristics of the East-Indians who are either too polite or too aggressive because of their ethnic style. But the professor could always make his point without confronting and being offensive. He relaxed people even when he argued with them. He always had his head on his shoulders.

The Interior Minister told the delegation in a meeting with them on 15 December 1911, that the East Indians were free to bring their families to Canada but on a 'through ship and there was no through ship'. The government never clearly spelt out whether these just demands of the East Indians had any sanctity in their scheme of things.

Vancouver East Indians' delegation met Lord Hardinge, the viceroy of India, on 20 December 1912, in Delhi and presented a charter of demands almost similar to those mentioned above and submitted to the government at Ottawa. But there was no satisfactory response from the Indian government as they did not like to exercise any pressure on the Canadian government.

In fact, the delegates found a streak of heartlessness, if not sadism, from the occupants of the citadels of power. They felt that to hope to achieve anything at that stage was like hoping to grow crops in the desert. Many of the sane voices were raised against the Canadian government's unreasonable restrictions. On 2 June 1913, Senator Douglas, Senator Bostock, Senator Davie and Senator Power of the Canadian Senate brought up the question of the Sikhs in Canada in the Upper House that they were being ill-treated. Senator Douglas said that the action of British Columbia against the Sikhs was un-Christian, un-British and un-grateful. The Sikhs were splendid men who have fought under the British flag. To inflict upon these men the cruelty of depriving them of the association of their wives was a thing unworthy of any part of the British Empire.[13] A well-meaning person from the United States wrote, "For many months I have been visiting the camps of the Sikhs and I am convinced that they have no equal in the labour market. They are superior workers. I am to note that the government of Canada that is a British territory is not allowing them to bring their families. We must not forget that the Sikhs are also British subjects. In the east they have been appointed on very responsible jobs. We talk of brotherhood of man but in practice we limit the brotherhood only to the whites. It is against humanity because our *Bible* says that in the eyes of God all people are equal. If we have faith in the *Bible* we must practice what we preach".

V.W. Baen, who pleaded the case of the Sikhs, wrote a long article in the *Victoria Times* that, "I can give hundreds of instances of the loyalty of the Sikhs towards their employers. They are not only very trustworthy but also very faithful and hard-working persons. I state with full confidence and responsibility that the Sikhs are superior to the workers of other communities. A Sikh is the most desirable person."

When the question of restricting the entry of the Sikh families into Canada began to gain momentum Lord Crewe, the Secretary of State for India stressed the need to safeguard the special rights of the British subjects. He said," If it is so, it amounts to injustice, because we are openly allowing the Chinese, the Japanese and the Russians to fetch their families. With this policy of discrimination we are harming the interests of the British Empire".

Sir Andrew Fraser, a senior officer of the British government in India, during his lecture in British Columbia, commented, "I believe that the Sikhs will become the most respected citizens of Canada, but the way we are treating them is shameful."

But unfortunately, by keeping its East Indian immigrants' families apart from them, the Canadian government gave a holiday to its nation's conscience and its healthy and vibrant society's humaneness.

After the return of the deputation from Ottawa a meeting was held on 29 January 1912, in Vancouver, and two resolutions were passed. First, about the right of the Sikh immigrants to bring their families to Canada and second, advising the Sikhs to fight for just rights together. Professor Teja Singh presented both the resolutions.

Many clergymen gave support to the East Indians' appeal to permit wives and children to enter Canada without the restrictions imposed by the 'continuous passage' order. The Ministry of Interior gave sympathetic hearing to the delegations but the whites feared that in case the rules were relaxed the East Indians would soon overrun the coast. The government agreed to revoke the 'direct passage' clause regarding the wives and children of 'better class of the East Indians'. From 'the better class' the government meant those East Indians who did not practise polygamy. Some mischievous whites had given to understand that the East Indians were polygamous. But this was far from truth. In an address delivered at the Canadian club in Vancouver on 10 July 1913, H. H. Stevens said that if a Hindu (Sikh) is allowed to bring over his family, he would bring here four girls as his daughters who would really be his wives. Stevens erroneously attributes polygamy to the Sikhs who never practised it.[14] Hardly a few people from some communities might have indulged in it. This practice had nothing to do with the Sikhs who were monogamous. The delegates were not satisfied with the government's response. Dr Sunder Singh came back from Ottawa and tried to communicate with some prominent people in India to wait on His Majesty, King George of the British Kingdom, who was then in India, and tell him that "We are British subjects. We seek from the government of Canada only the same treatment as given to the British subjects. We would not affect the Canadian labour market. Our people are farmers and they did not compete with the Canadian labour. We would till the soil and aid in developing the country."[15] But it seems that nothing came out of these efforts. The Sikh mission to Ottawa was not even remotely near success despite the delegates pleading their case very effectively. The federal government did not need rocket scientist to explain to them their simple demand. But the government's intentions were suspect and they refused to measure up to the gravity of the East Indian immigrants' problems.

In this tireless campaign against the East Indians Herbert H. Stevens— a rabid racist, who was always in search of this excuse or that to malign the East Indians, remarked that "the Indians were given to lying or deceiving, and it was impossible to believe them." The East Indians always rebutted his charges but in a mild language and they would never stoop so low as to match his senseless blustering, gruffy and antagonizing expressions and opinions. For such remarks history will judge H. Stevens harshly.

Stevens had supreme contempt for everything Indian. He considered Indians as enemies of the culture of the whites. Sticking to their Indian culture, he considered them degrading their Canadian culture. He was an arrogant and a heartless and evil-minded man but paradoxically a brilliant parliamentarian from B.C., belonging to the tribe of the Anglo-Saxons. His opposition to the causes of the Indians had no bounds. I admire his brilliance, but woefully regret his anti-Indian tirade. He was unwise, frank and inconsiderate in his blusters and could say any thing, in the Parliament and outside, as ugly as hell, against the whole of a big nation as India was even during the British domination. He believed in making incendiary speeches directly appealing to the emotions of the members of the Parliament and making no bones about hate politics that he practised. He spewed communal passions and accused the East Indian minority community of being intruders, warning them to return to the land of their birth. He seemed to have monopoly on venomous outbursts. He was lionized for his fearless utterances, which were most indiscreet, irresponsible, tactless and haughty. He probably failed to understand that when he was criticizing a community he was attacking them and when he was insulting them he was committing verbal violence on them. And all this could not be without repercussions. This author does not suggest defiling the memory of the dead. He believes in burying the sins of the dead with them.

During the *Komagata Maru* incident his role against the passengers' entry into Canada was most awful. Government officials like the immigration officer Malcolm Reid and Inspector Hopkinson were always at his beck and call and worked under his instructions.

The Vancouver Sun which was started on 12 February 1912, made slanderous remarks on 16 February 1912, that "the East Indian women should not be admitted as the safety of white women and children would eventually be placed in jeopardy through the increasing influx of the East Indians. The East Indians who lived in immediate vicinity of their colony lived in filth and squalor and the colony is worse than that existing in the slums of London...."[16]

Not only in 1912, even today, many whites in Canada live in much more filthier slums than where the East Indians lived then. Most of the East Indians, by nature, are scrupulously clean while most of the white people are, by nature, unclean and filthy whatever their living standard. Unfortunately, *The Vancouver Sun* has all through the decades been sarcastic and malicious towards the East Indians.

From every standard of ethical values it is highly immoral and morally criminal on the part of any government, even worth the name, to keep an immigrant separated permanently from his wife and children through a legislation. No civilized nation or cultured person would support such an uncivilized order which keeps the whole people from a civilized country in a torturous state of uncertainty for more than a decade under the pretext of the fallacious bogey of racial superiority.

There was a proposal from Prof. T. L. Walker of the Toronto University to either repatriate 3000 odd East Indians living in Canada to their country at government expense of two to three million dollars or they be permitted to bring their families to Canada.[17] The second part of the proposal was the only practicable solution of the problem.

Two Sikh women—Harnam Kaur, wife of Bhag Singh, President of the Khalsa Diwan Society, the Gurdwara of Vancouver, and Kartar Kaur wife of Balwant Singh, a priest and Secretary of the same Gurdwara, arrived in Vancouver along with their children, accompanied by their husbands. Since they had come through broken journey, the two women and their children were ordered to be deported. The editorial of *The Daily Province* of 28 February 1912, said that the Interior Department, after inquiry into the Sikh immigration in British Columbia, came to the conclusion that the rules against the entry of the Sikh women who sought to join their husbands in Canada should not be relaxed. The good of the white community and of the country at large demanded the exclusion of these people's families from the Canadian society.[18] The writ was filed in the Supreme Court of British Columbia against the deportation order of the two women and their children.

The National Council of Women of the province of Ontario passed a resolution requesting the government to end the Sikh women's immigration woe and to allow them to stay on. In case of taking unfavourable view of their suggestion they would propose to send the women back to India along with their husbands as it is cruelty to women to keep them away from their husbands and make children grow fatherlessly. Things dragged on for eight months. Before the Supreme Court of Canada could pronounce its judgement the Federal Immigration Department allowed the women and their children to remain in Canada as "an act of grace... and without establishing a precedent".[19]

"The attempt of exclusion formed a strong basis of an agitation against the inhumanity of separating husbands from their wives and children."[20]

Some sympathetic senators moved this question in the Senate. Senator Douglas described this action of the government as unethical and irreligious.[21]

H.H. Stevens, the crusader against the East Indians, blurted, "With a nucleus of 20,000 they would soon grow to such numbers as to constitute a permanent menace to the country. [In due course of time] we will have a race problem that will continue to grow in complicity and magnitude."[22] Stevens, who was a violent and a malicious antagonist of the East Indians' immigration to Canada further stated that" the Orientals have retarded the progress of this country". Despite his all out efforts for a long period of time, he could not reverse the process of history through a full-fledged hate campaign or through the legislature. He died in 1972, having lived up to a mature age of 94. With the passage of time, his extra sharp angularities must have been rubbed off, which he had been using for decades to cut into the flesh of the East Indians, totally ignorant or oblivious of their qualities of head and heart and their physical prowess or sturdy muscles which they used stoutly in the discharge of their duties as mill workers and farmers. Before his death he must have deeply regretted the unmerited venomous attacks inflicted on the East Indian community and must have seen with his own eyes the remarkable contribution made by them to the economic growth and various other fields of the country.

Reverting again to the question of immigration of the East Indians to Canada, the attitude of the media—*The Vancouver Sun* and *The Daily Province* (Vancouver), has again and again been that of a relentless fighter against the East Indians, expressed strongly through editorials in 1912 and 1913. According to them, "the dominant society wanted to undo the 'wrong' that had already been done. By keeping the women out, it hoped to purge Canada of the East Indian element within a generation. For the comfort and happiness of the generations that are to succeed us we must not permit their women to come in at all. The exclusion of the women would induce many men to leave Canada and the ones who refused to leave would be prevented from 'defiling the land' with their progeny."

A deputation comprising Nand Singh of Phillaur, Balwant Singh Khurdpur and Narain Singh Thikriwala left for England on 14 May 1913, to approach the home government in London to remove disabilities on immigration but without any fruitful result. England was not ready to put out the bush fires for the East Indians in Canada. After meeting the government officials in England the delegation left for India. They met Feroze Shah Mehta in Bombay and Mr. Natson, in Madras. At a meeting at Lahore they appointed a committee comprising Ram Bhaj Dutt, Mian Jalal Din and Mehar Singh Chawla to pursue the Canadian issues. The delegation also held a meeting with Michael O'Dwyer, Lt. Governor of the Punjab. They also met Kanwar Daljit Singh, Pt. Madan Mohan Malvia, Kanwar Harnam Singh, Joginder Singh, Joint Secretary of Singh Sabha, and some members of the viceroy's council. The delegation also attended a meeting of the Congress in Karachi. The Indian Congress passed a resolution supporting the demands of the Indians in Canada and sent a copy of the same to the Indian viceroy. The delegation voiced their grievances through media—the newspapers and magazines. But to their utter dismay all their efforts had no effect on the viceroy and the Indian British government machinery. They returned in 1914.

Later, Balwant Singh Khurdpur (1882-1917) was charged with his involvement in *Ghadar* movement and after his trial in Lahore jail , he was sentenced to death on 5 January 1917, and hanged on 16 March 1917. His son Hardayal Singh Atwal, the first Sikh child born in Canada on 28 August 1912, mostly lived in Duncan, B.C. as a perfect Sikh, died on 25 September 1996, at the age of 84. Throughout his life he remained a very respectable man in the Sikh community.

In view of the tough attitude of the Canadian government in respect of the orders-in-council the Sikhs were feeling sore about the separation of their families. Many of them preferred to go back to India permanently. After the declaration of the First World War in 1914 nearly half of the Sikhs left British Columbia for Punjab as job opportunities dwindled. In 1915 there were 1099 Punjabis in British Columbia. In 1918, the number fell as low as 700 in B.C. The 1921 census showed only 951 Punjabis in the province.

The exodus of the Sikhs from British Columbia continued unabated and by 1941 there were only seven hundred Sikh men and 165 Sikh women over 19 years of age in the province. According to the 1911 census there were only three Sikh women in this province. Due to economic depression in the late thirties and the World War-II (1939-45) only a few Sikhs immigrated to Canada as the table below shows. The number of immigrants from other countries was also affected by these considerations.

Year	East Indian Immigrants	Total Immigrants[23]
1936	13	11,643
1937	14	15,101
1938	14	17,244
1939	11	16,994
1940	6	11,324
1941	3	9,329
1942	0	7,576
1943	0	8,504
1944	0	12,801
1945	1	22,722

After repeated appeals to the governments of Canada, UK and India, the Sikhs in Canada succeeded in getting the restriction on the entry of wives and children (under eighteen years of age) lifted by the order-in-council of 26 March 1919. It was also due to the pressure from Britain which told that the policy of Canada was damaging to the British policy in India as the East Indians were getting very angry and rebellious towards the British Indian government. Now onwards the students, tourists and other non-immigrants were also allowed to come to Canada. The married East Indians registered in Canada could visit their families and relatives in India for a period of more than six months ordinarily allowed. Those unmarried men who came to India for marriage could have sufficient time to seek a wife and solemnize marriage.

After the ban on the entry of women was lifted vide Canadian government's order-in-council of 26 March 1919, only 172 women immigrated to Canada up to 31 March 1931, and during the next decade i.e. up to 31 March 1941 only sixty nine women. By 1940 nearly 70 per cent of the Sikhs in Canada had either returned to India or shifted to the United States, mostly to California.

Government data about the East Indians

The following letter addressed to Dr H.L. Keenleyside, Deputy Minister of Mines and Resources, Ottawa, provides information regarding the East Indian immigrant population in Canada according to the 1941 census report.

Chateau Laurier,
OTTAWA
16 March 1948

Dr H. L. Keenleyside,
Deputy Minister of Mines and Resources
OTTAWA

Dear Dr Keenleyside,
Further to my last interview with you with regard to the admission of the relations of Canadian citizens of Indian origin to Canada, I wish to submit the following facts based on the data attached hereto.

You will note that the total East Indian (mostly Sikh) population in Canada is 1394, of which 98% are domiciled in British Columbia, with 59% residing in Vancouver and Victoria. Out of this number, 70% are males and 30% are females that constitute an abnormality that is not conducive to the general welfare of any group of Canadian citizens, as it indicates a considerable disparity between the sexes. Another significant factor to take into consideration is that 25% of the total population are over 60 years of age and represent, in general, the immigrants who first arrived before the cessation of Indian immigration to Canada in 1908.

The community can be divided into three major age groups. The first group consists of those under 21 years of age, of which there are 35.7%, inclusive of 10% who are infants between the ages of one and four. In the second group, that is, those between the ages of 21 and 60, there are 39.3%, the majority of whom are the children of the original entrants. The last group is formed of those over 60, of which there are 25%.

As I indicated in my previous letter of 28 February, approximately 80% of the men are engaged in lumbering, either as wor' rs distributors or owners. The remaining 20% are for the most part farm

Family Units owning homes	Homes owned by the Sikhs and rented out	Businesses insured
200	102	85 %

It is interesting to note the high percentage of independently owned businesses in comparison with the general average for Canada.

If the members of the Sikh community in Canada are permitted to bring in their relations, as is now the case with Canadian citizens of European origin, it will give them the much needed assistance in their work in the primary industries of lumbering and agriculture.

The following figures taken at various census periods will indicate the decline of the East Indian population.

1911	1931	1941	1947 (essential)
5438	1400	1465	1394

There is no doubt also, that in the next ten years there will be a further natural decrease in the population through death, as 25% of the community are over 60. Most of these older men have no children, but have invested a great deal of money in various enterprises in Canada. If the relatives of these men are admitted, they will be able to assist them to carry on in their various business ventures and succeed them in case of their demise.

A favourable decision on this question will remove the last remaining discrimination against these Canadian citizens who are British subjects born either in Canada or the sister Dominion of India, and who, in the past, have rendered such invaluable service in developing the country and still continue to do so. I sincerely believe that in view of these facts that the East Indian community deserves a review and adjustment of their immigration problems by the Canadian government.

I know that you and your department have been exceedingly busy of late, especially due to your imminent departure for British Columbia. However, I would deeply appreciate it if you would give your usual sympathetic consideration to this matter, if it is at all possible, before your forthcoming trip to the West.

Population of East Indian Racial Origin, by Birth Place and Sex, Canada, 1941 Census

Birth Place	Male	Female	Total
Population	1059	406	1465
British Born	1050	396	1446
Canada Born	194	230	425
Prince Edward Island	-	1	1
Nova Scotia	7	6	13
Quebec	5	3	8
Ontario	4	9	13
Manitoba	-	2	2
Saskatchewan	-	1	1
Alberta	13	13	26
British Columbia	164	195	360

(Contd.)

British Isles	3	1	4
England and Wales	3	1	4
British possessions	853	165	1018
Foreign Born	9	7	16
United States	2	2	4
Europe	5	4	9
Hungary	5	3	8
Yugoslavia	-	1	1
Japan	-	1	1
Asia	1	1	2
Other	1	-	1
Other Countries	1	-	1
Not stated	-	3	3

Population of East Indian Racial Origin and Sex, Canada Provinces and Territories, 1941 Census

Province	Male	Female	Total
In Canada	1059	406	1465
Prince Edward Island	-	-	-
Nova Scotia	-10	-5	-15
New Brunswick	-	-	-
Quebec	17	12	29
Ontario	12	9	21
Manitoba	4	3	7
Saskatchewan	1	1	2
Alberta	30	18	48
British Columbia	985	358	1343
Yukon	-	-	-
Northwest Territories	-	-	-

Population of East Indian Racial Origin, by Five Year Age Gap Groups and Sex, Canada, 1941 Census

Age Group	Male	Female	Total
All ages	1059	406	1465
0-4	90	78	168
5-9	104	86	190
10-14	70	60	130
15-19	48	17	65

(Contd.)

20-24	37	13	50
25-29	47	37	84
30-34	64	29	93
35-39	54	30	84
40-44	33	17	50
45-49	46	15	61
50-54	160	12	172
55-59	126	5	131
60-64	101	3	104
65-69	43	3	46
70-74	25	-	25
75-79	6	-	6
80-84	5	-	5
85-89	-	1	1

Location of Population of East Indian Racial Origin in British Columbia, 1941 Census

Div No.	Sub-div	District Munici-palities	Male	Female	Total
Div. No.3	Sub-div A	Unorganized Parts	22	7	29
Div No.4	Sub-div A	Delta	29	3	32
		Fraser Mills	22	12	34
		Kent	16	8	24
		Surrey	22	2	24
	Cities	New Westminster	66	40	106
	Sub-division B	Burnaby	24	12	36
		Richmond	27	15	42
	Cities	Vancouver	222	81	303
Div No.5	Sub-div A				
		North Cowichan	13	13	26
		Saanich	47	33	80

(Contd.)

		Unorganized parts	164	53	217
	Cities	Victoria	108	30	138
	Sub-div C	Unorganiz-ed	59	1	60
	Cities	Port Alberni	26	-	26
Div No.6	Sub-div C	Unorganiz-ed parts	21	12	33
Total			888	322	1210

Sarjeet Singh Jagpal has given the figures of an unofficial census cond This survey showed that the total population of the Sikhs in Canada at that time was 1756 of whom 1715 — 98 per cent resided in

British Columbia. There is not too much of difference in the figures provided above from the government census report.

Place	Under 21	Over 21	Total Population
Kelowna	17	27	44
Port Hammond	8	8	16
Port Moody	5	14	19
Sardis	6	2	8
Mission	10	9	19
Abbotsford	11	15	26
Chilliwack	6	3	9
Agassiz	10	7	17
Kamloops	29	19	48
Cariboo	5	2	7
Nanaimo	0	1	1
Victoria	144	194	338
Hillcrest	12	42	54
Grand Forks	3	4	7
Coaldale	0	1	1
North Vancouver	3	40	43
Barnet	16	23	39
Vancouver	125	337	462
Youbou	0	42	42
Great Central	0	22	22

(Contd.)

Duncan	10	20	30
A.P.L. Alberni	3	13	16
Bloedel	3	12	15
Ladysmith	0	4	4
Sahtlam	5	4	9
Honeymoon Bay	20	27	47
Fraser Mills	20	24	44
Mohawk	0	14	14
Lulu Island			
(New Westminster)	21	23	44
Lulu Island (Queensborough)	33	26	59
Timberland	0	10	10
Cloverdale	6	5	11
Langley Prairie	0	5	5
Ladner	4	23	27
Sproat Lake	4	22	26
Paldi	53	62	115
Shawnigan Lake	6	3	9
Chemainus	3	4	7
Haney	5	3	8
Sinclair Mills	0	2	2
Calgary, Alberta			
(While Court, Alta) (Calaboo)	9	7	16
Montreal, Quebec	0	3	3
Toronto, Ontario	2	10	12
Total	**614**	**1142**	**1756**

The 1940s were good times for the Sikhs living in B.C. They had plentiful jobs. They were not required to go to war and their services were in good demand. Their trucking business prospered and their investments in real estate increased in value substantially.[24]

Immigration restrictions relaxed

In the spring of 1947, the Canadian Prime Minister Mackenzie King informed the Parliament of his government's decision to reopen Canada's doors to immigration. But his was not an unqualified support. The purpose of Canada's immigration policy, he declared, must be to "enlarge the population of the country. It would be dangerous for a small population to attempt to hold so great a heritage as ours." But he cautioned that "it is of utmost importance to relate immigration to absorptive capacity," and in his mind, Canada's capacity to absorb immigrants was tied not so much to the number of immigrants as to their ethnic or racial origins. The Prime Minister was only reflecting the national mood when he observed that, "the people of Canada do not wish to make a fundamental alteration in the character of their population through mass immigration." Discrimination and ethnic selectivity in immigration would remain. "It is not the fundamental human right of any alien to enter Canada. It is a privilege. It is a matter of domestic policy." There would be no lifting of restrictions against the East Indians' immigration. Preference in immigration was to be given to those who were easily able to assimilate into the existing Canadian society.

India obtained its independence in 1947 and it became a member of the commonwealth countries. Jawahar Lal Nehru, Prime Minister of India, visited Canada, accompanied by his daughter Ms. Indira Gandhi, in 1949.

Under the changed circumstances the immigration policy of Canada underwent a change in 1951. Canada established an annual quota of 150 for India over and above the sponsored immigrants, which included elderly parents, spouses and children under the age of 21. In 1957 the quota for India was raised to three hundred. But Canada always remained a difficult country for the East Indians to enter.

Though there was gradual relaxation in the restrictions imposed on the East Indians but they did not enjoy as yet all the rights and privileges which were enjoyed by the European immigrants and many other communities of the world living in Canada. For example, an immigrant from India was required to wait for five years before he could get Canadian citizenship. He could apply for the immigration of his spouse and children only after obtaining citizenship, while a European could apply as soon as he became a landed immigrant. This was a discriminatory rule. Kuldeep Singh Bains, on behalf of the East Indian Canadian Citizens Welfare Association sent the following letter to Indian Prime Minister Jawahar Lal Nehru. They solicited Indian Prime Minister's support in changing Canadian immigration laws that were discriminatory to the East Indians.

Pandit Jawhar Lal Nehru   June 30th, 1956
Prime Minister of India

Canadian citizens of the East Indian origin are deprived of the privilege, which is extended to other Canadians of bringing their relatives into Canada, notwithstanding our willingness to undertake such relatives will not become charge on the country.

Under the new immigration regulations, far more rights are granted to the legal residents of Canada from the Middle East countries such as Egypt, Israel, Lebanon and Turkey than to the Canadian citizens of the East Indian origin. This discrimination is still more rancorous and unjust because our country is an active and important member of the commonwealth.

Therefore, we appeal to you to urge the Right Honourable, the Prime Minister of Canada, to remove this unjust discrimination against the Canadian citizens of the East Indian origin, and to accord to us the right to bring to Canada our relatives, upon the same terms and conditions and to the same extent as enjoyed by the Canadians from other commonwealth countries.

Kuldeep Singh Bains
Secretary
East Indian Canadian Citizens Welfare Association

In 1962, the immigration policy was further relaxed and the skilled labour and professionals were freely allowed to come to Canada. The government encouraged the immigration of school teachers, engineers and doctors from India. Between 1961 and 1976 Canada's East Indian population increased about twenty times. In 1962 quota system was dropped and in 1967, the East Indians were given the same rights as the other citizens of Canada. They could sponsor their relatives under the new regulations. After 1967 a large number of immigrants from Britain entered Canada. Three quarters of the East Indians coming from Britain were the Sikhs. Quite a lot of the Sikhs came from East Africa during this time. During 1972-1976, hundreds of Sikhs migrated to Canada from Uganda, Kenya and Tanzania. These Sikhs spread to many parts of the country including Vancouver, Victoria, Toronto, Montreal, Edmonton, Calgary, Winnipeg, Kamloops, Kelowna, Prince George, Regina, Saskatoon, Halifax, Charlottetown, Hamilton, Kitchner, London (Ontario), St. Catherine, Windsor, Ottawa and Kingston.

The Sikh population rapidly grew in bigger cities. In the second half of the twentieth century, despite many handicaps, the foot prints of the East Indians speedily increased on the soil of Canada. At present more than half a million Indians are living in Canada and more than four hundred thousand of them are the Sikhs.

The Immigration Act of 1976 which became effective from 10th April 1978 was designed to administer and (a) to facilitate the reunion of Canadian citizens and landed immigrants with their close relatives abroad,

(b) to co-operate with other levels of government (especially the provinces) with respect to the settlement and admission of immigrants, (c) to ensure that visitors and immigrants to Canada are subject to non-discriminatory standards, (d) to fulfil Canada's international obligation to refugees and the persecuted, and (e) to foster strong economic Canada and protect the health, safety and good order of Canada.

All the above things sound very idealistic but at places and times these are away from reality. The reunification of the family does not include one's brother or sister, uncle, etc. At the Federal Progressive Conservative Party convention in September 1991 three draft resolutions, although defeated, were clear signals of sentiments opposed to immigrants: one draft resolution would have restricted where immigrants would live. Another would have extended the waiting period for citizenship from three to five years. The third would have made it Progressive Conservative Party policy to require the so-called economic or political refugees to leave Canada when "times in their homeland... have improved".[25] The bills of 1992 and 1993 to amend the Immigration Act could not stabilize any policy regarding the total annual quota of the immigrants to Canada at the rate of one per cent of the total population of the country. The age of the dependent children of the sponsored parents was reduced from 21 to 19 years. The top ten source countries of immigration to Canada in 1992 included India and the majority of the Indians were the Sikhs who were affected the most.

From the above resolutions it seems that there is not a sea of difference between the Canadian government's policies regarding immigration in the first half of the 20th century and the 1990s. Despite that the Canadian Prime Minister, Jean Chretien, said in 1993, "What sets Canada apart from every other country—what makes us a beacon of hope to so many of the world's people, is the welcome and encouragement we extend to those from other lands. People have come to Canada because they know that they can partake in the freedom, prosperity and beauty of its land without being pressured to leave behind all that they value of their cultural identity. By encouraging diversity Canadians have given our national life a distinctive flavour that is rarely found elsewhere".

Canada's record with respect to the acceptance of refugees has been one of the best in the world since 1950. As a relatively small country in terms of population Canada has taken a large share of the world's refugees.

Refugees are persons who leave their country for fear of persecution for reasons of race, religion, membership of a particular social or political group and migrate mostly illegally to another country and appeal for an asylum in that country. Hundreds of the East Indians sought permanent residence in Canada as refugees in the last quarter of the 20th century. Most of the cases were accepted even without legitimate travel papers. When these asylum-seekers enter liberal and sympathetic countries like Australia, Sweden and Holland, they find themselves in detention centres. In France they are not allowed to work. Though they are treated humanely in these countries but by comparison Canada is a refugee's paradise. The refugees arriving in this country are not forced to live in camps or detention centres. Since January 1994 they have the right to work. If they cannot find work they are entitled to welfare and full medical coverage. The average acceptance rate of major refugee accepting countries was 14 per cent as compared to more than 57 per cent of Canada in 1992. The East Indians' acceptance rate is fairly high. Canada's refugee system is comparatively generous, but it is far from perfect. There are always changes and improvements that can be made, making things more efficient and more humane.

Gerald Dirks has quoted in his book *Canada's Refugee Policy*, the following criticism of public interest groups:

"Expressed humanitarian concern by the Canadian government has been contradicted by lengthy processing and excessive security interrogations.... Canada is hardly humanitarian if in the execution of its policy, an adequate and speedy response to human need is superceded by the time-consuming procedures, partial measures for the oppressed and out of date and inappropriate security interrogations."[26]

To another category of the elderly East Indians—mostly the Sikhs, who approach the Canadian High Commissioner's office in Delhi for a visitor's visa to visit their children in Canada, in most of the cases, the visas are denied and unreasonably enough, the officials ask the applicants to apply for landed immigrant's visa. When the applicants argue that they do not mean to stay in Canada for a period longer than the one allowed them because they have families, property and close relatives back in their home country, their requests are turned down. The visa officers are governed by their whims to the chagrin of the applicants. An independent M.P. for Markham Stouffville, Ontario, told Parliament in April 1994 that at India's New Delhi visa office "mistakes are made by some officials on the application of the law and the result can be devastating". He cited the case of an 89-year-old woman who had been denied a visa to visit Canada. She was at one time a landed immigrant in Canada, but had returned to Indian and now wished to visit her son for a few months. This is not the solitary example. Many, many examples can be given.

Visa Problems for Indians

The visa problem is an unfinished, unsettled, unsatisfactory and an ever on-going agenda of the Canadian immigration office in New Delhi. Whether it is an immigration visa or visitor visa there is always a question mark on it, if these people are going to Canada on legitimate grounds. The applicants are considered guilty unless they prove themselves otherwise. This is matter of greater concern for the Indians. What they are deeply concerned about is their rights as Canadian citizens. If there is a marriage or death in a family and a close relative from India wants to participate in the happy or sad rituals will he be able to come here, sure? It is always uncertain. Many respectable East Indians who have been living in Canada for decades never let their relatives go through the harassment of immigration department to come and visit them in Canada, including their parents, brothers and sisters. It is simply unacceptable to them. They themselves choose to visit them in India thus saving them from the humiliation that they would suffer in Delhi. These matters have been brought to the notice of the Canadian government time and again but to no effect. Probably the bureaucracy is insensitive to the susceptibilities of the immigrants.

In the beginning of 1992 two MPs, who visited Delhi on a fact-finding mission to investigate problems with the issuing of immigration and visitor visas, submitted their recommendations to the immigration minister. To improve the processing procedures of visitors' visas the government must review its policy to ensure that all legitimate visitors receive visas without the current arbitrary denials for no apparent reasons, the MPs recommended. They also urged that parents travelling to Canada to see children or grand-children be given multiple entry, five years visas, to ensure that they may come and go without the necessity of applying for a new visa for each visit. They also recommended that the priests and *jathas* (religious groups) sponsored by temples be given priority and issued long-term visas. But nothing tangible has been noticed so far. [27]

Mohinderjit Singh Grewal, President of National Association of Canadians of Origins in India (Nacoi), John Kurien and Jasdev Singh Grewal, the three panelists in their brief at the Proceedings of the Standing Committee on multiculturalism at Parliament Hill said in 1987:

While under the law, Canadians may be equal but the treatment received from the governments is anything but equal. One area of particular concern to us is the way in which the Ministry of Immigration treats relatives of Canadians of origin in India. Let us note that we are not talking about independent immigrants. When the family reunification clause operates in such a way that spouses or old parents of a Canadian of European origin can come to Canada in a matter of days, while for those of origin in India it takes, in many cases, well over two years. We must say then that the government of Canada does not treat its citizens equally. If for my children's marriage my parents and brothers have formidable difficulties in obtaining a visitor's visa because my origins are in India, while those of European origin find a willing and eager consulate to facilitate their visits then I must insist that I am being treated as a second class citizen. It is believed that about 80% of the Indo-Canadians have gone through it. Their fate is very different—not just different, but very different because of religion, because of culture, because of colour. There are three or four things involved. For immigrants from European countries, there is only one culture, and may be there is a second, a little language. The refusal of visitor visas to the Indo-Canadians is out of palpable fear that these persons want to come to Canada not simply to visit but to stay. The immigration department should shed this fear, said John Kurien.

In the above brief Mohinderjit Singh Grewal said that Caucasian ethnic groups blend easily into the society at large, after a short period of adjustment, but coloured people remain distinct for ever. Thus, visible minorities are thought of as immigrants, generation after generation, while Caucasians become Canadians as soon as they step off the plane.

The presumptions under which the Minister of Immigration operates vis-a-vis those of origins in India—that a marriage is a marriage of convenience unless proven otherwise, that applicants for visitors' visas are not bonafide potential visitors unless proven otherwise—are so discriminatory that they should have no place in the administrative operations of a civilized society, and certainly not one which professes to uphold equality rights. The brutalisation of the Indo-Canadians through the activities of the Ministry of Immigration has become an intolerable affront to our dignity and rights in Canada. [28] The things are no better even ten years after, that is, in 1997.

The East Indians who immigrated to Canada have made one of the most important choices of their lives. With courage and hope they come to a new land to face great challenges of language, culture and realities of every day living. The choice is not easy, rather a very difficult one. Fortunately, they are not alone in their efforts to make new lives for themselves and their families. There is a spirit of caring in this huge country, which works very hard to ensure that when people have personal problems that they cannot handle alone, they get help. That caring spirit is exemplified by the United Way of the lower Mainland, which has been supporting through fund-raising, planning and providing a wide range of services.

When the immigrants intend to carry a big baggage of children with them, their complications and difficulties multiply. In undeveloped countries, baby-making industry is highly developed as against the highly developed countries.

The immigration bureaucrats generally deal with the immigrants heartlessly and often in an undignified manner. They often complain that the country is facing a glut of applicants in all categories and recommend to be more selective—to cream the market—and want to make the pool of people eligible, smaller.

As a matter of declared policy, the Canadians uncompromisingly reject a race-based immigration policy but are clearly uncomfortable with the shift from Europe to the Third World source countries like India. Canada can no longer attract thousands of skilled western Europeans because most of them now make the same or better wages than the Canadians and do not want to come here. Certain Canadians are eager to see the immigration level reduced from the Third World which constitutes close to 75 per cent of new arrivals each year. They argue that if Canada needs more people, the Canadians should have more children. They say that "we must decide whether we want Canada of the future to be made up of our children or of those brought from outside".[29]

In the next couple of decades the average family size in Canada will fall well below replacement level to 1.3 children per family. Without immigration Canada's current population would continue falling. Even if it is found desirable from an economic and social perspective that Canada's population remains at its current level, immigration would have to be increased significantly or programmes would have to be established to encourage the Canadians to have larger families.[30]

An effort should be made to increase public awareness and understanding of the contribution that the immigrants make to Canada. Immigration is a part of Canada's heritage, a part of its future. The immigrants contribute to the social and cultural enrichment of this country while providing specialized skills and new employment opportunities that benefit the economy. It is a public knowledge that the East Indians pay more taxes and use social programmes less. Most of the Indian immigrants are conversant with English before they land in Canada. The East Indian women are four times more likely than the Canadian-born women to work in product-fabricating jobs.

The Canadian government is proposing to increase the annual immigration quota to 500,000 from the current level of 225,000 with a government minister admitting that immigrants made an 'enormous contribution' to the nation's economic growth. According to a report in *The Toronto Star*, the plan to increase the immigration quota is the result of shortage of labour in many parts of the country, including Ontario, Manitoba and Saskatchewan provinces. In the past two years (i.e. in 1997 and 1998) the Immigration Department reportedly let in 50,000 immigrants less than the 225,000 ceiling.

Ms Elinor Kaplan, the new Minister for Citizenship and Immigration, seems to have greater sensitivity towards immigrants than her predecessor, Lucienne Robillard.

She was quoted as saying: "we have had tremendous success in our immigrant communities among new Canadians and they have created not only a success for themselves but for all of Canada."

Ms Kaplan reportedly said that she has already asked her department to develop new strategies to increase the annual immigration quota and that it needs to streamline the process to speed up the clearance of immigration applications.

"We need to make sure that we have the people here for the jobs that are being created today and will be created in the future," she stated, adding that all Liberal Party MPs "understand the importance of bringing people here that want to build this country."

"They know and I know that it brings prosperity. New immigrants bring their talents, their expertise, their creativity and ingenuity and their knowledge of the world," she said.

"Canada is a trading nation. Think of the human resource that we have and that understands all the cultures, have the linkages and speak the languages of the world. That is a fabulous resource for Canada. We want to harness that so we can continue to prosper and grow," Kaplan argued.

Kaplan has travelled to India several times. As former Ontario Minister of Health, she even attended *Diwali* functions of the Indian community here wearing a *saree*. *India Abroad News Service.* [31]

The Sikhs Immigrants have undoubtedly contributed more to Canada than they have received from it, in terms of hard-work, honesty, economic development and moral and social values. But their regret is that they have still to find a place in society that measures favourably with their dignified stature.

Dual Citizenship

The non-resident Indians (NRIs) are in a position and also interested to invest money in India. But they are not satisfied with the assurance of protection given by the government of India for their enterprises. The only solution for the necessary guarantee is the dual citizenship for which, both the demand from the NRIs and response from the government are half-hearted and lukewarm. The government should take a decision and go ahead with the process of granting dual citizenship so that the NRIs may feel that they are investing money in their own country rather than in a country to which they do not legally belong despite some of the government's concessional measures. The NRIs are always in a state of mental hesitancy or reluctance in respect of investments in India, thus depriving India from contributions of sizeably large sums of money, which the country badly needs. As against any difficulty confronting Indian government in granting dual citizenship, the financial gains would be tremendously larger to this country. The NRIs from the countries world over, including the USA, Canada, UK, Australia, European countries, Singapore and Malaysia would be coming forth to invest in different projects in India if they are provided with dual citizenship.

There is another aspect of the problem. The feeling of belongingness to ones ancestral land is deeply hurt when an NRI assumes foreign citizenship losing his own. If he were able to keep both—his original as well as foreign citizenship, it would keep him bonded to his motherland inseparably. In that case, dual citizenship works wonders. It is hoped that the Indian government will give due consideration to the NRIs' long standing and genuine demand of dual citizenship.

REFERENCES

1.   *Pacific Monthly*, Vol.17 of 1907.

2.   *Settlement Reports of the Punjab*, Civil and Military Gazette, Lahore, 38 of 28.2.1851.

3.   *Ibid.*, 39 of 28.2.1851.

4.   *The Daily Province*, Vancouver, 17 March 1908.

5.   *The Government Records of the year 1907-08*, 8 January 1908.

6.   *Canada Sessional Papers*—Vol. 17 (1907-08).

7.   *House of Commons Debates*, 1914, No.1233.

8.   Morse, Eric W., *'Immigration and Status of British East Indians in Canada'*, (unpublished thesis) pp 40-41, quoted by Khushwant Singh, *A History of the Sikhs*, Vol.2, 1839-1964, New Jersey, 1966, p. 171 fn.9.

9. *A news report from London*, 23 April 1909.
10. *The Daily Province*, Vancouver, 7 August, 1910.
11. James G. Chadney, *The Sikhs of Vancouver : Citizenship and Immigration Canada*, quoted by Bhagat Singh, *Canadian Society and Culture*, New Delhi, 1997, pp.405-06 and pp. 73-74.
12. Waiz, S.A. *Indians Abroad*, Bombay, 1927, p. 659.
13. *The Sansar* (an East Indian paper), Vol. I, No. 7., Victoria,B.C., June 1913.
14. *The Sansar*, Vol. I, No. 7., Victoria (B.C.), 20 July 1913.
15. *The Daily Province*, Vancouver, 16 and 18 December 1911.
16. *The Vancouver Sun*, 16 February 1912.
17. *Ibid.*, 29 February 1912.
18. *The Daily Province*, Vancouver, 28 February 1912.
19. *House of Commons Debates*, 1912, No. 2457.
20. Isemonger, F.C. and Slattery J., *An Account of the Ghadar Conspiracy*, Lahore, 1919, p.3.
21. Waiz, S.A., *op.cit.*, p. 663.
22. *The Daily Province*, Vancouver, 4 May 1912.
23. James G. Chadney, *The Sikhs of Vancouver : Citizenship and Immigration Canada*, quoted by Bhagat Singh, op.cit., pp. 405-06 and p.74.
24. Sarjeet Singh Jagpal, *Becoming Canadians*, Vancouver, pp. 131-32.
25. Joseph A Sanders, 'Hard Times for Multiculturalism, *The Forum* (Nacoi), Ottawa, August-September 1991, p.1.
26. Gerald Dirks, *Canada's Refugee Policy: Indifference or Opportunism?* Montreal and London, McGill - Queen's University Press, 1977, p.249.
27. 'Ottawa MPs make recommendations for improving immigration and visa services in India' *The Link*, 1 April 1992.
28. Mohinderjit Singh Grewal, and John Kurien of Nacoi presented Brief at the 'Proceedings of the Standing Committee on Multiculturalism at Parliament Hill ', *Forum*, Nacoi, Ottawa, Vol. 12, No.3 July-August 1987, p.3.
29. Paul Fromm, 'Government policy ignores views of majority,' *Ottawa Citizen*, 14 August 1990.
30. Victor Malerk, *Havens Gate - Canada's Immigration Fiasco*, Toronto, 1987, p.39.
31. Ajit Jain, 'Canada may raise immigrants' quota to 5 lakh' *The Tribune*, Chandigarh, 21 August 1999, p.9.

CHAPTER 7

RACIAL DISCRIMINATION —
A STIGMA ON HUMAN SOUL

"To behave as if visible minorities did not exist" is the chosen definition of racism. The dictionary meaning of 'racism' is a belief that race is the primary determinant of human traits and capacities and that racial differences produce an inherent superiority of a particular race. Most of the whites think that they are more of God's children than others and they look at their white skin as more precious and more divine than that of the blacks or browns. A white man believes, "you can never be as good as I am, whatever your qualifications and whatever money you make, because you are not white."

Every race on earth has brilliant members as well as average and below-average members. If intellectual capacity were based purely on a genetic blueprint there would be well-defined differences among the races and this is just not so. Race is not the measure of a person and when we use it for that we are on very shaky scientific ground. Beneath our different skins, we have many similarities. We all have hearts and minds, assets and liabilities and tendencies towards good and evil. When we can accept that there is really but one race, we will have taken important step towards eradicating the disease of racism.[1]

It is regrettably remarked that racism is still an unspent force in Canada. It has been the bane of this country's system since long. It is certainly the ugliest manifestation of discrimination. "The currents of racism in Canadian society run deep, they run smooth, lulling white Canadians into a complacency that will see racism anywhere else but in Canada."[2]

Racism is one of the world's great scourges. It is racist for one ethnic or racial group to try to enslave another. It is racist to attempt genocide against ethnic or racial groups or to harm individuals because of their race or ethnic background. It is racist to exclude people systematically from virtually any human activity on the basis of their racial or ethnic identity.

Different Forms of Racism

Frances Henry says that racism can take several forms. "Individual racism refers to conscious personal prejudice, institutional racism is that which is carried out by an individual because of others who are prejudiced; and structural racism has its base in the inequalities rooted in the operations of society at large."[3]

The variables that have the strongest relationship with racism are age, education, social and economic status and religion, with a clear finding that the older the people become the more racist are their views.[4] The relationship between education and racism is also strong, with a clear indication that racism decreases with education, and those with the least formal education scoring highest on the racism scale. Also the data showed a clear relationship between the low socio-economic status and the high racist attitudes. Henry was able to show that nearly two-thirds of those who are not religious fall into the youngest age group, and are most liberal in their attitudes to non-whites. And the majority of the older people of all religions fall into the racist categories.[5]

The East Indians, almost 98 per cent of them were the Jat Sikhs from the Punjab. They bore the brunt of racism in Canada right from the beginning of the 20th century. The Sikhs were the most visible among the visible immigrants because of their turbans and flowing beards and were very easy targets of the racist whites. Under all circumstances the whites wanted the Sikhs to be excluded from the country and they wanted to keep it a white country. Some whites that were sympathetic towards the Sikhs because of their having fought for the British Empire were favourably inclined to give them work. The Anti-Asiatic Riots (1907) and Asiatic Exclusion League were specifically aimed against the Sikhs. The legislature of British Columbia brought the 'Natal Act' into operation in 1907 and barred the Sikhs, who were tax-paying and law-abiding people, from voting in the municipal and provincial elections. The Sikhs had to fight for a right to vote during the next forty years till they got this right in 1947.

The 'direct passage rule' and keeping the families of the immigrants out of Canada were all due to racial considerations. The plan of the government of British Columbia to send the Sikhs to the British Honduras (1908) was a conspiracy to get rid of them exclusively based on racism. British Columbia government and people knew that the racial discrimination openly displayed by them against the Sikhs would result in unrest in India, thus upsetting the British Indian government. So, the Canadian whites were, at times, a little wary and tried to work their designs secretly. They gave to understand that they opposed Sikh immigration because of political and cultural differences and economic disparities. But it was not difficult to understand that the government's legislative measures and white people's designs to hit at immigration were simply racial in content. The Canadian journalism was no less communal in its writings. They were not anything other than a part of the white people and the Canadian system, which was embedded in racism. The white colour of the skin had indeed played havoc in the society that brought so much humiliation and misery to the East Indian immigrants. Rarely some sane voices would arise in the country against racism and plead for good treatment of the non-white immigrants, but were soon drowred in the din caused by the white racists and were silenced.

The Sikhs awaited for the change in their plight patiently but the change came tardily and even today by the end of the 20th century no one can assure that malady of racism has disappeared. It is very much there with no immediate or distant prospect of its ceasing to exist.

Speaking in the House of Commons, Gerry Weiner, Minister of State for Multiculturalism and Citizenship, stated in 1991 that " in any society plagued by racism and racial discrimination the struggle against these evils is important. Racism and racial discrimination have been and continue to be a burden on the soul of the nation. It is a disturbing reality that entire cultures are discriminated against, denigrated and exploited. The Canadian men and women treated as second-class citizens, living lives filled with bitterness, frustrated hopes and sorrows or, worse still, accepting that they are somehow deserving of the dehumanizing wrath of racism."

The above statement of the federal minister shows that some of the Canadian whites still stand where they were nearly a century back in respect of their attitude and treatment of the non-whites or the visible minorities of the country. In the meantime even the most backward rather savage communities of the world have learnt to value and respect people as equal human-beings irrespective of their colour and creed but these whites have not come out of their superiority grooves as yet.

It is a fact of history that racism has defiled the heavenly land of Canada. The whites had two faces: one unkind and sombre and the other benign and bright—the first for the non-whites and the second for the whites. This has been very unfortunate.

In the first quarter of the 20th century the Canadian whites had been all through making all-out efforts to keep the Sikhs out of their country but anyhow, they (the Sikhs) could hold out even under very odd and trying circumstances. They were paid less than whites in the mills and other establishments. If there was a dispute between a white and a non-white the case was generally decided in favour of the white by the establishment. If any body was to be retrenched it was an East Indian. Sometimes, the Sikhs were refused admittance to movie picture theatres under the pretence of their turbans obstructing the view of others. They made a rule that everyone should remove his headgear before entering the theatre house to which the Sikhs did not agree because of their religious convictions. The Sikhs often faced such problems in the second decade of the 20th century. H. A. Mills, Chief Investigator of the Immigration of the *Pacific Coast*, said in 1911, " They (the Sikhs) were the most undesirable of all Asiatics, and people of the pacific states were unanimous in their desire for their exclusion. The Asiatic Exclusion League gave some alarming figures of the Sikhs". The same year the *North American newspapers* wrote that their country was 'experiencing Sikh invasion' and 'a tide of turbans'. They wanted that the 'invasion' and the 'tide' should be stemmed with all the possible force.

There can be no hard and fast rules and measures to fight racial discrimination. When it is ingrained in the mind it is all the more difficult to get rid of it. In that case much can be done by the individual's own efforts. He should himself realize that good or bad human beings can be categorized not by the colour of their skin but by their personal qualities of goodness or badness. All races have good men as well as bad men. To differentiate their human qualities on the basis of their racial origin would apparently be an unsound and unbalanced judgment. A person racially discriminating against others lowers himself to a status that cannot normally be accorded to a human-being. He should be anything but a normal human-being.

The Sikhs in Canada suffered a lot at the hands of the white racists. In 1912, a British Columbia journal wrote that "the prejudice against a dark skin, which is the basis of that cowardly cry for 'white Canada', has forced the Sikh to quarter where he could and the only places where he could find accommodation have been in the slum districts of the cities.... Again the fact that the Sikhs have been unable to bring their wives and children has prevented them from organizing home life.... The cry of 'white Canada' does not commend itself to the clear thinker.... The British Empire has not been reared upon the policy of "a man is known by the colour of his skin".[6]

In those days many cases of glaring racial discrimination were, from time to time, brought before the British Columbia courts. One of such cases was that of one Bacha Singh who filed a writ petition in the Supreme Court of B.C. against the Northern Railway Company and the Steamship Company. He claimed that he could not get his wife from India because these travel companies refused to sell ticket for her to travel directly from India to Victoria. These companies were charged with racial discrimination against the Sikhs.[7]

The leading members of the Sikh community sent petitions and delegations to the Canadian federal government, wrote articles in journals and held mass meetings to get racial discrimination against them vacated. At the Imperial Conference in 1912 Lord Crewe, Secretary of State for India, asked the dominion government of Canada to make the entrance of the Sikhs more easy and pleasant. He further told them that, " If it became known that within those limits the East Indian subjects would receive a genuine welcome and would not be looked upon with suspicion, a great deal might be done to bring about better relations between India and the dominions. Until pleasant relations exist between the dominions and India, we are far from being a united empire."

Because of the rough treatment of the Sikhs by the Canadian government, the British government was apprehensive of unrest in India and so they desired of the Canadian government to be considerate and not unsympathetic and racially discriminating. But the Federal and British Columbia governments did not move from their stand for the time being. Dr Sundar Singh, who had earlier accompanied the delegation to Ottawa to meet the federal government officials in connection with the Sikh demands, was always busy in his efforts to elevate the members of his community in Canada, both on the platform and through the pages of his journal *Aryan*. Sundar Singh claimed that if a Sikh was good enough to fight for the Union Jack, as he had done, surely he was good enough to live at peace in the dominion of Canada. The Sikhs were the entire Aryan race, the same as the Canadians, whereas the Japanese and Chinese were Mongolians. He asserted that he was anxious to establish the principles of British fair-play than to gain admission for an unlimited number of his countrymen. He asked the government again and again to do away with the policy of racial discrimination against the Sikhs, but not to much advantage.

The whites were not prepared to relax their policy of racial discrimination towards the Sikhs who at times, in moments of intense pain, reacted sharply. The white press did not tolerate and under their racial pride hit hard against the Sikh immigrants and their native country India.

Hostile Media

The Vancouver Sun was a violent opponent of Sikh immigration especially inspired by its deep commitment to keep Canada a white colony. Referring to the resolution adopted by a Sikh gathering to protest against the exclusion of the wives and children of the Sikhs domiciled in Canada and sending of its copies to the Secretary of the Canadian Immigration Committee and to the Indian National Congress the editorial of this paper, of 25th June 1913, said that the tone of the letter accompanying the resolution was " so insolent and threatening that even if the Sikhs had a good case it must have been injured by them since their claim as British subjects, they should be allowed to plant themselves where they please and be considered as valid one."[8]

The editorial also quoted the letter that the Sikhs wrote as under: "The Japanese and Chinese empires have protected their subjects by treating them well but the British government of India have altogether sold us out. In about 1907, one Mr. Mackenzie King, either personally or by negotiations with the government of India, entered into an understanding which may be called a conspiracy against the whole nation of India, as a result no steamship company will book any Indian for Canada either at Indian ports or waypoints. Consequently, no merchant, no tourist, scholar, reformer, scientist, artist, educationist—let alone immigrant— has been allowed to proceed to Canada and this first condition of civilization and progress—namely, the interchange of ideas and ideals between nations through travel has been denied by the so called civilized British."[9]

The Vancouver Sun commenting on the above remarks of the Sikhs said, "It is going some lengths for members of a semi-barbarous race to characterize as—'so called civilized'—the people who have given India the only stable and enlightened government it ever possessed.... But more startling is the suggestion in the letter to the Indian National Congress that a commercial, social and political boycott should be directed by the East Indians against all British people and particularly against the Canadians, if the demands of the handful of the Sikhs of British Columbia are not complied with.... It is easy to understand that their attachment to British laws and British institutions is of the slightest and that they would gladly return to the old pre-British system under which justice was dealt out haphazardly."[10]

A British teacher's Indian student laments when he discovers the truth. As a student I shamefully agreed with my British teacher's view of the British Empire that they had brought the needed civilization to Indian people and had done kindness to them. The truth is that the British empire was based on the wrong and ugly idea that other people looking different and speaking different languages did not exist to be known as having meaning, hopes, aspirations and fears as real as any Anglo-Saxon but were inferior beings who existed, instead, to be used for Britain's own power, glory and wealth; and this centuries-old government policy caused horrors through mass-scale murders, hangings, mob-shootings just for their request to be liberated from the foreign bondage. And now, this white editor of a newspaper objects strongly to the use of an expression 'so called civilized people' by an angry sufferer, who pleads for his wife and children to be given to him, who are under indefinite segregation from him.

The above quoted editor of *The Vancouver Sun* seems to be suffering from an overdose of racial prejudice. I wish he had read his prime minister Wilfred Laurier's remarks about the ancient civilization of the Asian countries of which India comes foremost in that respect. He said in 1910, "Asia has been the cradle of the human race. There was a high condition of civilization when Europe was a mere geographical expression. There were nations enjoying a highly advanced civilization when our ancestors in Britain, in Gaul, and in Germany, were still naked savages roaming in the woods. Thousands of years ago some great cities and powerful governments in China, India, on the Tigris and Euphrates and other areas had risen".[11]

The editor of *The Vancouver Sun* called the Sikhs 'a semi-barbarous race' but the Canadian Prime Minister W. Laurier called the ancestors of the editor 'naked savages roaming in the woods'. But let me neutralize both the expressions. Both the Sikhs and the Canadian Anglo-Saxons, in 1910, were very respectable citizens of the world. They were fighting for their rights and privileges to which they were entitled in their own ways.

Segregation of the Sikhs

In the first half of the 20th century, the Sikhs had to face an open racial discrimination against them. This discrimination was very much there in the second half of this century also but it was covered under various pretexts.

In the earlier stages, the Sikhs faced racial discrimination and segregation. There can be quoted many examples of naked segregation to which the Sikhs were subjected. But a couple of cases can be cited here. One Mehar Singh came to Canada in 1907. In due course of time, through hard work and savings, he purchased a twenty-acre orchard in Kelowna. After his death in 1942, his family decided to sell the farm and purchase a house in the city to facilitate the education of their children. They struck a deal for a house for $ 6000, but they were prevented to shift into the new house because the white residents did not want the Sikhs in their neighbourhood. But the daring 25 years old daughter of Mehar Singh defied all the protests of the racists. The city council, after a heated discussion for weeks, and for fear of a political fall-out, allowed the Sikh family to move into the house.

The media covered the incident as under:

"Local residents, backed by several prominent organizations in the city, are protesting over the contemplated purchase of a house on Wolseley Avenue by a Sikh family on the grounds that if orientals settled in the neighbourhood, it would be the starting signal for more Far Eastern natives to move into the residential district, with the result that the area would slowly grow into a Sikh settlement, thereby lowering property values and causing general unpleasantness in the neighbourhood.... The young Sikh girl is adamant to go ahead and complete the deal....The protesting citizens pointed out that they are alarmed over the future, as the district may deteriorate into a Sikh settlement."[12] The young girl withstood all the pressure to shift over to some other site and ultimately the case was decided in her favour.

A similar situation cropped up when one Natha Singh Mattu decided to buy a house in the Shaughnessy area in Vancouver in 1941. His real estate agent told him that he would face resistance at the hands of the neighbours in completing the deal, because whites were not yet ready to accept the Sikhs as their neighbours. They felt that their security would be threatened and the prestigious status of their colony would be lowered. The whites belaboured under an absurd notion of their superiority just on the basis of their white skin. They were jealous and even today also they are when these whites find the East Indians living in mega houses and owning valuable properties. The Sikhs are not to blame if they work hard, earn more and live decently. To put their whole might into their work is an inalienable characteristic of the Sikhs. They have the natural or instinctive quality of starting from a scratch and rising to celestial heights.

Kapoor Singh went to Canada as an ordinary immigrant and struggled very hard to become a mill-owner and an industrialist. When he planned to establish a sawmill in Barnet in 1938 he was likely to face opposition and racial discrimination from the whites. He opened the mill in the name of a reliable white friend and named it as Modern Sawmills owned by J.T. Armstrong who later got it transferred in the name of Kapoor Singh and it was renamed Kapoor Sawmills. This is how the racial prejudice had to be encountered by the Sikhs in their early stages.

Wage Disparity

The discrimination in Canada was widespread and covered a lot of fields. In the mid-1930s government of B.C. stated that through a law they had decided to pay 35 cents an hour as minimum wages but 25 per cent of the workers would be paid 25 cents an hour. It was a clear racial prejudice against the East Indians as in every mill about 25 per cent of the mill-hands were the Sikhs. Some mills that employed more than 25 per cent, the Sikhs found themselves in a strange situation, as Alberta Lumber Company that had employed about fifty per cent non-whites i.e. Indians. But all the East Indians were paid at the rate of 25 cents per hour for the same work. This was a glaring discrimination. In certain mills this difference of 10 cents per hour between the wages of the East Indians and the whites remained for quite sometime.

Restrictions on the Sikhs' Entry into Public Places

Some weak-minded Sikhs who were totally ignorant of the Sikh code of conduct would go to the barber as soon as they landed in Vancouver or Victoria. They tell us that the white barbers would not cut the hair of the Sikhs because they did not like them and thus they were unfit to get service from the whites. How keenly we wish that the turbaned and bearded Sikhs had, at that movement, decided not to visit any barber any more in life again. And how wonderfully their humiliation would have permanently ended. The shoeshine men did not shine the shoes of the East Indians. They would say that they did not like the turbaned people.

There were certain theatres in Vancouver that would not let the turbaned Sikhs to get in. The Beacon Theatre and the Strand Theatre in Vancouver had signs displayed in front of the theatres that 'you are not allowed in if you have a beard and a turban'. There were certain establishments that refused to serve the Sikhs. Scott's Cafe on Granville Street did not allow the Sikhs to enter the cafe.

Racial prejudice was so high that the Sikhs, generally, would not go alone to the theatres or to the restaurants for meals. They would go in small groups, in the company of two or three friends.

There were many parlours that would not serve beer to the turbaned Sikhs, as to them the Sikhs were not desirable people. At certain small beer parlours, the Sikhs were seated in a separate room in the corner. Some big hotels, like the Vancouver Hotel, Ivanhoe Hotel on Main Street in Vancouver, did not serve the turbaned Sikhs. If a group of four or five Sikhs would go to these hotels the clean-shaven were served and waiters would refuse to serve the turbaned and the bearded Sikhs. Such racial discrimination was widespread in B.C. Archna Verma writes in her thesis titled 'Status and migration among Punjabis of Paldi, B.C.' that when once Mayo hunted around for a room in a small hotel in Sahtlam, he was refused accommodation. They told him that they did not accept people with beard and turban. He had to pass the night in the woods with one Sunder Singh who worked in CPR Railway. The Sikhs between 1920 and 1940 had suffered all the above discrimination, as some of the sufferers are still alive to tell the tales of their woe latent down their memory lane. They lived the moments of extreme humiliation and harassment hundreds of times. During that period of time, the Sikhs displayed great capacity to take blows but these blows gradually became unbearable. This apartheid policy was the manifestation of certain whites' inhumanity that was tolerated to be practised by some of the so-called civilized people of Canada.

Unlike today, when Sikh women, encouraged by government's policy of multiculturalism, can wear their ethnic dress in public, they had to wear western dress in the thirties or earlier. They had to keep their Punjabi dresses for use at home only. As was the practice, the Sikh women had to dress themselves like white women and were always required to keep their hair covered with scarf. Most of the women did it immediately after landing on Canadian soil. Thus, in dress the Canadianisation started soon after their arrival in Canada. It was believed in Sikh circles that the whites did not like or allow the Sikh women to come out of their homes in the Punjabi dress. It was probably in a bid to assimilate them in the Canadian society, to start with. It was strange for the white Canadian society even to adjust with the differences in the pattern of dress of a community hailing from a different land with their own culture.

Right from the beginning of the entry of the Sikhs into Canada they were entitled to vote in all elections. The British Columbia government got apprehensive of the role of the Sikhs in election and, therefore, through legislation in 1907, they debarred the Sikhs from their right to vote unless they were born of Anglo-Saxon parents. Till 1947, the Sikhs remained defranchised and excluded from participation in the political process of the province. This was totally an unjustified restriction imposed on the East Indians due to racial discrimination.

The Sikh students left schools as soon as an opportunity for a job came their way. They were not sure of a work after completing education. Having been defranchised since 1907 many jobs and professions had been blocked to them. Since the whites considered the Sikhs as foreigners and not real Canadians, most of the businesses would not hire them. The discriminatory hiring practices pushed most of the educated Sikhs out of British Columbia or they ended up as sawmill workers. Many Sikh Bachelor of Arts or Science and Master's degree holders from Canada itself pulled timber in the mills like illiterate people. It is a pity that even in the first half of the 20th century, when education was not so widespread in Canada as today, the Sikh doctors, lawyers or engineers could not get jobs especially due to the employing authorities' deep-seated racial prejudice.

Sarjeet Singh Jagpal who interviewed many early Sikh settlers in Canada writes, "The older the Sikhs, I talked to, have lived through decades of institutionalized discrimination, and they supported the community's long fight for the franchise and fairer immigration laws. But they were uncomfortable discussing racism and discrimination. They preferred not to talk about these things because they felt there was nothing to be gained by bringing up the unpleasant aspects of the past. The unfairness and injustice had not been directed just at them: "Look what happened to the poor Japanese, who lost everything."[13] Undoubtedly, racism has disfigured the face of the fairyland of Canada. Racism imprints the seal of ignomy on the societal edifice of the country that practises it. Lack of wisdom is racists' enemy and enmity with the non-whites is their disease.

Each pioneer had a bag of mixed emotions containing some great moments and some bitter experiences as in their laps were hidden countless chilly nights. It was they who scribbled the future of their progeny with their blood and tears. They always kept their dreams alive.

The old days will always remain in the hearts of the pioneers, in their souls and in their memories. It is not easy to deal with them. When we try to take a pioneer to his earlier days, he reports, "Don't connect me to the past—it is not even worth remembering." A little amusingly they say that they will not make a mistake of being in their 80s again as ill-health bothers them too much. They object too strongly, consult too long, adventure too little and repent too soon. They are now almost reduced to old burnt shells of men. When they fondly look to their ancestral homes back in India they view them as mausoleums of their early memories. With a deep sense of nostalgia they look too much over their shoulders into the past. When sitting alone they revisit their old and by gone days which are their valuable treasure to live on. When they immigrated to foreign countries they left their hearts back in the country of their birth. In fact, their home is where their heart is.

When they are asked about their anger on those who humiliated and tortured them mentally they graciously remark that 'forgiveness given to our tormentors is the gift that we give to ourselves.' The quality of forgiveness is the quality of great men indeed and not of ordinary human beings.

These tottering pioneers, who are very conscious of their health, smilingly tell that their first aim before retirement was wealth and the first aim after retirement was health. They jocularly remark that it is not the death that kills, it is the disease that kills and death is only subservient to disease which results from bad health. When told that the government cares about them through their pension, they remark that none ever cared for them in life. Their pension is only a delayed portion of their pay packet. It is not a gift.

These older Sikhs need to be expressly told that if they are hiding their past they are unfair to it. The pleasant and unpleasant memories of the past are a vital part of history which is bound to preserve them for future for those who are reaping rewards of the miseries and monstrous injustices their elders had gone through. These elders who are now travelling in the fast lane of their life-journey must open up and divulge all their experiences before they bang into the sunset of oblivion and the treasure of history within them gets cremated or buried unknown. Most of the pioneers are gradually disappearing into the portico of the history of the Canadian Sikhs.

In this distant land most of the Sikhs did not give up their religion and regard for their ethnic culture. They maintained their moral character and good social and family values throughout their life even in very odd and trying circumstances. Their devotional attachment with the moral and religious traditions that had been prized by their society so dearly over a long period of time transparently reflected their character, their personality and their spiritual strength. Those who bowed before pressure against their conscience and conviction and gave up the Sikh *rehat* (code of discipline) were weak, undaring and helpless species of humanity.

Soon after the Second World War the Canadian attitude began to show a slight change in their racial discrimination. Prompted by the tragic example of Nazi Germany, the Canadians began to examine their racial policies. But it was a transitory phenomenon as it clashed with the whites' in-born mindset.

In the second half of the 20th century things were no better but the whites practised racial discrimination through different methods. They covered their prejudice as if it was not there. But the clouds on the sky during the daytime cannot make people believe that the nightfall was thickening its darkness. However thick the clouds, the day can never be mistaken into a night. Even today, the racial discrimination in Canada is as strong as ever. All attempts to conceal it are bound to fail.

Do the Sikhs Steal the Whites' Jobs?

Some Canadians are prejudiced against the Sikh immigrants on the plea that they steal their jobs in the lumber mills and agricultural farms and they are a burden on the country's economy. But they should understand that "a bigger population means increased domestic markets for Canada's industries. A larger home market permits manufacturing firms to undertake longer, lower cost production runs, and it broadens the range of industry that can be undertaken economically; for both these reasons, population increase, in turn, improves Canada's competitive position in the world market. A bigger population also yields lower per capita costs of government transportation and communication, and stimulates the development of more specialized services"[14].

An immigration minister said that if the Canadians understood that the new-comers were creating rather than stealing jobs and that they enhanced rather than detracted from the economical and cultural life of the country they would welcome them.[15] The Sikh immigrants pay more taxes and use less social programmes. The Sikh immigrants are more qualified and less paid. They are more hard working, more honest, more responsible, and more loyal to the employer than those who are stricken with racism.

Some of the white racists discriminate against the new-comer Sikhs in Canada on the plea that they are uneducated people but the statistics demonstrate that the share of these Sikhs with university degrees is higher than the corresponding share for the Canadian-born people and immigrants from any other part of the world including the Europeans. But it is not hard to imagine how daunting it is to arrive in a strange country and find that the education and talent that earned a comfortable living at home, back in India, are hardly enough to rate a dishwashing job. Even, engineers, professors, school teachers and doctors cannot find work here in their fields even though they might be happy with the lowest entry-level position in this country. But how can they have job satisfaction? They cannot get a job because they have no Canadian experience or training. They do not qualify for unemployment insurance because they have not worked yet and they cannot take the training programmes because unemployment claimants have priority. It would not be too much to say that at the back of it racial prejudice works silently and steadily. If they are not employed from where would they get the Canadian experience? If all other requirements are more than adequately met can there be more fallacious reason for rejecting an Indian for not having previous Canadian experience?

The problem of recognition of academic qualifications and professional expertise obtained in India is a matter of great concern. Immigration from India has been extraordinarily selective. About 60 per cent of them are university graduates, a proportion not matched by any other major community in Canada as referred to above.

The smaller employers and private institutions in Canada do not have adequate information as to the quality of training and qualifications that the Indians possessed before landing in Canada. The Canadian government must have the norms of appropriate evaluation of qualifications from foreign universities and the same must be notified immediately after the arrival of these qualified people from the major sources of immigration to save them from unnecessary harassment.

It is a tragedy of human talent when First Class First in the University at M.A. level, M. Phil. and Ph. D.s and holders of other higher degrees from the prominent Indian or Asian Universities come to Canada to be told that their degrees are not recognized. Should I say that this is decidedly to keep the brilliant immigrants out to accommodate their own far less qualified mediocres. Those bright East Indians end up here as taxi-drivers, office secretaries, book keepers, farm and lumber mill workers, bus operators and restaurant waiters. The government of the country is a mute spectator of this tragedy and shocking wastage of high academic qualifications of the immigrants. In service or hiring, preference is given to the local grade 12 school chaps over the M.A.s and Ph.D.s from India. Can the Canadian system be more abusive than perpetrating such injustice on these so highly qualified people from outside Canada and ruining all the prospects of their promising careers?

Rosa Maria, a foreign-trained doctor said that during a Vancouver interview for a Saskatchewan position in the late 1980s, the doctor interviewer told her, "when we receive applications from foreign-trained graduates, we usually put the applications in the waste paper basket". The letters she received from various hospitals and the University of B.C.'s department of medicine were even blunter, stating that there were no residency positions for foreign-trained doctors no matter if they were now Canadians or landed immigrants. The foreign-trained doctors from category I countries—the U.S., Britain, Ireland, Australia, New Zealand and South Africa—have never had the trouble the so-called category II country doctors have had in getting placements. Lawyer David Luny remarked that, "The essential characteristic of all other countries is that they are non-Anglo-Saxon in nature and they have no relationship with Canada, the United States or the British commonwealth white dependency group. The evidence will show that in practice this constitutes discrimination on the basis of race, ancestry or place of origin." The plight of the foreign-trained doctors first came to light in the summer of 1990, when they went on hunger strike. That spurred the government to introduce two internships a year for foreign-trained doctors, but they are still not allowed to compete for +graduates, even if their exam scores are much better.[16] A look at the educational attainment of the Sikh immigrant youngsters, 15 to 24 years of age, shows that their attainment is higher than the Canadian average. In school system in Canada they were doing well. In spite of this, the non-white immigrant parents perceive that a policy of "demotivation is being practised by the school system through its counsellors, teachers and principals, who advise non-white children to pursue vocational studies rather than the academic path to a university".[17] From the majority group perspective, groups of racially and culturally different peoples have invaded the majority group's social and economic space. They are perceived as inferior 'strangers' who are a threat to the majority group's way of life.

At the university level also, their performance is remarkable. So on the plea of education there should be no prejudice and hostility towards the Sikhs. The Sikh immigrants have knowledge of Canada's official languages with 79 per cent conversant in English, four per cent in French and twelve per cent in both English and French. The East Indian immigrant women are four times more likely than Canadian-born women to work in product fabricating jobs. Thus we see that the Sikh immigrants, men and women, do much better in education and productive jobs as compared with the Canadian-borns. There is no ground for racial discrimination against them as they are above the Canadian standard of education and quality of their work.

Some of the present-day Canadians say that in the last quarter of the 20th century racism in Canada is only individualised, but this idea is, in fact, a myth and racism in this country is institutionalised as ever. Facts continue to exist as a palpable reality even if they are ignored. It has permeated in the blood of the whites and is deeply ingrained in the system. The opinion polls and surveys given in the following pages irrefutably establish it. By this, I do not suggest that all the whites are racists. Some of them are multiculturalists and above racism, no doubt. Instead of racial discrimination, human virtues in which most of the people are deficient should be institutionalised, in a sacred sense, on God's fair earth.

The whites consider themselves superior to the blacks or other visible minorities on grounds of colour of their skin. You do not have to scratch a white too deep to find racist views underneath. Undoubtedly, racism is the ugliest manifestation of discrimination. A young white woman who was exasperatedly separating two fighting dogs, snapped at the other canine owner, an East Indian woman: "Why don't you go back where you came from?" The instant rejoinder, "What are you, a native Indian? Why don't you go back where you came from?" drew applause from everybody within ear-shot.

All communities permanently living in Canada must be recognized as full-fledged citizens of the country. They are as much residents of Canada as Pope is resident of Vatican. One and all should accept this unassailable fact. But it is not so. The blacks or Afro-Americans or Afro-Canadians complain, and correctly so, that in spite of the images portrayed each week on the Bill Cosby Show, blacks remain outsiders in a country they have inhabited for more than four hundred years. Is it different with the Sikhs even having lived in Canada for a century? The government is not to blame for it. They have understood the reality of the situation and given equal status to all its citizens. The hard-core racists are not going to change. The only hope lies in the future when having played their innings the old racist fogies vacate for the new generations that are more understanding than the older ones.

Discrimination in Hiring

An unemployed woman filled an application at a job placement agency. The interviewer told her that she should remove the reference to her being from Jamaica. "You must not let them know that you are a black". The woman had excellent references and had been very successful at her job in Toronto. But in Vancouver the woman remained outside the work force for sometime since she would not remove the offending word. Such things happen invariably with all the communities including the Sikhs in Canada. It is sad that most white Canadians are not willing to acknowledge the fact that visible minorities are angry over their treatment or that there is a problem. They are not prepared to see that there is systematic injustice towards the people of colour. Victor Malarek writes, "But the facts of the matter in the day-to-day life are that there is as much racism and as much racial discrimination in employment in Canada as there is in every major industrial country in the world".[18]

To make the Employment Equity Act (1986) more effective, from time to time businesses have been desired by the respective provincial governments to come with specific plans to hire and promote traditional victims of discrimination, but not with much advantage to the groups for which this Act has been enacted. The majesty of law was violated with impunity. This Act was toothless because sanctions were not attached for non-performance or non-compliance. To test the discrimination, two persons with similar qualifications were sent for a gas station job. The white applicant was told that there was a job and he could leave his application or resume with them. The non-white that had preceded him by five minutes was told that there was no job. Minority-accented callers would not receive the same information about the position of a job as the whites. Employment discrimination appears not to be the result of a few bigoted employers. It had constantly been a hostage to the conspiracies of a large section of racists. Rather there is a system-wide bias against hiring non-whites. The most visible of the visibles—the Sikhs, are the hardest hit. Even when the white employer resorts to de-staffing the first onus falls on the visible minorities. The racists have been always encashing the colour-card. One only wonders how the country's policy makers expect to achieve the goal of speedier socio-economic justice without doing away with racial discrimination which moves on and on without a comma, a semicolon or a full stop. The employers must look beyond the narrow canvass of racial discrimination.

It is clearly noted that, when job applicants, who are qualified and well trained for the positions they seek, are denied access to employment because of the colour of their skins or their foreign accents, society loses the productive value of many of its members 'and it creates in them deep-seated frustration, bitterness and alienation. The long-term effects of these conditions create social unrest and disorder.' Government must take note of it and act stoutly.

Media Continues to be Unfair

Media's role in spreading racial discrimination has been no less biting. It has always been there because media's personnel have always been victims of structural racism. It has been generally perceived that media is not free of bias, preconception, thoughtlessness, stereotyping and narrow-mindedness. Its staff, who are of a certain age or race or ideology or economic stratum are not without a slant indulged in most of the matter published in the newspaper. These factors do influence the thinking patterns and sensibilities of the staff. Most newspapers refer thoughtlessly to the race, religion and country of the person whom they condemn in the story. A scandal relating to an East Indian is plastered all over the country's newspapers, specially mentioning the community to which he belongs. Through this mischief the media maligns and denigrates the whole community. It is absurd and mischievous to identify crime with a community. It seldom restrains itself from dumping garbage on visible minorities. It sparks a firestorm of public attention. For media good news is no news, only calamity or defamation sells. At times certain language is used to convey certain fixed motives in mind. They generally do not get out of it because they have to make their newspapers and TV programmes popular with the majority group of the society. Promoting their business outweighs all other considerations. When reporting the Third World countries and their people the motif of these westerners is showing them in poor and dreadful colours. They are described as having social disorder, political violence, political subversion, military combat, government corruption, human rights abuses, flawed development, primitivism and barbarism. These countries are narrated as having no stability, no harmony, no peace, no humanitarianism and no modernism and they are shown as uncivilized.[19]

People coming to Canada from these countries are linked with all the abuses that they dump on these countries. Media's aim is to sell their commodities in larger quantities. This anti-developing countries stance of such media is of poor quality and harmful to the world at large as it awfully disfigures the image of people coming to Canada from these countries. The media should stop this colonial ruler's strategy of maligning the captured countries to justify their rule. The Third World countries are making rapid strides to cover up the gap between the developed and developing countries. They need to be projected in good colours.

The June 1985 crash of Air India plane off the Irish coast had devastating effects on the East Indian community. The media speculation relentlessly focussed negatively on a large segment of Indian community. The Canadian media took it easy to condemn a whole community and tarnish its image with total immunity. The negative image adversely affected job situations, personal relations and day to day lives of many members of the community. Even a police officer remarked that some associations in Canada were fronts for terrorist groups. The media, print and electronic, and responsible people have always to function with restraint and not to unleash a campaign of hate against a whole community for the actions of a few. This attitude of the media must change in the interest of the country at large. The media cannot bring under gun the whole community without bringing in its trail repercussions unwholesome to the whole country as the innocent targets react sharply, when, indiscreetly, their dignity is hit and their self-respect is impaired.

The best we should do now is to confront racism vigorously, squeezing it out to the fringes of society where it exists as nothing more than a festering, but manageable sore. In the 1970s when the Sikhs came to Canada in a little larger numbers the whites got violent against them. They faced stark discrimination in respect of housing and work. There was a serious row between the Sikhs and the Euro-Canadians in Quesnel about the middle of 1971. There were violent incidents between the Sikhs and the whites in Fort St. James and some other places in 1973. The anti-Sikh incidents continued sporadically throughout 1970s. The Sikh schoolboys were harassed in the schools and outside. The cars of the Sikhs were damaged, their tires slashed, Sikh temples vandalized and desecrated, their houses looted and spray-painted with obscure racist remarks and abuses. The turbaned and the bearded Sikhs had to take special precautions when moving out. In Calgary the East Indian taxi-drivers alleged harassment at the hands of the police for defending themselves against the attacks of the hooligans. The Sikhs formed defence committees to confront racial riots and racial prejudice. Surrey (B.C.), Vancouver, and Toronto were, in a big way, planned targets of the rabid racists. The Sikhs emerged as strong defenders as they manly faced the onslaughts of the rioters.

The role of the media was stinking during these disturbed years. The visible minorities have invariably always been terribly whipped by the media. It always sensationalized the incidents, unjustifiably put blame on the Sikhs for being economically handicapped and consequently raking up trouble. It is unfortunate that in such situations the Canadian media never played a sobering role but took sides and exasperated the situations which is against the journalistic ethic.

Anti-hate Law

The British Columbia government amended the B.C. Human Rights Act in order to clamp down on the hate literature and the hate activities. Anita Hagen, Education Minister and Minister of Multiculturalism and Human Rights, said in June 1993, "Racial violence and racially motivated attacks are on the rise around the world. We do not want this kind of hatred to take root in British Columbia, a province of ethnic, cultural and religious diversity."[20] Prohibited grounds of discrimination in the Act include race, colour, ancestry, place of origin, religion, marital status, family status, physical or mental disability, sex, sexual orientation or age.

Hate is one of the ugliest words in English language but it is used very carelessly. It really damages the one who hates and not as much the one who is hated. If the spreading of hate grounded in racism is allowed to go unchecked, the whole of society will suffer in the long term. In fact, the very foundation of a free and democratic society will be undermined. In short terms, the victims of hate are, most often, those who are the least able to defend themselves. Hate is the antithesis of respect. Respect will bring a community together. Hate will tear it apart. It is the building of understanding that will be most effective guard against hatred and racism. This is where all Canadians must make a personal commitment and involve themselves individually.

Canada should feel proud of persons like Burnaby councillor Lee Rankin, one of those selected to be honoured with a special medal on the occasion of Canada's 125th anniversary, who said, "No, thanks." The reason being that one of the other recipients was a columnist who regularly attacked minorities, non-whites and immigrants, in his columns. Rankin refused to accept the medal because the columnist's commentary, "denigrates the contribution of non-whites to Canadian society in a way that appears calculated to foster contempt and hostility towards the non-whites."[21]

In his letter to the governor-general, Ray Hnatyshyn, Rankin wrote: "I am so profoundly disturbed that these medals were distributed with apparently so little regard to the credentials of the recipients, that I wish to dissociate myself from this medal."[22]

Racism strips people of their dignity. It robs the oppressed of their strength and their potential of growing to their fullest. It hurts, it wounds, it maims and it kills. It is a curse that affects both the racist and the victim of racism.

To determine the position of racism in Canada, *The Vancouver Sun* scanned the electronic libraries of several newspapers across Canada using the keyword 'racism' in English and 'racisme' in French, in 1991. The results showed that in the '*The Vancouver Sun*' the number of stories about racism increased from 95 in 1990 to 113 in 1991; in *The Toronto Star*, from 254 to 283; in *The Montreal Gazette* from 180 to 236 and in *La Presse* from 54 to 152.

Angus Reid Group's Poll on Racism

National poll of this Group that was conducted on racism in June-July 1991 gave very alarming signals issuing from the Canadian society at large. It revealed that racism was increasing and government must take steps to curb it otherwise assuming larger dimensions it would create serious concerns for the racial minorities. A large majority of respondents were for the assimilation of the ethnic minorities in the mainstream, forgetting their heritage culture at the earliest. The communities with which the respondents were not feeling comfortable included Pakistani and Arab Muslims, the Sikhs and West Indian Blacks.

In view of the above situation the urgent need of the hour is that plurality of the Canadian society must be protected. The society needs to be inoculated against racism. The majority group must say to the ethnic visible minority groups, 'we are you', otherwise, if the virus of racism is not stopped it will grow and grow and grow till it becomes uncontrollable.

Following is another recent sample of this terribly dehumanizing malady.

Decima Research Survey on Racism

A new survey conducted by the Decima Research released on 13th December 1993, found that:

Eighty six per cent of the Canadians believe that there is at least 'some racism' in Canada.

Three-quarters believe that racism is a serious problem.

More than half of Canadians believe that the level of racism has increased over the past five years.

Fifty four per cent of those surveyed believe that the current immigration policy allows "too many people of different races and cultures coming into Canada."

The survey finds that, "much of the concern about racism... stems from exposure to the media rather than direct exposure to or experience of racism on personal level." Television was cited as the major source for racial impressions.

Although seventy seven per cent of Canadians have been exposed to racism through television news reports, "just twenty two per cent have actually witnessed racism in the workplace and only eighteen per cent have witnessed racially motivated violence.

People of black or African origin face the greater discrimination, followed closely by native people, South Asians and the East Indians and then by other Asians. Eleven per cent believe that the Jews face the most discrimination and nine per cent believe that discrimination is primarily directed against the Muslims, Arabs and Lebanese people.[23]

The survey included 1200 respondents in its sample. It is considered accurate 19 out of 20 times or 95 per cent.

The situation as revealed by the above survey sends alarming signals. The government must actively watch it and should not allow it to assume threatening dimensions. Immigration department, judiciary, the police and the teachers and all such departments that have public dealings should set good examples to show fairness to all cultures. Before hiring, the applicants for these departments must be examined through such tests as can adequately and unmistakably discover their mental make-up and their attitude towards racism. Before starting to perform their duties they must have some sort of training in the principles of multiculturalism and basic knowledge of cultures of various minority groups which must be taken care of at the time of dealing with them.

Preconceived Notions of the Sikhs

The whites should not have a preconceived notion of the turbaned and bearded persons. It is a sad commentary on the officials of the immigration department that when four or five turbaned and bearded men are travelling in a car, at every check post or crossing between Canada and the United States the car is going to be stopped and pulled out of the lane for the checking of documents and search of the interior of the car including its trunk. Presumably every group of the Sikhs travelling together is considered a gang of smugglers or terrorists. No other car is stopped and checked like this. No doubt, those officials have every right to check a car but is that right meant to be exercised in the case of the Sikh travellers alone and not in the case of thousands of other travellers. Their mental attitude of suspecting all the Sikhs displays their mental sickness and it is sickening to the Sikhs.

When is this harassment and humiliation of the Sikhs going to stop? May I assure the immigration authorities that the Sikhs are more responsible and more law-abiding citizens than most of the other Canadian residents? Is the Sikhs' living in close neighbourhood of other communities for a century not enough to be able to know them thoroughly? The Sikhs are wonderful people with marvellous goodness and honesty, trustworthiness, hospitality, bravery and sacrifice ingrained in them. What else the white racists want of them? Do they still want to hear from a man of Anglo-

Saxon race? Sir Lepel Henry Griffin, a K.C.S.I. Officer, Chief Secretary of Punjab Government (1878) writes: "The Jat Sikh race is, for manliness, honesty, strength and courage, second to no race in the world."[24]

Summing up in the words of Margaret Cannon: "Canadians are doomed to fail if the existence of racism coiled in our hearts is not acknowledged, frankly and fully. We cannot otherwise hope to curb its power over us or reduce its violent place in our world. I would like to think that my children might live in a country that is free of racism, but I no longer believe that eradication is possible. We can limit the public damage; we can legislate public decency and put teeth into the laws. If we can, to some extent, regulate relationships among people, we cannot be so optimistic about making radical changes to the hearts and inner thoughts of men and women.... Racism is always there, and the hurt is like a stone in my heart."[25]

Sometimes racism is almost invisible because it is built into social structures and attitudes. It is an ongoing challenge to educate against it and create awareness in schools, the community and the media. The whites are cautioned to keep their ego under control. Any other benefits from its riddance apart, it is for the good of the country's social harmony.

Bush fires of racism have been burning in this country since the beginning of the twentieth century. In terms of racism, the Canadian white society seems change-resistant even today. But the East Indians did rise to the challenges of racism. If Canadian society refuses to be free from the racial discrimination it will be branded as one of the medieval societies of our times—an anachronism.

As late as December 1997, Justice Wally Oppal of Indian origin and of the B.C. Supreme Court said, "Racism is still prevalent. It is probably there more so now than it was 30 years ago. With the increased number of our people who have immigrated to Canada, there is an increased amount of racism because we are now perceived to be threats to certain segments of society. For that reason we have much to be concerned about."[26]

Racists are advised to shun the course of racism as it is in the interest of both the racists and the victims of racism as it is no more acceptable or tolerable to the latter. White supremacy has to die for humanity to live.

REFERENCES

1. John Langone, *Spreading Poison—A Book about Racism and Prejudice*, Little Brown and Company, New York, 1993, pp.13,15.
2. Marlene Nourbese Philip, *Frontiers*. Stratford. Ontario, 1992, p.12.
3. Frances Henry, 'The Demographic correlates of Racism in Toronto', *Black*

Presence in Multi-Ethnic Canada, ed. V. Doyley, Vancouver, Faculty of Education, U.B.C. , 1978, p.385.

4. *Ibid.*, p.392.

5. *Ibid.*, p.399.

6. *British Columbia Magazine*, 1912, edited by F.B. Vrooman.

7. *The Daily Province*, Vancouver, 19 and 22 November 1912.

8. *The Vancouver Sun*, 25 June 1913.

9. *Ibid.*

10. *Ibid.*

11. *The Daily Province*, Vancouver, 7 August 1910.

12. *The Kelowna Courier*, Kelowna, British Columbia, 22 August 1946, Vol.43, No.5.

13. Sarjeet Singh Jagpal, *Becoming Canadians*, Harbour Publishing, Vancouver, B.C.,1994, p.151.

14. Victor Malarek, *Haven's Gate—Canadian's Immigration Fiasco*, Toronto, 1987, p.33.

15. *Ibid.*,p.79.

16. Kim Bolan, 'Foreign doctors fight for rights', *The Vancouver Sun*, 26 October 1994.

17. W. Pitman, *Report on Race Relations in Metropolitan*, Toronto, 1978, p.175.

18. Victor Malarek, *op.cit.*, p.66.

19. Peter Dahlgren and Sumitra Chakrapani, 'The Third World on TV News: Western way of seeing the others', *Television Coverage of International Affairs*, edited by William Adams, New Jersey, Ablex, 1982.

20. 'B.C.'s Human Rights Act to get more bite', *The Link*, 9 June 1993.

21. Lee Rankin, 'You can keep your medal', *The Link*, 14 July 1993.

22. *Ibid.*

23. *Decima Research Survey*, released on 13 December 1993.

24. Lepel Griffin, *The Punjab Chiefs*, Lahore, 1890, p.64.

25. Margaret Cannon, *The Invisible Empire: Racism in Canada*, Toronto, 1995, pp.272-73.

26. Surj Rattan, 'Looking Back', *Mehfil*, An Indo-Canadian Magazine, Vancouver, December 1997, p.42.

CHAPTER 8
THE SIKHS VIS-A-VIS CANADIAN MULTICULTURALISM

Definitions of Mosaic and Melting Pot Ideologies

Before discussing this topic it would be worthwhile to define or explain a few terms that are important in the context of this subject as mosaic, multiculturalism, melting pot, assimilation and integration.

'Mosaic', literally means a picture or painting made by variously coloured material. The mosaic ideology as a model of reality is—one nation with many people and many cultures, that is, a diversified whole. The mosaic ideal means that members of all ethnocultural groups can maintain their ethnocultural distinctiveness.

Multiculturalism is a process that relates to diverse cultures. It is a set of social values that provides a basis for a new kind of universalism that legitimizes the incorporation of ethnic diversity in the general structure of society. Multiculturalism provides that all ethnocultural groups are held equal. Each individual possesses the right to identify or affiliate with the culture of his or her choice and yet retain full access to economic and social equality. No cultural identity is viewed as taking precedence over another, rather all are valued and encouraged for the contribution they make to society.

'Melting pot' is a procedure through which racial amalgamation and social and cultural mergers are going on at a place. Melting pot ideology is a process that aims at destroying the other traditional cultures and replacing them with some preferred one. It demands absorption or assimilation to the culture of the host society. And the immigrants must have no ethnic identity at all and they should forget their ancestry.

Assimilation as defined by Fleras and Elliot is one-way process of absorption—deliberate or unconscious, formal or informal, whereby the dominant sector attempts to undermine minority patterns of living, imposes its culture and institutions as the superior alternative. Assimilation is very much concerned with efforts to strip away the cultural basis of the subordinate society and transform minority members into patriotic and productive citizens. The cultural values and social patterns of the dominant group are defined as inevitable or desirable. Those of the subordinate are disparaged as inferior, childish, threatening, irrelevant and counter productive to both minority and societal interests.[1]

The supporters of assimilation are violent opponents of 'mosaic' and brand it as a 'visionless co-existence' and 'mosaic madness'. They believe that 'mosaic' creates an increasingly intolerable situation that threatens to dismember Canada into isolated fragments. Such thinking is awfully dangerous for Canada.

In the past as well as in the present the two ideologies of the 'melting pot' and 'multiculturalism ' have been working side by side with supporters for both of them. John Murray Gibbon says, "The Canadian race of the future is being superimposed on the original native Indian races and is being made up of over thirty European racial groups, each of which has its own history, customs and traditions. Some politicians want to see these merged as quickly as possible into one standard type, just as our neighbours in the United States are hurrying to make every citizen hundred per cent American. Others believe in trying to preserve for the future Canadian race the most worthwhile qualities and traditions that each racial group has brought with it.[2]

How should immigrants be incorporated into the recurring society? For some the melting pot is just another expression of assimilation to the values of the host society, for others it means that the host and the newcomers all melt into a new people.[3]

'Integration' is another term used in relation to this subject. Integration is the co-ordination with a society with equal membership or partnership, retaining ones separate identity, and ones cultural baggage. Integration into the society is acceptable to the Asian immigrants and it is desirable also.

In the light of the above ideologies we have to study here the situations faced by the Sikh immigrants from time to time during a hundred years of their existence in Canada, making strenuous efforts to protect their Sikh identity.

When the Sikhs started settling in Canada in the beginning of the

20th century, despite many restrictions, the concepts like that of mosaic ideology or multiculturalism were unknown to the white Canadians who held sway over Canada. Most of them were racist in the extreme and would not tolerate the presence of the Asians amidst them. They wanted the Asians to be out of Canada and if at all a few of them were to be allowed to stay on in their country they must immediately transform themselves into the external forms and life style of the white Canadians who presented themselves as a model for outsiders. But the bearded and the turbaned Sikhs would not give up their Sikh code of conduct to which they were religiously wedded. So they began to be more intolerable to the whites. Those Anglo-Saxons, who knew the Sikhs due to their earlier stay in India and mostly were sympathetic towards them, told the Canadians that the Sikhs would not assimilate in Canada.

The white Canadian employers could not deny the capacity of the Sikhs for hard and laborious work, though they felt uncomfortable with their Sikh appearance. Their white colour of the skin had a special value with the white people and their narrow- mindedness was in the extreme. The media was no less hostile to the Sikhs. The editorial of *The Vancouver Sun* published in its issue of 17 June 1913, exhibited the minds of the white people. It writes that, "there is the point of view of the white settler in this country who wishes to keep the country white with the white standards of living and morality. The vast majority of the intelligent population of this province will realise the danger to which British Columbia and more of Canada too, than British Columbia, will be exposed if we permit the immigration of the Sikhs with their families into the dominion.... They are not desirable people from any standpoint.... In the first place the white population will never be able to absorb them. They are not an assimilable people. Their religious beliefs render that impossible; their rooted habits are different from ours.... They will disturb the labour market here and they will create conditions that will injuriously affect the whole white population....We do not want a part of the Indian peninsula set down on this coast. We do not want an increasing colony of the Sikhs in our province.... They will not be allowed to obtain any permanent foothold as a race in this country."[4]

This newspaper clearly conveys that since the religious beliefs of the Sikhs would stand in the way of their assimilation into the Canadian society they would not be allowed to live in Canada. This is the melting pot ideology or the stark negation of the mosaic ideology or multiculturalism, which was not yet born in Canada at that time. Those who withstood the onslaughts of the soul-dead racists must have been very brave, tolerant and patiently enduring people.

Time and again the Canadian whites had been hitting very hard in the early years of the 20th century against the Sikhs. Henry H. Stevens—an M.P. from Vancouver said in 1911 that, "We in Canada, in common with all other self-governing dominions, have the right to say who shall and who shall not settle here; we contend that if we choose to say 'no' to the Hindus (the Sikhs) we are free to do so, and are not compelled to answer to any higher authority for our position than that of our own parliament.... Further our position or contention is strengthened by this fact, that the Sikhs are of a different race, standard of morals and ethical ideas, mental conceptions, traditions, history and culture, in every way different from us and cannot and will not assimilate."[5] The westerners saw their own societies as rational, modern and dynamic; they saw non-western societies as irrational, primitive, parochial and static. Western societies had evolved into modern nations whereas non-western societies remained tribal, mired as they were in their "ethnic" identities. It should not be difficult to see that this way of looking at non-western societies did not betray merely the arrogance and conceit of the colonial powers, it also facilitated their claim to retain colonies, or to act as "trustees" of the "pre-modern" (primitive) people who were incapable of governing themselves. The view, therefore, persisted until de-colonization was forced on these "civilized" countries on a worldwide "civilizing" mission.

Prof.T.L. Walker, of University of Toronto, a properly educated man, who should have a wider vision, made a negative approach like so many others. He said, 'While favouring exclusion, I do so solely on the ground that people so different in race as the Anglo-Saxons and the Sikhs can never live happily together in the territory and the introduction of such diverse elements must make nation-building exceedingly difficult, if not impossible".[6] Such highly educated snobs, with inflated ego, promoted racism. In his whole thesis irrelevance is the only relevance. Exponents of the melting pot ideology, like John Porter, pleaded strongly for the elimination of other cultures. If the Anglo-Saxons and the Sikhs could live together in Punjab for a century why could they not live together in Canada. When Prof. Walker made the above remarks the two were then living together in the Punjab and the Anglo-Saxons, by then, had come to know that the Sikhs were a great community. Nation-building does not depend on the homogeneity and at the same time inequality of its component parts but it depends on their being equal partners in all walks of country's life.

I have a few innocent questions to ask the host society in respect to the Sikh immigrants to Canada. Why do you want them to assimilate and thus reject their religious beliefs, their cultural heritage and the life style dear to them for centuries? Do you think that your culture is superiormost and a word from your mouth is a law of the land? Why don't you tolerate the best of the qualities that they prized in their native land and brought with them to their new homes? Why do you, so violently, like to strip the life-style of non-white citizens who are loyal to their new homeland, hard working, law abiding, peace- loving, co-operative, brave, sympathetic, highly honest and hospitable? Most races of an average country of the world do not have even half of these qualities. Come in close contact with these Sikhs and you will discover your baseless prejudice against them and the undignified and inhuman treatment you have been giving them over the decades and wonder over how they have been bearing all that with utmost forbearance and no ill-will against the perpetrators of all the unhappiness on them. They are saintly human-beings indeed. Their heritage culture has moulded them that way. Try to discover the miracles that their culture has been capable of unfolding before them. And, so ignorantly, some Canadians had wanted them to part with that great culture. Tell me sincerely, should they do it? I am sure you will say 'no' and they should not.

In the Canadian context, the mosaic was not given due recognition by the charter groups (English and French) in its early stages as pointed above and as applied to the immigrants the mosaic model was relegated to their private sphere of life. The protagonists of bilingualism (adoption of only two languages, English and French) and biculturalism (acceptance of only the English and the French cultures) relegated the non-English and non-French Canadians to the status of second class citizens. But the immigrants of the 'third force' demanded equal treatment. They vehemently stressed that "two official languages is one thing but to say that there are two cultures in Canada is a complete negation of the Canadian fact."[7]

John Diefenbaker, Prime Minister (1957-63) of the Progressive Conservative Party of Canada, said, "Canada was not a 'melting pot' in which the individuality of each element is destroyed in order to produce a new and totally different element. It is rather a garden into which have been transplanted the hardiest and brightest of flowers from many lands, each retaining in its new environment, the best of the qualities for which it was loved and prized in its native land".[8] Henry Cabot Lodge has beautifully said, "Let every man honour and love the land of his birth and race from which he springs and keep their memory green".

Prime Minister, Pierre Trudeau, announced a multicultural policy for Canada on 8 October 1971. He stated in Parliament that, "national unity, if it is to mean anything in the deep personal sense, must be founded on confidence in one's own individual identity, out of this can grow respect for that of others and a willingness to share ideas, attitudes and assumptions. A vigorous policy of multiculturalism will help to create this initial confidence."[9] He did not support the position that language and culture are indivisible. Thus, the federal governments rejected the notion that multiculturalism necessitates multi-lingualism and proposed that the multicultural policy be implemented within a bilingual framework. Trudeau told the Canadians: "two cultures, two languages, one vision, with room for the rest on the table." The Royal Commission on Bilingualism and Biculturalism in 1965 coined the term 'multiculturalism', though the mandate had mentioned the term 'cultural pluralism'. The two-founding-nation concept projected a colonial image of Canada, which was unacceptable to all the other immigrants, as this concept was blatantly opposed to the social cohesion necessary for the national harmony.

The Constitutional Reform Act of 1982 defined and expressed what Canada is; largely the fundamental character has been defined through the French-English linguistic duality of Canada. This is just an incomplete definition because it leaves out more than one third of the Canadians who are neither English nor French. They are disappointed and disheartened but are living with it a sort of grudgingly.

The Federal Government's Policy Statement on Multiculturalism' (8 October 1971)

This statement sets forth four objectives:

The government of Canada will support all of Canada's cultures and will seek to assist, resources permitting, development of those cultural groups which have demonstrated a desire and effort to continue to develop a capacity to grow and contribute to Canada as well as have a clear need for assistance.

The government will assist members of all cultural groups to overcome cultural barriers to full participation in Canadian society.

The government will promote creative encounters and interchange among all Canadian cultural groups in the interest of national unity.

The government will continue to assist immigrants to acquire at least one of Canada's official languages in order to become full participants in Canadian society.

The opponents of multiculturalism believe that emphasis on ethnic pluralism will prevent the creation of a coherent social structure supported by a set of values and beliefs about what Canada is and what it means to be Canadian. But Pierre Trudeau, Prime Minister of Canada, argued that multiculturalism would be integrative. He said, Canada would become "a special place, and a stronger place as well. Each of the many fibers contributes its own qualities and Canada gains strength from the combination".

The principles of a new multicultural policy included equality of opportunity, preservation and enhancement of cultural diversity, elimination of discrimination against the visible minorities, establishment of affirmative measures, enhancement of heritage languages and support for immigrant integration. But lack of accountability in the implementation of the policy of multiculturalism was openly flouted by the dominant society.

The former federal minister of multiculturalism, John Munro, said that multiculturalism is an exciting and valid concept. It is recognition of some fundamental facts about the nature of Canada. Besides English and French facts there are many more cultural facts. These many groups with their distinct values, problems and heritages cannot be ignored. In fairness, multiculturalism in Canada should include all peoples, residing in Canada and not just a select few".

At government level, with the passage of time, the concept of multiculturalism acquired strong acceptance though from time to time, it underwent changes at people's level. To a question Gerry Weiner, federal minister of multiculturalism and citizenship, in the conservative government, answered, "Pride in our origins, yes. Why not? What is wrong with preserving our cultural heritage; a heritage that enriches our society in so many ways? But not at the expense of respect and understanding for the culture of others".

Multiculturalism expresses the present reality of Canadian society, which is drawn from many parts of the world. Canada is a global community—home for many people of different races and cultures. Canadians are no longer of exclusively French or English origins. More than one-third (37 per cent) of the current population cannot trace their ancestry back to the French or English. Multiculturalism recognizes all Canadians as full and equal partners in Canadian society. The ultimate goal of multiculturalism is to make the people of this country fully Canadian and not fully homogeneous.

One thing the East Indians or the Punjabis do not want is to be 'de-

East Indianised' or 'de-Punjabi-ised'. They do not want 'to be just like everybody else'. They want to be free to keep as much of their own way of life as they themselves desire to keep, and to adopt what modern ways of white man's civilization as they wish to adopt.

Canada is ethnically and culturally a diverse country. In essence, to be Canadian is to be multicultural. Canada's heritage embraces all cultures. Cultural diversity is one of this country's most positive national characteristics. It is the belief of the sensible Canadians that more exposure to diverse cultures promotes tolerance, understanding and co-operation, giving them their Canadian identity. Canada is the world, in one country. It is a mixture of every race and culture, living together.

The government's commitment to the country's diversity is unambiguous but there are always some disturbing signals. Country's cherished policy of multiculturalism failed to destroy the monster of racism which has been killing innocent visible minorities in the past and is killing even at present unabshedly not by accident but by design.

Vis-à-vis Canadian government's concept and policy of multiculturalism as enunciated above, we examine below the practice and preservation of Sikh heritage culture in Canada.

Undoubtedly, the federal as well as the provincial governments are sincerely committed to multiculturalism but its opposition or disregard to it trickles down to the country's bureaucracy and officialdom. They, in the heart of their hearts do want the immigrants to lapse into assimilation. They do not cherish immigrants observing their own cultures and their life-styles. They want that the Sikhs should become Canadians but the Sikhs are undoubtedly Canadians. The very fact that they are living in Canada permanently is all that is needed for them to become Canadians. Those whites who are not comfortable with their turbans and beards want them to assimilate by getting themselves stripped of their turban and beard. These whites either do not understand the Canadian mosaic or refuse to accept it.

As the principles of multiculturalism enunciate the followers of the dominant culture must show full respect to the peoples with other cultures. The majority culture has no right to dominate the minority culture. Both are equal. The Sikh culture felt honoured when the Punjabi Market area (at Main Street) was officially recognized by the city of Vancouver by the installation of the Punjabi street signs in June 1993. Three blocks between 48th Avenue and 51st Avenue, on Main Street, now sport bright yellow and blue signs written in the *gurmukhi* script. The blue and yellow colours are embedded in Sikh psyche as religiously adopted colours. Mayor Gordon

Campbell looked very pleased as he congratulated the Indo-Canadian community for making a positive impact on Vancouver during their existence in this city for a century. "All of our (city) council is proud of the contributions you have made, "he said. Mayor Campbell and his council had shown the Sikh community and the Canadians at large that Canada was a country where all were welcome to promote their culture. And Canada is committed to multiculturalism to make the country a multicultural wonderland. In Surrey (B.C.) there is an area where mostly the Punjabis who run flourishing business, own shops and businesses. This market is called the Punjabi Bazaar and the road signs there had been displayed in both Punjabi (*gurmukhi* script) and English in June 1996.

Generally the press has been playing a negative role in regard to advancing the cause of multiculturalism. They sometimes link the minority-group immigrants to their ancestral country and project stereotyped and distorted stories. Their approach is almost always, as ever, negative, unsympathetic and prejudiced.

"T. Joseph Scanlan conducted a study, 'The Vancouver Sikhs' on crime stories which were published in *The Sun* and *The Province* between 1944 and 1974. There were stories about murder, stories about marriage rackets involving illegal immigration, stories about assault, bribery and rape. There were stories of families being evicted, stories about beatings and fights outside the Gurdwaras, stories on high level racial tensions in the community. What was missing was the kind of story to put this situation in context....The Sikhs were portrayed as a troublesome group. Scanlan arrived at two conclusions. The two newspapers appeared to have ignored a significant portion of the story of Vancouver Sikhs. Secondly, the press seems to have emphasized only one aspect of the story, the story of crime."[10]

They depict the Sikhs and their former home country India as very poor, primitive, unclean, unhealthy, unruly and politically and economically unstable and infested with so many other social ills. The Canadian media is generally ill informed and misinformed about India. Their sole purpose is to sell their stories about India and the Sikhs. One can test their knowledge of the Sikhs and Sikhism by putting very simple questions to them. Ask a reporter or an editor of a Canadian newspaper the name of the province from which the Sikhs hail and the language they speak there and a little bit about their religion. You will be surprised to know about their total ignorance. An elementary school boy who came to Canada from India only a few months back knows much more about Christianity and about the Canadian geography, city's super stores and the municipalities of the Greater Vancouver. The dismal ignorance of Canadian media betrays their lack of interest in the minority ethnic groups living in the country, their culture and life-style, their human qualities and their wonderful courage to have established a home in an alien land.

Most newspapers refer thoughtlessly to the race, religion and country of the person whom they condemn in the story. This has been done many a time in the cases of the Sikhs. When pointed out that they were bringing the whole community into disrepute they promised not to do it again but repeat it. They never do it in the case of a person from any other community. The press must take care that all communities and their cultures must be respected. An individual can commit faults and for that, only he is responsible individually. His community and its culture should not be blamed and placed under the gun. That is bad reporting and unjustifiable.

To promote multiculturalism in Canada the government must involve the schools and other educational institutions that should provide necessary information to the students about all the communities living in the country along with the cultures adopted by them. All cultures practised by ethnic groups, however small, deserve full respect from the majority group. At times, the members of the majority group deny such respect that is due to the Sikhs and their culture is denied to them.

A grade four Sikh child who was sporting full-grown hair on his head properly done up under a tightly fixed scarf was regularly bothered by some white chaps for his hair. He complained to his lady teacher about the harassment he was daily suffering at the hands of his schoolmates. The teacher told the child that the solution to the problem lay in the hands of his parents. How indiscreetly and absurdly she suggested that his parents should go in for the cutting of their child's hair and surrendering the child's religious symbol and pious heritage culture. The teacher displayed utterly unprofessional conduct towards her students. For the teacher's colossal ignorance of the religious culture of her Sikh students and her unwise suggestion to a student under her care, she does not deserve to be a school teacher. She is certainly in the wrong profession. She had undoubtedly abused the mosaic ideology adopted by Canada and supported the melting pot ideology of absorption and assimilation followed by the United States or the Canadian racists. Racial discrimination is unworthy of the society that holds its head high in the world community.

In pursuance of the federal government policy of multiculturalism or mosaic ideology, the Metro Toronto Police allowed the Sikh police officers, in 1986, to wear turbans and the other Sikh religious symbols when on duty. The central government permitted the Sikh RCMP to wear turban and other Sikh symbols during duty hours, with effect from 14 March 1990.

The Turban Issue

Multiculturalism wants to preserve for the future Canadian race the most worthwhile qualities and traditions that each racial group has brought with it. But some people want to merge these qualities as quickly as possible into one particular type.

Canada has been recognized as a global community home. As told earlier the ultimate goal of multiculturalism is to make the people of this country fully Canadian and not fully homogeneous. The present opposition towards it comes from the wrong presumption that ethnic groups are outside the mainstream of the Canadian society.

The Sikhs had been fighting for a long time for their right to wear a turban as a symbol of their religious code of conduct. Any opposition to it had to be fought against at the community level, as it did not concern an individual alone. The Sikhs know the Guru's commandments whose observance was sacrosanct with them

A Sikh who takes his meals with a turban off his head shall be under a Sikh taboo. This impresses upon a Sikh to attach absolute urgency to keep a turban on head while taking meals. And on no occasion he should go bareheaded in public.

During the Sikh-Afghan battles in the eighteenth century, as per a practice among the Sikhs they did not remove a turban from the head of a captured or defeated Afghan as they considered it an act of disgracing the captive and disrespecting his turban which, the Sikhs held in high esteem. The Sikhs who showed respect to the turban of the enemy could never tolerate getting their own turban dishonoured. The narrow racial perception of most of the people in the western countries has been causing vexation to the Sikh psyche again and again by raking the turban issue off and on.

A turban issue raised by the Royal Canadian Legions kicked up a clash of cultures. The refusal by the Surrey Newton branch of the legion to give admittance to the legion hall for five turbaned Sikh war veterans, all with chestful of war medals, after the Remembrance Day parade on 11 November 1993, unless they removed their turbans, raised a storm of protest from the well-meaning people—both the Sikhs and the non-Sikhs. What an enormous ignorance on the part of the officials of the legion regarding the Sikh turban. The Sikhs do not wear the turban only as a headgear but as an important fundamental symbol of their religious faith.

A Sikh is required to have full-grown hair on his head properly covered with a turban. The turban is an integral part of his dress. According to the religious code of conduct, the Sikh is never to remove his turban in any assembly of people or at any public place. If he does so, it would be an utter violation of his religious vow, disrespect to his hair and the assembly that he is in. Some ignorant people advise the Sikhs that "when in Rome do as the Romans do. If the Sikhs feel that they have to wear their turbans then let them go back to their country and do what they want to do." Let such Romans know that they are not living in the 17th century Rome, they are living in the 20th century Canada. Some Canadians advise the Sikhs that if they are not happy with the customs of Canada they should go back to their own country. What customs are these people talking of, English, French, German, Italian or Ukrainian or those of the native people to whom the country originally belongs. If they are not natives, how would their own medicine taste in their mouths if an aboriginal gives the same advice to them as they give to the Sikhs? How many of these people who cry out for preservation of traditions have ever cared to adopt some of the native practices to enrich Canadian entity. These people should know that they are living in a land where all but the aboriginals are the recent immigrants. The Canadian customs worth cultivating are those of tolerance, compassion, respect and understanding.

It is painful that a Sikh veteran who lost his comrades in war fighting with outstanding valour should be asked to surrender his own religious faith in a drinking club meeting to pay homage to the dead. These legions were founded as places to remember their old comrades and to raise money for their families if they needed financial help. But those feelings are not shared by the legion members of today. A Sikh wearing his religious headgear is not permitted inside the legion where other members can drink themselves to a drunken stupor. These legions are not churches or religious shrines. These are places for veterans to socialize and keep alive the memories of those who fought for their country. The Surrey councillor, Marvin Hunt, rightly said that, "the Sikh turban was never an issue when the commonwealth forces fought in Hong Kong, it was not an issue when they fought in North Africa or Germany, it was not an issue when they were decorated by the king or queen for their bravery and heroism in the midst of all the battles and all the wars they fought". It became an issue only when they came to remember and honour the dead. They were told that their contributions were valuable outside but not inside the legion halls. How sad it is!

If the turbaned Sikhs were good enough to eat, drink, sleep and fight along side legion members in the trenches why are they not good enough to socialize with them in the legion halls. Some legion members threatened that they would quit the club if the turbaned Sikhs were allowed to enter. There could be no better solution than this.

There could be no worse behaviour on the part of a legion that could not tolerate to be honoured by the presence of a 92-year old turbaned war veteran with the distinctive title of 'Order of the British Empire' (OBE), due to a preconceived prejudice. Could there be a greater dishonour shown to the British ruler who conferred this title?

The treatment meted out to the retired turbaned Sikh military officers is totally unacceptable to all fair-minded Canadians. Discrimination based on religion is wrong and contrary to the fundamentals of the Canadian society. None can make all the Canadians homogeneous and they will always have cultural differences, so there should be no intolerance. These brave men who have fought battles with courage and distinction to defend liberty all over the world should not be so unjustly denied their fundamental and cherished right of living by their religious code. If a turbaned Sikh MP can enter the Canadian Parliament without a finger rising towards him why can't a turbaned war veteran Sikh enter a legion hall just to sip a cup of tea?

There have been many sane voices all over Canada against Newton Branch's insulting and humiliating treatment of the Sikh veterans. Those who condemned their action included premiers, federal and provincial ministers, MPs, MLAs, mayors, teachers, old war veterans, human rights commissions, Ottawa's Dominion Command (of legions), legion members and the media. Most of the daily newspapers of the country wrote trenchant editorials.[11] The whites' individual voices of reason were not able to combine into a chorus of public opinion because most of the whites seemed friendly outwardly but not sincere inwardly.

Whether the Sikhs are able to go to the legions or not, the most dangerous thing for the Canadian society is the poison that certain people carry in their heads for the people who have a different faith and different cultural values. A society or organisation that discriminates on the basis of race, religion or gender is in its primitive stage of progress.

The turban has almost always been in the news at the national level in this country. Even as early as 1914 when the *Komagata Maru* brought 376 passengers (most of them turbaned Sikhs) to Vancouver there was an outcry in the town that 'the turbaned tide' should be rolled back from the shores of Vancouver.

The Sikhs had to struggle ceaselessly to get jobs in the USA, UK and

Canada with a turban on head. In 1982 Gur Sant Singh, an American convert to Sikhism, secured for himself and for many others the right to join the American army and police, keeping their Sikh symbols including turban intact.

Even Sikh children's parents had to fight to keep their wards in schools in the countries that declared to be supporters of multiculturalism.

Towards the end of 1993, three retired police officers challenged the 1990 decision of the federal government allowing the Sikh RCMP officers to wear a turban and its inclusion in the dress code. The plaintiffs clearly seemed to be using it as a cover for what may be called an 'essentially racist stand'. The turban trial was a judgement on multiculturalism or pluralism. It could have a far-reaching impact on the Sikhs. About four hundred thousand Sikhs are living in Canada with more than 70 per cent of them wearing turbans. The case was rejected by the court, allowing the Sikh police officers to wear turbans. Supreme Court of Canada's 15 February 1996 reaffirmation of a Sikh officer's right to wear a turban gave a strong moral and legal strength to the Sikhs to be able to preserve their identity. The Sikh culture and the dominant society culture are not opposed to each other. They are only different. Do we dislike different flowers, different-shaped houses or people with different hair-colours? No, we do not. Yearning for a uniform Canadianism is impossible to fulfil. So let no such vows be made. God shed his grace on Canada. This grace should never be abused.

Hard Hat Issue

A Sikh is prohibited from wearing a hat or cap on head in place of the turban or on it. Bhai Prahlad Singh's *Rehatnama* explicitly disallows a Sikh to wear a hat on head.

Once in the UK, the drivers of two-wheelers were required to drive only with a crash hat on head. The Sikhs objected to it as it was against their religious code of conduct. Winston Churchill, the former Prime Minister of England, supported their cause in the Parliament, telling the members of the House that the Sikhs had fought all the wars for the British with turbans on head, with their performance par excellence. He advised the government not to do anything that is in direct clash with their religious practices. Consequently the turbaned Sikh drivers of the two-wheelers were exempted from wearing the helmet. Interestingly, some clean-shaven Sikhs also started wearing turbans to avail exemption from wearing helmets.

A little earlier, during a battle between the Afghans and the British, the Sikh soldiers were asked to wear hard hats against the Afghan firing which they did from atop a hill. The British told the Sikhs that if they did not wear hard hats the number of casualties would be larger and the British would not be able to provide pensions to a larger number of turbaned Sikh soldiers. The Sikhs were said to have given in writing to the British that if casualties occur due to their turbans there would be no pension claims on their behalf. This strong conviction of the Sikhs against the wearing of hard hats persuaded the British to exempt them from wearing hard hats.

The Sikhs had to face this hard hat problem in every country again and again. Canada was no exception, but the Sikh struggle against wearing it had been uncompromisingly vehement and bitter as the foreign governments had been bound by their regulations and the Sikhs had been prohibited by their religious code of conduct.

Karnail Singh Bhinder—an *amritdhari* Sikh (one who had taken the baptism of the double-edged sword) and the UK trained electrician, joined the Canadian National Railways (CNR) in April 1974. The CNR prescribed the use of hard hat for its employees with effect from 30 November 1978. Karnail Singh refused to wear hard hat on or in place of turban as a matter of his religious faith. He was told by the CNR that if he did not comply with the rules of the Railways he would lose his job. Consequently he was put off his duties with effect from 6 December 1978,

In the western countries there is hardly any security of job. The employees can be fired even without notice but in countries like India, the people once entered into jobs become bulletproof.

Bhinder complained to the Canadian Human Rights Commission on 7 December 1978. The CNR explained that no discrimination was involved and wearing of the hard hat was a bonafide occupational requirement and the use of hard hat was necessary under the Canada Labour Code. It also entailed the safety issue under the Canada Transport Commission. But the emotional involvement of the Sikh community was a strong factor connected with the case.

The safety expert Dr Neuman whose opinion was sought in the matter told that the turban offered more protection than the hard hat to the front and rear of the head and the turban also keeps sticking to the head. But in the case of sharp protruding objects the hard hat could be more useful when the worker puts his head inside the confines of a panel.

The tribunal delivered a unanimous decision, in September 1981, that the complainant was the victim of discrimination because of his religion, though this religious discrimination was not intentional on the part of CNR. Bhinder was ordered to be reinstated with compensation of $14,500. The decision was a happy tiding for the Sikh community but a short-lived one.

The CNR made an appeal against this decision and the Federal Court awarded its ruling in a split 2-1 decision on 13 April 1983 that the Canadian Human Rights Act does not accommodate religious beliefs and the wearing of hard hat was a bonafide requirement. This decision was in utter violation of the letter and spirit of multiculturalism. It rudely shocked the whole Sikh community.

Karnail Singh and the Canadian Human Rights Commission appealed to the Supreme Court of Canada with half a dozen interveners. The appeal was dismissed on 17 December 1985 with a 5-2 split decision, announcing that there was no discrimination against Karnail Singh Bhinder when he was asked to wear hard hat by the employer as a measure of safety. C.J. Dickson, the Chief Justice of Canada and Justice J. Lamer gave the dissenting decision to the slight comfort of the Sikhs.

A member of the Federation of Sikh Societies of Canada, initiated a press conference with the remarks: " We have suffered a terrible blow from the verdict. It will take decades to recover from it, if we recover from it at all. Multiculturalism is reduced to song and dance and nothing more. The community is under siege. This disfunctionality of the government policies to integrate the visible minorities is obvious. The establishment is too strong for us to fight with and to win." The member used all the words to condemn the verdict except to say that it was a racist decision.

The Canadian Human Rights Commission's Chief Commissioner, Gordon Fairweather of the Canadian Human Rights Commission, wrote to the Minister of Justice on 10 February 1986: "It is the Commission's unanimous opinion that the failure of the Supreme Court of Canada, in its majority decision in Bhinder et al vs the Canadian National Railway rendered on 17 December 1985, to uphold the principle of reasonable accommodation, is an urgent matter.... This uncertainty will so significantly impede the Commission's work that it is of the utmost urgency and importance for Parliament to amend the Act to remove any doubt about the Act's authority in this regard. Therefore, the Commission recommends to Parliament that a provision be added to the Canadian Human Rights Act explicitly stating that it is a discriminatory practice to refuse to make reasonable accommodation for special needs or obligations related to a prohibited ground of discrimination."

Gordon Fairweather told the Parliament that "equal opportunity will not be established in country unless employers are required by law to accommodate differences." He said, 'legislative action is now crucial.' The Parliament did nothing in this respect. The Canadian Human Rights Commission's support of Karnail Singh Bhinder's taking complaint of religious discrimination against Canada to the United Nations also did not yield any results as the international body was of the view that the Parliament of Canada was the appropriate authority to deal with this matter. The Supreme Court decision in this case weakened the scope of human rights in Canada considerably. The government took no initiative to strengthen the legal basis of human rights through legislation. The political parties of the country also showed utter lack of interest in this respect.

To the dismay of the Sikh community, and the violation and neglect or observance of the policy of multiculturalism only in the breach, the hard hat Act remains unaltered and unresolved even up to the present day. If at places the employers exempt the use of hard hat in the case of turbaned Sikhs, it is availed by the Sikhs not as a matter of right but as a matter of grace or concession.

Motorcycle Safety Helmet Issue

Motor-cycle safety helmet issue cropped up in 1994. On 5 August 1994, one Avtar Singh Dhillon was refused to take test for driving a motorcycle by the Motor Vehicle Branch (MVB), Surrey, B.C. for not wearing a safety helmet.

Dhillon filed a case with the B.C. Council of Human Rights. He also wrote letters to Premier Mike Harcourt, some provincial ministers and MLAs on 17 February 1995, with copies of supporting letters from 40 Sikh Societies in B.C., telling them that many countries around the world that allowed Sikhs with turbans to ride motorcycles without wearing a safety helmet included the United Kingdom, Denmark, Australia, Malaysia, Hong Kong, Iraq and Singapore. He pleaded for permission to ride a motorcycle without wearing a helmet.

Upon hearing the counsel for the complainant Avtar Singh Dhillon and the counsel respondent Ministry of Transportation and Highways, Motor Vehicle Branch and counsel for the Deputy Chief Commissioner, B.C. and Human Rights Commission on 18th, 19th and 20th March 1997, the Human Rights Tribunal reserved decision upto 11 May 1999, when it announced that the complaint was justified and the Ministry of Transportation and Highways Minister Harry (Harbhajan Singh) Lali. The amendment allowed exemption to them from section 221 of the Motor Vehicle Act which requires motorcycle riders to wear a helmet.

Motorcycle Safety Helmet Exemption Regulation (of 20 July 1999) reads as under:-

The following persons are exempt from the requirements of section 221 of the Motor Vehicles Act.

a) a person who
   i) practises the Sikh religion and
   ii) has unshorn hair and habitually wears a turban composed of five or more square metres of cloth.

Kirpan Issue

The k*irpan* or sword or dagger is worn by a Sikh as a religious symbol and not as a weapon to be used to attack anybody with it. (Of course, its limited use exclusively in self-protection when attacked by someone with a weapon may not be ruled out).

Harbhajan Singh Pandori, a school teacher in the Peel Board of Education, was dismissed from his job as he refused to put off his *kirpan* while on duty in his school. He lodged a complaint on 21 June 1988 to the Ontario Human Rights Commission under the Ontario Human Rights Code, 1981. Two Sikh school boys were also involved in the case for wearing *kirpans*. The Commission got registered a case in the court against the Peel Board of Education. The Board of Inquiry, after due hearing in 1990 gave its ruling on 6 July 1990 that the Peel Board was guilty of restricting the religious rights of the Sikh students and the Sikh teacher.

The Peel Board had earlier applied to the Supreme Court of Ontario to quash the complaint pleading that the case was outside the jurisdiction of the Board of Inquiry. The Court rejected the Peel Board's application.

The issue before the court was of a very serious nature. Proscribing the wearing of a *kirpan* by the Sikhs was tantamount to depriving the Sikh students from getting education and the other *amritdhari* (baptised) Sikhs from pursuing the professions of their choice. On the other hand the Peel Board pleaded that for the maintenance of discipline in the school they had the right to ban all weapons in the school premises. The Peel Board considered the *kirpan* a weapon but the Sikhs insisted that it was not a weapon but a symbol of their faith. It was argued on behalf of the complainants that if at all the *kirpan* was going to be used for aggression many more things like knives, blades, forks, screw drivers or cutting instruments from the craftshop, baseball bat, or a hockey stick could be used much more easily than the *kirpan* that was worn under the Sikh wearer's clothing. The Human Rights Commissioner observed, "If society wants to protect the law-abiding above all, then, in my opinion, the Khalsa students rank high on the list of those to be protected." So the Peel Board's ban on the *kirpan* was a glaring denial of the constitutional right of the Sikhs to religious freedom.

The Commissioner issued an order that the Peel Board must withdraw the ban on the *kirpan* and the religious freedom and the safety of the students and teachers should be ensured. The Sikh teachers and students should wear a *kirpan* of a reasonable size and keep it under their clothing, further directing that in the event of a serious danger of violence in the school the principal may impose temporary and sparingly reasonable curb on the *kirpan*. The Peel Board of Education desisted from lodging an appeal against this decision in view of the strong public pressure.

The *kirpan* issue does not seem to have been settled in Canada once and for all. This issue had been raising its head again and again to the annoyance and anger of the Sikh community.

The above judgement regarding the *kirpan* had, unfortunately, no reference to the Multiculturalism Act or any other Act of Parliament to add strength or due legality to the decision. The Sikhs had to fight it out every time. In the adjoining country US and also in the UK this issue of wearing the *kirpan* by the Sikh students almost always remains alive.

The *kirpan* issue has not been exclusive only to the western countries where the Sikhs have mostly chosen to settle but animate in their native country India also. The Indian Constitution (Article 25, explanation I) provides that 'the wearing and carrying of *kirpan* shall be deemed to be included in the profession of the Sikh religion.' When a responsible Sikh elected from the Punjab to the Indian Parliament in 1989 with a record margin over his opponent wanted to enter the Parliament with his *kirpan* on his person he was not allowed to do so under a plea that he was carrying a weapon with him. Despite his arguing that the *kirpan* was a symbol of his religion, he was denied his constitutional right and was not allowed in with his *kirpan*. But Yasar Arafat of the Palestine Liberation Organisation was allowed to take on his person a loaded pistol and addressed the Indian Parliament. Undoubtedly, Yasar Arafat is a great and revered leader of Palestine. However, the Sikh MP referred to above was no less respectable Indian citizen who confided the trust of lakhs of people whom he represented.

In Indian Parliamentary election of 1999, the above referred to Sikh was again elected to the Lok Sabha (Indian Parliament) but on the insistence of his voters, he did not take up the *kirpan* issue. He visited Canada in April/May 2000 and entered the Canadian Parliament along with his *kirpan*. The Speaker of the Canadian Parliament expressed astonishment over the denial to a Sikh M.P. to carry *kirpan*, which is the religious symbol of the Sikhs, to the Indian Parliament.

It is a sad commentary on the Canadian government that when the Sikh community fights for their religious symbols and preservation of their valuable cultural heritage without causing any damage to other communities the government that upholds the policy of multiculturalism does not come forward to support them. They have to fight for their rights without the support of the government that enshrines in its constitution the protection of cultures of all its citizens. This indifferent attitude of the government loses the lustre of its policy of multiculturalism and in due course of time this policy of its great framers like Trudeau would be reduced to a meaningless item in the country's constitution.

Sikh Distinctiveness

Professor John W. Friesen feels that unlike most ethnocultural groups in Canada, the Sikh community has remained unaffected by the traditional campaign for assimilation waged by the dominant society. Gordon has delineated seven stages towards attaining complete assimilation. The Sikhs have essentially remained independent of even the first stage that suggests that members of an immigrant group should "change their cultural pattern (including religious belief and its observance) to that of the dominant society".[12]

Friesen says that there are probably two reasons for this, one, having to do with the success of the Sikh community in trying to maintain their own sub-cultural identity and the second, being the dominant society's very strong opposition to the Sikh ways. Foremost in the campaign to thwart Sikh assimilation is the public antagonism towards the Sikh 'uniform' particularly the practice that the loyal Sikhs are not to cut their hair (*kesh*) and they are required to carry a ceremonial sword (a *kirpan*). Growing long hair (including beards) necessitates the wearing of headgear like the turban, which was long ago, adopted by the Sikhs as a means of keeping their hair in place.

Friesen further remarks that it is difficult to understand why the Sikhs have had to be targets of such severe forms of public disapproval when it is primarily a question of differences in costume that sets them apart from the rest of the society. For the most part, the Sikhs live like other Canadians.

They are employed in traditional Canadian forms of business enterprises and in workplaces. They have good market value and work hard for their livelihood. They live in standard houses, engage in regular forms of socialising and like other Canadians attend the church of their choice. The Sikh temples look very different from church buildings constructed by other faiths and they tend to be very well maintained. The Sikh organizations have contributed heavily towards the Canadian national relief, the Mexico earthquake relief, the Ethiopian relief fund and the interfaith food bank, to name a few. Still in a survey conducted among the Sikhs in Vancouver in 1980, 52 per cent said that they had virtually no contact with other Canadians and only ten per cent said that they had a lot.

Friesen further says that the evidence is clear that the Sikhs are often targets of a form of racism that is virtually without any justifiable foundation. It also tends to enlarge their social distance from other Canadians.... In Canada it seems that the people are not yet free of the notion that human differences (even in costume) are always to be feared.[13]

Baljinder Singh Gill, Nacoi National President (1991), said:

"I am often told that if the community I represent wants to be Canadian, its members should act like Canadians. We are devoted to our families; we believe in hard work; we share responsibility in our community and participate enthusiastically in the political process; having come to Canada in search of peace, dignity and security, we are deeply committed to respect individual rights; we willingly make sacrifices so that our children can have a better life and children care for and respect their elder parents. How can these values be inimical to 'Canadian way of life'? Surely they are not less important than the clothes we wear or the religion we practise. In our experience this expression [Canadian way of life] is most often a coded way of saying that the quintessential Canadian is white and Christian. Canada cannot be sustained on rhetoric. Talk of equality is meaningless if individual Canadians are treated in an unequal manner because of where they come from."[14] Such a suggestion by the whites would be construed as intending aggression on the cultural freedom and distinct identity of the Sikhs.

The conflict of the future is between the West and the rest. The West is determined to extinguish the diversity. For example, America is exporting its way of life in order to extirpate or wipe out the world's diversity. It exports the products of its mass culture. One religion, one way of life, one entertainment—this is the US objective or their melting pot ideology that designs to undermine the values of traditional societies.

Today's young people of Indian origin have passports to two different worlds—to their own culture and to the western culture. Our regret is that the young are on their way to abandoning their own culture.

Despite all this the image of the Sikhs outside India is not that bad. But there is no denying the fact that the Indian embassies' contribution to the image building of the Sikhs abroad is almost negligible and sometimes negative. The Indian media abroad also keeps their eyes closed to the qualities of the Sikhs and they hardly write anything to help build their true image reflecting their honesty, hard work, sense of responsibility, dependability, self-respect, bravery, honour, gentleness and hospitality. I have every reason to blame the Indian missions abroad and the Indian media there for the poor image of the Sikhs if it is depicted with biases anywhere in the world.

For the Indian image abroad, as a whole, the above factors will also share the responsibility equally.

The Sikhs in Canada have been constantly making efforts for the retention of their identity. They want to keep the Sikh values. Religion is a vital ingredient and a source of internal strength to the Sikh community. Sometimes they feel that the preservation of the Sikh culture, its values and their identity are under a serious threat from external influences. Our identity must decay under a system which discourages to remember and respect our national past and our cultural values. It seems that the edifice of society's tolerance is crumbling.

To limelight their identity, the Sikhs often hold seminars and conferences in different parts of Canada as well as the U.K. and the U.S. They discuss their problems and find solutions to them through fruitful deliberations. Now, more than ever, they are conscious of protecting their identity and telling the non-Sikhs how dear it is to them. The Sikhs show full respect to other cultures and do want that their culture is fully respected. Do not show disrespect to the people who do not think as you do. It is the basic right of everybody to think, as he likes. The attitude of respect for all creeds is bred into the marrow of a Sikh's bones by the Sikh traditions. Multiculturalism is a great asset to the Canadian society.

Socialising with the Whites and the Other Non-Sikhs

Cultural bias is the horrible bane with which Canada rather all the western countries are afflicted. Socially the whites do not mix with the non-whites or visible minorities, probably due to some misplaced notion of their superiority based on colour of the skin. I have seen an undeclared policy of apartheid being practised in these countries. In the afternoons the whites are seen playing soccer or baseball in one corner of a park, the

Chinese in another and the East Indians in yet another corner. This presents an awful spectacle to an onlooker or a passer-by on his routine walk. When the whites and non-whites work together in a factory or a lumber mill or some other establishment their relationship is limited to their profession or their workplace and it seldom develops into a social relationship.

Even the Sikh people with education and no language problem will find friends among other Punjabis. Their cultural similarity and linguistic sameness make them more comfortable in each other's company. But it has a drawback to keep them away from other cultures and other people. In a way, they live and grow in isolation.

Besides, the Sikhs maintaining a liaison with their own community and its institutions to keep themselves abreast with all that is happening there, they must socialize with other communities of the country as well to gain greater acceptance. The socialization would help understand one another's culture better and the different communities would get friendly, co-operative and more sensitive to one another's susceptibilities and get much closer. Mixing with other Canadian people would save the Sikhs from living in isolation and would bring them into better recognition.

The Sikhs should participate in the meetings of the whites and the whites should be invited to the Sikh seminars and other functions. They should be welcomed to the religious programmes at the Sikh temples to listen to the discourses organized there. The whites should be taken to the *langar* (free community mess) and served with meals there and explained objectives behind it. They should be made to understand the import of the various Sikh religious and social institutions and told as to how many of these are based on the spiritual, material and social requirements of the needy human beings irrespective of their caste, colour or creed. Thus, they will have better understanding and respect for the Sikh heritage culture that they want to defend and promote.

The whites and the other non-Sikhs should be given a wide idea, about the Sikh Gurus, their teachings, Sikh scripture, Gurdwara, Sikh *sangat* (congregation), Sikh baptism, *sewa* (voluntary service), *ardas* (Sikh prayer), *kirtan* (recitation of the holy compositions), their Vatican (Harmandir Sahib, Amritsar) and other important cultural institutions. Gradually their discomfort regarding the Sikhs and their culture would change into deep regard and reverence. The whites' dislike for the Sikhs and their code of conduct arose from their stark ignorance of the significance of the same.

The senior school, college and university Sikh students can play an important role in acquainting their white friends or institution mates with at least the basic knowledge of the Sikhs and their cultural heritage. The elders can do the same at their level and contribute profitably to the betterment of their mutual relations. But according to the old maxim, 'Teacher, teach thyself,' the Sikh students and their elders must be well versed in the Sikh religion, Sikh history and culture and the Sikh values. Since the Sikhs have a different culture and if they want it to survive and want it to be preserved in their new homeland, a multicultural country, and desire to find a suitable place for it, they have to diffuse it among all the component elements of the society. If the Sikhs sleep over it their future generations will be won over by others and their ethnic identity would be forgotten and their past ancestry totally lost to them.

Despite government's commitment to keep Canada a multicultural country the white people are trying to outmatch others and ultimately assimilate all other cultural groups. Many recent opinion polls or surveys deliver this message in clear terms.

Canada is as dear to the Sikhs as it is to the Anglo-Saxons or the French and so is the Sikh culture dear to the Sikhs as the English culture and the French culture are dear to the English and the French respectively. Once George Bernard Shaw said, "He is a Briton, he thinks the customs of his tribe are the laws of the universe." So the distinct English society boasts of setting the political, social and cultural standards for everybody else in Canada. But they are accused by some people of the ethnocentrism and xenophobia, unique to the Anglo-Saxons. The English sometimes express unhappiness, when told in the name of multiculturalism, that anything they might do to try to inflict the English culture on others would violate the human rights of the ethnic Canadians to live, speak, eat, dress, dance and worship as they please. The English culture has every right like other cultures to survive as a sacred culture but has no right to forcibly assimilate other cultures that are also sacred to their followers. We cannot expect people who come to Canada to throw away their cultures and customs that are hundreds of years old. Neither it is desirable in the case of the Anglo-Saxons nor in the case of the Sikhs. The great policy of multiculturalism comes to their rescue. Long live the exponents and supporters of this policy!

Let me tell the advocates of the Anglo-Saxon culture alone, that the Canadian fabric does not consist of only white threads. The British must give up their pretensions to being the dominant culture. There should be no dominant culture in Canada. All cultures have equal rights to survive and flourish. The Canadian society will never lose its multicultural character. So the Canadians must learn to live with it. What was required was the desire on the part of the majority groups to live with the minorities as good neighbours and to let the benefits flow freely to all people.

Sikh Efforts to Promote their Culture and Values

In the Canadian Sikh society most of the Canadian-borns have not acquired the dominant voice in the families. They listen to their parents and for quite some time live under their care. Under their parents' guidance they marry within their own community and in most cases the marriage partners are searched from the Punjab. Such partnership lasts much longer and in most of the cases it lasts till death because marriage is considered a very sacred institution among the Sikhs. According to the Sikh *rahit* (code of conduct) marriage is a spiritual bond—unbreakable and life-lasting as against the marriage in the west where it is only a social agreement open to break any time. In the western society marriages break more easily than a glass breaks on a marble stone.

Despite the fact that there are more than half a million Indians including more than four hundred thousand Punjabi Sikhs in Canada, the libraries here, have almost no books on Sikh religion, Sikh history, Sikh culture and Punjabi literature on their shelves. Even the small libraries, if we can name this handful of books as libraries, attached to the Sikh Gurdwaras, have hardly any good titles in their meagre collections. It is unfortunate that the Gurdwara authorities are hardly interested in the purchase of good books on the above subjects. Library is a neglected part of their multifarious programmes. There are no other means of teaching history, culture and philosophy of Sikhism to the precariously placed Sikh youth than good books on these subjects. Recommend these books to the libraries and if they have any financial or other bottlenecks, purchase these books with money raised by collection and donate the same to the libraries.

To provide some useful glimpses of Sikh culture and Sikh religion to the non -Sikh Canadians more research should be done in the Canadian universities as is already being done in the University of British Columbia, University of Toronto and University of Michigan (USA). The Sikhs have done a good job by holding Sikh conferences in Canada almost every year since 1979. The Canadian department of multiculturalism had been very kind and thoughtful in providing financial assistance to organize these conferences mainly with a view to promoting Sikh culture and Sikh values and also holding deliberations on the various problems confronting the Sikh community.

For decades Punjabi had been taught in Canada to the youngsters at Gurdwara schools. The British Columbia Sikhs had been impressing upon the government for a long time that though Punjabi language might have been originated elsewhere, it is a language in Canada spoken by Canadian citizens and must not be treated only to be developed at community level. Ultimately the B.C. government included this language in the provincial list of examinable languages and approved a policy and curriculum under which it can be taught in the public schools with effect from the 1996-97 school year. The Sikh children, now, must possess the ability to read, write and speak the language which their parents or grandparents brought with them. They should be able to read their scripture in original through the medium of *gurmukhi* script. Introduction of Punjabi in schools, along with Japanese and Chinese languages, is a step forward in the development of the policy of multiculturalism. Thus, the Sikh children will also restore their connection with their only Punjabi-speaking grandparents. They will have access to the literature on their language, religion, culture and customs that have now become a part of their educational fabric.

It is remarked that since racism and lack of respect for a culture that is different than that of the majority group has been in the Canadian system for a long time, people require some time to get out of it. In fact, no effective way was found to bridge the yawning gap between the two principal ethnic groups, the whites and the non-whites. They need to be educated that the more they respect the cultures of others the more cultured they will be. Cultural diversity in a society is a more gorgeous phenomenon than cultural uniformity. Let such people shed off the narrow social grooves that always keep them tightly entangled and come into the variegated world of multicultural society.

But as things stand at present no miracle is expected to change the attitude of most of the morbid people. The country has to go a long way before people fully understand the intentions of the planners of multiculturalism. It is almost tantamount to a moral crime to pressurize a person to give up his social and cultural values and adopt that of the others. Even the new entrant with new cultural behaviour enriches the society that he enters. So long as this truth does not dawn upon the racists and opponents of multiculturalism the bliss of social grandeur will keep eluding us.

How wonderful it is that Canada represents almost every nation of this planet. It is universal in its composition. Diversity is an important asset. We should learn not to respect only similarities but also the differences with others. Multiculturalism is living with honour when there is no agreement on values. It is living well without hurting other people. Share your culture with others and vice versa and both of you will become culturally richer.

The social or cultural system of the Canadian Sikhs has endured over a century despite numerous strains and stresses. Now it can be expected that it would nòt face any danger of being eroded and replaced because in view of the falling birth rate and aging population of the country, the Sikh immigrants devoted to the Sikh code of culture, will continue pouring into Canada, day after day, month after month, year after year and decade after decade, thus supplying fresh water to the pool of the Canadian Sikhs and their Sikh culture and Sikh values. Their strength lies in their culture. The author does not mean to turn tables on any other culture. He only intends to portray here the Sikh culture which teaches them to always honour man's laws as well as God's laws. And the government's policy of multiculturalism will always aim at integration and not assimilation, at preservation and sharing of cultural heritage and elimination of barriers to full participation of all in the administrative, economic and political life of the country. The Sikhs have emerged as a global community with strong religious beliefs. They are enriching the larger communities while remaining true to their own moral and religious ideals. All religions have emphasised some values. Hinduism and Jainism emphasise non-violence, Buddhism compassion, Christianity love, Islam justice and Sikhism truthfulness, love and equality.

Multiculturalism Defended

The Tory Government's Multiculturalism and Citizenship Minister, Gerry Weiner strongly criticized the critics of multiculturalism. He says that we should not overlook or belittle what we have done and accomplished. Nor should we abandon our principles and ideals because there are some Canadians who do not know—or who refuse to know—and understand what we are doing and why.

It appears that critics of multiculturalism are as loud as ever and they are as wrong as ever. If the government introduces a new tax policy...or reforms criminal law...critics of that policy will be expected to argue their case on the facts. But when it comes to multiculturalism, it seems sufficient simply to say, 'I do not like it.'

Again and again, editorialists and columnists ask, "how can we succeed with multiculturalism dividing us?"

Gerry Weiner says that a few weeks ago, an editorial in a major daily newspaper in Atlantic Canada asked the following question: "Canadians look about the world and see bitter and bloody strife between different ethnic and religious groups, then seriously wonder if it makes sense to promote multiculturalism here. It is a tough question. Does it make sense to import ethnic strife rather than offer a haven for those attempting to escape it?" "It is not a 'tough' question. It is a stupid one! Where does the writer of this editorial get off equating multiculturalism with the importation of ethnic strife? Where is the reasoning? Where is the proof?" said Weiner.

Another writer in Vancouver defines multiculturalism as, "agreeing to disagree." Yet another in Kingston said, "Multiculturalism should not encourage one cultural group to isolate itself from the rest of their cultural neighbours." "These commentators gave no justification for their opinions. But if multiculturalism is so wrong and so disastrous, why are so many others studying us... and copying us? Why have so many governments around the world asked us for advice and implemented policies and programmes based on our initiatives?" said the minister.

Gerry Weiner said, "If we fund ethnocultural organizations— and the communities they represent— to stay apart from other Canadians, to create their own cultural ghettos, we do so because our experience shows that such funding actually helps the process of integration. Because it is through such community structures that we can identify problems to integrate, and act to eliminate them. Pride in our origins, yes. Why not? What is wrong with preserving our cultural heritage... a heritage that enriches our society in so many ways and though not at the expense of respect and understanding for the culture of others? That has never been our objective, nor is it the result of our policies, intended or otherwise."

"So much of our work, our programmes, are aimed at integration...and at the removal of the barriers that stand in its way. Why? Because only through integration can we guarantee equality of access of opportunity and of participation that leads to equality of citizenship. And it is only when you are part of something...that you really care about it and about its future. We still have a long way to go before all Canadians share fully in the equality of citizenship. So I think we all have a responsibility, those of us, who truly believe in multiculturalism, and what it has given our country—what it has yet to give."[15]

Robert Stanfield, the federal leader of the opposition referring to the government's programme as 'grudging acceptance' remarked, "If we really believe that Canadian pluralism should be encouraged and not merely tolerated, the government should work together with the various ethnic groups to help them survive, not simply as folklore, but as a living contributing element of the Canadian cultural mosaic."[16]

John Yaremko, the Ontario Provincial Secretary and Minister of Citizenship said in 1972, at a multicultural conference: "No other part of the globe, no other country, can claim a more culturally diversified society than we have here in this province (of Ontario). But does everyone really grasp that Ontario has more Canadians of German origin than Bonn, more of Italian origin than Florence or Rome, that Toronto has more Canadians of Greek origin than Sparta, that we have in our midst, fifty four ethnocultural groups, speaking a total of seventy two languages? ... Just as a hundred years ago the Canadian identity was moulded in the crucible of nationalism. It is now being tampered by the dynamics of multiculturalism."[17]

In earlier stages it was taken for granted that in Canada the immigrants would be and should be assimilated through public education as in the United States, and stress should be laid on compulsory school attendance. During that period, in Canada there was certainly no generosity displayed towards other nations and other cultures which would be necessary for the building of a cultural mosaic.

The editor of *The Montreal Gazette* wrote that the people must be aware of the voices that call ever so patriotically for a homogenized Canada. Those voices dominate many of the hot lines and public meetings of the citizens' forums on Canada's future. They speak some times directly and some times indirectly, of a dream country of uniform habits in which everybody should wear the same hat, speak the same language and love Canada in the same way. It is an impossible dream and even if it had been possible, every government must resist it. There can be no Canadian unity without diversity. The Canadian constitution commits the country to 'the preservation and enhancement of the multicultural heritage of the Canadians'. Yearning for a uniform Canadianism is impossible to fulfil. So no such vows should be made. Nor should there be any attempts to fit all Canadians into the same mould. It just would not work. French speaking Quebecers, for an obvious example, cannot and should not melt in the pot. And neither will melt a lot of other Canadians with strong and valued heritages from abroad or from their own regions. It is a trite, but true, that Canada is a mosaic. Such forums heed the assertions that bilingualism and multiculturalism interfere with a true Canadian identity. They are wrong. Bilingualism and multiculturalism are the true Canadian identity.[18]

To Canadian society's misfortune the whites could not accept the cultures of the immigrants as a part of the composite culture of the country.

They chose to practise racism, bias and bigotry against the visible minorities. Because of their distinct code of conduct the Sikhs are the most visible minority.

The founding-nations branded multiculturalism as divisive, anti-Canadian and anti-patriotic, but the 'distinct identity' status given to one community was bound to be discriminatory to the other communities and harmful for the country also as it showed them the path to sovereignty—their own separate independent state—cut óut of Canada. There should have been equal status and equal respect for all the cultures.

In India and the Soviet Union of Russia there have been dozens and dozens of different cultures—all enjoying equal positions and equal respect. Why could the Canadian whites not learn a lesson from them and many similar countries? Unfortunately, most of the whites believe that the colour of their skin gives them divinely ordained superiority to which others cannot lay any claim.

Prominent citizens of the country have time and again, stressed upon the implementation of the policy of multiculturalism in Canada.

John E. Cleghorn, President of the Royal Bank of Canada, speaking to the Toronto Board of Trade, in September 1993, said that Canada's mosaic of linguistic, cultural and regional experience constitutes one of Canada's strength and is not a reason for division. "Canada has gained an international reputation for being a generous and caring society. But we risk losing this enviable position if we cannot continue to capitalize on our diversity. We must do a better job of living side by side, accepting, respecting and valuing differences as building blocks instead of barricades". Cleghorn said, "Respect for others and for their individual differences allows every one to respond constructively and to appreciate and nurture the uniqueness of each and every one of us," he said.[19]

Unlike Cleghorn there are some in this country who believe that multiculturalism is divisive and should die. They would try to turn back the tide of reality. But let them be told that multiculturalism will stay alive and well and be preserved by every government.

The former Prime Minister, Kim Campbell said, "The objectives of our government's multicultural policy are to recognize the reality of Canada's cultural and ethnic diversity and to respond to it in a way that helps us realise our full potential as a society. Our predecessors did an adequate job of recognizing the reality, but their commitment did not extend to breaking down the barriers that robbed Canada of the full participation in its social, political and economic life of people from outside the historic mainstream.... I have always resisted the view that people must conform to some theoretical mainstream... to receive first class treatment from their government."[20]

Multiculturalism is the state policy of Canada for dealing with other races and ethnic groups. Most of the provincial governments have their own departments also to deal with multiculturalism. The principles of the policies of the provinces include encouragement to multiculturalism and to provide assistance to individuals and groups to increase opportunities to learn about their cultural heritage and the contributions of other groups in the province. The provincial governments recognize that over 50 per cent of the population has origins other than British or French. They recognize the ethnic and cultural diversity of their provinces and contribution from their pluralistic heritage. They recognize roles in increasing institutions in the provinces both public and private, to acknowledge and respond to the multicultural nature of society. The governments recognize multiculturalism as a province-wide concern and the need for the co-ordinating mechanism. The provincial governments are required to create climate in which multiculturalism readily applies to all constituents of the society.

At 1980 Sikh conference held at Ottawa, the guest speaker, Gordon Fairweather, Chief Commissioner of the Canadian Human Rights Commission, said in his inaugural address:

Every individual should have an equal opportunity with other individuals to make for himself or herself the life that he or she is able and wishes to have, consistent with his or her duties and obligations as a member of the society, without being hindered in or prevented from doing so by discriminatory practices, religion being one of them and national or ethnic origin as the other—besides so many others. Some well-meaning persons think like this but many others who suffer from attitudinal morbidity are difficult to tackle."[21] There is no substitute for mutual affection, understanding, tolerance and adjustment for the sake of country's harmony and unity.

Threat to Multiculturalism

It is a sad commentary on multiculturalism that no legislation could preserve the cultures and languages brought to Canada by the pioneer immigrants from different parts of the world. Of course, in very recent days some attempts have been made to teach some ethnic languages in some limited schools. It has still to be seen as to how successful these efforts would be. "Nor has multiculturalism brought about any equality of opportunity for all Canadians, regardless of time of arrival, cultural and linguistic differences and colour."[22]

One may wonder why there is growing intolerance towards a policy which, after all, is designed to promote harmony and peace? The answer may partially lie in the perception that the multiculturalism policies benefit only the non-white recent arrivals. Multiculturalism has become synonymous with ethnic, visible minorities and recent immigrants. This is both very unfair and very unfortunate.

No one terms the gathering of Scottish clans in Nova Scotia as a multiculturalism event while the 'Caribana' in Toronto is perceived as such. The Danish immigrants in New Brunswick can comfortably live in a town named 'New Denmark' while a Jew or a Sikh is hampered from participating in various legitimate work-related activities in Canada while sporting required religious symbols such as the turban.[23]

The members of the Association to Preserve English in Canada insist that multiculturalism is no more than a guise to destroy their mother tongue. Margaret Cannon writes that she met women in Vancouver who believed that having turbaned Sikhs in the Royal Canadian Mounted Police (RCMP) was a plot to destroy Canada.... "I had met people who lived their lives in the darkest corners of the human imagination and I thought that I had seen it all....I had seen racism first hand... In the great well of systems racism is thriving in Canada."

Gordon Fairweather gave a similar example in 1980: "I could not help remembering of a conversation that I had a couple of years ago in Kitchner, Ontario, with a man who was in the Canadian militia, fully dressed in the uniform and all regalia of Scotland, and he said to me, 'you at the Canadian Human Rights Commission are ruining the armed forces'. You are going to allow people who wear turban to be part of militia.' 'And I said to him that it seems to me somewhat extraordinary that a person in such an extraordinary uniform on, such as you have, would complain about your brother because after all we are all part of human fellowship. I said that to most of us that the costume that you have been allowed to share is a very extraordinary one. It took us little to debate and pushing back and forth and finally I am rather pleased to say that he got the message. But this business of attitudinal change, having people to understand differences and the differences are a precious part of one's dignity and it is really what we at the Human Rights Commission are all about."[24]

The whites may not be calling people nigger or chink or kike or raghead on the street, but they make it clear that the values they want enshrined in their institutions are the values of the founding races—whites, Catholic, Protestant, European culture, western philosophy, Margaret Cannon further told.[25]

Bharati Mukherjee, an East Indian scholar criticizes Canada for being more racist than the United States, but Neil Bissoonda, who was born in Trindidad and is of an East Indian origin and an outspoken critic of multiculturalism, does not share Bharati's position. He says, "She prefers the United States because there everything is up front. If an American does not like you for the colour of your skin, you will know it, whereas in Canada people will smile and be polite and not let you know it. And, therefore, Canada is a more racist country. I would much rather have racists behave in the Canadian way: smile and be polite.... Canadians, even when they are racist, realise that it is not a nice thing to be."

Bissoonda criticizing multiculturalism writes, "People, who arrive and find themselves living in their little ethnic community, never engage with society. That is what I think has to be avoided because a person ends up in a way caged by their cultural baggage. I know too many people from the Caribbean who insist on living here as if they were still back there, and then resenting being told that there are certain ways of doing things here."[26]

The problem of adjustment in the society is not a one way traffic. Surely the small groups of society must take an adjustment with the greater society in regard to their life style but the greater society also has to make an adjustment with the ways of the immigrants. Bissoonda's opinion, that the majority society's ways, their laws and their social rules should govern the minority society, cannot be popular among defenders of Canadian multicultural policy.

Angus Reid Group conducted a national poll in June-July 1991 on attitudes about multiculturalism. The poll revealed many points including the following:

Twenty eight per cent Canadians blamed official multiculturalism for the rising tide of racism.

Seventy nine per cent Canadians feel that schools are not doing a proper job of promoting ethnocultural tolerance.

Ninety per cent Canadians blame Canada's racism on immigrants who refuse to join the mainstream and, therefore, create ethnocultural ghettos.

Seventy seven per cent Canadians believe that multiculturalism will enrich Canadian culture.

Fifty five per cent believe that it is best if different ethnic or cultural backgrounds are forgotten as soon as possible.

Twelve per cent believe strongly that multiculturalism will destroy the Canadian way of life.

Sixty six per cent think that discrimination against non-whites is a problem in Canada.

On the whole Canadians feel less comfortable with people from the following groups: Indo-Pakistanis, the Sikhs, West-Indian Blacks, Arabs and other Muslims than they do with people of other groups.[27]

A new survey conducted by the Decima Research for the Canadian Council of Christians and Jews, released on 13 December 1993,[28] found that three of every four Canadians reject the notion of cultural diversity and think ethnic minorities should try harder to fit into the mainstream society. They believe that the multicultural mosaic is not working and should be replaced by a cultural melting pot of American style. Melting pot ideology means assimilation, that is, losing or merging ones identity into that of another. Canadians are frustrated with the traditional cultural mosaic in which ethnic groups are encouraged to retain their distinct cultures. They want a more homogenized society, the Decima report says.

"There is a relatively strong view that particular ethnic, racial or religious minorities must make efforts to adapt to Canada rather than insisting upon a maintenance of difference." The survey also shows that 74 per cent of the Canadians think that racism is a serious problem, leading the report to conclude that "while the population reports a strong rejection of any racist activity, it must balance this rejection with some views that are apparently... latently racist in themselves." The president of the Decima, Ned Goodman, said that he was surprised by the discovery that most Canadians have concluded that multiculturalism, as a government policy, is not working. This survey was conducted at the end of October 1993. It included 1200 respondents in its sample. It is considered accurate within 2.8 per cent, 19 out of 20 times.

Despite all the opposition to multiculturalism it is going to stay. The well-being of the country lies in its permanent and inalienable acceptance by the Canadians. This policy aims at assisting the preservation and enhancement of the multicultural heritage of the Canadians. And it recognizes the Canadian cultural identity of being pluralistic and multicultural. This policy prohibits discrimination based on race, national or ethnocultural origin, colour or religion, among other factors. It is due to this policy, besides some other factors, that Canada has been declared by the United Nations in 2000 for the sixth consecutive year, to be the best in the world.

REFERENCES

1. Augie Fleras and Jean Leonard Elliot, *The Challenges of Diversity, Multiculturalism in Canada*, Scarborough, Ontario, 1992, pp.60-61.

2. John Murray Gibbon, *Canadian Mosaic*, Toronto, 1938, p. vii.

3. John Porter, *The Measure of Canadian Society*, Toronto, 1979, p.141.

4. 'Editorial', *The Vancouver Sun*, 17 June 1913.

5. Henry H. Stevens, *Lectures on The Oriental Problem dealing with Asian Immigration*, 1911.

6. *The Daily Province*, Vancouver, 24 February 1912.

7. 'Ethnics attack biculturalism', *Toronto Telegram*, 16 December 1968.

8. Anna Galan (Ed.) *Multiculturalism for Canada*, Edmonton, 1979, p.6.

9. Pierre Trudeau, 'Statement on multicultural policy', in Canadian Parliament, on 8 October 197

10. Narindar Singh, *Canadian Sikhs*, Canadian Sikhs' Studies Institute, Ottawa,1994, p.88.

11. Bhagat Singh, *Canadian Society and Culture*, Vikas Publishing House, PVT, LTD., New Delhi, 1997, p.410.

12. Gordon, Milton M., *Assimilation in American Life : The Role of race, religion and national origins*, New York, Oxford University Press, 1964, p.70.

13. John W. Friesen, *When Cultures Clash*, Detselig Enterprises Ltd., Calgary Alberta, second edition, 1993, pp.189-90.

14. Baljinder Singh Gill, *The Forum*, a quarterly publication o f Nacoi, Ottawa, March 1991 p.5.

15. Gerry Weiner, 'Multiculturalism's critics are loud but wrong as ever' (a speech), *The Link*, 30 June 1993, pp.17-18.

16. Robert Stanfield (a speech), *The Globe and Mail*, Toronto, 1 May 1972.

17. *Press release of Minister's address*, office of the Provincial Secretary, Toronto, 20 March 1972 (quoted by John Porter, *The Measure of Canadian Society*, p.119).

18. Canadian scene, 'Diversity : the key to Canadian Unity', *The Link*, 16 August 1991, pp.1,4.

19. Canadian scene, 'Canada's diversity, a strength', *The Link*, 29 September 1993.

20. Kim Campbell, 'Committed to diversity', *The Link*, 19 June 1993.

21. Gordon Fairweather, *Proceedings—Sikh Conference*, 1980, The National Sikh Society, Ottawa, 1983, p.7.

22. Jean R. Burnet and Howard Palmer, 'Coming Canadians', *An Introduction to a History of Canada's Peoples*, McClelland and Steward, Multiculturalism Directorate. Ministry of Supply and Services. 1988.

23. B. Liddar, 'Multiculturalism under attack', *The Forum*, August-September 1991, p.9.

24. Gordon Fairweather, *op.cit.*, p.7.

25. Margaret Cannon, *The Invisible Empire : Racism in Canada*, Toronto, 1995, pp.266-67, 271.

26. Linda Hutcheson and Marion Richmond, *Other Solitudes* (Canadian Multicultural Fictions), Oxford University Press, Toronto, 1990, pp. 314,316.

27. Angus Reid Group, *Attitudes about Multiculturalism and Citizenship*, June-July 1991, 5-page report published by Multiculturalism and Citizenship, Canada.

28. Jack Kapica, 'Canadians want mosaic to melt, survey finds', *The Globe and Mail*, 14 December 1993, pp.A1-2; Allyson Jeffs, 'Notion of cultural diversity rejected by most Canadians,' *The Vancouver Sun*, 14 Decembe 1993, p.A5.

CHAPTER 9

PROFESSIONS AND
THE SIKH PROFESSIONALS

The first batches of immigrants to Canada were of agrarian background with little education. Many of them were retired military people who were disciplined and hardworking. In the beginning of the twentieth century the people of Punjab heard that Canada was a land of enormous wealth and the Canadians welcomed the new immigrants, providing them good opportunities of lucrative work. They needed people to develop their land. The land was freely available for permanent settlement. But as soon as these Sikhs and others entered Canada they found themselves disillusioned as the white population was hostile to them rather than befriending them as co-workers in the new land. For their humble living they ended up in railway track builders and as workers in logging and lumber industry.

Most of these East Indians were the Sikhs and in the early years their number in Canada was very small, hardly a few hundred. Since they were of enterprising disposition, they did not settle at one place and they were constantly on the move to Vancouver, Victoria, Seattle and Oregon. There was almost no problem in crossing over to America and from there to Canada as they had hundreds of kilometres open border between these two countries. Even today there are more than 70 million border crossings each year at about 130 such locations between these two sovereign states.

During those early years, the lumber mills accommodated the East Indians more than any other vocation.

Lumber Industry

Most of the early Sikh settlers lived in or around Vancouver so that they could have easy approach to the Sikh temple at 2nd Avenue in Vancouver. They found jobs in the lumber mills located around that area.

During the first decade of the 20th century the wages were very low, hardly ten cents an hour. A house could be purchased for less than three hundred dollars and during the First World War the prices for an average house were about five hundred dollars. A few of these mill workers lived in their own houses but most of them lived in the big bunkhouses attached to the mills, having five or six cook houses in each bunkhouse used by forty or fifty dwellers.

The sawmill bunkhouse built of wood was generally divided into ten to fifteen rooms with two beds in each room. There was a big hall in the middle of the bunkhouse with rooms on either side of the hall. At one end of the hall, there was a sitting area with a wood burning stove that provided heat to the hall. The owner of the mill, depending on the strength of the workers needing accommodation determined the number of the bunkhouses in the mill. People belonging to different communities—the Sikhs, Chinese, Japanese, Europeans, etc., lived in separate bunkhouses so that they could easily socialize with their own racial or heritage groups and prepare their favourite meals in their separate cookhouses.

The cookhouse was a separate building adjacent to the bunkhouse. An elderly Sikh, who prepared the meals for the workers and was compensated by the workers who earned wages, generally manned the cookhouse of the Sikh workers. The workers shared the grocery and the money to be paid to the cook, as he did not work in the mill.

The better off Sikhs lived in their own purchased or built houses. They sometimes rented portions of their houses to the new-comers or those who had not yet built or bought their own houses.

The enterprising Sikhs went in for contracts with the sawmills for hauling wood. The first such contract was executed with the Cedar Cove Sawmill. In the beginning they had the horses and buggies to haul the wood. Since 1918 they purchased trucks for the purpose. These truck-owners used to purchase the firewood from the sawmills and sold it to the users from house to house as the wood was burnt in the houses in those days. The sawdust also began to be used as a household fuel for cooking and heating purposes. Earlier the mill owners burnt the sawdust in the pits dug outside the mills. Now, a kind of funnel had been manufactured which could be fixed to the furnace and stove and the sawdust was burnt in it. The East Indians purchased trucks for their business. Most of the fuel dealers were single-truck self-operators. Some pushing and more enterprising people increased the number of trucks. Sohan Brothers in Burnaby possessed thirty fuel trucks. The Sikhs kept up visible presence in the fuel industry in Vancouver for many decades. By 1927 there were twenty-one fuel dealers in and around Vancouver and some five dozen of them operated in B.C.

In the early days about twelve Sikhs worked in the Cedar Cove Sawmill. Some of them worked in the Hemby Sawmills, Giroday Sawmills and Alberta Sawmills that were in or in the neighbourhood of Vancouver. Some of them worked in Robertson and Hackett Sawmill Ltd. These mills were located around the Granville Bridge. Robertson and Hackett Mill was on one side of the bridge and Giroday and Hemby mills were on the other side. These were the big mills and there were many small ones as well. The bigger ones had a variety of wood materials. The Robertson and Hackett Sawmill Co. Ltd. advertised "save time to get your building material in one place. There is a big advantage to you to get all your building material from one source. We are equipped to give you unusually efficient service because we carry 20 million feet of lumber in our yards and in addition have two huge warehouses stocked with such items as doors, shingles, interior finish, etc. We can give you prompt shipment by rail or boat direct from our mill or from our up-country retail yards at Kamloops, Penticton and Oliver."[1] This mill was established in 1888, in Vancouver, B.C. The above advertisement is quoted with a view to giving the readers an idea as to what type of material these lumber mills manufactured and supplied to the people. Some of the Sikhs always worked in this mill and helped the newcomers to join them. Similarly Alberta Sawmills also always employed the Sikhs along with others. The mill owners had good opinion about the performance of the Sikh workers. They had always one bunkhouse reserved for the Sikhs during the 1930s from which we can presume that at least thirty to forty Sikhs had always been working there during this period.

The East Indian mill workers got 30 to 35 cents an hour about the close of the first quarter of the 20th century. And also the records show that the Sikh workers at C.R. Lumber Mill, Golden, B.C. and Lumber Co., Savona, B.C. received from 2.75 dollars to 3.00 dollars a day in the year 1912. The new-comers or workers with less experience were paid $ 2.75 a day and the others $ 3.00 a day; that means for a period ranging between twelve and twenty years there was no change in rate of wages to the mill workers in Vancouver Island. These workers did not stick permanently to one place. They were always in search of better-paid jobs. They often changed their mills. They stuck to the same mills later when the mill workers formed their unions to fight for their rights— higher wages, seniority, medical coverage and some other such concessions.

Since during the early stages the main profession adopted by the Sikhs was lumbering they tried their hands at, taking on lease the operation of mills and logging camps or buying smaller mills. Because they had an experience of running the mills they purchased seven small sawmills and a couple of shingle mills in the Fraser Valley around Abbotsford and Chilliwack about 1915-16. These mills were, to start with, not purchased by individuals but in partnerships. The partners, who could be twenty-five or thirty, also worked in their mills. They did not get wages on daily or monthly basis like other workers. They shared or distributed the profits amongst themselves.

The East Indians were going headstrong into the lumber industry and farming. By 1922 they operated six lumber companies, seven logging camps, two shingle mills, fifty firewood distributorships and twenty-five farms in B.C.

In the third decade of the 20th century many mills were sold out by the white mill owners in B.C.'s distant areas because of the shortage of timber and moved to Vancouver Island where timber was available. Since the mills were sold at cheaper rates the Sikh dealers tried their luck at them, hoping that with their untiring efforts they would convert these deals into profitable business in due course of time and expand their financial opportunities which generally come the way of ambitious and risk-taking men. As a consequence a Sikh company became operative at Ladysmith and the Mayo Lumber Company was established at Duncan. Some other small mills also sprang up at other sites. Kapoor mill was set up at Barnet.

The owner of Mayo Lumber Company, Paldi, near Duncan, was Mayo Singh Manhas, born at village Paldi in district Hoshiarpur in 1890 in a poor Rajput family. In 1906 he came to Canada in search of an employment with little education. He started as a labourer on railways and sawmills and sometime later along with others he established a co-operative farming in Chilliwack, which was soon wound up. Gradually he worked out his way and built up in 1918 the most successful timber operation on Vancouver Island known as Mayo Lumber Co. Ltd., which included sawmill, logging and seasoning operations at McKay Lake near Duncan. A small mill town, named Paldi, after Mayo Singh's village in Punjab, grew up around the mill. Hundreds of men worked there and a large number of them were the Sikhs for whose regular religious service a small Gurdwara was built in 1918 and a larger one in 1928. Paldi town had its own school, a church, a Japanese temple, and homes for workers, community centre, a store, and its power system.

In due course of time Mayo Singh's Lumber Company business

became rip-roaring. He became a high substance Sikh industrialist in Canada. In 1925 he returned to India to find a spouse for himself. He married Bishan Kaur—a very charming lady, and returned to Canada the same year. In Canada he was known as 'modest Santa Claus' and one of 'the best known East Indians in Canada' due to his philanthropies down the years of his life. He gave a lot of gifts and donations to a lot of institutions for which he never sought or desired publicity. The long list of beneficiaries from Mayo Singh included St. Joseph's Hospital, Victoria (Canada); Royal Jubilee Hospital, Victoria; King's Daughters' Hospital, Duncan; General Hospital in Ladysmith (Canada); General Hospital Nanaimo (B.C.); Queen Alexandra Solarium, Mill Bay Children Aid Society (Canada); and B.C. Protestant Orphanage. He built a covered walk from the Nurses Home to St. Joseph's Hospital and it was known as 'Mayo Walk'. On his and his wife's birthdays he used to donate blankets, linen and one thousand pounds of turkey, etc., to every hospital for patients. He gifted a lot for the sick children and for their medicines wishing that no child should die in the dawn of his life. He gave a large amount to the Gurdwara at Anandpur Sahib (Punjab), for building a *sarai*. He gave lakhs of rupees to the educational institutions in the Punjab. He donated land and a large sum of money for a hospital at Paldi, Punjab.

Mayo Singh's wife Bishan Kaur, while on a visit to Punjab, died at Paldi in 1952, due to lack of medical attention. Moved by the irreparable loss of his wife Mayo Singh decided to build a hospital at Paldi so that no one else's dear one loses his or her life in the same way as his wife did.

The project of building the hospital was entrusted to Paldi village committee appointed by Mayo Singh and the Deputy Commissioner, Hoshiarpur. But no progress was made till he died in 1955 in Canada at the age of 65 due to separation of his most beloved wife, leaving behind four sons and two daughters. In 1956, Mayo family was moved to fulfil the wish of their late father. The project was taken up and the foundation stone of the hospital was laid by the then Punjab Chief Minister, Partap Singh Kairon, on 19 May 1957, and later on N.V. Gadgil, Governor of Punjab, inaugurated the hospital. Later the hospital was converted into Primary Health Unit.

A memorial bursary (scholarship) in the names of Cowichan Valley pioneer Mayo Singh and his daughter Joginder Kaur was established for the University of Victoria nursing students. His daughter was a long time member of the Cowichan District Hospital Senior Auxiliary.

The Mayo Lumber Co. Ltd. had three major ethnic groups—the East Indians, Japanese and Chinese, who had developed the township of Paldi.

They had lived in wonderful amity. The Mayo mill which was under the Sikh control had in its employment one hundred and eighty one Chinese, ninety-seven Sikhs, seventy-three Euro-Canadians and forty one Japanese in 1930. The close ties between the Japanese and the East Indians became most apparent during the 'sorry' part of Paldi's history when the war time Canadians regarded the settlement at Paldi, along with other Japanese-Canadian settlements, as shelters for potential spies and enemies. When Mayo Singh learned of the government order to evacuate Japanese families from Paldi he told the officials that he would take personal responsibility for the conduct of his friends and co-workers if they were allowed to stay. But none cared for his request. The Japanese were not released from the camps until 1947. By then the Mayo mill had closed down in their absence and the precious community ties fostered with neighbours and the spell of collective experiences at Paldi had been broken. The Paldi dwellers had dispersed in disgust. The place is now almost in ruins, houses and streets in total desertion. This author visited the place in 1991 and again in 1994 and found the Gurdwara in proper shape and functioning. On certain days, the Sikhs from Duncan, which is less than ten minutes' drive, come to the Paldi Gurdwara and hold celebrations there. This author found one Sikh family living there besides the Gurdwara *granthi*. One time pulsating township of Paldi now presents a ghostly spectacle, drowning the visitor into the morose and reflective waves that swept over the humming population of this hamlet that once enjoyed the warmth of the nature's protective hands.

Another prominent Sikh sawmill industrialist Kapoor Singh Sidhu established Kapoor Lumber Company, at Sooke Lake, B.C. near Victoria in the late 1920s. This mill had also a large logging camp at Shawnigan Lake. He had employed three hundred and fifty men in his mill and one third of them were the Sikhs. The workforce comprised the whites, Chinese, Japanese and the Sikhs; each one of the communities was in occupation of a separate camp. The mill had a store and its one-room school, which served the whole mill community. With the exception of two Sikh families all the Sikhs working there were single men.

The sawmill was situated in an isolated place. But it was provided with usual facilities attached to big mills, as bunkhouses, central halls, cookhouses, heating arrangements, washrooms, etc.

Kapoor Singh was a matriculate from High School Bajwara (near Hoshiarpur), Punjab, India and came to San Francisco in 1906. In search of employment he moved over to Canada and came in contact with Mayo Singh. Both of them, in partnership with some other Sikhs, bought a failing lumber mill in New Westminster in 1914. Through hard work they got some profit out of it and also gained experience of running a lumber mill. Later, both of them tried their luck in lumber industry separately and became very successful in this business. Both of them had blazing talent in lumber industry. They planned and moved on, never looking back. Only those people achieve their goals who ignore choice between the risk and reward.

Kapoor Singh was a highly cultured man with superior qualities of character and head and heart. Both Mayo Singh and Kapoor Singh liberally contributed to the Sikh community. They provided employment to the Sikh workers, always fought for equal rights, provided funds to the Sikh delegations sent to Ottawa to explain their problems to the federal government. They arranged lectures for the mill staff particularly on different aspects of Sikh religion. The Indian preachers visiting Canada or priests from the Vancouver and Victoria Gurdwaras were invited to the mill Gurdwara. Whenever India faced a disaster the mill workers raised money to be sent there for relief. [2]

Kapoor Singh had two daughters, who after having done their pre-medical courses from the University of British Columbia, shifted to the University of Toronto for further medical education. After becoming doctors they went to India and set up a hospital at their ancestral village Aaur, near Phillaur, in the present Nawanshahr district. Kapoor Singh was always a strong supporter of attaining higher education and equal rights for all. He was opposed to distinctions like 'a privileged class' and 'an unprivileged class' and was an advocate of equal status for men and women.

Another important Sikh community location was Hillcrest, four miles from Duncan (B.C.). At this place, Carlton Stone established Hillcrest Lumber Company in 1912. Soon after he employed the Sikhs in his mill he found that they were very hard working, honest, punctual and dependable people. From today they never mean tomorrow. They do not go to their work late or on time but in time. Such punctuality always abundantly pays a man in life. Lord Nelson, the great British naval officer and victor of the Battle of Trafalgar (1805) against Napoleon Bonaparte, told in reply to a question regarding the causes of his remarkable success in life, that he could not remember of any other thing except his always reaching the place of his duty fifteen minutes earlier than required. Carlton developed deep faith in the Sikhs. On their request Carlton built there a Gurdwara in 1935. Most of the Sikhs living in B.C. at one time or another had worked in the Hillcrest Lumber Company. So far as possible a job was not refused to a Sikh in that mill. In 1929 about 40 Sikhs worked in this mill. Later, at one time, the number of the Sikhs rose to about 70. Carlton had a heartload of goodwill for the Sikhs.

Besides the Sikhs, there were Chinese, Japanese and whites employed at Hillcrest. All communities were living in their separate bunkhouses. There were four Sikh families and all other Sikhs were living single. The owner of the mill, his manager and some whites lived there with their families. The owner of the mill had given some responsible jobs to the Sikhs and almost always accepted their suggestions in the day-to-day functioning of the mill. Carlton also valued their assistance in hiring men from the Sikh community. The Sikhs are straightforward and righteous people. Sycophancy is abhorrent to them as fearless persons never succumb to the demands from unethical 'superiors'. They rise in public esteem on the basis of their natural strength and performance. The Sikh workers felt that Carlton Stone represented the best qualities of the British race. He was a rose in the garden of thorns.

The *Guru Granth Sahib* installation ceremony in the Hillcrest Gurdwara on 7 September 1935 was very colourful, observed with all the decorum suitable to the occasion. The priest of the Vancouver Gurdwara accompanied by a large number of the Sikhs from Vancouver carried the holy *Guru Granth Sahib* through the steamer to Nanaimo from where they moved towards Duncan in the form of a big procession with nearly one hundred motor cars following. Passing through the streets of the town of Duncan the impressive procession reached Hillcrest. Many whites and members of the other communities participated in the procession and later ceremonies, making it a union of the East and West. The media extensively covered the gala procession and the ceremony.

The sizeable number of the Sikhs also worked in the following sawmills: The Dominion sawmill was located at the corner of Boundary Road and Marine Drive. About forty Sikhs worked there in the 1920s. The Fraser Mill, which was located in New Westminster near Maillardville, had between two hundred and three hundred Sikhs on its pay roll in 1925. Quite a fair number of them worked at the Industrial Timber Mills Ltd., Youbou, B.C. and the Bharat Lumber Company Ltd., Chase Creek, B.C. With the passage of time the number of mills grew and the growing Sikh population found employment in the mills. They could find work in the mills without difficulty because they had earned recognition and reputation as strong, efficient and trustworthy workers.

Union movement in Canada was an absolute need of the Sikhs who worked in the lumber industry. They had many problems including low wages as compared to those of the white workers, no promotions to higher-paying jobs and no security of service. All these issues had to be sorted out with the employers. Individuals could not achieve anything. Only the unions could make a dent into the hard attitudes of the mill owners.

Darshan Singh Sangha, a young and energetic Indian, made untiring efforts to unite these Sikh workers under the banner of 'International Wood Workers of America.' He was born in a Punjab village in 1919 to poor parents, in a peasant family. He intended to come to Canada to enroll in the University of British Columbia. His boat docked at Vancouver on his nineteenth birthday, 9 March 1938. He joined the university and later rose to an executive position in the International Wood Workers of America. He possessed a charming personality, was a fine speaker and a committed trade unionist. The East Indians respected his opinions and he was accepted as a leader of the people.

He says, "The first time I went into the mills to reorganize, I went to Mayo's mill, to Youbou and Honeymoon Bay. At first when I went into these mills it would seem that the only people that I could talk to were the ones that were slightly progressive. It was in 1944 that I began to inform people in-groups what the union was and what it would do and what its achievements are and why it is important to join the IWA (International Wood Workers of America). This is what I did in 1944 and 1945. Before that, in 1942 and 1943, I would go from one mill to the next mill talking to people individually. I would talk to those people that were militant and asked them to help me in this cause so that we could have small groups in these mills. My specific task for the first three years was to persuade the Hindustani people to join the union. Once I was offered a very nice job if I would agree to cease working with the union, in Mayo's mill, a job in the office (which I declined). The worker's trust and belief increased.... In 1946, the union gave the owners some demands: that wages be increased by 25 per cent, a forty-hour work week, time and a half for overtime and vacation time. There was to be union security, and union dues were to be deducted at the mill. These conditions being demanded by the union did not exist in any mill at this time.... There was (in 1946) a very big strike in B.C. and it was 100 per cent successful. I think the strike lasted thirty days." [3]

The Sikhs living in Canada always helped the newcomers in finding a job. They also helped their relatives who needed money urgently in face of an emergency in the family. Their fellow mill workers gave their cheques in time of such needs and this money was later returned to them when a person was in a position to do so. If in any mill, unfortunately, both parents died suddenly leaving behind small children, they were entrusted to some other family to raise them properly. They shared their sorrows and needs, thus decreasing their impact.

In the event of a loss of work because of the closure of mills, during the depression years, the Gurdwara committee advised the Sikhs not to ask for any relief from the government. The Gurdwara was there to help them in every way including the groceries and food of which the Gurdwara stores never ran short.

In true sense, in the early stages, the Sikh immigrants to Canada lived in a spirit of a joint family. When Bhag Singh, President of the Vancouver Gurdwara Committee, and his wife died with a gap of seven months in 1914, another family took care of their children. That spirit is deplorably missing now and the Canadian Sikh community is not so cohesive as it used to be half a century back.

In recent years lumber industrialists such as Doman and Asa Singh Johal have contributed considerably to the economy of the country and they gave huge donations to many institutions. The role of the Sikhs in promoting the lumber industry in Canada, particularly in British Columbia, has been remarkable.

I would like to give a brief account of the life history of Asa Singh Johal who rose from a humble mill worker to a big sawmill industrialist, a multimillionaire and a renowned philanthropist of Canada. It is the story of a man who rose to the top of the ladder, moving step by step, always looking into the aerial space rather than the mud below. It is a typical story of a man who attained eminence through grit and tenacity of purpose.

Asa Singh Johal received an honorary Degree in Law from the University of British Columbia (UBC) in 1990, an Order of British Columbia in 1991 and Order of Canada in 1992. He was on the Board of governors at UBC for two and a half years and a Director at Children's Hospital in Vancouver for seven years. He donated more than five million dollars to various institutions.

This account of Asa Singh Johal is based on the joint interview of Pritam Singh Aulakh and Balwinder Singh Brar with Asa Singh Johal and his wife Kashmir Kaur on 9 November 1999 at their residence 1026-W, 54th Avenue, Vancouver, and a write-up on Johal by Khurram Saeed, published in *Mehfil Magazine*, Burnaby (B.C.), October 1996.

Asa Singh was born on 17 August 1922 at village Jandiala in district Jalandhar, Punjab, India. His father Partap Singh, who had been working in Canada since 1906, had solemnised his marriage with Tej Kaur in the Punjab in 1920. Asa Singh was hardly one and a half years old when his parents moved from India to Vancouver in 1924 where his father worked as labour contractor. All the labourers lived in a bunkhouse but his father had a three-bed-room quarter adjoining the bunkhouse where they lived during 1926-27. He was doing well and he was one of three or four Indians who had cars.

Despite the fact that his father was well off financially Asa Singh had to join a second-rate school that segregated the visible minority students from the whites. The East Indian, Japanese and Chinese students had to go to a separate school because of racial discrimination. The visible minorities had to bear with it.

The East Indians knew that due to racial discrimination there was almost no chance of their getting a good job even after obtaining a fairly high education. As a result, their main concern was to look for a work and earn money. Asa Singh was not interested in learning and education and he dropped out of school after Grade-6, as he was mainly interested in making money. In the recession of the early 1930s Asa Singh's father lost everything. In around 1930, he moved to Whistler to find some regular work. The family lived there for six years. In 1936 Partap Singh shifted to New Westminster where he found work in the Canadian Western Lumber Company.

At the age of 14, Asa Singh got a part time summer job at the same mill where his father was working. A little later Asa Singh discontinued his studies and took a job, cleaning up around the plant of the mill, for 25 cents an hour. Soon after he was promoted as a lumber grader for 50 cents an hour, eight hours a day and six days a week.

In 1939 he purchased his first car for $1000. It was a brand new Chevrolet. At this time he was earning $100 a month, of which he gave $25 to his parents for his board and lodging and saved the rest. In 1940 he exchanged his car for a truck to start his own fuel supply business in which he earned $1000 a month, working more than 12 hours a day. A few months later he bought another truck and employed a driver for the same.

In 1948 at 26 he sold his business and left for India to find a bride. He married Kashmir Kaur, a 16-year old Punjabi girl. He had decided to sell his business and to re-establish it after returning from India as no body was prepared to care for it in his absence.

Because of his bitter experience of partnership in the Pioneer Fuel in 1955 he never entered partnership in his subsequent career. At the age of 40 (in 1962), he closed his business to find a new way to earn his livelihood. To the surprise of some people around him, Johal started the Terminal

Sawmills on Mitchell Island on three acres of land owned by his father, with the investment of $50,000. In the beginning , the mill started cutting 14,000 feet of lumber a day or 100 logs, with seven men in his employ. In mid-1990s Johal's mills would cut more than 400,000 feet of lumber, a day, or more than 3,000 logs and 300 lumberjacks were employed by him.

Since 1969 the Terminal Sawmills started earning considerable profit. In 1972, he purchased the Burke Lumber Company on Mitchell Island for $275,000. By mid-1970 Asa Singh became known as a wealthy industrialist.

In 1978, he purchased the Transco Mills located close to his first sawmill for $ 7 million. Soon thereafter he purchased property on the southern side of Ash Street along the Fraser River. In 1986, he purchased the Alan K. Lumber, out of bankruptcy for $ 11 million.

He established another sawmill in 1993 on the other side of the border, at Evertson (WA) USA, with 26 million US dollars, with the most modern plant.

Johal's income continued growing and in 1995 he hit $ 103 million in sales.

"The way things are going now, the timber supply is shrinking. His company plants more than 700,000 trees each year," Johal said in 1996.

Johal's commitment to donations on philanthropy started in 1990 when his youngest grandson, Rajiv, fell seriously ill and remained under treatment in B.C.'s Children's Hospital and recovered. The grandfather felt highly grateful to the hospital. "Healthy children are an asset to the country and when I see children in the hospital my heart melts," says Johal.

Since 1990 he has donated more than $2.5 million to the Children's Hospital including endowment of $1.5 million for research in cancer for children. In addition to his contributions to many organizations, he donates one hundred thousand dollars every year to the Children's Hospital.

Asa Singh and his wife Kashmir Kaur were among the 500 guests invited to the White House in 1996, on the occasion of the Children's Circle Programme where the donors to various children's hospitals throughout Northern America were to be honoured by President Bill Clinton and the First Lady Hillary Clinton. The Johal family was pleased to attend the function. He was also invited to similar conferences held annually, in Los Angles (US) in 1997, in Chicago (US) in 1998 and in Montreal (Canada) in 1999 but he could not attend any of these.

Johal donated more than one million dollars to the University of British

Columbia's (UBC) Forestry Department, most of the money in the form of scholarships to students of Forestry, and fifty thousand dollars for a chair in Punjabi Language, Literature and Sikh Studies, established at the UBC in 1985. He donated $1.6 million to the Indian Culture Centre of Canada, a Richmond Gurdwara that was built around 1993.

On 6 June 1999, B.C.'s Children's Hospital honoured Johal and his family and had put up a green chair in the hospital in their name and gave them a small green chair as insignia now preserved in his family room in a showcase.

Johal's two children—his son Darcy born in 1950 and his daughter Jiwan born in 1953, got their education up to Grade-12. For the last many years Darcy has been busy establishing his sawmills in Lithuania, bordering on Baltic, republic of USSR, 1940-91. He is trying to create his own lumber empire there.

Johal says that he wanted his grandchildren to start their careers from a scratch but he thinks he is spoiling them by providing all financial help and comfort without asking them any questions. He does not inquire as to what they were studying. He only bothers to pay their bills.

Johal is all praise for the pioneer Sikhs who had seen tough times and did wonderful things for their next generations.

He says that the total value of his business in 1999 could be around $200 million in sales.

Johal is a generous, unassuming, humble, hardworking, mellowed and a cool man. Today in the end of 1999, in his 78th year of life he looks after his wide-spread business and his word is the final in the major discussions of his company. He runs his business empire according to his own plans without much advice from outside. With a little education and almost no support, Johal was able to raise high fortunes, which he graciously shares with the needy institutions and individuals. He is a famous but not a hunted man. You can meet him anywhere.

The Chinese and Japanese who had been working in the mills side by side with the Sikhs, though slightly in weaker positions during the first half of the century, later changed over to other businesses and started paying more attention to the education of their children, who later found employments in almost all departments of the government and in all lucrative administrative positions. The Sikhs hardly came out of the mills and their children, with incomplete education, following them into the lumberyards, remained tied to the wood-logs, generation after generation. Even when the parents realized the importance of higher and vocational education for their children they could neither give them guidance themselves nor they could seek guidance from the right quarters. Hence they lagged behind in that respect and could not very much change from the blue collar to the white-collar jobs.

Farming

Most members of the first groups of Punjabi immigrants belonged to the Jat Sikh farming community. They had ample experience of cultivation of land as their ancestors had been doing it since ages. When they came to Canada cultivation of land was not a new vocation for them. They already knew how to make the land cultivable and fit to produce various crops.

These Sikhs had better knowledge of agriculture than that of the work in the lumber mills but they could not afford to purchase land and the equipment required for farming. Consequently, finding a job in a lumber mill became their first choice where they started receiving wages from the day they entered the lumber mill yard and without any investment, which was needed in farming. Thus, those who decided to take up farming started work as farm workers or tenants. They must earn money to be able to purchase land and thus, to start with, they took farms on lease or rent on partnership and co-operative basis. Later on, out of their profits and savings they purchased land to become owners of these farms. Though the land was cheap but the money was rare.

The Canadian people did not like the East Indians to enter the labour market, as they wanted it to be their own reserve. They had no objection for the Sikhs' to move to the farmland and develop new sites for cultivation. When Munshi Singh, a passenger of the *Komagata Maru* was sent as a test case before the Board of Inquiry, he was denied entry into Canada because he could not prove that he was not a labourer but a farmer. The Court of Appeal also upheld the same decision.

These farm hands from the Punjab worked in Abbotsford, Ladner, Kamloops, Pitt Meadows and some other places. The white farmers employed the East Indians at their personal farms and paid them fair wages as they found them hardworking and dutiful. Wherever they worked they left a deep impact of their physical capabilities on their employers. Those immigrant farmers who were not ambitious and lacked initiative continued working as farm labourers for decades together on very meagre wages and passed their lives in farm shacks as human vegetables. It was unfortunate that some of the whites who were impressed by the experience of these farmers expressed their inability to appoint them in their farms as they were foreigners, and it was a practice with them not to give work to those who were outsiders.

Some of the well to do Sikhs purchased farms in Mission and Chilliwack. Okanagan Valley also became an attractive place for the farming community. The Sikh farmers undertook fruit-growing and vegetable farming there. They mainly chose Kelowna and its surrounding areas for planting apple-orchards in particular and some other fruits in general about the mid-1920s. They developed the land, cleared the jungles and made it suitable for plantation. Through their hard and untiring physical labour and bending low on the hoe they turned wilderness into abundance. About half -a-dozen of them owned their own farms ranging from thirty to a hundred acres each. In the 1930s about a dozen more farmers joined them and finding their farming profitable more and more continued pouring into Kelowna.

Since 1930s was a period of depression, the work in the sawmills received a setback and some small businesses were closed, thus releasing the workers from the mills. During the harvesting season the unemployed people would go to Kelowna and other farming areas to earn their living. Kelowna and its surrounding areas including Vernon are still known for producing apples and mixed vegetables in large quantities that are exported to other parts of the country.

Kamloops was another place where some of the Sikh farmers found a comfortable haven in the mid-1930s. They had vegetable farms as big as fifty to a hundred acres and some of the Sikh farmers rented land for vegetable farming, which through their skill and industry was converted into a profitable business. Some of the Sikhs did farming in the province of Alberta as well. They, mostly, grew wheat for which the soil of certain areas was more suitable. They laboured on their farms wholeheartedly, making all efforts to have the maximum produce from the land. As farmers there is hardly any community in the world that can match them. They are deeply attached to their land and the hoe and to every little plant that they grow in their land. They can never tolerate their crops being ruined by anybody, may be the royal forces. They would come out to protect them, even by the use of force and even at the cost of their lives. The crops are so dear to the Sikh farmers.

About the middle of the century there were about fifty big farms under the ownership of the Sikhs in British Columbia. The farms in the Fraser Valley produced different types of berries and vegetables that were marketed in various towns and that accrued good profits to the Sikh owners. From 1970s onwards these farmers engaged labour contractors on certain conditions to supply labour during the harvesting seasons, especially when the vegetables and berries were ready to be plucked. The Sikh farmers dealt with the Punjabi contractors alone and the contractors dealt with the labour force. The contractors received payments from the farmers for the work done through their labour and made payments as per oral agreements made with the poor labourers.

The new East Indian immigrants, particularly the seniors, have no source of income immediately after landing in Canada and who are in search of work, are hired by the Indian contractors and taken to the farms at sunrise and brought back home at sunset. For the whole day they work on the farms, picking fruits, berries and vegetables. The contractors paid them at low rates under the threat that if they resent or object to low payments they would not receive records of employment that would enable them to collect unemployment insurance (UI) from the government. The farm labour contractors are supposed to pay the workers before the farmers pay them, in turn. But the contractors violate the rules and the workers remain quiet over it. The seasonal Sikh migratory labour comes to the Lower Mainland and to the Okanagan Valley from different parts of Canada to earn money and then to entitle themselves to unemployment allowance.

In a way, these farmers provide work to thousands of men and women who would be otherwise jobless because of language barrier and slump in the job market. Close to Canada, in California (USA) also, the Punjabis established themselves as very flourishing farmers. The Punjabis own about 90 per cent of the agricultural land and orchards around Yuba City. Didar Singh Bains, a resident of this town, is one of the richest farmers of America.

Some Sikh farmers have established large-scale dairy farms and they supply their produces to the near markets. Some of them set up roadside vegetable and fruit stalls near their farms and sell their produces themselves. The farmers are indeed a very hardworking community and they utilize every inch of their cultivable land to supplement their income.

Transport Industry

The Sikhs are known all over the world as very successful farmers and transporters. In cities everywhere the transportation is a profession adopted by the Sikhs as their first choice. They seem to have a special liking for driving automobiles.

In Canada too, in some of the big cities of the country the cab industry is controlled and run by the Sikhs. In Vancouver, the Yellow Cab Company, established in 1923, has been since decades, in the hands of the Punjabi Sikhs. This company has a large fleet of nearly two hundred cabs that are on the road for twenty-four hours. It has been generally noted that the Sikh operators are more disciplined, paying more regards to the rules and regulations of the company than those belonging to some other communities.

The whole operation is run in a scientific way. There is no hassle regarding the fare as all taxis are provided with the metres that keep showing the fare. Since the Sikh taxi operator is very hard working, he earns an average of $250 to $300 during his shift, exclusive of gas and other minor expenses incurred in connection with the car. The night shift drivers earn more as the other services of transportation are not so frequently available during night and secondly the club-goers travel to and from the clubs in the hired cabs alone as due to drinking bouts in the clubs they are not fit to drive their cars back home at mid-night. There is zero tolerance shown to a drunken driver. The police always wants the people to remember 'drink, drive, death'.

It is amusing to note that these law-abiding night cab-operators who are always at risk of facing the roughs of society are not allowed to keep anything like a weapon with them for self-protection while the offenders always move about with loaded guns concealed under their clothes. The police says that in the event of such a situation their help be sought. The criminals some times murder the cab operators and disappear in no time, and in all probability, the police will not be able to catch them. It is not understandable as to why the innocent victim is to remain unarmed and the offender freely moves about with a gun under his arm. Many night cab operators have lost their lives at the hands of these armed prowlers.

The Sikhs have successful taxi business in Vancouver, Calgary, Edmonton, Metro Toronto, Montreal, Ottawa and Winnipeg.

The cab operators have to work for about ten to twelve hours a day and, if they choose as the Sikh drivers generally do they work for seven days a week. Sikh taxi drivers are, by nature, more ambitious and money-minded than drivers are from most of the other communities. They put up more hours of work than others did. The whites earn and spend but the East Indians earn and save. The whites have a different attitude towards life and living as compared to the East Indians who care to make their progeny better off financially and they live frugally. The whites have, in that sense, no progeny to be concerned about. If the whites have enough for tomorrow they would suspend work today but the East Indians will go in for overtime. They hardly believe that Sunday means Sabbath day—a rest day.

But it is a matter of pride that the Sikhs seldom bring bad name to the community, whatever profession they adopt. They have a sense of Sikh community's dignity and honour, and noble traditions of honesty, responsibility, gentleness and dependability.

The cab industry that is mostly manned by the Sikhs is a very well organized public service institution in Canadian cities. In New York (USA) more than 10 per cent of the city's cabbies are Punjabi.

The Sikh drivers have also joined the transit system in all the big cities of the country. At present they have overcome the hurdle of turban and beard which earlier debarred them from even applying for the job of a bus driver. Due to persistent efforts of the Sikh organizations and arguing with the transit commissions on the plea of the government's policy of multiculturalism which declares that the members of all ethnocultural groups can maintain their distinctiveness and yet retain full access to economic and social equality, the Sikhs are accepted with Sikh symbols.

During duty hours they have been found capable of dealing with all emergent situations to the total satisfaction of the authorities. The qualities of a good driver—the courage, poise, presence of mind, swiftness in judgement and promptness in taking a decision, are inherent in the Sikh drivers.

A lot of the Sikhs are managing an independent profession of providing truck services in both light and heavy vehicles. These Sikh truckers carry loads from Vancouver to Calgary, Edmonton, Toronto, Ottawa, Montreal, Quebec, Winnipeg, Halifax, etc., and back and to distant parts of the United States and Mexico as an ambitious commercial enterprise. Canada is a land of distances. For example, the distance between Vancouver and Halifax is longer than the distance between Vancouver and Tokyo.

The Sikhs are very adventurous people and they drive their trucks on the highways covering thousands of miles in very inclement weathers to which they had not been used in their motherland, India. They are indeed marvellous people in respect of adjusting themselves to the conditions and circumstances in which they find themselves landed. Sometimes one trip alone keeps them on wheels for weeks together. Fatigue is alien to them and they seldom complain of the hardships they suffer in the course of their trips in the lands and among the people stranger to them. Trucking is a very desirable business with the Sikhs all over the world. Canada is no exception. When working locally the individual truckers pool their trucks and form a company. Sometimes these truckers own five or ten or fifteen trucks each and their company comprises forty or fifty or more trucks. The services of the Sikh truckers are always considered dependable, punctual and hassle-free. The Sikhs are, indeed, proud of their excellent services in all fields of their activities. Whoever has had any business with them is never disappointed. Rising equal to the expectations of the people is something practised by them religiously.

Real Estate

In all the big cities of Canada the Sikhs and Chinese own real estate business in particular. This business is very popular among the educated Sikh immigrants. They make good money through it. A few years earlier anybody could just enter the market in this profession but later those desirous of going in for this business were required to pass an examination conducted by an authorized agency and these days, in the B.C., it is done by the British Columbia University as it involves property dealings, big amounts of money, the banks and purchasers and sellers and the go-between or realtors. In education and passing tests the Sikhs are better than the Canadian-born whites.

The deal is struck between the parties through a realtor who gets commission for his services from the parties. Almost all types of purchases or sales are made through the intermediate agents. A realtor, sometimes purchases plots of land, builds houses on them and sells the same to the customers. At times he sells the plots to the people before or after these plots are developed for the construction of houses. He also arranges to sell the old built houses and gets his commission. This business is not always flourishing and prosperous as the occasional slump or recession in the market affects it adversely. The sale and purchase of properties get stuck for months and sometimes for years and the realtors become victims of reduced economic activity. Although the Sikhs, especially the Jat Sikhs are, by nature or instinctive inclinations not fit for real estate business or any business but they have proved themselves very successful realtors and businessmen in foreign lands. They are marvellously adjustable. They never do things half-heartedly as they put whole heart and soul into what they do and their work is never alien to their minds and in this habit lies the secret of an enduring success.

Police and Army

The Sikhs have been known as daring, brave and fearless and for these qualities they had proved their worth as first rank soldiers and warriors. In dealing with the roughs of the society the Sikh policemen would jump into hazardous situations not caring for their personal safety.

Colonel Eric John Swayne, governor of British Honduras, who had been in service in India, knew of the stuff the Sikhs were made of. After his visit to Vancouver in 1908 he wrote, "I asked some leading Sikhs at a conference to engage me twelve of their countrymen for the purpose of doing police duty at Belize, the capital city of British Honduras, as I had known the capabilities of Sikh policemen while I was in India." Despite the tempting terms offered to the Sikhs they refused to go to the unhealthy Honduras.

In its issue of 3 May 1945, *The Vancouver Sun* ran a story of the bravery of the Indian army as under:

Major Richard R. Tewson, Royal Artillery, speaking at a meeting of ·the Transportation and Customs Bureau of the Board of Trade, at Vancouver, said, "Indian troops are among the finest fighting men in the world. Indian army numbered 250,000 men. Of these the Sikhs had amazed Europeans by emerging as the finest dive bomber pilots in the world. We had tremendous co-operation from this army and there is no reason why we cannot have the same co-operation from the same people after the war."[4]

Despite this wonderful reputation the Sikh soldiers have not been in urgent demand of the Canadian army. In fact, Canada does not need big army, as they have no enemy to fight against. But as records show there had been a few Sikhs in the Canadian army. To quote one, Joginder Singh Manhas, signalman (K 812858) was released from the Canadian army on 5 November 1964, after a few years of service.

Now in 1990s there are some more people in the Canadian national army , air force and navy, some in the officers' ranks with turbans and beards intact. With the passage of time and the country's policy of multiculturalism rules have been liberalized and the Sikhs are fully eligible to join the army and the police in their Sikh form. In order to join these forces, as against the past practice, they have not to give up their faith and religious symbols.

The Sikhs succeeded in getting this change made in the dress code after a lot of efforts. In 1986 the Metro Toronto police allowed the Sikh police officers to wear turbans and other Sikh religious symbols during duty hours. About the middle of 1987 Royal Canadian Mounted Police (RCMP—the national police force) commissioner Norman Inkster recommended a provision for a baptised Sikh to be able to join the police force. Before this recommendation could reach the Solicitor-General Pierre Blais in June 1989 for further action, three women from Calgary started a vigorous anti-Sikh and anti-turban campaign. In Calgary the people clamoured loudly to 'keep the RCMP Canadian', displaying a picture of a

Sikh wearing turban in RCMP uniform with a line drawn across the figure. The anti-turban movement compromising on turban and other symbols spread to different parts of Canada. But this nefarious propaganda disheartened neither the government nor the Sikhs.

A Sikh delegation met the Solicitor General again to allow the Sikhs to join RCMP with turbans and other Sikh symbols. Prime Minister Mulroney supported the Sikh demand. On 14th March 1990, the Canadian Solicitor General announced in the House of Commons that the Canadian Sikhs would be able to joint the RCMP with Sikh religious symbols. On 11 May 1991, the first baptised Sikh Baltej Singh Dhillon was adorned as an RCMP officer sporting his turban and Sikh religious symbols at the graduating ceremony at the Regina Police Academy.

When a turbaned and bearded Sikh was allowed to join the RCMP in 1990 there were protests from some white racists that the permission to the Sikhs would negate and ruin the discipline in police force but the government, the law-court, the press and the sane Canadians stood firmly on the side of the Sikhs who eventually won. The court allowed the Sikh police officers to wear turbans and Sikh symbols. The Sikh culture and the Canadian white culture are not opposed to each other. They are pleasantly different. Young white Canadians are liberal and very tolerant to different cultures in the country but some 'oldies' are not.

At present, the Vancouver Police Department pursues its drive for recruiting visible minorities, particularly the Sikhs. The senior police officers come to the Sikh meetings and address them on the government's desire of the Sikhs joining the police force. The Sikh police personnel have been found to be more dutiful, efficient, daring and at the same time not without the milk of human kindness. They never behave heartlessly rather act with firmness and humaneness combined together as against the police of the developing countries where when police hauls up a person, he is not allowed to return home in one piece. There, the police behaves as torturers and not as protectors. In Canada preference for their recruitment is growing but the Canadian Sikhs are not coming forward in sufficient numbers as needed by the police department.

There were 54 members of the visible minorities in 1131 member Vancouver police department—20 Chinese, 19 Indo-Canadians, 7 aboriginals, 6 Japanese and 2 Blacks in December 1993. Prior to 1991 the Vancouver police accepted only Canadian citizens. However, the then new police chief Bill Marshall, took the major step of allowing landed immigrants also to join the force. Canada's policy of multiculturalism is opening doors into all jobs and economic opportunities for the Sikhs and others who had remained barred for decades after decades up till the recent past.

Education

In the second quarter of the 20th century some of the Sikh boys and girls joined the schools despite the advice of the seniors that it would not pay them in terms of jobs. Even after schooling they would end up pulling lumber in the sawmills and dishwashing in restaurants. They suffered political and economic disabilities and mental tortures even after a stay in the country for decades, by deprivation of the basic rights guaranteed to a country's citizen. From 1907 to 1947—for forty long years, they were denied the municipal, provincial and federal franchise in B.C. and as a result of that many professions were closed to them. They could not become trustees of schools and other improvement trusts and could also not be posted to the provincial public offices. The professions of law and pharmacy were also barred to them. Thus, education was no attraction to the Sikhs and consequently professions relating to education got outside their choice and as such education could not hold out any promise of a good and secure career to them.

We know a few names who were adequately qualified to get jobs in offices, schools or other establishments but they were refused to be considered. One Hazara Singh Garcha, who arrived in Canada in 1927 and obtained a degree of Master of Science in Agriculture, pulled lumber or worked on green chain like others who were illiterate. At that time, no Indian could get a job even if he was a lawyer or an engineer or a doctor.

The Hundal brothers reached Canada in 1913. Iqbal Singh Hundal got a Bachelor of Science degree in mechanical engineering from the University of Michigan in 1925 but could not get employment in Canada. He got a job as an aeronautical engineer in the U.S.A. His brother Jermeja Singh Hundal attended the University of British Columbia and then the Oregon State College but could not get employment in Canada and ultimately found work in Indian consulate's office in Los Angeles.

Ranjit Singh Mattu—a Canadian-born who graduated from the UBC in 1941 with a Bachelor of Arts degree in business and economics and was a national football player and a coach, had to work as supplier of fuel to industries. Canada had no respectable job for him. Ranjit Singh Hall graduated from the UBC in 1946, despite all the discouragement that he received from his sawmill co-workers. After 1947 when the ban on franchise for Indians was lifted he got a job with the federal government.

Dedar Singh Sihota graduated in 1949 with a Bachelor of Arts degree with economics and psychology as his major subjects. Later he got a degree in teaching and became the first Sikh teacher in Vancouver.

Mill owner Kapoor Singh Sidhu's two daughters—Jagdish Kaur and Sarjit Kaur, who obtained degrees in medical science from Toronto, went to India to set up a hospital in their ancestral village Aaur (Punjab), as their parents had desired.

After the 1950s some Canadian-born Indians got an education in law, medicine and engineering and through their merit, despite racial discrimination, could get jobs in Canada. Some of them after passing teacher's training courses joined the education department as school teachers and some, obtaining higher university education, became professors in the Canadian colleges and universities, some of them rising to the positions of chair-persons in their disciplines and deans of the university departments. In obtaining jobs they competed favourably with the whites—Europeans, British and others.

But the unfortunate part of it has been the clear and unconcealed prejudice against the Indian educated immigrants, however highly qualified they might have been, the preference was given to the Canadian whites in admission to the teacher's training courses and in the appointments as teachers. Despite all this we may find a small percentage of immigrant Sikh teachers in Canadian schools, colleges and universities. At present we have Sikh librarians, assistant librarians and restorers in the Canadian libraries as well.

The ire of the profession of education in Canada is that those Indian immigrants who aspire to be in this profession must pass through the Canadian system of obtaining and imparting education. Sometimes people with much higher qualifications and equally higher degrees of teachers' training courses from India are rejected simply because their education is not in accordance with Canadian system but they do not object to the British or European systems of education which are no less different from the Canadian system. They also demand Canadian experience. It is very unfortunate that the Canadian employers both in the public and private sectors follow closed shop practices and unfairly demand 'Canadian experience' despite the new immigrant applicant's adequate qualifications, as if the Canadian experience is available at a price from the super store. The applicants are wrongly told that their cases have been processed and found unsuitable and rejected. Sometimes their cases are rejected on the plea that they are over-qualified. These practices, to screen out the immigrants, are awfully unfair and unhealthy. Such employers must realise that their role is that of disservice and hindrance to the building of a strong Canada, through their unjust, fraudulent and racially discriminating attitude towards the new-comers who have adopted Canada as their new homeland.

Such unjustifiable prejudice cannot but belittle those white Canadians who under one pretext or another deprive the Indians of their rightful place in the social fabric of the country to which these immigrants genuinely belong. The code of discrimination is still closely sticking to some whites, while most of them are trying to shed off this evil and inhuman behaviour. But I am sorry to remark that this discrimination ingrained in the psyche of certain communities and groups of people is never going to be non-existent in all time to come. So we must learn to live with it.

Education Funding

The Canadian Society has always placed great importance on the post-secondary education. They came to realise in sixties that without the help of the parents themselves contributing to post-secondary education costs which are enormous it is very difficult for children to continue their higher education endevours.

Keeping this in mind some educationalists started scholarship plans which were deemed tax shelters in 1972. These are savings plans for post-secondary education. Parents save money through these plans upto child's age of 17 years. This plan matures at his/her age of 18 when the child graduates from the school. The principal amount returns on maturity and the child reaps the scholarship benefits (which include interest on the savings) for second, third and fourth years of education. Government also adds 20% on the first $2000, saved during a year per child, which is also used for child's education.

In 1983 a young Sikh man named Teshvinder Singh Chhachhi, a Business Management graduate and a great grandson of a prominent Sikh Chief Sir Sardar Nehal Singh Chhachhi, came to Canada and found that these education plans had great potential for the progress of the Indian immigrants and their future generations who could have the opportunities that they never had in India. He felt that there was a great need for these scholarship plans to be given to the Sikh families so that their children could go to colleges and universities without worrying about the cost. Mr. Chhachhi actively promoted these plans in his community and within a few years, with the help of his devoted team, he enrolled thousands of Sikh children in these plans.

Teshvinder Singh had a marvellous success in his enterprise. The company promoted him to be an Enrollment director in 1988. At the same time a new improved plan was launched which was called Heritage Scholarship Plan. Mr. Chhachhi's team in British Columbia became the company's best agency. Most enthusiastic persons on this team for the past 16 years, to whom he ungrudgingly owes credit for his remarkable success, have been his Associate Directors Mrs. Harleen Kaur Brar, Mrs. Mohinder Kaur Bhullar and Mr. Ajit Singh Anand.

Soon after, Mr Chhachhi was appointed by the Company as its Managing Enrollment Director for B.C. operations. His agency was given exclusive rights for British Columbia because this agency had become the best in the country for its operation. He enrolled the highest number of children each year ever since these plans were started in Canada.

Over a period of few years a team of five or six persons grew to over 400 people working for his agency which has attained the number one position and has been marked as the best and the most professional one in the country. Teshvinder Singh, with the help of his staff and co-operation of the registered children parents, had been able to give tens of thousands of Sikh children the opportunity to get post-secondary education, thus making them worthy, useful and very dignified members of the Canadian society.

Professionals

Besides school, college and university teachers there are some other categories of Sikh professionals in Canada that include doctors, engineers, information technology engineers and specialists, scientists, lawyers, notaries- public, accountants, pharmacists and nurses. Though the number of the Sikhs in these professions is small but they are represented in every profession. They are enterprising and gifted with a strong drive and initiative into new fields.

Doctors and Health Care

In the 1960s and 1970s the doctors with Indian qualifications settled in Canada without much difficulty. Later in 1980s the 'medical apartheid' came into being in B.C. The Canadian-educated and qualified doctors could straightway take up their profession, whereas doctors from India could not practice medicine in B.C. even though they had a degree in medicine. In 1991 they resorted to hunger strike and filed complaints with the B.C. and Canadian Human Rights Commissions but to no effect. These Indian-trained doctors had been required to have two years of post-graduate training, one year of which must be completed in Canada. The Indian doctors said that this requirement was discriminatory as medical graduates from English-speaking countries like South Africa and Great Britain were required only one year of post-graduate training.

President of the Committee for Racial Justice, Aziz Khaki, called the process a double standard and said that it was an example of blatant discrimination. "If there is a process, everyone should go through it," [5] he said. Steering Committee for foreign trained doctors spokesperson John Bitonti said that Canada was the only country in the world where doctors were discriminated against because of their place of origin. Forty per cent of the doctors in Canada were foreign-trained which meant that this problem was a recent one. In the 1990s about 97 per cent of foreign doctors, who applied for licensed practicing in B.C. were turned down, Doctor Bitonti told. [6]

Despite all the handicaps suffered by the East Indian doctors we have at present quite a number of them working in Canadian cities. There are family doctors, specialists and dentists running their clinics and many of them are working in hospitals and on the staff of other establishments. Some of them are very well known for their competence and high medical skill. There are lady-doctors who work as family doctors and specialists as well. The clientele of the Sikh family doctors is mainly from among the East Indians. The private practitioners have to be in competition with each other in the interest of their business.

According to the Revenue Canada's 1990 list of average assessed incomes, fees-for-service doctors including the East Indian doctors, were at the very top of the Canadian pay pile. In the fiscal year of 1991-92, 10 per cent of B.C.'s 6548 doctors, that is more than 600, billed the medical plan for more than $2,50,000 a year. Sixty-three of them billed the plan for more than $ 500,000 each and three of the doctors billed for more than $ 1 million each. The Prime Minister of Canada who fights long and hard to get into the Sussex Drive and who takes huge responsibilities earns $ 157,620 a year. [7]

Sure, doctors are well educated and they work hard but the same is true of many other less lucrative disciplines. Doctors may be important in their own way but what about the teachers who get about 40 to 50 thousand dollars a year? Are not the teachers as important as doctors and dentists in their own way? They shape lives and sometimes save lives. I would rate the teachers for worth way more than say the education minister. Do you suppose, I have said something unwelcome? If we desire a teacher to be more a nation-builder than a money-earner, cannot we expect a doctor to be a lifesaver more than a coffer-filler? Don't think I am uncharitable to a doctor. I am very grateful to his services but a little unconvinced of the income gaps between that of a doctor and a teacher or some one like him.

Nurses are also a category of professionals devoted to the service of suffering humanity and doing their utmost to alleviate the pain of the sick and the injured. Their services are remarkable but underestimated, under-appreciated and under-paid. Many Sikh women are engaged in this profession in the hospitals, nursing homes and in-home-supporting services. They are not only assisting the doctors in looking after the patients but also render the real service to the distressed and try to bring a ray of hope and long-forgotten smile on the face of the bed-ridden with no signs of recovery. Most of the Indian young women get education in nursing before their immigration to Canada as this profession is almost always in demand of qualified and experienced nurses.

Pharmacy is also an allied profession. It is a place where medicines are compounded or dispensed. The East Indian pharmacists have set up their drug stores and dispense medicines as prescribed by the family doctors. They also sell non-prescription medicines. They hold licenses to sell drugs. In order to obtain licence they have to pass a course in pharmacy from a recognized or affiliated institution. The pharmacists get medicines from the pharmaceutical companies at a discount and sell the same on a reasonable margin of profit.

The Sikh pharmacists generally engage the East Indians as drug dispensers or salesmen to facilitate services to customers from the Indian community. The pharmacists are employed in the hospitals also where they look after the stocks of medicines and supply or issue the same to the different sections or departments of the hospital.

Lawyers, Notaries-Public and Accountants

After 1947, the Sikh immigrants were allowed to join the law courses and qualified lawyers from outside Canada could also practise in this country. The children of the old-timers began to study law and adopt the profession but the Indian-qualified lawyers came into disfavour of the white Canadians. Those who came to Canada with a degree in law were not allowed to practise here. They were told by the UBC that their degree in the discipline could, at the most, help them to be admitted to the law courses along with the Canadian students.

In early 1990s, the law department of the University of Calgary told a Sikh law graduate from the Punjab University that he would be permitted to pass the complete law courses prescribed for a law degree, through correspondence courses and after obtaining the degree from the Calgary University he would have to work with a law firm in Calgary at least for three years before he would have the option to work independently and elsewhere in Canada. He did likewise and took a number of years to do the same. Such are the hurdles to which the Indians are subjected to keep them away from the profession. But still there are Sikh law graduates both men and women from India and Canada that are successfully practising law in this country.

Manmohan Singh (Moe) Sihota says, "Even in law, and I am talking about a decade ago now, if I wanted to phone a senior lawyer and ask him for advice on a particular file I could never find an Indo-Canadian that I could do that with. Today, that is not a problem.... In our era when you went to the Sikh temple on Sundays, men would talk about their experiences in the sawmills. When you go to the temple today you can kick the tires with other lawyers or other business people."[8] There are some law firms headed by Sikh lawyers established in Canada, that enjoy reputation for high professional efficiency. There was a Sikh law graduate who was elevated to the position of a British Columbia High Court Judge.

There are many Sikh law graduates from the Punjab who are working as notaries- public and accountants in the big cities of Canada where the Sikhs are living in large numbers. Most of the property transactions are done through the notaries. Some of them, starting from a scratch, have now set up big offices manned with quite a sizeable staff. They also help people in preparing and submitting their income tax returns and look to their allied problems. Sometimes they maintain and supervise the accounts of big firms and institutions. Some of these law graduates have specialized in immigration law and contest the immigrants' cases.

Politics and Politicians

As told earlier, from 1907 to 1947, the Indians living in B.C. were not allowed to vote in municipal, provincial and federal elections. This ban kept them outside the political arena of the province. They took long to get political awareness to be able to fight for their political rights and that fight took decades to get a right to vote. Thus, they had no participation in politics for forty years.

This bar on franchise was abolished in 1947 and there ushered an era of Sikh interest in the country's politics, and the candidates contesting elections began to approach the Sikh voters and their worth in the national life began to be recognized.

In due course of time, the Sikhs aligned themselves actively with the political parties and took part in the elections as candidates and as supporters of others. Politics for Indo-Canadians is not a 100-metre dash. It is a marathon race. To win a marathon race, it is necessary that one is sure-footed, remains cool and maintains a steady progress. As a result of this participation, they became municipal councillors, MLAs and MPs and rose to the positions of provincial and federal ministers, Attorney-General and mayor and shared power in the government. Naranjan Singh Grewal was the first Sikh elected to a city council in Mission, B.C. as early as 1950. In May 1997, he was the first Sikh Mayor elected to the city council of Mission. They were able to voice the problems of the minorities through municipal councils, provincial assemblies and the parliament. Dr Gulzar Singh Cheema, former MLA, Manitoba (elected in 1988), has put it emphatically that "Canadians of Sikh origin, have made tremendous progress in all aspects of life. Their achievements in public life are impressive and they have accomplished much needed respect and admiration in the mainstream community. Canada is one of the few countries outside India where during a short period of time, the Sikhs have reached a stage where being elected at all levels of government is no longer a dream but a reality. Canadians have shown their generosity and sense of egalitarianism by electing the Sikhs to represent them from the municipal halls to the House of Commons. All main stream political parties have established strong relationship with the Sikh community." Continuing further he remarks, "Many of today's political leaders have shown great courage of their convictions in responding to the Sikh community's need for representation at cabinet levels. The Prime Minister of Canada, The Right Honourable Jean Chretien, has given special meaning to the struggle, contribution and commitment by the Sikhs to this country by appointing Herb (Harbans Singh) Dhaliwal as minister of revenue."[9]

Gurbax Singh Malhi, a graduate from the Punjab University, and liberal MP from Ontario, along with (the present) federal Revenue Minister Harbans Singh Dhaliwal and former Ontario MP Jag Bhaduria made political history in 1993 when the trio became the first Indo-Canadians to be elected to Canada's parliament. Gurbax Singh with his hair and turban gave a new flavour to the House of Commons. In B.C. Manmohan Singh (Moe) Sihota, Harbhajan Singh (Harry) Lally, Ujjaldev Singh Dosanjh, and Satinder Kaur (Sindi) Hawkins are MLAs and Gurmant Singh Grewal is an MP from B.C. Gurbax Singh Malhi was again elected liberal MP from his old constituency. More Indo-Canadian names of MLAs from the other provinces can be added to the list in addition to the many municipal councillors from this community. They are performing their jobs wonderfully well. Now the community is no more left under-represented at provincial and federal levels.

It is just in place to give a little detailed account of Ujjaldev Singh Dosanjh. By becoming the first ever Indian rather the first Asian Premier of British Columbia—Canada's third largest province, Ujjaldev Singh Dosanjh, a Jat Sikh from the Punjab, has made history and carved out a niche in the B.C.'s hall of fame and has become an integral part of the Canadian history. He took oath of office on 24 February 2000. Before entering the powerful office of the Premier he had worked as Attorney-General and Home Minister of B.C. for four and a half years in the New Democratic Party (NDP) government and had been a member of B.C.'s Assembly for nine years.

At the time of oath-taking ceremony he said, "I started my journey on 31 December 1964, leaving India, little did I know, think or imagine that I would be standing before you being called Premier Dosanjh."

Ujjaldev Singh Dosanjh was born in 1947, in village Dosanjh Kalan, in district Jalandhar. After his early education at Phagwara (Punjab) he came to England from where he moved to Canada in 1968, where his life, in the beginning, was tough, awfully hard and uncomfortable. He worked as a janitor to start with. A little later he shifted to a lumber mill where his back got injured in an accident. He joined law course and obtained the degree of Barrister and Solicitor and started legal practice in Vancouver and also became social justice activist.

He has been a self-made man all the way. For his views he was beaten up allegedly by a Sikh with an iron bar in 1985 and had many stitches to his head.

During his pre-vote speech on 19 February 2000, he told that "a child from a dusty village in India can grow up to be the Premier of this great province seems a snap." He obtained victory over his rival contender Corky Evans for the Premiership scoring 769 out of 1319 votes. The Indian community in Canada took it as a matter of great honour and pride. Dosanjh is the 33rd Premier of a province created in 1871 and NDP's fourth leader in the past ten years. Some people think that as the first East Indian Premier 'he has a chance to improve the image of an immigrant group that is often misunderstood and has been repeatedly linked in the recent years to incidents of violence.' Despite his swearing in the name of the freedom fighters of the *Komagata Maru* some people point out that he was elected to lead the NDP and not represent the Sikhs. The Sikhs are capable, dedicated and sincere people. If they have a Sikh Premier in Canada today why not a Sikh Prime Minister tomorrow.

In the coming years, more people would be coming forward to actively participate in the politics of the country. The Indo-Canadians are passing through unique historical times. As seen above they are fast entering the decision-making agencies and active politics finding suitable berths in the provincial and federal ministries, showing their worth as administrators and dinning their voices into the ears of the governments.

At the government levels they pleaded for the protection of the ethnic cultures of the visible minorities and they would make a strong headway in breaking the cultural shell of the majority groups. The Sikh culture found its place and respectability in the Canadian society. It began to be realized that in the country's politics an active Sikh involvement was fairly significant vis-à-vis their population of above four hundred thousand people. The Sikhs currently in Canada constitute the same proportion to the country's total population as in India in the neighbourhood of 2 per cent. The Sikhs have their roots in a country that has the world's largest democracy and an advanced system of governance. The political experience of the educated Indian immigrants stood them in good stead in Canada. The political systems of both these countries are similar in many respects as they originated from the same British system. The East Indian immigrants had no difficulty in understanding and following the Canadian political system in which they could involve themselves without any problem and ado.

The Sikhs do not consider politics as a favourite pastime but a serious pursuit to enter the country's mainstream and meaningfully participate in its decision-making deliberations. Politics in the Indian community is a high form of calling, says Wally Oppal. The Sikh politicians do not deal only with their own community but they enlarge the sphere of their activity to engulf other communities or sections of the Canadian society but definitely not on the road to assimilation. Their cultural and religious distinctiveness will guarantee them their Sikh identity and the lack of this distinctiveness will bring death to their identity.

The politicians, the world over, are considered low in the estimation of the people as has been established by the opinion polls many a time. There is a new class of unprincipled politicians who function in opportunistic settings. They make false promises and have no qualms to tell lies. They sell dreams of rosy future. This is their pastime. All they have mastered is the manipulative politics of votes and notes. Hypocrisy is the hallmark of world's political culture. At the time of vote begging, they meet their voters with utmost humility but after the election they would never visit them for their full term, even in hours of their natural calamities, with a word of sympathy. They sometimes make indiscreet and contradictory statements, which they deny later. He is not a wise and tactful politician who says sort of unpalatable things today and can never take back or from which he cannot wriggle out next day. As soon as one chooses to withdraw from politics or is ignored by his party and the media, he ends up chasing his shadow to beat political isolation and ultimately rides off into his political sunset and oblivion. Fame in political life is utterly short-lived in this country. If you blink, you are going to miss the politician's moment of glory. Canadian politicians, though a much better lot, are sometimes no exception to the above observations.

In Canada, the voters eat politicians for breakfast if they once find that they have simply be-fooled them with false promises. They are always under a public microscope. The electors, here, have longer lasting memories and they do not forget and forgive their deceivers. The politicians and members of legislatures in Canada do not switch sides to receive extra-large chunk of the power cake as in India. They do not cling to their offices as a life-long business. When some genuine fault-finding finger rises against them they resign and quit politics. They do feel the pricks of their conscience. They do not believe that politics and power can open a magic door to happiness. Most of them, in fact, earn more when they are outside politics. It is exclusive to the Anglo-Saxon colonial masters, who had, once, been intoxicated with power and who had taste of authority in their blood, that they are not prepared to abandon politics that brings them power and authority. In Canada, as an instrument of election propaganda there is no practice of collecting mercenary crowds officially or by parties.

Some of the Canadian politicians are very intelligent and highly educated and qualified people but without any political antenna and not indulging in wheeler-dealer politics.

When an active politician, however corrupt, mean, racially biased or inefficient dies, it is a big news for the media but when the country's renowned scholar, an eminent writer or a prominent scientist or a professional dies, nobody cares to know about him and in most of the cases he passes away unnoticed, uneuologized and without a word of tribute. The western countries are also guilty of this indifferent attitude.

Engineers, Scientists, Technicians and Mechanics

Many Sikhs have obtained degrees in civil, electrical, computer Science and many other branches of engineering in Canada and found employment in the government and private sectors in the construction of roads, buildings and bridges and factories manufacturing diverse machinery and thermal plants and various other fields. Indian-qualified engineers had suffered a rough deal at the hands of the Canadians. They had to work in petty repairing garages, in small factories, manufacturing machine parts and in so many small works where illiterate persons would be as good as the qualified Indian engineers just to earn a living and the job satisfaction awfully lacked. The same treatment of these engineers holds true even today. Many Sikh immigrants, even those who were in professional and highly skilled technical occupations in their home countries have to take lower positions because of the lack of recognition of their qualifications and credentials by the Canadian governments and employers. The immigrants face difficulty in attaining recognition of professional status based on the past experience and achievements in their native country and their capabilities and contributions to their profession. The ridicule and downgrading of qualifications obtained in India leave lasting scars on the minds of educated and skilled immigrants. The long-term damage done to the individuals is beyond assessment. Some Canadian practices are far behind the time. These practices need urgent revisions to accommodate all the people of Canada.

Indian scientists have contributed to producing new and more useful appliances and tools through their persistent investigations and experiments. There are some scientists working in the universities and big research institutes in Canada. A lot of Sikh technicians are working in hospitals, laboratories, factories and research centres. They compete successfully with technicians of any other community or country.

The Sikhs are very efficient mechanics. They have set up their workshops in all the big cities across Canada. They have vehicle-repairing garages. They mend and fix all types of electrical equipment's, TV and videos, internal heating of houses, fans, stoves, refrigerators, etc. The immigrants are more mechanical-minded than education-minded. They seem to be more efficient and sharp in picking up and repairing faults in a big machine than correcting a small faulty sentence or a wrong spelling of an ordinary English or even a Punjabi word. The work situation in Canada has transformed their tendencies and mental attitudes to that effect. They feel that they can earn more through their hands than through the books they read. In their ancestral country India, these Jat Sikhs hardly undertake the profession of a mechanic or a plumber that they adopt with a notable success in Canada.

Banking

In recent years the Canadian Sikhs have paid attention to open banks and finance companies. The Khalsa Credit Union established in 1986, is a commendable Sikh enterprise, which in a short period, has expanded to its network of five branches with assets of over a hundred million dollars. Their business and credits are growing by rapid strides. The total staff comprises baptised Sikh officials. The depositors or shareholders have to fill up a form declaring that they are believers in the ten Sikh Gurus and the holy *Guru Granth Sahib*. This condition may be affecting the number of depositors or clients of the bank adversely but the Khalsa Credit Union is not going to compromise over the bank's total Sikh complexion. This bank assures all the facilities of banking as provided by other banks. Its Court of Directors, that takes all decisions regarding its functioning, is a democratically elected body. All its branches are, for the time being, set up in British Columbia and most of the Sikhs who intend to deposit money in banks patronize this bank in particular.

This bank may, in due course of time, open its branches in other parts of Canada where they can find enough number of depositors.

The hierarchy of this bank consists of the General Manager— controlling all the banks, branch managers, accounts officers and clerical staff. They provide instant service and despite the staff being typical Punjabis they have imbibed extra-politeness from the white Canadians— a quality which is most important adjunct to a successful business, especially in the western world.

A sizeable number of Sikhs, men and women, are working in other banks of Canada also. Every bank will, almost invariably, have at least one Punjabi official on their staff to deal with such Punjabi customers as have language problem, coming to have transaction with the bank. The banks have to do it not with a view to job equity but in the interest of their banking business.

Diverse Businesses

Some well to do Canadian Sikhs own hotels, restaurants and motels which are staffed by the Sikh men and women working on the jobs of cooking, serving, dish-washing and janitor services. In order to have good business the rooms, beds and furniture have to be kept very neat and tidy and other services up to an acceptable standard known to the users. Cooks and waiters are generally trained persons and the dishwashers, kitchen helpers, hotel workers and the janitors do not need any training and mostly they are from the new-comer illiterate women. They start from the lowest rung in respect of wages and whenever the business slows down the last on the list get laid off and they are referred to the unemployment office to get unemployment insurance (UI). All the hotels and motels managed by the Sikhs have the English speaking whites also on their reception and important service staff to attract customers.

Besides the East Indians the whites also visit these restaurants, though in small numbers, many of them to enjoy the Indian food which is much more spicy and tasty as compared to the western food. In these restaurants all types of food, western, Indian and East Asian, is available to the customers. The hotels and motels are a good source of employment for the freshly arrived East Indian women immigrants and it is next to finding work in the Sikh owned farms.

Some of the Sikh women continue working in hotels and restaurants for decades as for lack of knowledge of English they cannot shift to other vocations.

Since 1986, as a result of agitation by ethnic communities and immigrant women's and other human rights groups, the federal government has set aside special funding for English language training for immigrant women. Many women complain that these classes provide elementary lessons only that do not facilitate their entry into the labour market. Women's experience is, exacerbated due to sex segregation in the Canadian labour market. A female immigrant's first job in Canada, usually a low-skilled menial job, is treated as her Canadian experience and she is subsequently locked into similar kinds of jobs. Non-English speaking Sikh immigrant women take up employment that is low paid and without labour standard's protection. It generally suits the immigrant women's requirements as it can be fitted into their schedule of housework and childcare more easily than jobs with more rigid schedules. They do not have to use English as part of their work.

The East Indian women are recruited to industrial home- sewing, doing piecework in similarly isolated conditions within their own homes. They are also found in the lower jobs of manufacturing industries such as light manufacturing in textiles and garments, in plastic factories and in the retail trade. Frequently they are hired either by small operations owned by ethnic entrepreneurs such as small retail stores, super markets, etc., in the ethnic neighbourhoods or by large institutions employing dozens of workers with employees speaking the same language as the new recruits or employees. Occasionally in the garment industry if a woman shows initiative, works hard and learns a bit of English she may become an assistant to the supervisor. But most often women are confined to operating sewing machines. Men usually occupy the more prestigious positions, such as garment cutting and supervisory positions, and women are rarely promoted to them.

Women in the Indo-Canadian society are not given credit for their contributions to the development and enrichment of the Canadian society in areas like child raising and low entry-level jobs they undertake. They are the backbone of the low paid sectors, such as, caring professions and nursing. The Indo-Canadian women need to acquire a position in the household that will enable them to address their concerns. There is a discernible lack of choice for women in various areas of the household, finances, decision-making and many more as these areas have been traditionally male-dominated.

There are many travel agencies managed by the Sikhs and other Punjabis in the big cities of Canada. Thousands of the Punjabis who go to India every year purchase tickets from these agencies. As compared to the travel agencies run by the whites the rates of the Indian travel agents are comparatively low and competitive. Their services suit the Punjabi passengers. Language barrier keeps most of these passengers away from the English agencies. The Punjabi travel agents talk to their passengers in Punjabi and, as far as possible, they try to accommodate them in respect of their demand for a seat on a particular date or a particular flight.

Some well-built men, retired from the Indian army or police, are able to secure jobs as security guards in the offices, factories and stores. A workable knowledge of English may be necessary for such jobs.

Many of those who got their education in Canada right from the beginning and are able to match with others in merit can find jobs in government offices, telecommunication, railway, immigration and many other departments of the government.

There can hardly be a department not open to the Sikh citizens of Canada despite racism working stealthily or latently. They have only to compete with vigour and assert for their right to equal opportunity for their economic prosperity through jobs and businesses.

The East Indians generally man a large number of gas stations owned by the Sikhs. Small grocery stores are also attached to these gas stations that meet the simple needs of the travellers who stop there for getting gas for their vehicles. These stores generally provide coke, biscuits, juice, milk, coffee and so many other things of every day use. These stores are also a good source of income to the proprietors of the gas stations. Some of them own many gas stations. In the adjoining USA some of the Sikhs own a large number of gas stations each. Just to name one, Darshan Singh Dhaliwal is known as gas station king in Milwaukee (USA).

Those abroad have , by and large, established a good reputation for themselves even in hi-tech areas. Indians abroad are, undoubtedly a big success. Whether they are working in sophisticated sectors of medicine, computers, space-technology or as entrepreneurs in far off places in the USA, Canada and other global centres, they have made a mark. Back home, they have not been able to get the right kind of professional atmosphere for them to show their talent, drive, dynamism, discipline, hard work and overall entrepreneurial qualities.

Many East Indian immigrants, who entered the USA and Canada with a few dollars in their pockets became multimillionaires and billionaires in a few decades. We may include in them Chain Singh Sandhu, an industrialist, owner of NYX Inc., Detroit (Michigan), Jassie (Jaswinder) Singh, owner of electronics and Computer Software concerns in California and Jay Chaudhry, a businessman (USA) and Asa Singh Johal, Vancouver (Canada). Many such East Indians have created a prominent niche in these countries' economy and Hall of success through their indomitable spirit and unlimited dedication to work and right application of talent. Indian brain is among the most fertile and sharp in the world. We must find out why Indians could do so well abroad but not in the land of their birth.

The Sikhs are running stores that deal in groceries, cloth, crockeries, videotapes, music cassettes, photography, foodstuffs and a variety of other commodities. Indian sweets are also available in some shops. There are many gold and jewellery shops of the East Indians. The Sikhs own very large warehouses hoarding all kinds of construction material. They are also proprietors of large furniture and carpet stores in Vancouver, Toronto and in many other cities. The carpets are mostly imported from Belgium. The middle class furniture is manufactured locally in big cities of Canada and the high quality furniture is imported from Europe especially from Italy. In Greater Vancouver quite a number of big stores of these articles are owned by the Sikhs. The Main Street Punjabi market (Vancouver) that abounds in groceries, cloth, foodstuffs, etc., is exclusively in the hands of the Sikhs. Similarly there is a Sikh shopping centre or Mall in Surrey. The Punjabis own mega community halls that can accommodate thousands of people assembled to celebrate marriage parties or other functions.

The Indian-Canadian community made the most significant progress in the business sector during the last couple of decades, particularly in small businesses, especially in terms of creating jobs, higher in Greater Vancouver than perhaps in central Canada, through their skills, entrepreneurial abilities and hard work. They are never satisfied being under-achievers.

From the above study it is easy to conclude that there is hardly a profession or vocation that falls outside the reach or interest of the Sikhs. They have always and successfully tried their hands at multifarious works as a means of just earning livelihood, to start with, and later a decent living. They save even from the little they earn, for the rainy day. They are instinctively so disposed. In business, with the first step secured they proceed further.

Economic Contribution to Canada

The transformation of the Punjabis from a cheap source of labour to the creators of wealth is a remarkable story of human tenacity.

Through all the professions practised by the Sikhs as discussed above they have contributed to the country's economy in their own ways. The lumber industry, farming, transport, business, real estate, banking and the various vocations discussed in this chapter were productive of wealth that bettered the economic condition of the people.

The Indian immigrants have always paid more in taxes than they received in services. In comparison, the Canadian-born families pay less into the treasury in taxes than they use in services. Bluntly putting, the immigrants subsidize the Canadian-born population rather than burden them. They have been out-performing the resident-borns in terms of production that promotes the country's economy. Of late, we notice their shift from farms and lumber mills to the commercial and business enterprises, comparing favourably with other communities.

Indian-trained engineers, doctors, scientists, lawyers, nurses, etc., studied on the resources of India but their services were utilized by Canada—thus draining Indian talent to this country without spending anything on their education and training.

In permanent migration of technically trained professionals from less developed countries to more developed countries India suffered the most. The USA and Canada where most of scientific research takes place attracted bulk of India's best talent for which their native country received little or no return for the highly qualified, quality intellectual products. Imported human capital has made Canada and the USA the richest nations. The factors that compel the highly trained personnel to leave India include inadequate career growth opportunities, limited application of the acquired knowledge, unsatisfactory living conditions, lack of recognition and over-bossing bureaucracy.

It is a well-known fact that failure to recognize and reward true talent and merit pushed many scientists, professionals and scholars from India to western countries. Those who look beyond their own country for future advancement can be placed in two broad categories: The first category represents people of high calibre for whom the right opportunities do not exist in India. In the second category are those who have difficulty in finding a suitable opening within the country on the strength of their qualifications. Some people wrongly believe that brain drain is unnatural, anti-national and unpatriotic. An expert on the subject has drawn an apt analogy saying that, as water seeks its own level, people seek economic parity by migrating. As long as economic sense prevails people will continue to migrate within their own country and outside.

To some there is the ever-present spectre of unemployment which drives people to seek jobs outside the country. The lure of dollars may not be as much a reason to migrate as the corruption in India. Even the university toppers fail to get jobs without proper contact or bribing the selectors. One is made to work in humiliating conditions, where initiative and ideals are rewarded with frequent explanations, transfers, suspensions and even dismissals. Let us remember that no one wishes to leave ones country, relatives and friends and live amongst strangers, in a different, sometimes hostile, socio-cultural environment only for the sake of monetary gains. It is social discontent and professional frustration that compels one to leave ones near and dear ones.

When Indira Gandhi, Indian Prime Minister, complained about brain drain to the former Indian ambassador to the USA, Abid Husain, he quipped: "Brain drain is better than brain in the drain."

India's loss is certainly Canada's gain. This is a tremendous economic advantage or profit to Canada at the cost of the Indian immigrant's mother country. By attracting high-ranking professionally qualified and skilled people from the developing countries the western countries are committing a brain robbery.

Towards the end of 1994 the Canadian immigration minister proposed a dramatic cut of at least fifty thousand in Canada's annual immigration intake. But more immigrants mean more consumers and a boost to the economy. The advocates of increased immigration say, "A big population means increased domestic markets for our industries. A large home market permits manufacturing firms to undertake longer, lower-cost production runs and it broadens the range of industry we can take economically; for both these reasons, population increase in turn improves our competitive position in the markets. A bigger population also yields lower per-capita costs and stimulates the development of more specialized services."[10] Canadians must overcome their resistance to new-comers in order to meet future workplace needs and improve economic development. If Canada is to meet its requirements in future, its immigration policy needs a renewed economic focus. To rise equal to that position and meet the looming challenge to the country's economy, perhaps none are better than the Sikh immigrants. So their sustained immigration will enable Canadians to strengthen the size, composition and structure of the population and ensure an adequate supply of workers for the future. The Sikh immigrants are a richness that the country can economically benefit from. They must have their place in the economic set-up of this land to see them and the country in full bloom. Can majorities learn to value the contribution to national life of small distinct minorities? The Sikhs are indeed a unique community and none can match them in hard work, industry and devotion to duty which are gifts they have conferred upon Canada where they came to start new lives.

REFERENCES

1. Sarjeet Singh Jagpal (quoted), *Becoming Canadians*, Harbour Publishing, Vancouver, B.C. p.60.

2. *Ibid.*, p.70-71.

3. Sarjeet Singh (quoted), *op.cit.*, pp. 143-44.

4. *The Vancouver Sun*, 3 May 1945.

5. Stephanie Troughton, 'Medical apartheid', *The Vancouver Echo*, 10 July 1991.

6. *Ibid.*

7. Barbara Yaffe, *The Vancouver Sun*, 26 January 1994.

8. Surj Rattan, 'one hundred years', *Mehfil*, December 1977, pp.44-45.

9. Gulzar Singh Cheema, 'Contribution of the Sikhs in the Canadian Politics', *Canadian Sikh Centennial Celebrations Souvenir*, Vancouver, 1997, pp.33,34.

10. Victor Malarek, *Haven's Gate—Canada's Immigration Fiasco*, Macmillan of Canada, Toronto, 1987, p.33.

CHAPTER 10

THE KHALSA DIWAN SOCIETY, VANCOUVER — A POWERFUL INSTITUTION

Presumably the Khalsa Diwan Society, Vancouver, got its name from the Khalsa Diwan formed at Amritsar in 1883, jointly by the Singh Sabhas of Lahore and Amritsar. The sponsors of the Khalsa Diwan Society, seem to have a very clear picture of the programmes of the Singh Sabhas and the Khalsa Diwans and later the Chief Khalsa Diwan (formed in 1902). The Singh Sabhas and the Khalsa Diwans aimed at introducing Punjabi in *Gurmukhi* script, founding of new Khalsa schools and colleges, propagating Guru's mission, to do away with Brahmanical rituals, publishing books, journals and newspapers in Punjabi, making translations of the sacred works and inculcating pride in the Sikh youth in their tradition and history.

The Khalsa Diwan Society went further in some respects. The Punjab Singh Sabhas and the Khalsa Diwans worked in unison with the British rulers. They had no row with the government. But the Canadian Sikh or the East Indian immigrants had a clash with the majority groups and also the Canadian government over very vital issues that threatened the very existence of the East Indian immigrants. They were deprived of their rights to vote and debarred from bringing their families to Canada and were given utterly discriminating treatment in respect of housing, job opportunities, many civil rights and immigration laws.

For decades together the Khalsa Diwan Society worked as the sole representative body of the East Indians in the dominion of Canada. This society took upon itself to fight against all the difficulties that confronted the Indians—the Sikhs, the Hindus and the Muslims, relating to political, economic, social and religious problems.

Establishment of the Khalsa Diwan Society

The Khalsa Diwan Society, Vancouver, came into being on 22 July 1906, with the special efforts of Bhai Arjan Singh Malik. It was registered on 13 March 1909. Bhai Sewa Singh was its first president, Bhai Bhag Singh, first secretary-cum-treasurer and Bhai Bhola Singh second secretary and accountant. Sant Teja Singh, who arrived in Vancouver in October 1908, helped in framing certain important rules for the functioning of the Gurdwara in Vancouver. These rules formed the basis of the constitution of the Khalsa Diwan Society.

Constitution of the Khalsa Diwan Society

The corporate name of the society was 'The Khalsa Diwan Society'. The above office-bearers were to constitute the executive committee of the society until the first general meeting of the society was held. The future annual general meeting of the society was to be fixed on the first Sunday of April each year or at such other time as might be decided by a majority vote of the members present at any meeting. At the annual general meeting an executive committee consisting of five members was to be elected as president, secretary, treasurer, second secretary and accountant as referred to above. The executive committee could appoint additional members if needed and the management of the affairs of the society was vested in the executive committee. The society could be dissolved by resolution of a general meeting supported by the vote of a majority of the members of the society present at the meeting.

The objects of the society were:

a) To appoint ministers of the Sikh religion to officiate in B.C. and elsewhere,

b) to appoint missionaries of the Sikh religion to attend to scattered Sikh people in B.C. and elsewhere,

c) to manage the affairs of the Sikh temple at 1866, second Avenue, west, Vancouver.

The above constitution was approved and signed by the society's president Sewa Singh before a commissioner for taking affidavits within British Columbia, in the matter of the 'Benevolent Societies Act' and Amending Acts and in the matter of 'The Khalsa Diwan Society' (in the Dominion of Canada, county of Vancouver, Province of British Columbia) on 13 March 1909.

Rules and regulations for the management and conduct of the property and business of the Khalsa Diwan Society or any branches thereof were framed and approved on 7 February 1915, at a meeting. These were signed by the president and secretary, on 12 February 1915, and got registered in Victoria on 23 February 1915. These regulations comprising 51 items included, in detail, the objects, membership, meetings, voting by members, office bearers, etc., of the Khalsa Diwan Society.

The members of the society could be active or associate ones. Active members had to contribute one dollar per month towards the general fund of the society and the associate member was to contribute fifty cents per month. Only the active member had the right to vote at all general, special, annual or ordinary meetings of the society provided he had made full payment of his contribution, at least a day before the date of such meeting. The executive committee had the power to admit or refuse any applicant as either an active or associate member of the society. The committee could also reduce the privileges of any active members to those of associate members. For holding a meeting seven days notice to its members was necessary. To transact business a quorum of 25 members was essential.

The executive committee was to hold its meetings every three months at 1866-Second Avenue West, Vancouver, or at any other agreed place. If any other society desired to merge with this society it could do so by surrendering all the rights and privileges of that society to the Khalsa Diwan Society, Vancouver.

The society later named itself as 'Khalsa Diwan Society' deleting 'The' before its name. Through an extraordinary resolution passed on 13 January 1924, the society decided to hold election of the committee in future at the occasion of the anniversary celebration of the birthday of Guru Gobind Singh in place of first Sunday of April.

Through an extraordinary resolution passed on 13 February 1932, it was decided that the monthly dues (subscription for membership) should be reduced from $1-00 to 50 cents and from 50 cents to 25 cents on account of very hard times. This was only for the year 1932. Vide an amendment No. 53, made on 19 February 1933, the members of the executive committee, were required to pay one dollar a month and the other members were to pay only 25 cents a month.

Through an amendment No. 58 it was passed on 19 February 1933, that the body and existence of the Diwan (Khalsa Diwan Society) and the temple be kept functioning as long as there were even forty Sikhs in the province of British Columbia. A majority vote could not take any other action contrary to the above in this clause and if and when the temple was finally to be dissolved the cash and the property should revert to the ownership of the Shiromani Gurdwara Prabandhak Committee, Amritsar,

Punjab, India. The said property and cash could not be used for any other purpose.

By an extraordinary resolution passed unanimously on 18 June 1933, at an extraordinary general meeting of the members of the Khalsa Diwan Society, the by-law no. 58 of February 1933, which had reference to the transfer of the property of the temples to the Shromani Gurdwara Prabhandhak Committee, Amritsar (India) was revoked.

The members of the executive committee of the society were designated as directors of the society. In the early stages the directors were mostly mill workers or lumbermen, fuel dealers and farm workers who had lacklustre personalities which seemingly were not as tall as their interest in the work and sincerity for the community. Almost all of them were illiterate people who could not even properly put their signatures on the papers even in their own mother tongue script. Despite all such handicaps it was really great of them to have managed their community affairs so well. Literacy is indeed a great asset but illiteracy is not so great a drag as to deprive a man of his inherent intelligence and commonsense. Those illiterate Sikhs generally took very intelligent decisions that served the interests of the community in the best possible manner.

Some vital changes were effected in the constitution in 1942 and 1952, which resulted in creating unpleasant relationship between the principal Khalsa Diwan Society, Vancouver, and its branches. In due course of time, say from the 1960s onwards, educated and skilled men and professionals started coming to Canada. As a result, the Khalsa Diwan Society began to have on its executive committees doctors, engineers, realtors, teachers, accountants, office workers, mechanics, insurance agents, besides well- positioned skilled workers in the mills and factories.

From time to time the amendments in the constitution of the society continued to be made to bring it closer to the tenets and practices of Sikhism.

Through extraordinary resolutions passed on 28 September 1969, the Khalsa Diwan Society decided that the name of this body could be called 'The Society' where needed. And pursuant to the 'Societies Act' the society altered its objects which in future would aim to foster the spirit of fellowship and brotherhood amongst followers of Sikh religion and would create a spirit of goodwill with their fellow Canadians of all creeds, races and religions. They would instruct the children and youths of the Sikh community in the language of their ancestors and in history, philosophy, culture, heritage of the Sikhs and India as a whole. They would run schools for the purpose as elucidated in the aforesaid objectives. They were also to encourage the physical fitness of the children and the youth, and work for the moral, religious and social welfare of the members of the society.

The constitution of the society was modified and redrafted again and again, making it every time more comprehensive, defining the procedures of election, duties, responsibilities and powers of the office bearers or the directors of the society. Every time it was the object of these people to make the rules Sikh-oriented, as far as possible, but at the same time not partisan or against any other religion. These amendments included the ones for which resolutions were passed in the meetings of the society on the following dates: 5 December 1971, 20 June 1975, 27 January 1977, 30 December 1979, 27 December 1980, 18 October 1981, 31 December 1983 and 15 February 1986, some of which were got registered with the government and some of them got held up for disputes over them, as some of the changes effected in the constitution in 1952 and 1969 were not acceptable to many members of the Sikh *sangat*. The space here does not permit detailed discussion of the various items of the constitution and the innumerable amendments made through extraordinary resolutions.

The large number of amendments passed in 1969, 1986 and detailed redrafting of the constitution in October 1993 are available for study. In 1978 the executive committee of the Khalsa Diwan Society, Vancouver, was elected for the first time by a ballot voting system.

Through a special resolution passed in accordance with the by-laws of the society on 18 October 1981, it was resolved to amend by-laws of the Khalsa Diwan Society, Vancouver, B.C. Section 5 of Chapter X to be replaced as follows:

"Smoking, drinking, gambling and card playing shall strictly be prohibited in the boundaries of the Gurdwara and signs relating to it shall be displayed in the boundaries of the Gurudwara. Persons entering inside the temple in the presence of Sri *Guru Granth Sahib* ji, with shoes or uncovered head or under the influence of any kind of liquor shall strictly be prohibited. The executive shall have full powers and responsibility to enforce these conditions". In 1970 it was officially endorsed that in future the term 'the society' might be used for the Khalsa Diwan Society if and where needed.

All such special resolutions had to be sent for endorsement to the Registrar of Companies, Victoria, as these could be effective only with effect from the date the Registrar signed or accepted them. The incorporation number allotted to the Khalsa Diwan Society was 216 Soc or S 216 under which the society functions and corresponds with the government even today.

A special resolution was passed in accordance with the by-laws of the society on 31st December 1983, that the constitution of the Khalsa Diwan Society, Vancouver, B.C., relating to section I of the aims and objects, article-II of the constitution, be amended by deleting the same and substituting, therefore, as a new section-I as follows:

"To promote the teachings and philosophy of the Sikh religion as contained in Sri *Guru Granth Sahib* and in the writings of ten Gurus (Sri Guru Nanak Dev Ji to Sri Guru Gobind Singh Ji) and also to observe, maintain and promote Sikh religion and its traditions in accordance with the Sikh *rehat maryada* (the Sikh way of life) published by the Shiromani Gurdwara Prabandhak Committee, Amritsar, Punjab, India."

Through a special resolution on 23 April 1986, it was resolved that the constitution of the society be amended by deleting the words 'Sikh Temple' in object number 4 and substituting in their place the word 'Gurdwara', later Gurdwara Sahib. Many changes in the constitution and its by-laws were made in 1986.

The constitution was largely improved by amendments in 1993. It was made very exhaustive and comprehensive, discussing the society's purposes, membership (eligibility, qualifications and requirements) term of membership, rights and obligations of members, loss and restoration of membership, meetings of members, quorum, adjournment, voting, minutes of meetings, election of the executive committee, etc. These resolutions and by- laws were passed by the society on 30 October 1993, and were got registered in Victoria on 8 November 1993.

Financial Structure of the Society

In the early stages, the receipts or income of the society comprised the membership fee of the society's constituents and the donations of the Sikhs. Almost always the accounts of the society were kept above board and annually audited by the chartered auditors. During the early period the income of the society was low and so were their expenses. The statements were divided into two parts, receipts and disbursements.

Earlier disbursements included various items as *langer*, light, heat, water, office expenses, phone charges, religious books, etc., and in the later stages more items came to be included as *dharam prachar* (missionary work), Punjabi school, stationery and printing and postage, newspaper subscriptions, contributions to certain funds raised for India.

From the brief chart below we can discover regular rise in income and often rise in disbursements of the society, despite many handicaps.

Year	Income	Disbursement
1923	$10,424.58	$ 9,014.76
1925	$13,649.22	$12,989.02
1931	$17,413.56	$ 7,837.94
1967	$18,494.13	$11,106.70
1969	$28,123.22	$18,883.26
1974	$100,924.10	$99,815.94
1981	$442,886.00	$449,583.00
1986	$674,221.00	$723,826.00
1996	$2863,645.00	$2980,291.00

From the above figures we notice that until 1974, the expenses were kept below the income and with effect from 1981 disbursements were above the income, presumably due to more ambitious development plans of the society. The Sikhs gave donations generously whenever there was an appeal for money from the Gurdwara rostrum.

In the early stages the number of the contributors was very small. From 1908 to 1941 it fluctuated considerably. The population of the Sikhs was limited, hence their donations. The offerings made at the Gurdwara had a notable upward rise with the increase of the Sikh population in B.C. With the passage of time there was a remarkable rise in the financial position of the Sikhs because of their lucrative professions and higher educational accomplishments.

From 1904 to 1908 the number of the East Indians rose to 5185 and in 1911 the number fell down to 2342. In 1915, the number of the Sikhs dwindled to 1099 and in 1918; it came down to 700. The census of 1921 showed their number as 951 and in 1941 there were 700 Sikh men and 165 Sikh women over 19 years of age. So it is difficult to imagine how with this small Sikh population they maintained their society and the shrines. Even when their number was reduced so low they were never disheartened. Undoubtedly, the flame of faith in their religion burnt within them more florescently than it does today. The income suffered reduction when the job opportunities of the Sikhs declined. But their spirit for offerings to the society remained undiminished. That spirit was matchless. The Sikhs should be measured by the size of their hearts and not by the size of their bank accounts.

The Khalsa Diwan Society never turned their back to India — their ancestral land. Whenever Indian government or Indian people or Indian Gurdwara Committees were in need of financial aid the society never lagged behind. Whether there was famine, earthquake, war or a *morcha*, a delegation to be sent back to their home country or London or Ottawa, the society, besides collections and donations from the East Indians at large, contributed from its own funds as well.

In various fields—religious, social and political, the Khalsa Diwan Society made remarkable contributions, which deeply influenced the life of the Sikhs in particular and other Indians in general. The society served as a cementing force for the Sikh community. It was a centripetal force which kept the Sikhs attracted to it. Even when there were many more autonomous societies in Canada, the Khalsa Diwan Society, Vancouver, always played the role of the representative body of all the Canadian Sikhs. At every forum the Vancouver society, being the oldest in the country, had an edge over all others with its voice heard every where.

We may discuss the role of this society over its long period of time under the distinct categories of its activities.

Religious Role

In fact, to start with, the religious role of this society was its mainstay. The society built a Gurdwara at 2nd Avenue Vancouver, through the funds raised from the Sikhs, offered from their meagre income and inaugurated it on 19 January 1908. Regular congregations were held in the Gurdwara and the purchase of grocery and all the necessary arrangements of running the *langer* there were looked after by the society. Daily free mess was available to every one. Paid priests were employed to perform the routine Gurdwara services. When a priest was called from India his passage expenses were met by the society. Similarly when the temporary services of the *kirtani jathas*, *parcharaks* (preachers) and scholars of Sikh history to deliver lectures to the congregations in the Gurdwaras were requisitioned by the society from India their journey expenses were paid by the society itself and arrangements for their board and lodging in Vancouver were also made by them. As the records point out, the Khalsa Diwan Society contributed $ 148,000 (a rounded figure) to religious and educational funds in India and Canada up to 1921.

In 1921, the Khalsa Diwan Society remitted Sri Nankana Sahib *shahidi* fund collected at Vancouver to the Shiromani Gurdwara Prabandhak Committee, Amritsar.

The contributions were remitted telegraphically to the SGPC Amritsar, towards relief fund for the Sikhs who were wounded in the Guru Ka Bagh *morcha* in 1922.

C.F. Andrews, an English Christian missionary, saw with his own eyes the police brutalities on the Sikhs, in 1922, being committed during the Guru Ka Bagh *morcha*. He was deeply touched by it and pleaded the cause of the Sikhs with Lt. Governor of the Punjab, Michael O' Dyer, who stopped the action forthwith. Andrews was invited to Canada by the Khalsa Diwan Society Vancouver, in 1929, and met the expenses of his passage etc., from their funds.

Besides contributing to the needy religious places in India the society looked to the financial problems of the Gurdwaras in Canada and the U.S. as well. Very often this society gave financial aid to the societies at Victoria, New Westminster, Abbotsford, Fraser Mills, etc., to manage their affairs particularly relating to the Gurdwaras. For example, vide entry in the society's records the society donated $ 1000 to other Sikh temples in British Columbia. The Khalsa Diwan Society also contributed to the construction of the Gurdwara at Stockton, California, in 1927.

In all the Gurdwaras placed under the care of this society the recitation of *gurbani* or the holy compositions in the morning and evening was the daily routine. The *gurpurbs* or the anniversaries relating to the Gurus have always been observed by the society with absolute solemnity. In order to enlighten the congregation with the glorious past of the Sikh community lectures by the learned scholars were arranged by the society. *Amrit prachar* was often conducted by the society to keep the Khalsa spirit in radiant splendour.

When a *jatha* of ten persons was sent from Vancouver to participate in the Jaito *morcha* in Nabha State (India) their journey entailed an amount of $ 2889 that was paid by the Khalsa Diwan Society. An amount of $ 4000/- was also sent with the *shahidi jatha*, through a draft in the name of the *jathedar* of Sri Akal Takht, Amritsar. A sum of $ 700 was also sent to meet the contingent expenses of the *shahidi jatha*. The *jatha* comprising ten men had started from Vancouver on 13 July and from Victoria on 17 July 1924. Thirteen more Sikhs joined the *jatha* on their way to India at Shanghai. At Hong Kong four more and at Singapore ten and at Penang a few more joined them. The *jatha* reached Amritsar on 28 September 1924. People gave a rousing welcome to them at the railway station. This *jatha* gave a boost to the movement. The movement was assuming the complexion of an international problem. A few days later the leader and the deputy leader of this *jatha*, Bhai Bhagwan Singh and Bhai Harbans Singh respectively were arrested and after a brief trial were sentenced to imprisonment for two years on 15 December 1924, and a fine of a thousand rupees each was also imposed on them. The other members of the *jatha* reached Jaito on 21 February 1925, where they were taken into custody. The deadlock finally ended with the Akalis completing their 101 *akhandpaths* on 6 August 1925.

In view of the stringent financial position of the SGPC, Amritsar, a sum of $ 5000 was sent to overcome their crisis in 1924. A part of it was collected from the other B.C. societies.

An amount of $ 7700 was sent in 1924 and $ 3000 in 1927 to the Sikh temples in India as donations.

In response to an appeal from Sri Anandpur Sahib, the Khalsa Diwan Society gave financial help to them in 1924.

When after the conclusion of the *morcha*, an *akhandpath* was arranged at Gangsar (Jaito) in 1925, the society sent an amount of $ 200 to meet the expenses of the *akhandpath*.

A delegation was sent to Amritsar on a religious mission in 1982, incurring an expenditure of $11,981.

Very often, Sikh conferences were held at different places in Canada. The Khalsa Diwan Society had been invariably always sending its donations and delegates to attend the conferences where the topics relating to Sikhism were discussed and their problems highlighted. The preservation of the Sikh identity had been the main objective which society had always stoutly advocated.

The Khalsa Diwan Society took a great decision in 1969 to undertake a major project of building a splendid edifice of a Gurdwara at 8000, Ross Street, Vancouver, and shift to it from the old Gurdwara at 1866, 2nd Avenue, Vancouver.

2.75 acres of uninhabited municipal land on the Ross Street had been purchased for $ 75,000 by the society a little earlier.

The magnificent building of the Gurdwara was completed in the first week of April 1970 at the cost of $ 6,60,000. On the Baisakhi day of 1970 Sri *Guru Granth Sahib* was brought in procession from the old Gurdwara and installed in the new building.

It was a tragic and inexcusable decision on the part of the Khalsa Diwan Society to have sold a historic monument of the Sikh community— the old 2nd Avenue Gurdwara, Vancouver. It could have been retained or preserved as a Sikh memorial of an indomitable spirit of a matchless community on this earth. With this sacred shrine hundreds of Sikh community's momentous decisions and programmes were linked. This Gurdwara was the priceless repository of the unforgettable memories enshrined in its holy edifice that gave them strength for sixty long years to fight the injustice and aggression perpetrated against them by the white racial majority. This Gurdwara was the embodiment of the unique fortitude with which the dauntless pioneer Sikhs, bereft of their human and political rights, braved the ruthless onslaughts of the unfavourable times and hostile population.

The remarkable building of this Gurdwara was sold away for a few thousand bucks and an invaluable place of worship to which they had recourse for peace of mind and recouping of strength to fight for their inalienable rights was lost to them for ever.

Sometimes later in 1979 a big slice of land measuring 2.78 acres with a building on it, adjoining the Ross Street Gurdwara was purchased for a sum of $ 5,20,000. The new building was named Guru Amar Das Niwas, which began to be used as a Punjabi school, a Sikh library, a Sikh museum and the Gurdwara guest house. A part of it was marked to be used as a parking lot.

8000 - Ross Street Marine Drive, Vancouver, B.C. Sikh Temple, has always been the hub of all Sikh activity. Most of the programmes relating to Sikh religion and Sikh community were conducted there till more Gurdwaras in the Greater Vancouver were built. These Gurdwaras began to have their own independent committees and separate management. But for more than half a century the Khalsa Diwan Society held its total sway over the entire Sikh population of B.C. Voters came from distant places— sometimes covering hundreds of kms to cast their votes to elect the office-bearers or directors of the Khalsa Diwan Society.

Despite so many other Gurdwaras in Greater Vancouver and adjoining areas of B.C. the Khalsa Diwan Society of Ross Street enjoyed a distinct status among the Sikhs and the B.C. government. The glory of the Sikh *panth* in a foreign land remained preserved in the hands of the management of the Khalsa Diwan Society for nearly a century.

The *nagarkirtans* or religious processions started since 1979, are organized by the society. The local Sikhs and the people from the adjoining areas participate in the processions in thousands, displaying notable Sikh presence in Canada. These processions also give the non-Sikhs an idea of Sikh unity and an inalienable attachment with their religion, which they hold so dear to their hearts. The *nagarkirtan* displays a unique gaiety and splendour as participants wear their choicest and most colourful clothes.

As the procession marches on its marked route, the non-Sikhs, particularly the whites who come out of their houses and line up on the road to have a full view of the wonderful procession headed by a number of glamorously decorated floats, simply feel enchanted and enthralled by the celestial and unending rippling waves after waves of thousands and thousands of devoted marchers. Many of the viewers say that they had never seen such a spectacular procession moving in such a disciplined manner, every marcher brimming with a sort of divine bliss.

The society also organizes *gurmat* camps where they involve the young boys and girls who otherwise are likely to go astray under the influence of western culture. From time to time the Khalsa Diwan Society has been publishing and distributing Sikh literature, free of any charge, in the form of small booklets and magazines. For the last many years, the society's magazine, *Khalsa Diwan Gazette,* has been publishing articles on Sikh religion and Sikh history.

The Khalsa Diwan Society Vancouver's Resource Centre, first of its kind in Canada, built by the Sikhs, was constructed at the cost of about five million dollars and opened for use in July 1996. It comprises a Sikh library named Guru Hargobind Sahib Library to mark the 400th birthday of Guru Hargobind Sahib. This library sized 8004 square feet includes a slide room, audio visual room, a private study room, stacks for 15000 books, study carrels and reading areas. There is a Sikh museum, a commodious well furnished lounge for senior citizens with seating capacity of about 150 persons, to sit and chat over their past experiences in their new adopted home—Canada, and a little bit of their domestic problems which deeply bother some of them. This lounge includes a service kitchen as well. These senior citizens, who are held, as against the western society, in high esteem in Indian culture, always receive respectful treatment at the Resource Centre and are often rather almost always entertained with tea and various types of eatables. The centre is provided with dormitories/ residence including private accommodation for the *granthi* and *ragi* Singhs and visiting guests from around the world. The Resource Centre is dedicated to the first Sikh visitors to Vancouver in the year 1897.

The society has been purchasing, for its small library, religious books and calendars almost ever since its inception, spending hardly a few dollars every year as the records show. Though the necessary attention could not be paid to the library but it continued its existence over the decades. The main reason of inattention to the library could hardly be any other than the lack of readers—most of the immigrants being illiterate. Unluckily most of the Canadian Sikhs are not library - minded even today. High scholarship is almost rare among them.

Throughout its long history the purchase of the grocery for the *langar* has been one of the major expenses of the society. The *langar* is a very important institution of the Sikhs and its impact on the Sikhs and the non-Sikhs has been enormous and its role has been widely revolutionary.

Most of the records of the income and expenditure of the society year-wise are available with the society duly audited by the chartered accountants. The major items of expenditure have been listed below in a sample study:

Distribution	1982	1983	1984
Deg and Langar	$65,455.00	$73,300.00	$79,543.00
Dharam Parchar	14,930.00	16,936.00	15,719.00
Donations to other Institutions	17,063.00	24,547.00	33,941.00
Procession	13,286.00	13,387.00	9,758.00
Punjabi School	28,092.00	25,891.00	21,992.00

In the early stages also when there was no Punjabi school and no processions were taken out, *langar* was one of the major items of expenditure. For example, $ 2200/- (on *langar* in 1924), $ 984.28 (in 1925), $ 1721.39 (in 1929), $ 847.58 (in 1931) and $ 422 (in 1934).

Social Role

The social works also actively came within the purview of the Khalsa Diwan Society. The social services were extended beyond the limits of their religious and territorial boundaries. Whenever there was an appeal or need of financial help anywhere in this country or in the outside world, the society responded readily. Despite their scanty resources, their liberality was, allow me to say frankly, much more generous and instantaneous in those earlier times as compared to the society's response at present. It may be due to the present society's larger expenses in their multifarious activities regarding their shrines, the community and their financial constraints. The old spirit of sympathetic consideration of the needy has been undoubtedly slackened with the passage of time, though not totally missing. When there is an appeal to help in the calamitous situations caused by the nature's furious and unbounded wrath in any part of the world, this society and the Sikh community never fails to rise equal to the occasion They have been told by Sikhism that it is more blessed to give than to receive and the hands that help are holier than the lips that pray.

To give a deeper peep into the generous hearts of the pioneer Sikhs a few of the decisions taken by the society in the course of their cheqered span of life over the decades are given below. This information is based on the Khalsa Diwan Society's records. I suggest that records properly arranged, year-wise, filling up the gaps by tracing the missing links, may be kept in the library maintained in the Resource Centre. A few photocopies may be prepared for the use of the readers in the library itself. It is a very valuable record of the Canadian Sikh community's history. It must be treasured most carefully for future generations. A community without its old records is without its past. How would that past be built without the old records? Every nation has its past and future and without it their existence is ephemeral and volatile.

Through their orders of disenfranchisement in 1907 the Canadian government had deprived or strongly discouraged the East Indians from the study of law, pharmacy, medicine and engineering. It was really thoughtful of the Khalsa Diwan Society, Vancouver, to decide in 1909 to send Sikh students to the United States for higher studies in medicine, chemistry, engineering and agriculture on scholarships from the society. The names of such students who were of high moral character and upholders of the Sikh traditions were invited from the Chief Khalsa Diwan, Amritsar, to be supported for higher education.

To promote education, the Khalsa Diwan Society had earmarked 200 dollars for the Sikh Kanya Mahavidyala, Ferozepur, in 1910.

Bhag Singh, President of the Khalsa Diwan Society, Vancouver, lost his wife on 30 January 1914, and his daughter Karam Kaur was announced to be looked after by the society but a lady named Kartar Kaur took responsibility to raise her. She refused to accept any help from the society in the form of an allowance for bringing up the girl. On 5 September 1914, Bhag Singh was shot dead by Bela Singh and the Khalsa Diwan Society took upon itself the duty of looking after the education and all other requirements of his daughter from their own funds. She was sent to the Punjab to receive education at the Sikh Kanya Vidyala, Kairon, district Amritsar. The Khalsa Diwan Society met her expenses. Similarly two Sikh families suffered tragedies in the 1930s. Both parents lost their lives in these families and on the appeal of the Khalsa Diwan Society many members of the community came forward to look after their children. A childless woman took the girl to her family and raised her as her own while some other families raised the boys.

Shortly thereafter the Khalsa Diwan Society constituted an Orphans Committee to look after the upkeep and education of the orphan children.

In 1914, famine broke out in U.P. (India). Under the leadership of this society a U.P. Famine Relief Committee was formed in Vancouver that collected and remitted sums of money to India.

The Khalsa Diwan Society sent financial aid to the anti-apartheid movement in South Africa in 1914 and more help was promised to them to be sent after collection from the people.

This society sent a sum of 2,000 dollars as financial assistance to the California Diwan Society to meet an emergency requirement of funds for constructing approach roads to their Gurdwara at Stockton in 1918.

The executive committee of the Khalsa Diwan Society duly passed all amounts sanctioned as assistance to various institutions or individuals before these were sent. The general house of the society sanctioned an amount of $ 500 to be donated to the General Hospital, Vancouver in 1919. Besides that contribution many individual members also donated liberally to the hospital.

Jallianwala Bagh (Amritsar) massacre was a turning point in Indian history. From 13 April 1919, a new chapter in India's freedom movement started. Hundreds of unarmed and innocent people were shot dead by the orders of a mad military officer Brigadier R.E.H. Dyer. It is a lesson of history that the unprovoked suppression or the bullet that kills an innocent man ignites fire of rebellion, which cannot be extinguished easily. Jallianwala Bagh Memorial Fund was instituted to help the families whose bread-earners had been killed. The Khalsa Diwan Society sent their contribution to this fund in 1920.

The Khalsa Diwan Society remitted a sum of one thousand dollars to the Sikh League towards its Prisoners' Families Relief Fund in 1920.

The Khalsa Diwan Society came to the rescue of the students in Canada or the United States whenever Indian students were in trouble. In 1921, the students from Punjab (India) studying in Seattle were ordered by court to deposit certain amounts immediately. Those students were detained behind bars. They were likely to be deported in the event of their failure to deposit the amounts against their names as bail securities. The Khalsa Diwan Society, Vancouver, immediately discussed the matter. Many members of the society came forward to deposit the amounts as bail securities and the students were got released on bail.

The Khalsa Diwan Society sent in reply to a telegram from *Pardesi Khalsa* an amount of two thousand rupees telegraphically in 1921, to assist the paper that had fallen on bad days for want of funds.

In 1922, two Sikh students from the Punjab, namely, Kehar Singh Dhudeka and Achhar Singh Dhutt were detained by the government. The society arranged their bail security with the help of a lawyer. The funds were raised by the society to deposit the security amount and pay the lawyer's fee, keeping in view the welfare and education of the Sikh students from the Punjab. It was really admirable for the society to come to the rescue of the needy when none was there to help.

The same year, that is, in 1922, it was decided through a resolution by the society to provide a room as lodging to the students from the Punjab. This was in line with the society's policy of promoting education both in Canada and in India.

Donations were sent to the Earthquake Relief Fund, Japan, in 1923. And also as per 1923 report an amount of $ 1851.30 was given for charitable purposes.

It was resolved by the Khalsa Diwan Society to donate 2000 dollars to the General Hospital, Vancouver in 1924, in response to their appeal for financial help.

According to the report of 1925, disbursements show an amount of $ 3,800.27 under the item 'Orphans', a contribution made to orphanages.

In 1925, the society stood bail security of 500 dollars for one Bhai Aya Singh who had trouble with the Canadian law.

It was resolved at the meeting of the Khalsa Diwan Society by a majority vote to send a sum of 3000 dollars to the Khalsa High School, Sri Anandpur Sahib, as financial help in 1926. The money was immediately remitted to the said school.

When the Sikh population in Vancouver was reduced to a considerable extent and many of the Sikhs had shifted over to the USA due to economic crisis in Canada, the Khalsa Diwan Society was constrained to pass a resolution in March 1927 that no societies, *jathas* or organizations should be sent from anywhere, particularly from their home country to collect funds from Canada, as many Sikhs leaving Canada had caused dwindling of their income to a great extent. Besides that, they needed money for some of their own projects to be accomplished. They expressed regrets to their Indian brethren for their helplessness to raise funds for them and to send donations just on asking as they did earlier. This situation did not last long, nor did the fund-raising agencies take it seriously. They continued making requests for financial help and it continued to be given to them.

In 1929 the society donated a sum of 100 dollars to the General Hospital, Vancouver, and told them that if possible, this financial help of one hundred dollars would be continued regularly in the years to come. Some individual philanthropists like Mayo Singh donated very liberally to the hospitals. His beneficiaries included hospitals at Victoria, Duncan, Ladysmith, Nanaimo, etc. He sent large amounts to Gurdwaras and educational institutions in the Punjab. Kapoor Singh Sidhu also liberally contributed to the Sikh community. His two daughters, who were doctors, set up a hospital at their ancestral village Aaur near Phillaur, in Nawanshahr district (India).

At present i.e. in 1990s Asa Singh Johal is nationally known philanthropist. He donates millions of dollars to the hospitals and other denominational institutions in Canada. He was awarded the order of British Columbia and the order of Canada.

In 1935, the Khalsa Diwan Society sent donations to the Shromani Gurdwara Prabandhak Committee, Amritsar, to be forwarded to the Quetta Earthquake Relief Fund. The society sent contributions of $ 1500 to some societies in India in 1940.

From time to time people from the Punjab had been visiting Canada for collection of funds for various purposes including education, construction of Gurdwaras, raising of memorials, etc., and returned home with bulging purses. Such groups continued coming without any break and receiving large donations from the society and from the people on the society's appeal.

On the initiative of the Khalsa Diwan Society, Guru Nanak Temple Surrey sent 2100 dollars in 1978-79 towards Flood Relief Fund in India and also sent 3000 dollars to the Family Relief Fund of Baisakhi 1978 martyrs (Amritsar). In the year of 1978, on the appeal of the Khalsa Diwan Society, funds were raised and an amount of $ 8930 was sent to the government of India towards the Cyclone Relief Fund. The society had also contributed $ 2000 towards Indira Relief Fund to help the refugees from Bangladesh. As a measure of relief for the families of the Sikhs martyred in April 1978 at Amritsar, all societies and organizations of Canada raised a substantial amount of $ 60,000 and sent the same to India for distribution among the suffering families.

In commemoration of the Babbar Akalis who laid down their lives in the Punjab in 1924-26 the Khalsa Diwan Society holds games in Vancouver annually since 1933 inviting teams to participate in the tournament from India, the U.K., the U.S. and other countries besides team from different parts of Canada. Trophies are given to the winning teams. Earlier, more stress was laid on the Punjabi game of *kabbadi*. But of late, the society has introduced more games as volley ball, basket ball, soccer, floor hockey, field hockey, badminton, tennis and weight-lifting. These games are normally held on long weekend in May every year. There is always a very good arrangement of free mess (*langar*) close to the playgrounds, for the viewers and visitors. The expenses of the games, the board and lodging of the teams and some times their tickets to and from Canada are borne by the Khalsa Diwan Society. The bills generally rise to thousands of dollars.

This two or three-day game festival is a great attraction for the Greater Vancouverites in particular and the people of B.C. in general. In 1982,the Khalsa Diwan Society purchased 28 acres of land in Richmond, B.C. to build a sports complex. But for reasons best known to the organizers the building of the complex could not materialize so far.

The people or institutions in distress seeking immediate help from the Khalsa Diwan Society received instant attention. In the earlier stages, if some of the fresh immigrants were without any employment and had no means to fall back upon, they were advised by the society not to beg any help from the government. They should rather come to the society and get the needed help, free mess from the Guru's *langar* and other assistance from the society.

For individuals and also for the whole community, the Khalsa Diwan Society did all the necessary communications with India, Ottawa or the B.C. government. The society took care of their people's employment, housing, health and welfare problems. It actively helped the Sikhs to change their economic fortunes for the better.

In the earlier days when the number of the Sikhs in B.C. was small, the Sikhs of different towns generally shared the celebrations of their religious festivals. For Baisakhi they would assemble at Victoria, for Guru Gobind Singh's birth day celebrations they would assemble at Vancouver and for the celebration of Guru Nanak's birthday at Abbotsford. This was not a regular practice. They did it only sometimes.

In 1965 the society sent blankets worth $ 973.46 for distribution among the poor and needy in India. Giving charity, donations or contributions to the people in need is prized as a religious duty of the Sikhs. They must share their income with those who badly need it. This practice, among the Sikhs, seems to be a motivating impulse for *sarbat da bhala* (may peace and prosperity come to one and all).

Almost every annual report of disbursements of the Khalsa Diwan Society has on its list an item of 'donations' which sometimes amounts to thousands of dollars. For example, in 1981 the society sent donations of $ 31,367 to Gurdwara Hazur Sahib (India) and $ 27,505 to Gurdwara Tarn Taran (India) besides donations to other institutions to the tune of $ 13, 471, the same year—total yearly donations being $ 72,343. In the annual report of expenditure under the year 1984 the donations given amounted to $ 33,941/- and in the year 1987 to $ 20,346/-.

The Khalsa Diwan Society is never to refuse help whenever a needy person comes to them. This is one of the cardinal teachings of Sikhism that they observe in letter and spirit.

In 1993 a group of Sri Lanka tourists had to wait for four or five days at Vancouver before they could get flight for their return journey. The airport authorities sent them to Ross Street Gurdwara (Vancouver) where the Khalsa Diwan Society made free arrangement of their stay and food. The Gurdwaras always provide free food to the hungry and free accommodation to the homeless all over the world. Their holy Gurus had enjoined this noble practice upon the Sikhs.

The other Sikh societies, such as, the Guru Nanak Sikh Temple Society, Surrey, the Akali Singh Sikh Society, Vancouver, the Khalsa Diwan Society, Abbotsford, the Khalsa Diwan Society, Victoria, the Nanaksar Gur Sikh Temple Society and many others also help in religious as well as social programmes in India and in Canada. Since this chapter deals primarily with the activities and achievements of the Khalsa Diwan Society, Vancouver—the oldest society in Canada, much has not been said about the other Gurdwara societies in this study. Their role in the promotion and preservation of the Sikh values in true and pristine form is equally commendable. I wish, I could incorporate a chapter on the invaluable service rendered to the Sikh community by these societies.

The Akali Singh Sikh Society sent to government of India, during Indo-China war in 1962 a contribution of 25000 dollars. This society also sent 7000 dollars as help towards Andhra Cyclone Fund in 1978 and also contributed help of 4800 dollars to the families of Amritsar Sikh martyrs of Baisakhi 1978. The Khalsa Diwan Society is always ready to take part in any social work that can help the Sikh community in any way. The department of the RCMP started vocational training courses for visible minority summer employment programme in recent years. On the sponsorship of the Khalsa Diwan Society, Vancouver, many Sikh boys and girls got training and consequently were successful in getting employment.

The Khalsa Diwan Society, with the co-operation of Health Department, started a training course for running day care programmes in Guru Amar Das Niwas in Vancouver in 1995 where 19 Sikh girls received training. The society had also organized a successful seminar for such training in 1996. Many Sikh women participated in it and it helped them to run day care programmes, making it a good source of income for them.

To have better relations with other religions and communities the Khalsa Diwan Society almost invariably always sends its delegates to participate in interfaith and race relation programmes. At such functions the Sikh speakers explain the import of Sikh faith and tell them how Sikhism wishes well of everybody in the world. They profess friendship with everyone and hostility with none. They show full respect to every religion and in return expect full respect for their own.

Political Role

The pioneer Sikhs had to suffer innumerable physical hardships for a number of years. It is most regrettable that the restrictions on the Indian people, who chose to make Canada their home like the Anglo-Saxons, Germans, Italians, Ukrainians, Chinese, etc., continued to be slapped for decades after decades. All the above communities were free from any restrictions or prohibitions. Those who professed to be a very civilized nation of the world subjected the East Indians to such indignities, inhuman and barbaric behaviour as is totally unworthy of civilized people. Can a citizen of a country be deprived of his right to vote for forty long years? When a perpetrator of indignities loses a sense of justice his conscience dies and he becomes insensitive to the pricks of his conscience, which if preserved in an unimpaired form always gives the best message to the man. Conscience is the keeper of a virtuous man in a human body. Whenever you feel, you can listen its voice bringing to you the most virtuous course to follow. The next step or the choice to follow rests with you.

For full four decades, the Sikhs fought incessantly for their basic right of franchise. The Khalsa Diwan Society spearheaded the movement for franchise and pursued it with undiminished passion. They sent delegations to Ottawa, London and Delhi with ice-cold response to their vigorous demands. The society spent thousands of dollars on these trips. They argued for their rights fruitlessly at every level of government. But ultimately the good sense dawned on the Canadian government in 1947 when India won its independence.

The *Komagata Maru* was another confrontational issue that jolted the Sikh conscience all over the world. The refusal to the *Komagata Maru* passengers to land on the Canadian soil had political and social overtones. The Canadians wanted to keep their country white even by throwing to the winds the British citizens' (Indians') right to enter a British colony.

Under the guidance of the Khalsa Diwan Society the whites' conspiracy to rid themselves of the East Indians by sending them to Honduras was foiled by vigorous opposition of the Sikhs.

The whites considered their skin-colour divinely superior to that of the blacks and browns. This concept of the whites gave a crushing blow to the conscience of the non-whites over the centuries. The non-whites had to wage a ruthless struggle against this un-Christian, unethical and inhuman behaviour, which most unfortunately their white parents had instilled in their blood. The fight against racial discrimination was bitter and prolonged though the society's struggle promised them a victory in the end. But alas! The fight is still halfway. The discrimination based on colour of the skin still persists. It may be on its last legs as some optimistically feel, but it is there. It is difficult to predict as to when this ugly blemish and accursed stigma would disappear from the face of this earth.

We discuss below a few examples of the Khalsa Diwan Society's role in various fields just to give an idea as to how much our predecessors possessed the political acumen and how valiantly they fought and how with their slender resources they helped the movement for India's freedom and their struggle for their rights in their new homeland—Canada.

The Khalsa Diwan Society's records point out that during the Sikhs first quarter of a century in Canada, they were said to have spent around $ 147,463 until 1921, as assistance to the families of political prisoners ($ 2100), to political sufferers, ($ 30700), for the *Komagata Maru* affair ($ 50,000), on immigration cases ($ 30,000), and expenses on the deputations sent to Ottawa, London and India ($ 12000), on newspapers from India and Canada ($15000), the Congress—Tilak Swaraj Fund ($ 3333), and on sufferers from massacres ($ 4330).

For a tiny community in a foreign land not properly settled, contributing such huge amounts over a period of few years reflects their noble spirit of sharing their earnings with others and readiness to contribute to religious, social and political causes so dear to their hearts. If any other community in such circumstances had done so much for their people they might have received a much more glorified ovation and appreciation at the hands of their successors than these pioneers or our ancestors have received at our hands. I am simply charmed by their spirit of sacrifice and achievements in the face of horrifying odds. I salute them with all humility and respect at my command. It is due to their sufferings that our present generation enjoys opulence and abundance.

It was resolved in July 1920 by the Khalsa Diwan Society that contribution should be sent to Jallianwala Bagh Memorial Fund for the suffering families. A sum of ten thousand rupees was remitted for the purpose. Many people also remitted their contributions individually through cheques.

In June 1923, it was decided by the society that financial aid be sent to those such Sikh families in the Punjab whose bread-earners had been interned by the government in connection with the country's independence movement. For larger collections appeals were generally made to the congregations in the Gurdwaras for contributions which were readily given by the members of the *sangat*.

On an appeal from Sikh League, Jalandhar, for a donation of $ 1000 to defray the expenses of the League whose session had been proposed to be held on 17-19 October 1923, the amount was sent by the Khalsa Diwan Society Vancouver, immediately. Other Gurdwaras were also requested to earmark amounts for such conferences.

Similarly, the Swaraj Sabha approached the society for financial assistance which was remitted expeditiously. The Khalsa Diwan Society had never used the word 'no' for any appeal for financial aid from whichever corner of the world it came. This was extremely noble of the society; its liberality, generosity and humane approach had hardly any parallel in the world. *Sare jahan ka dard hamare dil mein hai* (The distress in the world pains our hearts).

The Akali *morchas* in the Punjab in the twenties of the twentieth century had both religious and political overtones. Government's interference in the affairs of the Sikh Gurdwaras was totally uncalled for and their attempt to put their own touts in control of the religious institutions of the Sikhs was tantamount to blasphemy. The Sikhs wanted to bring the Sikh shrines under the control of their own chosen or elected members, committed to the Sikh faith, and wanted of the government to make a law to this effect. The movement for such a demand entailed sufficient funds, which the Canadian Sikhs shared adequately.

In December 1925 the society unanimously resolved that funds raised towards the political and religious prisoners' relief fund be equitably distributed among the affected families of the Doaba, Malwa, Majha and the Babbar Akalis.

During this period thousands of dollars were sent to the ghadar party for their journals - *Ghadar* and *Ghadar di Goonj* by the Khalsa Diwan Society. Such donations were not recorded in the minute books. It seems that separate accounts were maintained and were not produced before the auditors, for checking, or if at all such contributions were placed under the item 'donations' without specifying the details of the donations, as some of the donations could be placed under objection by the chartered accountants or the government.

In May 1926, it was resolved by the society that in future the *akhandpath* of Sri Guru Granth Sahib would be performed in Vancouver on 23 May every year in memory of the Babbar Akali martyrs and the offerings collected on the occasion would be remitted to the families of the Babbar martyrs. On the first *akhandpath* held on the above date, total offerings were over 1000 dollars. The amount was sent to the families of martyr Kishan Singh Barring, District Jalandhar, and his companion martyrs.

The society decided in June 1926 that a sum of 45 dollars be sent to each of the Babbar families whose addresses were available. Efforts were made to trace the addresses of other families of the Babbars so that they might also be helped.

In June 1927, the Khalsa Diwan Society unanimously decided that a sum of $ 500 be remitted to the ghadar party. The money was sent immediately.

The society decided unanimously in September 1927 that an amount of $ 1000 be sent to the Sikh League, Hoshiarpur, and another $ 1000 be sent to the Nabha internees. The compliance was made immediately.

In January 1928 a sum of $ 500 was sent by the society to the families of the Babbar Akalis out of the Relief Fund raised in Vancouver.

In March 1929 a sum of one hundred dollars was sent to the families of the Babbar Akalis out of the Babbar Akali Relief Fund. Again in May 1929 the Khalsa Diwan Society decided to send money to all the families of the Babbars whose addresses had been traced by that time. It was desired by them that the families deserved maximum help and everybody should contribute as much as he could possibly do. A list of fifty families of the Babbars came up for consideration before the society. They decided to send 1500 dollars to these families and compliance was made immediately.

In January 1930, the society sent Rs.1000 towards the 44th session of the Indian National Congress that was being held at Lahore.

In 1930, a sum of 100 dollars was also donated towards the General Hospital Vancouver, B.C. and it was decided that if possible financial help of one hundred dollars be continued to be given to the hospital every year.

In May 1931 the son of Basant Singh Kangniwala had trouble with the immigration department. The Khalsa Diwan Society stood immigration security of 500 dollars for him.

In May 1931 the society unanimously decided to remit 500 dollars from the Babbar Akali Fund towards financial help of the Babbar Akalis in the Punjab. It seemed that the Khalsa Diwan Society was disposed towards the Babbars very emotionally and felt the pangs of the families of the Babbar martyrs very deeply. They were always ready towards rendering maximum financial help to their suffering families. These funds had been collected from the people in Canada and the USA and such funds as referred to earlier, presumably were kept outside the purview of the auditors as the same could create problems for them and the Indian government could list them as anti-government activists. But there was no doubt that almost every Sikh in Canada and the USA was anti-British and keenly aspired for their country's freedom from the yoke of the foreign rule. And since all could not jump into the battlefield they helped their liberation struggle through financial assistance without which no movement could carry out its programmes whether peaceful or violent.

The Khalsa Diwan Society remitted a sum of $ 1001.25 in 1971 for the Indira Defence Fund during Indo-Pak War.

A large number of distinguished people visited Vancouver and they were duly honoured, as was the practice with the Khalsa Diwan Society. A few of them may be briefly referred to here.

Annie Beasant, who was the President of International Theosophical Society based at Madras, visited Vancouver in 1909 and pleaded the cause of the East Indians' rights as citizens of Canada. Dr (Mrs.) Annie Beasant was probably the most remarkable woman on the world's surface at that time. She was an extremely cultured woman who knew and practised the best that has been said and thought in the world. She was a great, religious, cultural and educational reformer in England from 1875 to 1892 and in India from 1893 to 1913. Later she became the president of the Indian National Congress in 1917. She was appalled the way her own countrymen were treating Indians. Long before she came to India she had observed " We exploit Hindustan not for her benefit but for the benefit of our younger sons, our restless adventurers, our quarrelsome and never-do-well surplus population. At least for the sake of common honesty, let us drop our hypocritical mask and acknowledge that we seized India from lust of conquest, from the lowest and paltriest of desires". Her ideas moulded the lives of thousands of people. 'To hear her speak in public was to hear one of the most remarkable public speakers of the world'. Her words and voice could mesmerize her listeners.

H. H. Gaekwar of Baroda, Maharaja of Baroda, visited Vancouver in June 1910. Since he was a staunch supporter of the British *raj*, the Sikhs boycotted his visit and did not call him to the Sikh temple. The Maharaja of a minor state of Mourbhang in Bengal also visited Vancouver in 1910. He took no interest in the problems of the Indians and the Sikhs ignored him as well.

Ravindra Nath Tagore and Rev. F. Andrews visited Vancouver and Victoria in 1929. The Sikhs gave them rousing receptions. They were asked by the East Indians to see for themselves the unfair treatment given to them by the Canadian government. The Khalsa Diwan Societies of Vancouver and Victoria honoured them with *siropas* (robes of honour) and praised their contributions to the cause of the Indians in their country. But unfortunately they could not do anything positive towards softening the attitude of the government towards the Indians.

Pandit Jawahar Lal Nehru, Prime Minister of India, accompanied by his daughter Indira Gandhi, visited British Columbia in 1949. The Sikhs felt elated on their Prime Minister's visit to their adopted country—Canada. He was honoured by the Khalsa Diwan Society and was given a *siropa* at the Gurdwara. Pundit Nehru addressed the Indians at some places and pleaded strongly for their causes and problems but Canadian government had never been so soft as to make a change in its policy just for asking. They do things in their own tardy way. But with India having become independent changes had started taking place though slowly.

When Mrs. Indira Gandhi, Prime Minister of India, landed at Vancouver airport on 23 June 1973, she is said to have straightaway driven to the Sikh temple, at Ross Street, Vancouver, and offered $ 500 before the holy *Guru Granth Sahib*. Later she addressed a big gathering at Queen Elizabeth Theatre.

Many Akali leaders, *jathedars*, ministers, prominent Sikh historians, scholarly preachers, *ragis* and *dhadis* visited Vancouver in the 1970s and later. Vancouver is one of the most beautiful cities of the world with its top-class living standard. The visits of these dignitaries have been more with a view to having a look at the western life than to study the Sikh way of life in a bid to keep them on the right track if they happened to have gone astray. At that time, the Canadian Sikhs used to sit on chairs with uncovered heads in the holy presence of *Guru Granth Sahib* in a manner violative to the time-honoured Sikh *maryada* (code of discipline). These leaders and upholders of the Sikh *maryada* did not raise even their small fingers against the violations of the sacred Sikh practices. History never spares the errors of any body including its heroes who wrote it even with their blood.

Jathedars and preachers—the custodians of the Sikh *rahit maryada* and Sikh religion who visited Canada from 1970s to 1990s were found to be just ordinary men afflicted with ordinary human failings. Humility, selflessness and nobility of Sikh spirit deplorably lacked in them. None of them was even remotely associated with the spiritual stage that radiates the holy light of which they talked in the Gurdwaras. Sikh religion needs enlightened men to keep it among the top world religions. Those *jathedars* were more of politicians than of holy souls. My close contact with some of them disillusioned me horribly.

I pray that the Sikh code of conduct may be observed in letter and spirit and any violation of the same would lead to more violations and ultimately that may profane our holy traditions and damage the sublime dignity and supreme honour of our religion which we hold so dear and for which our ancestors made supreme sacrifices to save it from any sacrilege and blasphemy. We all are brothers-in-faith and we have to take all our religious decisions collectively and according to the accredited traditions laid down by our great mentors—our holy Gurus. We do not have a licence to change the Sikh code of conduct or its practices introduced by the Gurus, hundreds of years earlier. These practices were marked with universality in their application and not left to the choice or convenience of those who observe them. When once prescribed, the Sikhs resented violently even if the Guru himself—the creator of the order, happened to slightly violate any of them inadvertently to test his followers as to how strictly they complied with them or if they could note them being violated.

About the *rehat* (code of conduct) Guru Gobind Singh is said to have told his Sikhs:

Jab lag Khalsa rahai niara - tab lag tej diao main sara (So long as the Khalsa keeps a separate identity I shall confer all powers on it).

Jab eh gahe bipran ki reet, main na karon in ki parteet (When they adopt anti-Sikh practices I shall cease to have faith in them).

The challenge of modernity to Sikh religion has to be resisted otherwise, in due course of time, the Sikh religion and its *rehat* as propounded by our holy Gurus would change out of recognition. That would be the greatest tragedy in the realm of Sikhism—a world religion. Many Sikhs in the world are in a defiant mood with regard to their religious practices and many of them are well on the path of rebellion. Right, it is an age of reason and one is inclined to believe things if logically satisfied but spare the religion, which is only a matter of faith beyond the bounds of reason.

The Guru further said:

Rahni reha soi Sikh mera - oh sahib main us ka chera
(*Rehatnama* Prahlad Singh)

(He who lives according to the code of conduct prescribed for the Sikhs is my real Sikh. He is my master and I am his servant).

In the light of the Guru's above observations we are required to respectfully observe the *rehat* prescribed by our holy Gurus.

The Khalsa Diwan Society has been honouring visitors with *siropas*, purses, gold medals and *kirpans* at the Gurdwaras. The recipients of honours included Pandit Jawahar Lal Nehru, Mrs. Indira Gandhi, S. Kharak Singh, Chaman Lal Goswami, Bhai Piara Singh Langeri, Dr. Ravindra Nath Tagore, Rev. F. Andrews, Bhai Randhir Singh, Bhai Chet Singh *Granthi*, Dr D. P. Pandia and the Akali leaders and many more people whom the society found worthy of honour. Smt. Vijay Laxmi Pandit, sister of Pundit Jawahar Lal Nehru, who had come to the USA could not come to Vancouver because of certain restrictions imposed on her, was presented a robe of honour and a purse of $ 2000 at a conference held at San Francisco in 1944, by the Khalsa Diwan Society Abbotsford (Canada). The Khalsa Diwan Society made strenuous efforts to make her visit at Vancouver possible but the Canadian government stood in the way.

The dream of Gurdit Singh, the organizer of the *Komagata Maru* voyage to Canada in 1914, came true in his third generation when his granddaughter-in-law, Balbir Kaur Sandhu, landed on Canadian soil on 16 October 1996. The Khalsa Diwan Society honoured her on 3 November 1996, at the Ross Street Gurdwara, Vancouver.

The Khalsa Diwan Society, Vancouver, spent thousands of dollars on the reception and hospitality of the honourable visitors and on journey fares of many of them.

As pointed out earlier, the records of the Khalsa Diwan Society were not maintained in a systematic manner. Probably the managers or directors of the society did not realise that the history of the society and community to be written in the future would have to be based on the authentic records maintained by them.

Role of the Khalsa Diwan Society in many important events have not been discussed in detail in this chapter as these had been copiously referred to in other chapters. For example, the society's role in the *Komagata Maru* incident has been widely mentioned in the concerned chapter. The financial and legal assistance along with the supply of necessary food-stuffs and holding of meetings to arouse public support for the passengers of the *Komagata Maru* has found prominently conspicuous mention in the relevant chapter.

The long-drawn struggle of the Khalsa Diwan Society for the abrogation of orders-in-council debarring the Indians from entering Canada and waging an incessant fight for their right to vote for forty years is a woeful history. At every stage the society fought tooth and nail, never losing heart despite facing repeated discomfiture in achieving success in their objectives but feeling sure that ultimately the victory would be theirs and the rabidly disposed opponents would bow out of the field finding that the ceaseless struggle of the Sikhs for a right cause they were sure to meet their Waterloo on the Canadian soil. The Sikh struggle for franchise waged by the Khalsa Diwan Society with all the vehemence at their command and their final victory has been adequately discussed in the relevant chapters.

The ghadar movement had its birth in Canada, though later its tempo was built up in the adjoining country, the U.S. But the share of Canada in the movement and the sacrifices suffered by the Sikhs from Canada was no less. Canada supported the movement through men and money under the guidance of the Khalsa Diwan Society, Vancouver. Details have been discussed in the chapter on the ghadar movement.

In fact, the Khalsa Diwan Society, Vancouver, had been the hub of all the religious, social and political activities. All the problems of the individuals or, those of the community were referred to the society that deeply involved itself in them to find suitable solutions whether the cases were resolved at individual or community or court level. The Khalsa Diwan Society, was the only or the most effectively moving force in the total spectrum of life of the Sikh community in British Columbia. They have, undoubtedly, done the most to glorify and preserve the true image of Sikh identity. Its present status is no less impressive and effective than ever.

When politicians or other social organizations plan to have a contact with the Vancouver or B.C. Sikh population the most efficacious forum to meet them is the Khalsa Diwan Society, that uses the Gurdwara's rostrum to appeal to the congregation for their propaganda. Undoubtedly, the Khalsa Diwan Society, Vancouver, is at present, as ever, the most powerful institution of the Sikhs in Canada and a message from its stage has the largest appeal and the deepest effect.

In fact, the history of the Canadian Sikhs and the history of the Khalsa Diwan Society, Vancouver, are synonymous or one and the same thing. Have I said too much? The driving force of every Sikh movement in Canada, right from the times of the pioneer Sikhs to the present day emanated from none other than the Khalsa Diwan Society, Vancouver. All other Sikh societies came into being or started functioning effectively in the 1950s or after when most of the hardest battles had already been won by the Vancouver society. It never lost its initiative and maintained its status of leadership to which it has its rightful claim. It has been a permanent source of financial help to all the needy organizations the world over and particularly in India. It is amusing to note that as seen above the Sikh organizations in India had periodically sent leaders to obtain financial help for projects in India but no project has so far been thought of for the benefit of the Sikhs in Canada. The traffic has been one way only. For almost the whole century the Indian Sikh organizations have made no systematic effort to supply to libraries abroad books on Sikhism. Whatever little has been done by the non-resident Indian Sikhs it has been done through their individual or collective efforts.

Kartar Singh, an educated man, who periodically published in Canada a journal from June 1929 to September 1936, in English and Punjabi, titled, *India and Canada: A Journal of Interpretation and Information* ,wrote in 1929:

"It is a great joy to me to find that here in this distant land you still keep up your own religious faith and do not neglect your Sikh religion. That is the right thing to do if you want to remain in a distant country with moral character and good social and family traditions such as those which still remain in India itself.

"I am so glad to find that the Khalsa Diwan Society is the centre of your own life in British Columbia. That is quite right and proper and good. For without that binding link you are bound to fall to pieces. But if you keep this binding force of your own pure religious faith intact, then you will preserve your character also and your family life will be good and pure. You must cling together and help one another. Do not let any member of your community come to grief and ruin through your neglect." This message is as apt today as it was in 1929.

May I venture to remark that whatever the reasons, undoubtedly, the flame of faith for their religion and its practices burnt more brightly and radiantly within the pioneer Sikhs than it burns within the Sikhs of the present day. At present, efforts to promote and preserve Sikh religion in their new home land are sometimes more vigorously pursued than before but irrefutably the Sikh spirit in the earlier settlers was much more deepseated in the recesses of their hearts than we find it in the hearts of the present generation Sikhs. It is my painful regret.

The earlier Sikhs had been staunch believers in their faith. They insisted that faith never fails a person. It is we who fail, when we give up on our faith. Having faith in ourselves and our convictions gives the weakest of us the inner strength to endure and persevere in moments of adversity. It motivates us to do our best.

When all else fails, it is only faith and prayer that we can turn to. In moments of grief and pain, when there seems no light in the end of the tunnel, it is the faith that takes us through. Of all the virtues, faith helps us bear the pain and uncertainty of life. For it is faith that stands firmly rooted, unshaken by doubt and death.

The Khalsa Diwan Society, Vancouver, invited messages from some Canadian ministers and mayors for inclusion in its souvenir published in 1994. Giving a few words herein from their communications would not be out of place as these have direct bearing on the subject under discussion.

Jean Chretien, Prime Minister of Canada wrote:

"This publication will undoubtedly be a source of great pride as you reflect upon the Khalsa Diwan Society's proud history. Moreover, it will serve not only to educate Canadians about the Sikh community, but also to preserve vital cultural links from generation to generation. It is my hope that you will continue to foster fellowship among the members of your community, while at the same time contributing to a strong and harmonious Canada."

Herb (Harbans Singh) Dhaliwal, M.P. then Parliamentary Secretary to the Minister of Fisheries and Oceans, Federal Government of Canada said, "We owe a great debt to these pioneers for the difficulties they endured and challenges they met while settling in a new country. They are a vital part of our history and we are part of their legacy.... As a proud member of the Sikh community I congratulate the Khalsa Diwan Society...on the contribution they have made to Canada."

Mike Harcourt, then Premier of British Columbia said, "As Premier of British Columbia I am pleased and honoured to salute the Sikh community as it commemorates a century of events and accomplishments in Canada.

"This souvenir publication documents important developments in the Sikh community since the Khalsa Diwan Society's 1906 inception. It also celebrates the traditional, social, economic and religious roots of one of British Columbia's earliest immigrant communities. Indeed, we are proud of the leadership roles taken on by the Sikhs in B.C.'s social, economic and political life. The Sikh community has made and continues to make many positive contributions to our province".

Moe (Manmohan Singh) Sihota, then Minister of Environment and Multiculturalism, B.C. Canada, wrote:

"It is indeed a tremendous pleasure for me to honour the achievements of the Khalsa Diwan Society. The Sikhs have reason to be proud of their accomplishments and the contributions that they have made to British

Columbia since the first settlers arrived on its shores at the turn of this century. The Sikh presence has clearly enriched this province, and the lives of all British Colombians.

"Since its inception in 1906, the Khalsa Diwan Society, served as the beacon which guided the Sikh pioneers through the arduous first decades of the 20th century".

"The society fought for social and economic justice for fellow Sikhs at a time when racial intolerance and indifference was prevalent in our society. With determined and persistent efforts these pioneers were able to overcome these obstacles to win over their democratic rights and yet maintaining a pride and dignity that all British Colombians can be proud of".

"Future generations should never forget the hardships and challenges faced by our forebears, the Sikh pioneers, who settled in this province. The Khalsa Diwan Society was an integral part of that history. Its contributions as well as the contributions of its individual members can never be forgotten. I applaud the Sikh community and the Khalsa Diwan Society."

Philip W. Owen, Mayor of Vancouver, said,

"Vancouver is a city that is blessed not only by a beautiful physical setting, but also by the strength and spirit of the early pioneers who settled here.

"Our early Indo-Canadian immigrants who chose to make Vancouver their home played an important role in Vancouver's development as a truly international city. Since 1906, the Khalsa Diwan Society has helped maintain a strong religious and cultural base for Vancouver's Sikh community".

We often borrow from our tomorrows to pay our debt to our yesterdays. Our present and next generations are morally bound to pay our debt of gratitude to our pioneers who suffered immense misery and untold and incalculable hardships.

The Khalsa Diwan Society, Vancouver, celebrated its 90th anniversary on 26 September 1996. It was very thoughtful of the society to honour 43 men and women who had either come to Canada before 1936 or were born in Canada before that year, that is, those who had lived in Canada for 60 years or more.

Of late, the Khalsa Diwan Society, has been very conscious of maintaining and promoting the distinctiveness of the community in Canada as the Sikh image is creating its recognition all over the world very rapidly. Perhaps there is no part of the world where a Sikh in his full Sikh form is not known as a Sikh. The Sikh community is now a world community not exclusive to India or a few countries where they are living in larger numbers.

People all over the world are keen to know more and more about them. In 1995-96, besides others, students from Quebec (Canada), Japan, Korea, China, Washington University, Australia, New Zealand, and some groups of native students and Christian school students, came to the 8000 Ross street Gurdwara, Vancouver, to have deeper understanding of Sikhism. They were acquainted with the main teachings of Sikh religion and Sikh practices. The visiting groups enjoyed *Guru* ka *langar* immensely and admired the practice of free mess in the Gurdwaras.

In response to the Fraser area secondary school administrators' request, a meeting with the representatives from the Khalsa Diwan Society, in order to begin a dialogue as to how to help Indo-Canadian youth to be more successful at school was held on 16 October 1996. At the meeting it was decided that there is a need to work together in order to better understand school and community expectations pertaining to young people. This meeting was held in the Board Room of the Sikh Community Resource Centre, Vancouver, in which 25 members from both sides participated. The growing rapport between the school board and the East Indian community or the Khalsa Diwan Society was especially fruitful and gainful. The schools try to understand the problems of the East Indians in respect of their education and make efforts to remove their handicaps.

Canadian Sikhs have the great honour of having enjoyed the exciting occasion (10 October to 13 October 1997) of the centennial celebrations of our pioneers coming to Canada.

The Canadian whites who opposed the East Indian immigrants tooth and nail in earlier stages have now realized it full well that they are a richness that this country profits from. They are not just the people who snatched jobs from them or corrupted their life-style by introducing their own ways of living in the society. Now they feel that they have gained much from them in terms of hard work, honest dealings, utmost patience, super-gentleness, hospitality, and sense of self- respect and dignified behaviour.

The story of the Sikh pioneers to Canada during the early part of the twentieth century is at places horrifying and at places charming but this author lived with them for a century through records and their innocent self-told tales of living in Canada. I have never been at times more amused and at times more grieved in life than when listening to their bewitching and shocking experiences.

To link it with the centennial celebrations, I venture to repeat as already mentioned that the jawans of the Sikh regiment after participation in London in the celebrations of Queen Victoria's Diamond Jubilee in 1897, while on their way back home, reached Montreal by sea and from there arrived in Vancouver by train in the first week of October 1897. They moved about in Vancouver and the surrounding areas on horse-back. After a week's stay here they resumed their journey for India via Hong Kong, Shanghai and Singapore where some Sikhs, mostly retired army men were already living. These returning jawans met them and admired the scenic beauty of Canadian landscape and the prosperous living conditions of the people here and motivated and urged them to shift to Canada to better their prospects. Since then, the Sikhs started migrating to a new land in groups unmindful of the extreme difficulties that awaited them here. But the Sikhs being very hardy, enduring and adventurous people they did not bow or surrender before the hazardous odds confronting them in the new country. They braved hardships valiantly and weathered all storms almost always sailing against the winds. They seldom evade an impregnable situation but tear through it. It is their inherited trait. The 100 - year of the Sikhs in Canada is a living witness to it and a glowing tribute to their indomitable power of determination. Two big and impressive statues showing two Sikh soldiers riding horses have been installed near 8000 Ross Street Gurdwaras parking lot. These were built in imitation to two of the four Sikh horse-riders who were photographed moving about in Vancouver in 1897. These have been built by sculptures—Tara Singh and his son—on the request of the Khalsa Diwan Society, Vancouver. The inauguration ceremony of these statues was performed on 31 March 1996.

During the celebrations organized by "Canadian Sikhs Committee for Centennial Celebrations" which included the Khalsa Diwan Society of Vancouver and other Sikh Societies of the Lower Mainland organizations jointly from 10 October to 13 October 1997, the government of British Columbia and local governments of Lower Mainland recognized and declared as centennial celebration week of 'coming of the Sikh pioneers' to Canada and the 50th anniversary of enfranchisement.

Proclamations to this effect were put on record by the B.C. government and by the mayors of the cities of Vancouver, Burnaby, New Westminster, Surrey, Richmond, Abbotsford, Delta, Coqitlam, Port Coquitlam, Langley, West Vancouver, Pitt Meadows and Chilliwack.

And just as a specimen, a copy of Vancouver's proclamation is included in this book, as Vancouver has been the main centre of major activity of the Sikh community throughout the century of their stay in Canada.

Office of the Mayor
City of Vancouver

BRITISH COLUMBIA
Proclamation
"COMING OF THE SIKH PIONEERS TO CANADA WEEK"
WHEREAS
The first Sikhs arrived in British Columbia over a hundred years ago (1897) and contributed to the economic and social development of the Province;

AND WHEREAS
These early Sikh pioneers faced many challenges and hardships in their efforts to building their community and contributing to Canada;

AND WHEREAS
The Sikhs were finally extended the right to vote in 1947;

AND WHEREAS
The City of Vancouver, British Columbia, recognizes the contributions of these early pioneers, along with succeeding generations of South Asians, to the social, cultural, political and economic life of the province;

AND WHEREAS
The City of Vancouver, British Columbia, wishes to join with all citizens of the Province to recognize the 100th anniversary of the arrival of the Sikhs and the 50th anniversary of enfranchisement:

NOW, THEREFORE,
I, Philip Owen, Mayor of the City of Vancouver, DO HEREBY PROCLAIM the week of October 10th to October 17th, 1997 as
"COMING OF THE SIKH PIONEERS TO CANADA WEEK'
in the City of Vancouver.

Philip W. Owen
MAYOR

Summing up I have to remark that the Khalsa Diwan Society, Vancouver, was not only a committee that looked after the Vancouver Gurdwara but it was an institution that looked after the whole Sikh community. This society has led the Sikh community out of the valley of discrimination and gross injustices to a life of dignity and honour. It encompassed the Sikhs not only living in Vancouver but in the whole of North America and India and elsewhere. Its members remained linked with their roots, their culture, their language and religion. If a community or a nation loses its culture and its language they are lost to the world at large. Their identity would be lost.

The Khalsa Diwan Society has been doing its utmost to save the Sikh identity, Sikh heritage and its culture. In the future too they are believed to follow and preserve Sikhism, its practices and its values of social life. Besides the language of the country they live in they must not allow the mother tongue of their ancestors to disappear from use in their homes. If you are equipped with more languages you will surely be more cultured and to care for ones mother tongue is your moral and ethical duty.

I never mean to suggest that the Sikhs should live in Canada as an isolated community in respect of their language and culture. They must consider themselves as active members of the Canadian mainstream, integrating themselves in its programmes and social life but not assimilating themselves in the cultural mess of this country. They are not to divorce themselves from their ancestry and forget or replace their heritage values with those of the adopted country. When their culture is at divergent variance with that of the whites they must show full regard to theirs. They must respect and follow their own noble values of life, many of which, for their goodness, would be emulated by the non-Sikhs. Let the Khalsa Diwan Society be the flag-bearer of Sikhism and all the righteousness and the superb values that the Sikh religion embodies or enshrines in itself. Sikhism has emerged as one of the great religions of the world and the Khalsa Diwan Society, Vancouver, must keep its flame in its full glow and its glory ever in undiminished splendour.

The sweeping remarks about the Sikh community by Gurcharan Singh, former secretary of the Federation of Sikh Societies of Canada, need consideration here. We must sympathize with the inordinately disappointed and dejected writer who sounds a note of despondency and warning. On the superficial reading, the following lines about the Canadian Sikhs may not find favour with the Sikh community that is always wedded to optimism. But the note is an eye-opener and it intends to sound warning to the community.

"The Sikh community is poorly organized. Its building blocks —the Gurdwaras—which are situated across the country, need a stronger consolidation. The attempt made by the Federation of Sikh Societies of Canada need to be redefined more strongly — a type of a Canadian Gurdwaras Act like the one proposed by the Ontario Council of the Sikhs, is required. The other detriment for the Sikhs is the lack of intellectualism in the community. A cursory knowledge of social, cultural and religious matters is neither enough nor adequate to serve the community needs. Persons, with thorough, historically and traditionally correct (uncontroversial) and authoritative and specialized knowledge of social, cultural, religious and philosophic issues, relating to the community, are required. These people must be good, able and honest managers, teachers and communicators. When a professor of agriculture claims to be an authority on the Misal period or a doctor of psychiatry claims to be an expert on Sikh spiritualism many things can and do go wrong. There is a need of trained personnel in the art of management of Gurdwaras and propagation. Both scholarship and intellectualism is required. There is a remarkable lack of community spirit among the Sikhs. Loyalty to the cause is a rarity. Sheer opportunism and unscrupulous greed have become a norm. Quality in leadership is no longer a desirable or saleable commodity. Vulgarity, unethicalism and insensitivity have become the currency of value. Another aspect of impediment that the community suffers from is the lack of a defined objective and strategic planning. No goal is ever defined or stated and if it is there it is so broad and meaningless that it can hardly be considered as a challenge or a target. There is no sense of planning for any activity.

"Another fact is that there is no spirit of charity or philanthropy in the community. Their contribution to the public good is limited to the raising of Gurdwaras. The poor quality in the management, administration and maintenance of the Gurdwara does not perturb them. There is no accountability of any official of the Gurdwara which causes endless problems."[1]

The writer of the above lines is neither totally correct nor totally wrong in the context of present situation in Canada. His tilt to stark criticism of the community seems to have sprung from the unfulfilled high expectations that he nursed in the deep recesses of his heart. Generally our dreams never come true to our visualization fully. The community moves on and on towards the attainment of a goal set before it. The emotional agony of the writer is due to his deep reverential feelings for the community and we have every regard for these feelings.

In this article the writer has made a scholarly attempt to deal with some of the problems of the Sikhs but his approach slightly lacks optimism which is necessary to pull the community out of its shortcomings, if any. To brand a community suffering from all the ills present under the sun and to ignore its most valuable qualities may not be fair to it.

Let me say in the defence of the Sikhs that they are gifted with superb qualities of gentleness, honesty, self-respect, reliability, hospitality, humaneness, hard work, integrity and undaunted bravery that make them a people par excellence on this planet.

REFERENCE

1. Gurcharan Singh, 'The Sikhs and Multicultural Canada' *The Journal of Religious Studies*, Vol. XXIX, No.1. Spring 1998, Punjabi University, Patiala (India), pp.85-86.

CHAPTER 11
SIKH IDENTITY AND
ITS PRESERVATION IN CANADA

Sikh Identity

It is a matter of history that Guru Nanak's mission has been regarded as the promulgation of a new religion that remains distinct and complete in itself. The pattern of religious life produced by him endured unaffected over the centuries. The Guru did not identify himself with the existing forms of religion. The author of *Dabistan-i-Mazahib* (1645) informs us that "the disciples of Nanak do not read the *mantras* (scriptures) of the Hindus. They do not venerate their temples or idols nor do they esteem their *avtars*. They have no regard for the Sanskrit language which according to the Hindus is the speech of gods."[1] The Sikh insistence on the unity of God distinguished them from the Hindus and the Sikh belief in transmigration distinguished them from the Muslims. In the eyes of the author of *Dabistan*, the Sikhs of Guru Nanak or the Nanak *panthis* were a distinct entity. Their identity was based on their different doctrines, institutions and social attitudes including their sense of commitment to matters spiritual as well as temporal. This identity of the Sikhs was neither Hindu nor Muslim.

Guru Nanak discarded the contemporary forms of religious belief and ritualistic practices of the Hindus after he was convinced that he had something more valuable to offer. He adopted for himself and for his followers his own revealed compositions. This clearly meant the rejection of the old Hindu scriptural authority and also the Hindu deities and the scriptures of the contemporary religions.

According to Daljeet Singh, Sikh religion is independent and perfect in itself. To Guru Nanak, God is the ruler and protector of the universe.

He is the source of all values and virtues and He has interest in human life. To the Guru human deeds become all important: truthful living is higher than truth. The goal of life is not merely *nirvana* but carrying out the altruistic will of God. The *gurmukh* is the person who carries out God's will. Thus, Sikh ideology explains the dynamism and ethical activities of the Gurus and their followers. This gives distinctive identity to Sikhism and the Sikhs.[2]

Guru Nanak's highly sophisticated doctrine was that of *naam simran* (meditation of God) which reveals the presence of God all around and within oneself. It rejected idol worship, temples, pilgrimages, incarnation and the existing sacred scriptures. The message of *naam simran* was reinforced by the first four successors of Guru Nanak and consequently it was embodied in the *Adi Granth Sahib*. It gave them strength in all situations. Robert E. Humane said, "The Sikhs are a deeply devoted people and faith is an essential trait of their nature. An immense reserve of spiritual energy has been their strong asset in many a crisis during their 500 years old history."

We again refer to Daljeet Singh who believes that Sikhism is a class by itself. The Indian systems are dichotomous, drawing a clear line between spiritual and empirical life. These systems encourage asceticism, withdrawal and monasticism; they regard celibacy as a virtue, they consider woman as temptress; they value *ahimsa*; and they support the system of caste, untouchability and pollution. Islam and Judaism are a whole life systems, not dichotomous. But later in their history monasticism and asceticism appear as an important phenomenon. Christianity preaches involvement in life but prescribes non-resistance to violence and evil. Later on in its history we see monasteries and nunneries and still later a sort of dichotomy between religious and empirical life.

Sikhism is a whole life system, like Islam and Judaism but it is free from exclusiveness and leaves no room for withdrawal and monasticism. The Sikhs rejected the idea of renunciation. That was why they took either to agriculture or trades or services i.e. employment. Being productive, they could contribute towards Guru's treasury. 'Deliverance from the cycle of transmigration was to be achieved by remaining in the world not by withdrawing into ritual or ascetic seclusion'. This path to emancipation was open to men and women of all castes. The concept of *miri piri* and the ideal of *sant-sipahi* are an integral part of Sikhism. Asceticism, celibacy and downgrading of women are rejected in Sikhism together with caste ideology and *ahimsa*. Guru Nanak organized a whole life system of householders participating in all walks of life and remaining socially responsible. Thus, Sikhism from the very beginning was different from both the Indian and Semitic religions.[3]

In Sikh thought right or wrong are absolute and not relative concepts. In the sublime vision of the Gurus there is no room for ethical dualities, polarities or moral relativism.

No particular doctrines and devotional practices by themselves could create followers. The primary basis of the community of followers that gathered around Guru Nanak was his religiosity and personality that inspired veneration. His hymns had an attractive quality. To this legacy was added his decision to choose or nominate a successor, thus establishing a lineage and ensuring a succession that was recognized as legitimate till the death of the Tenth Master. This decision gave rudimentary organisation to the *panth* of Guru Nanak and ensured its continuing existence beyond his lifetime. The nomination of Angad to the Guruship was in the words of Indubhusan Banerjee "a fact of the profoundest significance."[4] Trumpp writes, "the disciples of Nanak would, no doubt, have soon dispersed, and gradually disappeared...if he had not taken care to appoint a successor before his death."[5]

Guru Angad took the holy compositions of his Master, Guru Nanak, and got them recorded in a special script called *gurmukhi*. A modified form of *bhatakshri* was adopted by Guru Nanak and was popularized among the Sikhs by Guru Angad as *gurmukhi* as it was used in recording the words fallen from the mouth of his Guru. Thus, the adoption of *gurmukhi* as the script for the sacred scripture was a prominent mark of distinction.

From the repeated references to the erection and use of *dharmsalas* it is clear that these buildings stood at the centre of the corporate life of the *panth* and much activity must have been conducted within them. These buildings obviously corresponded to the modern Gurdwara.[6] The *dharmsala* conferred a distinctive identity on the Nanak *panth*. The Vaishnavas had their temple, the *yogis* had their *asan*, the Muslims had their mosque, and the Nanak *panthis* had their *dharmsalas*. The *dharmsalas* of the early Sikh tradition developed into the Gurdwara of the eighteenth century. Erecting Gurdwaras at locations associated with particular events in the lives of the individual Gurus became common, particularly, after the establishment of the Sikh rule under the Sardars of the Sikh Misals. The *dharmsalas* continued as the centres for *kirtan* (singing of *gurbani*). Eventually, the term Gurdwara came into common currency. This was because the *sangat* that met in the *dharmsalas* came to be looked upon as the Guru. *Guru Granth Sahib*, that was ordained to be the Guru, came to be installed in the *dharmsala* and the place appropriately became the Guru's door (Gurdwara).[7] The change in term used for the sacred space reflected its enhanced importance in the eyes of the Sikhs as it got more intimately linked with the Guru. Wherever, Guru Nanak went during his missionary travels he established *sangats*, [8] with the instruction to his followers to build a place of congregation or *dharmsala* where they could regularly meet and sing the Lord's praises. Thus sprang up a network of *sangats* and *dharmsalas* that became centres of Sikh missionary activities. These centres were established in Kamrup (Assam), Bihar, Cuttack, Surat, Nanakmata (in the Kumaon Hills), Khatmandu, Jallalabad, Kabul and many other places. These *sangats* were supervised and presided over by persons generally appointed by the Guru himself. [9] These centres and *sangats* were established to ensure that practical shape was given to his ideals, through wider networking. The idea behind all this was to knit the Sikhs together as a separate *panth* or people. This system was unique in its formation and appeal.

The membership of the *sangat* organisation was open to all persons, men and women, whatever their social position. As these *sangats* grew with the passage of time, people hailing from different faiths, castes and walks of life came into their fold. Men belonging to high and low castes sat together without any distinction. The casteless assembly of the *sangat* gave it a distinct identity. The Guru gave the *sangat* a status superior to himself.

Another institution, that of *pangat* or *langar* (free common mess), originated almost simultaneously with that of *sangat*. It imparted a secular dimension to the *sangat*; added to the functional efficiency of the Sikh organisation; it translated the principle of equality into practice, making it obligatory for all people, whatever their status in life, to sit on the ground and eat together and finally it served as a cementing force among the followers of Sikhism. This institution of *langar* was wholly revolutionary in Guru Nanak's times. Not only *shudras* but also the Muslims could sit at the same level. This practice struck at a major aspect of caste, thereby advancing the process of defining a distinctive Sikh identity.

The process of integration of Sikhism went hand in hand with the enlargement of its ranks. As early as the time of Guru Amar Das—the Third Nanak, twenty-two *manjis* or dioceses were created which were centres for the spread of Sikhism.

From the time of Guru Amar Das, it began to be felt that the Sikhs should have their own seats of religion and pilgrimage so that it might not be necessary for them to go to the *tiraths* (the holy places of Hindus). A *baoli* (a well with *pacca* staircases reaching down to the water surface) was constructed at Goindwal under the instruction and personal supervision of Guru Amar Das. The water of this *baoli* was consecrated and a bath with this water was regarded as an act of great spiritual merit.

Indubhusan Banerjee writes, "Guru Angad had, no doubt, done something to give the Sikhs an individuality of their own but it was under Guru Amar Das that the difference between a Hindu and a Sikh became more pronounced and the Sikhs began, gradually, to drift away from the orthodox Hindu society and form a class, a sort of new brotherhood by themselves" [10] Thus, we see that with rapid strides, right from the beginning, the Nanak *panthis* were assuming a distinct Sikh identity.

The fourth Guru, Guru Ram Das, founded the town of Chak Ram Das which subsequently got its present name, Amritsar, from the holy waters of Pool of Immortality built there. The work on this tank commenced by Guru Ram Das, reached its completion under his son and successor Guru Arjan Dev, who, as well, built a Gurdwara in the centre of the tank calling it Harmandir that is, God's House. Thus, the Sikhs got a rallying centre at Amritsar where they could occasionally meet and maintain closer relationship with their brothers-in-faith. The Guru had conceived Harmandir, as the seat of spiritual power of the Sikh faith. It is a Sikh Vatican or Sikh Mecca with all the spiritual glories and divine aura surrounding it. Harmandir gave the Sikhs a distinct place of pilgrimage providing a noble Sikh identity to the Sikh religion.

Some Sikhs lived outside the Punjab or at distant places. Out of reverential feelings they made offerings to their spiritual guides. When they could not personally come to the Guru they sent their offerings through accredited missionaries called *masands*. The word *masand* is from Persian *masnad* meaning an elevated seat for which the *gaddi* was also used. As the Sikh preachers, being representatives of the Gurus, were offered higher seats or *gaddis* in congregations, they were called *masnads* or *masands*. With the extension of Sikh circles much beyond the Punjab, the *masand* system had come to replace the *manjis* of Guru Amar Das, which had been mostly confined to that province. The *masands* were not only collectors of offerings or *daswandh* but were preachers of religion is evident from the *Dabistan*.[11] As the fifth Guru had undertaken to raise public works of enormous dimensions that were sure to require and attract money, its collection and conveyance needed careful attention. The *masand* system was a distinct measure adopted by the Guru and it was discarded later when it became unnecessary or unwanted.

The Sikh scripture, *Guru Granth Sahib*, is the most emphatic pronouncement about the distinct and independent identity of Sikhism. Such an authentic compilation was needed because the Guru had 'a new thesis' to give to mankind. It closed the door to all possible controversies, and embodied a complete and final message. [12]

In the words of Arnold Toynbee—a great British historian, "The *Adi Granth* is remarkable for certain reasons. Of all known religious scriptures, this Book is the most highly venerated. It means more to the Sikhs than the *Quran* means to the Muslims, the *Bible* to the Christians and the *Torah* to the Jews. The *Adi Granth* is the Sikhs' perpetual Guru (spiritual guide).... The Sikh religion and its scriptures, the *Adi Granth*, will have something of a special value to say to the rest of the world."[13]

The Sikh scripture promises support for the spiritual emancipation of the devotee if he has unflinching trust in God and the Guru. Sikhism believes in the unity of God, God's self-existence, God as infinite, eternal and absolute, His omnipotence, His omnipresence, and His omniscience. To Sikhism everything in the universe is according to the Divine Ordinance or His *hukam*. Guru Nanak says:

What He wills He ordains,
To Him no one can give an order,
for He, O, Nanak, is the king of kings.
As He wills so we must live.

(Guru Granth Sahib, p. 6).

That is, there is absolute supremacy of Divine Will. Good and evil, happiness and misery, ignorance and enlightenment, ugliness and beauty are there, because the Lord wants them to be like that. The concept of the Divine rule working in every particle and every incident of the universe is precisely what is meant by the doctrine of *hukam*.

The Guru in Sikhism is a perfect prophet or messenger of God, in whom the light of God shines fully and visibly. He is not God but he is as perfect and sinless as God is. According to Guru Nanak, "The mysteries of God and His creation are known either to God or to the Guru (*Karte ki mit karta janai ke janai gur sura*) (Guru Nanak, *Onkar*-3).

The word Guru, etymologically means, *Gu*: darkness, *ru*: light or revelation. Thus, Guru means dispeller of darkness, revealer of light.

In the True Guru He has installed His own spirit,
Through him, God reveals Himself.

(Guru Nanak, *Asa di var*: 6).

The cultivation of faith on the part of a devotee is made possible through a scripture. Implicit trust in the Lord is not merely to put ones self under His shelter but to do so with the conviction that He is the ocean of mercy and so can be expected to redeem us.

The concept of grace is delineated in *gurbani* through various terms such as *kirpa, nadar, mehar, prasad, daya, bakhshish, karam* and so on. The Gurus impress upon their followers to take refuge in Him alone who will liberate them from all sins. The *gurbani* puts forth the view that *prasad* (grace) is given by the Lord to His devotees for the sheer joy of helping them. His *mehar* (kindness) is given free as a gift. Man's experience of grace comes, as an ever operating blessing of God which is a ray of divine beauty. When He casts His glance of power (*nadar*) the consequence for man is tranquility, mitigation of suffering and blissfulness.

The *gurbani* also clearly holds that an important pre-requisite for obtaining a vision of God is the true Guru's grace which sets the individual on the road to the consummation of his destiny. According to the Sikh scripture, our life itself is a gift of His *kirpa* (kindness). Therefore, it must be properly lived, that is, in a spirit of devotion and gratitude to God. The Sikh Gurus are clearly of the view that the grace of God can override the operation of the law of *karma* (actions or deeds) by which a man is destined to be rewarded or punished for his actions.

Guru Gobind Singh vested the spiritual part of Guruship in the *Adi Granth* and the secular one in the Khalsa or the *Guru panth*. The tenets enshrined in the *Guru Granth Sahib* were final and inviolable fundamental laws of Sikhism to be in no case altered. None could scrap the injunctions of the *Guru Granth Sahib*, and had, therefore, to remain within the framework of their holy teachings. To grow as an independent community and a distinct religion, the Sikhs needed scripture of distinct identity for all time to come. The compiler of the *Adi Granth* had all this in mind and his work was more than equal to his plans. Undoubtedly, it is unique and par excellence in its aim and appeal. After Guru Gobind Singh breathed his last the *Guru Granth Sahib* provided an alternative to the living Guru to ensure the continuity of Guruship as it carried the seal of the Guru's approval.

Guru Hargobind, the sixth Nanak, raised the institution of the Akal Takht. He blended religion and politics into one. The Guru told his Sikhs that as long as he was in the Harmandir he should be treated as a saint and when at the Akal Takht he should be looked upon as the temporal leader of the community. This clearly indicated the characters of the two places lying opposite each other. The Harmandir had been set up exclusively for spiritual programmes and the Akal Takht for secular matters.

With the martyrdom of Guru Arjan, under Guru Hargobind, the Sikhs assumed additional responsibilities of self-defence. The Guru had to play a dual role of a *mir* (an army leader) and a *pir* (a Guru). It added a new dimension with a new identity to Sikhism. The Sikhs called the Guru the *sachha padshah*, the true king, as against the temporal king who ruled only by the force of arms and concerned himself with the worldly actions of the people. [14] He introduced congregational prayers which added further religious fervour and social cohesion among the Sikhs and strengthened unity and co-operation between them. [15]

With the adoption of measures of self-defence by the Sikhs, tension with the state grew and led ultimately to open clashes.

The ninth Master, Guru Tegh Bahadur, by offering himself to the Mughal tyrant's sword at Delhi, registered his peaceful resistance against the policy of forcible conversion. The execution of the Guru was a staggering catastrophe in Sikh history and the minds of the Sikhs were rudely shaken. "Guru Teg Bahadur's was not a passive submission but a positive decision to confront an existing situation. A most comprehensive genius of the age undertook to answer the challenge of the time with all his moral strength. He brought to his response spiritual insight and discipline of the highest order. This martyrdom was no small happening. It was something of immense magnitude, of immense consequence." [16]

Guru Tegh Bahadur's execution "undoubtedly strengthened the resistance against the religious policy of Aurangzeb and at the same time prepared the way for the final stage in the evolution of Sikhism." [17] The Sikh community, at the martyrdom of Guru Tegh Bahadur, could hardly be expected to meet the challenge of the mighty Mughal government. A state of confrontation with the government was there and if the Sikhs were to survive, they could afford to ignore it only at their own risk. Consequently, the Sikhs imbibed a spirit of sacrifice for a noble cause for all time to come. History bears witness to the fact that when there is need for sacrifice whether for religion or for country's freedom, the Sikhs would always be found in the front ranks. Readiness for sacrifice for a genuine cause became a distinctive feature of the Sikh community.

Guru Gobind Singh strongly felt that the Sikhs needed further internal cohesion and external defence. He planned a measure to be executed in a dramatic manner that gave the Sikhs the final and distinct shape to their identity. Retaining the basic idea of administering *pahul* (baptism) to the Sikhs a new ceremony of giving the nectar of the double-edged sword (*khande ki pahul*) was introduced in place of the old practice. Guru Gobind Singh strengthened the organisation of the community by making steel an integral limb of a Sikh to fight tyranny and injustice. He invested the initiant with personal obligation of five Ks: *kesh* (hair duly covered with a turban), *kangha* (wooden comb worn in the hair), *kara* (a steel bangle), *kirpan* (a sword or dagger) and *kachha* (a pair of breeches which must not reach below the knees). This external *rahit* (code of discipline) gave the Sikhs an unalterable distinct identity for perpetuity.

Within a few days of initiating the Khalsa a little less than a lakh of people hailing from different parts of the country got themselves baptised. Thus he 'brought a new people into being and released a new dynamic force into the arena of Indian history.'

Guru Gobind Singh invested the *panth* with his personality. He told the Sikhs, 'Khalsa is my very self and I shall always live in the Khalsa'. The creation of the Khalsa was the crowning event in Guru Gobind Singh's life from the standpoint of both organisation and ideology. Organizationally, it completely eliminated the need of the order of the *masands* that 'had become corrupt, decrepit and creaky and needed to be replaced by a better system'. Ideologically, the creation of the Khalsa aimed at a well-balanced combination of the ideals of *bhagti* and *shakti* of moral and spiritual excellence and militant valour or heroism of the highest order. The use of a double-edged sword in the preparation of the *amrit* (baptismal nectar) was a psychological booster. The changing of names at the time of administering *amrit* was intended to revolutionize the psyche of the Sikhs.[18] The names of all the baptised Sikhs were now to end in the uniform appellation of 'Singh' meaning lion, "thus making lions out of humble disciples and raising them with one stroke to a position of equality with the noblest and most warlike class in India, for up to that time only the Rajputs bore the exalted title of Singh.... They were now to feel as good and as great as the members of the solar and the lunar dynasties."[19]

The compulsory wearing of *kirpan* (sword) being one of the injunctions of the Khalsa promoted the spirit of martial valour among the Sikhs. "They were taught as an article of faith to believe that God was always present in the general body of the Khalsa and that wherever even five Sikhs were assembled, the Guru would be with them."[20]

They were also told that they were born to conquer. The new salutation given to the Sikhs was *'Waheguru ji ka Khalsa, waheguru ji ki fateh'* (The Lord's is the Khalsa and the Lord's is the victory).

With the distinctive character and identity the Sikhs faced the challenges of the eighteenth century, retaining in full bloom the Khalsa features of Sikh identity and further made every effort to retain it whenever there was any threat to its form and distinctiveness.

Throughout the eighteenth century it was the Khalsa identity that had become the predominant Sikh identity. Harjot Oberoi wrongly believes that the Sikh peasantry resisted the mainly evolved Sikh norms of the Khalsa quality.[21] This author seems to have ignored the marvellous contribution made by the Sikh peasantry to the cause of Sikhism throughout the span of Sikh history. When Banda Singh Bahadur, after having been duly baptised at the hands of Guru Gobind Singh, came to the Punjab from the Deccan, he carved out a strong base in the villages to fight against the repression of the Mughals and to make a determined bid for the liberation of the land from the oppressive masters. We find a marked role of the peasants and the *zamindars* in the activities of Banda Singh who moved almost unchecked in the major parts of the Punjab. When he was captured in 1715 and taken to Delhi, all of his 740 baptised companions, who were mostly peasants, refused reprieve contemptuously whenever offered. They were deeply attached to Sikh code of conduct.

The Sikh peasantry mainly manned the Sikh movement, during the times of Zakariya Khan, Mir Mannu and Ahmad Shah Durrani. All the members of the *dals* and the Dal Khalsa were the Sikh peasants, who were, along with their leaders, baptised Sikhs. None could join their *derahs* without having been duly initiated to Sikhism. All the Sardars (rulers) of the Sikh Misals, including Maharaja Ranjit Singh's predecessors, belonged to peasantry. At no stage of Sikh history we find the Sikh peasantry faltering in their faith in Sikhism. To argue arbitrarily that after rising to the top by a ladder of religious faith and distinct identity the Sikh peasantry kicked the ladder down is historically unacceptable. Harjot Oberoi suggests that there were vague and unclear identities of the Sikhs till the closing years of the nineteenth century. If the Sikhs had no clear identity then to whom Emperor Bahadur Shah referred when he gave his following edict on 10 December 1710, that: *Nanak prastan ra har ja kih ba-yaband ba-qatl rasanand.*[22] (An edict ordering a wholesale genocide of the Sikhs (the worshippers of Nanak) wherever found). The same order was repeated a few years later by Emperor Farrukh Siyar.[23]

Who were these people, who under Banda Singh's leadership, shook one of the mightiest empires in the world to its very foundations with such terrible force that it was never able to re-establish its authority as firmly as before? Who were these people for whose heads prices had been fixed under Zakariya Khan (1726-45)? For whom did the punitive parties of Zakariya Khan comb the villages and forests and who were the people brought in chains every day, batches after batches, and publicly beheaded at Lahore at *nakhas* (horse market) now called Shahidganj? How could they be identified? Who were these people, when captured and offered choice between Islam and death chose the latter? And who were these people about whom once Zakariya Khan said, "By God, they live on grass and claim kingship." [24] It is a pity that certain writers cannot understand about the Sikhs today what Qazi Nur Muhammad understood in 1765, when he was in the Punjab for a short time during Ahmad Shah Durrani's seventh invasion, that "Guru Nanak was not a mere reformer but the founder of a new religion. The Sikhs are not from among the Hindus. They have a separate religion of their own. They are courageous like lions and do not make friends with adulterers and housebreakers. They never slay a coward and they are not plunderers." [25] Who were these people before whose religious zeal and determination the tact and skill of the greatest military genius of the time in Asia (Ahmad Shah Durrani, 1748-67) gave way and at whose hands, the Durrani bowed out of the province in abject humiliation while meeting his Waterloo in the Punjab? Who were these people who expelled from the Punjab its three masters: the Mughals, the Afghans and the Marathas and established their principalities and later under Ranjit Singh a kingdom as big as that of France? Did these people have vague and unclear identities?

As referred to earlier the Khalsa identity remained dominant throughout the eighteenth century with great emphasis on the Khalsa *rahit*. The Khalsa tradition was carried forward into the nineteenth century when Ranjit Singh became the Maharaja. The spirit and attitudes of the eighteenth century informed his administration. His coinage bore the image of Guru Nanak and his administration was known as *Sarkar-i- Khalsa*. The Maharaja being the offspring of the eighteenth century his state was an authentic extension of the eighteenth century Khalsa ideals. When Ranjit Singh became the Maharaja it must have seemed to many a fulfilment of *Raj karega Khalsa* prophecy, a final vindication of the eighteenth century belief that the Khalsa would rule.[26]

For Joseph Cunningham (1849) as much as for John Malcolm (1812), the Sikhs were distinct from the Hindus, if anything Cunningham is more emphatic about the predominance of the Khalsa identity among the Sikhs. This perception, says McLeod, is strongly supported by the contemporary Sikh literature.[27] Rattan Singh Bhangu's *Prachin Panth Parkash* (1841) vigorously affirmed the distinctive nature of the Khalsa identity and claimed that this was the identity which Guru Gobind Singh had his followers to adopt. Giani Gian Singh's *Panth Parkash* (1880) and his *Tawarikh Guru Khalsa* (1919) are a kind of extension of Rattan Singh Bhangu's work. Gian Singh's works can be regarded as an example of 'the sustained predominance of the Khalsa identity'. Similarly the *Prem*

Sumarg and the *Sau Sakhian* also emphasized the importance of the Khalsa identity.

As against the Khalsa the Sahajdharis cut their hair; they do not carry arms; they had a radically different line of succession; they did not accept *Guru Granth Sahib* as Guru, they had their own pilgrimage centres at places like Hardwar and Benaras. The model of Sikhism they enunciated diverged considerably from that of the Khalsa Sikhs. They had different codes of dress and modes of salvation. So what sort of Sikh identity can they project? They may be partly believers in Sikhism but not the followers of its code of conduct. The Gurus gave their Sikhs an identity with its final form of the Khalsa. They gave them a form and a practice to preserve that identity throughout all times; it may be seventeenth century or the twentieth century; it may be in India or Canada or UK; and it may be times of peace or times of war. The problems of identity are being created by people who only want to believe in Sikhism but do not want to live according to the tenets and practices of Sikhism.

By some ill-informed and prejudiced writers the use of terms like religious diversity in Sikhism, religious fluidity in the Sikh tradition, multiple or plural identities in Sikhism, is irresponsible and misleading. They try to awfully blur the Sikh identity and make a strenuous bid to disintegrate, disorganize and demolish the distinct Sikh identity, the doctrine enshrined in the Sikh scripture and the glory of Sikh history created by a determined community steeped in its religious direction and inspired by unshaken constancy in Sikh heritage. Distinguishing character or personality of an individual or a community or the sameness forms the basis of an identity. The negation of the sameness is the negation of an identity. But in the field of Sikh religion and that of its social growth the Sikh identity was unquestionable. 'The Sikh identity is not in any manner artificial, it is the one that was clearly created and proclaimed by the Gurus themselves'. An independent Sikh identity was fully formed in the Khalsa once for all. The Sikh identity took two centuries in its metamorphosis to assume its final shape in 1699. In the words of Gokal Chand Narang, "The seed which blossomed in the time of Guru Gobind Singh had been sown by Nanak, and watered by his successors. The sword, which carved the Khalsa's way to glory, was, undoubtedly, forged by Gobind (Singh) but the steel had been provided by Nanak."[28] All the Sikhs who wanted to be recruited in the British army had to undergo the Khalsa baptism and uphold the five symbols of the Khalsa. The British had realized that the Sikh soldiers were best in their performance when they were in their true form and spirit. Hence the British emphasized the real Sikh form for them.

The Sikhs have to keep their ideological base intact. They cannot allow it to be eroded. Any dilution, distortion or erosion of the Sikh identity may have a disastrous effect on the Sikh psyche. In the current socio-religious milieu in the foreign lands the Sikh traditions, values, culture and identity are, sometimes, confronted with a threatening spectre.

In order to maintain their true and natural stature, the Sikhs have to salvage their identity. Their socio-religious existence has to be safeguarded. It is necessary to simultaneously pursue both the existential and universal concerns of Sikhism. One cannot be pursued at the cost of other.

A cursory glance at the Sikh history reveals that the Sikhs have fought and laid down their lives for universal causes. They have suffered innumerable martyrdoms and made immense sacrifices to uphold certain fundamental and abiding values of human life like peace, harmony, love and freedom of conscience. It was only through the preservation of their identity and ideology that the Sikhs have pursued their cherished universal goals.

Preservation of Sikh Identity

In Canada, the Sikhs are conscious of the onslaughts on the Sikh identity from some people who want Sikh assimilation into the majority group of the Canadian society. Under the western influence the Sikh youth is not only breaking with the tradition bequeathed by the Sikh Gurus but is also opting out of the Indian way of life. Many Sikh boys use anglisized names as a mask to hide their identity. Particularly appalling is the trend marked among the children of highly educated and prosperous classes. But the Sikhs, as a whole, have already passed through difficult stages and are now out of any danger to their ancestral heritage because of the government's enlightened policy of multiculturalism. If the Jews have maintained their identity even after 2000 years of stresses and strains why not the Sikhs who have no such strains, rather have the support of the government.

Sikhisms' originality and distinctiveness is unmistakable. The Sikh Gurus adopted a critical attitude towards Hinduism, the Vedic scriptures, caste system and priesthood. Under Guru Nanak and his successors a new code of conduct and the revealed scripture, later enshrined in the *Guru Granth Sahib*, guided the Sikhs socially and spiritually. The Sikhs divested themselves of the Hindu code of conduct and emerged as a distinct community with a perfect religion of their own.

The Sikhs adopted Anand Marriage instead of Vedic marriage ceremony and performed their own rites and practices on naming of a child, turban-tying of a boy and baptising of their men and women. They discarded the Hindu *kirya* (death ceremony) in respect of the death of a Sikh and distributed sweet pudding after the *bhog* ceremony. The Sikhs carried a *kirpan* on their person instead of the Hindu sacred thread and a mark on the forehead.

The Sikh *amrit* ceremony was performed with the double-edged sword. The Guru told them that the baptised Sikhs should totally break away from their previous occupation, religion, ancestry and past actions and become new human beings. The Guru further told them that 'caste is non-sense' and no body should be asked his caste. But sadly enough, the castes and sub-castes did not die among the Sikhs.

The Sikhs not only assumed a distinct faith but also a distinct social structure and a distinct culture or a life style. In his outward appearance a Sikh is unique in the world, none can ever mistake him for some one other than a Sikh. With unshorn hair on his body and a turban on head he has a globally known appearance.

A young turbaned Sikh boy presented a garland to the crown prince Charles of England during the 300th year of the Khalsa celebration function in London 1999. The prince said, "My son always keep and respect your Sikh identity." This is a regardful recognition of the Sikh identity by the future King of England.

They have a common surname 'Singh' or lion and the Sikh ladies have 'Kaur' or princess at the end of their name. They have a different mode of salutation:

Waheguru ji ka Khalsa waheguru ji ki fateh (The Sikh or the Khalsa belongs to the wonderful Lord to whom also the victory belongs.) Their war cry is: *Jo bole so nihal sat sri akal* (He, who shouts loudly that God is true, will obtain His bliss.)

In their native province—Punjab (India) and also everywhere in the world, the Sikhs have their own first language—Punjabi and their own script—*gurmukhi*.

They have their own daily prayer in which they remember their Ten Masters and Holy Scriptures and they repeat the tale of joys and sufferings and achievements of the Sikh community. They remember every day "those who allowed themselves to be cut limb by limb, had their scalps off, were broken on the wheel, were sawn or flayed alive and all those who with the object of preserving the sanctity and independence of the Sikh shrines permitted themselves to be beaten, imprisoned, shot, maimed or burned alive." The Sikh prayer crystalises the history of the Sikh community. Over the centuries their prayers have comforted the tortured hearts and have given them strength to face hardships with unparalleled fortitude and perseverance.

The Sikhs urgently needed to be integrated for the preservation of their culture. If unfortunately, they fight amongst themselves over their religious *maryada* and get disintegrated, their precious and glorious culture and distinct identity will get shattered.

Efforts have been continuously underway in Canada to preserve their identity through various measures as have been discussed below.

Gurdwara-based Activities

The Gurdwara has been the nucleus of Sikh religious and cultural activities. When a number of Sikhs start living at a place their first requirements include a Gurdwara where they may be able to meet in the morning and evening for their prayers and singing of Lord's praises. The Gurdwara literally means the abode of the Guru or where the *Guru Granth Sahib* is installed. It becomes a rallying place for the Sikhs. It is here that they also discuss problems relating to the community, its development, and the retention of their religious *rehat* (code of discipline).

In 1904 one Bhai Arjan Singh Cheema brought *Guru Granth Sahib* to Canada and located it at a house in Port Moody. He belonged to village Malak, district Ludhiana. The old reports of the Khalsa Diwan Society reveal that he was a devoted Sikh who worked very hard for the community. He passed away at young age, on 22 July 1907. His early death was cruelty of fate and a great loss to the community. He had some knowledge of English, which he used in finding jobs for the new immigrants. He was an active member of the committee constituted to collect funds for the construction of a Gurdwara in Vancouver. But unfortunately he could not live to see it built.

Since the Sikhs first settled at Vancouver they laid the foundation stone of a Gurdwara at 1866 west, 2nd Avenue, in 1907. On 19 January 1908, the first *nagarkirtan* (religious procession) took place to celebrate the opening of this Gurdwara. Shortly thereafter, the Gurdwaras were built in Victoria, Fraser Mills and Abbotsford in 1912 and the Sikh temples at Paldi near Duncan (1918), Hillcrest (1935) and 8000-Ross Street, .Vancouver (1970) whose foundation stone was laid on 30 March 1969, and officially opened on 25 April 1970. At present there are about a hundred Gurdwaras across Canada, nearly half of them in British Columbia.

In every Gurdwara there is recitation of *gurbani* (holy composition of the Guru) in the morning and evening everyday. Most of the Sikhs, men and women, who are daily free or have time to attend the religious services there, may be for a short time. do attend the same. Generally there are brief programmes of expositions from the Holy Scripture every evening by a Sikh—a man or a woman, who has thoroughly studied the *bani*. On Sunday there are larger gatherings in the Gurdwaras where *kirtan, katha, dhadi* programmes and a couple of lectures, on Sikhism or Sikh history, are arranged.

The Gurdwara organizers may place before the congregation any problems confronting the community and after discussion may put the same to vote for decision which is always held in veneration as it receives the endorsement of the Guru (*Guru Granth Sahib*) in whose presence it is taken.

Generally there is an *akhandpath bhog* on Sunday at the Gurdwara. The *akhandpath* is either sponsored by a family or by the Gurdwara itself. In the congregation the *sangat*—men and women, may have a mixed seating arrangement but for the convenience of both, one side of the hall, generally the right side, facing the *Guru Granth Sahib*, is marked for the men and the left side for the women. In conducting the programmes in the Gurdwara, reciting from the holy *Granth* Sahib, performing *kirtan* or *katha*, both men and women have equal rights. It is in conformity with the teachings of the Sikh Gurus who proclaimed women as equal partners of men in all social and religious matters.

After the conclusion of the *bhog* of *akhandpath* and other items of the program *langar* is served in the basement hall of the Gurdwara. The food served in the Guru's *langar* is considered holy, and every Sikh keenly wants to partake of it. Contribution to the *langar* is taken as an act of religious import. Almost always, after religious functions or ceremonies in their families, the Sikhs arrange Guru's *langar* at their places, deeming it blissful and to the Guru's pleasure. At the big and historic Sikh shrines the individual Sikh families take upon themselves the *sewa* (voluntary service) of running the *langar* for the whole day at their personal expense. Generally the people have to wait for months for their turn because for such a holy service they have to be on the list which is sometimes very long one. This unique institution of free mess has earned the Sikhs a wide appreciation from all religious and social organizations or denominations of the world.

It was unfortunate rather sacrilegious that a few decades back some of the Canadian Sikhs used to sit in the Gurdwara on chairs in front of the holy *Guru Granth Sahib* with heads uncovered. It is not definitely known as to when this grossly non-reverential and outrageously unholy practice started in some Gurdwaras in Canada. A photograph of 1949 shows

Jawahar Lal Nehru, Prime Minister of India, addressing a congregation in a Gurdwara in Canada, in the presence of the holy *Guru Granth Sahib* with his head uncovered. Later he was presented with a *siropa* (role of honour) including a *kirpan* by the Gurdwara Prabandhaks or caretakers in the same position.

The practice to enter a Sikh temple with head covered was revived in 1974 by a special resolution, which was strictly applicable. The irreligious practice has now almost faded away with the exception of a single Gurdwara in B.C. In the Gurdwara, sitting on the carpet with head covered is an expression of respect for the Guru. I hope the *Guru Granth*, in the Gurdwara referred to above, will soon receive its due traditional respect from all its worshippers. All the Sikhs should venerate the time-honoured practice prescribed by the Gurus and followed over the centuries. The Christians have their separate religious concepts and practices and the Sikh practices should not be confused with theirs.

The *gurpurbs*, that is, the anniversaries, relating to the Gurus including the birth days of Guru Nanak, Guru Gobind Singh, the Baisakhi—the creation of the Khalsa, and martyrdom anniversaries of Guru Arjan, Guru Tegh Bahadur and Sahibzadas (sons of Guru Gobind Singh) are observed in all the Gurdwaras in Canada with due solemnity. Lectures regarding the anniversaries are delivered and people are linked with their glorious past.

The Khalsa Diwan Society celebrated the quincentenary birthday of Guru Nanak at its new Gurdwara at 8000-Ross Street, Vancouver, on 23 November 1969:

In 1995, in the Ross Street Gurdwara, Vancouver, Guru Hargobind's 400th birth anniversary was celebrated with great enthusiasm and devotion. *Kirtan darbars*, seminars, poetical symposiums, competitions on topics on Sikh religion and lectures on Sikhism marked the celebrations throughout the year.

On Baisakhi day, the *nagar kirtans* or religious processions are organized by the big Gurdwaras all over Canada. The annual Baisakhi *nagar kirtan* started in Vancouver in 1979 on the 500th birthday of Guru Amar Das Ji (the third Nanak of the Sikhs). Besides the local people, the Sikhs from the nearby towns participate in the procession. In Vancouver, the procession starts from the Ross Street Sikh Gurdwara and moving along a certain route, it reaches the Main Street market and returns to the starting point from a different route. The procession is headed by dozens of floats of different Sikh organizations. A large number of people join the procession on the route. They are lavishly entertained with juice, coke and other soft drinks besides various types of eatables on the way. The number of participants could be modestly estimated at a hundred thousand—men, women and children. This procession displays a unity of the community, a remarkable Sikh presence in the society and the distinct identity of the growing Sikh population in Canada. The Sikh procession deeply inspires a sense of wonder and splendour in the hearts of the viewers.

On Baisakhi day, *amrit* ceremony is conducted in almost all the Gurdwaras and hundreds of devoted Sikhs join the ranks of the baptised Singhs. The first *amrit* ceremony took place in Canada in 1908. According to the Khalsa Diwan Society's old records Bhai Mewa Singh Shaheed took *amrit* on 21 June 1908 and Balwant Singh, Bhag Singh and Waryam Singh were baptised on 28 June 1908. On 11 April 1909, eight men and two women took *amrit*. On the same day, that is on 11 April 1909, the marriage of Gian Singh (earlier named Munsha Singh) and Labh Kaur (earlier Annie Wright) was solemnised in the presence of Sant Teja Singh, according to the Sikh *rehat*. This was the first marriage that took place on the soil of Canada according to the Sikh rites. The *amrit* ceremony is not only exclusive to the Baisakhi day; it is performed on many other occasions and days of the year as well. In Vancouver, 95 Sikhs took *amrit* in 1995 and 130 people in less than a year in 1996 at the Ross Street Sikh Gurdwara alone. The *amrit* is prepared with double-edged sword by five beloved ones and the initiants take a pledge to keep five Ks and abide by the Khalsa *rahit* in letter and spirit and take a vow to maintain the distinction of their identity to their last breath.

Almost all the big Gurdwaras in Canada arrange periodically *gurmat* camps which provide education in Sikh religion, its teachings and philosophy, especially for the school-going boys and girls who are otherwise very likely to go astray from the path of Sikhism. These camps are arranged during the summer vacation. The Sikh scholars are invited to address the students on different topics of Sikhism and the Sikh history. During the lectures the participants are encouraged to ask questions to remove any doubts in their minds. Since the young men and women are more inquisitive and skeptical every effort is made to satisfy their queries.

In the end the participants are given prizes and medals for their performance. These camps are a regular annual feature of many Gurdwaras in Canada.

The Singh Sabha movement centenary was celebrated in 1974 with a tour of Sikh dignitaries around British Columbia. The aims and objects of the Singh Sabha were widely propagated in Canada by scholarly discourses and lectures in the Gurdwaras and at other forums. By a special resolution passed in 1974, it was decided that as against the irreligious practice followed in the past few years, all people entering the Gurdwara were strictly enjoined upon to cover their heads.

Ragis (reciters of *bani*) and *kathakars* (expositors of Sikhism) are called from India for a specific period to perform *kirtan* and give expositions on Sikh religion and its philosophy and enlighten the faithful in the Gurdwaras. The Shiromani Gurdwara Prabandhak Committee (SGPC) sent the first ragi *jatha*, led by Bhai Bakhshish Singh, which came to Canada, in 1975. In 1975 the tercentenary of Shri Guru Tegh Bahadur was commemorated with due solemnity. When the *ragis* are in greater demand in various Gurdwaras, the Gurdwara sponsors get their visas extended. Almost daily, they recite the hymns from the Holy Scripture in melodious and comforting tunes. The Guru's hymns are devotional in character. The *kirtan* arouses the listeners' feelings of devotion and creates oneness with God. Through *kirtan* (singing of *gurbani*), the Sikhs are kept tuned with their religion, and *katha* instills in the listeners the real import of Sikhism. With effect from 1993, a 24-hour radio programme featuring Sikh religion and *gurbani kirtan* started its transmission from Vancouver. It broadcasts across Canada and America via satellite. Their impact on the listeners is unique and it makes them distinctive in identity—people with matchless devotion and spiritual inspiration. Young boys and girls are also given training in *kirtan*. The *akhandpath* and Baisakhi day celebrations were held at the Parliament Building in Ottawa in 1994.

At the Gurdwaras an arrangement is made to give lessons in *kirtan* especially to the younger generations. To arouse further interest in them competitions in *kirtan* are held and prizes given. In 1993, 70 boys and girls participated in *kirtan* competition.

Some Gurdwaras provide lessons in reading the *Guru Granth Sahib* correctly. All these measures aim at promoting deep reverence for the Sikh tenets and practices. Among younger boys turban-tying competition is held and prizes are awarded to inspire due respect for the turban, which is worn not only as a headgear but also as an important fundamental symbol of their religious faith. The turban is a prominent symbol of Sikh identity. In 1993, 25 boys took part in the turban-tying competition.

To preach Sikhism, the Ross Street Gurdwara, Vancouver, has been publishing and distributing, in thousands, free of any charges, a magazine titled *Khalsa Diwan gazette* for the last many years. Its published special numbers include Baisakhi Number, *miri piri* Number. Dashmesh Number and *gaddi-nishini* Number of *Guru Granth Sahib*. Through valuable articles by scholars of Sikh religion and history its readers are kept abreast of knowledge of Sikhism and its distinctive features. Such literature is of highly persuasive value.

The Gurdwara is the hub of all religious and cultural activity. Almost all Sikh marriages are solemnised at the Gurdwara. The *akhandpath* or *sahajpath*, after the death in a family, is performed at the Gurdwara where the *bhog* ceremony is attended by a large gathering, followed by *kirtan*, *ardas* and distribution of *karah prashad*.

All ceremonies are conducted strictly in accordance with the Sikh *maryada* (code of conduct) and nowhere the Sikh identity is allowed to be alloyed, knowing full well the instructions of Guru Gobind Singh that so long as a Sikh keeps his identity distinct he would be given all the powers. "And whosoever lives according to the *rahit* prescribed for him, he is my master and I am his servant," said the Guru so graciously, ennobling his humble follower.

The Khalsa Diwan Society, Vancouver, has recently constructed a big Sikh community Resource Centre adjacent to the Ross Street Sikh Temple, Vancouver. Its foundation stone was laid on 24 July 1994 and its inauguration ceremony took place on 28 July 1996. Besides provision for many other things Sikh library and Sikh museum are also housed in this centre, which cater to the needs of the indulgent Sikh readers. A Sikh library is a most valuable asset for the promotion of the study of Sikh religion and the museum brings before the eyes of the viewers what happened away from them in the distant past.

The contribution of the Gurdwara in preserving the Sikh identity is undoubtedly the maximum as it covers many aspects of religious life of a Sikh and its impact on the community is deeper and longer-lasting as the Guru is central in all commandments issued to the Sikhs. The Gurdwara never means only the building in which the *Guru Granth Sahib* is installed, it also means the word of the Guru that removes darkness and provides light to the devotee. None can flout an edict issued from the Gurdwara as it is the Master's word and is infallible.

Sikh Societies

There is a widespread network of Sikh societies all over Canada. In British Columbia alone, there are more than forty Sikh societies which have been formed almost in all cities and towns that have some Sikh population including Vancouver, Burnaby, New Westminster, Pitt Meadow, Abbotsford. Mission, Victoria, Nanaimo. Duncan. Paldi, Campbell River. Merritt. Kamploops. Kelowna. Vernon, Penticton. Williams Lake. Prince George. Kitimat and Quesnel.

Often, one common goal that these societies had before them was, to start with, to build a Gurdwara for the Sikh community and organize regular religious functions and promote Sikhism.

The Sikh conference held in Toronto in 1979 records that "It is unanimously adopted at the plenary session that the planning committee for the conference shall assume the responsibility of a Task Force and work towards establishing a mechanism whereby the Sikhs in various centres can communicate on regular basis." This resolution was vigorously translated into action and such conferences became a regular feature of the Sikh community in Canada.

Gordon Fairweather, of Canadian Human Rights Commission said at the Sikh conference held in Ottawa in 1980 in his inaugural address, "We at the Canadian Human Rights Commission are particularly interested in the fact that from this meeting may well come a Federation of Sikh Societies of Canada, in other words a national group. I think that is important. If that goal is reached we at the Commission would be very happy because it will be important to us in the ongoing work that we have to do together.... I will set aside my notes and would say that from a national group and from the Canadian Human Rights Commission we surely together can pursue something. It will be a relentless battle because attitudinal changes are difficult."[29]

These societies hold frequent meetings to consider problems facing their particular localities or the Sikhs living in other parts of the country. They make united efforts to undo the injustice done to them. These societies, at their individual level, make plans, from time to time, for the protection of their ethnic identity. When the Sikhs are confronting a cause at national level these societies chalk out strategies collectively and plead their cause vigorously. For example, the Khalsa Diwan Society Vancouver's role in fighting for the rights of the Sikh community and in preserving the Sikh values has been marvellous, right from its inception in 1906. Now when the Sikhs have a sizeable number in the country and the Sikhs to represent them in the legislative assemblies and parliament they are deemed to have become a force to reckon with. In the past, for decades after decades, they had mutely suffered or their grumble was not audible to the authorities, and ultimately they created a place for them in the country's mainstream.

Their Sikh identity has all through been in a grave danger of obliteration at the hands of the hostile elements of the population but they could defend it with all the moral and spiritual strength at their command.

The Federation of Sikh Societies was formed in 1981. The principle objectives of this federation were to promote and preserve the Sikh religious values, its doctrines and practices and also to retain the cultural heritage of the Sikhs through co-ordination of various religious, cultural, Punjabi language and educational needs of the Sikhs in Canada. The federation was to take up the Sikh cause with the government when the occasion arose. Sikhism was to be preached among the Sikhs and vigorous efforts were to be made to save them from straying away from Sikhism under extraneous influences. It was not an easy job to fight against the strong tides of social change capable of sweeping away the existing social and religious values. This federation made many briefs on visible minorities, the Sikh turban and *kirpan* issues that were vital to the Sikh identity, to the relevant commissions and committees. In Canadian courts, in cases where the Sikhs were involved and were required to swear by their Holy Scripture the volumes of the *Guru Granth Sahib* were being used for the purpose. The Federation of Sikh Societies passed a resolution at the All Canada Sikh Convention (1983) in Ottawa that this court practice was contrary to the Sikh faith and should be discontinued forthwith. The courts were implored to return the volumes of the *Guru Granth Sahib* to the nearest Gurdwaras or the Federation for keeping them respectfully in proper places. The Federation of Sikh Societies with the support of the Sikh community across Canada and the Secretary of State for Multiculturalism established a Chair in Punjabi Language, Literature and Sikh studies at the University of British Columbia where close to 100 students take the Punjabi Language courses for credit at different levels

After a prolonged correspondence with the Attorney- General of British Columbia the Khalsa Diwan Society, Vancouver, retrieved thirty-six volumes of the *Guru Granth Sahib* from the courts of B.C. From some courts, copies of *Sundar Gutkas* were also collected by the society. Thus, with the efforts of the Federation of Societies, wrong and disrespectful practice of using the *Guru Granth Sahib* for swearing in the courts was stopped.

The International Sikh Youth Federation was established in Canada in 1984. The principal object of this federation was to spotlight the mission of the Sikh ideology, faith and life. They are committed to jealously guard their culture and faith as they have done during the last five hundred years. It was involved in preaching Sikh initiation or *amrit prachar* among the Sikhs. This Federation made frantic efforts to prevent the Sikh youths from committing crimes and indulging in the use of drugs.

The World Sikh Organisation (WSO) was conceived in 1983 in Ottawa and given shape in January 1985. In Canada the WSO pleaded strongly.

on behalf of the Sikhs, with the Human Rights Organisations and such other committees that dealt with racial justice, Sikh employment and refugee issues. This organisation stood very forcefully and effectively for the preservation of the Sikh symbols and Sikh distinctiveness. They pursued the Gurdwara-based activities vehemently and their thrust on the retention of the Sikh values has been intensely powerful and fervid.

In 1985 some educated Sikhs had set up the Macauliffe Institute of Sikh studies, in Toronto. This Institute aimed at serious scholarly pursuits in Sikh studies and educating people about Sikhism. It explained the importance of the Sikh *rehat* and salient doctrines of the Sikh religion to the Toronto police and to the school boards, to start with. The Institute impressed upon these departments to keep in view as to what Sikhism is and who the Sikhs were, while dealing with them. It also meant to make them aware of their own and other people's conscious and unconscious biases, behaviours and attitudes and the way in which they might adversely affect the Sikh community.

In 1987, this Institute helped the Toronto University in organizing the Sikh Conference. In 1988, the Institute itself organized a conference with the theme, "Sikh Canadians: The promise and the Challenge," in Toronto, primarily with a view to making the Sikh image distinct and worthy of respect.

The Canadian Sikh Studies Institute was established in 1989. This Institute presented a case on the Royal Canadian Mounted Police (RCMP) turban issue to the Solicitor- General, Pierre Blais, in February 1990, and through a symbolic signature campaign five thousand signatures were submitted to the Solicitor-General. This Institute also presented a paper on 'Canadian Sikhs' to the members of Parliament, enlightening them on the distinct Sikh identity over which no compromise could ever be made.

The Sikh presence in Canada is becoming increasingly visible. In order to know about Sikhism and its practices a large number of non-Sikh groups of students and teachers had been visiting the Gurdwaras very often. I have available with me a report of 8000 Ross Street Gurdwara Vancouver, for the year 1993. According to it about 50 groups comprising 1300 students belonging to different religions of the world accompanied by their teachers came to this Gurdwara in 1993. Fourteen of these groups belonged to the University of British Columbia with about 200 visitors. Four groups consisting of 190 students came from Columbia Bible College. A single big group of Saint Andrew School comprising 60 students and teachers also visited the Gurdwara. Besides them, students and teachers from Simon Fraser University, Langara College, Coventery College, Capilano College,

University Women Club, Senior Citizens groups of New Westminster, Trinity Western University Langley, Hillcrest community chapel Bellingham and Bellingham High School students had the honour to have visited the 8000 Ross Street Sikh Gurdwara, Vancouver.

All the students and teachers visiting the Gurdwara were curious to know about Sikhism and its practices. Invariably for every group coming to the Gurdwara lectures were arranged, free discussion conducted so that they could know as much as possible about Sikhism and about the community that professes this religion. These programmes were extremely fruitful for both the visitors and the hosts, in developing an understanding between them. In the end all the visitors were entertained with the sumptuous Indian meals at the *Guru ka langar* which they extremely relished. They admired the practice of free mess in the *Guru ka langar* and appreciated many other practices of the Sikhs.

During the same year, the Khalsa Diwan Society arranged the meetings with the School Board, Race Relations Committee and Canadian Racial Justice Committee, on the premises of Guru Amar Das Niwas, where the attending members were familiarised with the teachings of Sikhism and the code of conduct that the Sikhs were enjoined upon to follow strictly.

The Khalsa Diwan Society is never to refuse help whenever a needy person comes to them. This is one of the cardinal teachings of Sikhism, which they observe in letter and spirit. Any violation of the Sikh practices may not be taken lightly but as very deplorable negation and an anti-Sikh stance.

National Association of Canadians of Origin in India (Nacoi).

Nacoi was established in 1976 in Ottawa to provide a single common platform to voice the following concerns of Canadians of origin in India: to encourage Indo-Canadians to participate fully in Canadian society; to provide a forum for exchange of ideas, issues and common problems and protect their rights, to facilitate communication within the community and with other organizations; to assist them in the orientation and adaptation to Canadian milieu and also to bring about a better understanding of Canada and the Canadians; to formulate guidelines for improving their collective image and ensure due recognition of their contribution to Canada.

Indians may be of several different origins including the Punjabis, Bengalis, Tamils and the Sikhs in particular. They may have their own sectarian associations for purposes of their social, religious and cultural programmes. But Nacoi professes to be a cosmopolitan organisation representing all groups working for the good of all Canadians of origin in

India. The founders of this organisation primarily aimed at having the ear of the government to resolve their concerns.

It is a matter of history that Nacoi has almost always been headed and dominated by the Sikhs who are always there to spearhead such organizations and movements.

Nacoi is having a large number of chapters spread across Canada from coast to coast, from Victoria (B.C.) to St. Johns (New Foundland). Delegates hailing from all parts of the country attend its annual general meetings. In these meetings, spread over different sessions, discussions are held on various problems facing the Indo-Canadians. The annual conference or congress of Nacoi is held at a different place every year, lasting for two or three days.

Nacoi claims to have emerged as the national voice of the Indo-Canadian community as a whole. Because of the cultural, linguistic and religious diversity within the Indian community many individual organizations cater to different aspects of the community needs. But Nacoi claims to be an umbrella organisation that brings together all the divergent groups in pursuit of the common goals set before them. This organisation is not expected to be critical of the activities of any other association of any other Indian ethnic or religious group, because all those groups look to the interests of the Canadians of Indian origin, however limited their works or interests may be. So Nacoi's concerns are not supposed to come into clash with the concerns of any other group of the Indo-Canadians.

Nacoi has been vehemently pursuing with the federal or provincial governments the problems faced by Indians as those of under-representation on commissions, boards and senior positions in the bureaucracies of all the governments and their agencies and decision-making authorities.

Nacoi is also concerned about the invisibility of the visible minorities, immigration, employment equity, language, multiculturalism and racial discrimination. This organisation is seized of unity among the Indians to realise their objectives by changing the traditional attitude of the Indian community as many of them are still living mentally and emotionally in their native country and not recognizing themselves as Canadians. The Nacoi wants the Indians to become a part of the Canadian mainstream keeping intact their cultural heritage and their identity as distinct as ever, demonstrating their desire to be directly involved in the political, social and administrative structure of the country.

The membership of this organisation is open to anyone who belongs to any Indian community or religion as Sikhism or Hinduism or Christianity or Islam. All Indo-Canadian organizations can get themselves affiliated to local chapters of Nacoi. There are a large number of organizations in cities like Vancouver and Toronto, which have thousands of members who are affiliated to the local chapters. Even religious groups are affiliated to Nacoi at local levels and are a part of the organisation.

Nacoi has been lobbying all levels of government and presenting briefs to various commissions, legislative committees and task forces. This organisation has been striving for the recognition of the Indian degree-holders for employment in Canada in all fields as the talents of the Indo-Canadian doctors, engineers and other professionals and skilled workers are wasted because they cannot get accreditation to work in their field of expertise.

Nacoi has been trying to create mutually respectful relationships between the Indian ethnic communities and the police as incidents over the past many years in various urban centres have resulted in a confrontational attitude between community groups and the police force. To improve relations the best course is to hire more young members from these communities with diverse backgrounds, thus making police force to be multicultural.

Nacoi has been involving the young, both male and female, in the activities of the community's programmes by organizing youth seminars at different places in the country. This organisation has been pursuing with the Ethnocultural Council the speedy disposal of all cases of discrimination. Nacoi believes that unless more visible minorities are seen in government and the private sector, discrimination against visible minorities will continue unabated.

Nacoi has been again and again declaring that it belongs to all the Indo-Canadians who can make a difference by their involvement in it. All should work together for a better, stronger and united community. This organisation has been expressing deep concern that Indo-Canadian women face, in their society, domestic violence and battering within the household. It is a major problem and, unfortunately, transition houses in the big cities are filled regularly by women from this community. This organisation is making all-out efforts to reverse this trend.

Nacoi believes in persistent efforts to solve the community's problems, of course, never hoping for miracles to happen in this regard.

Nacoi brings out a quarterly *Forum* from Ottawa. It is just a leaflet or a newsletter of average ten pages. Such a large organisation, as Nacoi, should publish a periodical journal containing scholarly articles on different aspects of problems faced by the Indo-Canadians. A strong print media or highly informative literature is a great asset for any institution that deals so widely with the concerns of so potent a community.

Sikh Conferences

The Sikh conferences played an important role in focussing attention on Sikh problems and Sikh identity in Canada. The first Sikh Conference in Canada was held in Toronto in 1979. A large number of papers were read on issues relating to Sikh identity, Sikh professionals, Sikh women, relations of the Sikhs with other communities and education of Sikh children. This conference was followed by other Sikh conferences almost annually or with an interval of a couple of years. The Sikh conferences held on the soil of Canada in 1980s and 1990s were as under:

Sikh Conference, Ottawa (1980), All Canada Sikh Convention, Calgary (1981), The Heritage Conference, Ottawa (1981), All Canada Sikh Convention, Ottawa (1983), Regional Conference at Kamploops (July 1984), Regional Conference at Toronto (22 July 1984), Sikh Women's Seminar, Toronto (23 March 1985), Sikh symposium Toronto (25-26 May 1985), All Canada Sikh Convention, Victoria (9-10 November 1985), North American Sikh Convention Edmonton (1 September 1985), Academic Conference on Sikh Scholarship, Toronto (13-15 February 1987), 'Sikh Canadians: The Promise of the Challenge'—A symposium, Toronto (12-14 August 1988), International Conference on Sikh Studies, University of Toronto (24-25 November 1990), International Conference on Sikh Studies, University of British Columbia, Vancouver (2 December 1990) and some more conferences in Vancouver and Toronto in 1990s and many such conferences across the border in the U.S.A.

Scores of Sikh societies or organizations from across Canada sent their delegates to participate in these conferences. The delegates took with them to their respective societies the message of the deliberations of these conferences. Thus, the tempo of building and retaining the unmistakably conspicuous image of the Sikhs was kept.

The papers presented in the conferences exhibited a diverse range of topics relating to the religious and cultural needs of the Sikh community. These papers included: Heritage of Sikh culture. The problems of Sikh youth, Teachings of Sikhism, Teaching of Punjabi to Sikh children in Canada, Preservation of Sikhism in North America, Position of the Sikhs in the *Canadian Mosaic*, Difficulties faced by the community to maintain Sikh symbols and traditions, Response to negative coverage of the Sikhs in media. Role of women in Sikh society, The Khalsa and its universality, The Sikh Diaspora—its possible effects on Sikhism, Guru Nanak's ideology, Concept of *miri piri*, Concept of *charhdi kala*, Sikh identity—a continuing feature, kirpan and turban issues, Sikh practices, the Sikhs and racism, Sikh institutions. Spiritual concepts of Sikhism and Status of Sikh women in Canada.

It is gratifying to note rather it is a matter of pride that so many Sikh conferences had not been held anywhere else in the world in such a brief span of time. This reflects deep consciousness of the Sikhs in Canada regarding their serious concerns about their identity, their religion and their community as a whole.

Sikh Education

Since 1970, the Khalsa Diwan Society, Vancouver, had been making arrangements for the teaching of Punjabi (in *gurmukhi* script) at the Ross Street Sikh Temple, Vancouver, to the young Sikh children. In September 1972, Punjabi classes were started in the evening at David Thompson Secondary School, Vancouver. Later on, the Khalsa Elementary School, with a regular school board curriculum, was started in 1986, in Vancouver (and now with the addition of Khalsa High School in Surrey since 1992) with special arrangement of teaching Punjabi to the students and enjoining upon them and the school teachers the observance of Sikh *rehat* (code of conduct), thus encouraging and enabling the school children to grow up as committed Sikhs. On similar lines, the Dashmesh Khalsa School is functioning in Abbotsford.

Although Chinese and Punjabi are claimed to be in second and third places as mother tongues within the high school population of British Columbia, behind English, these had been relegated to after-school classes as if the Punjabi and the Chinese kids were going to stay an hour later for a language lesson. But they did. With the co-operation of the Vancouver School Board, after the school time, from 3.15 p.m. to 4.15 p.m. an arrangement was made to teach Punjabi in the following schools: Walter Moberley School, John Henderson School, Saxsmith School, Mackenzie School, Fleming School and Douglas School. The Khalsa Diwan Society arranged the Punjabi teachers. In 1993 about 500 Sikh students were studying Punjabi in these schools including those of Guru Amar Das Niwas School students.

Punjabi and Chinese are the languages spoken in the homes and businesses of the Canadians who form a significant part of the population of British Columbia and some other provinces. These are, in fact, the Canadian languages spoken by the Canadians; these might have originated elsewhere, just as other languages have. It is pleasing to note that British

Columbia reviewed its language policy so that people could move with the times and bring their language instruction in line with the changing face and needs of B.C. The British Columbia government included these languages in the provincial list of examinable languages from grade five to grade twelve. The government's commitment to teaching Punjabi in the schools will not only help protect and enhance the Sikh culture but through Punjabi Canada would be made richer culturally with the addition of one more language to the school curriculum.

On the British Columbia government's decision, in 1994, to introduce Punjabi in the school curriculum, Manmohan Singh (Moe) Sihota MLA, then minister in the B.C. government, said, "At the top of my list in things I wanted to accomplish during this New Democratic Party (NDP) government's days in office was to make sure that Punjab language instruction be available for future generations, so that those generations will have the ability to speak the language of their culture and would be able to pass it down to their children, so that those values are not lost. If you lose your language you lose your culture. it is a step towards true multiculturalism".

He continues further, "This is a historic, unprecedented and a very courageous decision on the part of this government and one that was long overdue. This decision says to the people of Chinese, Japanese and Indo-Canadian origin that there is a place for them in British Columbia. Things that are important to them—their language, culture and customs—are now part of their educational fabric, preserved forever." He especially looks towards the Punjabi youngsters for whom the language policy is crucial in maintaining their culture. Tragically, there are many second and third generation people from India, who have lost their ability to speak and write Punjabi, thus losing their touch or connection with their only Punjab speaking grand-parents. That is a tremendous loss, he said. "Our children need to know about our values in order to properly understand that they must possess the ability to speak the language which their parents brought to Canada."[30] Punjabi was started in the schools with effect from the 1996-97 school year. Of late, it has been an encouraging development that the Sikh parents take their Canadian-borns to India along with them, very often, to acquaint them with their parents' and grandparents' ancestral land and culture. These children visit the Gurdwaras there and familiarize themselves with the Sikh code of conduct and imbibe interest and respect for the same. Now, more than ever before, they are growing as Punjabi and Sikh children. though in a different environment, with the full or sufficient knowledge of their ethnic roots. It is hoped that the Sikh identity will be safe in their hands in the days to come, provided their parents play their wholesome role vigorously.

In 1983, the Federation of Sikh Societies of Canada conceived a plan of setting up a chair of Sikh studies at the University of British Columbia. The government of Canada promised to contribute matching financial assistance up to $ 350,000 to the collection of funds by the community. The Sikh Federation raised an amount of $ 350,000 and a chair in Punjabi Language, Literature and Sikh Studies was established in 1985 with the announcement of a Sikh chair by the Minister of Multiculturalism, David Crombie.

Similarly professorship in Sikhism was set up at the University of Toronto in the Department of South East Asian Studies, on the condition of raising $ 30,000, a year, by the Sikh community. These departments of Sikh studies were established with a view to promoting Sikh studies and Sikh culture. Due to some internal problems these chairs are in rough waters at present. The old incumbents working on these teaching assignments were made to quit as they fell short of the expectations of the Sikh community that raised funds to finance them.

Sikh Media

The media always plays an important role in awakening people to their rights and privileges. Right from the beginning of the twentieth century the leaders of the Canadian Sikhs have been making strenuous efforts to bring out weekly, fortnightly and monthly papers, highlighting their demands and injustices and prejudices suffered by them at the hands of government and the majority groups of the society. Since most of these papers did not enjoy sufficient patronage of the Sikh population in terms of financial help they could not survive long for want of funds. But efforts continued to be made through print again and again and generally by individuals through their limited resources to voice the grievances in respect of racial discrimination and denial of the very basic rights to which as members of society they were entitled. A few of papers that made their appearance in Canada during the twentieth century and disappeared in due course of time for want of readers and due to financial constraints may be listed below:

Dr Sundar Singh started a journal titled *Aryan* in 1909. Dr Sundar Singh and Kartar Singh published a journal, *Sansar* in 1912. In the fifties, Inderjit Singh Kohli started the *Indo-Canadian Times* magazine, which he continued to publish for 15 years until his retirement. Giani Tara Singh brought out a monthly magazine in Punjabi titled "The *Canadian Khalsa*.

Gian Singh published a quarterly magazine named *The Canadian Sikh* in Punjabi and English in 1961. Tara Singh Bains brought out a Punjabi weekly in 1969. It was closed after publishing 36 issues. Some others were: The *Canadian Qaumi Sandesh, Ekta, Lok Awaz, Purab Prakash, Lokta, Parivartan, Desh Sewak, The Punjabi Asia Times, Wangar, Watano Door, Pardesi Punjab, Western Sikh Samachar, Sikh Sansar* and many more.

Some of these papers were in Punjabi alone and some of them in both Punjabi and English. Because of limited circulation most of these papers were not financially viable.

At present, in Greater Vancouver, eight papers including *Indo Canadian Times, Punjabi Tribune, Charhdi kala* and *Sangarish* in Punjabi (*gurmukhi* script) and *The Link* and the *Indo Canadian Voice* in English are published regularly. These papers are weekly, bi-weekly and bi-monthly and often give the community news, news from India and a lot of advertisements relating to Indo-Canadians. These papers also publish some good articles on Sikhism and its practices, concerns of the Sikh youth, Sikh identity and measures to retain it. These papers which are the spokesmen of the Sikhs adequately bring to the Sikh readers as to what the Sikh community is up to and how the Sikhs have to maintain themselves in a dignified manner.

Some of these papers subsist on advertisements and are available to the readers at public places, free of any charges, and some of them are priced. As referred to earlier, the *Khalsa Diwan Society Gazette,* Vancouver, is periodically published, in thousands, and distributed without any charges. It, primarily, focuses on preaching Sikhism, its doctrines and practices; lives of Sikh Gurus and such events from the Sikh history as duly glorify the Sikh character and Sikh chivalry. This journal serves as a torchbearer of Sikh values. It contains articles both in Punjabi and English.

It is heartening to know that most of the Sikh families have a copy of these papers in their homes and at present, more than ever, they are anxious to remain abreast, in respect of information, of their community and the Sikh values.

The Sikhs also arrange to relay their religious and cultural programmes through TV cable channels.

Since 13 April 1996, the Khalsa Diwan Society, Vancouver, placed its Web Page on the Internet and is probably the first society among the Gurdwara Societies in Canada to have established the Web Page in 1996. Through Internet, the Khalsa Diwan Society is able to reach the *sangat* all over the world. It provides an opportunity to reach the younger audience that is possibly not present at the Sikh Gurdwara. This society's Home Page comprises four sections: (1) the Khalsa Diwan Society—that provides information about the Gurdwara, the Khalsa Diwan Punjabi School and the Khalsa Diwan Day Care Centre, the Sikh Community Resource Centre and the Sports Centre (2) the Canadian Sikh Pioneers—provides a historical perspective through biographical backgrounds on pioneers like Bhai Mewa Singh, Bhai Bhag Singh, Bhai Balwant Singh and Professor Sant Teja Singh (3) *Hukamnama* (Edict)—provides the *Hukamnama* from Harmandir Sahib (*Amrit*sar). And (4) Information—provides the latest information on programmes and events happening at the Khalsa Diwan Society, Vancouver. This Home Page is accessible from: http://WWW.Khalsa Diwan Soc.Vancouver.bc.ca/.

Isolated Sikh Families Brought within Fold

'Isolated Sikh families' here mean families living in small towns or places where the Sikh population is sparse and they do not form a viable unit. In such places, the Sikhs have their own problems. The children tend to forget their language, religion and culture sooner than the children living in larger centres of Sikh population, where they have the Gurdwaras duly provided with *kirtan*, lectures on Sikhism and the Gurdwara-based programmes and celebrations of the Sikh anniversaries. The Sikhs living in smaller places remain deprived of the above Sikh activities. Better-educated people living in small towns are considered to be more vulnerable to their new environment and they change their culture and life-style faster than the less educated people who take longer to integrate or assimilate into the new culture.

In an environment of different culture and different pattern of life-style only a person strongly committed to his own ethnic culture can stand unaffected. The others need to be supported to withstand the pressure of disparate or un-Sikh culture.

Efforts have been made by larger Sikh population centres to involve in their Sikh community programmes, the Sikhs living in isolated places. Those people are invited to bigger centres to participate in their religious and cultural functions. The *ragis* and *kathakars* are sent to these smaller places. The newspapers dedicated to the spread of Sikh religion and its practices are supplied to these people. Books on Sikhism are also sent to them from the libraries of main Sikh centres. Thus, they are made to realise that they belong to the Sikh community at large and it cares for their religious and cultural needs, and is deeply interested in the maintenance of their Sikh identity. The concerns of these scattered and marginalised families have been voiced during the various Sikh conferences and measures have been adopted from time to time to keep these families linked with the Sikh associations. It is larger community's duty to inform them that they might be 'lonely' but they are not 'alone', as they are a part of the larger community—only living at a little distant place. Creation of such a feeling will not allow them to drift away from their community.

Summing up, it is worthwhile to look at the whole range of a century that witnessed diverse changes in the Sikh identity in this country. As we see from the old pictures, the Sikh pioneers to Canada reached this new land with *sabat surat dastar sira* (untampered Sikh appearance and a turban on head). These enterprising immigrants, with irrepressible spirit and undying power of human endurance, maintained the Sikh form for decades.

Up to 1940s majority of the Sikhs retained most of their Sikh symbols including hair and turban. They bore the brunt of discrimination of the racists for their religious symbols bravely but when they gained some rights and privileges and white racists began to accept them with Sikh symbols in 1950s and onwards, the Sikhs unfortunately started discarding their valuable symbols of Sikh identity. I have before me an earlier photograph album of the generation that is now bordering on 70 or 80 years of age. Most of them remained in Sikh form for many years but now, sadly enough, most of them present un-Sikh appearance. It may be said after Bhai Vir Singh that *koi haria boot rahio ri* (only some rare plant remained green, all others dried up).

The author is constrained to point out this change when he is writing on the Sikh identity and its preservation in Canada. He has to study the stages through which, the Sikhs passed. He does not nurse any unpleasant feelings for this change but decidedly he is all respect for those who maintained their distinctive identity over the decades.

Then, in the 1980s and further the tide reversed its course and thousands of young men emerged in the Sikh form. The Gurdwaras became the focal points of Sikh solidarity after June 1984. A feeling of distinct Sikh identity gripped their mind and imagination. The Canadian government also needs to be thanked for removing all restrictions that barred the Sikhs from many public services on account of their Sikh symbols. If multiculturalism can have full play in Canada then this country is on its way to become wonderland.

The Western countries – the USA, Canada, UK and European countries, such as, Germany, Italy, France, etc., as well as Japan and Australia have been obliged to relax their immigration rules for future in respect of the traditional cultures of the immigrants in order to increase their working populations. According a UN study, European countries as well as Japan would need significant migration streams to maintain the size of their working age population over the next half a century in the face of a predicted birth rate decline and aging.

Many Western countries will need thousands and thousands of new immigrants annually. The Sikhs are advised to keep their identities intact in view of these added opportunities as there will be no external pressure to erode their cultural heritage.

REFERENCES

1.   Ardistani (also ascribed to Mohsin Fani), *Dabistan-i-Mazahib* (Persian, 1645), Nawal Kishore Press, Cawnpore, 1904, p.233.

2.   Daljeet Singh, 'The Sikh Identity', *Essentials of Sikhism*, Singh Brothers, Amritsar, 1944, p. 255-58.

3.   *Ibid.*, pp.259-61.

4.   Indubhusan Banerjee, *Evolution of the Khalsa*, Vol.I,2nd ed. Calcutta, p.146.

5.   Trumpp, *Adi Granth*, LXXVII, quoted by Indubhusan Banerjee, *op.cit.*,Vol.I,p.146.

6.   W. H McLeod, *The Evolution of the Sikh Community*, Oxford University Press, Delhi, 1975, p.31.

7.   W. H. McLeod, *Who is a Sikh ? The Problems of Sikh Identity*, Oxford Clarendon Press, Oxford, 1989, pp.56-57.

8.   Ghulam Husain Khan *Siyar-ul-Mutakherin* (Persian), 1781, Nawal Kishore Press, Cawnpore, 1897 (First printed in Calcutta, 1836),p.401; Bhai Gurdas, *Var* I, Pauri 27.

9.   Bhagat Singh, *Sikh Polity in the Eighteenth and Nineteenth Centuries*, Oriental Publishers, New Delhi, 1978, p.25.

10. Indubhusan Banerjee, *op.cit.*,p.183.

11. *Dabistan-i-Mazahib*, p.233.

12. Daljeet Singh, *op.cit.*, p.161-62.

13. Arnold Toynbee, *Foreword to the Sacred Writings of the Sikhs*, (Jodh Singh, Trilochan Singh, et al (ed.), G. Allen and Unvin Ltd., London,1960.

14. *Dabistan*, p.233.

15. *Dabistan*, p.239.

16. Harbans Singh, *Heritage of the Sikhs*. Delhi, 1983 (2nd ed.), p.84.

17. Indubhusan Banerjee, *op.cit.*, Vol. II, Calcutta, 1947, p.63.

18. Fauja Singh, Trilochan Singh, et al (ed.) *Sikhism*, Punjabi University, Patiala, 1969, p.32.

19.   Gokal Chand Narang. *Transformation of Sikhism*(5th ed.). Tribune Press. 1960, p.84.

20.   *Ibid.*, p.83.

21.   Harjot Oberoi, *The Construction of Religious Boundaries : Culture, Identity and Diversity in the Sikh Tradition*, Oxford University Press. Delhi. 1994, pp.47-48.

22.   *Akhbar-i-Darbar-i-Mualla*, 10 December 1710. The Persian manuscript is preserved in the private collection of Dr Ganda Singh, Patiala, now shifted to Punjabi University, Patiala. Translation into English by Dr Bhagat Singh, published in *The Panjab Past and Present*. Punjabi University, Patiala. Vol. XVIII-II, October 1984,pp.1-206.

23.   *Miftah-ul-Tawarikh* (Persian) p.398.

24.   Khushwaqat Rai, *Tarikh-i-Sikhan* (1811). MS.,GS.. Punjabi University, Patiala, p.44.

25.   Qazi Nur Muhammad, *Jangnama* (1765). edited by Ganda Singh, Amritsar, 1939,pp.6,12,55,57-58.

26.   W. H. McLeod, *Who is a Sikh? The Problems of Sikh Identity*, Oxford Clarendon Press, 1989, p.62.

27.   *Ibid.*, pp.66,67.

28.   Gokal Chand Narang, *op.cit.*,p.17.

29.   *Proceedings — Sikh Conference*, 1980, The National Society of Ottawa, Ontario, 1983, pp.6 and 8.

30.   Paul Dhillon, 'Sihota on Language Policy'. *The Link*. Vancouver, 20 July 1994, p.12.

CHAPTER 12

NEXT GENERATION SIKHS
IN CANADA

Next generation Sikhs mean the Sikh children and youth of the present generation. The present day youth will replace the present growing old generation. Here the future means 'now'. So what would be the next generation like will not be different from what we plan to make of our children at present. It is the parents and teachers who have to groom them into befitting successors of the present generation. Besides the roles of the teachers and parents, there are many other factors that will imperceptibly influence the next generation. The society and state polity is never static, it is always in the process of change and all individual Sikhs and non- Sikhs receive the impact of change.

In this chapter the whole spectrum of Sikh community is brought under review and an endeavour has been made to depict the emerging Sikh society in its multifarious activities with its positive and negative forms and trends. Since the author has tried to foresee the future of a community, he could have, under his personal biases, likes or dislikes, erred, at places, slightly, as the future is always uncertain and unpredictable. But let him assert that a historian is a prophet who knows the past, understands the present and can, more than anybody else, divine the future, well-nigh, correctly. To have historical perspective is the privilege, or more bluntly speaking, the monopoly of a historian. The author has also, at places, attempted to mark the path and set the trend for the next generation.

Education of the Sikh Youth

Language and culture are those two things as keep a community or a nation alive. In the earlier stages the Canadian government enlisted the services of the schools and the School Boards, as a plan to assimilate the Sikhs into the Canadian cultural mainstream.Education is the basic need of ones life right from the beginning. Sociologists believe that the mother tongue is the most important influence upon the development of our thought processes and perceptions of the world. Language is the basic factor in the growth of individuality. The mother tongue is the most effective medium in expressing ones needs, emotions and desires. Child's brain is gifted with a specialised capacity for learning languages. This specialisation begins to decrease after the age of nine. Dr. B. L. Whorf thinks that the social and cultural patterns of society determine the language styles.

It has been found that children experience the least amount of difficulty in learning the language of their parents. This is the correct method of language learning. Language does not have to be taught, it emerges in response to social needs. The translation method of language learning has many shortcomings.

Aldous Huxley holds a different but a plausible view. To him, every culture is rooted in a language—no speech, no culture. The universe, inhabited by accultured human beings, is largely homemade. Language is a device for denaturing Nature and making it comprehensible for human mind.

Thus, language conditions a person to a culture and a user or speaker of its language. So, according to Huxley, the Sikh children who do not learn Punjabi will remain stripped of lineal consciousness about Sikh culture. The 'realities' of these children will be different from the 'realities' of their Punjabi-speaking parents whose language was shaped by Punjabi culture. These children will have Punjabi genes but Canadian 'realities'.[1]

In a Canadian setting, the teaching of Punjabi to the children may not be possible to the extent that their conditioning could not be the same as that of their Indian-born Punjabi-speaking parents. But the parents can transmit their cultural heritage or conditioning to their children to a large extent. You cannot separate language and culture.

The children are very susceptible to learning. Their education should not be ignored. Teacher's role in child's life is very vital. The impressionable mind of the child accepts the views or perceptions of the teacher at once. So the teacher has to be very conscious of the learning needs of the child.

The first need of the Sikh student is the learning of Punjabi, which cannot be under-estimated. I suppose, Quebec has not been fighting for a separate state to win battles, subjugate people and make conquests over the territories of others. Their struggle has been to save the French culture, which is closely linked with the French language. Their first demand in their battle was the French language, which they won and got it a place along with English and their next and continuing fight is for the protection of their culture for themselves and for their future generations.

When the Jews immigrated to Palestine their first creation there was the Hebrew University to develop their language and culture. Canada and the USA have a closer link with each other and with the UK through the common language and common culture. I am not suggesting linguistic segregation but the development of a particular language and culture.

As the English language and culture are dear to the Anglo-Saxons, French language and culture are dear to the French, so are the Punjabi language and the Punjabi culture dear to the Sikhs.

In the early stages of the 20th century the Canadian government practised policy of cultural imperialism in respect of Canadian immigrants. One of the historians of the Toronto Board of Education wrote: "Free schools would make new arrivals into Canadians through coercion if necessary. The immigrant child would have to be separated from the influence of his parents between the ages of roughly five and twelve."[2]

Some decades later the School Board adopted a policy of cultural assimilation which was expressed by one of the officials of the Education Board as under: If immigrant children, of nations not Anglo-Saxon, were to be assimilated and made good citizens, it must be largely through education. Those children must attend their schools."[3] Under the cultural assimilation policy the Sikh students were obliged to shave beard, remove turbans and have hair close cropped, to graduate from a Canadian school. In so many picture albums of the Sikhs we can see the Sikh children growing into boys, sporting Sikh symbols, hair duly covered with turbans or scarfs. But when we see them in schools they are with distinct Sikh identities disappeared. Education was imparted through local day schools and residential schools. According to L. R. Bull's article 'Indian (native) residential schooling: The native perspective', published in the *Canadian Journal of Native Education*, 18 supplement, 1991, the schools which had been made available to the native people had been set up to eradicate native culture by changing the children and the adolescents. The students were often sent to schools located at long distances from their families with usually little contact between the students and their parents or relatives. Many old students of those schools recall that their culture, families and elders were unremittingly ridiculed. In many of these schools speaking an indigenous language was prohibited.

These residential schools brought about a painful alienation to many native students. Ovide Mercredi, Grand Chief of the Assembly of First Nations, while making a study of the impact of residential schools, in August 1994, remarked that the Indian residential schools were like the Nazi extermination camps for the Jews. He rejected the plea of the Catholic Church that the public opinion supported the residential schools at the time. This was like saying that the Germans supported what the Nazis did to the Jews,[4] he said.

Bob Overwald describes a very shocking experience at a residential school. He says:

"I have become almost totally conditioned to fit into southern society. On the other hand, for these many years have taken away from me, it has caused irrevocable damage to me as a Dene. It has caused a split between my parents and myself and that may never be healed; it has caused me to lose my Dene language and most significantly, it has left me in somewhat in a limbo — not quite fitting into Dene society and not quite fitting into white society either. These are just some of the many by-products of the system. God knows I would not wish them on anyone."[5]

The National Indian Brotherhood (NIB) clearly told the Canadian government that "the time has come for a radical change in Indian (native) education. Our aim is to make education relevant to the philosophy and needs of the native people. We want education to give our children a strong sense of identity with confidence in their personal worth and ability. We believe in education as a preparation for total living; as a means of free choice of where to live and work; and as a means of enabling us to participate fully in our own social, economic, political and educational advancement.... Decisions on specific issues can be made only in the context of the local control of education."[6]

Then came a change in the attitude of the Canadian government announcing the policy of multiculturalism in 1971 by Prime Minister Trudeau, declaring that there was no official culture in Canada; nor did any ethnic group take precedence over any other. He assured the cultural freedom of Canadians within a bilingual framework and also told that all cultural groups would be helped by the government to overcome all barriers to full participation in Canadian society. Thus the government promised that henceforth no ethnic group would be considered more important than another in the cultural, social, political and economic structure of Canada.

George W. Bancroft quoted in his paper read at the Sikh Conference (1979) at Toronto, the remarks of the Director of Education for Toronto, Duncan Greens, made at a Conference on Multiculturalism in Education in 1977. The director said that their support and encouragement of various cultures does not mean that they value their languages and cultural histories and that would be taught in schools and their national holidays would be celebrated and that these groups would represent on their decision-making bodies.

Bancroft told the director that the immigrants do feel and mean that their languages, their national holidays and cultural histories are important. To them English is no more important than Punjabi and Shakespeare is no more important than Tagore. Of course, the schools may not have enough time to teach the immigrants' languages in the Canadian schools. It may also be impracticable to celebrate every holiday in schools. It cannot be disputed that most of those holidays would lose their emotional and spiritual impact when one is out of the cultural milieu that celebrates them. The immigrant community or the ethnic group should celebrate them at their own level and their cultural histories should be provided in the schools as part of the total tapestry of human history.

And the immigrants also unhesitatingly mean that the various ethnic and racial groups must be represented in the important decision-making positions in the society. Why the chief of police in Toronto or Vancouver is not a Sikh Canadian? If he holds that position only then the Afro-Canadian boy or girl, every Chinese or Japanese will know that the Anglo-Saxon stranglehold on this position is broken and every Canadian can aspire to such positions.

The immigrants also do mean to get equality of opportunity. When a Chinese Canadian is appointed a High Commissioner to London or a French knowing Sikh Canadian to France, multiculturalism would be a Canadian reality.[7]

I believe that men or women from among the next generation Sikhs would be posted to such positions as referred to above. Things are swiftly moving in that direction. The next generation Sikhs need only to properly gear up, as these opportunities will certainly come their way.

The Sikh youth that are to succeed to the next generation will not have a comfortable walk over. To grow into a committed Sikh he has to strengthen his faith in the Sikh culture and the Sikh values. Besides his regular studies he has to furnish himself with literature on Sikhism. In Canada, he is handicapped considerably in that regard. Just a few titles on Sikh history and Sikhism may be available in the libraries here. A large number of books are published in English and Punjabi on this subject every year in India. There seems to be no arrangement of getting at least some of them on the shelves of the libraries in Canada.

There are small libraries attached to the big Gurdwaras but these are not properly equipped. The Gurdwara management generally does not spare or earmark funds for the books annually. The books on Sikh history, culture and religion are a great asset to the Gurdwara library and indeed, it is a crying need. Arrangements should be made to keep these books in circulation. For the benefit of the next or prospective readers these books should be received back in a stipulated time.

To keep the library functioning regularly a person can be appointed on a monthly salary basis. The funds so spent would be a very creative or productive investment to attract the young readers. The library section of the Sikh Community Resource Centre, Vancouver, is indeed a remarkably thoughtful addition to the Resource Centre. Needs of the library—its proper equipment with up-to-date Sikh literature would require the regular attention of some scholarly person or a committee of adequately educated persons. Efforts should be made to make library a proud institution of the community so that for all necessary references scholars should visit the library. The Khalsa Diwan Society, Vancouver, should aspire for the credit or distinction of making this library the largest collection of books on Sikh history, religion and culture in Canada and America.

The true University of these days is a collection of books. Habit of learning should be a life-long passion. The excitement of learning separates youth from old age. As long as you are learning or have lust for knowledge, you are not old. Your thirst for learning will not let your years overtake you. Books are more than kings' treasures that are filled not with gold, silver and precious stones but with riches more valuable than these— knowledge, noble thoughts and high ideals.

The Sikh youth should be encouraged especially by the parents to visit the Sikh libraries to draw books and journals on Sikhism and Sikh history. The study of these books would certainly strengthen him as a Sikh and inspire great confidence in him. These books will help him to comply with advice of Herb (Harbans Singh) Dhaliwal that "You do not know where you are going until you know where you came from."[8]

First, the Sikhs of Canada should know who they are and then make the Canadians learn who the Sikhs are, as most of them know nothing about them. The parents owe it to their children to be able to explain to them their roots and the culture and traditions that define their personality. Parents who were born in Canada have roots both in India and Canada, hence they were Indo-Canadians and they do a disservice to their children if they can not explain to them why people wear turbans or who Guru Nanak was or explain to them the struggles of their grand-parents.[9]

Indo-Canadians must not deny their roots because by doing that they would be subscribing to white dominance. To identify as Indo-Canadians or Sikhs would have much more power as a group if they do that. It is not to suggest that they are to promote ghettoisation. They need to strengthen themselves against racial victimisation and to find an equal status in society by discouraging the overwhelming preponderance of the majority group over others.

Among the Sikhs the aspirations for the retention of heritage is very strong. The transmittal of Sikh heritage background and religious beliefs and practices to the Sikh children is an indivisible part of their parental responsibilities. If the domestic environment is deficient in instilling the traditional and religious values in the Sikh youth no amount of external compensation would be sufficient. The youth should be grounded into very capable and committed members of the community. If the parents and teachers miss their duty today the youth will not find themselves equal to the challenges of tomorrow. They will remain teen-agers even at fifty.

Their faith in the moral and religious values of Sikhism must be kept alive in the day to day functioning of the Sikh family life. The parents should converse with the children in Punjabi—their mother tongue and the children should also communicate with each other in Punjabi, at home. Their ability in speaking in English while at school, in the market and in office is not going to get a setback at all, rather they would be adding another language, their mother language, to their knowledge of languages. The more languages they can fluently converse in, the more gifted or qualified they would be considered. Never feel shy to speak in your own mother tongue, which has a better claim on you than any other language. It must have been noted that all independent nations are not only privileged to speak in their mother tongue rather they are proud of it. Why the Punjabi youths fight shy of speaking in their mother tongue? Will the parents share some responsibility for it?

If you are not showing respect to yourself and your language, others are not going to show respect to you and your language. This respect will start from you. Always be proud of yourself and your language, your religion and culture, of course, never denigrating religion and culture of others.

In order to overcome their lack of confidence vis-à-vis the majority group youths the Sikh boys should play the same games that the others play. They should make full use of the community centres, sports functions, debates, cultural activities, camps and get-togethers in order to boost their confidence in their distinct identity.

They should study in the schools with predominantly majority group population with a feeling of pride for their distinctiveness and never with a sense of inferiority complex haunting them like an unreal goblin. This will help them overcome their feeling that they are socially unequal and culturally inferior.

The Sikhs should also establish their own socio-cultural community centres in all cities where they are settled in sizeable numbers. The members of the other communities should be invited to these centres to foster closer relations with them and exchange niceties of various cultures and also thus improving their community image with the Canadian environment. If under the impact of these potent measures, whose strong impact contributes wonderfully to the development of their personality, the Sikh youths enter the next generation, a respectable position for them is assured. They will have more vigour, greater confidence, larger adaptability to their environment and additional capability to meet their majority group peers at equal level with much more self-reliance than otherwise.

The first 20 years of a young person's life are very crucial in every respect—in getting education, in forming ones opinions, in developing ones perspectives, in building ones personality and in learning about the world around. It is believed that the period of these 20 years is longer half or a longer part of a person's life even if he or she lives up to 100 years. Do we need a nuclear scientist to explain this observation that the first part of one life's is most significant and most meaningful and it is to be lived with utmost care and sensibility?

It is gratifying to note that in consequence to economic prosperity now many Canadian Sikhs have access to higher education that their parents could not afford to get. It is a great advantage for the next generation.

The following survey was conducted by two scholars in Canada some twenty years back but in most of the items the answers hold good or relevant even today at the fag end of the twentieth century or the beginning of the twenty-first century.

Survey on Sikh parents regarding their children, language, religion and cultural needs is as under:[10]

Question	Yes %	No %	Unknown %	Remarks
L1 Do you want to retain your language?	98	2		

(contd.)

	Question	Once a week	Twice a week	Unknown	Remarks
L2	If language classes are arranged, how often in a week are you willing to take your child to School?	46	50	4	Not applicable

	Question	Yes %	No %	Unknown %	Remarks
L3	If you cannot take your child to class, are you willing to pay for the transportation?	98	2	0	Not applicable

	Question	Yes %	No %	Unknown	Remarks
L4	Are you prepared to pay for the teacher?	98	2	0	Not applicable

	Question	Reading only	Speaking only	Writing only	All three
L5	What level of language would you like your child to attain?		98		2

	Question	Yes %	No %	Unknown	Remarks
R1	Do you think present institutions provide adequate facilities for our children?	2	98	-	

	Question	Yes %	No %	Unknown	Remarks
R2	Would you like your child to have religious education?	98	2	-	

	Question	Gurbani %	Sikh Literature %	Punjabi Literature %	Remarks
R3	What level would you like your child to attain?	72	94	64	

Question	History	History in general (Indian History)	Sikh History	Remarks
	%	%	%	
R4 What level would you like your child to attain?	80	60	-	

Question	Yes %	No %	Unknown	Remarks
R5 Do you like the religious education to be combined with language education?	80	20	-	

Question	Yes %	No %	Unknown	Remarks
C1 Do you think Canadian cultural and social institutions fulfil your needs?	10	90		

Question	Yes %	No %	Unknown	Remarks
C2 Do you think we should have our own institutions to fulfil our needs	98	2		

Question	Educational %	Sports %	Cultural %	Religious %
C3 What kind of institutions would you like?	85	72	90	75

Stereotyping and generalising students from non-white countries by their white teachers has been a scandalous and dangerous approach to the personalities of these students. Some white teachers have been generally branding Asian or Indian parents as over-ambitious and over-estimating their wards, considering them fit to be doctors while they are not capable of making even an average score in their examinations. Some teachers consider the Asian immigrant students as inferior in quality and dim in intellect and understanding and undeserving for certain courses as science and medicine. They also consider them noisy, boisterous, and volatile and their parents want them to be beaten for unsatisfactory work. Such ridiculous generalisations manifest the teacher's awful lack of perception and sensitivity. The teacher's such stereotypic opinions of Indian or Asian students, as against the white or English students who are considered normal, mentally alert and capable of undertaking any courses, are simply bad and prejudiced judgements and totally unimaginative. They should ignore and discard such teachers who discourage them and act as a block in the path of their careers. The teacher is to light the candle in the students rather than curse the darkness in them.

Such teachers who mix race and education in that way merit to be impeached. They are a disgrace to the teaching procession. I pity the future of the students who happened to be educated by teachers with such dangerously morbid views. Such teachers are responsible for hampering the development and crushing the potential of the non-white Asian students. May God save our young students from these stereotypes so that as our next generation they succeed to the present one as free, frank and independent citizens of the country.

At present, the Sikhs have become a significant part of a multi-national diaspora—'seed scattered abroad' in all the countries of the world and compete successfully with everyone in every field.

Barriers to the Sikh Culture Broken Down

The Sikh symbols which had been a handicap for a Sikh to get hired for a job in the public and private sectors in Canada have been officially recognized, though at places these are being exploited under some unjustifiable excuses. A turban has been accepted as a religious headgear and a _kirpan_ (dagger) as a part of inseparable _rahit_ of a Sikh. For all government jobs including those in police and army a baptised Sikh with full-grown hair and a turban is acceptable provided he is otherwise fit and competent. He is not required to wear hard hat in his factory or mill while on duty. His turban has been considered an alternative to hard hat, and now the factory management understands that his religion does not allow him to wear hat on his head. A baptised Sikh wears _kirpan_ as an essential religious symbol. The government of Canada, through its policy of multiculturalism, has chosen not to deprive a Sikh from a job on that account. Thus, a Sikh living in Canada is a Canadian as well as a Sikh. Sikhism is his religion and Canada is his country and there is no contradiction and clash between these two factors. Canada in which these two things were considered to be incongruent is no more in existence. That was Canada of past and bygone days. So our present day youth and tomorrow's or next generation's full-fledged citizens will have no cultural barriers standing before them.

Whether born in Canada or educated here from an early age, the next generation Sikh youth will have equal opportunity without any barriers due to their race, religion, social background, gender or other differences. The society has to move in that direction with rapid pace. They will reach nowhere if they take one step forward and two steps backward. Instead, they have to take long strides if they have to compete with the toppers of the society in every field. Every dream has a price, higher the dream higher the price. If the East Indian parents fail to pay adequate attention to their children they will be found only as good as children in their thirties with larger physical growth. For such lack of mental development parents will have to take a major part of the blame.

Earlier, only the Christian church or court marriages were acceptable to the government. At present, the Sikhs can solemnise their marriages in the Sikh temples and a certificate to that effect from the Gurdwara priest holds good for all purposes of marriage. In respect of the Canadian social or cultural practices, the Sikhs may adopt such of them as are not in clash with their heritage practices because it is not always possible to keep away from the Canadian lifestyle. The changes in the new environment and a different country may include eating habits, social behaviour and relationship between the children and the parents. The child may call his parents daddy and mummy instead of *pitaji* and *mataji* but he would not call them by their first names. The deep abiding spiritual values that moulded the Sikhs are not going to change, as these values are a part of their cultural heritage. These should be retained. The Indian or the African society will not accept or tolerate a mother having children from two different men without getting married to them. They will not but brand her to be morally wrecked. They do not understand how men and women can live common-law and still be considered respectable. The present day practices of the western countries as living common-law and producing children without marriage and even some mothers not knowing who were the fathers of their children, have been abhorrent to certain societies over the centuries. Such Canadian practices will never be acceptable to the Indians and they will live without indulging in practices known as ignoble and base to an extreme degree.

Hooliganism, earlier resorted, to obstruct the celebrations of the Sikh festivals and anniversaries, is now a thing of the past. The racist cartoons that used to be printed in the daily English newspapers some decades earlier are no more tolerated. The editors of these papers now know it for sure. Now they will write what is right and not what pleases the majority at the cost of a minority. Thus, the Sikhs have the freedom to go ahead with the observance of their customs and rituals at the national or community level. In 1994, *akhandpath* and Baisakhi day celebrations were held at the Parliament Buildings at Ottawa.

The Sikhs are not under a threat to be assimilated into the majority mainstream and to forget or to reject their past. Now, they have their ethnic group newspapers, magazines, movies, records, tapes and TV channels available to them more than ever and thus their capacity to preserve their culture in this foreign land, adopted by them, has increased considerably.

Manmohan Singh (Moe) Sihota says, "Kids have a far greater level of pride in their culture, and denial of culture is not really as prevalent as when I was growing up. I look at the new generation, my kids, they speak Punjabi, they do Punjabi dancing, they watch Punjabi movies and listen to Punjabi music. If you take a look at a lot of other ethnic groups, they tend to lose their identity, whereas we can celebrate it."[11]

The present generation of the East Indians, born and brought up in Canada respects their culture as well as the cultures of other nations. The Indian youth is returning to his or her roots. They wish to learn Indian art, culture, folklore, etc. Most of these children know and enjoy *bhangra* and *gidha* and long to meet their relations back home. For this generation—it is a new journey of returning to their own culture. They are keen to visit places of historical and cultural interest in India, as India offers a lot to show them, perhaps much more than the western world—high mountains, large rivers, huge palaces and forts, marvellous temples and mausoleums, wonderful statues and sculptures, variegated cultures and life-styles, besides a variety of climates.

The Indian youth will be found hooked to the Indian channels on TV. It is another matter that the western television is not offering them anything worthwhile. The Indian youth attempts to catch the basic fabric and thread of the Indian culture in this process. Western society being very individualistic relationships cease to have any relevance. That emotional bond of relationships so much prevalent in each walk of life in India is completely missing in the Anglo-Saxon or the whole white society. Relationships and their understanding come naturally to children in India but the individualistic society of majority groups in Canada never allows such bonds to grow. Our Indian youth is able to understand this fact of life through a comparative study of Indian and western societies and they are opting, in large numbers, the Indian values of life. The Indian youth may go astray where parents happen to totally ignore them.

We are fully confident that the younger generations of the Sikhs are capable of establishing a strong and notable presence in the society. Our people are shining in various fields of activity as politics and business and many professions as education, law and medicine. More and more people from this community would be participating actively in politics and going in for higher education. This would inspire confidence in the Sikh community to be equal partners in the social, economic and political texture of the society. Why should a Sikh not be a governor of a province or governor-general of the country or its Prime Minister? Is it too much for a Sikh to aspire to be a governor when a man of Chinese origin could hold this office or a man of a foreign origin could be elevated to the office of the governor-general or a man of German origin could be the Prime Minister of Canada? Let me assure the Sikhs that they can justly feel that their dreams are not far off to be realised. So far, the Canadians Sikh community has been reactive whereas, now onwards, it is imperative for it to be proactive so as to make conscious efforts and to influence the events and developments at the national and international levels.

If the ability to fill these offices and unflinching loyalty to the state are the prerequisites then the country will not find the Canadian Sikhs lacking in them. So, such offices are within the pale of the next generation Sikhs. In future, they will aspire to achieve what they had never aspired to gain in the past. Unalloyed optimism and sincere aspiration will lead the community to achieve their goals. But they must retain their cultural distinctiveness, sublime character and noble qualities that they have inherited from their invaluable heritage. They must combat negative stereotypes and lay emphasis on the positive aspects of Indo-Canadian society to highlight its strength and virtues. Videos, portraying the Indo-Canadians positively should be produced for viewing in schools. Before anything else, they must show full regards to their self-respect, self-image and self-dignity. Thus, they will certainly grow to a full stature of an honoured and a perfect citizen of the country.

There was a time about the 1930s and even a little later when the Canadian-born Sikh students told their parents not to come to their school to see them as the white students might know that they were the East Indians. To be an East Indian was a stigma during that period of time. That is an ancient history now. Let them be proud of their ancestry and put the stamp of their distinct Sikh identity on the population chart of the country where other communities are unrecognizably mixed up in the crucible of assimilated section of society. Being distinctive is no drag on the Sikhs rather it should give them an edge on others. The Canadian society is definitely moving to think on these lines. The only thing for the

Sikhs to do is to have confidence in themselves or more precisely to shun lack of confidence. Indian experience of the Sikhs should help them. They are about 2 per cent of Indian population and are known as Sardars, meaning respectable leaders, and the Sikh population in Canada is almost in the same ratio, about 2 per cent. By the time the next Sikh generation comes in the saddle they will be feeling much more comfortable, much more aggressive in the pursuit of their goals and much more intimately acquainted with their roots and much more entrenched in various fields of the Canadian life with greater and rip-roaring success. My optimism is linked with the Sikh regard for their distinctive identity.

Perennial Source of Heritage Culture

The Canadian society needs permanent inflow of immigrants to make up their numbers that are regularly on the decline because of the white population's decrease in birth rate. No wonder, men and women in the West refuse to bring out new human beings into this world. They see no purpose in rearing up a new generation. "What for?" they ask.

Tens of thousands of women in the west refuse to be mothers today. Why go through the pain and drudgery? There will be millions to follow them. The trend is catching. Where family has no role to play, there will be no need for children. The women are getting firm on it day after day. The Sikhs from India will certainly be coming to Canada as immigrants in the family class or as skilled workers or in the professionals' category along with their families. They would keep on refreshing the Sikh culture and Sikh values in Canada.

The Sikhs immigrating to Canada is a continuing process without any let-up unless there are some sort of totally unusual circumstances prevailing in the country. The new immigrants, who are wedded to the Sikh religion, culture and Sikh values keep sticking to it for quite sometime after their arrival in Canada. We may notice slight change in their eating and drinking habits, social behaviour and style of life after years. In these days, in cities, they would be able to get the same environment that they left behind in India. Almost the similar Indian media, similar Punjabi speaking earlier immigrants, similar Gurdwara-based programmes similar social ceremonies and similar celebration of festivals. Before they tend to slightly change to the new culture another batch of the Sikhs would be landing in Canada to live in their neighbourhood. In fact, we find new arrivals on everyday basis.

Thus, the Sikh heritage culture would not face any challenge or threat of losing its essential features in any way in this country. We can maintain Sikh society, with its cultural and religious values intact, in this new land which the Sikhs chose to adopt. Even very old immigrants never feel that they are alienated or distant from their cultural heritage which is ingrained in their emotional system or mental constitution and the newcomers also feel quite at home in their new environment. The interaction of the old and the new immigrants keeps the Canadian Sikh society in a state of perpetual freshness and newness.

Sikh Relations with Other Communities

Sometimes the rapid immigration of the East Indians arouses racial animosity among the whites. The change in the attitude of the whites is generally linked to the economy. Their media also gets hostile. It is felt that if there is greater socialisation between the Sikhs and the whites the image of the Sikhs in the society and the relationship between the two can improve considerably. Often, the lack of communication between them creates misunderstandings.

The closer intermingling of communities would definitely give each other the message that none of them would like to conform to an imposed cultural mould. In every free society like that of Canada everybody can live according to his own traditions, beliefs and practices that will have no effect on the lifestyle of others. Their social relations will remain unaffected, without causing any emotional disturbance. This fact can amply be brought home to them through socialisation.

There is a large number of skilled, unskilled and professional Sikhs rubbing shoulders with the whites everyday and everywhere. They (the Sikhs) would never feel comfortable or satisfied with the position of a stranger for them and their children for all time to come in the country of their permanent residence.

Mixing with all other communities that had been slow earlier must be accelerated as an urgent need of the Sikhs. The familiarity with each other would remove most of the misunderstandings and would lead them in establishing a harmonious and much better relations among them. They can start just with a respectful nod of greeting to a neighbour and then a smile, which is a gift, we all can afford to give. In their own interest, the Sikhs are advised to come forward and shake hands with people of other communities and give up living in isolation. They should know about others and let others know about them more intimately. They must make more and more friends and pull down the curtain that hangs between them.

The Sikhs should speak about their religion and culture at church, schools and social gatherings and expose the good qualities of their culture to others.

On an evening walk a Sikh met two Christian priests in America. One of them asked whether he was a Hindu. He replied, "I am a Sikh." "Then you are a fool," said one of them. The Sikh asked him what he actually meant. The Christian missionary replied, "Christ was only one, the whole world knows him. You had ten Gurus and two of them martyred. What have you done to make them known to others?" This one-minute conversation is an eye-opener for the whole Sikh community. The Sikhs must tell to the others as to who they are and who have been their spiritual mentors. The Sikhs must actively participate in the ·multicultural programmes and express appreciation for the cultures of others. The Sikh culture would definitely find better response from others. The Sikh communication with the other members of the Canadian community will go a long way in creating cordial and friendly relations with each other.

This is a fact of life that the invisibility of visible minorities projects an image of non-belonging to the young in the Indo-Canadian community. The image of non-belonging and the implicit lower performance expectations from them by the system tend to undermine their morale, reduce pride in heritage and diminish the desire to maintain it. This has to be reversed. The government of a country which is committed to multiculturalism has a moral and political obligation to give adequate representation to the minorities at all levels of government and use the levers of governmental machinery in assuring that due representation is there in non-governmental positions as well.

The Sikhs should be active partners in the various community organizations as neighbourhood organisation, school association, parents association, taxpayers association and voluntary service association. All communities should have joint sports, folklore and art programmes for closer ties and better understanding of each other. To have equal status with any other community in the Canadian society, the Sikhs must fully participate in all walks of private and public life of the country. Under no circumstances they should carry the notion in their head that their status has anything to do with the number of their population. It depends on the overall character of the community—their honesty in dealings, intrinsic quality of hardworking, the unshaken pride in their heritage culture, their total trustworthiness, deep sense of humanity, innate kindness and humility. These qualities are inherent in the Sikh character. With these noble attributes practised by the Sikhs no power on earth can stop them from attaining a status in society that would be seen with envy by any other community, however large their number and however glorious their imperial past. The Sikhs in Canada have to be conscious of their unblemished image. They do not need to make any change in themselves to become Canadians. They are in Canada and therefore, they are Canadians. They are the Sikhs at the same time. Their next generations have remarkable future in their adopted country—Canada. The fortunes will not come to them as a gift on a plate; they will have to strive for the same.

Dr Frances Henry wrongly believed that Indo-Canadians were arrogant and they did not like to mix with others. They had some other reasons including racial discrimination, language barriers, poor economic condition, low social status and the Anglo-Saxons' pride for having been rulers. Now most of these factors are melting away to the advantage of the minority groups who are recently coming into their own.

The Sikhs are mixing freely with all other communities in political activities. They are gaining recognition and building position in politics and becoming important components of societal fabric and political system and participating in decision-making bodies, impressing upon people as of what worth or mettle they really are. Understanding is the shortest distance between the two persons or the two communities or the races.

The Sikhs on Path to Prosperity

During the earlier stages of their settlement in Canada, the Sikhs were severely handicapped in many ways. Because they had remained disenfranchised up to 1947, they were legally debarred from higher education as in the subjects of law and medicine and thus from the government or the public services as well. Economically most of the Sikhs had been just vegetating and subsisting only on labour excepting a couple of mill owners. As restrictions relaxed, with the passage of time, and avenues for better jobs and lucrative professions opened up, their economic condition improved. They expanded their businesses, purchased bigger farms and competed with the majority groups in many vocations. Through hard labour and industry they bettered their economic prospects considerably, knowing full well that there was no get-quick-rich magic formula.

At present, there is hardly a profession that the Sikhs have not entered. They have become successful house builders and realtors, business magnates, industrialists, doctors, engineers, hi-tech professionals, lawyers, politicians, educationists and are on the high-income-earners lists.

All the Sikhs are not that affluent. Most of them are in the middle income range and are straining every nerve to get better financially. Their characteristic quality of hardworking and industrious disposition always stands them in good stead. The Indians are habitually economical; they earn more and spend less; they stick to their code and culture of saving, however meagre their income. Saving is their great asset.

The low-income groups among the Sikhs are also struggling to supplement their income through some legitimate means as working overtime and going in for two shifts or working on different assignments. They always prefer work to unemployment insurance (UI). They would hardly be seen doing nothing on weekends. They do not go on pleasure trips or for boating in lakes or for holidaying at the sea-resorts. When they can spare a few days from their jobs or busy routine businesses they make a hurried trip to the Punjab—back homeland, to see their relatives or visit their holy places in India. ,

All categories of the Sikhs are in hot pursuit of bringing prosperity to themselves and their progeny. Very much contrary to the thinking of the whites the Indians save for their children—the next generation. The motto of the whites is 'live rich than die rich', as against the thinking of the East Indians. Money can work for you but it cannot think for you. It is you who are to decide as to how to utilize it. Man makes money by using his brain and loses it listening to his heart. Generally, the Indo-Canadians use their brain rather than heart in respect of money. Despite their best efforts, they may be property-rich and are not yet cash-rich. What their parents and grandparents could not afford would be within an easy reach of the next generation. For our tomorrow they sacrificed their yesterday.

The whites' notion of keeping Canada a white man's country has long been shattered and the visible minorities have carved out a suitable niche for them in this wonderland. A space for the Sikhs in the country is now no less assured. In every passing decade their grip on the economy is tightening and like so many other immigrant communities their feet are getting firm in the soil. Surely we shall find next generation Sikhs as equal partners in the country's glorious future. Retaining their identity and cultural heritage, they will no longer be living in splendid isolation in their newly adopted country.

The Sikhs are Permanent Settlers

When the Sikhs came to Canada in the beginning of the 20th century they came alone, without families, and they did not plan to stay here permanently. They wanted to earn money and return to their mother country where their families and relatives lived. By 1907 their number in Canada was 5179 but when placed under restrictions some of them shifted over to America and many of them returned to India. As per census of 1941 their number in Canada was hardly 1465. With the liberalisation of immigration rules their number began to grow. Most of them came accompanied by their families. In that case there was no hurry to go back, rather they decided to tie their future with their new homes. In due course of time their parents also joined them. They have purchased or built houses in their adopted country and have equipped them with all the needed amenities of life. They took a firm decision to return to their country no more. Most of them had already sold their properties back in India. Of course, they kept their links with their relatives whom they occasionally visited. Most of the families now settled in Canada have almost nothing to fall back upon in India. They are financially better off in their new homes, enjoying better facilities and better living standards in Canada.

They have left India for good and settled in Canada permanently. No one prefers to go from a developed country to an undeveloped one. Whatever fortunes they aspire in life are to be obtained from this land. So let us believe that they are the Canadian Sikhs for all time to come. They belong to all the coming generations. Their heritage culture has an inherent power to withstand the evil influences if any, that could possibly sweep the country over the coming years. The Afro-Americans have been living in their adopted country for many centuries still the code of their heritage culture is sticking on them tightly, and they have never tended to change it for the American culture. It would be true of the Canadian and American Sikhs as well. With all the corruption, fraud, lack of sincerity and a thousand and one social ills prevalent in India I am not too proud to be an Indian and yet, in terms of my Sikh cultural heritage and social values, I would not like to be anything else. The Sikh response to Sikh culture would always be positive. They will show due respect to other cultures and would in return like their culture to be respected by others.

The Problems of The Immigrant Sikh Youth

A paper, raising a discussion on the problems of an immigrant youth, was presented by Raghbir Singh Samagh[12] at the Sikh Conference held in 1980 at Toronto. He focussed on the issue as to how the young Sikh immigrant student would walk into the next generation and be able to perpetuate the religious, moral, social and cultural values of the Sikhs. The youth is doubtful of his own identity. The youth is in constant conflict with himself, peers, home and society. The youth is always in the process of making decisions regarding the acceptance or rejection of the norms set by his peers, his parents and society as a whole, still wants to be normal and not to be different. According to the author of the paper if that student plunges into the host culture and rejects his own culture he would be alienated to his parents and relatives and he will lose his family's love and support. If he sticks to his original culture he will not be able to make friends in school. There exist no such problems as have been posed or created above. The young man creates unnecessary miseries for himself through unreal suppositions and involves himself in the same. If ever a peer or peers bully him and no help from police or teacher, or friends is handy, he should courageously protect himself against them rather than yield meekly.

To me the problem is not that serious now, around the close of the century, as it was twenty years back. Since then much water has run underneath the bridge. If the Sikh youth is prepared to accept his peers as they are why should they not accept him as he is. The peers are no bodies to set the norms for others. They can do it for themselves. A Sikh boy with his turban and hair might have seemed slightly different for a few days in the beginning if the whites had never seen the Sikhs earlier. But a Sikh has never been a stranger in Canada since the beginning of the 20th century. He is as much a Sikh as Pope is a Catholic. Unfortunately, the Sikhs had not been adequately told as to who they were and what was their heritage culture. If the immigrant student had been duly informed he would never have had a problem. To his peers there is nothing new or unacceptable about him. To be friendly with others turban poses no problem. If it does, it is their problem and not of the Sikh young man. Friendship, which the Sikh youth seeks with his peers, does not demand the surrender of his faith and his ethnic culture. He should be proud of himself and his heritage culture. Inferiority feelings commonly start from the careless or inadequate attention received from parents in childhood. The kids growing with low self-esteem are more susceptible to negative peer pressure. They should straightway unburden themselves of these troubling thoughts. The greatest loss is the loss of self-regard and self-confidence.

At present the school teacher and the non-Sikh students are supposed to know why a Sikh student ties a turban and grows hair. So there should be no conflict in the mind of the immigrant student today. He should feel comfortable with his hair and turban as he felt when studying in India with the Muslim, Christian and Hindu peers of diverse cultural backgrounds.

If at all, the immigrant youth may have problems of other types as English language with different accent and different system of education. In Indian system the discipline is rigid, the choice of courses is limited, the student-teacher relations are strictly authoritative, and the teacher knows the social and cultural background of the students. And the Canadian system offers liberal discipline, unlimited choice of academic courses and free and frank student-teacher relations and the teacher knows little of his immigrant student's cultural and educational background. This difference poses hesitation from both sides in opening a communication channel. But there are no insurmountable problems and he will overcome them soon. He should hang on his dreams.

The immigrant student should mingle with his peers with full confidence of acceptability. He should join the sports clubs or health clubs and participate in all the school activities of his choice. He should make friends in his school and feel free and unreserved with them. Friends are ones hidden treasures. The white friends will be of immense help to them in many ways. They are no more narrow-minded now as some of them were a generation back. The white young men are less spacing from the visible minorities now. They are much better informed about the Sikhs at present. Since the last fifteen years, the Sikhs have come to their own and their image as a Sikh is gaining respectability in the society at large. The Sikhs themselves must value Sikhism first, only then the others would follow suit. Otherwise, there is no magic solution to this problem.

Areas of Sikh Concern

To the community's great dismay, the Sikhs are top newsmakers in the big cities of Canada these days. Many of them live by the gun. It is amusing to note that in Canada domestic dogs are registered with the government but the guns are not.

Of late, it has been noticed that the Sikh youths, who are product of bad company, are getting involved in bone-chilling crimes. American trends of crime often jump the border into Canada and there is no escape from it as America's impact is terribly strong. As a result of groupism there have been murders among them. This criminal practice may not be older than a decade or so. A part of the Sikh youths plays truant in educational institutions and ultimately they become dropouts. When they have nothing to do, no job, no source of income which they badly need, they join gangs, raise money by foul means and turn to booze or alcohol and drugs and so many other vices seep into their system. In many cases they take to drugs in school itself. Experts have noted that kids are more likely to engage in anti-social activities and objectionable behaviour when they are part of a gang. Trouble with law is their daily routine.

It has been found that parents often find it difficult to talk to their children about drugs and alcohol that run their life. Young people must communicate with their parents, teachers, doctors or friends to seek help to get out of evil habits and save themselves to live fuller and richer lives as respectable and law-abiding citizens.

On the other hand the parents also cannot abdicate their role. The deeper their kids indulge in vices the more difficult it would be to pull them out. So the sooner the parents step in, the better. The kids ignored by parents move towards deviant peer groups. There should be authoritative parenting rather than authoritarian parenting. The former involves discussion between the kids and the parents as against the latter where parents dictate a set of rules without going in for dialogue.

The adolescents, on their part, do know that their parents are the most important people in their lives and are most sincerely concerned about them right from their hearts. Therefore, they must seek parental advice and assistance without any hesitation.

The young must be made to understand that alcohol has ruined more marriages, wrecked more careers, damaged more children and caused more misery than any single thing we know. Those who are not giving up excessive drinking immediately they are walking straight to their death. So the sooner one gives up drinking, the better. The best time to quit drinking is before you start it. The world's greatest fire can be extinguished by pouring a cup of water at the right time.

The East Indians drink at night parties and drive back home in drunken condition. A drunken driver is like a loaded gun or detonated bomb that may create terrible havoc any moment. Should we presume that a drunk driver is a fatalist as, generally, his first accident is his last accident. Nothing in life is risk-free except death that awaits a drunk driver.

The East Indians may learn to evade tragic happenings from the whites who go to the night clubs or night parties, in taxis, where they drink and return home in taxis rather than in their own cars. There are things you cannot put a price on. Safety is one of them.

In Canada, an average Indian woman's life is extremely hard. Their husbands expect them to behave like women in India and yet work in a western society. They are expected to cook, look after the home, rear children and also fulfil the rigorous demands of work outside. Indian men have hardly changed and it is the women who have to bear the brunt. Indian women have been robbed of that family status which they achieve back home naturally. One day she becomes senior and is elevated to the status of a grandmother (*dadi* or *nani*) or aunt (*tai* or *chachi*) or elder brother's wife (*bhabi*) who is loved and respected by all. But in Canada children grow in an alien world deserting all values unless Indian parents have made extraordinary efforts to inculcate Indian values in them. Their grandchildren, thus inflicting mental pain on them in the fag end of their lives do not properly respect most of these elderly women.

Sometimes Indian women are badly treated by their husbands. Domestic violence in the Sikh community sometimes assumes awful dimensions. Wife-beating and spouse-murdering is not a restricted domain for them. Spousal violence of alarming magnitude has been hidden in the homes of its victims and perpetrators. The position of women and men as wives and husbands has been historically structured as a hierarchy in which men possessed and controlled women. A woman is, sadly, treated as an object of desire and consumption not only by the male but also, unfortunately, by a woman, in her self-perception.

Marriage is a very sacred bond and much better than any of other alternatives. Respect the sanctity of the institution of marriage. Women will respond very positively. They are more sensitive to the signals of life. Why don't you accept that woman is the best thing God created? The old social practice had the unjustified approval of use of physical force against them. Sometimes women are subjected to violence because they object to their husband's spending money on drinking, gambling or nightclubs. Some women suffer violence for years together silently and secretly. These women remain physically passive. Many of them believe that if they try to hit back it just gets worse. These women are often beaten, verbally abused, psychologically terrorised and murdered by their husbands. They convert their homes into a war zone. Their whole life seems crashing on them. The effects of domestic violence on a woman's mental health and well-being can be just as serious as physical injuries or even worse. Let such husbands be told that men make houses and women make homes and home is not the place where we only live but a place where we become what we are. The home must be protected from disruption under all circumstances, and made a safe place for the family to live a happier life. A woman's role in home is invaluable. None can correctly calculate the value of the unpaid household work performed by them. Women's empowerment is necessary to pull them out of their inferior status in the family. The Indo-Canadian homes should be saved from the invasion of sex and violence culture of the West. The Sikh women have been assured equal position in the family by their religion. Why should women always carry with their names the tag of their husbands' family names and not otherwise?

The children who witness assaults on their mothers can also be seriously affected. They are at risk, of being assaulted themselves, of developing adjustment problems during childhood and adolescence and of continuing cycle of violence. If you hit a child on the back he is hurt in the heart. The children are a very sensitive stuff. Be merciful to them. Mothers care and spend more on their children than the fathers do. So, for their sake the mothers work harder and make greater sacrifices and suffer greater humiliations and cruelties at the hands of their husbands, suffering abusive relationship all their life. The Indo-Canadian women cannot even remotely be charged with infidelity. But many married white women's heartbeats are in other men's chests. As against a white child no body can ever say about an Indian child as 'mama's baby and papa's may be'. Congratulating a white woman on her new-born babe, a woman remarked, " Thank God, he looks like his father". Will the man feel small if told that the man descended from the monkey and woman from the angels? Thus, does she not deserve better treatment and superior regards? As a mark of respect Indian women walk three steps behind men but western white women walk all over them. Everybody commits faults. Men who do not forgive women for their little faults will never enjoy their great virtues.

It bedims the image of the whole community when an old man of 70 takes with him to Canada a bride of 20 years old from the Punjab. This is an immoral act of immense gravity that makes the head of every Indo-Canadian hang in utter shame. They cannot absolve themselves by simply giving the old man a licence of freedom of choice. What is socially debased, perverted or unchaste deserves condemnation. Every society has its culture, its norms, its values and it is not anybody's business to violate them. Society cannot exist if its accepted values are not protected. At the moment, I have no stringent suggestion to offer to deal with the people who flout the time-honoured norms of society but such people do need to be handled at societal level and in a way that conveys the public displeasure and social abhorrence to the present culprits and the future offenders.

The Sikh community's internal groupism resulting in abiding animosity has been plaguing the Sikh society at large. This hostility between different groups is centred in the Gurdwaras and the Gurdwara-based programmes including elections to religious bodies. Sikhism preached from the Sikh Gurdwara gives its followers the message of harmony and brotherhood of man. If in the Gurdwara itself they do something otherwise they are the violators of the sanctity of the sacred temple and the teachings imparted from its altar. The activities of the Sikhs in the Gurdwara are in the service of the Guru and any counter-activity is an act of gross disservice to the holy Master. Seeking Guru's bliss is supreme in the Sikh's life.

When they hold meetings in the Gurdwaras, these are not kissy-huggy meetings rather these are awful gatherings of warring rival groups. I hang my head in shame when the Sikhs wrangle for religion, fight for it, die for it but not live for (according to) it. They choose the holy Gurdwara as a venue for their fighting. And in the eyes of non-Sikhs they make a mockery of themselves and the electronic media or silver screen flashes their sabre-rattling in the Gurdwara, all over the world. I appeal to my Sikh brethren to observe utmost restraint in religious matters and iron out their differences according to the Sikh *maryada* (code of conduct) in the sacrosanct presence of the holy *Guru Granth Sahib*. To have best results there should be collective response to collective issues. Groupism will lead the community nowhere. This is a golden lesson learnt by the progressive communities through practice and experience.

Canadian Sikh Seniors

There has been a recent study titled *The Voice of Indo-Canadian Seniors* conducted by Calvin Lee and Ina Cheung for 'Orientation Adjustment Services for Immigration Society' (OASIS) in 1993, relating to a part of Greater Vancouver. In general, it depicts the condition of the Indo-Canadian seniors all over Canada. The overwhelming majority of the Indo-Canadians is the Jat Sikhs from the Punjab—an affluent state of India.

Three groups of seniors emerge distinctly. They are: (a) the professional and educated group, (b) the semi-literate group, (c) the illiterate group. The first group comprises mainly of the former civil servants, educators, military and police officers. They have good command of English language, both written and spoken, besides their own heritage language (Punjabi) as well as one or two other Indian languages. They actively participate in the mainstream services and the community services by volunteering as counsellors, interpreters and organizers of the seniors' societies. These seniors are largely independent and have the support and respect from their family members and the community.

The second or the semi-literate group comprises farmers, farm owners or former petty workers and employees in various vocations in their country. These people can read and write in their own heritage language. They can speak fair to fractured English and can read and write this language at a minimal level. They attend Indo-Canadian seniors' society groups and gather information about Canada and their mother country through mutual intercourse. They have almost no contact with the mainstream society. They often work in low status jobs as parking-lot attendants, janitors and farm workers.

The third or the illiterate group comprises former land cultivators or farm owners from the Punjab villages. These people are mostly illiterate even in their own language— Punjabi. They cannot speak or read or write English, and because of age-factor, have no motivation to learn it. They work mostly as farm labourers in summer and collect unemployment insurance (UI) in winter. They interact with people in their own community. They get support from the Indo-Canadian seniors' society groups for their personal difficulties. This group faces transportation, language and financial difficulties. The women of this group are mainly homebound with household and child-caring responsibilities.

The majority of the seniors immigrated as 'family class'—their sons or daughters sponsored more than 80 per cent of them. The seniors in the first group are quite independent and have little or no difficulty in adapting to their new environment. The more skilled in English, the less difficulties in adaptation to their new homeland. The groups two and three, that is, the semi-literate and illiterate have to confront a lot of difficulties and challenges in this country.

The language barriers and lack of knowledge of other cultures make them uncomfortable when mixing with other cultural and mainstream groups.

Back in India, the father is usually consulted on matters relating to finance, land investments and business. In Canada, he finds the *bapucracy* (rule of the father) ending, as his opinion is no more sought by his son. The mother looks after all the household affairs and the social aspects of life. But this role of authority and respect by the family is drastically diminished and reversed when the parents immigrate to Canada. Lacking in the knowledge of the life-style of their new country the parents are no longer the advisers and the authority figures in the family. Their children make all the decisions pertaining to their life, household affairs and particularly on finance. The parents, who were once on the top of the hierarchy of the family in their home country, are now at the bottom. For many, their dreams and idealism of uniting with their family and retiring in a rich and stable country are shattered. Their reduced status has a devastating effect on their self-esteem, self-confidence and mental health.[13] These seniors often feel that if faith in them is lost and their honour is dead they are over-living. If they cannot live the way they want to live they do not want to live any more. But most unwillingly they resign to their lot. It is a reality of life that aging portends loss of intellect, attractiveness and independence and loss of love. In old age there is nobody around to endorse and approve the fact of his or her existence. Old people feel hurt more deeply and more quickly and their young sons have hardly a sense to understand it and sympathize with them. In old age negative traits outnumber positive traits by about two to one. The old—an irritated lot, protest too soon, too much and too loudly. These nowhere people do deserve our utmost care and consideration. The young must bear with them.

Financial problem is another source of discontentment for the Indo-Canadian Sikh seniors. In India most of these elderly people owned land and many of them continue to own it, land which had passed on to them through the generations. There, the cost of living was fairly low as compared to Canada. They were not rich by Canadian standards. But they had a place of their own and were financially independent. Upon migration to Canada they are no longer landowners, have no money and no income.

Many of them are forced to work. Language barriers and illiteracy limit their choices of employment. Most Canadian employers who do not recognize their education and experiences from India, due to some false notions of their superior education, discriminate against even the fairly educated people. Most of these men have no choice and end up with taking low status jobs such as security guards, parking-lot attendants and farm labourers.

About 25 per cent of the farm workers are seniors. Many of them have no money in deposit. Working in the farm gives them pocket money—a little additional income. Although farm labour is hard work and many of the working conditions are not ideal, working in the farm allows the seniors to get out in the open air and socialize among their community group.

The sponsors of the 'family class' have to be financially responsible for the approved migrants for a minimum of ten years. This ten-year condition creates barriers for the seniors from becoming financially independent and receiving old age security pension, bus pass and continuing care services. One can be young without money but cannot be old without it. In old age seniors are needed to be active rather than productive, otherwise a perpetual holiday is a good working definition of hell.

Health includes the physical, mental, emotional and total well-being of an individual. No doubt, medical care in Canada is far better than in

India. The Indo-Canadian seniors will seek help only when they are physically ill. They rarely seek emotional and psychological help. As referred to earlier many factors devastate them terribly. They suffer the mental stress themselves and hardly share it with anyone else. The change from an independent role to a dependent and helpless role in a new society coupled with language barriers and isolation exercises a ruinous effect on their health.

Individualism has broken up the family in the East. Today the West has nuclear families. Upwardly mobile children and grandchildren have no obligation to look after the parents who generally end up in old age homes to be looked after at state expense. In what way is this an improvement on the joint family system? It deprives man of his emotions. It drains him of his love and affection. In India, as in Asia, in general, the family is the basic unit of society. The West pays lip-service to the family. But it is like a fetish—the West has lost interest and faith in the family.

The trend among the East Indians to send their senior citizens to the nursing homes is deemed as most horrible by the Sikh seniors as it ill-agrees with their old practice of living in joint families despite the fact, that there too, though, they sometimes live alone but they are not lonely. Their stay in their homes is becoming intolerable to the third generation children of the family. This treatment is suicidal to the Sikh elderly citizens who cannot stand isolation and boredom in the health care centres. The best prescription for their ailing health is keeping them in the homes where they had lived for decades. No doubt, there is a perception gap in the old and the young but that has to be plugged to the extent that the old are made to feel restful and cheerful in their homes as our Indian culture rightfully emphasizes. They should be considered something much more than the ghosts of dying men. There is need to impress upon the youngsters that the best place for the 'doting oldies' is their home in the company of their children and grand-children who have to look after them as their heritage culture enjoins upon them. We have to take every care that these seniors die in peace of mind rather than in ghastly agony. In old age, living within the embrace of the family is immeasurably soothing and comforting.

I quote below from the United Nations International Plan on Action on Aging:

"The human race is characterized by a long childhood and by a long old age. Throughout history, this has enabled older persons to educate the younger and pass on the values to them. This role has ensured man's survival and progress. The presence of the elderly in the family homes, the neighbourhood and in all forms of social life still teaches us an irreplaceable lesson of humanity. Not only by his life, but also indeed by his death, the older person teaches us all a lesson. Through grief, the survivors come to understand that the dead do continue to participate in the human community, by the results of their labour, the work and institutions they leave behind them, and the memory of their words and deeds. This may encourage us to regard our own death with greater serenity and to grow more fully aware of the responsibilities toward future generations."

Summing up the discussion in this chapter and the progress being made by the Sikhs it can be clearly visualized that the next generation Sikhs are destined to do much better than foreseen. The Sikhs have always shown better results than expected in all walks of their activity. Their vision, planning, determination and effort have made their achievements par excellence. 'Distinction' is their motto and they have always proved themselves equal to it. They are a people alien to lagging behind. To them their goal is never unachievable. Their future in Canada is bound to get them a remarkable place bedecked with laurels which they eminently deserve and sure to win.

REFERENCES

1. S. S. Sodhi, 'Implications of not teaching Punjabi to Sikh children in Canada', *Proceedings—Sikh Conference*, 1980, the National Sikh Society of Ottawa, Ontario, 1983, p.250.

2. Toronto Board of Education, *We are all Immigrants to this Place*, Toronto, 1976, p.26.

3. *Ibid.*, p.27.

4. William Johnson, 'Indian (native) Schools—how bad', *The Vancouver Sun*, 18 August 1994, p.A15.

5. Bob Overwald, 'The Schools', in M. Watkins (ed.) *Dene Nation—The Colony Within*, University of Toronto Press, Toronto, 1977.

6. National Indian Brotherhood, *Indian (native) control of Indian Education*, Ottawa, 1972, p.3.

7. George W. Bancroft, 'On the transplanting, transformation or preservation of roots: Sikh children and their education', *Proceedings of the Sikh Conference*, 1979, Toronto, The Sikh Social and Educational Society, Willowdale, Ontario, pp.60-61.

8. Surj Rattan, 'Looking back', *Mehfil*, December 1997, p.51.

9. *Ibid.*, p.45.

10. Joginder Singh Kalsi and Dr Mohinder Singh Grover. 'How Sikh Parents

view the Language. Religious and Cultural needs of their Children', *Proceedings of the Sikh Conference*, 1979, Toronto, p.72.

11. Surj Rattan, *op.cit.*, p.44.

12. Raghbir Singh Samagh, 'The Problems of the Sikh Youth', *Proceedings—Sikh Conference*, 1980, The National Sikh Society of Ottawa, Ontario, 1983, pp.180-89.

13. Calvin Lee and Ina Cheong, *The Voice of Indo-Canadian Seniors*, Vancouver, p.23.

CHAPTER 13

RELIGIOUS HERITAGE OF THE SIKHS AND THEIR TRANSFORMATION THROUGH IT

The Sikh Gurus had a few things in common with their contemporary reformers who were making efforts to purify the existing religious practices. But those reformers seem to have been deeply impressed with the nothingness of the body and life and they considered it unworthy of a thought to build up a new order of society. In the words of Joseph Davey Cunningham, "They aimed chiefly at emancipation from priest craft, or from the grossness of idolatry and polytheism.... They perfected forms of dissent rather than planted germs of nations, and their sects remain to this day as they left them. It was reserved for Nanak to perceive the true principles of reform, and to lay those broad foundations which enabled his successor Gobind (Singh) to fire the minds of his countrymen with a new nationality, and to give practical effect to the doctrine that the lowest is equal with the highest, in race as in creed, in political rights as in religious hopes."[1]

Sikhism, unlike Hinduism and Buddhism takes a positive view of the human-being and his body. Man, the highest and the noblest of God's creation, is not merely a handful of dust but the repository and the medium of the Lord's message. The human body is not an unclean vessel but the temple of God worthy of reverence and adoration. And woman, the mother of mighty heroes is elevated to the highest position in the hierarchy of human beings. This attitude towards man, woman and body is possible because Sikhism is a religion rooted in material and human reality. Sikhism does not dismiss the world out of hand as mere *maya* or illusion.

Sikhism ennobles the simple virtues of life such as purity, contentment, continence, service and sacrifice. It inculcates in man the fear of God. It upholds the dignity of man and labour. Untouchability, perhaps the greatest single crime against God and humanity is given no comfort or quarter. In

Sikhism a life of action is strongly commended as against a life of passivity, escape and abdication. A Sikh is a sharer of the riches of life but he never loses sight of the ultimate reality. That is why the metaphor of the lotus is often used in the Sikh scriptures when the paradox of purity amidst dirt is to be highlighted.

Distinctive form and symbols of Sikhism have often intrigued those who are unacquainted with Sikh history and Sikh doctrines. The wearing of the beard and full grown, unshorn hair on head, covered with turban, has never been quite understood or appreciated by many. Sikhism is the only religion in the world to insist on this practice. All ceremonies and rites are expressive and affirmative in character and they embody and communicate abstract meanings and values in concrete shape.

One of the notable things about Sikhism is its inherent eclecticism and resilience. It has a capacity to take heterogeneous doctrines and resolve them into a coherent, positive and distinctive philosophy.

Sikhism, though formally consecrated and institutionalized after Guru Nanak, carried from its inception a kinetic potential capable of encountering and overcoming the difficulties each new religion has to face. From the time of its initiation by Guru Nanak to its ritual consecration by Guru Gobind Singh, a period of about 200 years, Sikhism acquired not only its distinctive church, institutions, scriptures and symbols but also an unmistakable form. Sikhism has all the attributes and graces of major world religions.

Universalism as Sikh value pattern is its stout pillar, Sikhism has never been ethnicity-specific and a region-specific religion. The different ethnicities of the first five beloved ones initiated into the order of the Khalsa through the holy *amrit* by Guru Gobind Singh clearly mean that this religion is not bound down to a particular ethnicity or a particular region. The whole of the earth planet being revered as 'mother' by Guru Nanak, there is no specific 'holy land' conceived as such in Sikhism, thus making de-regionalization and de-ethinicization the corner stone of Sikhism.

This religion is universal in another sense also. In the daily prayer, a Sikh wishes *sarbat da bhala* (peace and prosperity for one and all), thus making the entire humanity in their reckoning.

Sikhism is a thoroughly modern and progressive religion. From the very outset it rejected orthodoxy, formalism and feudalistic values. It sought to liberate man and make him conscious of its high vocation and high destiny. Such a revolutionary creed was bound to create a new race of men and women leonine in appearance, vigorous, open, spontaneous and full of life, with their eyes on the stars.

The Ten Masters

Guru Nanak (1469-1539) was the founder of the Sikhs faith. His revelation came directly from God. He had a direct vision of the truth. He preached the unity of God, His Omnipresence and Omnipotence. The Guru told the people that the means to attain Him included self-surrender and worship of His Name. He advised people to abide pure amidst the impurities of the world, to have faith in the universal brotherhood, to live a householder's life, to reject the invidious distinctions of caste, and to reject empty rituals. The term 'Guru' means the spiritual mentor of his followers. Guru Nanak's religion remains a revealed, distinct and complete religion in itself. He showed little appreciation for the established orders of his time and did not identify himself with the existing forms of religion. In his philosophy an ideal man is a free, fearless and a moral being. He wanted to evolve a new social system, which had to be different from that of the Hindus and Muslims. It was clear to him that without mental and spiritual liberation there was no possibility of converting a man into a moral man. And so long as he was the member of the parent community, he could not be liberated. Therefore, there was a great need of a distinct social group that he created. In the words of Fredric Pincott, "He taught that all men are equal before God, that there is no high, no low, no privileged, no outcast, all are equal both in race and in creed, in political rights and in religious aspirations." [2]

It is well known that humanism, liberalism, pluralism and universalism are the fundamental values of Sikhism. Guru Nanak's vision enshrines in it a global society based on equality, fraternity, justice and peaceful co-existence.

When the great scholar Max Muller was asked to give Guru Nanak's teachings in one sentence, he said, "Nanak preached harmony", who believed that harmony and not violence was the only effective and strong basis of living together in this conflict-torn world, there being no other escape route. Guru Nanak felt that violence stemmed or issued from underdeveloped human mind and the low cultural level of society. Therefore, he vehemently advocated the brotherhood of man and fatherhood of God.

Guru Angad (1539-1552) was the immediate successor of Guru Nanak. He popularized *Gurmukhi* letters to be used as a script for the hymns of the Gurus. He condemned asceticism and collected and preserved the spiritual writings of Guru Nanak. The *langar* or free mess was further developed under him.

Guru Amar Das (1552-1574) was the successor of Guru Angad and his senior in age by twenty-five years. Guru Amar Das initiated the Sikhs into new ceremonies regarding birth, marriage and death and enthusiastically pursued and promoted the institution of *langar* (community kitchen) making it obligatory for every visitor to partake of the common repast before seeing him. This was evidently to disabuse his visitors of the old caste prejudices. He proclaimed the sanctity of human life and forbade the practice of *sati* or immolation of widows at the funeral pyre of their dead husbands. As referred to earlier, according to Indubhusan Banerjee, "Guru Angad had, no doubt, done something to give the Sikhs an individuality of their own but it was under Amar Das that the difference between a Hindu and a Sikh became more pronounced and the Sikhs began, gradually, to drift away from the orthodox Hindu society and form a class, a sort of new brotherhood, by themselves."[3]

Guru Amar Das divided his spiritual domain into 22 bishoprics or dioceses called *manjis*, each being placed under the charge of a devoted Sikh, whose duty it was to preach the mission of the Sikh Gurus and to keep the local body in touch with the centre.

Guru Ram Das (1574-1581), the Fourth Master, developed Guru Ka Chak (Amritsar) as the seat of Sikh faith. This town became the religious capital of the Sikhs. Pilgrims arrived there in large numbers. Guru Ram Das laid special stress on the invaluable virtue of rendering voluntary service (*sewa*) to the people. As subsequent history witnessed, Amritsar played a significant part in the development of Sikhism. The Sikhs received tremendous inspiration from this place in their struggle for liberation from the Mughals and Afghans.

Under Guru Arjan Dev (1581-1606), the fifth Guru, Sikhism became more firmly established. Its religion and social ideals received telling affirmation in practice. It added to its orbit more concrete and permanent symbols and its administration became more cohesive. Guru Arjan gave Sikhism its scripture, *The Granth Sahib*, and its main place of worship, the Amritsar shrine. He taught, by example, humility and sacrifice. He was the first martyr of the Sikh faith. The work of the first four Gurus was preparatory. It assumed a more definitive form in the hands of Guru Arjan.[4]

Guru Hargobind (1606-1644), who succeeded his father, framed a policy of militarizing the community. Under him, the Sikhs assumed certain additional responsibilities. Guru Arjan's martyrdom marked a turning point in the history of the Sikh faith. Instead of rosary and other saintly emblems of spiritual inheritance, his son Guru Hargobind wore a warrior's equipment for the ceremonies of succession. He sanctified steel as a will to resistance of tyranny. He put on two swords declaring one to be the symbol of his spiritual and the other that of his temporal investiture.[5]

The Guru sat at Akal Bunga (later called Akal Takht) and administered justice to his followers. The Guru had no political objectives to achieve and the military character added to the Sikh movement was purely a measure of self-defence.

Guru Har Rai (1644-1661), the seventh Guru, preached humility and disfavoured a clash with anyone though he kept the style of Guru Hargobind. The Guru kept the daily practice of his predecessors including the *langar*, which continued to be the central factor in the social transformation that Sikhism had initiated. The Guru chose for himself the simplest fare, which was earned by the labour of his own hands.

Guru Har Krishan (1661-1664) succeeded to Guruship at the early age of five. He had a rare ability in explaining passages from the holy *Granth*. Emperor Aurangzeb summoned the Guru to Delhi where he was stricken with smallpox and died in March 1664 at the age of 8.

Guru Teg Bahadur (1664-1675), the ninth Guru, and the youngest child of Guru Hargobind succeeded his grandson Guru Har Krishan. On false and totally untenable charge of inciting the peasantry of the Punjab for rebellion against the Mughal government, he was arrested, taken to Delhi and martyred on 11 November 1675, under the orders of Emperor Aurangzeb.

Guru Tegh Bahadur, by offering himself to the Mughal tyrant's sword at Delhi, registered his peaceful resistance against the policy of forcible conversion. The martyrdom of the Guru was a staggering catastrophe in Sikh history. According to Harbans Singh "The martyrdom was no small happening. It was something of immense magnitude, of immense consequence. A most sensitive and comprehensive genius of the age undertook to answer the challenge of the time with all his moral strength. He brought to his response spiritual insight and discipline of the highest order, a living experience which bespoke love, compassion and humility and inheritance, descending from Guru Nanak, symbolising the ideals of faith, self-giving service and freedom. The choice was deliberately made. It was no passive submission but a positive decision to confront an existing situation."[6]

Guru Gobind Singh (1675-1708) felt that the Sikhs needed reorganization in order to bring about internal cohesion and provide external defence. He baptised his followers with *amrit* (nectar) prepared with a double-edged sword and made steel an integral limb of a Sikh and thus evolved out of the Sikhs a powerful engine of revolution, a force to fight tyranny and injustice.

Guru Gobind Singh invested the Khalsa *panth* (Sikh community) with his personality or, in other words, the Khalsa *panth,* was to be the Guru in future. He told the Sikhs, "I have bestowed the Guruship on the Khalsa. Khalsa is my very self and I will always live in the Khalsa."[7] Of his close identification with his Sikhs, the Guru provided a unique example at the initiation ceremony in which he, the supreme head of the religious organisation, voluntarily surrendered his authority to his disciples and adopted the unusual procedure of being baptised by the same disciples, who a short while ago, had been baptised by him. He undertook to abide by the same *rehat* (code of conduct) as had been enjoined upon the Sikhs to follow. Although the Guru himself designed the Khalsa, yet the Guru was so much charmed and fascinated by his own creation that he saluted it, as his own ideal and master. He had introduced a sort of spiritual socialism in the field of religion.

Guru Gobind Singh bifurcated Guruship—investing spiritual guidance in the *Guru Granth* and the leadership of the community in the Khalsa *panth* itself. In other words the temporal sovereignty was vested in the Panth, Guru Panth, and the divine sovereignty in the *Adi Granth*, thereby institutionalizing it as the *Guru Granth Sahib*. He had to suffer extreme sacrifices for the glory of the *panth*. He made a humble submission to his father to face the challenge of the Mughal oppression. All his four sons suffered martyrdom at the hands of the oppressive and cruel Mughal government. Children survive their parents but when parents survive their children it is a heart-shattering tragedy. His own martyrdom was also due to a Mughal government-deputed assassin.

During all the 42-years of his life span he never bowed before injustice and suppression by the government. Many battles were inflicted on him, which he fought in the spirit of *dharam-yudh* (a holy war) against the unrighteousness or the enemies of righteousness and goodness. He used force for a legitimate and noble cause and as a last resort.

Guru Granth Sahib

Guru Arjan, the fifth Guru, was a saint, a poet and a scholar of rare piety and spiritual insight and marvellous literary acumen. He was the compiler of the *Adi Granth*, the revealed Sikh scripture which embodies, in addition to his own writings, the spiritual compositions of his predecessors, a number of other Indian saints, some of them coming from the so called low and untouchable castes.

While compiling the *Adi Granth* (in 1604) Guru Arjan kept a certain spiritual ideology in mind. For him the essential thing was the expression of the fundamental truth and the harmonious unity of spiritual emotion and thought. And only those compositions that came up to his standard were incorporated in it without any other consideration.

In the words of Macauliffe, "Guru Arjan felt the necessity of laying down rules for the guidance of his followers in the performance of their daily religious duties and expiratory rites. This course wc ald reduce his religion to consistency, and hinder divergent tenets and rituals. That consummation, however, could only be attained when the exact words of the Guru were permanently recorded in one grand volume."[8] To save adulteration in the holy texts of the Gurus and to keep them in their pure form, Guru Arjan preserved their holy composition in the form of *Guru Granth Sahib*. If those compositions were left to the memory of the devotees, in due course of time, the same would get corrupted and then vanish. So, the collection and compilation of the same was essential in the interest of Sikhism. It was also realised that in order to make the Sikhs an independent community with a religion of their own they must have their own separate holy Book.

In the *Adi Granth* Guru Arjan's contribution was the biggest, including some of the sublimest pieces like the 'Sukhmani'. *The Granth Sahib* mainly consists of *shaloks, shabads* and *pauris*. It contains 974 hymns of Guru Nanak, 61 hymns of Guru Angad, 907 of Guru Amar Das, 679 of Guru Ram Das and 2216 of Guru Arjan himself. Later on 116 *shabads* and 2 *shaloks* of Guru Tegh Bahadur were added to it. The hymns of fifteen saints and Bhagats and fifteen Bhatts or minstrels were also incorporated in the holy *Granth*. The compositions of Satta, Balwand, Mardana and Sunder are also included in this holy Book. Thus we see that besides the Gurus a large number of Bhagats found place for their composition in the *Adi Granth* and were thus immortalized through the inclusion of their compositions in the immortal holy *Granth*.

It is arranged according to 31 ragas or musical measures. Those ragas were rejected which were calculated to work the mind to extremes of joy or sadness, e.g. *megh* and *h??ol, jog* and *deepak*. Its arrangement was a marvel of scholarly fastidiousness.

The *Adi Granth* mainly rather exclusively deals with the religious and spiritual matters. It is the *Bible* of the Sikhs. As referred to above it contains the teachings of Guru Nanak and his successors and of many other elevated souls from among the Hindu and Muslim saints. Most of the hymns of this holy *Granth* are in praise of the Almighty God. This *Granth* is the treasure of spiritual knowledge from which a man of any community, any religion, any country and any age can equally benefit.

Dr Trumpp says, "Prayer to the Supreme is hardly ever mentioned in the *Granth*." This statement is simply absurd as literally hundreds of prayers to the Supreme could be produced from this holy Book. In fact this holy *Granth* is a long prayer before God and a long song in His praise.

The holy *Granth* deals with the instruction regarding a pious, honest and spiritually elevated living. It aims to help the seekers of truth and to praise those who sincerely meditate on His Name. The hymns establish a deep spiritual unity between man and God. Its hymns chanted in deep reverence and devotion inspire the minds of listeners to lofty ideas of pure living and high thinking. This *Granth* is a source of divine wisdom and spiritual bliss.

Guru Gobind Singh, the Tenth Master, before he breathed his last, as mentioned earlier, divided the institution of Guruship, vesting the spiritual part of it in the *Adi Granth* as finalized by him and the secular one in the Khalsa. The former was to be the *Guru Granth* and the latter was to be the *Guru panth*. Thus ending the personal Guruship, the succession passed to the *Guru Granth Sahib* in perpetuity. The line of personal Gurus could not have continued forever. It was only through the Word that the Guruship could be made everlasting. The *Guru Granth Sahib* was henceforth—for all time to come—the Guru for the Sikhs. The Guru enjoined the Sikhs to own the holy *Granth* equal with the Guru and make no distinction between the two. "He who would wish to see the Guru's Word let him read the *Granth* with love and attention." It was ceremonially installed in the centre of the inner sanctuary of Harmandir Sahib on 16 August 1604. For the Sikhs the Guru is the holy teacher, the prophet, under direct commission from God. The *Guru Granth Sahib* is the continuing visible manifestation of the Guru. The Sikhs live their religion in response to it. It is the focal point of the Sikh devotion. It is the living source of authority, the ultimate guide for the spiritual and moral path pointed by the Gurus. Whatever is in harmony with its tenor and spirit will be acceptable, whatever not, is rejectable. Guidance is sought from it on doctrine, on the tenets of the faith. The holy *Guru Granth Sahib*, with its cosmopolitan or universal appeal, continued guiding the Sikhs with its comprehensive outlook and respect for all other religions and regard for people belonging to different castes and classes.

The tenets enshrined in the *Guru Granth Sahib* were final and inviolable fundamental laws of Sikhism to be in no case altered. The Khalsa, being the product of the Guru, naturally could not have the authority to scrap the injunctions of the *Guru Granth Sahib* and had, therefore, to remain within the framework of its holy teachings.

Primarily, the *Guru Granth Sahib* is a collection of revealed compositions of spiritual experience that speaks about the Will or Word of God. All compositions embody supplication in praise of God, the Supreme Being. In the words of Arnold Toynbee—a great British historian, "The *Adi Granth* is remarkable for certain reasons. Of all known religious scriptures, this Book is the most highly venerated. It means more to the Sikhs than the *Quran* means to the Muslims, the *Bible* to the Christians and the *Torah* to the Jews. The *Adi Granth* is the Sikhs' perpetual Guru (spiritual guide).... The Sikh religion and its scriptures, the *Adi Granth*, will have something of a special value to say to the rest of the world."⁹ *The Guru Granth Sahib* is the only scripture in the world that has been supremely exalted and given divine status of a living Guru and is worshipped as such by the Sikhs. The landmark judgement of the Supreme Court of India delivered on 29 March 2000 considered *Guru Granth Sahib* as jurisdic person. The judgement further read: *"Guru Granth Sahib* cannot be equated with any other sacred book such as the *Gita*, the *Bible* or the *Quran* or with an idol."

The Sikh Gurus transformed the heritage and deeply coloured their teachings with love of God.

Dasam Granth

It is the second revered Book of the Sikhs. Most of its compositions were written at Paonta Sahib and Anandpur Sahib. There are various versions of this *Granth* and scholars are divided in their views on its authentic version. Dasam *Granth* is a large collection of miscellaneous writings. It is controversial whether all its compositions have been authored by Guru Gobind Singh. According to all available evidence it was compiled at Damadama Sahib (Talwandi Sabo) by Bhai Mani Singh—a very learned Sikh and later custodian of Harmandir Sahib (Amritsar), who was later martyred by the orders of the Lahore government in 1734, twenty-six years after the death of Guru Gobind Singh.

The contents of this *Granth* may be divided into four parts. The first part is autobiographical. The *Vachitra Natak* is an account of the Guru himself, of his genealogy, of his previous incarnation as ascetic in the Himalayas and his earlier battles. This part also contains *zafarnama*, the defiant epistle addressed to the Mughal Emperor Aurangzeb.

The second part may comprise the *Jap Sahib*, the *Akal Ustat*, *Gian Prabodh* and *Shabad Hazare*.

The third part may include *Sawaiyye* and *Shastar nam mala* (inventory of the weapons).

The fourth part provides a lengthy account of legends and anecdotes—the *Tria Charitar*. Of the standard printed edition the first part covers 73 pages, second part 68 pages, third part 96 pages and the fourth part 1185 pages which includes *Krishna Avtar* covering 316 pages and *Tria Charitar* 580 pages. The language of this *Granth* is predominantly Braj with sprinkle of Persian, Punjabi and Khari Boli. *Dasam Granth*, besides its spiritual ethos, is a historical source of critical importance for any analysis of the evolution of the Sikh *panth*.[10]

The musical notes are at times martial in appeal and at other times soothing and peaceful. The poetic genius of Guru Gobind Singh, combined with sublime music and singing, created the most melodious and inspiring patterns of spiritual compositions.

Gurdwara (Sikh Church)

It is a place where the holy *Guru Granth Sahib* is installed. Everybody is admitted to it without any reservation. Anybody entering the Gurdwara (Guru's house) is expected to bow before the *Guru Granth Sahib* and make some offering which is, of course, voluntary. People enter from the front and after making obeisance to the *Guru Granth Sahib*, take their seats on the carpet. Generally the women sit on the left and men to the right facing the dais on which the *Guru Granth Sahib* is seated.

The *granthi* (reader or reciter) or officiant sits behind the *Guru Granth Sahib* and waves a *chauri* (flywhisk) as a sign of respect. Any man or woman who is able to recite the revealed *bani* (holy scripture) can perform the reverential duty. The k*irtan* (devotional singing) interspersed with *katha* (exposition) is performed by the *ragis* (reciters).

All the people, men and women, are required to cover their heads at the time of entering the Gurdwara, and bow before the *Guru Granth Sahib* with folded hands, expressing utmost humility and respect for the Guru. Towards the conclusion of the programme conducted in the presence of the holy *Guru Granth Sahib, ardas* (prayer) is offered with all members of the congregation standing with folded hands. Then the *wak* or the Guru's word is solicited. There is always a special decorum observed in the presence of the *Guru Granth Sahib* in the Gurdwara. It is believed that the holy presence of the Guru prevails inside the Gurdwara.

At the end of all the ceremonies inside the Gurdwara, *karah prasad* or the holy pudding is distributed to everybody present there and free meals are served in the *langar* (community mess) attached to the Gurdwara. Every Sikh makes it a point to visit the Gurdwara as often as he can do.

The role of the Gurdwara in keeping the Sikhs on the right path is, unquestionably, tremendous. The Gurdwara is the hub of the Sikh community's activities—religious, social and political. It is a central place where people of all religious and political affiliations may assemble and participate in the deliberations confronting the community. None can object to anybody's entry into the Gurdwara, as it is a place to which every person is privileged to come.

It is a Gurdwara, formerly called dharamsala, where all the religious functions of the community are celebrated including the *gurpurbs* (anniversaries relating to the Gurus). The *kirtan* from the holy hymns, *katha* (expositions) and lectures on the Sikh history are regularly conducted. Most of the Sikh marriages are solemnised in the Gurdwara. *The sadharan paths* and the *akhandpaths* and finally the *bhogs* and congregational *ardas* include the routine programmes performed in the Gurdwara.

The *amrit-prachar* or baptismal ceremonies of the Sikhs are also occasionally arranged in the Gurdwara. Caste distinctions, which, unfortunately, the Sikhs have not so far shed off outside the Gurdwara, have no place within its precincts. Inside the Gurdwara all are equal irrespective of their social status, caste, colour or creed. The Gurdwara has a pattern of conduct that is strictly observed by the Sikhs both individually and collectively. None is privileged to flout any part of the Sikh *maryada* (code of conduct) prescribed for the Gurdwara.

The Gurdwara is a very holy place for the Sikhs. They donate liberally to build, renovate or repair the Gurdwara buildings. The Harmandir Sahib (Amritsar) was damaged and pulled down by the Afghan invaders thrice but the Sikhs raised and repaired it at their earliest opportunity. The Gurdwara is certainly a radiating centre of the Sikh culture and a strong cementing force or bond of *panthic* unity. But of late, some Sikhs in the western hemisphere are fighting over how to make the Gurdwara relevant to the present and future generations. This is very unfortunate. The centuries-old Gurdwara *maryada* introduced by the Gurus has been and will be relevant to all ages and in all countries. The role of the Gurdwara in keeping the Sikhs on the right path is, undoubtedly, tremendous, and its sanctity is undiminished as ever.

Sangat and Sadh Sangat

The word *sangat* means, an assembly or meeting together. The fundamental object behind the organisation of the *sangats* was to guide the followers of the Guru to mould their lives according to the teachings of the Master. Guru Nanak has defined *sat sangat* (congregation of the true ones) as "the society where the praises of the Supreme Lord alone are expounded."[11]

Bhai Gurdas, a contemporary of the fifth and sixth Gurus, and Saint Paul of the Sikhs, tells us that "of all associations the most fruitful was that with the Guru's Sikhs, who were the holiest of the holy."[12] He was so highly impressed with the piety and virtuousness of the Sikhs of his days that he sees in their congregation (*satsang*) an image of Heaven, the abode of All-truth.[13] Another name used for the Sikh congregation was *sadh-sangat*, the assembly of the *sadhus* or saints. The *sadh sangat* came to mean a very respectful Sikh congregation that daily assembled around the Guru or his nominee, mostly for religious purposes and matters of the community interest were not excluded from its deliberations.

In these assemblies or organized fellowships of the Sikhs they sang the Guru's hymns in praise and adoration of the Almighty Father which imperceptibly leads the receptive mind of the devotee to a life of virtue and service. As such, the institution of *sangat* aimed at the spiritual advancement of the Sikhs.

Once some *yogis* asked Guru Nanak to work a miracle. He replied that he could do so through two things—the Word and the Assembly.[14] Thus, Guru Nanak considered the assembly or the organized fellowship to be the proper medium for the communication of his message. Wherever Guru Nanak went during his missionary travels, he established *sangats*[15] with the instructions to his followers to build a place of congregation or dharamsala where they could regularly meet and sing the Lord's praises. Thus sprang up a network of *sangats* and dharamsalas that became centres of Sikh missionary activities.

Sangats Open to All

The membership of the *sangat* organisation was open to all persons, men and women, whatever their social position. People of all castes, high or low sat together in the *sangat* without any distinction. This casteless get-to-gather gave the Sikhs a strong feeling of brotherhood of man.

The number of the followers of the Sikh faith increased considerably by Guru Amar Das's time. The number of the *sangats* also multiplied. Many Muslims are also said to have started coming into the *sangats* and later Guru Arjan had many Muslims as his followers to whom Jahangir has referred in his autobiography[16]. As told above the number of the *sangats* had increased considerably, Guru Amar Das found it difficult to supervise them personally. He, therefore, divided the Sikh spiritual domain into twenty two bishoprics which were named *manjis*, as the preacher sat on a *manji* (cot) at the time of giving a spiritual discourse. These *manjis* were, in fact, local *sangats* placed under the charge of a devoted Sikh whose duty it was to preach the mission of the Guru and to keep the local body in touch with the centre—the headquarters of the Guru.

Sangats Meet the Financial Needs of the Guru's Projects

In order to collect money from the *sangats* established in different parts of the country Guru Arjan organized the *masand* system. The word *masand* is the corrupted form of *masnad* or *masnad-i-ali* meaning high official seat. Preachers being the representatives of the Guru, were offered higher seats in congregations, therefore, they were called the *masands*.

The *masand* not only gathered the tithes from the Sikhs away from the important centres but also propagated the religion of Guru Nanak[17] and according to *Dabistan* the *masands* had appointed their deputies also.[18] The *masands* rendered accounts of their collections to the Guru in the month of Baisakh. The Guru received substantial amounts of money and many other precious gifts from the *sangats*. Guru's control over the entire Sikh organisation of the *sangats* through the *masands* ensured the solidarity of the Sikh community. "Wherever a Sikh might be, he was brought under a *sangat* and through it made to realise that a Sikh is not only to look to his individual character but is also to shoulder his responsibilities as a part of the corporate body of the *panth*."[19] These *sangats* were not loose and incoherent units but had been a closely-knit system.

It was through the unstinted support of the Sikh *sangats* that Guru Arjan could found towns like Sri Hargobindpur, Tarn Taran and Kartarpur and could complete the tanks and temples in Amritsar and Tarn Taran and a *baoli* in the Dabbi Bazaar in Lahore. The *sangats* not only actively participated in the physical labour involved in the projects but also played a vital role in their planning, execution and administration.

Sangats Supplied Horses and Weapons to Guru Hargobind

Under Guru Hargobind the *sangats* assumed certain additional responsibilities consequent upon the martyrdom of Guru Arjan. Guru Hargobind sent a word to his *masands* to ask the Sikhs to bring arms and horses as a part of their offerings. In response to the Guru's demand the Sikhs made the necessary compliance and they also came to join the Guru's forces. By supplying the Guru with the weapons of war, horses and fighting men, the inoffensive and peaceable *sangats* assumed a different complexion. These *sangats* from that time onwards became the feeding depots of the financial and military requirements of the Gurus. Undoubtedly, the Gurus had no political objective to achieve and the militant character or trend given to the Sikh movement was purely a measure of self-defence against the religious bigotry of the ruling class.

Identification between the Guru and the Sangat

There was a growing identification between the Guru and the *sangat* and thus the *sangat* began to acquire great sanctity until the whole spiritual authority was transferred to them after Guru Gobind Singh when the Sikh *panth* came to assume the personality of the Guru. The spiritual character of the *sangat* had begun to appear much earlier. Bhai Gurdas said, one disciple is a single Sikh, two form a holy association, but where there are five present, there is God himself."[20] Guru Ram Das declared, "The Guru is a Sikh and the Sikh who practises the Guru's word is at one with the Guru."[21]

On the one hand Senapat identifies the Guru with God and on the other he identifies the *sangat* with the Guru. In this way, a divine character is attributed to the collective body of the *sangat* that became sacrosanct and authoritative for the individual members of the congregation. The *sangat* played a vital role in the integration of the community. As the tradition goes the Gurus rated the *sangat* above the Guru and used to say that where the Guru was equal to 20 parts the *sangat* was equal to 21 parts. According to *Dabistan*, whenever a Sikh had a wish to be fulfilled he made a request to the assembly and then it was referred to the Guru or invoked to God. And whenever the Guru had a wish to be fulfilled, he also placed it before the *sangat* considering it spiritually competent to get it granted through an efficacious prayer to that effect.[22]

The *sangat* played an important part in the life of a Sikh in keeping him to the right path. It was fully competent to punish or forgive his faults and lapses.[23]

Guru's Headquarters in Contact with the Sangats

Almost all the Gurus kept contacts with their local and distant *sangats*.[24] If they did not find time to visit them personally, they would address them by letters very often, telling them to observe the discipline of the *sangat*, invited them to their headquarters and also asked them to send certain things including money, weapons, horses, oxen, camels and elephants, as we read in the *Hukamnamas*.[25]

Some Sangats Placed under the Direct Control of the Gurus

The *sangats* whose presiding leaders turned out to be corrupt were taken over under the direct control of the Guru himself. The Guru told them that they had been made 'Khalsa', that is, taken under his personal supervision. Here the word 'Khalsa' is used in a symbolic and technical sense. The Khalsa is an Arabic word in its origin with 'Khalis' as its root. The 'Khalsa' was used for the territory or land or property controlled by the king himself, the revenue of which was deposited directly into the royal treasury without any share or interference of a landlord. The Gurus have also used this term with special meanings attached to it, thereby doing away with the intermediary *masands*. Guru Hargobind used this term for the *sangat* of the east saying, The *sangat* of Patna is Sri Guru's Khalsa.[26] Guru Gobind Singh used this term very often, in his *Hukamnamas* for many *sangats* as "you are my Khalsa" and "*sangat* is my Khalsa."[27] Besides this use of the term, Guru Gobind Singh gave a collective name of 'Khalsa' to all those persons who went through the baptismal ceremony initiated by him on 30 March 1699.

Important Centres of the Sangats outside Punjab

During the course of his missionary travels Guru Nanak established *sangats* in Kamrup (Assam), Bihar, Cuttock, Surat, Nanakmata (in the Kumaon Hills), Khatmandu, Jallalabad, Kabul and many other places. The discovery of a few letters and manuscripts at Dhaka by G. B. Singh has clearly established that by the year 1666, "prosperous *sangats* flourished at Sylhet, Chitagong, Sondip and Lashkar besides the one at Sutrapur. By the time of Guru Gobind Singh Dhaka had earned the title of 'the home of Sikhism'"[28] It may also be mentioned that "Sikh temples still exist at Rameshwar, Salur, Bhaker and Shivaji in Madras and Colombo in Ceylon. Old Sikh temples also exist at Burhanpur, Surat, Bombay, Amraoti and Nirmal (district Adilabad in Hydrabad State).[29]

Some of the important centres of Sikh *sangats* outside the Punjab referred to in the *Hukamnamas* include Patna, Sylhet, Chitagong, Jamalpur, Dehradun, Benaras, Bhawanipur, Monghyr and Mirzapur.

Summing up, it may be remarked that spiritually the *sangats* helped the Sikhs in maturing their beliefs according to the instructions of the Gurus. Socially, they provided opportunity to the people of all castes and creeds, high and low, rich and poor, to meet and sit together as equals. And politically, the *sangats* developed among the Sikhs strong democratic tradition.[30]

Pangat or Guru Ka Langar

In the Sikh terminology *pangat* means a row of men sitting together to partake *langar* or food from a common kitchen. The need of a common mess was felt for the reason that as an institution it possessed the potentiality of a valuable instrument of social reform in a setting where caste taboos prevented people from sitting and eating together. Hence from the very outset the institution of *langar* was integrally associated with that of the *sangat*. The Sikhs voluntarily made provisions for the *langar*. The Sikhs shared their earnings with the needy. Ganesh Das Badehra writes, "If a hungry person approached a Sikh for food he was served with it even if the Sikh himself were to go without it. And in order to entertain the visitor the Sikh would even pawn his clothes and utensils."[31] According to Malcolm, at the time of initiation a Sikh is told that "whatever he has received from God it is his duty to share with others," because the provisions belong to the Guru and the service in the *langar* is the privilege of the Sikhs.

The *pangat* proved a vital means of social cohesion and integration. It was a big step towards bettering the lot of the downtrodden and untouchables and under-privileged section of the people, who had been groaning under the weight of socio-economic inequalities and religious discriminations prevalent in the society.

The *langar* provided avenues of selfless service through the collection of rations and fuel, grinding of grains, cooking the vegetables and food, serving the meals and water, and washing or cleaning the dishes, utensils and the dining halls.

Under Guru Nanak's successors, the *pangat* or Guru's *langar* developed into a very powerful institution, entailing far-reaching significance and consequences. Guru Nanak's successor, Guru Angad, who had served in the Guru's *langar* for quite sometime and had deeply acquainted himself with the experience of running a *langar*, enjoying the bliss that was its natural outcome. Guru Angad used to bring provisions for the *langar* and did all odd jobs as commanded by his Master. After Guru Angad shifted from Kartarpur to Khadur, the Guru's wife *Mata* Khivi supervised the common kitchen there. The *langar* supplied delicious dishes like rice boiled in milk and *ghee* as written by Satta and Balwand.[32]

o

According to Gokal Chand Narang the institution of *langar* was the first such institution among the Sikhs that taught them the first lesson of contributing towards a common fund.[33]

The *Guru ka langar* became a great institution under Guru Amar Das who shifted his headquarters to Goindwal in the present district of Tarn Taran (Punjab). As was the practice with Guru Angad, ' the Third Master, also lived on very simple food like boiled rice and lentils, got with his own small earnings but his public mess was daily provided with supplies of butter, refined flour and sugar.'[34] Guru Amar Das insisted that any one who wanted to see him had first to accept his hospitality by eating with his followers. The Mughal Emperor Akbar and Raja of Haripur who came to see the Guru had to dine at the Guru's free mess before having a meeting with the Guru. Akbar's offer of a grant of land to meet the requirements of the Guru's *langar* was politely refused by the Guru, telling the emperor that it was run by the voluntary offerings of the visitors.

Guru Ram Das, the Fourth Master, and later Guru Arjan, the Fifth Guru, and his wife *mata* Ganga also served in the *langar,* distributing food to the visitors, fanning them in hot weather. Serving in the *langar* was considered a work of noble virtue and through it one learnt to be humble, tolerant and generous. *Guru ka langar* continued feeding the hungry under all the Gurus.

During Guru Gobind Singh's days a large number of pilgrims visited the Guru at Anandpur. Besides Guru's *langar*, there were some other *langars* as well run by certain Sikhs in their houses. Some of these *langars* were not run according to the instructions of the Guru. The Guru often visited these *langars* in disguise to have first hand knowledge of their functioning. Some of them worked only for a short time and some started very late and thus not rendering satisfactory service. Only Bhai Nand Lal's *langar* served meals quickly and even at odd hours. The Guru referred to his visit to various *langars* and their faulty functioning. He told them that when the cooked food ran short and a hungry man came and asked for food, whosoever feeds him feeds the Guru. Turning away a hungry man from ones door amounted to turning away the Guru himself. By Guru Gobind Singh's time the *langar* had become an inseparable adjunct of the *sangat* or the congregation. There was no consummation of the programmes of the congregation without the *langar* following it.

Banda Singh Bahadur (1708-16) introduced an official seal for his state documents and letters patent. It contained the following inscription:

Deg-o-tegh-o-fateh-o-nusrat bedirang, yaft az Nanak Guru Gobind Singh.[35]

(The kettle and the sword (symbols of *langar* and power) victory and ready patronage have been obtained from the Gurus—Nanak and Gobind Singh.)

The above inscription lays stress on two things—*langar* and sword, both got from Guru Nanak and Guru Gobind Singh. Degh or cauldron is the symbol of feeding the hungry and *tegh* or sword is the symbol of protecting the weak and helpless.

To sum up, the institution of *langar* was maintained by the Sikhs as a sacred one. In all the big Gurdwaras there is an arrangement of running the *langar* regularly. In some Gurdwaras the food is available for twenty four hours a day. The Sikhs voluntarily bring provisions including *ghee* (butter), milk, pulses, vegetables, sweets, flour, etc., to the Guru's kitchen. The food served in the *langar* is considered sacred, blessed by the Guru. The food distributed is the same for every one without any distinction, which if made, destroys the concept behind it.

Indubhusan Banerjee observed that the institution of *langar* proved a powerful aid in the propagation work. Besides serving as an asylum for the poor it also became a great instrument for advertisement and popularity and 'it gave a definite direction to the charities of the Guru's followers'. It served as a great bond of union among the Sikhs and also helped to mitigate caste prejudices, to some extent, as all those who came to have their food in the *langar* had to take it together irrespective of caste or creed.[36]

Sikh Ardas

Prayer is a very much natural and necessary outcome of a person's belief in God. Martin Luther said, "Faith is prayer and nothing but prayer. He who does not pray or call upon God in his hour of need, surely does not think of Him as God nor does he give Him, the honour that is His due". Mystics believe that "our end is to seek, find and ultimately be one with God, and prayer is the means to achieve that end." To the godly persons the religious impulse is essentially the impulse to pray and the non-praying man is rightly considered to be religiously dead.

The Sikh practice of prayer is an important way to invoke the divine grace. Prayer involves commitment to God, faith in Him and in His goodness. Here the devotee experiences God as living reality. In prayer man is waiting on God. The Sikh prayer is psychologically in the conversation form. It is a dialogue between the person who prays and Him who is being addressed. The worshipper holds conversation with God in his prayer and solicits His response. Undoubtedly, the prayer enhances the well being of the prayee and supplements his energies wonderfully. The prayee believes that his purpose will be fulfilled. The Sikhs have unbounded and limitless faith in the efficacy of prayer. Most of the hymns of the *Guru Granth Sahib* are in the form of supplication or prayer to God.

The Sikh Gurus taught their followers to address prayers direct to God, the Supreme Being, as against the earlier man who invoked the lower divinities to intercede for him. His prayers were addressed to various gods, deities and minor spirits of nature as winds, thunder, fire, evil spirits and even to their ancestors. He prayed to get rid of fears from the natural calamities. People in earlier times tried to approach God through rituals, deities, sacrifices, spells and priests. But a Sikh approaches God direct through his invocation and through a direct communication with Him. It is generally believed that fear may be the impelling and hope as the releasing motive of prayer. Another factor that motivates prayer is to obtain forgiveness for sinful acts. Man is always liable to sin. He is victim of 'I-ness', considering himself more important than the Supreme Lord. Such thinking lands him in sin and when he realizes of his folly he attempts to absolve himself of this state of utter unrighteousness through prayer. The Sikhs have full faith in the efficacy of a sincere prayer coming right from the deep recesses of devoted hearts.

"If a Sikh has something to be done he should pray to God for help to accomplish it." says the Guru.[37] The Sikh is again and again told by the Gurus that God is merciful and kind and fulfils the wishes of his devotees. He looks after their works. His help must always be sought through prayer, which uplifts the human soul to the vicinity of the Almighty. Prayer renews our resolve to always remain on the path of God and to remain in the service of His creation. In an hour of extreme stress in life prayer proves a source of stability in our shaken personality and mental disturbance.

Ardas is a sanskrit word. *Ard* means 'seek' and *as* means desire, thereby *ardas* means to wish ones desire to be fulfilled. Some scholars believe that it is the corrupted or contracted form of Persian word *arzdasht*, a petition or an address from an inferior to a superior or a higher authority for favour of granting one something he desires. According to the Sikh faith when a person needs some of his desires to be fulfilled he should make a submission only to God. Guru Gobind Singh told his Sikhs categorically that he never demanded anything from the gods or goddesses. He always solicited the Almighty Father.

The congregational prayer added religious fervour among the Sikhs and strengthened unity and co-operation between them.[38]

Need for Regular Prayer

Prayer is a thing more of the heart than of the tongue. The effectiveness of the prayer does not so much lie in the beauty of the language employed or the style of expression as the earnestness and the humility of the heart from where the prayer springs up. This is especially true in the case of an individual prayer. But the prayer offered in large congregations on special occasions marked with deeply sentimental moments, dealing extensively with the past glories, the present and future aspirations of the community, needs to be said in a phraseology that carries the appeal deep to the heart. In that case, the spontaneous flow of words and ideas keep the listener's mind tuned to the theme and keeps the concentration of his mind unbroken.

The Nature of the Sikh Prayer

A Sikh meditation and prayer aim at the advancement and welfare of the individual as well as the Sikh community at large. The individual should not mean individualistic; it should be taken as personal and his prayer for the community should not be taken as communal. It is not that. A community is a part of the world as a whole. When a Sikh prays— *jahan jahan Khalsa sahib, tahan tahan rachhia riayat* (May His protection be extended to the Khalsa wherever they are). This protection for the Khalsa is sought in the context of larger sense and a larger population of the world. To explain it more clearly we hear in the same prayer, the Sikhs praying to God for the peace and prosperity for all in the world— *tere bhane sarbat da bhala* (In thy will may peace and prosperity come to one and all). The Sikh community has given effect to this core assertion of the Sikh religion. Unshaken confidence in their destiny would enable them to whole-heartedly direct their energies to ushering in a new era of a grand collectivism at the global level in which all would get equal opportunities for free and unfettered growth of their personality.

The Sikh Gurus wanted that their followers should mainly pray for things which render service to the soul and help man to advance on spiritual plane. Guru Nanak requested the Lord to give him contentment, humility and His Name. And instead of asking for worldly things the Sikh must put his trust in God and entreat Him to do what He deems best for him.

The Contents of a Set-form of the Sikh Prayer

The first part of the *ardas* comprises the invocation to God and the Gurus up to Guru Tegh Bahadur, the ninth Guru, followed by a couple of lines referring to Guru Gobind Singh and to the *Guru Granth Sahib*. Then there is mention of the valiant deeds of the five beloved ones, the four sons of Guru Gobind Singh and the forty saved ones. The congregation is then asked to think of the men and women who sacrificed their lives for the sake of *dharama*, suffering extreme tortures at the hands of the enemies. Then the participants in the *ardas* are asked to preserve the sanctity of their holy places. Then they are reminded of their five *takhts*, the seats of holy authority, and various Gurdwaras. The congregation is then reminded that the *ardas* was being offered for and on behalf of the *Sarbat Khalsa*, the entire community. May the *panth* be ever victorious. May the great sword be ever helpful and may the Khalsa always triumph and prosper. Further in the prayer the Lord is beseeched that the Sikh banners and mansions may remain in existence forever and ever, and may righteousness triumph. May the Khalsa be humble in mind and exalted in understanding. May the Timeless Himself guide the Sikhs and protect their honour.

The Almighty Father is beseeched to save them—his Sikhs, from lust, wrath, greed, wordly attachment and arrogance and grant them to love His feet. May He grant them peace and happiness day and night. The prayees address the Merciful Almighty Lord who is the honour of the unhonoured, strength of the weak and shelter of the shelterless, for forgiveness of their sins and for the fulfilment of the wishes of all.

In the end, God is implored through Nanak that His glory be always and forever on the increase and in His Will, may peace and prosperity come to one and all in the world. In the course of prayer the person offering *ardas* may mention in all humility the purpose for which the personal or congregational prayer was being said.

The brave martyrs in the Sikh history have been mentioned in the *ardas* and the glories of their brave deeds and their sacrifices for the cause of the *panth* and the suffering humanity are remembered by thousands and thousands of men and women every day. In the *ardas*, the Sikhs daily pray to God for granting them an eternal privilege to have bath in the holy *sarovar* and access to the holy Golden Temple. The Sikh prayer repeats its permanent commitment that no power on earth would be allowed to damage the holy complex of the Sikh shrine at Amritsar. And the Sikh banners may keep flying forever.

The Sikh prayer is usually followed by the couplet *agia bhayi Akal ki tabhi chalaio panth, sabh Sikhan ko hukam hai, Guru manio Granth*, that commands all the Sikhs to recognize the *Granth* [*Guru Granth Sahib*] as the Guru. The *Granth* should be taken as the visible body of the Gurus.

A couplet sung by the congregation immediately after the *ardas* has been offered says:

Raj karega Khalsa aqi rahe na koe, khwar hoe sab milenge, bache sharan jo hoai. (The Khalsa shall rule; no hostile refractory shall exist. Frustrated, they shall all submit and those who come and seek shelter shall be saved).

This couplet clearly refers to the days of the later Mughals from Emperor Bahadur Shah to Shah Alam-II (1707 to 1771). This couplet seems to have been composed and first sung during the days of Banda Singh Bahadur (1710-16) who was the first Sikh political leader to declare the independence of his people in the Punjab. The Sikhs survived despite immense sufferings and sacrifices and far from lying low, the Sikhs announced *raj karega Khalsa, aqi rahe na koe*. The Sikh slogan *raj karega Khalsa* gave the Sikhs immense strength and confidence that they were destined to rule their country and the frustrated enemies would ultimately submit before them. The *raj karega Khalsa* is a part of their past aspirations and traditions to save their motherland against the foreign rulers and foreign invaders. And now its recitation reminds them of their duties and responsibilities towards the entire family of their motherland to which they belong.

The *ardas* has been providing great strength to the Sikhs over the centuries. They always received peace of mind and spiritual solace from prayer. Through prayer they are regularly reminded of their glorious past replete with the feats of high dignity and sacrifice. It prepares them for any sacrifices and enhances a deep respect and devotion for those who suffered tremendously for their brethren. Over the centuries this prayer has comforted the tortured hearts and enabled the Sikhs to face hardships with unparalleled fortitude and perseverance. All that is most glorious and most wonderful in the Sikh religion and the Sikh community is the direct result of the Sikh prayer and the unshakable faith in its efficacy. The Sikh prayer, undoubtedly, presents the Sikh history most thrillingly and it is the monument of the undiminished glory and greatness of the Sikh *panth*. The story of their marvellous past would continue to be narrated before them again and again through the *ardas* in the years to come, so that the old spirit is always kept fresh and radiant in the hearts of the Sikhs. Thus, the Sikh prayer is unique in its effect on the minds of the people when they stand with folded hands in the presence of their Guru, before their Almighty Father.

Harmandir Sahib (Golden Temple)

The Harmandir at Amritsar is a living symbol of the spiritual and historical traditions of the Sikhs. The serene and immaculate beauty of

Harmandir, the Abode of God, also called the Golden Temple, rising like lotus from the surrounding waters of the holy reservoir of nectar, bewitches and enchants the visitor. The Guru himself writes in the *Guru Granth Sahib*, "I have seen all places but in beauty it far surpasses all the known edifices of the world."[39] Throughout the Sikh history, no place, not even the birthplace of Guru Nanak, the founder of the Sikh religion, can claim the continuing role in the Sikh history as the Golden Temple complex, which assumed the position of a symbol representing the life and soul of the whole Sikh community. The foundation of the Harmandir complex has been the most significant achievement of the Sikh Gurus as a centre of inspiration and action for the Sikhs. Soon after its foundation the temple became an unparalleled establishment as a place of pilgrimage. The building of this holy temple was constructed in the middle of the *sarovar* (holy tank) under the direct control and supervision of Guru Arjan Dev.

The Harmandir Sahib is an object of striking architectural beauty. It was during 1577-1581 that the fourth Guru, Guru Ram Das, constructed the pool of nectar at Amritsar. The Fifth Master, Guru Arjan, who had conceived the idea of building a sacred shrine for his followers envisioned that the Harmandir would be a repository of the Sikh religion. The Guru chose to build a small structure in the centre of the *sarovar* as a shrine. The Guru kept the plinth of the Harmandir at a level lower than the surrounding buildings and provided it with four entrances implying that all the people, the members of all the four castes in Indian society as well as the members of different faiths of the world will have equal access to the holy temple.

This pool of immortality is almost a square measuring 510 feet by 490 feet, the depth of the pool being 17 feet. Steps go down into the pool meant for bathing. The Harmandir got its name of *Swaran Mandir* (Golden Temple) when its upper part sheathed in richly embossed and highly decorated sheets was covered with gold all around during Maharaja Ranjit Singh's period.

Every visitor feels a spiritual environment of divine presence within the complex. The Guru had conceived the Harmandir as the seat of spiritual power of the Sikh faith. It is a Sikh Vatican with all the spiritual glory and divine aura surrounding it.

The Harmandir played a very important role in the Sikh struggle for independence in the eighteenth century. The Harmandir was desecrated and destroyed by the Afghan invaders thrice i.e. in A.D.1757, 1762 and 1764 and was finally built in 1765. Phoenix-like the holy edifice reappeared, completely falsifying the pronouncements of the enemies that the Sikhs had disappeared from the corridors of history. The more the Durrani invader tried to destroy the temple and tank the bolder and more defiant and powerful the Sikhs grew. The Harmandir, to the Sikhs, was a symbol of their national unity and independence. The people flock to the *sanctum sanctorum* from all over the world for reasons ranging from curiosity to salvation. The Harmandir is a thing of beauty and has always served as a refuge, as a healer and as a provider of spiritual peace par excellence.

The Akal Takht

With Guru Arjan's martyrdom and under the changed circumstances the dire need of a place was felt where the Sikhs should assemble in the presence of the Guru and discuss their secular affairs and hold deliberations for their self-preservation. Since the Harmandir could not be used for this purpose, Guru Hargobind ordered in 1609, the construction of a place at a distance of about 100 yards from the Harmandir. The place was named *Akal Bunga* (The house of the Lord) or the Akal Takht.

There, Guru Hargobind used to discuss the social and military problems of the Sikh community. Sitting on this 'throne' he would watch the wrestling bouts and military feats of his disciples performed in the open courtyard in front of the Akal Takht. It was here that the Guru also used to receive presents and offerings of weapons and horses from his followers and particularly from the *masands* who brought the same from their respective *sangats* for the Guru. It was here that the Sikhs presented their personal disputes before the Guru and got them settled.

There is a great significance in the Akal Takht being constructed a few paces away from the Harmandir. The Akal Takht symbolized Sikh politics while the Harmandir signified religion. Each of the two is visible from the other end so that people sitting in the Harmandir would remember their involvement in politics and vice versa. Religion and politics were thus blended into one by Guru Hargobind.[40] It is also said that the Guru told his Sikhs that as long as he was in the Harmandir he should be treated as a saint and when at the Akal Takht he should be looked upon as the temporal leader of the community.

Since the days of the sixth Nanak the Akal Takht has remained the seat of the temporal authority of the Sikhs. During the eighteenth century when the Sikhs were forced to resort to the forests, it was used as the rallying place. The meetings of the *Sarbat Khalsa* (a general gathering of the Sikhs) were held here usually during the Baisakhi and Diwali festivals. The Akal Takht served as a very important forum for the Sikh struggle and for their liberation. Sitting in front of the *Guru Granth Sahib* at the Akal Takht they proceeded to consider the dangers with which they were threatened. They settled their plans and strategy for averting the danger and chose the generals who were to lead their armies against the enemy. It was at the Akal Takht that the *Sarbat Khalsa* elected the *jathedar* or the chief leader of the Dal Khalsa. Throughout the eighteenth century the Akal Takht was the hub of the Sikh politics and it gave direction to the activities of the Dal Khalsa. They would visit the revered place and seek blessings from there before launching their campaigns.[41]

Jassa Singh Ahluwalia maintained the files of the Misals at the Akal Takht. Thus, it served as a record office also during the days of ascendancy of the Sikh power.

Almost all the Muslim and English historians have failed to note the distinction between the respective functions of the Harmandir and the Akal Takht. They have always taken the Akal Takht as a part of the Harmandir or its annexe. Khushwaqat Rai, who completed his *Tawarikh-i-Sikhan* in 1811, has noticed the difference while writing about Jaswant Rao Holkar's visit to Amritsar in 1805. According to him, Holkar made an offering of a sum of rupees five hundred each at the Harmandir and the Akal Takht. He was given a *siropa* (robe of honour) at the Harmandir and a sword and a shield at the Akal Takht. This clearly indicated the characters of the two places lying opposite each other. The Harmandir has been set up exclusively for spiritual programmes and the Akal Takht primarily for secular matters.

With the rise of Ranjit Singh as a sovereign ruler, the Punjab came to be consolidated and the foreign invaders ceased to endanger the country and the community. So during Ranjit Singh's period the rule of the Akal Takht fell into disuse so far as the political affairs were concerned. But at the same time when the Akal Takht found the Maharaja going astray and that affected his image as a ruler, he was called by the *jathedar* of the Akal Takht and punishment was proposed. The Maharaja accepted the punishment without the least resistance, rather in all humility. Nobody could be above the decisions taken at this place, not even the great Maharaja. Ranjit Singh paid his homage to the Akal Takht not simply as a force that he could not afford to ignore or control, but as the ultimate source of strength and stability to the state he was engaged to build.

When Emperor Jahangir visited Amritsar and offered to complete the building of the Akal Takht at his own expense, Guru Hargobind declined the offer saying, "Let me and my Sikhs raise this throne of God with the labour of our own bodies and with the contributions from our own little resources. I wish to make it a symbol of my Sikhs' service and sacrifice, and not a monument to a king's generosity."

The first storey of its present building (one that was severely damaged and partly demolished during the army attack at the Golden Temple complex in June 1984) was built during the rule of the Sikh Misals in 1774 and the building was later completed during the period of Maharaja Ranjit Singh. After the demolition of the Akal Takht in 1984, the Indian government rebuilt it at its own expense. But the Sikhs did not accept the new edifice, as it was not built by the voluntary services of the Sikhs. The Indian government-built edifice was demolished and the Sikhs in accordance with the Sikh traditions rebuilt it.

Besides being a token of the Sikh identity the Akal Takht has always served as a Sikh mass meeting venue, as an arbiter of community disputes and a source of enormous inspiration. Throughout the whole range of Sikh history it has intensely throbbed as a living presence.

As in the past, so even today, the Akal Takht is used as a venue for political and secular deliberations of the Sikh community. The sacrosanct character of the decisions taken there has remained unchanged over the centuries, ever since its establishment by Guru Hargobind. The Harmandir Sahib and the Akal Takht, facing each other with a little gap, symbolize synthesis of the spiritual and the temporal.

The Gurmata

In the Punjabi language the word *mata*, literally means opinion or resolution. When a resolution concerning the Sikh *panth* is placed before a congregation in the presence of the *Guru Granth Sahib* and after dispassionate and unbiased deliberations, when some decision is arrived at with common consent and is confirmed by a formal prayer followed by the recital of a hymn from the *Guru Granth Sahib*, it is called the *gurmata*.[44] The *gurmata* guided the Sikhs to take unanimous decisions in the presence of the holy *Guru Granth Sahib*. The *gurmata* or decision had the endorsement or sanction of the Guru. The practice of the *gurmata* kept the leaders of the community under restraint and did not allow them to become autocratic. Through the *gurmata* the will of the community prevailed.

In the eighteenth century, ordinarily the Sikhs tried to meet twice a year during the Baisakhi and Diwali festivals (that is, in April and October) at the Akal Takht and discussed their problems and passed the *gurmatas*.[45] But they would also meet on other occasions as and when some urgent matter of political importance had to be discussed or some imminent danger threatened the country or any large expedition was to be undertaken. At the time of their meeting at Amritsar, the Sikhs assembled in the open space in front of the Akal Takht. A *gurmata* was always passed by an assembly of the Sikhs, giving to each member of the community, a sense of participation. The basic ideas kept before them by the members of the assembly were those of equality, unanimity and responsibility. The idea of equality entitled every member of the community including women, to attend and participate in the deliberations of the assemblies. This right of participation in the discussions had to be exercised personally and directly and not through elected or nominated representatives. The principle of unanimity was based on the belief that the Khalsa was an embodiment of the holy Guru and that all their assemblies were made sanctimonious by the Guru's presence in them. Therefore, all collective deliberations were conducted in an objective manner. Different viewpoints could be expressed but as bound by a solemn pledge of being united in the presence of the Guru, the resolutions were carried unanimously. The principle of responsibility involved in this practice was useful and necessary in so far as it kept the leadership on guard.

The resolutions were not voted upon individually or passed by the majority but were carried unanimously. Through the *gurmata* the *Sarbat Khalsa* elected the *jathedar* or the chief leader of the Dal Khalsa and chose agents who were entrusted with powers to negotiate with others on behalf of the Sikhs. Second, by the *gurmata*, the Sikhs decided the foreign policy to be pursued by them. Third, they drew up plans of military operations against the common enemies of the community. Fourth, they took measures for the spread of the Sikh faith and the management of the Gurdwaras.

Although there existed no means to enforce obedience to the *gurmata* passed at the Akal Takht, yet there was never an occasion known to history when such a decision was flouted. The decisions taken in the presence of the *Guru Granth Sahib* had behind them the religious sanction, the force of which was greater than that of a military dictator. The Sikhs obeyed these decisions even at the cost of their lives. They believed that the *gurmata* or the decision of the council had the spiritual sanction of the Guru.[46]

This simple constitution of the Sikh commonwealth was sufficient to preserve the Khalsa through turbulent times. We read in the contemporary records about very important *gurmatas* passed by the Sikhs in 1726, 1748, 1761,1762,1764,1765, 1766,1798, and 1805. These *gurmatas* related to the security of the Sikhs, their campaigns against their enemies, avenging the murders of the prominent leaders of the Sikhs and fighting pitched battles against the foreign invaders like Nadir Shah and Ahmad Shah Durrani.

The *gurmata* was a symbol of the inherent strength of the unity of the Khalsa. The institutions of the *Sarbat Khalsa* and the *gurmata*, which have an ethical base and are democratic in character, have exercised a very potent unifying force on the Sikhs since the eighteenth century.

TRANSFORMATION THROUGH SIKHISM

The main inspiration for the Sikh code of conduct came from the teachings of the Sikh Gurus. The whole outlook of the community was influenced by religion and their social and political behaviour was guided by the views of the Gurus. Religion is the righteous and noble way of life and a system of values and as such Sikhism is a set of co-ordinated doctrines serving as an ideal to be achieved and practised by its followers. Sikhism sets forth purity of life as the highest object of human endeavour. Loyalty, chastity, honesty, justice, mercy and temperance are among the virtues on which vital stress is laid. Guru Nanak taught, 'Truth is higher but higher still is truthful living.' Religious purity, if it is to be meaningful, must be complementary to ethical purity, which can be attained only through a life of dedicated service to fellow-beings. The Sikh Gurus repeatedly emphasized equality in the ranks of the society. Our lack of faith in the brotherhood of man blurs our vision and we fall into the habit of lending greater weight to dis-similarities than to similarities.

When the Sikhs became rulers, they made all efforts in keeping with the traditions of the Gurus to actively promote and rigidly enforce morality and righteousness in the conduct of their affairs.

In the light of the ideals of Sikhism we examine here, not very strictly but a little generously as to how faithfully the Sikh men, women and rulers abided by the prescribed code of conduct and underwent metamorphosis.

The Sikh Women

Sikhism worked as potent force to plead the cause of the emancipation of Indian womanhood. The Gurus advocated equal status for women with men, in all spheres of life. They repudiated the old and deep-seated belief that a woman was inferior to man and condemned the social evils of *purdah*, infanticide and *sati* (self-immolation of a woman on the funeral pyre of her dead husband). Guru Nanak sang:

From women is our birth,
In the women's womb are we shaped,
Women are our friends,
And from the woman is the family,
If one woman dies, we seek another,
Through a woman are the bonds of the world,
O, why call women evil,
Who giveth birth to kings.
(Var Asa Mohalla I, *Guru Granth Sahib*, p.473).

As against many religions, Sikhism believed that a woman, who was the pivot of the household, was the helping hand of man in the achievement of salvation. Guru Nanak's sister Bibi Nanaki was a lady of high calibre and spiritual elevation. Guru Angad's wife *mata* Khivi, managed the *langar* at the Gurus' place. Guru Angad's daughter, Bibi Amaro, was a noble lady who transformed the life of Guru Amar Das. Guru Amar Das's daughter Bibi Bhani's dedicated life was a perennial source of inspiration to all womenfolk of the Sikhs. Guru Gobind Singh's mother, *mata* Gujri proved equal to the very trying and difficult days through which she passed and became an embodiment of supreme sacrifice. Guru Gobind Singh's spouse *mata* Sahib Devan (Kaur) played the role of the Khalsa's mother.

Many ladies like Deep Kaur, Anup Kaur and *mata* Bhag Kaur, through their marvellous deeds inspired the coming generations as a result of which innumerable Sikh women performed most daring deeds in the battle-field and also in the field of diplomacy in the eighteenth and nineteenth centuries.

The Sikh traditions of bravery and sterling qualities brought about a total transformation in the Sikh women's overall personality and mental attitude towards chivalry, self-respect and high sense of dignity. In the words of William Francklin, "Instances indeed have not infrequently occurred in which these Sikh women have actually taken up arms to defend their habitations from the desultory attacks of the enemy and throughout the contest behaved themselves with an intrepidity of spirit, highly praise-worthy."[47]

The Sikh Gurus honoured the women-folk as the symbol of domestic harmony and happiness, social cohesion and unity. The wives of the Sikh Gurus, by serving in and running the *langar* (free mess) and by preaching high ideals of equality, love and sacrifice, set examples worthy of emulation by other women.

The status of the Sikh ladies, as compared to the Hindu and Muslim ladies was, undoubtedly, much superior. They were able to stand by the side of their husbands in difficult situations.

The Sikh women had a manly demeanour and had a reputation of chastity. When an occasion arose, the Sikh ladies of the royal houses actively participated in state affairs. They occasionally took charge of state administration and their contribution to the Sikh polity as rulers, regents, administrators and advisers had been creditable indeed, "The Sikh ladies ruled with vigour and diplomacy," says General Gordon.[48] To quote Griffin, "The Sikh women have, on occasions, shown themselves the equal of men in wisdom and administrative ability".[49] Usually the dowager *ranis* were involved in commendable works. Rani Sada Kaur, widow of Sardar Gurbakhsh Singh Kanaihya and mother-in-law of Maharaja Ranjit Singh, was well versed in the affairs of the state and commanded her soldiers in the battle-field.[50] She was a very shrewd lady with a thorough grasp of state- craft.

Mai Desan, widow of Charhat Singh Sukarchakia, was a great administrator, an experienced and a wise diplomat who conducted the civil and military affairs dexterously.[52] Her administration was better than that of men. Rani Rattan Kaur, widow of Tara Singh Ghaiba was a brave and able lady who kept the Lahore Darbar forces at bay for quite sometime till the gate-keepers were bribed by the Lahore Darbar army.[53] Mai Sukhan, the widow of Gulab Singh Bhangi, strongly defended the town of Amritsar against Ranjit Singh for some time.[54] Dharam Kaur, wife of Dal Singh of Akalgarh, after her husband's imprisonment by Ranjit Singh, mounted guns on the walls of her fort and fought against the Lahore Darbar forces.[55] Rani Chand Kaur, widow of Maharaja Kharak Singh and Rani Jindan, widow of Maharaja Ranjit Singh, played important roles in the Lahore Darbar politics, though Rani Jindan was too young to be widow at the age of 22 and too young to die at the age of 46.

After Sardar Baghel Singh's death in 1802, his two widows, Ram Kaur and Rattan Kaur looked after their territories very well.

From the Patiala House also many names like that of Mai Fato, wife of Sardar Ala Singh, Rani Rajinder Kaur, Rani Aas Kaur and Sahib Kaur may be mentioned. Rajinder Kaur, the first cousin sister of Raja Amar Singh of Patiala, was a highly self-respecting, determined and brave woman. In the words of Lepel Griffin, "Rani Rajinder (Kaur) was one of the most remarkable women of her age. She possessed all the virtues which men pretend are their own—courage, perseverance and sagacity—without any mixture of the weakness which men attribute to women."[56] Sahib Kaur was proclaimed as Prime Minister of Patiala at the age of 18. She managed the affairs, both in office and in the battlefield, wonderfully well. Later, when his cousin, Fateh Singh imprisoned her husband Jaimal Singh

Kanaihya, she hastened to Fatehgarh at the head of a strong force and got her husband released.

In 1794, when the commander of the Maratha forces coming northwards, sent a message to Sahib Kaur, the Prime Minster of Patiala, for submission, she preferred to settle the issue in the battlefield. The armies came to grips near Ambala. She infused new spirit in her disheartened soldiers, led a surprise attack on the Marathas, and in the words of John J. Pool, "With mingled feelings of fear and respect they (Marathas) turned their forces homeward and gave up the expedition. Thus, Patiala was saved by the skill and daring of Rani Sahib Kaur."[57] She died at the age of 26.

The role of Rani Desan of Nabha and Daya Kaur of Ambala, in shaping the destinies of their territories, was no less noteworthy. About Rani Daya Kaur (1786-1823) Lepel Griffin writes, "She was an excellent ruler and her estate was one of the best managed in the protected territory."[58]

These ladies were well known for their administrative acumen, grasp of political situations and dexterity in handling and organizing defence. The above achievements of the Sikh ladies were indisputably the result of inspiration they drew from Sikhism—its ideals and *rehat*. Sikhism equally worked its miracles on the Sikh women in all walks of life.

The Baptised Singhs

Retaining the basic idea of administering *pahul* to the Sikhs, a new ceremony of giving the nectar in place of the old practice, which some of the people had started misusing to create independent followings of their own, was started by Guru Gobind Singh.

Within a few days of adoption of the dramatic procedure of initiating the Khalsa, many thousands (to some almost bordering on a lakh)[59] people hailing from different parts of the country got themselves baptised. It worked wonders in abolishing the old distinctions. After initiation, a person could claim and was readily given the status equal to any other member of the Khalsa *panth*.[60]

In the words of Teja Singh and Ganda Singh, "Even the people who had been considered as dregs of humanity were changed as if by magic into something rich and strange. The sweepers, barbers and confectioners, who had never so much as touched the sword and whose whole generations had lived as grovelling slaves of the so called high classes, became, under the stimulating leadership of Guru Gobind Singh, doughty warriors who never shrank from fear and who were ready to rush into the jaws of death at the bidding of the Guru."[61]

Dr S Radhakrishnan said that Guru Gobind Singh "raised the Khalsa to defy religious intolerance, religious persecution and political inequality.... Those who grovelled in the dust rose proud, defiant and invincible in the form of the Khalsa. They bore all sufferings and unnamable tortures cheerfully and unflinchingly.... India is at long last free. This freedom is the crown and climax and a logical corollary to the Sikh Gurus' and the Khalsa's terrific sacrifices and heroic exploits." [61A]

Guru Gobind Singh brought a new people into being and released a new dynamic force into the arena of Indian history. The complete charge of the temporal leadership was given to the Sikhs in 1708 during the last moments of his earthly existence.

By converting the *Guru sangat* into the Khalsa the creator of the Khalsa raised his creation to a status superior to himself when he said:

It is due to them that I am holding an exalted place.
I was born to serve them.
Through them I reached eminence.
What would I have been without their kind and ready help.
There are millions of insignificant people like me. [62]

According to Senapat, the aim of Guru Gobind Singh in initiating the Sikhs with the double-edged sword or founding the Khalsa *panth*, was to build up a community that would live a virtuous life and be able to rescue the people from evil-doers and the tyrants. [63] The basic character of the Sikh *panth* to be good and virtuous was never allowed to be changed. Once the Sikhs asked Guru Gobind Singh why the Sikh rules of conduct prohibited them from carrying away the women of the Muslims as captives as a retaliatory measure. To this the Guru replied, "I wish to raise the *panth*—the Sikh community, to a much higher plane and not to push it down into the depths of hell." In their struggle for independence or sovereignty the Sikhs always maintained this lofty ideal of the Guru.

According to Gokal Chand Narang, "Guru Gobind Singh was the first Indian leader who taught democratic principles and made his followers regard each other as *Bhai* or brother and act by *gurmata* or general councils". [64]

This new practice of baptism brought with it tremendous changes in the Sikh code of conduct. In the words of Muhammad Latif, "Guru Gobind Singh instituted a new code of law which not only treated of religious subjects, but infused a spirit of valour and emulation into the minds of his followers and inflamed them with zeal for deeds of heroism and bravery in the field. He incorporated in it a narrative of his own exploits in a glowing and even hyperbolical style. He placed the four great sects of the Hindus on the same level and declared that none was greater than the other, thus adding materially to the strength of his nation. He laid the foundation stone of that vast fabric which the Sikh nation was not longer after, enabled to build on the ruins of the Muhammadan power in the Punjab and emancipated his tribe from foreign thraldom and persecution, giving it the character and rank of a military nation."[65]

The Tenth Master brought Guruship on a level with his followers. It was a revolutionary and democratic step when in 1699, after initiation, he solemnly undertook to abide by the same discipline that had been enjoined upon the Sikhs to follow.

The Khalsa commonwealth did not belong to any individual, not even to the Guru—the creator of the order, but it belonged to those who constituted it. In this way a new type of democracy took birth in this land. The Khalsa, as combined body of the Sikhs, was made the supreme authority among the Sikhs in all matters.

J. D. Cunningham writes, "The last apostle of the Sikhs did not live to see his own ends accomplished, but he effectively roused the dormant energies of a vanquished people and filled them with a lofty, although fitful longing for social freedom and national ascendancy, the proper adjuncts of that purity of worship which had been preached by Nanak. Guru Gobind Singh saw what was yet vital and he resumed it with Promethean fire. A living spirit possesses the whole Sikh people, and the impress of Gobind Singh has not only elevated and altered the constitution of their minds, but has operated materially and given amplitude to their physical frames. The features and external form of a whole people have been modified, and a Sikh chief is not more distinguishable by his stately person and free and manly bearing, than a minister of his faith is by a lofty thoughtfulness of look, which marks the fervour of his soul, and his persuasion of the near presence of the divinity."[66]

The Sikhs are peerless, gifted with nobility of character, sublimity of humanity and are matchless in kindness of disposition. Guru Gobind Singh told his followers that the force by itself was no evil, it was its misuse that made it so. He felt that ideals of humility and surrender had no appeal to a tyrant whose soul was deadened by repeated acts of oppression and who used and understood the language of cold steel alone. He was thoroughly convinced that force had to be met by force and that is why he almost deified the sword. He considered it to be the hand of God to punish the evildoers with:

Sword, thou art the protector of the saints.
Thou art the scourage of the wicked;
Scatterer of sinners, I take refuge in thee,
Hail to the Creator, Saviour and Sustainer;
Hail to thee, Supreme.[67]

This must not be understood to mean that Guru Gobind Singh believed in the dictum that 'might is right.' It was assumed that the wielder of sword must be imbused with a divine mission. It should be used for the protection of the oppressed and for the furtherance of righteous acts. The sword used for such purposes signifies divine beneficence. Guru Gobind Singh symbolized God in the weapons of war. He is presented as the punisher of the evil and destroyer of the tyrant. But if the sword is used for oppression and for the attainment of power, it loses all its significance. Even where the use of the sword is permissible, it is to be used, only as a last resort. "When all other means have failed, it is but righteous to take to the sword."[68]

The Guru expected of the baptised Sikhs to fight only a holy war (*dharamyudh*) against the enemies of righteousness and for the protection of good virtues. With the Sikh gospel to light their path, the Sikhs were opposed to religious bigotry and communal hostility. The Sikhs had, in the first half of the eighteenth century, suffered a lot at the hands of the fanatical Mughal rulers of the Punjab but when they took over the control of the Punjab they were not revengeful or intolerant towards the Muslims as such. What they had disliked in the Mughal government, they would not do that themselves. It was really noble of them to have so soon forgotten about the wounds inflicted on them in the recent past. It was in keeping with the traditions of their Gurus.

Qazi Nur Muhammad, who accompanied Ahmad Shah Durrani to the Punjab in the winter of 1764-65, during the Afghan invader's seventh invasion, has given an account of the Durrani's invasion. He has recorded therein his own first hand impressions of the character and fighting qualities of the baptised Sikhs. The Qazi in his intense hatred for them as opponents of the Afghans trying to establish their power in the Punjab uses abusive language. But he was impressed by the lofty character and bravery of the Sikhs in their struggle for freedom. He says, "Do not call the Sikhs 'dogs' because they are lions and are courageous like lions in the field of battle. In no case would they slay a coward nor would they put an obstacle in the way of a fugitive. They do not plunder the wealth or ornaments of a woman, be she a well-to-do lady or a humble servant. There is no adultery among them nor are these people given to thieving nor there are housebreakers among them. They do not make friends with adulterers and housebreakers. They are not from the Hindus. They have a separate religion of their own.[69] The Sikh character's transparency is unquestionable. They are the same in the light as well as in the darkness that offers limitless opportunity and freedom to get astray.

The new organisation, Guru Gobind Singh's *magnum opus* was, in the words of Indubhusan Banerjee, "a fully democratic compact community armed to the teeth struggling to maintain what is right and fighting incessantly tyranny and injustice in all their forms." [70] The baptised Sikhs— the Khalsa, was charged with the responsibility of promoting, with force if necessary, the cause of righteousness. One of the most interesting features of the Khalsa was the idea of commonwealth. Before Guru Gobind Singh breathed his last he had taken every possible care to promote the corporate aspect of the Khalsa brotherhood. "It was in Sikhism", says Banerjee, "that a sense of corporate unity gradually evolved."[71] Guru Gobind Singh, after the creation of the Khalsa, advised the Sikhs to take decisions, or pass *gurmatas* through a council and this measure gave a form of federative republic to the Sikhs.[72]

Thus, we see that the community was united and integrated through baptism or *amrit* prepared by the double-edged sword. All members of the community enjoyed equal privileges with one another. By receiving *amrit* from the *panj piaras* (five beloved ones) the Guru had exploded the myth of his superiority to his followers. This equality with one another, common external appearance, common leadership and common aspirations bound the Sikhs together into a compact mass, raising their strength manifold. With that strength they fought against the Afghan invaders, Mughal highhandedness and British rulers.

The Sikh Jats

From the rough tribals the Jats were chiseled by the teachings of the Sikh Gurus into marvellous people with qualities of superb gentleness, hospitality, honesty and unique bravery. Whenever some new invaders or travellers came to the Punjab through the passes of the North-West Frontier of this province many of them chose to settle down here, finding it a better place to live. Thus, Punjab became the permanent home of the Pathans, Balochs, Ghakhars, Afghans, Turks, etc. Many castes, communities or tribes already lived in the Punjab. The Jats were more prominent among them. The scholars hold different opinions about their origin. James Tod believes that the Jats were related to different Rajput families of Rajasthan. Some believe that they were the Scythians from Central Asia and some others say that they belonged to the Jertik tribe that has been mentioned in the Mahabharat. Still some others think that they had their origin in the Indian Aryans who came to the Punjab from Rajasthan as we believe of the Phulkians.

With the advent of Muslims into the Punjab some of the Jats accepted Islam under the invaders' sword. According to Indubhusan Banerjee, Guru Arjan is said to have converted almost the entire Jat peasantry of the Majha tract and there could be little doubt that by the time of Guru Hargobind the Jats, formed by far, the preponderant element in the Sikh community. The character of the Jats imperceptibly modified the Sikh system as it was bound to do.[73] We had Sikh Jats, Hindu Jats and Muslim Jats, most of them having common sub-castes or *gotras*. We have Bajwas, Manns, Gills, Tiwanas, Chatthas, etc., among the Sikh, Hindu and Muslim Jats. There was a sizeable chunk of the Jats who remained outside the pale of Sikhism; most of them beyond the boundaries of the Punjab especially in the present U.P., Rajasthan and Haryana states who came to be known as Hindu Jats. They remained outside the influence of Sikhism. They could not become the pride of the community as the Sikh Jats. Most of the Muslim Jats are in Pakistan and some of them are in India as well.

Professor Irfan Habib, of Aligarh University, believes that these Jats of the Punjab can be traced to a pastoral people of the same name who appear in old archival records dating from the period between the seventh and ninth centuries and who were distinguished by a notable absence of social or economic stratification. From Sind these Jats moved northwards via Multan into the Punjab and eastwards across the Jamuna River. In the course of their migration they changed from pastoralists to peasant cultivators. Their inherited egalitarian traditions attracted them to the teachings of the Sikh Gurus, who gave them positions of high authority in the new *panth*.[74]

The role of the Jats was of considerable importance in the Khalsa *panth*, particularly for the developments that took place during the seventeenth and eighteenth centuries with the change or shift from the Khatri to the Jat leadership in the community. The author of the *Dabistan-i-Mazahib* noted that though the Gurus had been the Khatris, they had made the Khatris subservient to the Jats who were considered a low caste among the Vaishyas. As a result of this change most of the big *masands* of the Guru were the Sikh Jats.[75]

The new features of Sikhism came to represent the dominance of the

Jat culture that Guru Gobind Singh proclaimed in 1699 as the essentials of Sikhism. Love of freedom and warlike spirit of the Jats could no longer be denied a place within the system.[76]

Irfan Habib further remarks that the Jats were the peasants in the seventeenth and eighteenth centuries who had to bear a heavy burden of land revenue and a great degree of oppression of the ruling classes of the Mughal empire. This situation was bound to provoke peasant revolts. Thus, the militant development of the Sikh community during the seventeenth and eighteenth centuries can have one major explanation in this resort to armed violence by the Jat peasantry, when the economic pressure became increasingly intolerable.[77]

The economic pressure on the Sikh Jats could be one of the reasons for arraying themselves on the side of Banda Singh Bahadur, converting his movement into an agrarian revolution, as Khushwant Singh believes.[78] It may be partly true but more powerful reason was the religious persecutions suffered by the Sikhs at the hands of the Mughal government. It led the Sikh Jat peasantry to take up arms under the leadership of Banda Singh to replace the tyrannical government. Banda Singh was, indeed, very lucky to have such spirited and fearless Sikh Jats, known for their intrepidity and sacrifice, as his followers.

After Banda Singh's execution on 10 June 1716, with brief intervals of respite here and there, the history of the Sikhs is a record of a great struggle between the Jat Caesars on one side and the Mughals or the Afghans on the other. It ultimately resulted in the occupation of the Punjab by the Sikhs about the middle of the sixties of the eighteenth century. During the prolonged Sikh struggle for their liberation from the foreign yoke, the rural Jat peasants headed the fighting wing of the movement and also helped these fighters for liberation by providing protection, supplying them with means of living, hiding them in their houses in small batches and joining their ranks.[79]

By their tribal characteristics these Sikh Jats were unamenable to a despotic rule, still more to a hostile foreign rule. They were much more democratic than others in governing their villages. They had less reverence for hereditary rights and had a preference for elected headmen.[80] On becoming the Sikhs, the Sikh democratic traditions strengthened their views. Earlier they were known for their total disapproval of monarchic principles and gave their strong preference for self-governing commonwealth. In ancient times they were known as *arashtra* or kingless. Later on, under the Sikhs, when they had a Sardarship or kingship it was of a totally different nature. Their rulers sat with them on the ground and talked to them as friends. A Sikh ruler always considered himself as one of them and not infallible.

George Campbell, a civilian officer, who had been looking after the administration of the Sikh states after they came into the hands of the British, writes that Mehraj, now in Bathinda district of Punjab, remained an independent republic till it came under the British protection. "It continued to be a completely independent self-governing republic down to my time—the only real, well-established republic that I know in India. It was diplomatically recognized as a state and had its own state administration and state justice. There was no chief or hereditary ruler. The state was ruled by its *panches* or elders." [81] Mehraj was a Sikh Jat republic, functioning efficiently about the middle of the nineteenth century when Campbell took charge.

Campbell further writes, "I remember one strong village (of the Sikh Jats) in Kaithal, which for generations had made it a point of honour never to admit a government officer within their walls. The villages were almost all walled and fortified. The inhabitants of the village paid the revenue over the wall and that was enough." [82] Campbell further writes:

"My experience of the village institutions on the Satluj, where perhaps they are at their best, made me appreciate them very much indeed and I think that they were not only good for India but for some other countries as well. In fact, I can deliberately say that far from imposing any ideas on these people it was from them that I learnt ideas of local self government which I retain to this day and which I have brought with me to my native country." [83] The Sikh Jats learnt it from the Sikh Gurus that they must take all decisions through the village *panchayats*, elected democratically. They always followed the teachings of the Sikh Gurus in letter and spirit.

These Sikh Jats committed to their religion have also been nostalgically disposed towards their land and could never tolerate to part with it. When they were dispossessed of it and made to wander in the jungles it was natural that they should try to come back to the lands which they and their ancestors had been ploughing for generations. The impulse for revenge or vindication of personal honour, traditionally regarded as a trait of Jats, was a major factor in their determination to strongly resist their enemies or opponents. And in a bid to get political freedom they had paralyzed the Mughal power in the Punjab and consequently the Mughals had abdicated for all intents and purposes. These Sikh Jats could not allow the opportunist foreign invaders—the Afghans, to steal a march over them in establishing sovereignty in the province. They strongly sustained their struggle through very terrifying spells of time in the eighteenth century and then rose to their political apogee in the form of the kingdom of the Punjab. Being the sons of the soil and through a long drawn struggle for independence and a series of sacrifices, the Sikh Jats had a genuine case for the possession of the Punjab both on moral and legal grounds. The Jats remain as ever a rural community heavily committed to agriculture and deeply devoted to Sikhism.

Maharaja Ranjit Singh had a judicious discrimination in the selection of his officials. He was shrewd enough to understand that the Sikh Jats were pre-eminently a fighting class (besides being agriculturists) and as such could nowhere be more profitably employed than in the national defence.

Ibbetson wrote in 1833, "The Jats are the backbone of the Punjab by character and physique as well as by locality. They are stalwart, sturdy yeomen of great independence, industry and agricultural skill and collectively form perhaps the finest peasantry in India".[84] However sturdy the Jats may have been in the British experience the Sikh Jats have offered much more than their competence and skill in two fields—agriculture and military. Their participation in politics, transport, industry and sports has also been remarkable.

It is through Sikhism that their experience as rulers and their dominance in rural Punjab has elevated them well above their humble origins. In terms of status no Sikh Jat feels inferior to any one on earth and never considers him downtrodden.[85]

To conclude, their determined courage and unconquerable spirit of resistance always kept their flame in high splendour. Sikhism moulded the Jats into a marvellous community. They are very sturdy, exuberant and matchlessly hardworking. Persecutions could never bend their spirits. It is an unforgettable lesson of history that persecution stimulates the spirit that it designs to suppress.

Their integrity is aboveboard, tested through the centuries and established as irrefutable fact of history. Integrity to them means matching words and feelings with thoughts and actions. Duplicity, breaking promises, distorting the truth, snooping, manipulating people and situations to suit ones personal ends, all denoting lack of integrity, are alien to a Sikh Jat character. To them integrity is the foundation of all goodness and greatness. Their internal strength that emerges from it eliminates any tendencies to impress others through credentials, possessions and status symbols. Even in deep crises they conduct themselves with utmost grace and dignity. These people have brought with them these qualities or characteristic traits from ages in their blood, further ennobled by the teachings of the Sikh Gurus. History has taken a glaring note of it through their marvellous role during the march of the past times.

Writing about the Sikh Jats Khushwant Singh says, "It was the *baptised keshdhari* (having full grown hair on head) Jats who had been the chief instruments of the Sikh rise to power and consequently became the land-owning aristocracy during the rule of Maharaja Ranjit Singh. Under British rule, Jats maintained their position as the premier caste among the Sikhs superior to the Brahmans, the Kashatriyas (from whom the Gurus had sprung) and the Vaishyas, this position was not achieved by Muslim or Hindu Jats in their respective communities."[86]

Lepel Griffin, an Indian Civil Service Officer, could not miss to note and make insightful remarks that "The Jat race is, for manliness, honesty, strength and courage, second to no race in the world."[87] It is a very well deserved glorification of their character at the hands of the above British author.

The Sikh Rulers

The main springs of the ideas of the Sikh chiefs were the teachings of the Gurus. The Khalsa ideals served as beacon light for the Sikh chiefs. Whenever the people felt their leaders likely to stray away, out of ignorance, from their ideals, they showed them the right path. The chiefs dared not, therefore, defy the Sikh code of conduct. Guru Gobind Singh gave the final shape to the *panth* or the Khalsa commonwealth that was considered by all the Sikhs as a very sacred creation of the Gurus. The respect for the creation of the Khalsa was so great that none could ever think of doing any thing in violation to the tenets laid down for the members of the *panth*.

In respect of their duties towards the Khalsa commonwealth, no Sikh, including the Sikh chiefs, enjoyed any exception. None could pose to be above the *panth*. No single individual or a group of individuals could be considered as superior or equal to the entire body of the community. No Sardar could ever think like the Mughal ruler that he belonged to a different category and was one specially blessed and destined by God to rule over others and exercise and enjoy some special and superior rights and privileges vis-a-vis the whole of the *panth*. He always kept before his mind that his position was not due to any of his personal qualities but was due to the grace of the Guru and the Khalsa. The Sikh chiefs, time and again, declared that they were the humble servants of the *Panth*, subservient to its will, working for the good and pleasure of the Khalsa commonwealth.

To take *amrit* (baptism of the double-edged sword) and become a member of the Khalsa was required of every Sikh. He who was not duly baptised could not be elected as their leader. They all had to adopt the *rahit* (code of conduct) or discipline of the Khalsa and abide by it. Jassa Singh Ahluwalia received *amrit* from Sardar Kapur Singh[88] and Raja Amar Singh Phulkian prided in having received it at the hands of Jassa Singh Ahluwalia.[89] The founder of the Kanaihya Misal, Amar Singh Sanghania (Kingra), considered it absolutely necessary to baptise a person into a 'Singh' before accepting him into his *derah* or camp. Similarly, Charhat Singh's essential condition for recruitment to his contingent was that the incumbent must be a duly baptised 'Singh'. Those who were not already initiated into Sikhism with the baptism of the double-edged sword were baptised by him before joining his ranks.[90] The Sardars of the Misals were generally known by the appellation of *Singh Sahib*.

The Gurus had enjoined upon the Sikhs to take their decision through *panchayats* or councils, and all important decisions relating to common interests of the community must have the approval of those for whom they were meant. The Sikh chiefs were alive to the democratic ideals inculcated by the Gurus and they followed them to the best of their power. The *gurmata* was a strong expression of this ideal of democratising the *panth*ic decisions. The practice of electing a leader of the Misal in the earlier stages and electing the leader of the Dal Khalsa were in pursuance and fulfilment of the same ideal of republican and democratic spirit of the Khalsa.

The Sikh chiefs ruled in the name of the Guru and the Khalsa as is apparent from their coins. An important aspect of their victory over their enemies was that it was the triumph not of any individual leader or leaders but of the Khalsa or the Sikh commonwealth. No wonder, therefore, the Sardars founded their states and attributed their successes to the Gurus whom they believed to be the real founders and masters of their commonwealth.

The Sikh rulers had fully realised that 'dominion can subsist in spite of mischief but cannot endure with the existence of injustice'. However crude the methods of investigation and trial they might have adopted, the Sikh chiefs were known for their love of justice. Every ruler at the time of his investiture solemnly promised in the presence of the *Guru Granth Sahib* to always keep before him, in the performance of his duties, the Sikh code of conduct, the law of the land and the customs of the society.

The Gurus placed a high standard of war morality before the Sikhs and the former punctiliously observed it. "They never harassed the old, infirm and women, "says Qazi Nur Muhammad in his *Jangnama*.[91] Polier wrote that, "it is true that they seldom kill in cold blood or make slaves."[92]

And "during any intestine disputes their soldiery never molests the husbandmen."[93]

Under the influence of the teachings of the Sikh Gurus, the Sikhs had disregarded the caste distinctions, difference of high and low, untouchability, etc. In the matter of origin, growth and development of the Misals the castes had no place. No Misal was named after any caste or sub-caste of any chief or Misaldar. The leaders of the Misals originally belonged to the peasant, carpenter or any other profession; it was immaterial with the Sikhs. The leader should be a member of the Khalsa. The *amrit* or the Sikh baptism had elevated them all to the same level and made them members of the same casteless Khalsa fraternity.

The examples of the Gurus provided the guidelines for their followers. Kapur Singh Faizullapuria was tipped by the *sangat* for the title of *nawab* offered by the governor of Lahore, when he was fanning the Sikh congregation. The Sikh Sardars and Misaldars always kept before them the motto: "The service of humanity is the service of God". The Sikh rulers were well known for performing *sewa* in the Gurdwaras and the other holy places.

The chiefs always maintained their free kitchens to supply food to the way-farers as well as to the poor and the needy and they paid special attention to this part of the service in the event of a famine.[94] The famine of 1783 occurred in Budh Singh's time. He is said to have sold all his property to feed the people with grains from the proceeds.[95]

It is interesting to know that the Sikh Sardars who were so well known in the art of war were no less adept in the art of peace. Sardar Jassa Singh Ahluwalia, Ala Singh Phulkian, Lehna Singh Bhangi and Charhat Singh Sukarchakia were, no doubt, great soldiers, but as history bears witness, they knew well how to bring about conditions of settled life and peace. In the words of the author of the *Gujrat gazetteer*, "the names of Sardar Gujjar Singh and Sahib Singh are often in the mouths of the people, who look back to their rule without the smallest bitterness. They seem, indeed to have followed an enlightened liberal policy, sparing no effort, to induce the people, harried by twenty years of constant spoliation, to settle down, once more, to peaceful occupation."[96]

As emerges from the achievements and human qualities of the Sikh Misal Sardars of the eighteenth century they were gifted, in western analogy, with Caesar's arm, Plato's brain and Christ's heart.

We generally find the Sikh rulers equating and identifying themselves with their soldiers and declaring themselves as the humblest servants of their subjects. From the letters exchanged between the Sardars (collected by Dalpat Rai in 1794-95) we notice that almost invariably all the Sardars or the rulers of the Sikh Misals were addressed as '*Singh sahib*', 'Bhai Sahib' or 'Khalsa jio'. For example, Bhai Fateh Singh, Bhai Amar Singh, Bhai Gulab Singh (ff 44-45), Khalsa Jai Singh (f 17), Bhai Ranjit Singh jio (f 104) and *Singh sahib* Bhai Sahib Dal Singh jio (f-13). These titles were applicable to every member of the Sikh gentry. The Sikh rulers liked to be addressed by these plain and simple titles, which as referred to above maintained their identities with the Sikhs.[97] *Nawab* Kapur Singh, Jassa Singh Ahluwalia, the '*Sultan-ul-Qaum*' and Sardar Ala Singh, are not the solitary examples to be found amongst the wonderful Sikh rulers who were thoroughly committed to the teachings of the Gurus.

As Mahraja Ranjit Singh was the offspring of the eighteenth century, he did not depart from the deep influence or impress of Sikhism on the conduct of his predecessors. He never acted in opposition to the wishes of his people who could express themselves in his favour or against him. Although the full-ledged king of the Punjab, he refused to sit on a throne. Even when he reached the summit of his power he never arrogated to himself the distinction of an absolute sovereign. Rather, in speech, writing and action, he represented himself as a member of the Sikh community. Under him we observe a complete departure from the accepted traditions of oriental courts where protocol was rigidly observed to keep the monarch as far away from the subjects as possible. But Ranjit Singh kept himself in close touch with his people.

As in the case of Sardars of the eighteenth century the Maharaja also did not rule in his own name or in the name of his family or Misal. He wielded power in the name of the Khalsa. "In the early days Ranjit Singh liked to be addressed by the plain and simple title of "*Singh sahib*", a title applicable to any member of the Sikh gentry. The old Sikh chiefs even addressed him, occasionally, as 'brother'[98]. He always felt that he was holding that office through the Guru's kindness before whom he bowed as his servant.

As the tradition goes, once his Prime Minister Dhyan Singh told the Maharaja that as he was their ruler he should not tie a cloth around his waist like the humble servants. The Maharaja enquired, "In whose name the coin is struck?" Dhyan Singh told that it was in the name of Guru Nanak. The Maharaja smilingly told him that the ruler was the one in whose name the coins were struck and Ranjit Singh was only the humble servant of that ruler. He considered himself to be the *kookar* (dog) at the door of the Guru and the *Panth*. He is also said to have called himself a *raptia* (reporter-cum-watchman). The Maharaja would often proclaim himself to be nothing more than just the drum (*Ranjit nigara*) of Guru Gobind Singh, adding that his purpose was only to assert the supremacy of the Khalsa. He never arrogated to himself any high-sounding titles but on the contrary, adopted the impersonal title of Sarkar, denoting the government responsible for law and order. The princes were addressed as Khalsa Kharak Singh, Khalsa Sher Singh and Khalsa Naunihal Singh. This shows the Maharaja's attachment to the Khalsa.

In referring to his government, he always used the term Khalsa ji or *Sarkar-i-Khalsa* as he felt that he was the founder of a kingdom that derived its legitimacy from the Khalsa commonwealth, the mystic entity in which resides all sovereign powers. And verily all his diplomatic correspondence was carried on in the name of the Khalsa. His coins did not bear his effigy or his name. His principal coin was called Nanakshahi (of Nanak). He named his chief forts after the names of the Gurus, for example, the fort of Gobindgarh at Amritsar was built in the name of Guru Gobind Singh and the garden of Rambagh laid out in Amritsar was named after Guru Ram Das. The official form of salutation in the whole of the state was *Waheguru ji ka Khalsa, waheguru ji ki fateh*—the Khalsa belonged to the Lord and victory also belonged to Him. All official oath-taking ceremonies were performed in the presence of the Holy Book—the *Guru Granth Sahib*.[99]

Ranjit Singh rejected the prevalent theory of the ruler's infallibility. He, it seems, remembered the words of Guru Nanak: "*Bhullan andar sabh ko abhull Guru Kartar*" that is, every one is fallible and Supreme Creator alone is infallible, and therefore, he never behaved like an infallible autocrat. We have two orders preserved in the family archives of the Fakir Brothers at Lahore. Fakir Waheed-ud-Din, the great grandson of Fakir Nur-ud-Din, has published the photographic copies of original (in Persian) in 'The Real Ranjit Singh' (facing pp.31-32).

One of the *farmans* (orders) is addressed to Syed Fakir Nurud-Din— the governor of Lahore, in 1825. It was as under:

It is decreed by His Highness (the Maharaja) that no person in the city should practise high-handedness and oppression on the people. Even if His Highness himself should issue an inappropriate order against any resident of Lahore it should be brought to the notice of His Highness so that the order may be amended.

Second *farman* issued in 1831 was addressed to Sardar Amir Singh and Fakir Nur-ud-Din. It reads as under:

If His Highness (the Maharaja) or his son Prince Kharak Singh or Prime Minister Dhyan Singh or Raja Suchet Singh or any other Sardar commits an inappropriate act he should be told to refrain from committing inappropriate acts. If they do not desist from that it should be brought to the notice of His Highness.

Through these *farmans*, as we see, the Maharaja authorized Syed Fakir Nur-ud-Din and Sardar Amir Singh of Lahore to withhold and bring to his notice for amendment any order of the Maharaja himself, of the royal princes, the Prime Minister or of the chief Sardars if in the opinion of the Syed or the Sardar, it was inappropriate and against the interests of the people. These *farmans* are certainly unique in as much as they throw over board the time-honoured legal fiction upon which the fact of kingship is based—that the king can do no wrong. These are perhaps, the only orders of its kind in history issued by a king authorizing a subordinate officer of the state to withhold any order issued by the king himself which in the opinion of that officer, appeared to him to be inappropriate and oppressive.

All the Sikh rulers had been religious but not communal. In the words of George Campbell "They were not exclusive and unduly prejudiced in favour of their own people but employed capable Mohammdans and others almost as freely as the Sikhs."[100] Ali-ud-Din Mufti writes that Lehna Singh Bhangi gave turbans and bestowed honours on *qazis* and *muftis* on the occasion of *Id*.[101] William Francklin bears witness to the fact that 'the Sikhs allow foreigners of every description to join their standard and to sit in their company.[102] It was Sikhism that bestowed on the Sikhs these noble qualities of humility, humaneness, respect and regard for all people irrespective of their caste, colour or creed, as sons of the same Almighty Father.

Summing up we may say that with the Sikh gospel to light their path, the Sikhs were instinctively opposed to the religious bigotry and communal hostility. Far from retaliating in a spirit of fanaticism, the Sikhs followed the policy of perfect toleration towards those who did not belong to their faith. As the Sikhs had fought for freedom to profess the faith of their choice, they respected this right for other people as well, when they came to assume the government of the country.

The Sikh religion does not accept anybody entitled to superior status because of his birth in a so-called higher family. It discarded the ancient Hindu restriction on the low caste *shudras* studying the Holy Scriptures. Among the Sikhs, we find many people who were *shudras* by birth but on becoming the Sikhs acted as Sikh preachers and soldiers. The Jats, who were unamenable to any discipline before their conversion to Sikhism, became noble people after accepting Sikh faith. They never committed outrage on women and torture on men and they never compromised over morality. The Sikh Gurus emancipated the Sikh women from male chauvinism and from the rigid social and moral barriers erected against them by the dictators (of social and moral commandments) like Manu, the law-giver. Through Sikhism, a woman grew and evolved into a distinguished entity as characterized by Sikh scriptures. Sikhism provides that women have equality in worship, equality in society, freedom in wielding arms, freedom of speech and preaching, freedom to act as a priest and freedom from superstitions and empty rituals.

REFERENCES

1. J. D. Cunningham, *A History of the Sikhs* (1849), Delhi 1955, p.34.

2. Fredric Pincott, *The Sikh Religion* (A symposium), Calcutta, 1958,p.74.

3. Indubhusan Banerjee, *Evolution of the Khalsa* , Vol. I, 2nd edition, Calcutta, 1961, p.183.

4. Harbans Singh, *Heritage of the Sikhs*, 2nd ed. Delhi, 1983, p.41.

5. Macauliffe, M.A., *The Sikh Religion*, Vol. IV, Oxford, 1909, p.2; Teja Singh and Ganda Singh, *A Short History of the Sikhs*, Bombay, 1950, p.109.

6. Harbans Singh, *op.cit.*, p.84.

7. Senapat, *Sri Gursobha* (1711), Patiala, 1967, Adhya 18, verses 806-07; cf., Ganesh Das Badehra, *Char Bagh-i-Punjab* (1855), Amritsar, 1965, p.155.

8. Macauliffe, *op.cit.*, Vol. III, p.66.

9. Arnold Toynbee, *Foreword to the Sacred Writings of the Sikhs*, Jodh Singh, Trilochan Singh et al (ed.) G. Allen and Unvin Ltd., London, 1960.

10. McLeod, *Evolution of the Sikh Community*, Oxford University Press, Delhi, 1975, p.81.

11. Sri Rag Mahalla I, *Adi Granth*, p.72.

12. Bhai Gurdas, k*abit*, 57.

13. *Ibid.*, *kabits*, 124-26.

14. *Ibid.*

15. Ghulam Husain Khan, *Siyar-ul-Mutakherin* (1782), Nawal Kishore Press, Cawnpore, 1897, p.401; Bhai Gurdas, *Var* I, Pauri 27.

16. *Tuzuk-i-Jahangiri*, Nawal Kishore Press, Cawnpore, n.d.p.35; Rogers and Beveridge, translation of *Tuzuk*, Vol. I, p.72.

17. *Dabistan-i-Mazahib* (1645), Nawal Kishore Press, Cawnpore, 1904, p.233.

18. *Ibid.*

19. Indubhusan Banerjee, *Evolution of the Khalsa*, Vol. I, Calcutta 1961, (2nd ed.), p.259.

20. Bhai Gurdas, *Var 3*, Pauri II.

21. *Asa Chhand, Mahalla IV.*

22. *Dabistan*, p.239; Senapat, *Sri Gursobha* (1711), chapter V chhand 61.

23. Senapat, *op.cit.,* (Ganda Singh edited), p.39.

24. *Hukamname* (of the Sikh Gurus), Ganda Singh edited, Punjabi University, Patiala, 1967, Nos. 37, 43-46, 49, 54-55, 63, 65.

25. *Ibid.,* No.3.

26. *Ibid.,* No.8.

27. *Ibid.,* Nos. 46,48,50.

28. Indubhusan Banerjee, *op.cit.,* p.258.

29. Ibbetson, Denzil C., Edward Maclagan and Rose, H.A., *Glossary of Punjab Tribes and Castes,* Vol. I, Lahore, 1919, pp.687-88.

30. Bhagat Singh, *Sikh Polity in the Eighteenth and Nineteenth Centuries,* New Delhi, 1978, p.38.

31. Ganesh Das Badehra, *Char Bagh-i-Punjab* (1855), Khalsa College, Amritsar, 1965, p.112.

32. Satta and Balwand, *'Ramkali Ki Var'*, *Adi Granth*, pp. 966-68.

33. Gokal Chand Narang, *Transformation of Sikhism*, 5th ed., p.48.

34. Satta and Balwand, *op.cit.,* pp.966-68.

35. Teja Singh and Ganda Singh, *A Short History of the Sikhs,* Orient Longmans, Ltd., Bombay, 1950, p.87.

36. Indubhusan Banerjee, *op.cit.,* pp.158-59.

37. V*ar Sri Rag* IV.

38. *Dabistan-i-Mazahib* (1645), Cawnpore, 1904, p.239.

39. *Guru Granth Sahib*, p.1362.

40. Surrinder Singh, *The Sikh Gurus and their Shrines*, Delhi, 1967, p.182.

41. Bhagat Singh, *A History of the Sikh Misals*, Punjabi University, Patiala, 1993, p.394.

42. Khushwaqat Rai, *Tarikh-i-Sikhan* (Persian 1911) MS., Ganda Singh Private Collection, Punjabi University, Patiala, p.147.

43. Bhagat Singh, *Sikh Polity in the Eighteenth and Nineteenth Centuries,* Oriental Publishers and Distributors, New Delhi, 1978, p.178.

44. Bhagat Singh, *A History of the Sikh Misals,* Patiala, 1993, pp. 384-85.

45. Bhagat Singh, *Sikh Polity in the Eighteenth and Nineteenth Centuries,* New Delhi, 1978, pp.109-10.

46. Malcolm, *Sketch of the Sikhs*, London, 1812, p.115.

47. Francklin. 'The Sikhs and their Country', reprinted in the *Early European Accounts of the Sikhs*, (ed. Ganda Singh), Calcutta, 1962, p.105.

48. Gordon, *The Sikhs,* London, 1904, p.84.

49. Lepel Griffin, *Ranjit Singh,* Oxford, 1905, pp.62-63.

50. Ahmad Shah Batalia, *Appendix* to Sohan Lal's *Umdat-ut-Tawarikh,* Dafter I, Lahore, 1885. p.25.

51. *Ibid.*

52. Sita Ram Kohli, *Ranjit Singh*, Allahabad, 1933, pp.33-34.

53. Gian Singh, *Tawarikh Guru Khalsa*, Patiala reprint, 1970, p.253.

54. *Ibid.*,p.231.

55. *Ibid.*,p.294.

56. Lepel Griffin *op.cit.*,p.67.

57. J. Pool, *Women's Influence in the East*, London, 1892, pp. 234-37.

58. Lepel Griffin, *op.cit.*,p.93.

59. Teja Singh and Ganda Singh, *A Short History of the Sikhs*, Bombay, 1950, p.69.

60. J. D. Cunningham, *A History of the Sikhs* (1849), Delhi, 1955, pp. 63-64.

61. Teja Singh and Ganda Singh, *op.cit.*,pp.71-72; cf., Ali-ud-Din Mufti, Ibratnama (1854), Vol. I, Lahore, 1961, p. 344.

61A. Quoted by Mary Pat Fisher *'Living Religions*, 4th Edition, Prentice Hall, 1999, p. 401.

62. Guru Gobind Singh, *Gian Prabodh*, Padshahi 10, Sawaya 545.

63. Senapat, *op.cit.*, Chhands, 129-30, p. 21.

64. Gokal Chand Narang, *op.cit.*, p.33.

65. Muhammad Latif, *History of the Punjab*, Lahore, ed. 1916, pp.46-47.

66. J. D. Cunningham, *op.cit.*, p.75.

67. Guru Gobind Singh, *Vachitra Natak*, Adhya I, Chhand 2.

68. Guru Gobind Singh, *Zafarnama*, Verse 22.

69. Qazi Nur Muhammad, *Jangnama* (1765), (edited by Ganda Singh), Amritsar, 1939, pp.6,12,55,57-58.

70. Indubhusan Banerjee, *Evolution of the Khalsa*, Vol. II, Calcutta 1947, p.119.

71. *Ibid.*, p.119.

72. *Ibid.*, p.52.

73. *Ibid.*,p.21.

74. Irfan Habib, *Proceedings of Punjab History Conference*, Patiala, 1971, p.54.

75. Zulfiqar Ardistani Maubid (Mohsin Fani) *Dabistan-i-Mazahib*, (1645), Cawnpore, 1904, p.233.

76. Indubhusan Banerjee, *op.cit.*, Vol. II, p.124.

77. Irfan Habib, op.cit.,p.54.

78. Khuswant Singh, *History of the Sikhs*, Vol. I, Princeton, London 1964, (chapter on Banda Singh).

79. Ahmad Shah Batalia. *appendix* to the first daftar of Sohan Lal Suri's *Umdat-ut-Tawarikh*, Lahore, 1885, p.13.

80. William Irvine, *Later Mughals*, Vol. I, (1707-1720), Calcutta, 1922, p.83.

81. George Campbell, *Memoirs of My Indian Career*, Vol. I, London, 1893, p.42-43.

82. *Ibid.*, pp.52-53.

83. *Ibid.*, p. 82.

84. Ibbetson, *Census of Punjab*,, 1881, Vol. I, Book-I, Lahore, 1882, p.229.

85. W. H. McLeod, *The Evolution of the Sikh Community*, Delhi, 1975, p.96.

86. Khushwant Singh, *A History of the Sikhs*, Vol.2, 1839-1964, Princeton, New Jersey, 1966, p.120.

87. Lepel Griffin, *The Punjab Chiefs*, Lahore, 1890, p.64.

88. Rattan Singh Bhangu, *Prachin Panth Parkash* (1841), Wazir Hind Press, Amritsar, ed. 1939, p.204.

89. Ramjas, *Tawarikh-i-Riast* Kapurthala, Vol. I, 1897, p.150.

90. Sohan Lal Suri, *op.cit.*, Daftar-II, p.5; Bute Shah, *Tawarikh-i-Punjab*, Daftar V (1848), MS., Ganda Singh, pp.2-3.

91. Qazi Nur Muhammad, *op.cit.*, MS., Ganda Singh p. 158.

92. Polier, 'An Account of the Sikhs', reproduced in the *Early European Accounts of the Sikhs* (ed. Ganda Singh), Calcutta, 1962. p.61.

93. Brown, 'Introduction, History of the Origin and Progress of the Sikhs' reprinted in the *Early European Accounts of the Sikhs*, edited, Ganda Singh, Calcutta, 1962. p.17.

94. *Ludhiana District Gazetteer* Lahore (1888-1890), p.72.

95. *Montgomery District Gazetteer* Lahore (1833-84),p.34.

96. *Gujrat District Gazetteer* (1892-93), Lahore, pp.21-22.

97. Dalpat Rai (ed.) *Amir-ul-Imla* or *Muntkhab-ul-haqaia*, MS., Ganda Singh Personal Collection, Patiala, (now at Punjabi University, Patiala).

98. Faqir Waheed-ud-Din, *The Real Ranjit Singh*, Karachi, 1965, p.29.

99. Bhagat Singh, *Maharaja Ranjit Singh and His Times*, New Delhi, 1990, pp 173-74.

100. George Campbell, *op.cit.*, Vol. I, p.180.

101. Ali-ud-Din Mufti, *Ibratnama* (1854) Lahore, 1961, 2 Vols, Vol.I,p.240.

102. Francklin, *Memoirs of George Thomas*, Calcutta, 1803, p.75.

GLOSSARY

Abhyasi	One who is regularly given to meditation.
Adi Granth	The Sikh scripture, the holy *Guru Granth Sahib*.
Ahimsa	Cult of non-violence.
Akal Takht	The throne of the Almighty, the highest seat of authority in the religious hierarchy and temporal and political matters of the Sikhs. It is built in Amritsar.
Akali	A member of the Akali or Nihang order of the Sikhs, literally meaning 'an immortal'.
Akhandpath	Non-stop recitation of the holy *Guru Granth Sahib* performed by a team of *granthis* or *pathis* as readers.
Amrit	Sikh baptism of the double-edged sword, nectar of immortality, also called *khande ki pahul*.
Amrit prachar	Sikh missionary activity for initiation to the Khalsa fold, holy ceremony of administering *amrit*.
Arashtra	Kingless, people who spurned to be ruled by a ruler or king.
Ardas	A prayer, supplication, representation, solicitation, a request or offering made by the Sikhs to the Guru.
Arzdasht	A representation, petition to a superior for grant of some favours.
Asan	Yogic posture, a body posture, abode of *yogis*,

	a seat, a carpet or rug on which some people sit to perform their worship.
Ashram	Abode, hermitage, residence of men belonging to a certain cult, institution of a religious order.
Babbar Akali	A radical section of the Akali reformers who organized themselves into a militant group who planned to paralyse or liquidate the supporters of the British bureaucracy. This movement lasted from 1922 to 1925 in a few districts of the Punjab.
Bagh	A garden, in context of Akali movement in the Punjab it relates to a particular *bagh* (Guru Ka Bagh), Amritsar.
Bahadur	Brave, courageous, high-spirited, champion, a hero; also a title of honour affixed to the names as Banda Singh Bahadur.
Baisakhi	The first day of the month of Baisakh, an important festival of rural Punjab, celebrating the advent of harvesting season, generally falling in the second week of April.
Bande matram	It was the national anthem of the ghadar party, meaning 'hail mother', a salute to the motherland.
Bani	Holy hymns, Guru's word recorded in the *Adi Granth*.
Baoli	A well with stairs going down to the water.
Bhagti/Bhakti	The doctrine of worship of God through loving adoration.
Bhai	Literally a 'brother', also a title of sanctity and respectability among the Sikhs.
Bhangi	An addict to *bhang* (Marijuana) - an intoxicating preparation of hemp. Bhangi Misal took its name from its leader's nick name Bhangi — an adict to hemp.
Bhangra	A particular type of dance of joy performed by the Punjabi youth.
Bhog	A ritual or a concluding part of a holy ceremony, conclusion of *path* (recitation) of Guru Granth Sahib.

434 *Canadian Sikhs Through a Century (1897-1997)*

Bible	Christian scripture.
Chachi	Aunt.
Charhdi Kala	Being in high spirits.
Chauri	A fly-whisk generally made of long white hair of the tail of yak. It is used as a mark of respect for royal or holy persons or holy scripture to be waved over them.
Chhota ghallughara	Small holocaust in which about seven thousand Sikhs were killed in June 1746.
Dadi	A grand-mother.
Dal Khalsa	The word *dal* is a Punjabi expression meaning a horde and suggests the notion of a group with a definite mission of fighting against their enemies. Dal Khalsa means the Sikh force or their national army.
Daswand/Daswandh	A Sikh term for tithe (one tenth of the income) paid by the true Sikhs for the Guru's fund or an offering made by the Sikhs for charitable purposes.
Degh	Holy pudding or holy food.
Derah	An abode, a camp, barracks of Sikh troops or a place where *sadhus* or *faqirs* live.
Dhadi	One who plays on a kind of tambourine, the ballad singer.
Dharam/Dharama	Righteousness, the moral law, code of conduct in life that sustains the soul, the doctrine.
Dharam prachar	Preaching religious or holy teachings.
Dharamsala	The abode of dharama, generally the Sikh Gurdwara or Sikh place of worship, a place of religious assemblage, a rest house for pilgrims.
Dharamyudh	Crusade, a holy war.
Diwali	The Indian festival of lights celebrated in commemoration of the return of Lord Rama from his exile and the release of Guru Hargobind from the fort of Gwalior, usually falling towards the end of October or the beginning of November.
Doaba	A territory lying between two rivers; in the Punjab particularly the one between the rivers Satluj and Beas.

Durbar/Darbar	A court, an elevated place, a government.
Farman	A Royal command, an order, a mandate, an edict.
Fateh	Success, victory.
Gaddi	A dignified place or a place on higher plane for the Guru or a ruler to sit on, throne.
Ghadar	Rebellion or revolt.
Ghadar di gunj	Echoes of rebellion, a call for revolt.
Ghallughara	Holocaust, destruction or loss of human life in an attack or battle.
Ghee	Purified butter.
Giani	One possessing *gian*, knowledge or wisdom; a Sikh theologian, a reputed Sikh scholar.
Gidha/Giddah	A popular dance, accompanied by clapping of hands, performed by the young Punjabi girls with vigorous physical movements.
Got/gotra	Sub-caste.
Granth/Granth Sahib	Literally a book but here used for the holy Book of the Sikhs.
Granthi	The reader or reciter of the holy *Granth* of the Sikhs. The Sikh priest; the functionary in charge of a Gurdwara.
Gurbani	Guru's word, the sacred hymns of the Sikh scriptures.
Gurdwara	Guru's abode, Sikh temple.
Gurmat	Guru's commandments, Guru's philosophy, religious ideology of the Sikh Gurus.
Gurmata	The word *mata* in Punjabi language means a resolution. When it is passed in an assembly of the Sikhs in the presence of the holy *Guru Granth Sahib* it is believed to have been endorsed by the Guru and is called *gurmata*, a resolution of the *Sarbat Khalsa*.
Gurmukh	A pious man, one who follows Guru's commandments.
Gurmukhi	Proceeding from the mouth of the Guru, Punjabi script, modified and popularized by Guru Angad for the writing of the Sikh scriptures.
Gurpurb	Commemoration of birth and death

	anniversaries of the Sikh Gurus and other events in their lives.
Guru	A spiritual preceptor or a guide, a religious teacher, title of the founders of Sikh religion.
Guru gaddi	Spiritual throne of the Sikh Gurus.
Gurughar	Guru's abode, Gurdwara, a Sikh temple.
Guru Granth Sahib	The holy book of the Sikhs called the *Adi Granth/Guru Granth Sahib* compiled by Guru Arjan Dev in 1604.
Guru Ka Bagh	The garden planted by the Guru or planted in his name or named after the Guru.
Guru Ka Langar	Free community mess attached to the Sikh Gurdwara.
Guru panth	Collective community of the Sikhs vested with powers of Guruship after Guru Gobind Singh's death.
Hakam	An officer, a magistrate, a ruler.
Harmandir Sahib	The temple of God, the central Sikh shrine in Amritsar, also known as Golden Temple, also called Darbar Sahib.
Hukamnama	Letter, epistle, order of the Guru, an order, a decree,command, a letter issued by the Guru.
Id	A religious festival of the Muslims.
Inqlab Zindabad	May the cult of revolution be ever alive, a slogan adopted by the revolutionaries during India's struggle for independence.
Jagyasi	One given to meditation.
Jangnama	A diary or record of a battle.
Jat	A virile community in the Punjab. They are mostly the Sikhs. There are Muslim and Hindu Jats also who live in the western or Pakistan Punjab and in Rajasthan and U.P. respectively
Jatha	A band, a group, military detachment.
Jathedar	A group leader, commander of a band. At present a leader or an organizer of the Akali Dal or Akali Party.
Kabbadi	A sports game particularly popular in the villages, involving strength of the players' muscles.

Kachha	A pair of shorts, mandatory for a baptised Singh. It is one of the five Ks.
Kangha	A comb used to clean the hair on the head of a Sikh and to impart an orderly arrangement to it.
Kara	Steel bracelet, one of the five Sikh symbols.
Karah prasad	Sacred pudding dispensed in the Gurdwaras.
Katha	Exposition of religious text, preaching, explaining the holy scriptures.
Kathakar	One who gives an exposition of a religious text. One who explains the ideology of a religion.
Kesh	The unshorn hair on the head of a Sikh, one of the five Sikh symbols which the Sikhs are required to keep.
Keshdhari	One who has uncut hair on ones head.
Khalsa	The brotherhood of the baptised Sikhs, particularly those conforming to the instructions of Guru Gobind Singh; The land held or administered directly by government or the sovereign.
Khalsa Diwan	The Khalsa Diwan (formed in 1883) was the general *sabha* or association of the Sikh societies formed for the propagation of Sikhism.
Khalsa panth	The Sikh community.
Khande ki pahul	Initiation of the double-edged sword, particularly in reference to the Khalsa initiation or baptism.
Kirpan	A sword, particularly one worn by the baptised Sikh.
Kirtan	Devotional music, singing of holy hymns in praise of God, generally by a group to the accompaniment of musical instruments.
Kirtan Darbar	A program organized for singing of holy songs.
Lambardar/Numbardar	The village official who collected the revenue from the farmers and deposited in the state treasury.
Langar	Community kitchen, free mess, generally attached to a Gurdwara where food is served to all regardless of caste or creed.

Mahant	The in-charge or a superior of a religious institution, manager and head of a religious centre.
Maharaja	The great king, king of kings, a supreme sovereign.
Mahatma	A saint, a saintly person.
Majha	Literally the middle country, usually referring to the territory of Lahore and Amritsar districts lying between the rivers Beas and Ravi.
Malwa	Land of the Malweis or Malois, the plain tract extending to the south and south-east of the Satluj river, particularly the areas occupied by Ferozepore, Muktsar, Moga, Ludhiana and Patiala districts of Punjab.
Manji	Literally a cot, a Sikh preaching centre established by Guru Amar Das — the third Guru, a diocese.
Manji pratha	A system through which the areas of Sikh population were divided into 22 parts, each part placed under a preacher appointed by the Guru.
Mantra	Scriptures, hymns, spiritual instructions.
Marjada/Maryada	A code of conduct, basic tenets of a religion.
Masand	An agent or representative of the Sikh Guru, the holder of a diocese or *manji*.
Masnad	It is a Persian word, meaning an elevated seat. As the Sikh preachers, being representatives of the Gurus, were offered high seats they began to be called *masnads* or *masands*.
Masnad-i-ali	A representative of a higher authority or the Guru.
Mata	Counsel, advice, decision, opinion.
Mata	Mother, a title of respect given to elderly ladies.
Maya	Cosmic illusion, delusion, a power of nature which veils the reality and thus produces an illusion or an error in ones mind.
Miri piri	Miri signifies temporal and piri signifies spiritual authority. *Mir* means an army leader or a general and pir means a spiritual leader or a saint. Guru Hargobind assumed the double

	role of a temporal and spiritual leader of the Sikhs.
Misal	The Sikh confederacy, Sikh military band in the eighteenth century, also used for the territory or troops of a Sikh Sardar, an equal, a file.
Misaldar	Belonging to a Sikh Misal; holder of a portion of a Misal, the ruler of the Misal being designated as Sardar.
Morcha	Agitation, organized political or religious campaign.
Mufti	Pronouncer of a *fatwa* or verdict according to Muslim religious law.
Nagar Kirtan	A Sikh procession to the accompaniment of singing holy songs or hymns.
Nakhas	A horse-market.
Naam	The divine Name of God.
Naam Simran	Repeating the holy Name of God or meditating on the Supreme Being.
Nanak prastan	Worshippers or followers of Guru Nanak, believers in the teachings of Guru Nanak.
Nawab	A noble, the governor, the viceroy, a lord, an influential man.
Nirvana	A state of oblivion to care, pain, or external reality, the final beatitude sought especially in Buddhism through the extinction of desire and individual consciousness, salvation, or liberation from the cycle of birth and death.
Nishan Sahib	Sikh flag flown over a Gurdwara, a standard or flag.
Pacca/pucca	Solid, built of baked bricks.
Padshah	King, sovereign, lord, also Supreme Being, an epithet used by the Sikhs for addressing their Gurus.
Pagri	A turban.
Pahul	The rite of Sikh baptism, Sikh initiation, baptism of the Khalsa.
Panch/punch	A member of the *panchayat*, a prominent person in a village or a community, an elected representative of the people.

Panchayat — A court of arbitration consisting of five or more members chosen by the parties themselves, the lowest rung in the hierarchy of judicial administration.

Pangat — A row, particularly for inter-dining.

Panj piaras/pyaras — The five chosen ones who were given the first *pahul* at the inauguration of the ceremony of this practice by Guru Gobind Singh on the historic Baisakhi day of 30 March 1699 at Anandpur Sahib.

Panth — A sect, a community, this title designates the Sikh community.

Parchar — Publicity, propagation of any matter or religion, propaganda, religious publicity.

Parcharak — A person engaged in religious publicity or propaganda.

Pardah/purdah — A curtain, a screen, screening women from the sight of men, veil, seclusion particularly observed by Muslim women.

Parsad/Parshad — A food or sweets offered to God or a deity.

Path — Reading or reciting the holy Book as an act of devotion, also to study a lesson.

Patwari — A village accountant, a revenue official.

Pauri — Staircase, steps, a stanza.

Pir — A spiritual guide among the Muslims, a Guru.

Pitaji — Father.

Punjab — 'Punj' means five, 'ab' means water or 'waters' and Punjab means a land of five rivers, an area or territory through which five rivers —Satluj, Beas, Ravi, Chenab and Jhelum flow.

Punjabi — Language spoken by the people of Punjab, a person belonging to the Punjab state.

Punjabi Suba — Punjabi-speaking state.

Qazi — A judge, a magistrate who administers justice according to Islamic law.

Quran — Holy scripture of the Muslims.

Rag — A musical note, a tune.

Ragi — A musician, a singer of *ragas*, a musician employed to sing holy hymns in the praise of God in the Sikh Gurdwara.

Raj	A kingdom, government, rule, sovereignty.
Raja	A king, a prince, a title of high rank.
Raj Karega Khalsa	The Khalsa shall rule. This slogan refers to the days of the later Mughals, first sung during the days of Banda Singh Bahadur (1710-16) and continued to be sung during the Sikh struggle for independence in the first half of the eighteenth century and made a part of the Sikh prayer by them.
Ramgarhia	First used for Jassa Singh, occupant of the fortress of Ram Rauni and later began to be used for all those people who belonged to his sub-caste. Hence a misnomer.
Rani	A queen, a princess.
Ranjit nigara	A drum beaten during Guru Gobind Singh's time was named as such.
Raptia	A reporter-cum-watchman.
Rehat/Rahit	Rules or code of conduct of the Khalsa, way of living, morals, principles.
Rehat maryada	Rites, rituals, customs, mode of worship, religious observances.
Sabat surat	An appearance (of a Sikh) that is untampered with, hair on head and beard unshorn, with turban on head.
Sacha	True, just, righteous.
Sacha padshah	The true king as against the temporal king, as the Sikhs called their Guru by this designation.
Sadh	A saint, a holy person, a religious person, a *faqir*, a righteous and virtuous man.
Sadh-sangat	The assembly of the *sadhus* or saints.
Sadhu	A mendicant, renunciant, ascetic, a saint.
Safed	White.
Safedposh/safaidposh	A person wearing white clothes, an influential man, a government protege during the British rule, who had an eye on a number of villages and secretly reported to the government about the anti-British activities if any in the area under his surveillance. He was a government agent.
Sahib	An owner, possessor, a gentleman, chief,

	governor, ruler, lord, master, a title of God.
Sangat	Congregation, a holy assembly, company, a place of meeting.
Sant	A holy man, a sadhu.
Sant-Sipahi	A saint soldier, one who combines in him a double role of a saint and a soldier, as was adopted by Guru Hargobind—the sixth Nanak.
Sarai	Inn.
Sarbat da bhala	The welfare and well-being of all.
Sarbat Khalsa	The whole Sikh community, the entire Khalsa *panth*.
Sardar	Chieftain, head of a Misal, the term is now commonly used as title of address for all Sikh men.
Sarkari-i-Khalsa	Government of the Khalsa, in referring to his government Maharaja Ranjit Singh always used the term *Sarkar-i-Khalsa* as he felt that he was the founder of a kingdom which derived its legitimacy from the Khalsa commonwealth.
Sarover	A tank, a holy tank, attached to a Gurdwara.
Sati	Self-immolation, a wife who burns herself on the funeral pyre of her deceased husband.
Satsang	The fellowship of true believers, congregation, assembly of true ones.
Sewa	Dedicated community service, voluntary service.
Sewadar	One who renders voluntary service, a servant to his superiors, a Gurdwara attendant, also an employee of a Sikh temple.
Shabad	A hymn, a holy song.
Shahidganj	A place where committed men or devoted Sikhs had been martyred.
Shahidi	Martyrdom, to obtain the status or degree of martyrdom.
Shahidi jatha	The Sikh volunteers who joined various agitations launched by the Akali Dal from time to time with a solemn vow to stake their life for their mission.
Shakti	Power, to use force to attain ones objective, physical prowess, spiritual energy or potency.

SGPC	Shiromani Gurdwara Prabandhak Committee, the highest administrative body to manage the Gurdwaras.
Shudra	A serf, slave, a person doing menial work, the lowest caste in the caste hierarchy in India, untouchables, scheduled caste or *harijans*.
Sidhi pag	Straight turban, turban tied in a particular style by the Kukas or Namdharis.
Sikh	Sikh (Sanskrit *shishya*) means a disciple, a learner, a follower of the Sikh religious order founded by Guru Nanak.
Singh	Lion, the title assumed by all members of the Khalsa.
Singh Sahib	A respectable title of a baptised Sikh who strictly observes Sikh *rehat*.
Singh Sabha	A movement comprising several local Sikh societies dedicated to religious, social and educational reforms amongst the Sikhs. The first Singh Sabha was founded at Amritsar in 1873.
Siropa	A robe of honour given by the Gurdwaras to VIP visitors or by Sikh associations or foundations to eminent persons for their outstanding contributions to the community or the Sikh religion.
Suba	A province, a state.
Subedar	The governor of a *suba*, the chief of a province.
Subedari	Governorship.
Sudharanpath/ Sadharanpath	Recitation or reading of the complete *Guru Granth Sahib* without fixing any time limit. Interruption is permissible as against the non-stop *akhandpath*.
Sunder Gutka	A portion of *Guru Granth Sahib*, printed separately in the form of a *pothi* or a book.
Swaran Mandir	Golden Temple.
Takht	Throne, seat of royal or spiritual authority.
Tegh	A *kirpan*, sword.
Tirath	A sacred place, a place of pilgrimage.
Torah	Scriptures of the Jews.
Trishul	Three pronged sharp iron javelin kept as a

	religious symbol by certain Hindu cults and used as a weapon when so required.
Wadda Ghallughara	Great holocaust which entailed huge human loss of the Sikhs on 5 February 1762, fighting against Ahmad Shah Duranni the Afghan invader.
Waheguru	Wonderful Lord, God, Supreme Being.
Wak	A random reading from the *Guru Granth Sahib*, taking that *shabad* or stanza as Guru's commandment for that time or occasion.
Yogi	One who practises self-discipline, also one who belongs to one of the sects of yoga.
Zaildar	One who looked after the activities of a group of villages; he attended on higher officials of the government.
Zamindar	A landlord, a farmer, land owner.

SELECT INDEX